FIGHTING ON THE CULTURAL FRONT

*A Nancy Bernkopf Tucker and Warren I. Cohen Book on
American–East Asian Relations*

NANCY BERNKOPF TUCKER
and WARREN I. COHEN
Books on American–East Asian Relations

Edited by
Thomas J. Christensen
Mark Philip Bradley
Rosemary Foot

John T. Downey, Thomas J. Christensen, and Jack Lee Downey,
Lost in the Cold War: The Story of Jack Downey, America's Longest-Held POW

Anne F. Thurston, ed., *Engaging China: Fifty Years of Sino-American Relations*

Andrew B. Kennedy, *The Conflicted Superpower:*
America's Collaboration with China and India in Global Innovation

Jeanne Guillemin, *Hidden Atrocities:*
Japanese Germ Warfare and American Obstruction of Justice at the Tokyo Trial

Michael J. Green, *By More Than Providence:*
Grand Strategy and American Power in the Asia Pacific Since 1783

Nancy Bernkopf Tucker was a historian of American diplomacy whose work focused on American–East Asian relations. She published seven books, including the prize-winning Uncertain Friendships: Taiwan, Hong Kong, and the United States, 1945–1992. *Her articles and essays appeared in countless journals and anthologies, including the* American Historical Review, Diplomatic History, Foreign Affairs, *and the* Journal of American History. *In addition to teaching at Colgate and Georgetown (where she was the first woman to be awarded tenure in the School of Foreign Service), she served on the China desk of the Department of State and in the American embassy in Beijing. When the Office of the Director of National Intelligence was created, she was chosen to serve as the first Assistant Deputy Director of National Intelligence for Analytic Integrity and Standards and Ombudsman, and she was awarded the National Intelligence Medal of Achievement in 2007. To honor her, in 2012 the Woodrow Wilson International Center for Scholars established an annual Nancy Bernkopf Tucker Memorial Lecture on U.S.–East Asian Relations.*

Warren I. Cohen is University Distinguished Professor Emeritus at Michigan State University and the University of Maryland, Baltimore County, and a senior scholar in the Asia Program of the Woodrow Wilson Center. He has written thirteen books and edited eight others. He served as a line officer in the U.S. Pacific Fleet, editor of Diplomatic History, *president of the Society for Historians of American Foreign Relations, and chairman of the Department of State Advisory Committee on Historical Diplomatic Documentation. In addition to scholarly publications, he has written for the* Atlantic, *the* Baltimore Sun, *the* Christian Science Monitor, Dissent, Foreign Affairs, *the* International Herald Tribune, *the* Los Angeles Times, The Nation, *the* New York Times, *the* Times Literary Supplement, *and the* Washington Post. *He has also been a consultant on Chinese affairs to various government organizations.*

Fighting on the Cultural Front

U.S.–CHINA RELATIONS
IN THE COLD WAR

Hongshan Li

Columbia University Press
New York

Columbia University Press
Publishers Since 1893
New York Chichester, West Sussex
cup.columbia.edu
Copyright © 2024 Columbia University Press
All rights reserved

Library of Congress Cataloging-in-Publication Data
Names: Li, Hongshan, author.
Title: Fighting on the cultural front : U.S.–China relations in the Cold War / Hongshan Li.
Other titles: U.S.-China relations in the Cold War
Description: New York : Columbia University Press, [2023] | Series: A Nancy Bernkopf Tucker and Warren I. Cohen book on American-East Asian relations | Includes bibliographical references and index.
Identifiers: LCCN 2023020609 (print) | LCCN 2023020610 (ebook) | ISBN 9780231207041 (hardback) | ISBN 9780231207058 (trade paperback) | ISBN 9780231556781 (ebook)
Subjects: LCSH: United States—Relations—China. | China—Relations—United States. | United States—Cultural policy—History—20th century. | China—Cultural policy—History—20th century. | Cold War.
Classification: LCC E183.8.C5 L312 2023 (print) | LCC E183.8.C5 (ebook) | DDC 327.73051—dc23/eng/20230607
LC record available at https://lccn.loc.gov/2023020609
LC ebook record available at https://lccn.loc.gov/2023020610

Cover design: Milenda Nan Ok Lee
Cover photo: Chinese Communist Party chairman Mao Zedong signs *Quotations from Chairman Mao* for Robert Williams, an African American civil rights fighter residing in China, on October 1, 1966. Bentley Historical Library, University of Michigan, Ann Arbor.

For my wife, Liu Yang, and my son, Ran

Contents

List of Abbreviations   xi

Introduction: Beating Plowshares into Swords   1

    I   Drawing the Sword   13

    II   Cutting All Ties   50

    III   Fighting Over the Stranded   84

    IV   Building a Cultural Bastion   123

    V   Faking the Exchange   161

    VI   Setting a New Pattern   201

    VII   Forging the Black Blade   242

    VIII   Lowering the Sword   280

Epilogue: Beyond Rattling   321

Acknowledgments 335
Notes 339
Bibliography 419
Index 433

Abbreviations

ACEACS	Advisory Committee on Emergency Aid to Chinese Students
ACLU	American Civil Liberties Union
ACSW	Association of Chinese Science Workers
AP	Associated Press
CAS	Chinese Academy of Science
CBS	Columbia Broadcasting System
CCAS	Committee of Concerned Asian Scholars
CCP	Chinese Communist Party
CCPCC	Chinese Communist Party Central Committee
CCPDWP	Committee of the Chinese People Defending World Peace
CIIA	China Institute in America
CIT	California Institute of Technology
CNAST	Chinese National Association of Science and Technology
CNSC	Chinese National Sports Commission
CNTTT	Chinese National Table Tennis Team
CORE	Congress of Racial Equality
CPACRFN	Chinese People's Association of Cultural Relations with Foreign Nations
CPAFFN	Chinese People's Association for Friendship with Foreign Nations

CPPCC	Chinese People's Political Consultative Conference
CPVA	Chinese People's Volunteer Army
CSCA	Chinese Students Christian Association in North America
CSCPRC	Committee on Scholarly Communications with the People's Republic of China
CUSA	Council for United States Aid
ECA	Economic Cooperation Administration
FBI	Federal Bureau of Investigation
FOA	Foreign Operations Administration
GPCR	Great Proletarian Cultural Revolution
ICA	International Cooperation Administration
IIE	Institute of International Education
INS	Immigration and Naturalization Services
JCRR	Joint Commission for Rural Reconstruction
KKK	Ku Klux Klan
MFA	Ministry of Foreign Affairs
MOE	Ministry of Education
MSA	Mutual Security Agency
NAACP	National Association for the Advancement of Colored People
NAFSA	National Association of Foreign Student Advisors
NBC	National Broadcasting Company
NCUSCR	National Committee on United States-China Relations
OCAC	Overseas Chinese Affairs Commission
PLA	People's Liberation Army
PRC	People's Republic of China
PUMC	Peking Union Medical College
RAM	Revolutionary Action Movement
RNA	Republic of New Africa
SFLI	Shanghai Foreign Language Institute
SNCC	Students Nonviolent Coordinating Committee
UBCCC	United Board for Christian Colleges in China
UPI	United Press International
USACEE	United States Advisory Commission on Educational Exchange

USIS	United States Information Service
USOE	United States Office of Education
USTTT	United States Table Tennis Team
VOA	Voice of America

FIGHTING ON THE CULTURAL FRONT

Introduction

Beating Plowshares into Swords

As archenemies in the Cold War, the People's Republic of China (PRC) and the United States engaged each other not only in bloody military conflicts, intriguing diplomatic maneuvers, and a prolonged trade embargo but also in fierce battles on the cultural front. With the termination of all existing cultural ties between the two nations and the establishment of various new cultural contacts aimed at attacking and isolating each other, Sino-American cultural interactions were transformed from mostly a constructive force in the making of bilateral relations into sharp swords constantly wielded in hot as well as cold wars since the late 1940s. It was those constant battles on the cultural front that expanded and aggravated the confrontation between the two sides throughout the Cold War years. When Beijing and Washington finally allowed and even facilitated the establishment and expansion of cultural exchange as part of their effort to normalize diplomatic relations between the two countries in the 1970s, the swords were only lowered rather than beaten back into plowshares, making clashes on the cultural front a constant phenomenon in the following decades. As a result, the dramatic transformation of U.S.-China cultural interactions in the Cold War not only altered the trajectory of the history of Sino-American cultural relations but also shaped the Cold War experience shared by the Americans and the Chinese, who still cope with its aftermath. A careful investigation of the beginning, evolution, and impact of the Sino-American confrontation on the cultural front from the late 1940s to the late 1970s fills a gap in the study of the U.S.-China Cold War and sheds new light on the history of Sino-American cultural relations.

Just like interactions between any other two nations, U.S.-China relations are intercultural because each nation is a "cultural system."[1] A cultural system or culture generally refers to a way of life shared by a human community over time. Each culture is composed of two interconnected and evolving components: the material and the immaterial. While architecture, fashion, food, and furniture are good examples for the former, art, belief, customs, education, literature, philosophy, religion, values, and the like belong to the latter. Given its inclusive nature, culture not only plays a decisive role in shaping a nation's perception for and policy toward other nations but also constitutes the core of international interactions, since most if not all of them are cultural in nature. The centrality of culture in the making of U.S.-China relations is most visible because China, as one of the oldest continuous civilizations in the world, has an enduring cultural legacy, and the United States, as the first republic in modern world history, is built on clearly articulated ideals and values embodied in the Declaration of Independence and the Constitution rather than on race, blood, or soil.[2] Beginning with the arrival of American merchants and sailors in Guangzhou aboard the *Empress of China* in 1784, cultural interactions grew into the oldest, strongest, and most consequential dimension in U.S.-China relations by the end of the 1940s.

Three clear trends emerged in the cultural interactions between the United States and China prior to the late 1940s. First was the constant expansion of Sino-American cultural interactions despite a few minor setbacks. When the first American merchants and missionaries arrived in China in the late eighteenth and early nineteenth centuries their numbers were small, and their activities were restricted because of the sharp differences between the two cultures and strong opposition from the Qing court as well as local people, especially those with traditional educations and views. For the same reasons, only a handful of Chinese students sailed to the United States for education in the mid-1840s. However, by the late 1940s there were hundreds of American cultural institutions, including schools, colleges, hospitals, churches, and publishers, in China and more than six thousand Chinese students and scholars studying and working in the United States, making the two countries the greatest cultural relations partners in the world. Second was increasing government involvement in bilateral cultural interactions. While the Qing court was transformed from a resolute opponent to an active sponsor and regulator, Washington acted as a supporter and facilitator from the very beginning. Both governments greatly elevated their involvement in the first half of the twentieth century when they worked out the return of part of the Boxer indemnity for educational purposes and then signed the first Fulbright agreement. As a result, cultural exchange became a preferred instrument to alleviate diplomatic crises between the two nations.[3]

Third was the continued improvement in mutual knowledge and understanding that resulted from the constant expansion of cultural interactions. When American and Chinese merchants met for the first time in 1784, they knew practically nothing about each other.[4] After a century of cultural interactions, the Americans had learned a lot about Chinese art, literature, philosophy, and history. At the same time, the Chinese people had adopted a modern educational system after the American model and embraced "Mr. D," democracy, and "Mr. S," science, introduced by Chinese students studying in the United States in the mid-1910s. Partly because of the popularity of those ideals, Chinese Communist leader Mao Zedong signed an agreement proposed by Patrick Hurley, the special envoy of President Franklin Roosevelt, in November 1944. Mao agreed to accept, at least on paper, a united national government of the people, by the people, and for the people, adopt progressive and democratic policies, and guarantee justice and freedom of thought, press, speech, assembly, and residence.[5] Although mostly a tactic used to strengthen the Communists' position in the fight for national power, Mao's approval of such an important political document, drafted by an American politician and filled with American ideals, clearly demonstrated that even Mao was familiar with those terms and used them to his advantage.

The strong historical trends in U.S.-China cultural interactions formed since the late eighteenth century were stopped and reversed in the late 1940s and early 1950s with the Chinese Communists' rise to power. They started to ban Americans from entering Communist-controlled areas and restricted the activities of those American reporters and missionaries already there while still fighting against Nationalist forces in China's civil war. As soon as the PRC entered the Korean War, Beijing took steps to nationalize all cultural institutions with American affiliations and to eradicate American cultural presence and influence in China. At the same time, Washington provided financial aid to Chinese students stranded in the United States and imposed a strict travel ban on Communist China. With hostilities persisting after a truce was reached in Korea, both sides established new cultural contacts with carefully selected partners in the 1950s and 1960s as part of their fight against each other, ushering in a new era in bilateral cultural relations. As Washington quickly developed strong and broad cultural ties with Taiwan as part of its effort to transform the island into an anticommunist bastion in Asia, Beijing kept inviting individual American citizens for short visits or extended stays. Their visits not only directly challenged the travel ban imposed by the U.S. government but also gave Beijing the opportunity to influence them and use them in the PRC's anti-American propaganda. Although the rapprochement did lead to the normalization of diplomatic relations between the two nations, hostility toward each other's ideals and values remained largely unchanged. As a result, despite the impressive growth of cultural exchange programs and the sharp increase in participants, confrontation on the cultural front persisted, and cultural interactions between the two nations continued to be used by both governments as a weapon against each other during and after the 1970s.

Why were the historical trends in Sino-American cultural relations reversed during the Cold War, and why did the United States and the PRC become mortal enemies on the cultural front? How did the two sides utilize cultural interactions as weapons against each other in the Cold War years? What impact did the Sino-American confrontation on the cultural front have in shaping U.S.-China Cold War relations and rebuilding bilateral cultural ties during as well as after the rapprochement? Clear answers to these important questions will help us better understand not only the cause, process, and impact of the transformation of Sino-American cultural interactions in the Cold War but also the complexity of U.S.-China relations during those tumultuous years. More important, they will help reveal exactly how power and policy were shaped by culture and cultural contacts and interactions were used by states as weapons. Despite the publication of numerous brilliant studies on the long history of Sino-American cultural relations and the intense hostility between the two countries in the Cold War in the past few decades, clear and comprehensive answers to these questions remain elusive.

The long and intriguing history of U.S.-China cultural relations has attracted attention from many scholars. However, most of the existing scholarship has concentrated on Sino-American cultural relations before the late 1940s.[6] Studies on Cold War U.S.-China cultural relations have remained few in number and limited in scope.⁷ Largely as a result of the lack of access to government and institutional archives, those scholars who did venture into research on U.S.-China cultural interactions in the Cold War years tended to approach the subject from the American side, focus mostly on American cultural interactions with Taiwan and Hong Kong, and give most credit to private foundations, religious organizations, and universities for the establishment of those new cultural ties, overlooking the role played by the U.S. government as well as the Chinese Communist regime.⁸ When some scholars did direct their insightful investigations to Beijing's interactions with foreigners, including Americans, during the Cold War, they either completely neglected or paid only scarce attention to those Americans, especially African Americans, who flocked to the PRC in the 1950s and 1960s.⁹

While researchers on Sino-American cultural relations have left the Cold War years lightly cultivated, scholars in the field of U.S.-China Cold War have generally overlooked the confrontation on the cultural front between the two sides. Most of the studies on U.S.-China relations during the Cold War have focused on military conflicts, diplomatic maneuvers, and economic embargo. While providing thorough examination and penetrating analysis on state-to-state interactions between the two Cold War foes, they have neglected the engagement on the cultural front that involved state as well as nonstate players.¹⁰ The emergence and growth of cultural Cold War scholarship since the 1990s have effectively expanded the scope of Cold War studies by putting the spotlight on the war of words and cultural exchange among countries belonging to the two opposing camps. However, almost all the existing cultural Cold War studies focus on interactions between the United States and the Soviet Union, leaving the PRC out.¹¹ Some recent studies have broadened and deepened our understanding of U.S.-China Cold War relations through sharp examination of the perceptions and misperceptions of American policymakers, radical African American activists, and concerned Asian scholars.¹² While doing a great job in revealing the crucial role played by nonstate players in shaping U.S.-China relations in the Cold War, they have suffered somewhat from the lack of a wider scope or a clearer historical context.

As the first close examination of U.S.-China cultural interactions in the Cold War, this book scrutinizes the role played by state as well as nonstate participants in the confrontation on the cultural front from both sides. Through analysis of the goals, strategies, tactics, and mechanisms developed by those players in their Cold War cultural interactions and the evaluation of the impact of the cultural-front confrontation, this book dissects the transformation of Sino-American cultural interactions from a mostly constructive instrument prior to the late 1940s to a destructive weapon thereafter. While drawing as much as possible from existing scholarship on the subject, this book relies heavily on primary sources collected from national, local, and institutional archives as well as libraries in the United States, the PRC, and Taiwan. Many of the primary sources have never or rarely been used by other scholars before. It is based on the critical reading and analysis of these rich primary as well as secondary sources that three major themes are developed and emphasized.

First, the PRC and the United States entered and continued their confrontation on the cultural front after the late 1940s not only because they were foes in "hot" wars but also because each viewed the ideas and values espoused and disseminated by the other as real threats to its security and survival. To U.S. government officials as well as private citizens, American ideas and values centered on self-government, liberty, and equality were not only the core of the American culture but also the foundation for the world order established by the United States and its allies after World War II. That was why Washington sided with Jiang Jieshi (Chiang Kai-shek) in China's civil war, resumed military and economic aid to the Nationalist government in Taiwan once the Korean War broke out, offered emergency aid to Chinese students in the United States, and did everything possible to stop Chinese Communist ideological as well as cultural penetration in other Asian countries. For CCP leaders, American ideas and values were inimical to their revolution, which was aimed at not only seizing national power through armed struggle but also establishing absolute ideological and cultural control over the Chinese people so as to perpetuate Communist rule. Thus, they characterized American cultural activities in China as cultural aggression while still fighting the civil war, adopted policies to take over American cultural institutions in China before the PRC was founded, terminated all cultural ties with the United States, launched national movements to eradicate American cultural influence in China after their entrance into the Korean War, and kept fighting against the "peaceful evolution" (*heping yanbian*) encouraged by Washington in the following years and decades. The confrontation on the cultural front continued when Beijing was determined to keep American ideas and values out while taking in as much American science, technology, and capital as possible after the normalization of diplomatic relations between the two nations.

Second, with different political and social systems built on opposing ideas and values, the PRC and the United States confronted each other on the cultural front in markedly different ways by developing different mechanisms and patterns in cultural interactions during the Cold War. As a democratic nation deeply rooted in the rule of law, Washington fought Chinese Communist penetration and influence mostly through adopting various laws and regulations, including a travel ban on mainland China, emergency aid to Chinese students and scholars, prohibition of some Chinese students and scholars from returning to China during the Korean War, and assistance to the education of overseas Chinese in Taiwan. In sharp contrast, Beijing kept eradicating American cultural influences and resisting "peaceful evolution" through violent political movements and tight ideological control that openly violated the basic rights and human dignity of numerous Chinese, especially intellectuals, students, scholars, scientists, artists, and journalists. Having terminated all the old cultural ties, both the PRC and U.S. governments built new ones in different ways. While refusing to recognize the CCP government in Beijing, Washington took steps to directly engage Chinese students and scholars in the United States and establish cultural and educational relations with Taiwan, creating a new pattern in and adding a new dimension to U.S.-China cultural relations. At the same time, Beijing, despite its insistence on closing the door to regular cultural interactions with the United States, invited a small number of carefully chosen Americans to visit and even work in China in the 1950s and the 1960s, building a new type of state-to-people interaction aimed at isolating the U.S. government and disseminating Maoist revolutionary theories and tactics to Americans. It was during this period that Beijing institutionalized a set of mechanisms in selecting, controlling, and utilizing Americans involved in cultural interactions with the PRC.

Third, the U.S.-China confrontation on the cultural front had profound and lasting impact on the Cold War experience of the American as well as the Chinese people and on Sino-American relations before and after the normalization of diplomatic ties between the two countries. In the name of repelling cultural aggression, Beijing not only terminated all cultural ties with the United States but also took over all American cultural institutions in China, banned American movies and radio, dismembered all

American missionary colleges, replaced China's American-modeled educational system with Soviet-styled schools and curriculum, and established the CCP's absolute control over all media and educational, cultural, and art institutions, something that no other ruler in Chinese history had ever achieved. While the Chinese people experienced the most drastic cultural seismic shift in Chinese history in the name of stopping American cultural aggression, the American people had almost unchecked exposure to Chinese Communist propaganda during the Cold War years. Taking advantage of the constitutional rights enjoyed by American citizens, media, and other cultural institutions, Beijing managed to disseminate its revolutionary theories and distribute its official publications, including *Quotations from Chairman Mao* and other books, journals, newspapers, and films, among the American public. American students, workers, intellectuals, and radical activists, white as well as Black, were especially targeted so that Beijing could influence their views toward the PRC and their political activities in the United States. Determined to adhere to its socialist orientation and maintain its absolute control over the nation, the CCP continued to use the same mechanisms developed in the previous decades in fighting against American values and managing American visitors after the normalization of diplomatic relations between the two nations. As a result, strict restrictions on at least some areas of Sino-American cultural interactions continued to exist, and the confrontation on the cultural front between the two sides remained constant after 1979.

Chronologically arranged, this book can be divided into three parts. The first part, comprising the first three chapters, focuses on the termination of existing cultural ties between the two countries and its aftermath. Chapter 1 shows that the Chinese Communists and the United States became open enemies on the cultural front in the late 1940s before they entered direct military confrontation and economic embargo. Setting out to take over the national government and establish absolute ideological and cultural control, CCP leaders saw American cultural activities in China as aggression and adopted a plan to restrict and eventually eliminate the American cultural presence even before they took complete control of mainland China. Their first actions included a ban on American journalists and restrictions on American missionary colleges in the areas under their control in the late 1940s. At the same time, Washington responded to financial difficulties faced by Chinese students in the United States and the CCP's ideological penetration among them with emergency aid to

Chinese students and an anticommunist ideological campaign to make sure that Chinese students could continue their education and remain friendly to the United States as well as its ideas and values.

Chapter 2 investigates the termination of existing Sino-American cultural ties during the Korean War. Immediately after the Chinese People's Volunteer Army (CPVA) crossed the Yalu River, Mao launched a national campaign aimed at stopping American cultural aggression and eradicating pro-American sentiments among the Chinese people. Taking advantage of Washington's ban on transmitting funds from the United States to the PRC, Beijing seized all cultural, educational, medical, and philanthropic institutions operated or subsidized by American organizations. After forcing students and faculty members to go through devastating thought reform (*sixiang gaizao*), the CCP merged the dismembered missionary colleges with other Chinese institutions and put all colleges and schools under the CCP's absolute control. All cultural ties between mainland China and the United States were completely cut off for the first time in history when Washington increased its aid to Chinese students and scholars in the United States, prohibited some of them from returning to their homeland, and imposed a strict travel ban on Communist China.

Chapter 3 explores the maneuvers made by Beijing and Washington in competing for Chinese students and scholars stranded in the United States. With more than five thousand Chinese students remaining in the United States after the Korean War, Beijing made their return one of the key issues at ambassadorial talks with the United States in Geneva in the mid-1950s and launched a national campaign to get them back. However, various political movements launched by Beijing to denounce and punish intellectuals, including those returned from the United States, made it clear that the PRC, despite its desire to use the expertise of American-trained Chinese students and scholars, could not tolerate any returnees with the slightest bourgeois ideals and values. In sharp contrast, Washington, while following existing law and offering assistance to qualified Chinese students for their return to mainland China, created favorable conditions for those who decided to pursue further education or employment in the United States. As a result, the vast majority of them chose to stay in the United States permanently, breaking the century-long tradition of almost all Chinese students' returning home immediately after graduation.

Part II centers on the new cultural interactions established by state as well as nonstate players at the height of the Cold War. Chapter 4 examines the new cultural interactions fostered by Washington and Taipei in the 1950s. While breaking all cultural ties with the Communist regime on mainland China, Washington quickly developed special programs to train students and technicians from Taiwan right after the Korean War broke out. This new cultural tie was further strengthened after Vice President Richard Nixon announced Washington's plan to turn the island into an anticommunist military as well as cultural bastion during his visit to Taiwan in late 1953. Beginning in 1954, Taipei, with generous funding from Washington, dramatically expanded education for overseas Chinese in Taiwan, supported vocational education, and established cooperation between Taiwanese and American colleges. These programs not only helped the Nationalist regime consolidate its control in Taiwan and turn the island into an unsinkable aircraft carrier but also served as a counterattack on Communist China's cultural expansion and infiltration in Asia.

Chapter 5 analyzes the tricky interactions among Beijing, Washington, and American journalists as well as media companies in the mid-1950s that further demonstrated both governments' commitment to keeping officially sanctioned cultural exchange between the two nations as dead as could be. As part of the PRC's effort to instigate antigovernment sentiment among the American people and get the United States out of Taiwan, Beijing invited some Americans, including journalists, to visit mainland China in the mid-1950s. Although the first group of eighteen American reporters turned down Beijing's invitations under pressure from the U.S. government, three journalists did defy the travel ban and went to the PRC in December 1956, forcing Washington to modify its position and authorize a few dozen American reporters to visit the PRC in 1957. Although Beijing had just hosted an American youth delegation, it refused to admit any American reporters who were now authorized by the State Department to visit the PRC on the grounds that Washington denied reciprocal treatment for Chinese reporters. With no real interest in an exchange of journalists, Beijing and Washington simply used the episode as an opportunity to attack and isolate each other.

Chapter 6 discusses Beijing's interaction with individual U.S. citizens in the Cold War and the new mechanisms developed to control and utilize them. Despite its official ban on the admission of American visitors and rejection of the exchange of journalists sanctioned by Washington, the PRC government kept inviting a carefully selected small group of American citizens for short visits or extended stays. With all the state resources under its control, Beijing perfectioned and institutionalized a set of sophisticated mechanisms in hosting those Americans, including journalists, writers, teachers, language experts, and civil rights activists, turning most of them into an instrument to attack the U.S. government and disseminate Maoist theories and strategies to the American public. It was through its interactions with these American citizens that Beijing not only added a new dimension to the U.S.-China cultural relations but also turned China from student to teacher in the Sino-American cultural interaction.

Chapter 7 scrutinizes the special effort made by Beijing to export its revolutionary ideology to the United States through building an alliance with African American activists during the Cold War years. As part of its fight for leadership of the world revolution and response to American involvement in Taiwan as well as Southeast Asia, Beijing invited an unprecedentedly large number of African Americans to visit the PRC in the 1950s and the 1960s. Having failed to sell his revolutionary views to W. E. B. Du Bois in 1959, Mao found a viable ally in Robert Williams, an African American activist known for leading an armed self-defense movement in North Carolina. Taking advantage of requests from Williams, Mao issued a statement in August 1963 not only to show his support for the African American struggle but also to make it part of the world revolution he led. It was after his visits to the PRC that Williams wrote a large number of articles on Black revolution, printed numerous quotations from Mao's *Little Red Book* in his newsletters, and became the most vocal advocate of Maoist revolutionary ideology in the United States.

The third part, containing chapter 8 and the epilogue, traces the brief de-escalation of the confrontation on the cultural front and the reestablishment of "normal" cultural exchange between the two countries after the early 1970s. Chapter 8 reveals that both Beijing and Washington sought to improve relations with each other through reestablishing cultural ties in the late 1960s and early 1970s as part of their effort to cope with the increasing threat from the Soviet Union. Robert Williams's return to the United States to fight legal charges against him in court in 1969 marked his abandonment of Maoist revolutionary ideology, removing an obstacle to rapprochement between the two sides. The exchange visits of the American and Chinese table tennis teams ushered in a new era when some of the old cultural ties were rebuilt and new exchanges were established. However, the early exchanges, participated in by thousands of Americans and hundreds of Chinese, mostly scholars, scientists, artists, journalists, athletes, doctors, remained small in scale, short in duration, selective in category, and unofficial in status, mostly because of intervention from the PRC government.

The epilogue offers a brief look at the expansion of cultural exchange and the continued confrontation on the cultural front between the United States and the PRC since the late 1970s. After the normalization of diplomatic relations, both Beijing and Washington continued and even intensified their involvement in and support for cultural exchange. However, while contributing to the rapid growth and expansion of cultural exchange programs in some areas, the two governments remained hostile to each other's ideas and values. Holding onto its tight control over all cultural institutions and activities, Beijing did everything possible to prevent so-called bourgeois spiritual pollution (*jingshen wuran*) from the United States while absorbing as much American science, technology, capital, and management as possible. Because Washington insisted on the inclusion of American ideas and values as an integral part of the Sino-American cultural exchange, continued confrontation on the cultural front between the two sides became inevitable.

CHAPTER I

Drawing the Sword

As soon as World War II came to an end, civil war between the Nationalists and the Communists broke out in China. Despite massive military and economic aid from the United States, the Nationalist government led by Jiang Jieshi (Chiang Kai-shek) was defeated and forced to flee to Taiwan. Besides the permanent alteration of China's political map, the Communists' victory brought drastic changes to Sino-American cultural relations. The Chinese Communist Party (CCP) began to take steps to ban the operation of American journalists and impose restrictions on American cultural institutions as more cities came under its control later in the war. Soon after the PRC was established in October 1949, the new Communist government adopted stricter regulations, making it difficult if not impossible for those American institutions to function as they had. While unable to stop the Chinese Communists from imposing various restrictions on individual U.S. citizens and cultural institutions in China, Washington made a strenuous effort to preserve at least part of the existing cultural ties between the two nations by offering emergency aid directly to thousands of Chinese students stranded in the United States. At the same time, the State Department launched an ideological campaign against Communist penetration and influence among those students. As a result, Communist China and the United States started to confront each other on the cultural front before they entered into direct and massive military conflict.

The early clashes on the cultural front clearly demonstrated that the Chinese Communists and the United States had ended their brief alliance formed in the war against Japan and became open enemies. Such a drastic change was caused partly by Washington's support for Jiang in the civil war and partly by the vast American cultural presence in China, which was perceived by the CCP as a major threat to the revolution led by it. The Chinese Communist revolution entered a new era after the Rectification Movement (Zhengfeng Yundong) in Yanan with the emergence of Mao Zedong as the undisputable paramount leader and Mao Zedong Thought as the guiding principle for the CCP. Under Mao's leadership, the CCP was determined not only to overthrow the Nationalist rule and establish a new central government under its leadership but also to build a new society with a new revolutionary culture that would perpetuate its rule.[1] Emboldened by what it had achieved in Yanan and other base areas under its control, the CCP set out to duplicate that success throughout the whole nation, beginning in the civil war. In order to build a so-called new society ruled by one party and guided by one thought, the CCPCC decided to restrict and eventually eliminate all American cultural institutions and organizations that had been disseminating American ideals and values in China. The CCP's determination to carry its revolution to a complete victory and Washington's commitment to preserving American ideas and values through salvaging existing cultural ties and to countering Communist penetration in the United States made Sino-American confrontation on the cultural front inevitable.

Becoming Enemies Again

When the civil war between the Communists and the Nationalists reopened only months after the Japanese surrendered, it was not a mere resumption of the military struggle between the two old political foes that had originated in the late 1920s. The United States became an integral part of this conflict when it continued to provide military and economic aid to Jiang Jieshi, an American ally in World War II. By blaming the United States for stirring domestic warfare, the CCP was able to characterize this new phase of the civil war as a national revolution against Jiang's dictatorial rule as well as American colonization and aggression. Such a characterization allowed the Chinese Communists to shift responsibility for this unpopular war to their opponents and justify their adoption of a hostile policy toward the United States. As the limited collaboration between the Chinese Communists and Washington in World War II came to an end, the United States was resurrected as the enemy of the CCP, as it had been before the war against Japan broke out.

Born as part of the world communist movement, the CCP had set the destruction of imperialism and feudalism as its primary goal since its founding in 1921. The United States became the enemy of the Chinese Communists not only because it was one of the major capitalist and imperialist countries, but also because it kept supporting the warlord and the Nationalist regimes that were the enemies of the CCP-led Chinese revolution. The CCP continued its constant attack at the United States in its propaganda until late 1935 when it was instructed by the Communist International to establish the broadest antifascist international united front. At a meeting held in December 1935, the CCP Politburo decided to take necessary steps to reach understanding, seek compromise, establish diplomatic relations, and sign alliance agreements with all nations, parties, and individuals who were against the Japanese imperialists and their lackies.[2] In his interview with Edgar Snow, an American reporter visiting Communist-controlled northern Shanxi Province in July 1937, Mao emphasized that imperialist Japan was the enemy not only of the Chinese people but also of all peace-loving peoples in the world, including the Americans. He hoped that the Americans and the Chinese could form an anti-Japanese united front. The CCP began to actively seek American military support after the Japanese attack on Pearl Harbor. Mao even welcomed the American Military Observation Group to Yanan and asked the U.S. government to establish a consulate in the Communist capital in July 1944. He issued numerous orders to Communist troops to cooperate fully with the American military forces in their reconnaissance activities and projected future landing on China's eastern coast.[3]

The brief collaboration between the Chinese Communists and the U.S. government came to an end when Washington continued to support Jiang after he rejected the agreement proposed by Hurley and signed by Mao in mid-1945. The United States soon became an enemy of the Chinese Communists again as it was blamed for reigniting the civil war. In an order issued on November 7, 1945, Mao declared that a nationwide civil war had already existed because the Nationalists, with assistance from the United States, had mobilized all their forces in attacking the liberated areas. It was in that context that the CCP mandated reducing rents for farmland and improving production in all liberated areas to "overcome all difficulties, support the war effort, and win the victory."[4] In an interview with Anna Louise Strong, another American journalist, in August 1946, Mao identified the American reactionaries as a threat to China as well as the Soviet Union and pointed out that they had also started to attack the American people, politically and economically oppressing the working class. He called upon the American people to rise and resist attacks from American reactionaries. He also emphasized that although the Chinese people would suffer for a long time under joint attacks from the American imperialists and Chinese reactionaries, all of them would ultimately be defeated because they were "paper tigers."[5] In his conversation with Archibald Steele, another American journalist, about a month later, Mao sharply denounced Washington for its oppression of democratic forces in China and its effort to turn China into an American colony through strengthening Jiang and supporting his murderous policies.[6]

Once the United States was identified as an enemy, the Chinese Communist leaders began to include the defeat of American imperialist aggression as part of their revolutionary goal. Despite fierce military offensives launched by the Nationalist army, Mao predicted in early 1947 that a great revolution against imperialism and feudalism would soon arrive in China and that the revolution would prevail because the policies adopted by the American imperialists and their lackey, Jiang Jieshi, left the Chinese people with no other choice but to fight back.[7] In an article published in late 1948 to celebrate the thirty-first anniversary of the October Revolution in Russia, Mao accused American imperialism of replacing Germany, Italy, and Japan in madly preparing a new world war and becoming the greatest threat to the whole world. He called on revolutionary forces all over the world to unite and oppose American imperialist aggression. He also vowed that the CCP would unite all revolutionary forces in China so that they could expel the American imperialist aggressors and overthrow the reactionary rule of the Nationalist Party.[8]

Since there was a limited American military presence in China after the repatriation of Japanese troops in the wake of World War II, concrete actions taken by the Chinese Communists focused mostly on exerting increasingly tight restrictions on individual Americans and American institutions engaging in cultural interactions in China. Those actions became necessary and urgent for the CCP partly because more cities with a large number of Americans living and working there fell under its control beginning in 1948, partly because it was determined to establish absolute control over all cultural institutions and activities in the newly liberated areas as it had done in its base areas in the previous decade. Although its ultimate goal was to exterminate American cultural influence in China and unify the thought of the Chinese people under Mao's teachings, its early restrictions were relatively mild because of the difficulty of the task and their own vulnerable position in the war at the time. In early 1948, the Chinese Communist Party Central Committee (CCPCC) instructed the People's Liberation Army (PLA) not to confiscate or destroy churches, schools, hospitals, nurseries, and nursing homes operated by foreign residents. Those institutions, the CCPCC ordered, should be allowed to continue their business as long as they followed the laws issued by the new government and did not engage in any espionage or sabotage activities.[9] However, once victory in the civil war was within reach for the Communists in late 1948, the CCPCC issued strict orders to ban foreign reports from liberated areas and prohibit foreigners from publishing newspapers or magazines there without approval from the CCPCC. It justified its new action by asserting that "the vast majority of these propaganda apparatus are controlled by the reactionaries" and "are the instruments used by certain class, parties, and social organizations to carry out class struggle."[10]

Since most of the foreign journalists were Americans and most of the major publications were American-owned, the CCPCC's new restrictions not only reflected the principles of what historian Gao Hua called Maoist journalism (*Maoshi xinwenxue*), which treated all news media as an instrument for class struggle, but also marked a reversal of its position on cultural interactions with the United States adopted a few years earlier.[11] In summer 1944, the CCPCC gave a warm reception to a large group of foreign journalists, mostly Americans, and invited China's allies, mainly the United States, to establish diplomatic as well as government news offices, set up news bureaus, and have correspondents stationed in Yanan. It also instructed that dispatches sent by journalists, except those that leaked military secrecy or slandered the government, not be stopped or censored so as to show the difference between the CCP and the Nationalist Party. It even allowed foreign priests to enter the border area controlled by the CCP and ordered the return of church buildings, houses, and other properties to them.[12] In December 1945 the CCPCC issued another instruction directing all its subordinating units to assist American journalists in their reporting on their region. The purpose was to "give the Americans a friendly impression which can have relatively progressive influence on U.S. policy toward China."[13]

Treating the United States as their foremost enemy and imposing further restrictions on American cultural institutions as well as activities in China were integrated into the foreign policy formulated by the Communist leaders for the new national government in early 1949. Mao made it clear in his speech at the CCPCC Politburo meeting on January 6 that the new government under the leadership of the CCP would not seek recognition from imperialist countries and that what it should be busy doing was to establish diplomatic relations with the Soviet Union and other democratic countries.[14] Approved by the Politburo, this position, known as "leaning to one side" (*yibian dao*), became one of the three pillars of CCP foreign policy. In another speech delivered a few days later, Mao warned his colleagues that Washington had adopted a new two-pronged China strategy. On the one hand, it continued to support the remnant Nationalist military forces and local warlords in resisting the PLA. On the other hand, it sent its lackeys to penetrate the revolutionary camp to destroy the revolution from inside by organizing so-called opposing factions. He called on his comrades to heighten their vigilance and defeat the imperialist plot. In order to achieve that goal, he listed seventeen tasks for 1949. One of them was to ensure that education at all levels, news reporting, literature, and art would meet the needs of the current revolutionary situation and tasks.[15]

In order to implement the foreign policy decisions made at the Politburo meeting, the CCPCC issued a number of orders immediately. The first order went out on January 18, 1949, imposing strict regulation on the press from imperialist countries in China and on dispatches sent by them. It stipulated that all private outlets in the country should not set up devices to receive dispatches from the foreign press and that all state or private newspapers and magazines should not publish dispatches sent by the press from imperialist countries. International news, it ordered, would come from Xinhua headquarters (Xinhua Zongshe). Local authorities were also instructed to clearly explain to the people that all news agencies in imperialist countries, such as the United Press International (UPI), the Associated Press (AP), and the United States Information Service, were the instruments of imperialist aggression and were always hostile to the liberation cause of the Chinese people; thus they should absolutely not be allowed to have their dispatches published publicly and freely in the liberated areas. The strict regulation of them, it emphasized, was needed to serve the interests of the Chinese people.[16]

A more comprehensive instruction on foreign affairs with major revisions and additions made by Mao was issued by the CCPCC on January 19. Its focus was to lay out two additional major principles of the CCP's foreign policy.[17] The first was not to recognize representatives from imperialist countries currently in China as formal diplomatic personnel, not only because the new government did not have formal diplomatic relations with those nations at the time but also because most of those nations' governments, especially the imperialist U.S. government, were assisting the reactionary Nationalist regime and opposing the liberation of the Chinese people. The second stated that all privileges enjoyed by the imperialists in China should be terminated and the independence of the Chinese people should be achieved when the Nationalist regime was overthrown, even though particular steps for implementation should be taken with discretion based on the nature and conditions of specific issues.[18] These two positions were soon shared by Mao with Anastas Mikoyan, the special envoy of Joseph Stalin who was visiting CCP headquarters in Xibaipo, Hebei Province, in late January and early February 1949. Mao called the first position "starting fresh" (*lingqi luzao*) and the second "cleaning house" (*dasao fangzi*). In order to avoid any misunderstanding on the second term, Mao elaborated that China, like a dirty house, was filled with trash, dirt, flea, bedbugs, and lice. It had to be thoroughly cleaned, well ordered, and nicely furnished after the liberation, Mao asserted, before guests could be invited and entertained. He did make an exception for "true friends" who were welcome to enter the house earlier and give a helping hand to the housecleaning.[19] Together with "leaning to one side," which Mao also elaborated to Mikoyan, these interlinked principles would serve as guidelines for the CCP's foreign policy in the following years, if not decades.

The CCPCC's January 19 instruction also included more concrete directives on various specific issues. The first, revised by Mao, made it clear that the American military attachés should be put under house arrest and guarded by PLA soldiers because the new government did not recognize any foreign countries that had diplomatic relations with the Nationalist regime and were assisting Jiang in the civil war. About one-third of the directives were about the handling of foreign cultural, educational, religious institutions, news agencies, and foreigners working in those areas.

According to these directives, no new foreign individuals or cultural institutions would be permitted in the liberated areas. Although foreign missionaries, schools, and hospitals already in the liberated areas were allowed to continue their operations, the new directives required all schools operated by foreigners to have Chinese principals, report their financial sources, and set their courses by following the new government regulations. Hospitals operated by foreigners had to be supervised by the new government. While requiring foreign newspapers and magazines to register, the CCPCC instructed that their applications be turned down and their publications stopped. Foreign news agencies should be banned from issuing reports and operating telegraph machines, and foreign journalists would not be authorized to conduct interviews or send out reports.[20] Since most of those foreign schools, hospitals, and news agencies were operated by Americans and the largest group of foreign journalists were U.S. citizens, the increasingly tough restrictions imposed by the CCP brought immediate and drastic changes on U.S.-China cultural relations.

The new Communist government's restrictions on American media and cultural institutions were toughened when it started to impose tight control over all newspapers, magazines, and presses in major cities as soon as they came under its rule. Only weeks after the PLA took over Beijing, the Military Control Commission (MCC) (Junshi Guanzhi Weiyuanhui), with the approval of the CCPCC, issued "Temporary Procedures for the Registration of Newspapers, Magazines, and Presses in Beijing." The MCC required that all newspapers, magazines, and presses apply for registration and their publishers, editors, and managers clearly state their political positions, experiences, and relations with various political parties, organization, and factions. All existing newspapers, magazines, and presses were also ordered to submit their publications in the past year with their registration applications for official review. Only those that had applied and received temporary registrations issued by the MCC could continue their publication and operation in the city. They were prohibited from any activities in violation of the laws adopted by the people's government and the MCC, engaging in any propaganda against the people's democratic cause, leaking state or military secrets, and conducting propaganda through fabricating rumors or slandering.[21] The order issued by the Beijing MCC clearly showed that banning and limiting the operation of foreign presses and reporters were an integral part of the CCP's effort to establish absolute control over all media and other cultural institutions in China.

Mao again emphasized the importance of gaining such a control at the Second Plenary of the Seventh National Congress of the CCP held in early March 1949. In his opening speech, Mao stressed that the foreseeable nationwide victory was "only the first step in the ten-thousand-*li*-long march." "While the enemies with guns have been wiped out," Mao warned, "the enemies without guns are still there and they will fight desperately against us." Therefore, he urged his comrades to learn to carry out political, economic, and cultural struggles against the imperialists, the Nationalists, and the bourgeoisie in the cities. He told them that if they failed to learn how to fight the enemies on those fronts and win those battles, they would not be able to stay in power and would eventually lose. In order to win those battles, Mao insisted that the Communist government give no recognition to the legal status of foreign diplomats or agencies, close all foreign propaganda institutions in China, and exert immediate control over foreign trade. As for the imperialist economic and cultural enterprises, they would be allowed to exist temporarily. However, Mao emphasized, they should be "under our supervision and control, waiting for resolution after we have won the national victory."[22]

Mao's call on preparing for and carrying out a resolute fight against enemies on the cultural and ideological fronts was anything but new for veteran Communist leaders attending the meeting. While serving as the interim director of the Nationalist Party's Propaganda Department during the first united front between the Communists and the Nationalists, Mao founded the *Political Weekly* (*Zhengzhi Zhoubao*) in 1925. Besides acting as its editor, Mao wrote more than twenty essays for the magazine in the first month as part of the counterattack on reactionary propaganda from the enemies of the revolution, including imperialism in the world, national as well as local warlords in China, the comprador class, and local tyrants.[23] After the collapse of the first united front in 1927, Mao led the Autumn Uprising in Hunan Province and established the Red Army with Zhu De and other Communist leaders. Since the very beginning of the armed revolution, Mao made propaganda a primary task for the Red Army and established propaganda units at all levels to mobilize the people and attack the enemy on the cultural front.[24] The CCP continued and even intensified its attack on the Nationalist regime on the cultural and ideological fronts during the war against Japan. Taking advantage of the establishment of the second united front between the Nationalists and the Communists, the CCP published newspapers and magazines, including the *Xinhua Ribao* (New China Daily), the *Qunzhong* (The Masses) weekly, in Nationalist-controlled areas; disseminated the writings of Mao Zedong and other Communists leaders through its presses and other venues; and promoted the so-called progressive culture by organizing various performance troupes and holding numerous rallies and forums attended by artists, writers, scholars, and students.[25] Once the war against Japan came to an end, Mao immediately ordered sending cadres to Wuhan, Nanjing, Hong Kong, and Shanghai as soon as possible so that they could publish newspapers as well as magazines, establish news agencies, bookstores, printing houses, and work in theaters, movie industry, and schools before the arrival of the Nationalists.[26]

While leading the Red Army and the CCP in fighting their enemies on the cultural front, Mao also launched numerous campaigns against what he called erroneous thoughts within the CCP. With support from the CCPCC, Mao called the Ninth CCP Convention of the Fourth Army in December 1929 to correct the various nonproletarian thoughts in the Red Army, including extreme democracy (*jiduan minzhu zhuyi*), absolute egalitarianism (*juedui pingjun zhuyi*), subjectivism (*zhuguan zhuyi*), and individualism (*geren zhuyi*).[27] As soon as the Red Army settled down in Northern Shanxi after the Long March, Mao urged all CCP members as well as other revolutionaries to pick up the weapon of thought struggle (*sixiang douzheng*) and fight against liberalism (*ziyou zhuyi*), which, according to Mao, was rooted in bourgeois selfishness and fundamental conflict with Marxism and was favored by the enemies of the CCP.[28] In order to eradicate liberalism among CCP members and end the phenomenon of a hundred different sayings for a hundred individuals (*bairen baishuo*) in Yanan, Mao launched the rectification movement (*zhengfeng yundong*) in 1942.[29] In his speech at the Yanan Literature and Art Forum, Mao emphasized that there were many fronts in the struggle for the liberation of the Chinese people and that a cultural army (*wenhua de jundui*) "is indispensable in uniting ourselves and overwhelming the enemies."[30] In order to be part of this cultural army, all artists, writers, and other intellectuals, Mao insisted, had to go through thought reform and shift their stand from the bourgeois to the proletarian side.

Mao's speech immediately became the most important guiding document of the rectification movement. After formal publication of the speech in *Jiefang Ribao* in October 1943, the CCPCC issued two circulars instructing all Party officials and members to carefully study it and apply its principles to their work in every department, since Mao's speech was the reification and Sinicization of Marxism and Leninism.[31] It was through the strenuous rectification movement that Mao was able not only to consolidate his absolute control over the army and the Party but also to establish Mao Zedong Thought as the guiding principle of the CCP and the Chinese revolution. In his speech delivered on July 5, 1943, Wang Jiaxiang, one of the top leaders of CCP, credited the formulation of the correct anti-Japanese war strategy and policy to brilliant leader Mao Zedong and declared that "Mao Zedong Thought is Marxism, Leninism, Bolshevism, and Communism in China."[32] The Constitution of the CCP adopted at its Seventh National Congress in 1945 clearly stated for the first time that the CCP "takes Mao Zedong Thought as the guiding principle for all its work."[33] Once Mao Zedong Thought was elevated to the only correct thought for the CCP and the nation, American institutions and influence in China became the chief enemy of Mao and the Party because they cherished democratic ideals and freedom of thought, speech, press, association, and religion.

Mao's rise as the paramount leader as well as the only thinker in the CCP marked the beginning of a new era in the Chinese revolution led by it.[34] In addition to the overthrow of the Nationalist government with an armed revolution, the CCP set out to unify the thoughts as well as actions of all Chinese under Mao, creating a so-called new society and a new cultural system. Although the CCP had started to deny basic rights, including the right of independent thinking, to its members and the Chinese people living in the areas under its control during the rectification movement, Mao continued to attack Jiang by demanding more freedom and democracy from the Nationalist government. In his reply to questions raised by Chinese and foreign reporters, mostly Americans, who were visiting Yanan in June 1944, Mao insisted that what the CCP wanted from the Nationalist government was democracy in all areas. He emphasized that badly needed political unification should be established on the foundation of freedom of speech, press, assembly, and association and of a democratically elected government.[35] While most American reporters liked what they heard from Mao and wrote favorable reports on Mao and Communist forces, Theodore White, an American journalist who arrived in Yanan a few months later, had a slightly different impression of the Communist leader. White observed that the godhood of Mao had already been recognized, and when he preached like Jesus, all others, including Zhou Enlai, carefully listened and took notes. Naturally, White was treated as a student in his interview with Mao, who instructed him all the way through. Mao also told White that in the new Communist China "anyone could be able to publish in any newspaper whatever he wanted—except 'enemy of the people.' "[36] White later regretted that he forgot asking Mao who would define what an enemy of the people was. However, a clear answer was provided in the orders issued by the CCP in late 1948 and early 1949.

Skirmishing on the Cultural Front

Local Communist authorities strictly followed Mao's call for fighting enemies on the cultural front and the CCPCC's repeated instructions on the same subject. Some of the earliest actions took place in Beijing soon after the nation's cultural capital came under Communist control on January 31, 1949. Unhappy with reports written in early February by some American journalists who likened the warm reception given to the PLA by Beijing residents to the welcome received by the Mongol and Manchu conquerors when they entered the city centuries ago, *People's Daily* (*Renmin Ribao*), the main organ of the CCP, published an article on February 12 denouncing their reports as a slander and claiming that the Chinese people had the right to refute their nonsense.[37] Two days later, it published an article listing the statements from workers, students, professors, and other intellectuals condemning those reports and demanded the expulsion of American journalists from the city and the liberated area.[38] Two weeks later the same newspaper printed the order issued by the Beijing MCC banning all activities of foreign news agencies and reporters and prohibiting foreigners from publishing newspapers as well as magazines in the city. It also listed the names of seventeen foreign reporters in the city at the time. With ten of them working for the AP, UPI, *New York Times*, *Look* magazine, *Chicago Daily Tribune*, *Hartford Times*, and the like, American reporters were obviously the main targets of the MCC's new regulation.[39]

Similar actions were taken by the CCP in other major cities under its control and reported to Joseph Stalin by Liu Shaoqi, vice chairman of the CCP, who went to Moscow in July 1949 seeking Soviet support. In order to help Stalin have a better understanding of the revolution led by the CCP,

Liu wrote a lengthy report elaborating the CCPCC's positions and policies on various issues. As part of his effort to prove the revolutionary nature of the CCP, Liu informed Stalin that the CCPCC had decided to stop the activities of foreign newspapers, magazines, news agencies, and reporters in China and that the decision would be carried out in all locations.[40] Stalin highly praised the policies adopted by the CCP and commented that the center of the revolution was moving to the east.

About the same time when Liu forwarded his report to Stalin, the CCP expanded its actions to include U.S. government offices in major cities now under its control. In late July, the MCCs in Beijing, Shanghai, Tianjin, Nanjing, and Wuhan ordered all U.S. Information Service (USIS) offices located in their jurisdictions to immediately stop all activities including news releases, display of books and newspapers, movie showings, art exhibits, library services, and musical concerts.[41] The Communist regime's ban on American news agencies and reporters received a quick rebuff from Secretary of State Dean Acheson. In a letter transmitting the comprehensive examination of U.S. policy toward China to President Harry Truman on July 30, he praised the responsiveness of the American government to "an informed and critical public opinion" and pointed out that "it is precisely this informed and critical public opinion which totalitarian governments . . . cannot endure and do not tolerate."[42] Mao fired back immediately, asserting that the "informed and critical public opinion" in the United States represented by newspapers, news agencies, magazines, and radio stations were controlled by the Republican and Democratic parties and always lied to the people. He reaffirmed that the Chinese Communists would not endure or tolerate the calumny, and that it was why they "have closed imperialist information offices, banned imperialist news agencies from releasing news reports to Chinese newspapers, and refused to allow them to continue poisoning the soul of the Chinese people."[43]

While shutting down USIS offices and banning the activities of American journalists, local Communist authorities did allow most American-subsidized cultural and educational institutions to maintain their routine operations. When the PLA took over the western suburbs of Beijing in December 1948, it sent a young officer to Yenching University, one of the best-known American missionary colleges in China. After delivering a short speech on the bright future of the university the young officer departed, leaving Lu Zhiwei (Luh Chi-wei), the chairman of the Administrative Committee of Yenching, in control.[44] On February 26, 1949, the

Board of Managers of Yenching University met in Shanghai and officially appointed Lu as Yenching's superintendent.[45] Under Lu's leadership, Yenching had a rather smooth transition, at least in his view, during the power shift in China. Thus, Lu urged the United Board for Christian Higher Education in China (UBCHEC), located in New York, to keep sending funds and instructors to Yenching.[46] Ling Xianyang, the University of Shanghai (Hujiang Daxue) president, was the only Christian college administrator who was forced out of office in this transitional period. His removal, taking place right after the PLA entered Shanghai, was mostly the result of his close ties with the Nationalist regime and harsh policy toward the student movement.[47]

The CCP allowed American-subsidized cultural and educational institutions in China to continue their operations mostly because it wanted to maintain order in cities newly taken over by the PLA and win support from scholars as well as students in these institutions. As soon as the Thirteenth Corps of the PLA took over the western suburbs of Beijing, it posted a public announcement at the front gate of Qinghua University ordering all military as well as government officials to strengthen the protection of the university and urging the university administration and all students to continue their educational routine, concentrate on their studies, and maintain order.[48] The Communist leaders were fully aware that the political chaos that helped bring down the Nationalist regime was partially caused by college students demonstrating in city streets. They wanted to make sure that the same thing would not happen under their watch. At the same time they made an effort to win over leading intellectuals, including those teaching at American-subsidized missionary colleges. When the CCP organized the first Chinese People's Political Consultative Conference (CPPCC) in September 1949, it invited many prominent professors from missionary colleges. Led by Lu Zhiwei, nine Yenching professors attended that historical conference, the most among all colleges in China. It was at that conference that the first government of the PRC was elected and the Common Program (Gongtong Gangling), which would serve as the constitution of China in the next five years, was approved. Lu himself became an elected member of the National Committee of CPPCC, which would serve as a constitutional convention until 1954.

While preparing for the first CPPCC, Mao intensified his attack on U.S. government policy as well as American cultural aggression. In response to the publication of the *White Paper on U.S.-China Relations* by the State

Department, Mao wrote an editorial for the New China News Agency on August 14, 1949, pointing out that the United States had not only given money and guns to Jiang Jieshi to fight the civil war and kill Chinese for the Americans but also had launched political, economic, and cultural aggression against the Chinese people.[49] In another editorial published about two weeks later, Mao openly called Dean Acheson a liar when the secretary of state claimed that American religious, philanthropic, and cultural enterprises, including the return of part of the Boxer indemnity to be used to educate Chinese students, were a demonstration of friendship toward the Chinese. Mao stressed that compared to other imperialist nations the United States had for a long time focused more on "spiritual aggression" (*jingshen qinglue*), extending from religious to philanthropic and then to cultural enterprises. He even listed ten missionary colleges run by the Americans and used Leighton Stuart, the founder and former president of Yenching University, as examples to show the close ties between the missionaries and the U.S. government. He also mocked American friendship by pointing out that the United States first joined the Allied Forces of eight powers in defeating China and forced the Qing government to pay the Boxer indemnity. Then it returned part of that indemnity to educate Chinese students for spiritual aggression.[50] Thus, he called on the Chinese people to dismiss any illusions of a friendly relationship with the United States and prepare to fight the American imperialists for a long period.[51]

The Common Program approved by the first CPPCC clearly reflected the CCP's determination to fight the United States on the cultural front and provided the legal foundation for the new government to do so. According to the Common Program, the main task for the new government in education was to eradicate feudal, compradorial, and fascist ideologies. Thus, the government should take planned and gradual steps to reform the old educational system, contents, and methods.[52] The CCP had already stopped all political indoctrination courses imposed by the Nationalist Party, such as the Party Doctrine (*Dangyi*) and the Three Principles of the People (*Sanmin Zhuyi*) in all cities as soon as they came under its control. Now based on the Common Program, it required all students as well as teachers, including those in Christian colleges and schools, to participate in the nationwide political study movement (*zhengzhi xuexi yundong*). Special workshops were organized for faculty members and new political courses, including the history of social development, political economics, and the new democracy, were required for students.[53] Yenching, while claiming that it opened fall semester in 1949 with academic and religious freedom unimpaired, had to comply with a "suggestion from the People's Government." Like all other colleges in China, it added three new courses: Principles of New Democracy, History of Chinese Society, and Marxism-Leninism and the Philosophy of History to its curriculum to present Marxist viewpoints on these subjects. However, the university took comfort in the fact that these courses were taught by instructors who were not members of the CCP.[54] In addition to these new courses, Yenching students were required to attend study camps organized by the Communist government at Qinghua University.[55]

Although the curricular changes and study camps were imposed by the new government with non–Party members taking about half of the ministerial positions, real control was in the hands of the CCP. Prior to the establishment of the people's government, the Propaganda Department (Xuanchuanbu) of the CCPCC was in charge of all cultural and educational affairs. It had added offices to manage radio broadcasters, publications, and motion pictures near the end of the civil war. Once the new central government was established, the CCPCC issued an instruction in December 1949 to turn all these offices into parts of the state apparatus. The Xinhua News Agency (Xinhuashe) morphed into the national news agency. While the broadcast section became the Bureau of Broadcasting (Guangboju) under the Information Administration (Xinwen Zongshu), the motion picture section was renamed the Motion Picture Bureau (Dianyingju) reporting to the Ministry of Culture. The Committee on Publications was turned into the Bureau of Publications (Chubanju), and the Xinhua Bookstore became the national bookstore, both under the Publications Administration (Chuban Zongshu). The purpose of these new arrangements, the instruction continued, was to allow the government to play its role in managing cultural and educational affairs under the leadership of the CCPCC. With most administrative responsibilities removed, the Propaganda Department was to focus more on ideological struggle, its leadership in propaganda, and the formulation of policies on culture and education. In the end, all regional Party leaders were required to report to the CCPCC all important cultural and educational issues and to request instructions before any action was taken.[56]

As major military campaigns gradually came to an end, the new central government began to take steps to reform the educational system, including missionary schools. At the first national conference on education held in December 1949, Ma Xulun, the minister of education, asserted that since the old education in China served imperialists and feudal compradors it should be thoroughly reformed. Fundamental changes, he insisted, were needed in the educational system, curriculum, textbooks, teaching methods, and faculty. He did repeat what had been stated in the Common Program: that these reforms should be carried out gradually with planned steps.[57] All the meeting participants agreed that strengthening government control and management of private schools, including missionary institutions, in the newly liberated areas had become an important and urgent issue.[58] In order to achieve that goal, the Ministry of Education (MOE), with the approval of the Executive Council (Zhengwuyuan), held the first National Conference on Higher Education in early June 1950. It was at this conference that five important regulations and resolutions were adopted.[59] Approved by the Executive Council on July 28, these regulations and resolutions gave the MOE authority over all higher education institutions except military academies in the nation; laid out the mission, admission, curriculum, organization, and administration for colleges and universities; and banned faculty representatives from the Administrative Committee (Xiaowu Weiyuanhui) while giving the president power to approve resolutions passed by the committee.[60] As a result, academic independence and shared governance, the hallmarks of modern Western higher educational institutions and practices enjoyed by college professors in many Chinese universities, came to an end.

The Temporary Regulations for Private Higher Education Institutions were most relevant to missionary colleges and universities in China. They began by requiring all private colleges and universities, including missionary institutions, to follow all regulations therein in setting missions, goals, the academic system, curriculum, and instructional and administrative organizations. It also clearly spelled out that the administration, finance, and property ownership of private colleges had to be under Chinese control. All private colleges and universities must apply for registration, which had to be reviewed by the regional government offices and approved by the MOE. While presidents and vice presidents of private colleges and universities were appointed by the board of directors, the appointments had to be verified and approved by regional government offices and filed with the MOE. Private colleges were prohibited from making religious subjects required courses or forcing students to participate in religious ceremonies or activities. Most important, the MOE had the authority to require private colleges and universities to change their boards of directors, replace their presidents, reorganize them, or shut them down.[61] These regulations not only put all Christian colleges under the Communist government's complete control but also cleared the way for their eventual termination.

The strict requirements set in the Temporary Regulations for Private Higher Education Institutions were part of CCP's effort to limit American cultural activities in China and weaken the American cultural influence among the Chinese. While the National Conference on Higher Education was in progress, the CCP opened its Third Plenary of the Seventh National Congress in Beijing. In his speech at the meeting, Mao clearly listed the reactionary forces in the missionary schools established by imperialists and religious circles in China and the reactionary forces in the cultural and educational institutions inherited from the Nationalist regime as enemies of the CCP. He warned his comrades that the struggle against these enemies would be tremendously fierce and unprecedented in the history.[62] On August 19, the CCPCC issued an instruction on Catholic and Christian churches, laying out its policy toward missionary schools and Christian religion. The instruction opened with an accusation that Catholic and Christian churches had been an instrument used by imperialists in cultural aggression in China and that some of church members were imperialist spies. Since the imperialists had failed in their political and economic aggression, they, the instruction asserted, were trying to maintain their hold on the churches and use them to maintain imperialist influence in China and conduct espionage activities. Thus, the CCPCC instruction prohibited churches from preaching the Gospel outside of church buildings and banning all church activities in the areas where land reform was conducted. In the same breath, the CCPCC warned the churches not to publish any materials slandering the people's democracy in China. As for the missionary schools, CCPCC viewed them as private enterprises and ordered them to make political studies required courses and religious subjects electives.[63]

Once the new laws and regulations were adopted, they were seriously implemented and those who dared to challenge them were severely punished. While most missionary cultural and educational institutions in China chose to follow the strict regulations issued by the new government, the Catholic Church decided to defend its control over Fu Jen (Furen), the Catholic University in Beijing. In early July, the Church representative wrote to Chen Yuan, president of Fu Jen, informing him that the $144,000 subsidy would be provided for the university only after the Catholic

Church was allowed to appoint a new board of directors, veto any personnel decisions, and maintain ownership of the church building. Later, it also demanded the firing of five professors. When the Chinese government refused to accept the conditions, the Catholic Church decided to withhold the money from the university on August 1. Chen turned to the government for assistance and received funding from the MOE. After the Catholic Church rejected the terms offered by Ma Xulun in late September, the MOE, with authorization from Premier Zhou Enlai, decided to take over Fu Jen University on October 12. Chen Yuan was appointed by the MOE as president of the new National Fu Jen University. Ma Xulun asserted that the takeover was done to protect China's educational sovereignty (*jiaoyu zhuquan*).[64]

While enforcing the regulations set for missionary colleges and universities, the Communist regime did not nationalize all of them immediately at the time. In his instruction to the MOE on taking over Fu Jen, Zhou Enlai emphasized that "missionary schools can continue to run as long as they follow the laws adopted by the Central People's Government and the Common Program."[65] Even after CCP leaders had decided to send CPVA to Korea to confront United Nations forces led by the United States, Zhou told the officials attending the Fifty-Third meeting of the Executive Council on October 6, 1950, that other missionary schools, mostly established and subsidized by the Americans, should be allowed to continue their operations.[66] The Communist leaders were reluctant to end the operations of all American missionary cultural and educational institutions at the time for various reasons. First, the CCP still had to focus on destroying the remnant Nationalist forces on the mainland and establishing order in the newly liberated areas in 1950. Thus Mao, while seeing reactionary forces in the missionary schools as an enemy, warned his comrades not to "strike in all four directions."[67] Second, faced with more urgent needs to finish military campaigns and bring economic recovery to major cities devastated by the war, the new regime lacked the financial resources to take over and run all private schools, which counted for about half of all educational institutions in the nation.[68] Third, since missionary colleges were among the best in China, the Communist regime still had to depend on them in producing a large number of highly trained experts for the nation's economic reconstruction. Fourth and last, with their strong reputation and record, missionary colleges and universities were still able to attract many Chinese students even after many new restrictions were imposed on them. Yenching actually had a record enrollment of about 1,200 for fall 1950 because a large number of well-qualified students chose it over state-run colleges.[69] Some Yenching faculty members were so confident that they reported to the UBCHEC in fall 1950 that Yenching was still very much alive and that its contribution was desired for at least ten or twenty years.[70]

Those Yenching faculty members would reach a completely different conclusion if they had read the CCP documents, especially the report sent by Liu Shaoqi to Stalin a year earlier. Liu informed Stalin that the CCPCC had decided to allow the schools and hospitals owned by imperialist countries to continue their activity on condition that they "abide by our laws." However, he also emphasized that "we shall not permit the opening of new schools or hospitals in China," and "once we are able to run these educational institutions and hospitals by ourselves, we shall take them over." Actually, while foreign religious organizations were allowed to continue their activities, antireligious propaganda, Liu added, was carried out and the lands of religious missions and churches were confiscated and distributed with the consent of the believers.[71] The defeat of the Nationalists in the civil war and the establishment of the PRC helped the CCP get closer to its goal. The American cultural, educational, religious, and philanthropic institutions in China were actually living on borrowed time.

Extending Emergency Aid

Treated by the CCP as an enemy in China's civil war, Washington was unable to do anything to stop the Chinese Communists from banning American presses and restricting American institutions and citizens in other cultural activities. It was forced to suspend the Fulbright program with China in August 1949 because the fleeing Nationalist government was no longer able to make payments for surplus war materials bought from the United States at the end of World War II.[72] What Washington could and did do to keep the Sino-American cultural interactions alive was to offer assistance to thousands of Chinese students who came to the United States in the wake of World War II and began to face increasing financial distress in 1948 because of runaway inflation in China and the collapse of the Nationalist government. Although the Emergency Aid Program to Chinese students was inspired by U.S. government assistance to Chinese students during World War II, it was distinctly different from the very beginning and quickly morphed from a mostly humanitarian measure into an instrument for Washington to salvage existing cultural ties with China and preserve anticommunist leaders for the Chinese people. In addition to offering an unprecedentedly large amount of financial aid directly to Chinese students, the State Department had to launch a covert anticommunist ideological campaign to counter the CCP's infiltration and influence in the United States. As a result, the United States and the Chinese Communists entered battles on the cultural front on both sides of the Pacific.

Washington became aware of the financial difficulties faced by an increasingly large number of Chinese students in the United States in mid-1948 and alerted the Nationalist government immediately. Having received a letter from Laurence Duggen, director of the Institute of International Education (IIE), sharing his concerns on financial difficulties encountered by students from China, the Department of State forwarded the letter to the American embassy in Nanjing on June 15, 1948, instructing it to raise the issue with the Chinese government.[73] The initial response from the Nationalist government was slow and disappointing. On September 13, 1948, the MOE sent a letter to presidents of 139 American colleges and universities informing them that it was now against government policy to grant a special exchange rate to self-supporting Chinese students studying abroad. Aware that some students would be unable to continue their studies because of this policy change, the MOE decided to have those students recalled and instructed them to apply for a government travel subsidy of $400 each from the Chinese embassy before December 31, 1948.[74] Later, the MOE extended the deadline for the application to February 28, 1949, and offered limited relief and loans to certified self-supporting students. However, the MOE made it clear that these provisions did not apply to the uncertified self-sponsored students, the largest cohort of Chinese students in the United States at the time.[75]

Extremely concerned with the deteriorating conditions in China and unhappy with the Nationalist government's decisions, most Chinese students refused to return to their war-torn homeland before they could complete their education in the United States. Unable to receive financial support from their government or families, they began to seek assistance from all possible American sources. Many of them applied for and received financial aid from universities and private organizations. With limited resources, many colleges and universities soon ran out of funds and had to turn to the federal government for help. Beginning in September 1948, the

Department of State and the Office of Education received numerous letters reporting the plight of the Chinese students and requesting information about the Chinese student aid program. Although Congress had just passed the Information and Educational Exchange Act, popularly known as the Smith-Mundt Act, which made educational exchange an "essential part of the conduct of this Nation's foreign affairs," no substantial funds were appropriated for its implementation.[76] Although deeply concerned with the financial difficulties faced by many international students, especially those from China, the Office of Education set aside a meager $15,000 to assist them. Over half of the amount, $8,000, was offered as a grant-in-aid to Chinese students in fall 1948. Administered by the China Institute in America (CIIA), a nongovernmental entity in New York City, each recipient got no more than $100.[77] The Office of Education informed Chih Meng, director of CIIA, on December 3 that it had no more funds to be used for the aid program. With 140 applications still on hand, the CIIA estimated that a total of $70,000 was needed by those students in the first half of 1949.[78]

Fully aware of the seriousness of the situation, Meng turned to the Department of State for help. Having served on the committee that administered its assistance to Chinese students in the United States during World War II, Meng had developed very close working relations with many officials and was "held in high regard" by them.[79] He informed officials from the Division of Exchange of People at a meeting on December 31, 1948, that about 2,500 Chinese students in the United States would be in need of financial aid by February 1949. Based on the estimate provided by the National Association of Foreign Student Advisors (NAFSA), $1.25 million would be needed to support those students beyond the maximum local resources and part-time employment for the next six months. Since assistance from the Chinese government was minimal and most students could not complete their education by February 1949, Meng hoped that the State Department would be able to secure funds for them.[80] Ten days later, Meng sent another letter to George Marshall, the secretary of state, asking him to "take immediate steps to extend emergency aid to Chinese students in the United States." He pointed out that the "emergency that exists today exceeds in magnitude that arose [sic] shortly after the outbreak of war in the Pacific about eight years ago."[81]

Meng's in-person presentation and persuasive pleading pushed the State Department to further its discussion with the Economic Cooperation

Administration (ECA) on possible aid to Chinese students. After meetings among State Department officials and with Meng, Francis Colligan, acting director of the Office of Educational Exchange, sent a letter on January 14 to Harland Cleveland, director of its China Program, telling him that a great many Chinese students were already in serious need. He blamed the Chinese government for providing only $100,000 to cover transportation expenses for certain Chinese students who wanted to return to their homeland without making "any money available to relieve the needs of worthy Chinese students who have been cut off from their source of support in China." He believed that "political as well as humanitarian considerations require that a serious effort be made to furnish financial assistance for these young Chinese, many of whom will be among the leaders of their generation after their return to China." Since "the Department is quite without any means of contributing directly to the alleviation of the distress of the Chinese students," he suggested informally that the ECA "consider the feasibility of a special allocation, from its China Program funds, of $500,000 to be allocated for immediate use, with appropriate safeguards on behalf of needy Chinese students now stranded in the United States." He also informed Cleveland that the department had sent a telegram to the American embassy in Nanjing regarding the proposal and was waiting for its reaction as well as that of the Chinese government.[82]

The response from the Chinese Nationalist government came on February 12, 1949, when V. K. Wellington Koo (Gu Weijun), its ambassador to the United States, sent an official request to Paul Hoffman, administrator of the ECA. Koo asked Hoffman to transfer $500,000, part of the economic aid already appropriated by Congress for China's postwar reconstruction, to the State Department as initial funding for an emergency aid program for Chinese students.[83] Upon receiving positive reactions from the Chinese government and the ECA, the State Department took immediate steps to develop a formal policy regarding the use of federal funds in assisting destitute foreign students in general and the Chinese students in particular. Based on the joint survey conducted by the NAFSA and the IIE, the State Department adopted a policy with three major components on February 24, 1949. First, the department should support the allocation of $500,000 from the ECA as requested by the Chinese government for immediate emergency aid to selected Chinese students. Second, the department should continue to actively "explore means to an effective and early solution of the recent problem," including approaching the Chinese government for more funds to help students complete their education and return to China, seeking an emergency deficiency appropriation under the Smith-Mundt Act, and receiving additional funds allocated by the ECA. Third, all funds provided by federal agencies for assisting Chinese students should be allocated to the Department of State, and, as it had done during World War II, it would transfer the funds "to competent public and/or private agencies for their direct administration under the supervision of the Department."[84] It was clear that the Department of State still wanted to find other resources for prolonged assistance to Chinese students and keep itself away from direct interaction with Chinese students by using a nongovernmental entity to administer the aid program.

The State Department took many factors into consideration in formulating the policy. William Johnstone Jr., director of the Office of Educational Exchange, listed the major ones in his memo to George Allen, assistant secretary of state for public relations, on February 28. He emphasized that the Department of State had offered assistance to Chinese students in similar situations to complete their studies in the United States during World War II and that the legal staff of the ECA had agreed that the present appropriation language was sufficient enough to permit the funds to be used to assist Chinese students working in certain scientific and technical fields. He also pointed out that the federal assistance to Chinese students would release private funds that could be used to help the remaining students who could not qualify for assistance under the ECA legislation and that it would cost the American public more in the long run if no federal assistance was provided and many Chinese students were allowed to become public charges. More important, if these Chinese students did become public charges, he argued, there might be a serious public relations reaction since ample warning had been sent to the State Department by colleges and other institutions. He reminded Allen that many congresspeople, who had received inquiries from their constituents, had already been asking his office for solutions.[85] Johnstone's memo clearly revealed that the State Department officials were concerned mostly about the legality of the emergency aid program for the destitute Chinese students and the possible public relations fallout if no assistance was offered to them.

Once the new policy regarding assistance to the Chinese students was adopted, the State Department shared it immediately with other government agencies and won quick support from them. Because of the urgent nature of the issue, the ECA was informed of the department's decision verbally on the afternoon of February 28.[86] The policy statement was also presented to the United States Advisory Commission on Educational Exchange (USACEE), which met in the same afternoon, discussing the problem of destitute students. After careful review, the commission endorsed the new policy adopted by the State Department. However, it emphasized that "no grants of Federal funds shall be made to these Chinese students which do not include travel funds for the return of the students to the country of their origin or which are not accompanied by proof that clear and dependable arrangements will be made for their return."[87] The special emphasis included in the USACEE endorsement demonstrated clearly that it wanted to achieve two goals with the emergency aid program. These two goals ostensibly mirrored the two pillars of U.S. government policy toward Chinese students and educational exchange with China set at the beginning of the twentieth century. One was to help as many Chinese students complete their education in the United States as possible. The other was to make sure that they would all return to China after graduating.

Through candid and detailed discussions, the State Department and the ECA worked out an operational plan to achieve those two goals. Since the appropriation for the new emergency aid program was from the China Aid Act of 1948, the ECA insisted that the original intent of the law be closely followed, and the State Department agreed with it completely.[88] In a joint press release issued on March 30, 1949, the two agencies made it clear that the emergency aid program was "designed to enable qualified Chinese students to achieve immediate professional objectives in certain scientific and technical fields, and to enable them to return China as soon as possible to make use of the knowledge and skills acquired in the United States."[89] Concrete rules and regulations on the operation of the Emergency Aid Program were announced by the two agencies on April 7. According to the rules, all applicants had to meet six qualifications. The last one required each applicant to "sign a pledge to return to China where he can apply his skills when his education is finished."[90]

However, the State Department was soon forced to make some changes in its operation of the emergency aid program. One was to accept the recommendation from the Bureau of the Budget to administer the aid by itself because of the program's size and significance.[91] As a result, the State Department gave up its original plan to allow IIE to run the program. Instead, it set up a new Special Project Section with a staff of ten people in the Federal Programs Branch, Division of Exchange of Persons, to do the job.[92] Another was to adjust the language in the return pledge. The State Department began to realize that after Chinese Communist forces crossed the Yangtze River, the "situation in China may make it impossible for this Government to insist that Chinese nationals, students or otherwise, return immediately to that country." George Allen sent a letter to Hoffman on May 28 proposing a revision of the previous administrative decision that required immediate return of emergency aid recipients to China after reaching "an appropriate stopping place" in their education.[93] After some discussion between officials from both agencies, an agreement was reached and the revised pledge required Chinese students to "return to China as soon as practicable" after the termination of their awards.[94] While returning to China remained a key requirement for Chinese students to receive emergency aid from the U.S. government, they were given some flexibility in the timing of their return so that they would not be forced to go to Communist-controlled areas.

The Program of Emergency Aid to Chinese Students officially began when the ECA transferred the $500,000 to the Department of State on April 1, 1949. Despite the restrictive requirements, the program attracted many applicants. By May 19, 258 Chinese students were approved for the emergency aid and 205 of them, about 80 percent of the total, also received travel grants that would cover the expenses for their homebound journey.[95] On September 22, the entire sum of $500,000 was committed to assisting 613 Chinese students. A total of 311 of them had reached what the Department of States considered to be "suitable educational objectives" in the summer. The rest would receive assistance through February 1950. Among these 302 students, about 78 percent, 234 to be exact, were approved to receive travel grants. Those students who did not request travel grants claimed that their return journey would be covered by their own sponsors. By the end of the year, about a dozen students returned to China with travel grants provided by the U.S. government.[96]

Providing emergency aid to Chinese students in the United States was nothing new for Washington in the history of Sino-American educational exchange.[97] What was new about this program was that, in addition to the direct operation by the U.S. government, it required the aid recipients to pledge their return to China, offered travel grants for students to go back to their homeland, and disqualified Chinese Communists and their sympathizers from aid.[98] Alarmed at Communist activities among Chinese students in the United States, the State Department adopted a policy that from the very beginning refused funding "to applicants who are known to have undesirable political affiliation" and stated that "every effort is being made to eliminate such persons from the program."[99] In addition to asking a university representative, either the president or the international student advisor, to certify the "correctness of every application" and "consider personal qualifications" of each applicant, it required "confidential statements from three references for each applicant for assistance." Based on its own experience, the department believed that these "references are in general frank and revealing." Once all the application materials were received, the State Department would have its own Security Office check the name of each applicant against the lists of Chinese Communists provided by the Office of the National Intelligence, the Federal Bureau of Investigation (FBI), the Office of Strategic Service, and the House Un-American Activities Committee. While confident of catching any active Communists among Chinese students through comparing these lists, it also allowed a representative from the Chinese embassy to go over the applications regularly, believing that this representative would identify and report any known Communists among the applicants.[100] Although the State Department stopped opening Chinese applicants' files to Nationalist diplomats in late 1949, it continued to do everything possible to prevent Communists from taking advantage of the emergency aid program.[101]

Launching an Anticommunist Ideological Campaign

It became apparent as soon as the Emergency Aid Program started that its initial funding was too small in size and too restrictive by limiting grants only to students in technical fields. The Advisory Committee on Emergency Aid to Chinese Students (ACEACS) recommended at its first meeting held on May 13, 1949, that State Department officials "make known to legislators the critical nature of the existing situation and suggest appropriate legislation" for extra funding.[102] Accepting the committee's recommendation, Assistant Secretary Allen wrote a letter to Senator Scott Lucas confirming that the $500,000 now available for emergency aid to Chinese students was insufficient. He also pointed out that "in principle there should be no distinction as to field of study." While indicating the State Department's desire to have legislation for extra funding open to all qualified

Chinese students, he emphasized that the "procedure would involve a return to China where feasible."[103] Although legislators were divided on whether military or economic assistance should be provided to the collapsing Nationalist regime, there was strong support from both the Democratic and Republican parties for emergency aid to Chinese students in the United States. The House of Representatives voted 254 to 46 to pass House Resolution 5602 on August 1, 1949, setting aside $4 million from the remaining funds provided by the 1948 China Aid Act to continue the relief of the stranded students. Although the Senate failed to act on the bill, both houses approved a similar conference report on September 28, providing the same amount for the Emergency Aid Program.[104] The act was signed into law by President Harry S. Truman on October 6, 1949, only days after the founding of the PRC.

The new legislation not only provided badly needed financial resources to continue and expand emergency aid to Chinese students, but it also added a new dimension to its mission. Members of the House of Representatives recognized that "the immediate purpose of legislation is a humanitarian one—to provide urgently needed financial assistance to Chinese students in the United States." However, they pointed out that from the standpoint of long-range foreign policy "there is an equally compelling reason for assisting these men and women." Having had an opportunity to observe and experience the democratic way of life in the United States, these students, the lawmakers believed, "are in a unique position to exert a profound influence on the future course of their country." Fully aware of the leadership status traditionally held by scholars in Chinese society, they pointed out that "it is in the interest of the United States to assist these individuals who can play such a vital role in shaping China's future."[105] Walter Judd, a Republican representative from Minnesota, told the public that the new legislation would permit Chinese students to "become advocates of our system as opposed to the Communists."[106] It is clear that Congress wanted to use the program as a powerful instrument to counter the expanding Communist influence on Chinese communities on both sides of the Pacific. Charged with the responsibility of managing the Emergency Aid Program, the Department of State had to take action to fulfill the new mandate given by Congress.

The clearly stated desire of Congress to expand emergency aid against the backdrop of the Communist victory in China forced many officials to discuss whether and how the State Department should undertake responsibility for sending friendly Chinese students back to their homeland. Thomas Fisher, director of the newly established Special Project Section, argued that taking that responsibility "is as important if not more so than issuing the grants." He believed that the three thousand Chinese students in the United States, together with other friends already in China, "may very well be the difference between our success and failure in China ten to twenty years from now." He pointed out that about 90 percent of all the Chinese students in the United States fell into one of four categories: graduates of Christian colleges, recipients of the Nationalist government grants, employees of the Chinese government, and children of American-educated parents. Therefore, he was confident that they "not only know something of western culture, but are also friendly toward the democratic and economic framework within which our social system works." As for the best means by which the State Department could discharge such a responsibility, he recommended that the open operation should be left to university representatives, graduate deans, and the community. A department representative could attend meetings, teas, and other activities to show the government's interest in Chinese students. However, the department should stay away from the enforcement of the return pledge made by students and the "security" aspect of the program.[107]

The discussion on how to handle Chinese students in the United States gained intensity after Francis Sayre, a consultant working for Philip Jessup, the U.S. ambassador at large, circulated a letter among senior officials on October 3, two days after the establishment of the PRC. In his letter, Sayre recommended that the Department of State "should lose no time in planning and putting into operation an aggressive ideological campaign in China." Since large-scale military assistance to the Nationalist forces in China was now futile, the United States, he urged, should organize and pursue an ideological campaign "constituting a vigorous offensive for the great principles of democracy and liberal humanitarianism." His campaign comprised setting up a center to train Chinese students so that they could return to China as "cadres" in an infiltration movement; providing personal assistance to Chinese students to "remedy their pitiable economic situation"; sending American visiting professors and students to China; bringing Chinese students to the United States with funds provided by Washington; helping liberal Chinese writers publish periodicals, pamphlets, and books in Chinese; strengthening the Voice of America (VOA); and supporting and stimulating major cities in China to become centers of ideological activities. After receiving Sayre's letter, Howland Sargeant, deputy assistant secretary of public affairs, gathered the directors of related offices for a meeting on October 7 to discuss the anticommunist ideological campaign proposed by Sayre.[108]

After a candid and long discussion, a consensus emerged among midlevel State Department officials who were involved in managing the Emergency Aid Program. They all agreed that the department had the responsibility to achieve both objectives set by Congress. In addition to helping Chinese students meet their financial needs, actions should be taken by the State Department to "strengthen and encourage democratic forces in China."[109] They supported such actions because they were all well aware of the fact that the Communist press in China was "violently anti-American in its outlook" and that Chinese Communists were working hard among students in this country to win them over.[110] However, most State Department officials rejected Sayre's idea to get the State Department openly involved in any concrete activities, especially those in mainland China. Oliver J. Caldwell, director of the Federal Program Branch, disapproved Sayre's recommendations for the department to disseminate the "true facts" about Communist control of China and follow up with the students after their return to their homeland because "relations of this nature should be spontaneous and cannot be legislated."[111] Thus, Caldwell concluded that any "overt attempt on the part of the United States Government to mould or influence the thinking of Chinese students in the United States would inevitably be reported to the Peoples' Government, and, in all probability, distorted and used as a propaganda weapon." Similar rejections came from Teg Grondahl, who pointed out that distributing anticommunist materials in China "approaches a clandestine operation and might be in the province of an organization other than ours." He also believed that sending similar materials to Chinese students in the United States by the Department was troublesome because they could be automatically discounted by the recipients as propaganda.[112] Therefore, most of them agreed that "the Department can be most successful in working with Chinese students in this country if it works indirectly through appropriate private channels."[113]

While disapproving most of Sayre's action plan, the midlevel officials came up with approaches and mechanisms that would keep the ideological campaign going without the State Department's taking part in any overt activities. Grondahl advised that the approach adopted by the department be "an American one rather than an aping of communist method of intensive indoctrination." The right mechanism, he insisted, was to "get the Chinese students to identify themselves with the communities in which they are temporarily living."[114] After careful examination, Richard Cook, director of the Office of Education Exchange, concluded that "a good deal of work is actually being done in this field by private agencies and individuals." He recognized that three agencies, the NAFSA, the Committee on Friendly Relations Among Foreign Students, and the CIIA, had been "particularly active in fostering activities which tend to orient Chinese students toward American ideals." These agencies helped find homes in good American families for Chinese students, assisted them in locating jobs, and secured cooperation from local groups for them. Similar work, Cook pointed out, had also been done by churches and communities. As for the State Department, staff members of the Office of Educational Exchange had kept in touch with the situation and given "discreet advice to individuals and organizations when such advice has been sought." He acknowledged that some of the most productive activities "have in this manner received an unofficial impetus as a result of the advice thus given."[115]

The predominant view shared by most officials formed the foundation of the State Department's policy for the ideological campaign. As recommended, the department made every effort to avoid overt involvement in any activities aimed at Chinese students. At the same time, it did increase contacts with university representatives and encouraged them as well as leaders of other organizations to treat Chinese students in the friendliest manner. William C. Johnstone proposed a meeting with presidents from more than a dozen universities to solicit their views on how to deal with Chinese students so as to "strengthen and encourage democratic forces in China." He wanted to push universities and colleges to take actions in three areas. The first was to ensure that Chinese students "have ample opportunity to gain an understanding of American democratic institutions and life through visits to American communalities and homes, participation in American student activities, and close relations with faculty members." The second was to have Chinese students "join in discussion groups where the importance of free institutions, free debate and free speech is stressed." The last was to encourage "rapprochement between faculty members and American students and Chinese students who show qualities of leadership." The State Department, Johnstone recommended, might offer indirect assistance to university and college newspapers and magazines on their campuses in providing information for Chinese students that "will enable them to get a better balanced view of the situation in China than they get in the Communist press and which would provide them with the arguments with which to combat Communist philosophy."[116] The proposal from Johnstone and initiatives from his colleagues won strong support from the State Department.

The need for the anticommunist ideological campaign was reinforced with the increase of activities and influence of Chinese Communists in the United States. The State Department received an FBI report in November 1949 on its investigation of the Chinese Students Christian Association in North America (CSCA), one of the most popular organizations among the Chinese students with more than nine hundred members. The FBI concluded that Mrs. Siu May Ting, the CSCA's new general secretary, was "openly pro-Communist" and "very active in establishing a Communist tinge at the CSCA conference" held at Camp Ockanickon, Medford Lake, New Jersey, in June 1949. Chinese students attending the conference, according to the FBI, on the whole "seemed willing and even eager to cooperate with the Chinese Communists."[117] Although Thomas Fisher did not agree that all 126 Chinese students attending the conference were Communists or Communist sympathizers, the State Department did nothing to stop the FBI from declaring CSCA and the Association of Chinese Science Workers (ACSW), another popular Chinese student organization, as pro-Communist subversive groups (figure 1.1). This forced the ACSW to dissolve in September 1950 and the CSCA in early summer 1951.[118]

The FBI's assessment of the ties between these two organizations and the CCP was rather accurate. Having had some of its members studying and working in the United States as early as 1927, the CCP sent more members to America during and after World War II. Following the rules of the Communist International, all CCP members in the United States were organized as the Chinese Bureau of the Communist Party of the United States of America (CPUSA). Although the CPUSA was a legal political party in the United States, the Chinese Communists were instructed to keep their membership secret. The CCP was able to directly contact and control its members in the United States after the Communist International was dissolved in 1943. Under the instruction of Dong Biwu, who represented the CCP at the UN Conference on International Organizations in San Francisco in 1945, a leading group headed by Xu Yongying was established to guide CCP activities in the United States. Their major tasks

Figure 1.1 Attendees at the Annual Conference of the Association of Chinese Science Workers in Chicago in 1950.
Source: Chinese People's Political Consultative Conference, Beijing, China.

included continuing the propaganda work among Chinese Americans, publishing the *China Daily News* (*Huaqiao Ribao*), managing CCP members coming to the United States, and translating Mao's writings and CCPCC's documents.[119] Members of the CCP's leading group, including Pu Shouchang and Xu Min, had actively participated in CSCA activities since the mid-1940s. Through publishing CSCA newsletters, giving speeches at CSCA summer camps, and organizing discussion sessions they attacked the Nationalist government and encouraged students to return to parts of China under the CCP's control. Some CCP members, including Tu Guangzhi and Hou Xianglin, were elected CSCA officials.[120] After the arrest of Huang Baotong, a CSCA member and former leader of ACSW's New York branch, for overstaying his visa in the spring of 1951, the CSCA leadership decided to stop its activities to ensure the safety of its leaders and members.[121]

The intensified Chinese Communist propaganda attack on the United States after the formation of the Sino-Soviet alliance and the outbreak of the Korean War gave further impetus to the State Department's ideological campaign. Many department officials were deeply disturbed after *People's Daily* reported that thirty American-trained students attended a meeting held at the Yale Nursing School in Changsha, Hunan Province, on July 23, speaking one after another about the "pretentious democratic and charitable activities in the United States." They told the audience that "the colored people in the United States are greatly oppressed and discriminated." They also revealed that since many American soldiers were lured into service with the beauty of the places where they would go and the pretty girls there, they, these students claimed, "suffered from shellshock during the war." They all agreed that "American imperialism was outwardly strong but inwardly weak" and that it was "not to be at all feared."[122] Reports like this forced those officials to think harder about what could be done in the United States to counter Chinese Communist propaganda. Thomas Fisher believed that the State Department had been "at least remiss in not giving more time and attention" to Communism among Chinese grantees. He recommended that the Department pay to place some of the five hundred mature and advanced Chinese scholars in the United States in at least twenty-five universities to educate and direct young grantees.[123]

Through a new round of discussion, the predominant view reached by State Department officials earlier in the year was solidified. Johnstone reaffirmed that it was the State Department's responsibility to strengthen democratic forces in China by encouraging friendly feelings toward the United States and promoting fuller understanding of democratic principles and practices among Chinese grantees. However, he insisted that direct propaganda run by the State Department and special summer centers would not work well. Instead, he recommended two existing programs. One was the "big-brother" program on some campuses that assigned an American student to a foreign student, proving highly successful in breaking down social barriers. The other was a program started in Mt. Vernon, New York, that organized families to adopt individual Chinese students, offer them financial assistance through job placements, and draw them into close contact with American life. He held onto his belief that whether Chinese students would have favorable attitudes toward the United States depended primarily upon the local and intellectual climate. What the State Department should do, he concluded, was to find means to bring it to the attention of community and academic leaders.[124]

Encouraged by the U.S. government, more American organizations, communities, and individuals reached out to Chinese students. While appreciating the emergency aid offered to Chinese students, the CIIA urged the State Department to find ways to assist those who did not receive government grants and who had completed their educational programs so that "they may not become factors of ill-will."[125] Besides its advice to the State

Department, the CIIA sent its staff members to visit students at numerous universities, provided counseling to them through the mail, and raised funds for emergency medical care for students in need. Taking advantage of its contacts with many American industries, businesses, and communities throughout the country, the CIIA started to offer placement service for Chinese students in 1950. With grants from the United Board of Christian Colleges in China and the National Council of the Churches of Christ of the United States of America, the CIIA established its Department of Placement in July 1951. By early 1953, the department accepted more than two thousand registrations, interviewed about two thousand individuals, made more than forty-four hundred job referrals, and placed about seven hundred applicants. Working with the Tsinghua Teaching and Research Fellowship Program established by Y. C. Mei, the CIIA helped three Chinese scholars receive appointments at American colleges and offered research fellowships to six scholars by March 1953. The goal, as CIIA Director Chih Meng pointed out, was to "conserve this group of highly trained Chinese scholars as a reservoir of democratic leadership for the Free China of tomorrow."[126]

Similar efforts were made by other American institutions and organizations, with profound impact on Chinese students in the United States. According to a study of Chinese students conducted in fall 1953, all but three of the 107 Chinese students participating in the research were members of at least one community group such as a church, professional society, Chinese student and alumni service organization, social club, Young Men's Christian Association branch, and the like. About 88 percent of the students participating in the survey had been guests in American homes and about 59 percent of them had lived with American families. The vast majority of them believed that the American people in the communities where they lived were either very friendly or friendly toward them.[127] It is clear that Chinese students were not only the recipients of generous financial assistance from the U.S. government but also the main targets of the covert ideological campaign launched by the State Department. Although almost all State Department officials agreed that it was their responsibility to fight the Chinese Communist influence on both sides of the Pacific with the Emergency Aid Program, they committed to winning the hearts and minds of Chinese students and scholars through providing generous assistance, adjusting the immigration regulations, and increasing their exposure to local communities and families.

While organizing the ideological campaign behind the scenes, many State Department officials began to see the need to revise the policy toward Chinese students in the United States. Besides increasing public criticism and the difficulties in forcing the Chinese students back to China, the signing of the Sino-Soviet Treaty of Friendship, Alliance and Mutual Assistance on February 14, 1950, and the ejection of American diplomats from their Beijing offices soon after added urgency to the matter. In his speech delivered on March 15, 1950, Secretary of State Dean Atchison blamed the Communist regime for forcing American diplomats out of China, exposed the unequal nature of the new Sino-Soviet treaty, vowed to maintain the friends of the Chinese people, and warned them against the danger that would be caused by the aggressive and subversive adventures led by their new rulers beyond their borders.[128] A couple of weeks after Atchison's speech, John Byers, based on discussions among the officials involved in the Emergency Aid Program, recommended that policy changes be included in the proposed legislation that would provide extra funding for the program. He emphasized that the program "can no longer be considered one of educational relief to stranded Chinese students." Instead, it "should be considered as a program designed to salvage certain intangible values in terms of human relationships in China and in neighboring areas of the Far East." The program should be designed, he insisted, to serve the national interest and provide "in the event of war, a group of highly trained Chinese students available for various services in the Far East." In accordance with the new nature and function of the emergency aid program, he wanted the new legislation to extend visas for all academic persons of Chinese nationality, waive legal restrictions prohibiting them from gainful employment, and eliminate taxes on scholarships and funds received by Chinese students under $1,500.[129]

Byers' recommendations received strong support from other officials and quick approval from the State Department. Senior officials started to share the department's new position with other government agencies and lawmakers immediately. In his letter to Frederick Lawton, director of the Bureau of the Budget, Assistant Secretary of State Jack McFall reiterated the State Department's desire that "provision be made in behalf of Chinese academic personnel, now in the United States and liable to deportation," so that they would not be forced to return to China and "place their skills at the disposal of the present Chinese Communist regime." He further confirmed that the department "is of the opinion that it would be prejudicial to the interest of the United States either to oblige such persons to serve that regime against their wishes, or to prevent them from support [sic] themselves within the United States," especially when employment was available to them.[130]

Through close collaboration with lawmakers, the State Department was able to have all its major recommendations incorporated in the China Area Aid Act of 1950. Signed into law by President Truman on June 5, 1950, three weeks before the United States entered the war in Korea, the new legislation authorized another $6 million to support the Emergency Aid Program. Like its predecessor, the new law authorized the secretary of state to use the funds to cover "tuitions, subsistence, transportation, and emergency medical care" for grant recipients. Unlike the previous law, the new legislation provided assistance for the first time to Chinese scholars teaching or researching in the United States. It also permitted the State Department to use part of the fund to bring Chinese students and scholars stranded in Hong Kong and other nations to the United States. By summer 1950, more than three thousand Chinese students and scholars received emergency aid from the U.S. government.[131] More important, the new law included an instruction to the attorney general directing him to "promulgate regulations providing that such selected citizens of China who have been admitted for the purpose of study in the U.S., shall be granted permission to accept employment upon application filed with the Commissioner of Immigration and Naturalization."[132] By including such an instruction in the new law, Congress clearly revealed its intention to adjust the existing immigration policy to make extended stay in the United States a legal option for the Chinese students. Once implemented, it would add a new weapon to the arsenal for the anticommunist ideological campaign against the Chinese and turn the Emergency Aid Program into an instrument in keeping a large number of American-trained talents from returning to their homeland and serving the Communist regime.

CHAPTER II

Cutting All Ties

The outbreak of the Korean War, especially the entrance of the Chinese People's Volunteer Army (CPVA) into the conflict in October 1950, drastically heightened the confrontation between the PRC and the United States on the military as well as cultural fronts. In addition to sending the Seventh Fleet to the Taiwan Strait and resuming military aid to the Nationalist regime in Taiwan, Washington suspended the transfer of funds from the United States to mainland China, effectively cutting off subsidies for Christian colleges and other American cultural, educational, and religious institutions there. Later, it also banned American citizens from traveling to Communist China and prohibited some Chinese students and scholars specializing in science and technology from returning to their homeland. The CCP started a carefully planned nationwide political campaign aimed at eradicating loving-America, worshiping-America, and fearing-America sentiments among the Chinese people immediately after the CPVA launched its first attacks on American forces in North Korea. Taking advantage of Washington's decision to freeze all Chinese assets in the United States and ban the transfer of funds to mainland China, Beijing immediately nationalized all American-subsidized cultural, medical, relief, and religious institutions; dismantled all Christian colleges; banned American movies, radio, and other cultural presence; and established tight control over all cultural and educational institutions in mainland China. By taking these measures, the two governments reversed their role from facilitator to exterminator in U.S.-China cultural relations, striving to cut all cultural ties between the two nations.

The termination of cultural ties between the two nations and the obliteration of the American cultural presence in China, besides reversing the historical trend of constant expansion of cultural exchange between the two nations, shaped the Cold War experience for Americans as well as the Chinese people. By launching a nationwide anti-American movement the CCP was able not only to mobilize the Chinese people to support its war effort against the United States in Korea but also to impose thought reform on them, especially the intellectuals, bring fundamental changes to the Chinese educational system, and establish its complete control over all cultural, educational, and religious institutions in China. While unable to help Kim Il-sung unify Korea or drive the American forces out of the Korean Peninsula when the armistice was signed in July 1953, Beijing did manage to eliminate the American cultural presence in China, alter China's educational system, and change the orientation of Chinese culture. The fundamental changes brought by the Communist regime to Chinese culture, especially its subjugation to the state, and to Sino-American cultural relations within such a short period of time was made possible largely because of its effective exploitation of the surging nationalist spirit during the Korean War, its ruthless exertion of state power, and its skillful utilization of various mass movements aimed at humiliating and remolding Chinese intellectuals. The patterns established by both sides in fighting their enemy on the cultural front in the early 1950s would be followed in the coming years and decades.

Stopping Cultural Aggression

The prediction made by Yenching faculty members about the future of their institution was soon proved too optimistic. The fate of American-subsidized cultural, educational, medical, and philanthropic institutions in China began to take a sharp turn as Mao decided to send the CPVA to face the United Nations forces led by the United States in Korea in early October 1950. Beijing's decision to enter the war was made after long and heated debates among top CCP leaders, with Mao overruling the initial majority objection. It was relatively easy for Mao to get support from his comrades since they had developed a tradition in the past decade or so to allow him to make strategic decisions even if they overrode the majority opinion. However, Mao and his comrades were fully aware that it would be much more difficult to convince the Chinese people, especially those intellectuals who had lived under the Nationalist regime for a long time and those who had received educations in missionary schools in China and at colleges in the United States. Many feared American military and economic might, wondering whether it was the right decision for China to confront the United States militarily in Korea right after so many years of war in their own country and before the economy had recovered.[1] Some, with deep understanding of American history and politics, even doubted that the war in Korea was started by the United States or that Washington planned to invade China, as CCP leaders asserted. Therefore, Mao and his comrades believed that it was essential to find a way to get rid of all those doubts and erase the positive feelings shared by many Chinese toward the United States if they wanted to win the war.

While actively preparing for military actions in Korea, CCP leaders took steps to attack Washington's mistreatment of Chinese students in the United States and plan a national movement to eradicate American cultural influence in China. The detention and arrest of a few Chinese students and scholars in the United States or on their way home offered Beijing a good opportunity to launch attacks on Washington on the cultural front. Although most Chinese students who wanted to return to China were able to do so without any problem even after the war broke out in Korea, a handful of them began to experience delay in their homeward journey and some were even detained in fall 1950. Qian Xuesen (Tsien Hshue-shen), a leading scholar in jet propulsion at the California Institute of Technology (CIT), decided to go back to China after he was investigated by the FBI on his involvement with the CPUSA in the early 1940s and lost his security clearance in mid-1950 largely because of the ongoing investigation. After further consultation with his friends and colleagues, he changed his mind and canceled his flight to China, but not before packers had found "suspicious" materials in his luggage and sent them to law enforcement agencies. Qian, with help from his colleagues at CIT and his lawyer, was able to clear all charges against him of stealing government secrets. However, he was still arrested on September 6 for lying about his CPUSA membership when reentering into the United States in 1947, a violation of the new Subversive Control Act of 1950. The Immigration and Naturalization Services (INS) wanted to deport Qian as required by the immigration law.

Instead of accepting the deportation, Qian mounted a legal battle in the United States to clear his name. As a result, Iris Chang pointed out, Qian, who had tried desperately months earlier to leave the United States, "was now fighting for the privilege to stay."[2] On September 12, 1950, only days after Qian's arrest, three Chinese scholars, Zhao Zhongyao, Shen Shanjong, and Luo Shijun, were detained in Japan on their way back to China, accused of stealing American defense secrets.[3]

These cases caught immediate attention from the Ministry of Foreign Affairs (MFA) directly under Premier Zhou Enlai. Based on the information gathered from recent returnees, Ling Qing, head of the American and Australian Affairs Division, concluded in his October 5 report that it might not be appropriate for the MFA to issue an official statement denouncing the U.S. government for mistreating Chinese students, since the detained scholars had all been accused of taking secret government documents.[4] He was also concerned that a government statement might threaten the safety of these detained Chinese scholars and worsen their cases. Sharing Ling's concern, Ke Bainian of the American and Australian Affairs Division ordered a letter to be sent to the Chinese Academy of Science (CAS), which had employed a large number of returned scholars and supervised all science-related organizations. In its letter of October 9, the MFA made it clear that while it was inappropriate for the PRC government to issue an official statement, it was necessary for civil societies and nongovernmental institutions to promulgate public denouncements and protests.[5] Following the MFA's instruction, the Chinese National Council of Professional Associations of Natural Science sent protest telegrams to the United Nations, the World Association of Scientists, and President Harry Truman on October 17.[6] Simultaneously, more than 180 Chinese students who had recently returned from the United States also telegraphed the UN and Secretary of State Dean Acheson to express their anger. They denounced the U.S. government for preventing Chinese students and scholars from returning to their homeland and violating the human rights promoted by the UN.[7]

Although the protest against the detention of Chinese students and scholars was strong, it was not enough to justify a war with the United States. CCP leaders had to make the Chinese people believe that the United States was the chief enemy of the whole nation before they could have their full backing in the war. In order to achieve that goal, Zhou met with Guo Moruo, Ma Xulun, Zhang Bojun, and Wang Kunlun, all leading non-Communist intellectuals working in the new coalition government on October 21 and 23. He shared with them CCP leaders' decision to assist North Korea in its war against the United States, discussed all the issues related to launching the Resist America and Aid Korea (KangMei YuanChao) movement, listened to their concerns, answered their questions, and asked them to help explain the CCP's decision to other noncommunist friends.[8] On October 24, Zhou delivered a speech at the first meeting of the Standing Committee of the Chinese People's Political Consultative Conference (CPPCC), making the first public appeal to the noncommunist intellectuals for their support for the Resist America and Aid Korea campaign. He justified the CCP's decision by accusing the United States of following the old path taken by the Japanese since the mid-1890s in invading China: occupying Korea first and then taking over the Northeast (Manchuria). While it took Japan more than forty years to get to China proper, it would take the United States, Zhou warned, four or five years to accomplish the same. In addition to setting "the fire of war in front of our door," the United States, Zhou pointed out, had also drawn its defense line along the Taiwan Strait. By sending its Seventh Fleet there, the United States clearly showed its hostility toward China. Thus, it was necessary for the PRC, Zhou concluded, to send troops to Korea to stop the American aggressors.[9]

Only hours after Zhou's speech at the CPPCC, the CPVA launched its first attack on American and South Korean forces in North Korea, marking China's official entrance in the war. While carefully planning military maneuvers in Korea, CCP leaders instructed the Propaganda Department of the CCPCC to draft a directive for a nationwide propaganda campaign on current affairs. After receiving revisions and approvals from Mao as well as Zhou, the CCPCC issued the directive on October 26, 1950.[10] It required the immediate start of a nationwide propaganda movement aimed at "making our people understand the current situation, establishing confidence in victory, and breaking the fearing-America mentality." Such a movement, the directive asserted, was necessary because the U.S. Army had expanded its aggression in Korea and invaded Taiwan, seriously threatening China's security.[11]

The movement was designed to make the Chinese people understand why the PRC could not ignore the expansion of the American invasion in Korea. Its ultimate goal was to "completely destroy the reactionary loving-America thinking and the erroneous fearing-America mentality so that an attitude characterized by hating, contemning, and despising American imperialism can prevail." In order to achieve this goal, it set out to clearly show that the United States was the enemy of China as well as the whole world, and at the same time a paper tiger. The directive listed sixteen past and current American aggressions against China to prove that the United States was the enemy of China and enumerated various crimes committed by the Americans, characterizing the United States as the enemy of world peace, democracy, and culture. The directive also required that internal discussions (*neibu taolun*), the main method of the campaign, start from Korean issues and then move on to denounce loving-America and fearing-America sentiments, with individuals encouraged to have free debates to completely resolve their "thought problems."[12]

Following the CCPCC's instruction, all provinces and cities immediately launched the fiercest and best-organized anti-American movement in modern Chinese history. The intellectuals, especially those who had received education in American schools either in the United States or in China, became obvious targets of the new national campaign. They were among the first to make public statements to support the Resist America and Aid Korea movement and denounce the American military invasion in Korea and cultural encroachment on China. On November 1, 1950, more than 370 teachers at Peking University, many educated at missionary schools in China or colleges in the United States, sent a letter to Mao Zedong denouncing American aggression. They also expressed support for Zhou Enlai's public statement that China could not ignore the open invasion of its neighbor. In the end, they pledged their complete trust in Mao and promised to make their greatest effort to defend their motherland.[13] On November 4, several Yenching professors published statements to express their "boundless anger" toward the American imperialists' expansion of the war. One of them was Yan Jingyao, chairman of the Political Science Department, who graduated from Yenching in 1929 and earned his doctorate from the University of Chicago in 1934. He accused the American imperialists of stabbing China with three knives: one striking Taiwan, another Korea and China's Northeast, and the last Vietnam. In order to stop American aggression, the Chinese people, Yan appealed, should wholeheartedly support the government's policy and follow the CCP and the people's leader, Chairman Mao.[14]

Besides public denouncements, various concrete actions were taken to support the Communist government and reject American cultural influence. On November 7, members of four units of the Shanghai Filmmakers Union held a forum to show their support for the ban on American movies in the city imposed the day before. They argued that the Americans poisoned the Chinese people with two or three dozen movies a year, making it difficult to show Chinese or Soviet films. In the past five years, American companies made more than $56 million with their movies in the city of Shanghai alone. That amount, they calculated, would be enough to make 2,800 Chinese films. In addition to their support for the ban of American movies, they vowed to cooperate with the Resist America and Aid Korea movement and start a patriotic contest to make progressive movies. Part of their plan was to make short anti-American films to expose crimes committed by Americans.[15] On November 14, forty movie theaters stopped showing American movies.[16] Having already done the same in late February as a response to the bombing of coastal cities by the U.S. Air Force, the leaders of cinema industry in Beijing held a meeting on November 24 and passed a resolution reiterating their determination to continue the ban on American movies and increase showings of Chinese and Soviet films.[17] By the end of the year, American movies were completely expelled from Chinese cinemas.[18]

The Voice of America (VOA), a radio network operated by the U.S. government, was another target in the movement. At a meeting held on November 21 to celebrate the success of the first two weeks of the propaganda movement at Beijing Normal University, the Biology Department initiated a campaign to stop listening to the VOA and collected signatures among union members to support its proposal. At Peking University, on November 23, all 961 faculty and staff members signed a convention refusing to listen to the VOA and issued a statement to call on the people of the nation to do the same. They opened their statement by telling the Chinese people that "the American imperialists used the vicious and shameless VOA to spread rumors and twist information, attempting to numb our mind in addition to military invasion." They urged that while the CPVA was heroically fighting the American imperialist robbers in Korea, people should voluntarily refuse to listen to the VOA so as to destroy imperialist ideological aggression. They published their convention so that it could be used by others throughout the nation.[19] On the same day, more than fifty faculty members at Fu Jen University held a meeting and agreed unanimously to sign a statement to urge the government to ban listening to the VOA.[20] Their statement was published in the *Guangming Daily* two days later.[21]

Focusing sharply on mobilizing the Chinese in the early stage of the movement, the CCPCC directive did not mention American-subsidized cultural, educational, medical, or philanthropic institutions in China. As late as October 28, Zhou assured Lu Zhiwei that Yenching University could continue to accept subsidies from the United States. He justified the decision by allegedly saying, "water from a robber's spring can be used for irrigation."[22] However, Beijing soon changed its position as the anti-American movement was pushed forward rapidly and the confrontation between the United States and PRC on the cultural front intensified. While happy with the quick rise of the anti-American tide in schools and factories, the Party Committee of Beijing reported that strong worshiping-America and fearing-America sentiments continued to exist among some professors, capitalists, Christians, and missionary school students. One female student at Yenching University, it cited, openly stated that she could not hate the United States no matter how hard she tried. Thus, it concluded, greater effort had to be made to cleanse such pro-American sentiments. On November 5, the committee established a headquarters to better guide the movement locally.[23]

Besides resistance from faculty and students at the missionary colleges in China, a speech before the Security Council made by Warren Austin, U.S. ambassador to the United States, pushed the confrontation between the United States and China to the forefront. After PRC representative Wu Xiuquan attacked American aggression in his speech at the UN on November 28, Austin spoke to repudiate Wu's points by laying out the facts of "the long and close friendship" between the two peoples. He listed John Hay's Open Door Notes, Washington's opposition to Japan's Twenty-One Demands, and its assistance in China's rise to the status of a great power in World War II to prove that the "preservation of China's territorial and administrative entity has been a major tenet of American policy ever since relations were first established between the two Governments in 1844." He also reminded the audience of American economic aid by noting that the United States sent about $1.7 billion to China since 1937 beyond lend-lease and military assistance. The greatest emphasis, however, was put by Austin on the close cultural relations developed between the two nations in the preceding 150 years, observing that Americans had been supporting 203 hospitals, 82 nursing schools, a number of other medical institutions, and 320 orphanages in China. He also pointed out that one-eighth of all college graduates in China had received their educations at one of the thirteen colleges established by American Protestant missions. He proudly named all those colleges and their location to show "how they are spread out over the Flowery Kingdom." Some other outstanding American-endowed colleges, including the Union Medical College, Fu Jen University, and Qinghua University in Beijing, Yale-in-China in Changsha, and the Nankai University of Economics in Tianjin, were also mentioned. After listing all these educational institutions, Austin concluded that "they are not evidence of a bloodthirsty aggressor."[24]

Austin's goal was to fill what he called "a gaping void between the facts as seen by most of the world and the facts as claimed by the authorities of Peiping." However, the detailed facts listed in his speech aroused unprecedented attacks from Beijing on American cultural and educational activities in China. The earliest responses came from Chinese educators working at missionary colleges in China. William P. Fenn, associate executive secretary of the United Board for Christian Colleges in China (UBCCC), sent a letter to Austin on December 8, sharing a telegram from Wu Yifang, president of Ginling College, and Li Fang-hsuen, the acting president of University of Nanking. They informed the UBCCC that "our faculties and staffs protest Austin citing Chinese Christian Colleges in political speech [at the] Security Council [on] November 28." Fenn believed that the message from these leading educators was not a repudiation of American ties or denial of the fact that the Christian colleges were expressions of American friendship. Rather, what they objected to was the inclusion of their institutions in "what is considered a 'political' speech." Fenn explained that in view of the Communist suspicion of all American-supported institutions as 'tools of Capitalist imperialism," one should not be surprised at such sensitivities. Fenn personally doubted the "wisdom of detailing publicly all we have done for China." His reasoning was that "our friends know; the Communists are not moved by sentiment."[25]

The Chinese Christian educators' concerns were soon proved well founded. While continuing to denounce American armed invasions in Taiwan and Korea, Beijing, taking advantage of Austin's speech at the Security Council, immediately shifted the focus of the propaganda movement from supporting the war effort in Korea to stopping the so-called American cultural aggression in China. On December 10, eight missionary middle schools in Beijing held a rally to protest Austin's speech at the UN.[26] On the same day, a professor from Yenching University testified at a rally that the purpose for American imperialists to establish schools in China was cultural aggression.[27] Seizing the opportunity offered by Austin's speech, Chinese Christians intensified their push for self-government, self-support, and self-proselytization. Started at the beginning of the Korean

War, the movement was aimed at eradicating imperialist influence on the Christian church in China and enhancing patriotic spirit among Chinese Christians. Mao instructed CCP officials to give support to the Three-Self Movement (Sanzi Yundong) as early as July 19, 1950.[28] With approval from top CCP leaders, the Three-Self Declaration written by Wu Yaozong was published by *People's Daily* on September 12. On October 21, Mao ordered that another article written by Wu on how to further reform the Christian church be broadcast on state radio.[29] Soon a national movement was started to collect signatures to support the new reformation declaration. Now with a new focus on terminating religious ties with imperialist countries, more than 27,000 people signed the Three-Self Declaration by December 12.[30] On December 13, Christian organizations, missionary schools and hospitals, and students returned from the United Sates organized a demonstration in Beijing, protesting the "shameless lies" made by Austin in his speech and exposing the crimes committed by American imperialists in their cultural aggression in China. *Guangming Daily* published a commentary on December 20 to praise the patriotic action and called on Christians throughout the nation to do the same.[31]

In addition to the demonstrations and declarations, many articles were written to repudiate Austin's claim of American friendship with the Chinese. One of them was written by Wei Zichu and published in the *Guangming Daily* on December 25. Under the title "American Imperialist Religious and Cultural Aggression in China," Wei provided a long survey of American religious, educational, medical enterprises in China. He pointed out that the American missionaries had close ties with Washington and committed to spreading the frivolous American bourgeois lifestyle rather than honest proselytization. He also denounced missionary schools for transplanting American curriculum to China and training compatriots who at the end were more suitable to work for American companies and the Nationalist reactionary institutions.[32]

Having taken mostly the form of moral denunciation until the end of December, the campaign against American cultural aggression made a sharp turn after Washington decided to impose harsher commercial and financial sanctions against the PRC. Washington's decision was made over objections from the State Department. Once the war started in Korea, Washington immediately imposed an embargo on all exports to North Korea and persuaded American companies and European allies to stop shipping oil products to the PRC.[33] The limited restriction on trade with

China was challenged when the CPVA entered the war in Korea on October 25, 1950. Despite strong demands from the Department of Defense and the Treasury, the State Department opposed unilateral embargo, since it would alienate allies and have no positive effect on the existing licensing system. It was also concerned that such an action would place "in *acute* jeopardy the safety of the American missionaries in China which are virtually the last and only foothold which the United States retains in China."[34] The State Department gave up its position only when the Joint Chiefs of Staff openly stated that they, "from the military point of view, do not concur in the recommendation by the Department of State." They unequivocally believed that the "policy proposed by the Department of State will not serve United States security interests and is incompatible with the present United States military effort." Thus they demanded "at once full unilateral trade embargo, together with financial freezing measures against Communist China."[35] Dean Acheson reluctantly backed down and joined the treasury secretary in issuing an order on December 16 to impose the blockade, freeze Chinese assets in the United States, and make it unlawful to send money to mainland China without a license.[36]

These tougher sanctions brought sharp criticism from Christian educators in China. Fenn sent a letter to Dean Rusk, the assistant secretary of state, stating that the Treasury Department's regulation governing the transmission of funds to Communist China had immediate and serious impact on the work of the UBCCC. He reported that no funds had been transferred since December 17 to twelve Christian colleges in China. Although these colleges might be able to survive the semester, Fenn warned, they would have trouble continuing in the next semester "without the financial support that has in the past assured their independence." He predicted that they would most likely end up like Fu Jen when American aid was withdrawn. Therefore, the UBCCC wished to explore the possibility of securing a license from the government that would permit it to continue financial aid "because of values and gains that cannot be measured by ordinary standards of immediate military, political, and commercial gain and loss."[37] In his reply, Rusk told Fenn that the State Department was conscious of the impact of the Treasury Department's order on the UBCCC and other similar American institutions engaged in philanthropic activities in China. He let Fenn know that the Treasury and State Department were giving urgent consideration to the problems of how "the historic interest of this country in preserving the values which those institutions represent can be reconciled" under present circumstances. He thus advised Fenn to send a letter to the Treasury Department to express UBCCC's concern.[38] UBCCC followed Rusk's advice and requested of Treasury a license for transferring funds to China.

The countermeasures from Beijing were swift and resolute. On December 28, Premier Zhou Enlai issued a brief order to immediately put all American government and company assets in China under the control of the Chinese government and freeze the deposits of the U.S. government and private citizens in all Chinese banks.[39] At the meeting of the Executive Council held the next day, Zhou was rather happy to tell the officials that "we have estimated that it would take us three to four years to drive the remnant American imperialist forces completely out of China." However, the U.S. government's freeze of Chinese assets, Zhou continued, "has given us such a great opportunity that we can drive the remnant American imperialist forces completely out of China earlier." The order he had issued the day before, Zhou pointed out, was thus a heavy blow to American imperialism.[40]

It was at the same meeting that Vice Premier Guo Moruo laid out the plan and policy for taking over American-subsidized cultural, educational, and relief institutions. Guo pointed out that the American imperialists, besides committing political, economic, and armed aggression, had especially focused on cultural aggression for a very long time. This, Guo claimed, was done through subsidizing religious, educational, cultural, and medical institutions and publication, relief, and other enterprises in China. Since those entities had been used to spiritually enslave the Chinese people, he proposed that they either be taken over by the Chinese government as state enterprises or run as private enterprises completely controlled by Chinese citizens. He specifically recommended that American-subsidized relief institutions be taken over by the General Relief Association for the Chinese People and that Chinese religious organizations receiving American subsidies be operated completely by Chinese Christians.[41] Officials attending the Executive Council meeting unanimously approved the policy proposed by Guo and authorized the Cultural and Educational Commission of the Executive Council to work with other ministries in adopting necessary implementation methods to stop American imperialist cultural aggression in China completely.[42]

The Executive Council meeting also approved the Decree on the Registration of the Foreign Subsidized and Managed Cultural, Educational,

Relief Institutions and Religious Organizations, which listed seven categories of institutions and organizations that were required to register with the government. They included schools, colleges, kindergartens, hospitals, clinics, orphanages, nursing homes, newspapers, presses, bookstores, libraries, museums, research institutes, and more. All these institutions and organizations had to register not only with the administrative authorities in their trade but also with the provincial or municipal governments that had jurisdictions over their localities. In addition to closely following the Common Program and other government laws as well as orders, they were also required to report to the government their work and financial conditions every six months and inform the government before they transferred any funds or received any money from foreign countries. If any institution or organization failed to report or provide accurate information, it would be punished by the government. The notorious offenders would be taken over, reorganized, or even closed by the government. The registration period would end three months after issuance of the decree, and any institution that failed to register by that time would be punished by the local government. Most important, all these cultural, educational, relief, and religious institutions and organizations could apply to cancel their registrations once they had cut off their ties with foreign nations. The Cultural and Educational Commission was again authorized to adopt specific policies to implement the decree.[43]

The Executive Council's resolutions and decrees received strong support from American-subsidized missionary schools immediately. The Administrative Affairs Committee, the Union, and the Student Association of Yenching University held a joint forum on December 31. They issued a declaration on behalf of the faculty, staff, and students to support the recent orders and policies issued by the Executive Council. They praised the government decision to control American assets, freeze American deposits, and take over American-subsidized organizations. These measures, they believed, eradicated the bane of American imperialist cultural and economic aggression in China and brought a thorough and final end to the century-long American imperialist cultural aggression against the Chinese people.[44] On the same day, the teachers, students, staff members, and workers of the Bridgeman Middle School for Girls issued a unanimous statement to support the decisions made by the Executive Council. They accused the American imperialists of using churches and schools to poison the minds of the Chinese people so that they would forget their motherland

and serve as slaves of the United States for generations. Now they wanted to smash American cultural aggression after driving American military and political forces out of China.[45] It is worth noting that the language used in these statements was very similar to and even an exact copy of the editorial published in *People's Daily* on December 30, marking the beginning of the "unification of thoughts" (*tongyi sixiang*) among the Chinese people under the CCP.[46]

In addition to public endorsements from faculty, staff, and students at American-subsidized colleges and schools, the Chinese media offered theoretical justification for the new government policy. In an editorial published on January 5, 1951, the *Guangming Daily* emphasized that the nation was in the middle of the hard Resist America and Aid Korea struggle. In order to win that struggle so that American imperialists would never dare invade China again, national defense needed to be greatly strengthened. As national defense construction became the top priority, education should do its part to cooperate. The broadly defined national defense education, the editorial pointed out, should include the resolute eradication of remnant loving-America, worshiping-America, and fearing-America sentiments and suppressing scholarship-for-scholarship's-sake or science-for-science's-sake ideas.[47] This editorial clearly demonstrated that when the American policymakers used the trade and financial sanctions as an instrument in fighting the Korean War, the CCP leaders responded with an all-out attack on the American cultural and educational presence in China. By taking over all American-subsidized or American-managed cultural, educational, religious, and philanthropic institutions and organizations in China, Beijing was able not only to expel all American imperialist aggression forces from China and mobilize the nation to fight the American military forces in the Korean War but also to position itself to terminate all cultural ties with the United States and gain complete control over all cultural, educational, and religious institutions in the country.

Remaking the Colleges

As soon as Washington imposed financial sanctions against the PRC, Beijing first moved swiftly to force American-subsidized institutions and organizations to cut off financial as well as administrative ties with their sponsors in the United States. Then it took carefully planned steps to put them under Chinese control. Following the instruction from the Executive Council, the Ministry of Education (MOE) issued a directive on January 11, 1951, laying out guidelines and timelines for the process. It required that an investigation of all missionary schools receiving foreign subsidies in the country be conducted first and reports on colleges submitted by the end of the month. Taking over all American-subsidized schools, it projected, should be completed by the end of the year. It instructed that missionary schools that had completely or mostly depended on American subsidies be turned into state-run institutions if their funding was cut off and no private Chinese citizens volunteered to take them over. Missionary schools that depended only partially on American subsidies should become private institutions, and the government might provide appropriate subsidies if they had financial difficulties. The directive made it clear that all American board directors be fired and that no Americans be allowed to take any administrative positions at the schools. However, American teachers, except those with what the CCP deemed reactionary speeches and behaviors, were permitted to stay in their jobs. Those who did not want to stay were allowed to leave. It promised that all the Chinese presidents, teachers, staff members, and workers would keep their positions, that all schools would remain in their locations, and that no mergers of colleges or reorganization of schools or departments would take place during the process. For all American-subsidized missionary schools, the government would lend them money if their foreign funds failed to come in before the takeover was completed.[48] Three days later, the Cultural and Educational Commission of the Executive Council published specific policies for registration.[49]

With these concrete guidelines in place, the takeover of American-subsidized cultural and educational institutions formally began. The MOE held a special meeting with representatives from all foreign-subsidized colleges, except one business school in Chongqing, from January 16 to 22 to discuss the issues involved in taking over the schools. Ma Xulun, the minister of education, reassured the attendees that they should not worry about relocation, merger, or reorganization of schools or departments after the nationalization. Having gone through group discussions and one-on-one talks, the representatives worked out three types of plans for taking over American-subsidized colleges and submitted them to the Executive Council for approval. The first would take over some colleges immediately and turn them into state-run institutions. The second would allow some other

American-subsidized institutions to temporarily maintain their private college status and prepare to become state-run institutions in the future. And the third would permit the rest to continue their operations as private institutions with reorganization of the board of directors and reappointments of administrators to make sure that they were under complete Chinese control.[50]

While attending the meeting, all representatives from the American-subsidized colleges issued statements to reiterate their support for the nationalization and their denunciation of American cultural aggression. Lu Zhiwei recognized that the American imperialists were the chief bullies, and he now understood why the American-subsidized schools should be nationalized first. Huang Fu, the vice president of Huachung University, asserted that China's fight against American imperialism was not limited to the military front. Having used all missionary colleges as the stronghold of their cultural aggression, the American imperialists, Huang pointed out, were the most vicious cultural aggressors. He vowed to wage a strenuous fight against the American imperialists, completely eradicate the influence of American imperialist cultural aggression, and turn his university into a people's university.[51]

In addition to their public statements, the representatives demonstrated their support for the nationalization of the American-subsidized colleges by rejecting the resumption of financial assistance from the United States during the meeting. After earnest communication with the U.S. government, the UBCCC received the license from the Department of Treasury to transfer $75,000 a month to the PRC to support missionary colleges.[52] It immediately sent telegrams to their presidents, inviting them to meet with William Fenn in Hong Kong on February 19 to arrange the transfer of subsidies. The presidents ignored the invitation and reported it to the government.[53] By ignoring the offer from UBCCC to continue its subsidies, Yenching and other missionary colleges in China effectively cut off their financial ties with their American sponsor. What they were waiting for now was to turn over complete control of their institutions to the PRC government.

The Peking Union Medical College (PUMC) was the first American-subsidized educational institution taken over by the PRC government. As a medical school, the PUMC was taken over by the Ministry of Health. At a rally attended by many high-ranking officials and over a thousand teachers, students, staff members, and workers on January 20, 1951, He Cheng, the deputy minister of health, declared that all faculty and staff members would remain employed at their current positions with the same pay. The existing curriculum would also be maintained. He believed that the Chinese people had the ability and confidence to better manage the PUMC after ridding it of American imperialist influence. Qian Junrui, the deputy minister of education who also spoke at rally, called on all faculty members and students to completely cut off economic, political, and ideological ties with American imperialists.[54] The PUMC was chosen to be the first for nationalization partly because of its reputation and partly because of Beijing's urgent needs for high-quality medical service during the war. By the end of the 1940s, the PUMC, generously funded by the Rockefeller Foundation and closely modeled after the Johns Hopkins University Medical School, had become the best among its peers in Asia. Faced with heavy casualties suffered in the Korean War, the CCP leaders were forced to conscript the top medical experts working at the PUMC and its hospitals. As soon as it was taken over, many scientists and doctors of the PUMC were drafted to work for the Resist America and Aid Korea movement.[55]

About three weeks later, Yenching University, which had received subsidies from the UBCCC for twenty-two years, was taken over by the MOE. Lu Zhiwei announced at the rally attended by all the faculty members and students on February 12, 1951, that "from now on Yenching University is completely and will forever be the Chinese people's university in name, in fact, in funding source, and in teaching philosophy and methodology." During his speech, Lu read the second telegram from the UBCCC that it could send funds immediately to Yenching as long as it was willing to receive the transfer. Having sharply denounced the American imperialists for their cultural aggression against China, he publicly announced his decision to ignore the offer and gave the telegram to Ma Xulun. Ma, speaking after Lu, pointed out that the American imperialism, as a paper tiger, had already been poked in the Korean War. However, the remnant poison from its cultural aggression in China still needed to be completely eradicated. He hoped that faculty members and students at Yenching would work hard to complete that glorious task. He then announced that Lu was appointed president of the newly nationalized Yenching University. The MOE also sent five officials to Yenching to assist Lu in completing the turnover.[56]

Taking over the PUMC and Yenching University set examples for all other foreign- and especially American-subsidized educational institutions in China. By the end of April, all twenty foreign-subsidized colleges, with seventeen receiving subsidies from American sponsors, were taken over by the Chinese. Of the American subsidized-colleges, ten were taken over by the central government and seven were turned into private institutions with government subsidies. The PRC government put in over 62 trillion yuan to support those colleges. Among 515 foreign-subsidized middle schools, 255 received financial support from the United States. Foreign-subsidized primary schools, more than 1,100 in total, were taken over by the end of the year. The MOE proudly reported that the takeover had turned hundreds of educational institutions from instruments of imperialist cultural aggression into educational enterprises serving the Chinese people. More important, this process, the MOE claimed, greatly elevated the political consciousness of teachers, students, staff members, and workers. They now understood the significance of recovering educational sovereignty, realized the greatness of the people's motherland, cut off economic ties with the American imperialists, drew a clear ideological line against the enemy, and looked down on and hated America. Thus, the ministry concluded, taking over the American-subsidized educational institutions was a great victory for the Chinese people.[57]

While the nationalization of American-subsidized educational institutions was taking place, other American-subsidized cultural, medical, philanthropic, and religious institutions and organizations went through similar processes. On February 12, 1951, the Ministry of Health held a meeting in Beijing to take over ten additional American-subsidized hospitals and twelve hospitals receiving subsidies from other foreign nations in northern China. When the meeting came to an end on February 16, the ministry announced that five American-subsidized hospitals were taken over by the government, one was turned into a private hospital operated by Chinese, and four were owned and run jointly by the Chinese government and private citizens.[58] All other American-subsidized medical institutions were taken over by regional government offices throughout China. The Central China regional government alone took over twenty-five American-subsidized hospitals.

In order to better manage the takeover of religious organizations, the Cultural and Educational Commission of the Executive Council established the Office of Religious Affairs in February. On April 16, that office held a meeting with representatives from American-subsidized Christian organizations to work out the plan for their nationalization. At the end of the six-day meeting, the representatives unanimously approved the nationalization measures, organized the Chinese Christian Committee on Resist America and Aid Korea and the Three-Self Reform Movement, and sent a banner as well as a telegram to Mao Zedong expressing their gratitude and admiration. Eighteen representatives who spoke at the meeting denounced the American imperialists in the church and demanded harsh punishment of some Chinese Christian leaders who were accused as traitors. Having confessed that they had been poisoned and duped by the imperialists in the past, all representatives vowed to cut off ties with the American imperialists completely and permanently and establish Chinese people's own church.[59]

The Executive Council also established a special commission to manage the nationalization of American-subsidized relief institutions. The commission gathered more than a hundred representatives from national as well as regional relief institutions in Beijing for a meeting on April 26. Xie Juezai, director of the commission, pointed out in his opening speech that imperialists carried out aggression and destroyed Chinese children's lives under the guise of "relief," "charity," and "religion." Thus, this kind of "relief," Xie asserted, should be exterminated and all Chinese staff members of the existing relief institutions should be united to provide new China's own relief and welfare.[60] At the end of the meeting, the representatives agreed that national relief and welfare organizations would be reorganized or taken over by the National Association of Relief for the Chinese People (NARCP) led by Madam Song Qingling. Local relief institutions would be assisted or taken over by the NARCP local branches.[61] By the end of April, all American-subsidized educational, medical, relief, and religious institutions and organizations were taken over by the Chinese government or private entities. The century-old cultural ties between the two nations were cut off for the first time through the direct intervention of the Chinese Communist government.

For CCP leaders, nationalization of American-subsidized institutions and organizations in China was just the first step. As one of the speakers at the Yenching University rally on February 12, Qian Junrui again emphasized that nationalization meant more than cutting off financial ties with the American imperialists. Repeating the point made at the PUMC rally, Qian told his audience that it was easy to cut off economic ties with the United States. However, it would be relatively more difficult to completely break ideological ties with American imperialism. He expected everyone at Yenching University to expel American imperialist influences from their minds and lives. Yenching, he declared, would become a real people's university only after the American imperialist cultural influence was completely eradicated.[62]

Following the instructions from the MOE, Yenching and all other American-subsidized colleges immediately launched a thought-education (*sixiang jiaoyu*) movement after nationalization. While continuing to expose the crimes of the American imperialist cultural aggression, the movement put greater emphasis on self-examination and self-criticism on how each individual was influenced by the poisonous American culture.[63] Lu Zhiwei took the lead by publishing an article in the *Guangming Daily* on February 13, 1951. He first pointed out that the growth of Yenching showed a history of increasing collaboration between Leighton Stewart and reactionary forces. The most common method used in American cultural aggression, Lu now realized, was to spread the American way of life. He recognized that he failed miserably since he himself accepted it unconsciously. He also acknowledged that his earlier self-criticism was not deep enough and that he was unable to see the danger of American cultural aggression. He confessed that he could not hate American imperialism because he had never hated anyone or any class before. Thus, he denigrated himself as an individual who was politically backward and acted as "a small child in the revolutionary cause." Born in bad families, Yenching administrators and faculty members, Lu believed, would have a better understanding of the difficulty of thought reform. However, he vouched that they would have the greatest determination to eradicate American imperialist cultural aggression in China.[64] After four meetings with two to three hundreds attendants each, a university-wide meeting was held on March 8, 1951, allowing professor, students, workers to get onstage to tell the audience how American cultural aggression made them lose their love for China, indulge themselves in the decadent American way of life, and became worshipers of the United States. After tearful denouncement and self-criticism, the speakers all vowed to intensify their thought reform so that they could better serve the people.[65]

Emboldened by its successes in the Korean War as well as nationalization of American-subsidized institutions, the PRC government pushed reform of China's educational system. Beijing's first attempt to remake China's education, especially its colleges and universities, after the Soviet model began in mid-1950. Its initial effort largely failed because of strong resistance from faculty members who still preferred the America-style liberal arts education offered at comprehensive universities.[66] Hardened by the initial setback and empowered by the newly obtained control over all colleges and universities, the Executive Council adopted the Resolution on the Educational System Reform on August 10, 1951, and made it public on October 1, 1951. Comprehensive reform was needed, according to PRC leaders, because the existing educational system, adopted in 1922 after the American model, was semifeudal and semicolonial in nature. Ma Xulun pointed out that the major problems of the existing system were the absence of training schools for cadres and various remedial schools for working adults, the bilevel elementary education structure that impeded working-class children, and lack of status for technical training schools needed for national reconstruction.[67] The new educational system established by the resolution addressed those issues by making the cadre and adult training schools an integral part of the school system, replacing bilevel elementary education with a single five-year program, and sharply increasing specialized technological education at both the secondary and college levels.[68] Drawing the lesson from the setback suffered a year earlier, the Executive Council delayed issuing the resolution until existing obstacles were removed with a further step, which forced all college faculty members to participate in a new phase of thought reform beginning in fall 1951. While recognizing the enhancement of their political consciousness, the CCP believed that they retained Euro-American bourgeois ideology in their educational philosophy, research methods, and work styles, hindering the implementation of Marxism and Leninism in higher education.[69] An opportunity came when Ma Yinchu, an American-trained economist who was recently appointed president of Peking University, sent a letter to Zhou Enlai in early September. Ma invited Zhou and nine other top CCP leaders, including Mao Zedong, Liu Shaoqi, and Zhu De, to be instructors for the study movement at Peking University. While recognizing Ma's effort at the study movement and agreeing to send several officials to the university for some speeches, Mao turned down the invitation.[70] Zhou accepted it, though, and gave a long talk to more than three thousand faculty members from twenty colleges and universities in Beijing and Tianjin. In addition to faculty members from Peking University, those from Yenching University, PUMC, and several other former American-subsidized institutions were prominent among the audience. Zhou used his own experience to demonstrate the necessity for intellectuals to reform their thoughts in order to become part of the working class and acquire revolutionary views and methods.[71]

Once Zhou made such an open scrutiny of his own thought-reform process, it became difficult if not impossible for any intellectuals in the nation to find any excuse to keep themselves away from or silent in the movement. Jiang Yinen, chair of the Department of Journalism at Yenching University, was deeply ashamed after hearing Zhou's talk on thought reform. He realized that it would be impossible to become a teacher working for the people without thorough thought reform. Thus, he confessed that he worshiped American democracy as well as freedom after receiving an American imperialist education for many years and often approached many issues from a reactionary class position because of his bourgeois family. Inspired by Zhou's report, Jiang vowed to thoroughly repudiate his old thoughts and establish a correct working-class standpoint so that he could be reformed and become a teacher truly working for the people.[72]

In addition to sending Zhou out as a persuasive personal example for thought reform, Mao delivered several speeches to elevate the movement to another level in the following months. In his speech given at the CPPCC on October 23, Mao reminded the audience that he had proposed to start a self-education and self-reform movement with the use of criticism and self-criticism as its main tool in June 1950. Happy to see his proposal becoming reality, he told the audience that "thought reform, especially that for various kinds of intellectuals, is one of the key preconditions for the realization of thorough democratic reforms and gradual industrialization in our country."[73] After many rounds of revisions, Mao approved and issued the Directive from the Chinese Communist Party Central Committee on Thought Reform and Organizational Cleansing in All Schools on November 30.[74] Having pointed out that schools were important institutions to train cadres and educate the people, the directive emphasized that the Party and the people's government must work systematically to "eradicate reactionary remnants at schools and gradually put all schools under the leadership of the Party." To achieve that goal, the CCPCC required that all colleges as well as all secondary and elementary schools start planning and carrying out preliminary thought reform among all faculty members and students at high schools and colleges within a year or two. Once that was accomplished, a loyalty movement (*zhongcheng yundong*) should follow so that reactionaries among college students would be identified. Another goal for thought reform, the directive made it clear, was to prepare the schools for educational reform, including changes in school systems, curriculum, and academic as well as administrative organization.[75]

Under heavy pressure from the CCP, faculty members at colleges and universities were forced to conduct sharp self-criticism (*ziwo piping*) and receive strong criticism from their peers as well as students. Many well-known scholars were forced to publish their self-criticism in newspapers. In his self-criticism published in the *Guangming Daily* on November 17, 1951, Deng Jiadong, chair of the Department of Internal Medicine, recognized that the PUMC was a stronghold of American imperialist cultural aggression and that its faculty members were the instruments for such an aggression. Thus, both the college and the faculty members, Deng believed, had greater needs for reform. He went on to denounce the old PUMC for training its students to know the greatness of only their college and not their nation, making its educational and administrative systems meet only American needs, and designing its curriculum to produce graduates who became salespersons for loving-America and worshiping-America sentiments and the American lifestyle.[76] Similar public self-criticism was made by Deng's colleague Xu Yingkui, chair of the Neurology Department of the PUMC. Xu confessed that he chose to attend the PUMC because of his worship for America and his desire to have other people beg for his help. He exposed that the PUMC's teaching was inferior, service bad, and research useless. Thus he vowed to cut off all ideological ties with the old PUMC and make contributions to the construction of a new PUMC devoted to serving the people.[77] Most faculty members, like those at Yenching, had to go through this self-criticism and criticism process in their own departments and universities, a process known as "bathing" (*xizao*).[78] By February 23, 1952, more than 110 faculty members made public self-criticisms at Yenching. While seventy-eight received approval from students, twenty-three faced sharp rebukes and were forced to go through extra rounds of self-criticism.[79] This kind of experience was extremely humiliating to faculty members because in the context of traditional Chinese culture a teacher enjoyed the same status as a father to a student.

As soon as the thought-reform movement started, the MOE relaunched its reorganization of colleges and departments (*yuanxi tiaozheng*), first in eastern China and among engineering schools. By mid-November, all colleges and departments in eastern China had gone through the reorganization process. Based on the merger of Guanghua (Kuanghua) and Daxia universities and with the absorption of the Department of Music from the

University of Shanghai, the new East China Normal University was established in Shanghai. In Nanjing, through the merger of two former American-subsidized institutions, the University of Nanking and the Ginling University, the new National Jinling University was born. A similar action was taken in Fujian Province, the Hua Nan College, another former American-subsidized institution, was merged with a local college, becoming the new Fuzhou University.[80] Early in the month, the MOE gathered the deans of all engineering schools for a meeting in Beijing. At the end of the meeting, they worked out a reorganization plan that would turn a number of comprehensive universities such as Qinghua and Zhejiang into engineering institutes. According to the plan, some new specialized technology institutes, including Aviation Institute in Beijing, the Mining and Metallurgy Institute in Changsha, would be established. The most obvious victim of this reorganization was Yenching University. Its engineering departments would be absorbed by Qinghua, its humanities, science, and law schools would go to Peking University, and its name would be eliminated. The plan also required all engineering schools to establish a political adviser (*zhengzhi fudaoyuan*) system in charge of political studies and thought reform.[81]

Since almost all the faculty members had publicly denounced American cultural aggression and the American educational system in the thought-reform movement, the MOE had no trouble in enforcing its reorganization plan this time. Beginning in April, many universities held mass rallies to show their resolute support for the reorganization of colleges and departments. On May 19, the MOE formally announced its decision to merge most of Fu Jen University's departments with Beijing Normal University to form a new normal university. Fu Jen's facilities became the north campus, and its name was dropped.[82] Chen Yuan, president of Fu Jen, issued a statement on June 7 accepting the reorganization decision and pledging to complete the task under the leadership of Chairman Mao and the CCP.[83] Chen was appointed president of the new Beijing Normal University and remained in that position until 1971, a rare case among administrators of American-subsidized colleges. On June 29, more than seven hundred faculty members from five universities—Beijing Normal, Fujen, Qinghua, Yenching, and Peking—that would form the new Peking University held a joint rally. They passed a resolution to send a salutary telegram to Chairman Mao, pledging to strengthen their unity and implement the reorganization plan. Their pledge was delivered to Mao on July 1, 1952, as a present for the thirty-first anniversary of the CCP.[84]

By mid-September about three-quarters of colleges and universities, mostly in northern and eastern China, had completed their reorganization. The rest went through the same process in 1953 without any trouble. When the reorganization was completed at the end of 1953, the total number of higher education institutions in China was reduced from 201 to 182. While only fourteen comprehensive universities survived, the number of specialized colleges increased sharply, including thirty-nine industrial institutes, thirty-one normal colleges, twenty-nine colleges of agriculture and forestry, twenty-nine medical and pharmaceutical colleges, fifteen art institutes, eight language institutes, and five athletic institutes.[85] This reorganization of colleges and departments not only marked Beijing's adoption of the Soviet model of higher education, which emphasized specialized practical training, but also brought fundamental changes to Sino-American educational relations. It was through the reorganization that all former American-subsidized colleges, except the PUMC, were broken up in pieces and absorbed by other colleges and universities.[86] For example, Peking University, besides absorbing departments in the arts and sciences of Yenching University, relocated from its old and cramped campus in the center of the city to the beautiful and spacious Yenching campus in the northwestern suburbs. As a result, Yenching, one of the best private universities in China, quickly became a historical memory.

Most important, the reorganization made it possible for the CCP to establish absolute control over all colleges and universities in China. In addition to the harsh criticism and removal of most administrators at the former American-subsidized colleges, the university affairs council (*xiaowu weiyuanhui*), the most powerful administrative entity at Chinese colleges and universities that allowed faculty members to exert influence and control over their own institutions, was removed from the organizational chart of all colleges. Greater power was given to the president, who was appointed by the PRC government and advised if not supervised by the CCP Committee secretary. In many cases, Party secretaries held the position of president at the same time. Jiang Nanxiang, who was appointed Party committee secretary and president of Qinghua University in December 1952, was a good example. Although he had no training in engineering, Jiang was sent to lead the top engineering college in China and stayed in that position for fourteen years. Having clearly told faculty, students, and staff that he was entrusted by the CCP and the government to work at Qinghua, he emphasized that trust in the CCP's leadership and truthful implementation of all policies adopted by the CCP would guarantee the successful completion of educational reform at Qinghua.[87] As soon as the office of the president was up and running, he established the Department of Political Guidance (Zhengzhi Fudaochu), which would work among the students on behalf of the CCP.[88] With committees and branches established at all colleges and universities, the CCP gained complete control over higher education in China. The imposition of CCP control and the new Soviet educational system received little resistance from faculty and staff, partly because of lessons they learned from the thought-reform movement and partly because of their new dependence on their work units for jobs, income, housing, medical care, and other services.

Reversing the Trend

When Beijing took swift actions to take over all American-subsidized cultural institutions and eradicate American cultural influence in the PRC, the U.S. attorney general, despite clear instructions from Congress, was slow to formulate the new regulation that would permit Chinese students to seek employment after their graduation so that they did not have to return immediately to their homeland. The delay was caused mostly by the different interpretations that officials in the Department of Justice had of the new law. They believed that the legislation meant that Chinese students could be employed only during the summer. Once they graduated, the Chinese students would lose their student status and thus could not be employed according to the existing laws. The Justice Department officials were also concerned that the Chinese students might stop working and seek government assistance after receiving permission to remain in the United States.[89] With a completely different interpretation, State Department officials had to work hard to rid of what they believed to be "misinterpretations" held by their counterparts in the Department of Justice. Between June 1950 and April 1951, the State Department sent numerous inquiries to the attorney general and the Immigration and Naturalization Service (INS) commissioner.[90] Many nongovernmental organizations and individuals, including Chinese students, also sent letters to the State Department and Justice Department, demanding the immediate adoption of the new regulation as required by the recent legislation.[91]

While waiting for the new regulation to be promulgated by the attorney general, the State Department decided to modify the Emergency Aid Program as its response to "the rapidly changing international situation." After the CPVA entered the Korean War, Thomas Fisher appealed to his colleagues that Chinese students should not be encouraged to return to China to make their technical skills available to an unfriendly regime. Instead, he recommended that a "provision should be made to allow these students to remain in the United States indefinitely and thereby conserve in this country a reservoir of potential political leaders of China who may at a later date make material contributions toward the rebuilding of a regime in China friendly to the United States." Before any action was taken by the Department of Justice or Congress, the State Department decided on January 1, 1951, to eliminate the pledge imposed on Chinese students that required them to return to China.[92] As a result, Chinese students no longer had to go back to their homeland after the completion of their educational programs in the United States.

Under pressure from Congress, the Department of State, and the public, the attorney general finally announced the new immigration regulation on April 9, 1951. It provided that any citizens of China who had been admitted temporarily to the United States and selected by the secretary of state to participate in the educational and training program authorized by the China Area Aid Act of 1950 "may be permitted to accept employment in the United States during the period he is a participant in such program." It also provided that if a student who "remains in the United States after he has completed his participation in such program, he may accept employment in the United States if he makes application to the district director having jurisdiction over his place of residence for the permission to accept employment, and such application is approved." The only condition was that the student submit a report every three months to the INS district director, reporting his current address and the nature and place of his employment.[93] By allowing Chinese students to seek employment and remain in the United States after graduation, this new regulation marked the beginning of a gradual change in American policy toward Chinese students and the transformation of U.S. immigration policy into what Meredith Oyen called "a direct tool of foreign policy" in the Cold War.[94]

However, State Department officials soon realized that making employment an option for the stranded Chinese students and scholars was not enough, especially as military concerns grew with the increasingly tense situation in Korea. At the request of the Office of Chinese Affairs, representatives from different divisions met on June 12, 1951. They discussed the necessity of preventing the "return to Communist countries of aliens now in the United States who possess information or skills vital to the security of the United States." Their focus was on Chinese students, professors, researchers, and visitors because of their large number and the likeliness of their returning to China. Although all participants agreed that something must be done, they eventually decided that under the present regulations "it would be impossible to prevent any one of the Chinese student groups from returning to China."[95]

What was considered impossible by State Department officials was effected by the Department of Justice. Based on a law passed by Congress on May 22, 1918, and on Presidential Proclamation No. 2523 issued on November 14, 1941, Benjamin Habberton, acting commissioner of the INS, sent an instruction to all district directors on September 28, 1951, ordering them to prevent the departure of Chinese nationals with scientific training. That order was replaced by another letter sent by him on October 9, 1951. The revised instruction stated that "until such time as a more specific policy is formulated, this Service will endeavor to prevent the departure, for destinations in Communist-dominated countries, of Chinese nationals whose scientific education or training might be of military assistance to a potential enemy." It clarified that scientific training referred to education and training in any of the physical sciences, such as chemistry, physics, engineering, mathematics, and medicine, that "might be of value in a war effort." If a Chinese national fitting the description intended to depart for a Communist-dominated country, he "should be served immediately with a written order not to depart." The Chinese national who received such an order, according to the instructions given by Habberton, should not depart or attempt to depart from the United States until he was notified that the order had been revoked. If anyone willfully violated any of the provisions of the law, that person would be fined not more than $5,000 or imprisoned for not more than five years, or both.[96]

Permitting Chinese students to accept employment in the United States and prohibiting some from leaving the country, all within a few months, represented a complete reversal of Washington's policy. However, Washington implemented its new policy with care and discretion. On the one hand, the INS stopped forcing Chinese students to return to China and issued a permit to any Chinese student who had obtained employment after graduation. State Department officials encouraged Chinese students to stay in the United States by continuing providing emergency aid to Chinese students and assisting them in finding jobs. Taking advantage of the new American policies, most Chinese students pursued as much education as they could, making them the best-educated ethnic group in the United States. With mostly graduate education in science, engineering, technology, mathematics, and medicine, most of them had no difficulty in finding employment after completing their educational programs. He Guozhu, who obtained his PhD in physics from University of Norte Dame in 1951, received a telegram from the INS while waiting for his ticket back to China informing him that he was not allowed to leave the United States. He easily got a job in one of the physics research institutes at the University of Chicago conducting research in biological physics.[97] Li Hengde received his detention order from the INS in October 1951 while he was still working toward his PhD in physics at the University of Pennsylvania. Because of his active role in the Association of Chinese Science Workers (ACSW), he was not allowed to continue his research project sponsored by U.S. Navy. However, he was able to get financial support by taking some other research projects from R. M. Brick, his advisor at the University of Pennsylvania, until his graduation in 1953.[98]

On the other hand, Washington continued to assist Chinese students return to China even after detention orders were issued in September 1951. Besides travel grants offered by the Emergency Aid Program, the State Department kept providing other services through its Orientation and Service Center (OSC) in San Francisco. From August 1 to September 29, 1950, the OSC assisted 139 Chinese students, covering room and board or stays in a local YMCA. Twenty-six of those students departed for China on board SS *President Cleveland* on August 9.[99] A larger group, with 128 Chinese students, scholars, and their family members, sailed for Hong Kong on board SS *President Wilson* (figure 2.1) on August 27. Sixty-three of them had received services from the OSC. Deng Jiaxian (Teng Chia-Hsien), Tu Guangzhi (Tu Kuang-Chi), Tu Guangnan (Tu Kuang-Nan), Lu Shanhua (Lu Shan-Hua), and Jin Yinchang (Chin Yin-Ch'ang) were among those on the OSC list. Another thirty-five Chinese students who had received assistance from the OSC, including Chen Tianchi (Chen Tien-Chih), Wu Liangyong (Wu Lianyong), Zhang Qingnian (Chang Ching-Nien), and Ji Chaozhu (Chi Chao-Chu) departed San Francisco on SS *President Cleveland*, on September 21.[100] Deng (figure 2.2), with a PhD in physics from

Figure 2.1 Chinese students returning to their homeland on board *President Wilson*, August 31, 1950.
Source: Chinese People's Political Consultative Conference, Beijing, China.

Figure 2.2 Deng Jiaxian graduating with a doctoral degree in physics from Purdue University on August 20, 1950.
Source: Chinese Central Television, Beijing, China.

Purdue University, continued his research in nuclear physics and became the leading scientist in the development of China's atomic and hydrogen bombs. He was awarded posthumously the Two Bombs and One Satellite Meritorious Award for his contribution to China's military science in 1999.[101] Ji, an undergraduate at Harvard University, finished his college education at Qinghua University and joined the Chinese team in truce negotiations in Korea. After working as the English interpreter for Zhou and Mao, he became China's ambassador to Great Britain and undersecretary general of the United Nations.[102]

When the SS *President Cleveland* docked in Honolulu on September 25, nine Chinese students were taken away by INS officials because of their training and education in science, engineering, and medicine. After receiving clear instructions from Washington, the officials issued detention orders to Wang Liangneng and six other students, making them the first to be affected by the recent policy change. However, Wu Yi and Li Baokun, trained in biology and traffic control respectively, were allowed to resume their journey back to China.[103] The experience of Wu and Li illustrated that the INS wanted to keep only Chinese students with education and training in physical sciences, which might be of value in a war effort, from leaving. With a rather narrow interpretation of physical sciences, only a relatively small number of detention orders were issued to Chinese students. According to the State Department's record, among 434 Chinese students who applied for permission to leave the United States, about 120 were rejected by the INS and served with detention orders.[104] Li Hengde, one of the Chinese students who started an organized effort to win their rights to return to the PRC, also believed that only 120 or so Chinese students received detention orders from the INS.[105]

The door for most Chinese students and scholars to return to their homeland was kept open even after the detention policy was adopted by a confluence of different forces. The first was the strong commitment of many officials to traditional U.S. policies. As the State Department pushed for the new regulation that would allow Chinese students to accept employment and have extended stay in the United States after graduation, Oliver Clubb, chief of the Office of Chinese Affairs, reminded his colleagues that historically the U.S.-China educational exchange was conducted under two principles. One was that "the purpose and value of the training of Chinese students in this country have been the utilization in China of the knowledge and general ideas acquired in the U.S." The other was that "these students have been subject to the standard immigration laws." While recognizing that some students might fear a return to China under Communist control, he insisted that "it is our belief that the two basic points mentioned above should continue to be basic in our policy toward the Chinese students in this country." By doing so, he believed, the United States "would avoid to the extent possible the questionable procedure of bringing the students to the U.S. to be trained for (if they desired) residence in the U.S. and to assume a status which is clearly contrary to the basic intent of our immigration laws (which have prescribed quotas for those who will take up permanent residence)."[106]

The second was the limited legislative authorization. While allowing Chinese students to apply for work permits, the new regulation released by the attorney general in April 1951 clearly stated that "nothing in this part shall be construed as granting to or conferring upon the alien any other status, exemptions, or privileges under the immigration laws of the United States."[107] As a result, Chinese students had to find employment immediately after graduation and return to China if they failed get jobs since they were not allowed to change their nonimmigrant status. In response to such an intriguing situation, Fisher proposed a two-pronged strategy. On the one hand, the State Department should continue to provide a haven for those who wished to remain in the United States until such time as they might safely return to China. On the other hand, the Department should keep providing travel funds for "those Chinese students who have, or will have, received help under this program" to return to China.[108]

The third was Washington's strong desire to win friendly feelings from the Chinese students in the United States. Although most Chinese students made it clear that they wanted to extend their stay and return to China only when it was safe for them to do so, there were still a considerable number of them eager to go back to their homeland to be with their families and work for their country. Fully aware of the stand of these students, most policymakers, including State Department officials and congresspeople, did not want to force them to become the so-called involuntary refugees. They were worried that the good feelings of many Chinese students would be lost if they were not allowed to go back to China. That would defeat the purpose of educating them in the United States and push them to the Communist side. Therefore, the U.S. government continued to help Chinese students, except the 120 plus with detention orders, to return to their homeland even at the height of the Korean War.

Despite the generous help offered by the U.S. government, only a few Chinese students and scholars chose to return to mainland China during the Korean War. Wu Liangkun, a PhD candidate in English at University of Chicago, was one of them. He decided to return to China in 1951 without finishing his dissertation after receiving a job offer from President Lu Zhiwei of Yenching University to replace an American professor of English who had left China because of the war. Tsung-tao Lee (Zhengdao Li), his good friend at the University of Chicago, went to San Francisco to see him off. Having taken a photo together, Wu asked Lee, "Why aren't you coming home to serve the new China?" Lee, who had received his doctoral degree the previous year and was teaching at University of California at Berkeley, answered with a knowing smile, as Wu recollected, "I don't want to have my brain washed by others."[109] Wu began to understand what Lee meant only when he was forced to go through thought reform weeks after his return to China and sent to Nankai University in Tianjin after Yenching University was dismantled. Wu was persecuted at Nankai for resisting "brainwashing" and labeled an ultrarightist for demanding freedom of speech and independent thinking. Lee joined Columbia University as an assistant professor in 1953. He and Chen-ning Yang (Zhenning Yang), another Chinese scholar prohibited from returning to the PRC, completed their research and won the Nobel Prize in physics in 1957.[110]

While most Chinese students and scholars continued to focus on their educational programs, research projects, and new jobs after receiving INS order prohibiting them from returning to Communist China, a few, mostly former leaders or active members of the ACSW, protested and fought for their rights to return to their homeland. Li Hengde, the former editor of the ACSW newsletter, and several of his friends started to contact each other and organize activities against the detention order in early 1952. They found twenty-plus Chinese students and scholars who shared the desire to challenge detention and return to China in Philadelphia, Baltimore, New York, Boston, and Chicago. Li first sent protest letters to the INS, demanding that he be allowed to go back to China immediately because he came to the United States only for education and his parents were still there. He insisted that it was inhumane to keep him in the United States simply because China was involved in the Korean War. He also contemplated suing the INS for prohibiting him from returning to his homeland, though he did not have enough financial resources to support such a fight. Under advice from a sympathetic American lawyer, Li and his comrades sought assistance from the Chinese Communist government and progressive organizations in the United States. Li managed to get Clarence Pickett, a well-known Quaker leader, and the American Civil Liberties Union (ACLU) to write letters to President Dwight Eisenhower and other U.S. government officials sharing their concerns on the detention of Chinese students and scholars. The U.S. government sent polite replies to Pickett and the ACLU acknowledging their concern and promising a solution in the future.[111] However, no detention order was revoked for any Chinese students or scholars until 1955, two years after the truce was reached in Korea.

CHAPTER III

Fighting Over the Stranded

Although most Chinese students and scholars in the United States were free to return to their homeland throughout the Korean War, the vast majority, about five thousand, chose to stay. As the war ground to a halt, the issue of the stranded students resurfaced as an increasingly contentious problem in U.S.-China relations. Beijing formally raised the issue at the Geneva Conference in 1954, accusing Washington of detaining and mistreating Chinese students in the United States. While vehemently denying Beijing's accusation, Washington took steps to revise its wartime policy and gradually revoked restraining orders imposed on all Chinese students and scholars as part of its effort to win the release of U.S. citizens, including missionaries, imprisoned in the PRC. Despite Washington's revocation of the detention orders in mid-June 1955, there was no substantial increase in Chinese students and scholars returning to mainland China. Disbelieving Washington's decision on its detention orders, Beijing kept demanding that the U.S. government permit all Chinese students to return home freely and made the repatriation of nationals the top priority at the Sino-American ambassadorial talks begun in August 1955. Although an agreement on repatriation was reached in September 1955, the number of Chinese students and scholars returning to their homeland dwindled to a trickle in the second half of the 1950s, while some U.S. citizens remained in jail in China. Unsatisfied with the results, Washington constantly accused the PRC of violating the repatriation agreement.

At the same time, Beijing continued to attack the U.S. government for blocking Chinese students from returning to China.

Beijing and Washington elevated the matter of Chinese students and scholars stranded in the United States to a major issue in Sino-American relations by the mid-1950s, with different goals as well as approaches. Although Washington did not want to see these American-trained experts go back to China to serve the hostile Communist regime, it still rescinded the restriction orders in order to remove an obstacle to the release of American citizens detained in the PRC. Beijing raised the issue at the Geneva Conference, hoping to get Washington into direct bilateral negotiations that might lead to solutions to major issues between the two sides. While obeying the existing laws and giving Chinese students and scholars the freedom to return to their homeland, Washington adopted new laws and regulations to allow Chinese students and scholars to extend their stay in the United States. Following its own political playbook, Beijing launched a national campaign to get all Chinese students and scholars in the United States back to China. The reluctance of Chinese students and scholars to return was largely the result of the constant political movements launched by the CCP aimed at Chinese intellectuals, including those who had returned from the United States. With the return of Chinese students coming to an almost complete stop in the late 1950s, educational exchange, the strongest tie in U.S.-China cultural relations, was finally cut off. The decision made by most Chinese students and scholars in the 1950s to stay in the United States permanently not only brought drastic changes to their lives but also heightened the U.S.-China confrontation on the cultural front in the Cold War.

Making Return a Major Issue

Although military actions came to a stop in Korea in July 1953, the armistice did not officially end the war or eliminate hostilities between Beijing and Washington. More important, the bloody war experience shared by the Americans and the Chinese continued to shape their attitudes and strategies toward each other. On the one hand, they kept viewing each other as their most dangerous enemy and took various steps to contain or prevent possible expansion or invasion from the other side. On the other hand, they became aware that it was extremely difficult if not impossible for either side to win a prolonged military confrontation against the other.[1] Thus, both Beijing and Washington were forced to make strenuous efforts to avoid another hot war with each other and find nonmilitary solutions to the urgent as well as thorny issues they faced in the mid-1950s.

The Geneva Conference attended by all major powers to settle outstanding issues from the Korean War and the First Indochina War in April 1954 offered an opportunity. For Beijing, the liberation of Taiwan became its top priority after the truce was reached in Korea. In October 1953, Mao Zedong asked the CCP Central Military Committee to concentrate all its resources to resolve the Taiwan issue. Vice President Richard Nixon's visit to Taiwan in November 1953 and the formal proposal by Jiang Jieshi (Chiang Kai-shek) for a mutual defense treaty with the United States in January 1954 made the liberation of Taiwan an even more urgent task for Beijing. Mao told his colleagues at the enlarged Politburo meeting on July 7, 1954, that Taiwan was one of the key issues in the PRC's relations with the United States, saying, "we should sabotage the possibility of the United States' signing a treaty with Taiwan." In a telegram to Zhou Enlai, Mao warned that "we are going to make a major political mistake if we do not take up this task or start a series of programs to work on it now."[2] In addition to military planning and preparation, Mao proposed to start a propaganda campaign focusing on denouncing the American bullying of Taiwan and Jiang Jieshi's selling off the nation.[3] Since it was impossible to drive the American military out of South Korea or liberate Taiwan with the heavy American military presence there, Beijing had to sit with Washington at the negotiation table to have a chance, no matter how slim it might be, for a peaceful withdrawal of American forces from those areas. Washington, while deeply concerned with the threat posed by the Chinese Communists in Asia, was committed to having American citizens jailed in the PRC returned to the United States as soon as possible. The need to tackle these and other thorny problems made direct negotiations between the two sides at the Geneva Conference possible.[4]

Although both Beijing and Washington sent delegations to Geneva, neither side had planned or expected to start a direct talk on Chinese students stranded in the United States and American citizens detained in China. Supporting Moscow's initiative for an international conference to discuss the situation in Korea and Indochina, Beijing sent a large delegation to the Geneva Conference, led by Zhou Enlai.[5] Having not expected to have formal bilateral interactions with the Americans in Geneva, the Chinese did not plan to raise the issue of Chinese students in the United States at the conference.[6] Because of the existing hostility between the two sides, the American delegation did not want to have direct meetings with the Chinese diplomats in Geneva, either. However, under heavy domestic pressure, the State Department tried to get more information on or even the release of the American citizens detained in China at the conference. Sticking to its nonrecognition policy, the American delegation used Humphrey Trevelyan, the British chargé d'affaires in Beijing, and the International Red Cross (IRC) as intermediaries for that purpose.[7] In their communication with potential intermediaries, the American diplomats quickly realized that their Chinese counterparts would probably react to the IRC probe concerning American civilians detained in China by raising the question of the Chinese in the United States. Huang Hua, the adviser to and spokesman for the Chinese delegation, had told a reporter that the Americans were held in China as hostages for the fifty Chinese students whom the United States blocked from returning to their homeland.[8]

Agreeing with the assessment of the delegation in Geneva on Beijing's possible response to the American request for the release of U.S. citizens detained in China, the State Department took immediate steps to end the detention of a small number of Chinese students and scholars. One of the first things that it did was to persuade the Interdepartmental Committee of Internal Security to make a recommendation to the attorney general for a reappraisal of all the Chinese students and scholars who were detained in the United States. The review recommended that future detention be imposed "only if the return to the Communist China would substantially injure [the] defense of [the] United States." John Foster Dulles told the American delegation in Geneva with confidence that the attorney general would agree and start the necessary procedure at once, since most of those detainees were teaching at colleges or working in private labs. However, he emphasized that the recommendation was made on the assumption that the repeal would result in the reciprocal release of American citizens held in Communist China.[9] By taking this preemptive action, Washington turned the Chinese students stranded in the United States into an instrument in its effort to win the release of the Americans detained in China.

The issue came up first at a meeting on May 17 between Humphrey Trevelyan and Huan Xiang, advisor to the Chinese delegation and director of the Division of European Affairs of the Ministry of Foreign Affairs (MFA). The two met to settle the issue of British nationals in China. When

Trevelyan touched on an American working for a British firm, Huan replied immediately that he belonged to a separate category because of his nationality. In answering Trevelyan's inquiry on China's policy toward American citizens in China, Huan stated that all Americans who had not violated Chinese laws were free to leave China. However, he quickly added that there were also Chinese detained in the United States. As an experienced diplomat, Trevelyan immediately realized that the Chinese had given a "possible bargaining area" when the detained Americans and Chinese were mentioned in the same breath. Encouraged by his meeting with Huan, Trevelyan finally agreed to play an intermediary role in the negotiation between the United States and the PRC on detained Americans as well as Chinese. However, he would take the role only when the U.S. government was prepared in principle to allow the detained Chinese the freedom to go wherever they wished.[10] With the reappraisal of detained Chinese students in the United States already in motion, Dulles immediately authorized the American delegation to ask the British diplomat to find out whether Beijing would accept him as an intermediary between the PRC and the United States.[11] Trevelyan did ask Huan whether the PRC government would like to have him working as an intermediary at their meeting on May 19. Huan did not answer because he had no authority to make such a decision.[12]

Trevelyan's inquiry took the Chinese delegation by surprise, forcing Zhou Enlai to hastily work out a strategy to cope with the new situation. After prolonged discussion with his assistants deep into the night, Zhou concluded that the PRC should not reject contact with the Americans. Instead, the Chinese delegation, he decided, should take advantage of the American desire to win the release of the Americans detained in China to open a channel for direct contact.[13] Zhou and his comrades knew clearly that they had to negotiate with the Americans directly if they wanted to have any of the major issues between the two nations resolved. The direct talks would also give them the opportunity to articulate their views and observe as well as attack the United States whenever it was necessary.[14] Therefore, in the strategy newly adopted by Zhou there was no place for Trevelyan as the intermediary.

The Chinese delegation quickly took calculated steps to implement its new strategy. In his international press briefing on May 26, Huang Hua told reporters that all Americans were free to leave China as long as they did not have any unsettled criminal or civil cases. He also informed them that more than 1,500 Americans had left China since 1950. At the same time Huang claimed that the American government oppressed Chinese people, especially students, in the United States and forcibly detained them. He even accused the U.S. government of confiscating passports from Chinese students in 1951, making it impossible for them to leave the country. In the end, he demanded that Washington stop the detention and mistreatment of Chinese students and restore their right to return to their homeland.[15] Huang's statement not only offered a defense for Beijing's handling of American citizens in China, but it also officially raised the detention of Chinese students in the United States as a major issue in Sino-American relations. By doing so, the Chinese delegation built itself solid ground for direct negotiation with its American counterpart. Huang told the journalists that if the U.S. government intended to discuss the issue of the Americans in China, it should enter into direct contact with the Chinese delegation at the conference.[16]

The Chinese delegation put more pressure on the U.S. government when Huan met with Trevelyan on May 28. Having reiterated all the major points made by Huang two days ago, Huan formally informed Trevelyan that the Chinese would not reject negotiation on the issues if the Americans had the desire to do so. Since both the Chinese and the American delegations were in Geneva, the Americans, Huan suggested, could make the request to the Chinese delegation directly or through Trevelyan. Although the Chinese did not keep Trevelyan out of the loop, Huan made it clear that his government preferred to deal with the Americans directly. Fully aware of the true intention of the Chinese, Trevelyan had no choice but to tell Huan that he agreed that it would be better if the Americans and the Chinese could talk directly to each other without him in between.[17] After passing the message from the Chinese to the American delegation, Trevelyan made it clear that further effort by himself alone on this matter would be unproductive and suggested that members of the American delegation accompany him at the next meeting.[18]

Faced with the new moves made by the Chinese delegation, the Americans were forced to make quick and difficult adjustments. The American delegation issued a statement on May 29 to refute all the major points Huang made at his press conference. It denounced Beijing for ignoring Washington's effort to obtain information about American citizens detained in China and lashed out at Huang's accusations about Chinese nationals residing in the United States, calling them either "without foundation in facts" or a "grave distortion of the facts." It pointed out that among 434 Chinese students who applied for exit visas, only 120 were denied for security reasons during the war, and the rest were allowed to leave the United States. The delegation also emphasized that the denial of departure for selected students was based on the American law and that none of them had been "imprisoned, detained, or mistreated." Instead, they all enjoyed freedom of movement, communication, and employment. It also announced that the Attorney General "is now restudying the cases of these 120" and that those who still wished to leave the United States "will have their status given careful review."[19] The American response demonstrated that Beijing was successful in making Chinese students in the United States a major issue between the two nations and forcing Washington to take a defensive position.

The State Department had trouble figuring out how to respond to the Chinese proposal for a direct meeting between the two sides. Walter Smith, undersecretary of state, who led the American delegation after Dulles returned to the United States, recommended that in order to ascertain whether there was any possibility to obtain the release of at least some Americans on a reasonable basis, it would be necessary to have at least one meeting with the Chinese diplomats. In order to minimize possible political impact, he proposed that Trevelyan accompany the members of the American legation.[20] Despite the careful arrangement Smith proposed, Dulles still did not like the idea of directly meeting with the Chinese diplomats. To him, it was clear that the Chinese Communists were attempting to use the prisoner issue to bring about direct negotiations between the two sides. He doubted the desirability of this course of action because it would cause many negative comments and be mistaken as a step toward recognition. Thus, he suggested that the delegation refrain from sending representatives to negotiate with the Chinese Communists and let Trevelyan make further efforts as an intermediary.[21] Dulles's rejection forced the American delegation to cancel the meeting with the Chinese already arranged through Trevelyan.[22]

Unwilling to give up the opportunity presented at the Geneva Conference, Smith continued to push for at least one meeting with Chinese diplomats. Emphasizing that Trevelyan would not serve as an intermediary for the United States because of opposition from the Chinese, Smith urged that three factors should be considered in making the decision. He believed that if the United States refused to meet with the Chinese diplomats it would be blamed for lack of action on imprisoned Americans in China, prejudice Trevelyan's efforts on behalf of Americans in Beijing, and miss an opportunity to obtain release of a substantial number of the Americans detained in China. He recommended that if the State Department authorized direct negotiations, Walter Robertson, assistant secretary for Far Eastern affairs, would hold appropriate rank to represent the United States.[23]

Smith's recommendation received strong opposition from Everett F. Drumright, deputy assistant secretary of state for Far Eastern affairs. Drumright built his opposition on three major points. He argued that the high-level meetings recommended by Smith would have negative political implications such as de facto recognition, do little to improve the prospects of the Americans detained in China, especially when the United States was not prepared to force the Chinese students in this country to go back to mainland China, and make it more difficult for Washington to justify the abandonment of its well-established position against negotiation with the Chinese Communists as a central government. Thus, Drumright recommended that Dulles give no authorization for direct negotiations and instruct the American delegation to urge Trevelyan to continue to represent American interests.[24]

The opposing recommendations from Smith and Drumright made it extremely difficult for Dulles to finalize his decision. He called James Hagerty, press secretary to President Eisenhower, on the morning of June 3, seeking advice on direct negotiations with the Chinese Communists. Hagerty was able to alleviate if not eradicate most of Dulles's concerns by telling him that the United States should take any possible steps to obtain the release of the Americans detained in Communist China, that the start of such a discussion could not be construed as the opening of a negotiation for official diplomatic recognition, and that a special statement could be issued in Geneva to emphasize that the negotiations had nothing to do with diplomatic recognition.[25] Only hours after his phone conversation with Hagerty, Dulles authorized Smith to have a member of the American delegation accompany Trevelyan in at least one meeting with the Chinese Communists to discuss the release of the Americans detained in mainland China. However, he replaced Robertson with Alexis Johnson, the American ambassador to Czechoslovakia, who had negotiated with the Chinese Communists in Korea.[26]

While the American delegation was waiting for Dulles's authorization, Zhou sent a telegram to Beijing seeking approval for the Chinese delegation's direct contact with American diplomats in Geneva. Zhou informed Mao that the American delegation, through the British, had expressed its willingness to have direct talks with the Chinese delegation. However, no concrete move had been made since they were still waiting for instruction from Washington. Zhou recommended that if the Americans did agree to talk the Chinese delegation should enter negotiations with them, with the Chinese students detained in the United States as the top issue. If the Americans did not want to have any contact with the Chinese delegation, the delegation, Zhou proposed, would issue another statement to illustrate Beijing's policy toward Americans in China and expose the unjustified detention of the Chinese students.[27] To Zhou, by making the Chinese students the top issue Beijing could put itself in an advantageous position no matter whether Washington agreed to hold direct negotiations or not. The CCPCC agreed with Zhou's analysis and approved his action plan.[28]

With approval from Dulles, the American delegation scheduled the first meeting with Chinese diplomats through Trevelyan. Meeting in a small conference room at the Palais des Nations on June 5, Trevelyan introduced Johnson to Wang Bingnan, the Chinese representative. Still waiting for instructions from Beijing, Wang limited the discussion at the first meeting to procedural issues. However, he did give Johnson some hope by emphasizing that now with the establishment of direct contact between the two sides, it would be much easier to solve substantive issues.[29] Although unhappy with the result of the first meeting, Smith sought Dulles's approval for one or two more meetings with the Chinese because they had committed to entering substantive discussion at the next meeting. However, he was prepared to break contact if no positive results were achieved by the third meeting.[30] In order to minimize the negative political impact of the first meeting, the American delegation issued another statement on the same day, declaring that the meeting with the Chinese diplomats took place because of its obligation to protect the welfare of American citizens and that the contact in no way "implies United States accordance with any measure of diplomatic recognition to the Red Chinese regime."[31]

The discussion on substantive issues did begin at the second meeting on June 19. Johnson opened the meeting by pointing out that there were fifty-four American civilians and twenty-nine military personnel detained in China. He then gave the list of their names to Wang and demanded their release as soon as possible. Wang, while denying that China had ever prevented anyone from leaving the country except those who had violated Chinese law, promised to study the list provided by Johnson and comment on it at the next meeting. When asked whether Communist China had any provision for issuing pardons or commuting sentences which might permit early release of the imprisoned Americans, Wang again promised to look into the issue and reply at the next meeting. One bright spot of the second meeting was the Chinese decision to allow letters and small parcels to be transmitted to Americans imprisoned in China. However, Wang refused to discuss Chinese students in the United States at the same meeting and rejected Johnson's proposal to have Trevelyan at the next meeting.[32]

Both the American delegation and the State Department were fully aware of the PRC's intention and worked out a strategy to cope with it. Smith told the State Department that the delegation had ignored the political innuendos made by the Chinese and stuck to concrete questions relating to the detained Americans. While clearly listing what the delegation would do at the third meeting, Smith assured the State Department that they intended to "keep in mind the importance of not derogating from our recognition of the Nationalist [Government] as [the Government] which represents and protects interests of Chinese Nationals in US." Smith recommended that bilateral talks continue after the next meeting and estimated that two or three more meetings might be needed to achieve satisfactory results. As for the strategy to deal with Chinese accusations, Smith suggested that the United States avoid heading into anything like person-for-person exchange. Instead, it should state its principle that any alien Chinese were free to depart for any destination, including Communist China, and demand that the Chinese provide the names of those Chinese students, other than the 120 legally banned from leaving the United States, whom they had claimed were prohibited from departure. This time, Smith's recommendation received full approval, and Johnson was authorized to continue the talks with the Chinese as long as he considered that they were serving a useful purpose.[33]

The Chinese students in the United States finally became the focal point at the third bilateral meeting held on June 15. Wang again accused the U.S. government of forcibly detaining and mistreating Chinese students. Johnson repudiated Wang's accusations by reiterating all the major points made in the statement issued by the American delegation on May 29. Claiming that most Chinese students now residing in the United States no longer wanted to go back to their homeland, Johnson asked Wang to provide the names of those who wanted to return to China but were prohibited from doing so. Wang immediately presented five cases to prove that Qian Xuesen, Zhao Zhongyao, Zhao Mindiao, Wang Liangneng, and Huang Qibao had been prevented from leaving the United States between 1950 and 1952. Johnson responded that he had never heard of those cases and promised to investigate them. He also stated that he would recommend that his government further study those 120 students whose departure had been prohibited. Unsatisfied with Johnson's promise, Wang proposed that a joint statement be drafted to declare that Chinese and U.S. citizens should have complete freedom to return to their homeland. Johnson declined his proposal.[34]

Although no substantive results came out of the first three meetings with the Chinese, the American delegation believed that the chances of the release of Americans detained in China would be increased if some Chinese students with detention orders were permitted to leave the United States. Therefore, Smith recommended that one more meeting be scheduled to arrange the future transmission of information on the status of the detained Americans in China as well as the Chinese in the United States. He also wanted to tell the Chinese at the next meeting that ten or so Chinese had been approved to leave the United States and the review of the other cases was continuing. The purpose, Smith told the State Department, was to put certain psychological pressure on the Chinese so that they were forced to release some Americans after investigation.[35] Dulles approved Smith's recommendation and called Attorney General Herbert Brownell Jr., asking him to let ten to fifteen Chinese students go before the Geneva Conference came to an end. Brownell told Dulles that he could lift the ban on those Chinese students as long as the Department of Defense could certify that these students would not be of substantial aid to Communist China. To him, all but one of the 124 Chinese students and scholars who had been barred from leaving the United States could be allowed to depart.[36] Dulles immediately sent a letter to Brownell to formally start the process that would issue exit permits to those Chinese students who still desired to go back to mainland China.[37]

The swift step taken by Dulles not only showed his desire to use Chinese students in the United States as a bargain chip to win the release of American citizens detained in China, but it also put the American delegation in a better position in negotiating with the Chinese. Having failed to persuade Johnson to issue a joint statement on the repatriation at the June 15 meeting, Wang informed Chester Ronning, a Canadian delegate at the Geneva Conference, that Andy Machenzie, a Royal Canadian Air Force pilot who was shot down by friendly fire and captured by the Chinese in December 1952, was held with American flyers. However, his release, Wang made clear, depended in part on the current negotiations with the American delegation. Wang also mentioned that China wanted the Americans to announce that Chinese in the United States were free to return home. Ronning shared this information with the American delegation and told them that the Chinese might release the flyers if Washington made some gesture on the detained Chinese students and scholars. The American delegation passed the information to the State Department and proposed a seven-point response. One of them was to tell the Chinese officials that they would be informed of the results of the review of detained Chinese students who wanted to return to their homeland.[38] The delegation got what it asked for when the State Department sent the names of fifteen Chinese students whose cases had been reviewed and to whom exit permits were granted.[39]

Johnson and Wang had their last meeting at the Geneva Conference on June 21. Johnson told Wang that the U.S. government had completed the preliminary review of those Chinese students whose departure had been denied. According to the information gathered by the U.S. government, about half of those students had changed their minds and decided to stay in the United States. Among those who still wanted to return to China, fifteen were found eligible to leave. Their names were then given to Wang, who expressed gratitude for their release. However, he hoped that the number would not be limited to those Johnson named and requested the American delegation to provide the names of all 120 Chinese students whose exit permissions had been denied. In return, Wang provided information on a few Americans detained in China and assured Johnson that all cases of detained Americans could be properly settled in light of the progress of the negotiation between the two sides in Geneva. Wang again turned to the issuance of a joint communiqué committing both governments and presented a draft of the agreement to be signed by both sides. Johnson rejected Wang's proposal by informing him that the American delegation would issue a statement covering similar points. Having failed to get Johnson to agree on a joint statement, Wang asked to keep the content of the communiqué part of a "common record" of the meeting to demonstrate the mutual understanding reached by the two sides. He also proposed that both sides have a third country take charge of the interests of nationals in the other country. Johnson turned down both of Wang's new requests and told him that further discussion between the two was no longer necessary. The formal talks between the two nations at the Geneva Conference came to a stop, as the State Department had planned.[40]

Despite numerous rejections from the Americans and their clear desire to end direct bilateral contact, the Chinese delegation refused to give up. Wang kept the communication open by rejecting Trevelyan as an intermediary, as Johnson had proposed at the end of the June 21 meeting. Instead, he insisted that staff officers be appointed by the two sides to continue contact in Geneva after the conference. Unwilling to cut off the source of more information on Americans detained in China, Johnson accepted Wang's proposal and recommended that Alfred Jenkins of the Office of Chinese Affairs be sent to Geneva to maintain contact with the Chinese Communists.[41] Dulles approved Johnson's recommendation and ordered that only inquiries on those Chinese who wanted to return to mainland China should be answered at those meetings.[42]

The first meeting between the staff officers was held on July 21, the last day of the Geneva Conference. It was at this meeting that Pu Shan, the Chinese representative, informed Jenkins that exit permits for six Americans in China had been approved. Having provided something that Washington had been awaiting for a long time, Pu quickly turned to Jenkins asking whether he had any information concerning Chinese students in the United States. Although unprepared to present names of additional Chinese students permitted to leave the United States, Jenkins was able to inform Pu that all fifteen students on the list handed to Wang at the last meeting had been notified of the decision. Unsatisfied with the answer, Pu demanded that the right of Chinese nationals to leave the United States for their own country be observed speedily. Since it was the last day of the Geneva Conference, Jenkins proposed continuing contact between the two sides in order to exchange information relating not only to Americans in China but also to those Chinese students desiring to return to mainland China.[43] Jenkins's action clearly demonstrated that Washington recognized the Chinese students stranded in the United States as a major issue in Sino-American relations and was willing to use it as an instrument to maintain direct contact with Beijing and win the release of Americans detained in China.

Giving Them All Back

Beijing's decision to grant exit permits to six Americans in China not only gave the American policymakers new hope to get more Americans detained in China back, but it also made them believe that the release of the Americans detained in China was tied with the rescission of the restriction orders against Chinese students and scholars in the United States. They quickly came to realize that the most effective way to get more Americans detained in China released was to continue direct meetings with the Chinese and use the return of the Chinese students as leverage. Johnson actually started to plan another meeting the next day. Since both sides had agreed that meetings should be called only when there was new information on the detained Americans or Chinese to be exchanged, Johnson sought approval from the State Department to release fewer than a dozen Chinese students in the United States so that he could formally request a meeting with the Chinese. With the approval from Dulles, a meeting was called by the American side and John Shillock, Consul for the United States in Geneva, met with his Chinese counterpart Xia Fei (Hsiah Fei), on July 28, 1954. Shillock provided the names of seven Chinese students whose departure permits were granted before he inquired information on Americans imprisoned in China. However, Xia offered nothing.[44] In October, Shillock called another meeting. As he had done in July, Shillock provided Xia with names of five additional Chinese students whose departure had been authorized and informed him that six Chinese students had left the United States and five other students had made arrangements for their return to China.[45] Although no new information on Americans imprisoned or detained in the PRC was provided, this meeting was important since it took place at the height of the first Taiwan Strait Crisis.

Despite the lack of success, Washington continued to find ways to increase the chance to win the release of Americans detained in China and derail attacks from the PRC government as well as protests from the Chinese students in the United States. This task gained greater urgency after groups of Chinese students sent petition letters to elected leaders, civil societies, news media in the United States, and top UN officials. Inspired by the direct negotiations between the United States and the PRC on the repatriation of nationals at the Geneva Conference, twenty-six Chinese students, mostly from eastern cities, sent a letter to President Eisenhower on August 5, 1954, demanding the repeal of the restraining order against any Chinese student and the right of each to "leave the United States whenever he so chooses." They told him that most of the students had been separated from their families for seven years and that they had suffered an "ever increasing agony that verges on despair, since no immediate return could be foreseen."[46] On September 2, nine Chinese students from western states sent another letter to President Eisenhower, reemphasizing that they came to the United States to pursue advanced education and what they learned at the universities were open to the public and involved no secrets. Thus, they asked to be allowed to travel freely.[47] Having heard nothing from Eisenhower, thirty-one Chinese students sent a letter to Dag Hammarskjöld, secretary general of the UN, on December 16 requesting that he use his "good office to bring about appropriate action on our behalf."[48]

The petition letters from the Chinese students intensified media's attention and coverage on the subject. The AP and the UPI had reported on Huang Hua's accusation that the U.S. government forcibly detained five thousand Chinese students and the State Department's acknowledgement that some one hundred Chinese students were detained by the Department of Justice.[49] Once the petition letters from Chinese students were publicized, more reporters asked related questions at press conferences, and many newspapers published stories on those students. Acknowledging the letter to him at a press conference on August 11, President Eisenhower recognized that "it had been a troublesome question." However, he emphasized that exit permits had been issued to some of the detained students and promised that at the end "they were starting to go back."[50] The *New York Times* not only reported the letter to Hammarskjöld but also carried a UPI story on eight Chinese students who volunteered to exchange themselves for eleven American airmen imprisoned as spies in China.[51] This constant media coverage kept the issue of the Chinese students in the spotlight and put increasing pressure on the U.S. government.

Unsatisfied with the lack of progress in winning the release of Americans detained in China, the State Department had to take more dramatic steps. On April 1, 1955, Dulles informed President Eisenhower that the State Department had thoroughly considered the issue of the detention of technically trained Chinese students in the United States in relation to the problem of Americans imprisoned in Communist China. The conclusion was that the detention of those Chinese students "would not contribute to the release of the imprisoned Americans" and the revocation of all the detention orders "would enable the U.S. to press its case against the Chinese Communists more effectively in the United Nations and elsewhere." The State Department notified the INS that it had no objection to the departure of any students who had been found eligible to leave the country and that it concurred in the rescission of restraining orders issued against seventy-four Chinese students. He went further to state that while cases of technically trained Chinese students who wished to return to mainland China would continue to be screened, few if any applicants under the present criteria would be denied permission to depart.[52] The next day the State Department issued a press release announcing that on March 31 the INS had rescinded restraining orders on seventy-six Chinese students who were now free to depart. It also stated that the INS would complete its review of the remaining few cases shortly.[53] While insisting that the action was not part of a deal reached with Beijing, Henry Suydam, a State Department press officer, made it clear that the United States "would like Americans of all categories in China to be released for whatever reasons might appeal to the Red Chinese authorities."[54]

As soon as the decision to lift the restraining order against the seventy-six Chinese students was made public, Franklin Gowen, the U.S. consul general in Geneva, requested and had a meeting with Shen Ping, his Chinese counterpart, on April 8. After presenting the text of the April 2 press release to Shen, Gowen categorically rejected "Chinese Communists' groundless allegations about illegal, inhuman and oppressive treatment of Chinese students" in the United States. He also took every occasion to impress upon Shen and his associates the "very grave and deep indignation and resentment [of the] American people and my government at the pitiful plight [of] Americans detained in Red China." Having deplored the Chinese Communists for their failure to furnish satisfactory and prompt information regarding the welfare of those Americans, he emphasized the excellent treatment consistently extended to the Chinese students by the U.S. government. While promising to send the press release to his government, Shen immediately pointed out that five thousand Chinese students were still in the United States and demanded that the "US Government must grant permission [to] our students to return [to] their homeland and must not refuse their applications [to] leave U.S." Shen also asked for the names of the seventy-six Chinese students and their departure dates. Having heard Gowen's claim that half of the Chinese students who had been denied permission to leave no longer wanted to return to China, Shen expressed disbelief and wanted to find out why they did not wish to go back to China.[55]

The interaction with the Chinese representative in Geneva in April pushed the State Department to remove the issue of the detained Chinese students as a hurdle to the release of Americans imprisoned in China. Having completed the review of all but two cases of Chinese students whose departure had been denied, the State Department instructed Gowen to request another meeting with Shen in order to present to him a revised list of the Americans detained in China and inform him of the rescission of detention orders against all Chinese students who desired to leave the United States. However, it did tell Gowen that all restraining orders previously issued had been rescinded except for two individuals who no longer wished to leave the United States. At the meeting held on May 30, Gowen passed the newest information on the rescission of all detention orders against Chinese students to Shèn Ping and repeated his request for prompt, detailed, and up-to-date news regarding the welfare and whereabouts of the Americans detained in China. In response, Shen declared that the Military Tribunal of Supreme Court of the PRC had ordered four U.S. Air Force pilots who were shot down by the Chinese in 1952 and 1953 to be immediately expelled from China. Gowen, while expressing appreciation, demanded again that all Americans in Red China be released.[56] The State Department did the same, expressing earnest hope that the release of the four fliers "signifies the intention of the Chinese Communist Regime to act swiftly" to free the other fifty-two Americans held in China.[57]

Although not quite satisfied with Beijing's response, the State Department continued to push for the revocation of the restraining orders against the last two Chinese scholars. The Office of Far Eastern Affairs recommended in a memo to Dulles on June 2 that steps to be taken to rescind the restrictions on the two Chinese "students" who were still under the detention order.[58] The recommendation found strong support from President Eisenhower. At a meeting with Eisenhower on June 10, Dulles proposed a hard-nosed position on the eleven airmen held by the PRC. However, Eisenhower did not believe that the United States had much room to maneuver because of the issue of the Chinese students in the United States.

He pointed out that "the Chinese had come here with an implied understanding that they would be allowed to go home." When Dulles defended the detention of Chinese students, Eisenhower still believed that "we had not been able to live up to part ourselves." Thus, he told Dulles that "we should let all of the Chinese go back." Seeing an opportunity, Dulles informed the president that the Defense Department was still dubious about two Chinese "students." Both Qian Xuesen, a renowned scientist in rocket propulsion, and David Wang (Wang Kexin), a scientist who had worked on the Nike rocket project, were believed to be in possession of highly classified information. Eisenhower responded that this should not be an obstacle and that the information they possessed might not be valuable.[59]

Once President Eisenhower made his attitude clear, Dulles took immediate action to push for the completion of the review of these two Chinese "students." He called Deputy Secretary of Defense Robert Anderson on June 11, telling him of the president's "give them all back attitude" and urging him to discuss the matter with Eisenhower. Andrew Goodpaster, the staff secretary and liaison officer of the Defense Department to the White House, did talk with President Eisenhower, who approved the Defense Department's decision to release the two Chinese "students" on June 13.[60] With that presidential approval, the detention order against the last two Chinese students in the United States was finally lifted. Now all Chinese students, including those with technical training, were free to leave. The issue of Chinese students detained in the United States was resolved, at least in the U.S. government's view. The only missing step was the delivery of the official decision to the two Chinese citizens, neither of whom wanted to go back to their homeland.[61]

The information received by the State Department was not completely inaccurate. David Wang made it clear that he would not return to mainland China under Communist rule and in May 1955 sought to change his legal status from student to immigrant with assistance from the Nationalist consulate general in Los Angeles.[62] However, Qian Xuesen, who had fought hard against his deportation, did change his mind and started to seek assistance for his return to mainland China. Unaware that President Eisenhower had just approved the rescission of the detention order against him, Qian, after making a routine report to the INS office on June 15, 1955, sneaked into a coffee shop and wrote a letter to Chen Shutong, a family friend and vice chairman of the National People's Congress. After acknowledging that his misjudgments led to his detention in the United States, Qian told Chen that he had been thinking of going back to China to participate in the great reconstruction and preparing for it by working hard on his research. He also informed Chen that Washington lied when it claimed that all Chinese students who wanted to go back to China had been allowed to do so. He emphasized that beside himself some other Chinese scholars, including Guo Yonghuai, a professor at Cornell University, still could not return to China. Thus, he advised that Americans detained in China not be released until all these Chinese scholars had returned to their homeland. Qian asked Chen and the government to forgive him, stressing that he had been anxiously waiting for liberation and did not want to miss any opportunity.[63] Qian did not make any complaints about living or working conditions in the United States in his letter. Actually, he was very productive in his research during this period, publishing numerous papers and a book on engineering cybernetics. Besides regular teaching and graduate student supervision, he served as the director of the Guggenheim Propulsion Institute at California Institute of Technology.[64] However, accused of being a Communist Party member and unable to refute the charge, Qian was barred from any defense-related research and banned from traveling beyond the county's borders while appealing in court.

The State Department also continued to provide financial assistance to cover the travel expenses for those returning to mainland China as required by law. In its April 2 press release, the State Department reminded those Chinese students who wished to return to the Far East and were eligible for travel grants that they must be in actual travel status on or before June 30, 1955, since the emergency aid program for Chinese students would terminate on that day as planned.[65] Earlier in the year, the State Department officials had decided to offer travel aid to those Chinese students who had just gained permission to leave the United States as long as they still had financial need and were not leaders of either the Chinese Students Christian Association in North America (CSCA) or the Association of Chinese Science Workers (ACSW). In order to make sure that the applicants were able to receive the grant and start their travel before June 30, the State Department decided to waive a full national agency check and replace it with an internal current security file check for applicants who were going to Hong Kong or the mainland. As for the grantees who were seeking to return to Taiwan, they would not be required to have such a check because it was extremely difficult to go from Taiwan to mainland China, and the

Nationalist government made thorough investigations before issuing any entry permit.[66]

Once established, the policy was implemented immediately by the State Department. After conducting a quick review in late May, the State Department ascertained that fifty-five of the seventy-six students who had received clearance from the INS were technically eligible for travel grants. It cleared thirty-three for travel requests and prepared to present twelve additional cases to the Suitability Committee for consideration. The rest either had sufficient funds to cover their own trips or were still under security review. Many of the qualified applicants did return to China in 1955.[67] Although it is still difficult to identify everyone who among the returnees had received travel requests, the State Department record did show that between April 1 and June 30, 1955, eighteen grant recipients applied and received travel requests for trips back to mainland China.[68]

Despite Washington's revocation of all the restraining orders against Chinese students, no extra Americans were released by Beijing after May 1955. In order to increase the chance to get all Americans detained in China released and preserve the de facto cease-fire in the Taiwan Strait, Washington decided to accept the proposal made by Zhou Enlai at the Bandung Conference in April 1955 to establish direct talks between the two nations.[69] In a letter to Indian Prime Minister Jawaharlal Nehru, who had worked as an intermediary to reduce the tension between the United States and the PRC, Eisenhower suggested that both sides send representatives of ambassadorial rank to meet in Geneva. He made it clear that the representatives should "deal in the first instance with the question of the citizens of each of our countries in the territory of the other who wanted to return." He recognized that this topic had already been "discussed intermittently at Geneva, at the consular level, with some, though meager, results." He indicated that further progress on this matter could lead to discussion of other topics as long as they did not involve the rights of Taiwan.[70] A similar message was passed to the PRC through the British embassy in Beijing. After an exchange of communications between the two sides through the British, Beijing and Washington issued an identical statement on July 25, announcing that bilateral ambassadorial talks between the two sides would start in Geneva on August 1. The talks were designed to settle the matter of "the repatriation of civilians who desire to return to their respective countries and to facilitate discussion and settlement of certain other practical matters now at issue between both sides."[71] This agenda closely reflected the crux of Washington's original proposal. Since all Chinese students in the United States were free to return to China, the only civilians who needed to be repatriated, the State Department officials believed, were the Americans still detained in China.

Keeping the Issue Alive

When Zhou proposed direct talks with the United States at the Bandung Conference on April 23, 1955, he made it clear that the goal was to reduce tensions in the Far East, especially the Taiwan Strait. Even after the agreement on the agenda of the ambassadorial talks was publicly announced by both governments, Zhou still believed that the talks should focus sharply on substantive matters, including laying the foundation for negotiating détente in the Taiwan Strait, lifting the embargo against the PRC, withdrawing the American armed forces from Taiwan and Taiwan Strait, and ending foreign sabotage in China.[72] However, Dulles, while hoping to maintain a "talking" relationship with Beijing to make it less likely for the PRC to attack Taiwan, insisted that the repatriation of U.S. civilians be put at the top of the agenda for the ambassadorial talks in Geneva.[73] Beijing quickly accepted Dulles's proposal, partly because it believed that Chinese students in the United States still did not have the freedom to return to their homeland and partly because it wanted desperately to get Washington into higher-level direct talks to have an opportunity to tackle key issues, including tensions in the Taiwan Strait.[74]

Busy dealing with the crisis caused by its shelling of Jinmen beginning on September 3, 1954, Beijing took limited actions to get Chinese students back from the United States. Besides keeping pressure on Washington to lift the detention order against all the Chinese students in the United States through the staff-level meetings in Geneva, Beijing focused on collecting information on those Chinese students and reporting on their activities. The MFA's Division of American and Australian Affairs started to collect foreign news reports on Chinese students in the United States during the Geneva Conference and continued after the conference ended. By October 23, 1954, it had twenty-one items in the section of American newspaper reports on the contacts between the PRC and the United States, fifteen reports on Chinese students petitioning for the permission to leave the United States, and sixty letters from Chinese students in the

United States and their relatives in China.[75] However, the PRC government offered little concrete assistance to Chinese students in the United States after the Geneva Conference, forcing many of them to turn to the U.S. government for financial support.

Beijing began to contemplate offering concrete assistance to Chinese students in the United States for their return to China only after the State Department's news release was issued on April 2, 1955. That release not only announced that the detention orders for seventy-six Chinese students were lifted but also reminded Chinese students that the emergency aid would be terminated on June 30, since most of them had already completed their educational programs. Even though the termination date was set in 1953 and publicized in 1954, the Division of American and Australian Affairs seemed surprised when the text of the news release arrived in Beijing. After careful study, the division concluded that the release of seventy-six Chinese students was merely propaganda and termination of emergency aid would make it difficult if not impossible for Chinese students to continue their education and return home, since they had been depending on U.S. government grants to cover their tuition and transportation. It recommended that the PRC government, while demanding the return of all Chinese students without any time restriction, provide travel subsidies to returning students depending on their needs. The travel subsidies, the division proposed, should be disseminated through the Indian or Soviet embassies in the United States. The division believed that those steps would be advantageous for the PRC government because they would have a positive impact among the Chinese people, especially the Chinese students in the United States, expose Washington's inhumane behavior, and obtain technical experts needed for the national reconstruction. The division also considered the potential problems of those steps, including the cost of the subsidies and a possible influx of spies. However, it believed that the advantages overweighed the problems, since the cost was limited to half a million U.S. dollars and the spies among the returning students would be manageable.[76]

The MFA quickly approved the division's recommendations. The policy stood out in several unique ways. First, since the Communist leaders did not believe the U.S. government's assurances that it had lifted the restraining order, Beijing kept making the free return of all Chinese students a major issue in its negotiations with Washington in the following months and years. By doing so, it inadvertently gave an extra bargaining chip to Washington, since it had already done what Beijing was demanding. Second, while showing some interest in obtaining well-trained experts in science and technology for the construction of a powerful Communist nation, the main goal for Beijing to get students in the United States back to China was to further enhance its political position and use the issue to attack Washington. The Chinese officials' concern over the relatively small cost associated with travel subsidies for the returning students showed that the welfare of these students and their reunion with families in China were not really top priorities for the PRC government. Third, despite their well-publicized effort to get back all the Chinese students in the United States, PRC officials continued to show their deep distrust of the returnees and treated them as a security risk. They were willing to allow the students to return only because they believed that they could manage that risk.

Once approved, the policy was implemented in the bilateral talks in Geneva and beyond. Although Gowen had already made it clear at the meeting on May 30 that all Chinese students still in the United States were "entirely free to return to Communist China," Shen Ping, following the instruction from Beijing, emphasized again at the meeting on June 23 that no student, including those who had knowledge of special techniques, should be prevented from returning to China.[77] He denounced the U.S. government for giving them only one month to leave the country and demanded it give Chinese students sufficient time to receive funds for passage and make necessary travel arrangements. Having reiterated what he had stated at the previous meeting, Gowen pointed out that some students did not return to China because they voluntarily elected to remain in the United States or to go to countries other than Communist China.[78] However, that kind of explanation was not acceptable to the Communist leaders, who saw few Chinese students return to China. According to the information gathered by the MFA on July 11, 1955, only sixty-seven Chinese students had gone back to China since the Geneva Conference was held a year earlier. Among the forty-four students who wrote petition letters to Eisenhower and Hammarskjöld, a mere sixteen of them had returned by that time.[79]

In addition to maintaining pressure at the talks in Geneva, Zhou Enlai took steps to make sure that similar demands were presented to top American policymakers through various international intermediaries. At a meeting with the Indian ambassador in Beijing on July 7, Zhou pointed out that the PRC had already released four American pilots and complained that

Washington had not made appropriate moves on the Chinese students detained in the United States. He voiced concern that since Washington required the Chinese students to leave the United States by September 6, they might not be able to return to China even if they were permitted to depart before the deadline because of the lack of funding for transportation. Thus, Zhou emphasized that it was essential for China to have a third country look after of its interests in the United States, including dissemination of travel funds among Chinese students there.[80] In order to make sure that his message would be communicated to Washington accurately, Zhou sent a telegram to Krishna Menon, the Indian representative at the UN, on July 14, repeating his demands that Washington revoke the unreasonable requirements and that India be allowed to look after the interests of Chinese nationals in the United States.[81]

Beijing's demands on more actions to be taken by Washington to release all the Chinese students in the United States did reach top American officials. At a meeting with Dulles on July 6, Menon, while continuing to push for direct talks between Beijing and Washington, suggested that the question of the Americans in China and the Chinese in the United States be "disposed of" first. He asked Dulles whether it would be possible for the secretary to make a public declaration stating that all Chinese nationals in the United States were free to return to China if the PRC released the American fliers. Dulles must be surprised to hear this peculiar request, since the detention orders against Chinese students had already been lifted and the information had been given to Shen Ping at Geneva talks. He knew clearly that there was nothing to prevent him from making such a statement since it did not deviate from the new policy toward the Chinese students in the United States. However, Dulles, as an experienced diplomat, immediately saw the advantage of being ambiguous. He told Menon that he would rather present such a public declaration after the direct talks started. This would not only put Washington in a stronger position in the coming negotiations, but also make it better prepared for a possible agreement between the two sides, since he had already anticipated that the Chinese would like to see tangible results come out of the direct talks.[82] Beijing's persistent fight for a right that Chinese students in the United States had already obtained inadvertently set a trap for itself and gave its opponent a strong bargaining chip for free.

Despite its repeated complaints, Beijing had trouble finding any concrete evidence to prove the continued detention of Chinese students in the

United States after April 1955. The arrival of Qian's letter in July offered Beijing what it believed to be the strongest evidence to support its accusation. As soon as Qian's letter arrived in Beijing via his sister in Belgium, Chen Shutong immediately passed it on to Zhu Kezhen, a meteorologist and the vice president of the Chinese Academy of Science (CAS). Having no power to do anything concrete for Qian himself, Zhu forwarded two letters, one from Qian and the other from Qian's father, with his own note to Zhang Jiafu, the secretary of the CCP Committee at CAS on July 12. Zhang then sent the three letters to Chen Yi, the vice premier at the time, on July 21, asking the MFA's Information Division to conduct a thorough investigation of Qian and then decide whether it was necessary to make an effort to get him back. Chen Yi forwarded the letters to Zhang Hanfu, the deputy minister of foreign affairs, instructing him to handle the issue. After a careful study of Qian's background, Xu Yongying completed a formal three-part report on July 29. Xu believed that given Qian's status as a renowned rocket scientist the United States might still not be willing to release him easily. However, since Washington had accepted Zhou's proposal to hold direct talks between the two nations, it might let Qian go and use Qian's return to win the release of more Americans detained in China. Therefore, Xu recommended that Qian's case not be mentioned at the ambassadorial talks starting in August if his return was certain by that time. If there was no information on Qian's return, his case should be raised in Geneva when the issue of Chinese students in the United States was discussed. If Washington agreed to permit Qian to depart the United States, that would be the end of the issue. If the response from the American side was negative, the request for his release should be presented with clear reasoning.[83]

The MFA approved Xu's proposal and sent clear instructions to Ambassador Wang Bingnan in Geneva. Following the instructions from the MFA, Wang raised the issue of Chinese students in the United States at the second meeting on August 2.[84] He first accused Washington of intentionally setting September 6 as the deadline for Chinese students to leave the United States to force those who could not meet the deadline to apply for permanent residency. Then he presented four proposals to safeguard the interest of each other's citizens in the other country, including providing the names of each other's nationals, the repeal of all prohibitions and time limits imposed by the U.S. government on Chinese students, and the designation of a third country to take charge affairs of nationals of each country and assist their return. Johnson, while agreeing to study Wang's proposals carefully, stated that the concern that the PRC government had regarding the Chinese students in the United States appeared to be based "largely on misunderstanding of [the] true situation." He told Wang that he was authorized to assure the PRC government that the United States imposed no restraints on Chinese civilians who desired to go to mainland China. He even invited Wang to let him know if any Chinese student was prevented from departing and promised to have the case investigated immediately once it was received. Instead of presenting any specific cases, Wang promised to carefully study Johnson's statement and reply at the next meeting.[85]

While Beijing refused to believe the repeated statements made by the U.S. government on its new policy toward Chinese students, the Nationalist government became seriously concerned. It sought assistance from the State Department to prevent Chinese students and scholars from returning to mainland China. Although the State Department wanted to see the Nationalist regime adopt policies to encourage and incentivize Chinese students to go to Taiwan, it insisted that neither the U.S. government nor any institutions had the power to force anyone to travel to a destination against his will.[86] Unable to get any help from Washington, the Nationalist government had to depend on its own diplomats and supporters in the United States to collect information on those Chinese students who wished to return to mainland China and do everything possible to keep them in the United States or send them to Taiwan. It was not until May 1956 when the Ministry of Education of the Nationalist government finally came up with the name list of the eighty Chinese students who had been cleared to leave the United States about a year ago. Even at that time, it still did not have all the essential information about those Chinese students, including the Chinese names of thirty of them.[87]

With little trust in Washington's adherence to its publicly announced new policy and great concern over the Nationalist effort to prevent the Chinese students from returning to the PRC, Beijing was determined to act as the legal protector for those Chinese students and get as many of them back as possible. To the PRC government, it was only natural for it to assume such a role since it had already overthrown the Nationalist government and established solid control over all of China except for Taiwan and a few smaller islands. However, Washington viewed the issue from a completely different perspective. Still recognizing the Nationalist regime in Taiwan as the only legal government for China, Washington vehemently rejected Beijing's request for the names of all Chinese nationals in the United States. Dulles reminded Johnson that providing a list to the PRC would subject many Chinese who still held allegiance to the Nationalist government and their relatives in China to harassment and violated the American policy not to provide any foreign government with information on its nationals in the United States. Johnson did give Wang the names of the seventy-six students who were permitted to leave the United States on April 2 at the meeting held on August 4. However, Dulles quickly turned the representation arrangement requested by Beijing into a bargaining chip. In his telegram to Johnson on August 5, Dulles announced that the State Department would authorize the Indian embassy in the United States to facilitate travel for Chinese students who desired to return to mainland China and to transmit funds for that purpose only when Beijing permitted American citizens in China to depart the country.[88]

In order to strengthen its position on the need for a third country to represent the interest of Chinese students in the United States, Beijing, on August 7, sent Wang a long statement that was read at the meeting the next day. The statement listed grievances regarding Chinese students in the United States whose return to China was disrupted or prevented. Qian Xuesen's case was used as an example to support the claim.[89] Besides Qian, Wang also gave Johnson the names of forty-four students who were among the seventy-six students permitted to leave the United States in April yet were still not back to China. Johnson came to the meeting well prepared. Fully aware that the INS had sent a letter to Qian on August 4, informing him that he was now free to leave the United States if he chose to do so, Johnson was able to state again with confidence that restrictions on Chinese students, including Qian, were "now rescinded and all without exception [are] free [to] depart if [they] desire." Unable to repudiate Johnson's statement with convincing evidence, Wang went back to the proposal made in the past two meetings, demanding that a third country look after the affairs of Chinese nationals in the United States."[90] Johnson quickly detected Beijing's adhesion to the representation arrangement aimed to help Chinese students return to China, and Dulles used it to Washington's advantage. By the end of the fifth meeting held on August 11, it had become clear for Johnson that the representation arrangement had become the only item on Beijing's agenda for the first round of the talks and that the Americans would take no further action until an agreement on the matter was reached.[91] By linking the representation arrangement to the issue of Americans detained in China, Beijing handed Washington another bargaining chip.

Quickly, Johnson began to toughen his position in the negotiation for the agreement on representation management. Under direct instructions from Dulles, he rejected Wang's proposal that would allow the PRC government and family members to initiate investigations on Chinese students in the United States. He also insisted that the arrangement be publicized as a unilateral statement rather than a formal agreement jointly announced by the two sides. More important, he openly told Wang that he expected that any statement coming out from Chinese side would include not only their actions with regard to Americans in China, but also the "categorical statement similar to that we have made concerning [the] departure [of] Chinese." It is true that Johnson did offer to include such a categorical statement regarding Chinese students in the United States as part of the proposed American text.[92] However, since Washington had already made that statement many times, it did not need to take any new action, whereas the PRC government would be forced to commit to the release of all Americans in China. Thus, Johnson could not help but praise the tactics adopted by the State Department to keep the "representation arrangement as bait for [the] release [of the] Americans has paid dividend."[93] Although Dulles later agreed to make a small concession that would allow a joint statement on the representation arrangement, he ordered Johnson to "hold tenaciously to our basic position on [the] return of all [the] detained nationals as [a] part of any agreement on representation before we proceed to discussion of Item 2 of Agenda." Knowing that Wang was eager to obtain the representation arrangement, Dulles ordered Johnson to maintain unremitting pressure on Wang for accepting the Department's principle.[94]

After tough negotiations over the course of a month, an agreement on repatriation was announced on September 10, 1955, with Beijing accepting almost all the terms presented by Johnson. First, Beijing gave up its original plan to have a real joint agreement on the repatriation of nationals formally signed by the two governments and announced simultaneously in both capitals. Instead, it accepted the format of the agreed announcement proposed by Johnson that let the two ambassadors in Geneva inform each other of the measures that his government would take regarding the return of nationals to their respective countries. Second, Beijing, as demanded by Johnson, included a categorical statement in the agreement that both governments recognized that the Chinese in the United States and the Americans in China who desired to return to their respective countries were entitled to do so. Third, under the pressure from Washington, Beijing kept the promise made by Zhou Enlai and accepted the text stating that both governments had adopted and would further adopt appropriate measures so that the nationals of both countries could expeditiously exercise their right to return. Last, Beijing agreed that only when a Chinese in the United States "believes that contrary to the declared policy of the United States he is encountering obstruction in departure, he may so inform the Embassy of the Republic of India in the United States and request it make representation on his behalf to the United States government."[95] Although Washington made no major concessions, Beijing still considered the agreed announcement a significant success because it believed that it finally forced Washington to permit all Chinese students, including those with practical training, to return to the PRC.

Reaping Mixed Results

Washington strictly followed the only agreement reached by the two sides at the ambassadorial talks partly because it had already lifted the restraining orders on all the Chinese students and scholars and partly because it did not want to give Beijing any excuse to keep holding American citizens in China. As soon as the agreed announcement was made public, the State Department authorized the Indian embassy to represent any Chinese students if their return to mainland China was prevented by the U.S. government and transfer travel subsidies from the PRC to those students who desired to go back to their homeland. At the same time, it publicized the agreed announcement in all media in the United States, including Chinese-language newspapers. It even followed the advice of the Indian embassy and posted copies of the agreed announcement at 36,000 post offices. On December 16, 1955, the State Department issued a press release asking that anyone who had any knowledge of any Chinese who felt his return was obstructed to communicate with it or the Indian embassy.[96] While some Chinese students and scholars, including Qian Xuesen and his family, returned to mainland China by using their own resources, some others did seek financial assistance from the Indian embassy. According to the Indian Foreign Minister, Beijing provided $50,000 as subsidies for Chinese students to cover their travel expenses. Between March 1956 and December 1959, the Indian embassy assisted about ninety Chinese students and their family members to return to China.[97] However, none of them needed the representation of the Indian embassy, which, according to a State Department document prepared in October 1956, had not brought to its attention any Chinese whose departure from the United States had been prevented.[98]

Washington's enforcement of the agreed announcement was so rigorous that the Nationalist government was unable to get real assistance from its ally in keeping the Chinese students and scholars from returning to mainland China. According to information gathered by the Nationalist consulate in San Francisco, Chinese students who had received exit permits from the State Department could leave the United States freely as promised by Washington in the agreed announcement. They only needed to obtain sailing permits from the local Internal Revenue Service (IRS) office to prove that they did not owe any taxes to the U.S. government. The IRS refused to reveal the names of any foreigners who had applied for sailing permits except when needed by court investigation. It was only after numerous requests that Zhang Zichang, the consul general of the Republic of China in San Francisco, managed to obtain from the INS the list of all Chinese on board of SS *President Wilson* departing for Hong Kong on January 8, 1956.[99] In all other cases, Nationalist diplomats were unable to get any information from the U.S. government. They had to find out the names and itineraries of those departing students through their own channels and often got the information only after those students had departed long before.

While fulfilling its promise to allow all the Chinese students and scholars to leave the United States if they chose to do so, Washington kept pressing Beijing to do the same expeditiously for all American citizens detained in China. Beijing offered some hope when it announced the release of eleven American airmen at the first meeting of the ambassadorial talks held in Geneva on August 1 and twelve more Americans on September 10 when the Agreed Announcement was issued. According to Wang Bingnan, the first group of Americans was released to produce a good beginning for the talks, and the second group was let go to bring tough negotiations on repatriation to an end so that both sides could quickly enter the second phase of the talks.[100] However, no additional releases were made after six Americans were freed by Beijing late 1955. Holding Beijing responsible for honoring the agreement reached by the two sides, Washington constantly demanded the release of all the remaining Americans, including those imprisoned, in the PRC. It showed no interest in reaching any new agreements until Beijing fulfilled all its obligations under the agreed announcement. Unhappy with the lack of progress on practical issues and afraid of losing its last bargaining chip in the direct negotiations with Washington, Beijing refused to release any Americans on the grounds of national sovereignty and adherence to the Chinese law. By October 1956, the Department of State began to realize that it could not accomplish all its goals and partial success was the best that it could achieve.[101]

Beijing's disappointment was much greater since it had always believed that the lack of return of Chinese students was caused by the restriction order imposed by the U.S. government. With the public announcement of Washington's promise to permit free departure to all Chinese students in the United States, Beijing expected to see throngs of Chinese students and scholars pour back to their homeland. Although Qian Xuesen and his family returned to China with twenty-plus other Chinese students and scholars in September 1955 (figure 3.1), the total number of Chinese students who went back to their homeland remained small in late 1955 and early 1956. In response to this disappointing situation, Beijing first launched fierce attacks on the U.S. government, accusing it of blocking Chinese students from returning to China. The *People's Daily* challenged Washington's claim that Chinese students in the United States had been free to leave the country since April in an editorial published on August 24, 1955.[102] On December 31, it published five letters from relatives of Chinese students in the United States denouncing the U.S. government for blocking their loved ones from returning to China.[103] Although none of the students told their family members in their letters that their return was blocked by the U.S government after September 10, it did not prevent the newspaper from using them as examples of its claim that thousands of Chinese students in the United States still could not freely express their desire or go back to their homeland three months after the repatriation agreement was reached.[104]

Besides relentless attacks on Washington, Beijing launched a nationwide movement in early 1956 to intensify its effort to get as many Chinese students and scholars back from the United States as possible. The movement was based on the report presented to Zhou Enlai by the Special Work Group of Getting Students Back from the United States (Zhengqu LiuMei

Figure 3.1 Qian Xuesen and his family returning to China on board *President Cleveland*, September 1955.
Source: Chinese People's Political Consultative Conference, Beijing, China.

Xuesheng Huiguo Tebie Gongzuo Xiaozu) on January 27, 1956. Comprising top officials from several ministries and coordinated by the Second Office of the State Council, the work group was established to achieve the goal set by Zhou that the PRC should get one thousand Chinese students back from capitalist countries in 1956.[105] Its report also included the contents of another study submitted earlier by Xu Yongying, director of American and Australian Affairs.[106] Relying mostly on conversations with Qian Xuesen and other recent returnees, the work group divided all the Chinese students in the United States into four categories. Those who were willing to return belonged to the first. Those who wanted to return but had practical difficulties to do so were the second. Those who had real concerns about their future in the PRC fell into the third. And those who did not want to return to mainland China were counted as the fourth. Based on the information gathered by the work group, only about 630 students in the United States had expressed willingness to return. While recognizing the difficulty of getting one thousand Chinese students back to China, the group believed that the goal was still achievable if several measures were taken. It recommended compiling a list of Chinese students in the United States, having returnees and relatives send letters to them, launching a diplomatic campaign against the U.S. government's obstructing repatriation, finding ways to ease the return trip for Chinese students, and improving the reception of and employment for the returnees.[107]

With approval from Zhou, the recommendations from the Special Work Group were implemented immediately. The ministries of interior, higher education, and public security issued a joint circular in February 1956, starting a nationwide campaign to register all Chinese students who were still in capitalist countries. Reflecting the urgency and importance of the project, the departments of civil affairs, public security, and education of Hubei Province first sent a telegram on March 31, 1956, instructing the Civil Affairs Bureau (Minzhengju) in all major cities to publish an announcement in local newspapers for five days. Family members of Chinese students in capitalist countries were either to go to the Civil Affairs Bureau to fill out the registration form or to complete the registration through mail. Similar joint committees were established at all levels to manage the campaign. In another joint circular issued on April 10, all major cities in Hubei Province were required to report on the establishment of the special joint committees and the progress of the project within five days.

In the future, similar reports should be made to the provincial commission on the twentieth of each month.[108]

In order to better guide the national campaign, the ministries of higher education, public security, foreign affairs, and interior issued an internal circular providing instructions on major related issues on June 26, 1956. It was in this circular that these government offices stated for the first time that the U.S. government dared not interfere with the Chinese students who desired to return to China and that no persecution occurred when Chinese students sought assistance from the Indian embassy in the United States. The circular emphasized that Chinese students should be able to leave the United States without seeking approval from the American government, could receive subsidies for return fare and transportation of luggage no matter whether they had financial difficulties or not, and would receive subsidies and job assignments within a month or so after their return. It also instructed that students' family members and friends in China should write them frequently, informing them of the situation at home and helping them resolve to return to the motherland. The letters could be mailed locally or sent to the Ministry of Higher Education so that they could be put in the mail abroad. If necessary, postage could be subsidized by local civil affairs bureaus.[109]

While most of the letter writing, especially those done by family members and friends, was organized by local governments, the MFA did its part to help. Some sensitive letters were sent to its offices overseas for safe mailing. On July 11, 1956, Wang Ren and eleven other returned students wrote a letter to those who were still in the United States. Having spent two or three months in Communist China, Wang and his friends wrote that all those who had returned to the motherland had found jobs, that married couples were not forced to be separated, and that there was no theft, no inflation, no fear. Impressed by the content of the letter, officials at the MOE sent it to the MFA, asking MFA officials to send the letter to the United States and had it published in the *Overseas Chinese Daily* there. The MFA honored the request by sending the article to America via the Chinese embassy in Switzerland to avoid possible interception by the U.S. government.[110]

As soon as the registration of Chinese students in the capitalist countries was completed, Beijing took another step to win the return of Chinese students and scholars in the United States. On September 8, 1956, the ministries of higher education, interior, and public security issued another joint circular instructing societies for family members of Chinese students in the United States to be established in major cities such as Beijing, Tianjin, Shanghai, Wuhan, Guangzhou, and Chongqing, where a large number of them resided. The mission of those societies was to maintain contact with the family members of Chinese students who were still in the United States, get information on the communications between family members and those students, report difficulties in winning their return, and provide assistance to overcome those difficulties. The societies and forums should be founded by the end of September, and they should report their activities on the fifteenth of each month beginning in October. The chairs and vice chairs for the societies and forums should be selected from politically progressive family members or moderate representatives.[111] Following the instructions, the Work Group for the Return of the Students in Capitalist Countries, which was established in Beijing in September 1956, organized friendship groups (*lianyi xiaozu*) for relatives of Chinese students in the United States in all neighborhood communities and colleges in the city. It also held several social gatherings for relatives of students in the United States and invited Zhou Enlai to deliver a speech at one of the meetings.[112] With the establishment of these work groups and friendship societies in all other major cities, the national movement to get Chinese students back from the United States and other capitalist countries was elevated to a new level.

Despite all the efforts made by Beijing, the number of Chinese students who returned to China from the United States after the ambassadorial talks began in Geneva remained small. According to a report compiled by the MFA, only 198 Chinese students and 36 of their family members returned from the United States between 1956 and 1958. Among those returnees, 147 paid travel expenses with their own funds and 87 received travel subsidies from Beijing through the Indian embassy in Washington.[113] Although Zhou gave it a positive spin when he told Chinese officials at a conference in the late 1950s that the ambassadorial talks were worthwhile just by bringing back Qian Xuesen, such a low return rate eventually forced Beijing to end the national movement aimed at Chinese students in the United States.[114] With only twenty-eight students going back to China in 1958, mostly in the early months, the National Association of Science and Technology (NAST) issued a circular on December 6, announcing that management of the work of getting back Chinese students from capitalist countries would now be "lowered" (*xiafang*) to provinces and municipalities. While claiming that measures were taken to give greater incentive to local governments and to improve efficiency, NAST clearly instructed the local authorities to choose the students carefully and prohibited them from promising returned students offices or offering other incentives. Having warned the provincial governments that more spies were among the returning students, it ordered that political review of the returnees by public security departments be intensified.[115] By lowering the management responsibility to provincial governments and keeping the focus on catching spies, getting students back from the United States was no longer a key task of the PRC government.

Although Beijing blamed and attacked the U.S. government for the lack of the return of Chinese students, the Communist regime itself was the real culprit. The tactics Beijing used to get them back and the humiliating treatment the returnees received kept most of the Chinese students and scholars in the United States from returning to their homeland. While the letters that poured in from mainland China did lure some students to return to their motherland, these letters caused deep concern and even severe fear among most of them. Many became more determined to prolong their stay in the United States after receiving the letters. Chou Wen-te, a professor of civil engineering at the University of Illinois, Urbana, had received many letters from Chinese officials and his wife in China by March 1956. He dared not tell his family members that he did not want to return to China at the time for fear that it might be used against his wife. Deeply troubled by those letters, he sought advice from the State Department. Interested in seeing the letters themselves, State Department officials invited him to Washington. Although it is unknown what was discussed at the meeting, Chou continued to stay in the United States and asked the State Department to help him bring his wife and two children from Hong Kong in 1957. He visited the State Department again with an appointment set through Senator Paul Douglass's office on August 19 to make an in-person appeal for assistance. The advice received by him from the State Department was to contact the U.S. consulate in Hong Kong, prepare documents proving his relationship with his wife and children, and wait for an extremely long period for visas because of the limited quota—105 a year—for Chinese immigrants.[116]

While most students, like Chou, kept their decision to extend their stay in the United States to themselves to avoid getting their relatives in China into trouble, some Chinese students and scholars publicly expressed their attitude and opinions. Having heard Beijing's proposal to have a third country investigate and represent the Chinese students and scholars in the United States, sixty-three Chinese students and professionals in San Francisco area sent a letter to President Eisenhower on September 9, 1955, urging him to reject Beijing's proposal at the ambassadorial talks in Geneva. They emphasized that the Chinese Communists came to power through violence and turned mainland China into a country of terror and fear. They especially pointed out that by depriving freedom of religion, ignoring human rights, humiliating scholars and intellectuals, and brainwashing the whole population, "the rulers of Red China have sought to control the mind of those who had once learned to think independently." It was for these reasons that they refused to go back to mainland China. The students urged the U.S. government to continue the fight against any demand of forceable repatriation and object to being investigated by any third power in respect to their willingness to go back to their homeland.[117] Although they failed to stop Washington from accepting the agreed announcement on repatriation, the State Department did reassure them that it would not allow any country to investigate Chinese in the United States or force any of them to return to mainland China.[118]

The fear caused by the "letter barrage" was amplified by the wide media coverage in the United States. The *Houston Press* reported on June 8, 1956, that as the flow of letters from mainland China multiplied in recent weeks, even an obscure Chinese student living in New York City had received a letter from Ambassador Wang Bingnan. Wang told the student that his parents residing in a village in mainland China wanted him to return home. Wang invited the student to write to him in Geneva to get more detailed information and advised him to contact the Indian embassy if he ran into any trouble in departing the United States.[119] Jack Lotte of the International News Service also observed that agents of Red China were waging a special pressure drive "aimed at forcing Chinese physicists, electronics, aviation and engineering specialists, now studying in this country, to go home." According to the information provided by Chinese welfare agencies, letters, phone calls, and personal visits were employed in nationwide "psychological warfare" against hand-picked targets. Lotte reported that those scientists received almost identical letters from relatives urging them to place the special skills they acquired in America at the disposal of the Communist government. The letters promised all returnees with "ideal jobs" and pledged them no harm. Although the FBI was called in to combat this widespread "operation terror," its probe was hindered by fear among the Chinese students for the safety of their relatives in China.[120]

The greatest fear was generated by numerous political movements launched by the CCP after 1949 that targeted intellectuals, especially those educated in the United States. Right after the thought-reform movement, which forced almost all the intellectuals returned from the United States to publicly denounce American cultural aggression in China, a nationwide movement was launched in 1954 against Hu Shi, one of the most influential scholars with an American education. With Hu living in the United States at the time, such a massive attack on him caused strong resentment and fear among Chinese students who had the greatest respect for Hu. When Mao turned a rectification movement against some CCP officials into an anti-rightist movement aimed at hundreds of thousands of outspoken intellectuals in 1957, numerous scholars returned from the United States became top targets. Zeng Zhaolun, the deputy minister of higher education; Qian Weichang, the vice president of Qinghua University; Luo Longji, the vice chairman of the Democratic League; and many others were publicly denounced as rightists and removed from their offices. Fu Ying, a professor of chemistry at Peking University who returned to China in 1950, was attacked repeatedly by the CCP branch in his department. He was forced to write an article, "Surrender to the Truth" (Xiang Zhenli Touxiang) and have it published in the *People's Daily* and other newspapers in May 1958. Besides sharp denunciation of his pro-American bourgeois thoughts, he vowed to love and follow the Communist Party and make every effort to become a working-class red expert.[121] Xu Zhangben, a professor in physics at Qinghua University who signed the petition letter to President Eisenhower and went back to China in 1955, received more severe punishment. He was arrested and jailed as an antirevolutionary (*fangeming*) because he attempted to establish a Labor Party and challenged Marxism as the guiding principle for China in 1957.[122]

As the Chinese students returning from the United States dwindled to a trickle in the late 1950s, the last remnant of the old cultural and educational ties between the two nations built in the past century dissolved. Since Beijing did make an effort to get those students back to China and Washington lifted all the detention orders against them in mid-1955, the lack of return of the Chinese students to their homeland was largely the result of decisions made by those students themselves. When they decided to extend their stay in the United States after completing their educational programs, they broke the century-old pattern followed by almost all of their predecessors, who returned to China immediately after their graduation. Blaming Washington for its failure to get all or even most of the Chinese students in the United States back, Beijing refused to release all the Americans imprisoned in China, which in turn hampered negotiations with Washington on Taiwan and other substantive issues. The fight over the stranded Chinese students in the United States not only helped complete the termination of cultural ties between the two nations but also broadened and deepened hostility between the two Cold War foes.

CHAPTER IV

Building a Cultural Bastion

While ushering in the termination of cultural ties between the United States and mainland China, the Korean War gave birth to new cultural interactions between the United States and Taiwan, which remained under the control of the Nationalist government. The sudden attack launched by North Korea against the South in late June 1950 forced Washington to reassess the strategic significance of Taiwan and readjust its policy toward the Nationalist regime. In order to prevent Taiwan from falling into the hands of the Chinese Communists, Washington not only immediately resumed military and economic aid to the Nationalist government but also offered technical assistance, including a special program to train students and technical experts in the United States. As part of its effort to ensure the military security and economic stability of the island, Washington took further steps to establish and expand engineering, agricultural, and vocational education programs in Taiwan, further strengthening educational and cultural ties with its born-again ally. As soon as military actions in Korea came to a stop, Washington stepped in to help Taipei expand education for overseas Chinese and revitalize schools, especially colleges and universities, in Taiwan as a response to the cultural, economic, political, and diplomatic offensives launched by Beijing. The collaboration between the two Cold War allies on the cultural front, while strengthening the military and economic security of Taiwan, turned the island into a bastion against Chinese Communist cultural expansion.

Following the tradition established in previous decades, some high school graduates and college students, mostly mainlanders who had just relocated to Taiwan with the Nationalist government, started to pursue higher education in the United States through applying for and receiving scholarships from American colleges and universities as early as 1950. However, it was the visible hand that played a predominant role in establishing and expanding the new cultural and educational ties between the United States and Taiwan during the Cold War. With greater resources and flexibility, the new foreign assistance agencies established in the Cold War, such as the Economic Cooperation Administration (ECA), Mutual Security Agency (MSA), and Foreign Operations Administration (FOA), supplanted the State Department as the leading player in sponsoring and managing major educational and cultural programs with Taiwan. Adhering to their missions, these agencies planned and implemented various programs to achieve their strategic goals. If the early technical training for experts from Taiwan in the United States and the promotion of vocational education at home were aimed at keeping the island from falling into the hands of the Chinese Communists, the expansion of overseas Chinese education was designed to counter Chinese Communist ideological as well as cultural penetration in Southeast Asia. Sticking to its Cold War strategy, Washington also tried through various cultural and educational programs to keep its Chinese ally's attention on political as well as economic developments rather than on retaking the mainland by force. Although reluctant to divert precious resources to nonmilitary programs, Taipei collaborated with Washington on the cultural front partly because its security depended very much on its alliance with the United States and partly because the improvement of education was also deemed essential for its military as well as economic successes. With the rapid expansion of cultural and educational ties, Washington and Taipei grew into strong allies in confronting Communist China on the cultural front.

Starting with Technical Training

Although Taiwan was returned to China at the end of World War II, U.S. cultural interaction with the island province remained minimal prior to the outbreak of the Korean War. Having accepted the surrender of the Japanese, who had ruled the island as a colony for half a century, the Nationalist government was occupied with the task of establishing effective control over a population that was quickly disillusioned by the new victorious master. Thus, it did not bother to include the province in the Fulbright Program or other educational exchanges with the United States. When the Nationalists were soundly defeated and forced to flee to Taiwan in December 1949, Washington completely lost its confidence in the regime and was prepared to accept the Chinese Communist conquest of Taiwan within months. President Harry S. Truman made it clear in a special statement issued on January 5, 1950, that the United States, with "no predatory design on Formosa [i.e., Taiwan] or on any other Chinese territory," "will not pursue a course which will lead to involvement in the civil conflict in China." He emphasized that the U.S. government "will not provide military aid or advice to Chinese forces on Formosa" and that economic assistance provided by the ECA under the existing legislative authority would be the only aid that the Nationalist regime would receive from the United States.[1] Secretary of State Dean Acheson further clarified that the ECA had only limited programs in Taiwan, including the supply of fertilizer for the spring crop, the purchase of oil for refineries on the island, and assistance to keep "power plants and other factories in repair and in operation."[2]

The State Department strictly followed President Truman's order in the coming months. On February 8, Acheson instructed the American embassy in Taipei to immediately send a strong written protest to the Ministry of Foreign Affairs (MFA) over the Nationalist air force's bombing of Shanghai on February 6, which caused extensive damage to American property, including the Shanghai Power Company. He emphasized that American aviation equipment was not supplied to the Chinese government for the "use against its own defenseless people or civilian property in heavily populated areas." He pointed out that the employment of American-supplied equipment in this manner "can only result in inflaming populace against Chi[nese] Gov[ernmen]t and in turn against US."[3] When Foreign Minister Yeh Kung-chao (Ye Gongchao) defended the bombing and promised early warning before similar attacks in the future, Robert C. Strong, the American chargé d'affaires at Taipei, refused to accept such an arrangement and warned Yeh that "serious difficulties would arise if such things continued."[4]

Although disgusted by President Truman's January 5 statement and unhappy with Washington's request to refrain from bombing coastal cities on the mainland, the Nationalist government had no choice but to try repeatedly to seek assistance from the United States. While most of the procurements that predated Truman's statement did go through, almost all requests from Taipei for additional assistance were turned down. In March, the State Department blocked the shipment of twenty-five M-4 Sherman tanks and twenty-five F-5 jet fighters to Taiwan by rejecting Taipei's application for export licenses for these items.[5] Taipei tried to find ways to improve its relations with Washington and obtain more assistance from the United States for the defense of Taiwan by sending Hollington Tong (Dong Xianguang), a member of the Central Advisory Committee of the Nationalist Party and general manager of the China Broadcasting Corporation, to Washington. Although he was able to meet with John Foster Dulles, then the consultant to the secretary of state, Dulles's response was negative and blunt. Tong was told that this was not a matter "where there was any possibility of any sort of a bargaining arrangement." When Tong asked whether the United States would change its policy if the Nationalist forces were able to defend the island for a certain period of time, he was lectured that the Nationalists should fight for their own cause, not for a change of American attitude.[6]

Having failed to win military assistance from Washington, some Nationalist officials tried to obtain American aid in other nonmilitary areas. In mid-April, K. C. Wu (Wu Guozhen), governor of Taiwan Province, sent a letter to the Council for United States Aid proposing to set aside $200,000 of the $6 million of ECA funds designated for emergency aid to Chinese students in the United States as a scholarship to send twenty men and women from Taiwan for advanced education and training. He recognized that graduates from both Taiwan and the mainland who were then on the island had little opportunity to pursue further studies in their fields. Thus, he suggested that those candidates be university graduates in agriculture, engineering, science, or medicine. He even emphasized that fourteen native Taiwanese would be included in the program to show his efforts to improve relations between the Nationalist government and local people, as Washington urged.[7] A number of Nationalist leaders backed Wu's proposal, but it failed to get a positive response from the Department of State. The department, based on its interpretation of congressional intent for the emergency aid, insisted that the special funds be used only to help Chinese students in the United States. More important, it strongly believed that Communist forces would most likely take over Taiwan in the summer of 1950. Accepting the recommendation of the embassy in Taipei, the State Department advised American citizens to withdraw from Taiwan on May 19 and ordered the evacuation of American diplomats and other government employees on the island on May 26.[8] By the end of May, top State Department officials had reached consensus that the fall of Taiwan was inevitable and the United States would do nothing to assist Jiang Jieshi (Chiang Kai-shek) in preventing it.[9]

Drastic changes began to take place once the Korean War broke out on June 25, 1950. To Truman and his advisors, the attack on South Korea "makes it plain beyond any doubt that communism has passed beyond the use of subversion to conquer independent nations and will now use armed invasion and war." In these circumstances, Communist occupation of Taiwan, Truman believed, "would be a direct threat to the security of the Pacific area and to United States forces performing their lawful and necessary functions in that area." Therefore, he managed to persuade the United Nations Security Council to pass a resolution on July 27, demanding that North Korean forces cease hostilities and withdraw to the thirty-eighth parallel. On the same day, he not only instructed U.S. military forces to give South Korean troops cover and support but also ordered the Seventh Fleet to "prevent any attacks on Formosa."[10] This action marked a complete reversal of Washington's policy toward Taiwan. Preventing the island from falling into the hands of the Chinese Communists became the new top strategic goal of the United States in the Far East during and after the Korean War. However, Truman also called on the Nationalist government on Taiwan to "cease all air and sea operations against the mainland" to keep the United States from being dragged into direct military confrontation with Chinese Communist forces. He made it clear that his request was more than mere advice, since the Seventh Fleet was instructed to "see that this is done."[11] Before the statement was released to the press, Acheson had instructed Strong to inform Jiang of Truman's order and request his full cooperation.[12] Jiang, although unhappy with the American action, did issue a cease-fire order the next day and sent a positive reply to Washington on July 29.[13]

As Taiwan's strategic significance elevated, the U.S. government began to increase its military aid to the Nationalist regime. Secretary of Defense Louis A. Johnson recommended on July 19 that the Nationalist government be authorized to purchase with its own funds any material under the control of the United States, including tanks and jet aircrafts. The purpose, Johnson made it clear, was to "increase the capacity and will of the Chinese Nationalist forces to fight."[14] Within days, the Joint Chiefs of Staff proposed that immediate military aid should be provided to the Nationalist government because it believed that Taiwan's security could not be provided by the Seventh Fleet alone, given its greater responsibility in the heated fight in Korea and that over half a million Nationalist soldiers had to prepare to resist possible Communist attacks.[15] Acheson concurred with Johnson's recommendation on July 24, and the National Security Council listed military grant aid to the Chinese Nationalist forces as one of the steps that the U.S. government should take immediately. On August 25 Truman informed Acheson that over $14 million from funds under the Mutual Defense Assistance Act had been allocated to the Department of State for military aid to Taiwan.[16] In addition to military aid, economic and technological assistance were also provided to stabilize the economy and sustain the Nationalist forces in Taiwan. In early August 1950, General Douglas MacArthur made it clear that he hoped to see the ECA "continue its economic work so that Formosa can become increasingly important in trade relations with Japan and in the improvement of the economic life of the Formosans."[17]

After the Chinese Communists entered the war in Korea in late October, more military, economic, and technical aid was extended to the Nationalist government. For fiscal year 1951, beginning on July 1, 1950, the U.S. government not only included Taiwan in its foreign aid budget but also increased the amount of aid to the island from $40 million to $97.7 million. In the following three fiscal years, American economic aid to Taiwan amounted to $81, $105.5, and $125.5 million respectively.[18] As soon as President Truman signed the Mutual Security Act into law on October 10, 1951, the new MSA replaced the ECA in administering American military, economic, and technical assistance to friendly nations to contain Communist expansion. Taiwan became one of the top recipients of American aid in the following years.

The changed situation and increasing American aid made it necessary and possible to expand cultural interactions between the two reconnected allies in the 1950s and 1960s. At the beginning of the 1950s, agriculture was still the largest sector in Taiwan's economy, and the vast majority of the Taiwanese were farmers. As the agency largely responsible for helping the Nationalist government strengthen and grow the economy in Taiwan, the ECA paid great attention to agriculture and worked closely with the Joint Commission for Rural Reconstruction (JCRR) to improve farming on the island. However, the ECA officials were troubled by criticism from local farmers that the agricultural program supervised by the JCRR was staffed completely by mainland Chinese. Some ECA officials even thought of having a Taiwanese replace James Yen, who was resigning from the JCRR, as commissioner. But they could not find a Taiwanese meeting the qualifications for that job, since the local people had not been given positions of responsibility under decades of Japanese rule that would train and qualify them for more active participation.[19] In order to amend the situation, Jim Ivy of the ECA sent a memorandum to John B. Nason, deputy chief of the ECA mission in Taipei, on August 4, recommending a program to send qualified Taiwanese as well as mainland Chinese to the United States for further technical training in agriculture, animal husbandry, and political science. He revealed that the JCRR was willing to finance a modest scholarship program focusing mostly on agriculture with its own funds.[20] A few days later, Ivy and Nason met with two officials from the State Department to discuss whether the $6 million earmarked for the emergency aid to Chinese students could be used for the proposed Taiwan program. The State Department officials were surprised by the proposal and requested more time to consider it before a definitive answer could be given.[21]

While the State Department was still contemplating, the ECA went ahead with the program planning in collaboration with the JCRR. Such collaboration was natural since Raymond T. Moyer, chief of the ECA mission, was also one of the two American commissioners of the JCRR.[22] At the request of JCRR, Owen L. Dawson, the economic counselor at the American embassy; Shen Zonghan, one of the three Chinese JCRR commissioners; and Jiang Yanshi, the JCRR assistant executive officer, completed a four-part outline for the leadership training program. The program planned to send forty high school graduates and sixty college graduates to receive education and practical training in the United States in health, engineering, agricultural science, economics and sociology, natural science, and arts and literature. The purpose of the program, the outline clearly stated, was to grant scholarships to students, largely Taiwanese, for advanced training in the United States "so as to better prepare them for assuming responsibilities of carrying out reconstruction work in the future."[23] After careful consideration, the ECA mission in Taipei decided to join the JCRR in sending students from Taiwan to the United States for undergraduate, graduate, and "on-the-job" training in technical fields directly related to needs on Taiwan beginning in February 1951. However, it proposed to limit the number of students to forty for the initial program, with twenty for practical training and twenty for undergraduate or graduate education. Fully aware that this would be the first time a large number of Taiwanese students would be sent to the United States, the ECA mission emphasized that "it is essential that this group receive personal attention." Still unclear about the State Department's attitude, ECA officials agreed to further explore the possibilities of using the funds the department administered.[24]

Another round of efforts to win the State Department's permission to use part of the Chinese student emergency aid fund to bring students to the United States for specialized training ended without any success. R. Allen Griffin, director of the ECA Far East Program Division, send a letter to William C. Johnstone Jr., director of the State Department Office of Educational Exchange, on October 20 expressing hope that the Department of State could cover the cost for twenty students from Taiwan to receive education in the United States. He stressed that having "even a few students from Formosa in this way will have a remarkable effect in creating good will for the United States."[25] The initial response from Johnstone was again noncommittal. He claimed that the ECA's proposal would involve policy discussion at a higher level, and thus he could only assure Griffin at the moment that "the Department will give every consideration to your suggestion."[26] Having heard nothing from the State Department for several weeks, ECA officials began to have serious doubt about its willingness to "relax its clutch on the funds allocated to them for our program" and proposed either to allocate more funds to them for this specific program or to have the ECA's Technical Assistance Division do it.[27]

When Moyer sent another letter to ECA headquarters in Washington on November 28, requesting early action on the leadership training program, William C. Foster, the new ECA administrator, approved the program in principle without the State Department's commitment to the cost-sharing proposal. In his telegram sent to Taipei on December 6, 1950, he instructed Moyer to initiate discussion with the Nationalist government agency as soon as possible so that the formal application for technical assistance could be submitted and selection of candidates for the program could be started. While approving all the major parts and procedures of the program, Foster proposed two modifications to Moyer's proposal. One was to replace students in literature with students in science. The other was to give the lowest priority to the five students in economics and sociology.[28] While Foster's approval for the program was welcomed, the second suggestion aroused internal criticism. One ECA official pointed out that such a suggestion implied that it would be better to train a man in technology than in social science. He argued that the technologist must operate in society and that a technician, "without any sophistication in human relations or in the economic or political implications of technological development, can be as much of hazard to society as a bomb in the hands of a child." Thus, he recommended that students in economics and social science have equal priority with students in natural science.[29] Shannon McCune, deputy director of the Far East Program Division, defended Foster's position by pointing out that such modification was necessary because the State Department refused to finance or administer that part of the program. Now as an ECA "technical assistance" project, it was stretching a point, he argued, to include them at all.[30] As a result, literature and economics were eliminated from the subject fields covered by the leadership training program.

Once approval from Foster was received, the leadership training program was fast-tracked. The Committee on ECA/JCRR Scholarship was soon organized with members from the JCRR, various Nationalist government offices, the National Taiwan University, and the American embassy. Chaired by Chiang Monlin (Jiang Menglin), JCRR director, the committee accepted the original plan approved by ECA headquarters and passed fifteen resolutions at its first meeting on December 20. These resolutions further clarified the qualifications for candidates, laid out the selection procedures, and set January 20, 1951, as the application deadline.[31] At its second meeting held on January 15, the committee extended the deadline to February 10, approved the draft of the public announcement of the program, and persuaded the Ministry of Education (MOE) to exempt candidates from the government regulation that allowed only students with two years of college education to go abroad for advanced education and training.[32] Right before the program was made public, the State Department finally gave its full support for the ECA program to bring up to one hundred persons from Taiwan to the United States in the current year.[33] Livingston T. Merchant, deputy assistant secretary for Far Eastern Affairs, emphasized that the training would be specialized and "closely related to the economic development of Taiwan rather than the conventional study courses." He hoped that the ECA would move ahead rapidly and coordinate its activities with the Division of Exchange of Persons in the State Department so as to obtain the benefits of that division's past experience in this field. However, he did not say a word about financing the program.[34]

Without substantive commitment from the State Department, the ECA assumed the new position in educational exchange and went on with the training program immediately. Following the specially designed selection process, 709 applicants completed preliminary examinations in Chinese and English on February 27. The ECA/JCRR Scholarship Committee agreed at its fourth meeting to set different standards for Taiwanese and mainlanders so that the three-to-one ratio set by the ECA could be achieved. For the Taiwanese candidates in agriculture, they would need 25 points to enter the next round of examinations and 30 points for all other fields. For the mainlanders, they would need 50 points to make the cut for the next round of examinations in agriculture, engineering, and public health. With these standards, 111 Taiwanese and 230 mainlanders became eligible for the field specific written tests given between March 25 and 27. After all the examinations were graded, the working committee carefully studied the results and agreed to set different passing standards for Taiwanese and mainlander candidates, since the former again received lower grades than the latter. It was based on these different standards that seventy-four candidates, forty-six Taiwanese and twenty-eight mainlanders, were chosen for the oral examination conducted by a special subcommittee.[35] In the end, thirty-six students passed the oral examination, including eleven in agriculture, seven in engineering, eight in public health, four in natural science, and six in social science.[36]

The Scholarship Committee managed to keep the number of Taiwanese and mainlanders as close to three-to-one ratio as possible. Of the thirty-six candidates, twenty-six were born in Taiwan, a bit over 72 percent of the total. One of the Taiwanese candidates was Lee Teng-hui (Li Deng-hui), who, at age of twenty-eight, was recommended by the Provincial Department of Agriculture and Forestry to pursue graduate education in marketing and pricing in agriculture in the United States. Although he had studied at Kyoto Imperial University during World War II, he was still qualified for the Scholarship Program because it exempted those candidates who had attended colleges in Japan, special treatment designed to benefit mostly the native Taiwanese. However, Lee was hit by tuberculosis in summer 1951, preventing him from going to the United States with his group as scheduled in the fall. When Lee finally recovered in January 1952, Hubert G. Schenck, chief of the MSA mission in Taipei, informed headquarters and requested confirmation for his visa and decision on his destination in the United States.[37] Within ten days, the MSA made arrangements for Lee to attend the University of Iowa for a year and informed the mission in Taipei that the spring semester would begin in March.[38] With the destination and date in hand, the mission booked tickets for Lee in February to make sure that he arrived in Washington, DC, on March 17 and forwarded detailed flight information to headquarters.[39] Lee spent a year at the University of Iowa and received his master's degree before returning to Taiwan in 1953.[40]

Lee Teng-hui was not the only Taiwanese student who received such close personal attention and care. In order to make sure that the students and trainees from Taiwan had happy and rewarding experiences in the United States, the ECA hired Consultants, Incorporated, a private company based in Boston, to provide comprehensive services. Consultants organized a ten-day long orientation program in Chicago to better prepare the students and trainees for their education and training in this country. Besides discussions on subjects such as American social customs, secondary and higher education in the States, and American labor organizations, special arrangements were made for them to visit universities, colleges, government offices, factories, farms, and so forth. The deepest impression for many students came from their visits to American homes. Peng Guiling, one of the trainees born in Taipei, reported that he really enjoyed the visit and "found that the life in the States was so bright and free that all people could enjoy their lives very much." He also hoped that he could have more opportunities to visit American families so that he could "understand the States more rightly and deeply."[41] Once all the students and trainees started their programs, the company requested that they send in a monthly report so that it could include some of the contents in the *Cosin Commentator*, a newsletter published to serve them. With the first issue printed on October 24, 1951, the newsletter not only allowed students to share their activities with each other but also provided a venue for the company to answer questions from students and share important information with them. It was through this newsletter that the students and trainees were informed that they did not need to register with the INS, that they could go to the

Chamber of Commerce for more information on local institutions and activities, and that their visa extension applications were handled by the ECA. The reports from students and trainees were sent to ECA headquarters and then forwarded to Taipei to be examined by the ECA mission and the JCRR.[42] Under such close supervision, all students and trainees completed their programs and returned to Taiwan on time.

The successful completion of the first ECA/JCRR scholarship program provided a model for the implementation of American technical assistance to Taiwan throughout the 1950s. Under the Mutual Security Act, American economic aid to Taiwan had three components. The first was defense support, which covered the construction of road, bridges, dams, and power stations aimed at strengthening Taiwan's defense abilities. The second was technical cooperation, which was designed to share technical knowledge and skills with Taiwan so that it could more effectively develop its economy and improve the living standards of its people. The third was the use of funds generated from selling surplus agricultural commodities purchased from the United States with American aid money to develop Taiwan's agriculture and industry. In addition to the huge demand for well-trained specialists created by numerous defense support projects, technical cooperation itself needed a large number of experts to cover vast areas including land reform, agricultural production, industrial modernization, public health, vocational education, rural electrification, improvement of the fishery and forestry sectors, and so on. Sending key individuals involved in MSA projects in Taiwan to the United States for short-term practical training became an effective way to meet the needs for skilled experts in technical and other fields. In order to better coordinate the technical training, the Council for United States Aid (CUSA) of the Executive Yuan joined the MSA and the JCRR in establishing the U.S. Aid Technical Assistance Committee (USATAC). The committee reviewed proposals from the Nationalist government, recommended annual plans to MSA headquarters in Washington, and implemented the programs approved by the MSA. Between 1951 and 1958, Taiwan sent 1,087 individuals to the United States for technical training and education as part of the American technical assistance package. While the largest cohort, 242 in total, came from agriculture, tens if not hundreds of selected individuals in manufacturing, transportation, electrical power generation, vocational education, and public health also participated in various training programs.[43]

As the ECA and its successor, the MSA, sent an unprecedentedly large number of technical trainees from Taiwan to the United States, the State Department also brought some students, scholars, and teachers, although in a much smaller number, across the Pacific. In 1951, the State Department's exchange of persons program sponsored eight students and four scholars to pursue graduate education or conduct research in humanities, social sciences, law, journalism, natural science, and medicine. While the number of graduate students was reduced to five in 1952, the Department of State started an English teacher-training program that sent nine teachers to Columbia University and the University of Michigan.[44] Such a small number of individuals involved in the State Department's nontechnical programs caused strong concern on the part of Karl L. Rankin, the American ambassador in Taipei. In a letter to the State Department on November 4, 1953, he presented a survey on the exchange of persons in Taiwan and lamented that almost nothing had been done in the field of information media or in the humanities. He thus recommended that "all of the present resources of the Department be used in those neglected fields and that every possible effort be made, through an increased appropriation under Public Law 402 and through the early reactivation of the Fulbright Program to strengthen the program."[45] Agreeing with Rankin's assessment and recommendation, the State Department started to put greater attention to and more resources in bringing more students, teachers, scholars, artists, and others in nontechnical fields to the United States in the following years. However, given its limited resources and the lack of interest from the Nationalist government, the State Department was never able to get nearly as many individuals in Taiwan involved in its programs as ECA or MSA did.

Promoting Vocational Education

Encouraged by its early success, the ECA and its successor, the MSA, came up with a more ambitious plan to train a much greater number of capable technicians, skilled farmers, and engineers locally. The goal was to further strengthen Taiwan's economy and sustainability by expanding and modernizing its industry and agriculture. The core of the plan was to dramatically increase the offer of vocational training in agriculture and industry on the island. The first step taken by the ECA was to improve and expand vocational teacher-education programs at the Provincial Teachers' College. The ECA believed that its first goal could be achieved by pairing the college with an "affiliating" American university so that the vocational schools in Taiwan could soon be staffed with well-trained and qualified teachers.[46]

The initial response from the Nationalist government was mixed. The JCRR's attitude was not encouraging, since it believed that the time was not ripe for the MSA's affiliation programs, given the poor condition of colleges in Taiwan. In addition, it already had a different plan set for agricultural teachers training in Taiwan. Despite the lack of interest from JCRR, the MSA kept pushing its program forward. In order to seek cooperation from the Nationalist government and get firsthand information, Clarence R. Decker, assistant director, and J. Russell Andrus, education advisor to the Far East Program Division, the latter accompanied by Wayne O. Reed, assistant commissioner of education, visited Taiwan in June and July respectively. After meetings with Chinese officials and visiting schools and colleges in Taiwan, the American visitors became more confident in their educational program. Writing to Tien-fong Cheng (Cheng Tianfang), the minister of education, after his visit, Decker emphasized that "education is the basic approach to all of our long-time problems."[47] More than happy to agree with Decker on this point, Cheng took the opportunity to ask the MSA to be "kind enough to provide us every possible aid."[48] Wu Kuo-chen showed appreciation in his letter to Andrus and Reed even before they could return home, thanking them for their offer to "bring about contact of affiliation between Taiwan and a leading American engineering institution" and their readiness to help Taiwan with "technical assistance as well as equipment in the vocational field."[49]

With most Chinese officials on its side, the MSA took immediate steps to identify an American university that would be willing to get involved in the educational program in Taiwan. Assisted by the United States Office of Education (USOE), MSA officials offered four American institutions as potential partners in the affiliation program.[50] Pennsylvania State College was chosen not only because it was on USOE list and the top choice for Taiwan Teachers College, but also because its leaders showed strong interest in the program. After a few meetings between MSA officials and top Penn State administrators, S. Lewis Land, director of vocational teacher education, was chosen as a consultant by the MSA and sent to Taiwan for a survey on the island's need for vocational teacher education. Based on the information gathered through meetings with government officials, college and vocational school administrators, and staff of the MSA mission in Taiwan, Land submitted a twenty-four-page report on December 8, 1952. His major findings, shared in his written as well as oral reports, were that teacher training in industrial fields was urgently needed and would have immediate impact upon the economy. Thus, he recommended that a Department of Industrial Education and a Department of Home Economic Education be established at Taiwan Teachers College to offer in-service training for more than two thousand teachers employed in the fourteen industrial schools and five home economics schools, and preservice training for teachers to meet the needs for future expansion and improvement of vocational training in junior and senior high schools. As for the agricultural aspect of the program, Land concluded that it had been properly placed in the hands of the JCRR and agricultural teacher training should not be carried out by the Taiwan Teachers College. Based on Land's report, the MSA mission in Taipei recommended that the JCRR handle the investigations on the needs for vocational training in agriculture and that the contract with Pennsylvania State College be expedited.[51]

While still working on the industrial education project, the MSA started to find a university in the United States to help improve engineering education in Taiwan. Engineering education came into focus at a meeting between American officials and Wu Kuo-chen on July 26, 1952. They agreed that an engineering contract would be highly appropriate and that the Taiwan Engineering College, the best of its kind on the island according to Wu, should be the top choice if such a contract moved forward.[52] Eager to play a crucial role in the collaboration with an American university in improving engineering education in Taiwan, Ta-Kuin Tsing (Qin Dajun), president of the college, wrote an introduction to the information pamphlet about the college and submitted it to the MSA in September 1952, openly seeking encouragement and help from "our friends."[53] In transmitting the pamphlet to the MSA headquarters, C. L. Terrel, deputy chief of the MSA mission to China, made it clear that the mission believed that "developing a local college based upon the American methods" was "probably the most effective method, from a long run point of view" in supplying Taiwan with the "necessary engineers and trained industrial management." While recognizing the importance of in-service training programs offered by foreign advisers, the mission insisted that "a permanent establishment on Taiwan is also necessary and will give considerable future returns to any investment made at present."[54]

A procedure similar to that applied to the Taiwan Teachers College was followed by the Taiwan Engineering College and other institutions in building their affiliation relations with American colleges. Based on the wishes of Taiwan Engineering College, the MSA first contacted the CIT and worked out a rough agreement with the administration.[55] When the CIT administration reversed its position because of opposition from its board of trustees, the MSA turned to Purdue University after consulting with President Tsing.[56] Fortunately, Purdue administrators, especially Frederick L. Hovde, the president, and Andrey A. Potter, the dean of engineering, showed strong enthusiasm after their meeting with Andrus in Washington, DC.[57] They quickly sent R. Norris Shreve to Taiwan in December to conduct a survey on engineering education. Once the survey was completed, Purdue University signed the contract to commit itself as the affiliation institution with the Engineering College of Taiwan by following the model set by Pennsylvania State College. By the end of 1954, the Medical College and Agricultural College of the National Taiwan University also established affiliation relations with Columbia University and the University of California respectively.[58] Although their cooperation was with colleges in Taiwan, the American universities and colleges signed their contracts with the MSA as required. Such an arrangement allowed the U.S. government to make sure that the collaboration between the colleges on both sides of the Pacific would be effective and efficient and more important would meet its strategic needs.

With Pennsylvania State College and Purdue University on board, the MSA was able to start implementing vocational and engineering education programs in early 1953. On February 3, Emmett Brown, education officer of the MSA mission in Taipei, submitted a two-year plan to headquarters requesting five and eighteen staff members from the two American colleges for fiscal year 1953 and 1954 respectively.[59] Because of the limitations of the MSA's and FOA's budget and the availability of faculty members from the American colleges, the exact number of American experts sent to Taiwan was adjusted when the contracts were signed with Purdue University and Pennsylvania State College. Following the contracts, Purdue University had four faculty members at Taiwan Engineering College and Pennsylvania State College had two at the Taiwan Teachers College, helping the Chinese faculty further developing their institutions. In addition to $323,000 budgeted for personnel expenses, the MSA set aside a similar amount to support the improvement effort at the institutions in

Taiwan.⁶⁰ With funds from the MSA and the FOA, these two institutions were able to build new classrooms and laboratories, rehabilitate old ones, purchase new equipment and books, and send thirty Chinese faculty members to their affiliating American colleges to study for a year by mid-1955. A new Department of Mining and Metallurgy was established at the Taiwan Engineering College, while a new Department of Industrial Education was founded at the Taiwan Teachers College. New instructional methods were adopted at the Taiwanese institutions as a result of this cooperation. To assist in the adoption of new teaching methods, a new Educational Material Center was established at the Teachers College, providing up-to-date instructional materials as well as services from audiovisual and curriculum laboratory sections.⁶¹ The MSA also worked with the JCRR in helping the College of Agriculture at Taichung (Taizhong) establish a Department of Agricultural Education.

While working on the college affiliation projects aimed at improving engineering, industrial, and agricultural education, great effort was made at reforming and rebuilding the industrial and agricultural vocational education in Taiwan. The MSA mission to Taiwan specially created the position of vocational education adviser to provide guidance for such an effort. One existing vocational school was turned into a pilot school in 1952 to start the conversion from an engineering-type curriculum to one focusing on trades that were needed by the industries in Taiwan.⁶² Soon, the new curriculum was adopted by seven more schools selected by the MSA as model schools. With funding provided by the MSA, these schools obtained new equipment, lengthened factory internship for their students, and sent instructors to the United States for in-service training. Between 1952 and 1963, Taiwan's industrial vocational education received more than US$2.5 million and more than 66 million in New Taiwan Currency (NTC) from the United States. The improved industrial vocational schools were able to increase their enrollment by nine times during the same period, supplying industries in Taiwan with an unprecedentedly large number of well-trained technicians.⁶³

The MSA implemented a similar agricultural vocational education program beginning in 1954. It brought in an American expert in agricultural vocational education and had him work with two counterparts from the MOE in developing an experimental program. The new program was first tried out at four pilot agricultural vocational schools, and then twenty-one more schools were selected to participate. The MSA helped all the schools to get new equipment and set a new specialty, integrated agriculture (*zonghe nongye*). By the early 1960s, these schools were able to graduate more than five thousand students each year.[64]

The close cooperation between Washington and Taipei in improving vocational industrial education in Taiwan did not prevent the two sides from setting different goals for the educational programs. As the recipient of massive American military, economic, and technical aid since the outbreak of the Korean War, the Nationalist regime wanted to utilize the resources provided by the United States not only to strengthen its hold on Taiwan and other islands under its control but also to reconquer mainland China through military actions. Jiang Jieshi proposed military attacks on the mainland many times in his talks with visiting top American officials and generals during the Korean War. When Ta-Kuin Tsing introduced the Taiwan College of Engineering to the MSA, he made it clear that his institution was established to "train technical young men for the economic development along the modern lines of the island province of Taiwan in preparation for the reconstruction of continental China when conditions permit."[65] In his opening remarks at the Conference on Industrial Training Programs held on October 20, 1952, T. K. Chang, minister of economic affairs, reminded the attendees that "when we return to the mainland we will need still more trained men." He asked them two questions: "Do we have enough trained labor?" and "How many more do we need to train to go back to mainland?"[66]

However, Washington, while committed to assisting the Nationalist government in defending Taiwan, was always clear that its military, economic, and technical assistance was defensive in nature. This was determined by the Mutual Security Act, aimed at strengthening "the mutual security and individual and collective defense of the free world, to develop their resources in the interest of their security and independence and the national interest of the United States, and to facilitate the effective participation of those countries in the United Nations system for collective security."[67] Thus, Washington, while rejecting Jiang's proposals for major military actions against the Chinese Communist forces, generally ignored Chinese officials' effort to include educational programs as part of their grand plan to regain control of the mainland and stuck closely to the strategic goal set by the Mutual Security Act. In his speech at the Sino-American Conference on Vocational Industrial Education, Schenck likened the economy of Taiwan to an eagle and insisted that it had to have two wings:

a strong agriculture wing and a strong industrial wing. With these two wings, Schenck asserted, the economy of Taiwan could "soar above the storms of the day." While the agricultural wing of the Taiwan eagle was strong and getting stronger, the industrial wing must catch up. The joint effort had given it strength. But it still must be taught to fly with the new strength. Here, Schenck insisted, was where "education comes to the fore."[68]

While constantly rejecting Taipei's attempt to integrate the American economic and technical assistance as part of its effort to militarily reconquer mainland China, Washington never limited educational programs to economic purposes. When planning their educational programs for Taiwan, ECA and MSA officials always kept in mind political development in mainland China and acted accordingly. As the leadership training program was taking shape, R. Allen Griffin, ECA director of the Far East Program Division, reminded Moyer that one of the objectives for ECA activities in Taiwan was to compete with Chinese Communists in winning over the local students. He recognized that the Communists had succeeded in working their way effectively into the student classes and derived "their most vociferous support today from the student class, especially those that were in secondary schools when the Communists took over." Thus, he believed that the ECA should scientifically and imaginatively go after that field and this objective should be as carefully programed as any other objectives. Having dismissed the effectiveness of customary or typical propaganda means, Griffin proposed that "a special effort should be made to bring the students of our countries into our camp" and that part of it could be done by increasing association with them and their teachers.[69] The vocational education programs, in addition to their economic impact, did offer such a venue for the Americans to associate with young students as well as teachers in Taiwan, making them a useful instrument in resisting Communist influence.

The generous assistance provided by the MSA to the Taiwan Teachers College and College of Engineering for the improvement of vocational and engineering education spurred the National Taiwan University, the flagship institution in higher education in the island, to seek larger-scale aid from Washington. On July 2, 1953, National Taiwan University sent a letter to the MSA asking for $3 million to expand its operation. Many top Chinese government officials supported the plea. However, the MSA's first response was negative, pointing out that the proposal was not sufficiently prepared and that the Nationalist government was shifting its responsibility for higher education to Washington.[70] Undeterred by the discouraging comments from MSA officials in Taipei, Chiang Monlin sent a letter directly to Moyer, now MSA's regional director for the Far East, on September 17, 1953. After seeking collaboration between the college of agriculture of his university and an American institution, Chiang again expressed the interest of the Nationalist government in strengthening the entire National Taiwan University. In the reply to his former colleague at the JCRR, Moyer did not close the door on Jiang's first request. However, as for Jiang's second request, he made it clear that U.S. aid to education in Taiwan had gone as far as it could "when contracts covering assistance to a College of Engineering, Vocational Education and a College of Agriculture are in effect."[71] A couple of weeks later, J. Russell Andrus, now acting chief of the Education Division in the Office of Public Services, further clarified MSA policy on this matter. He emphasized that no assistance should be provided for the engineering college of Taiwan University because the MSA's policy "calls for help to only one institution in a given field in any one country." Since Purdue University had already been working with the Industrial College in Tainan, he insisted that no exception be made for the Republic of China.[72]

Expanding Education for Overseas Chinese

Despite the initial rejection from the MSA and the FOA, the National Taiwan University soon became the biggest recipient of American aid beginning in fall 1954. All other colleges and many high schools in Taiwan also received significant assistance from the U.S. government at the same time. Such a dramatic increase of American aid to a large number of educational institutions was made possible because of Washington's decision to expand its collaboration with Taipei from vocational, technical, and engineering education to education for overseas Chinese. With generous assistance from Washington, new classrooms, dormitories, student activity centers, and other buildings were constructed, and laboratories, libraries, audiovisual equipment were updated to rapidly increase the enrollment of overseas Chinese at colleges and secondary schools in Taiwan. This new focus on education for overseas Chinese not only effectively expanded American aid to Taiwan's education but also marked a shift of Washington's strategic priority in 1953. With the defense of Taiwan secured and the Korean War halted, American policymakers became less worried about the fall of the island to the Communist China or its military aggression. Instead, they started to take steps to help Taiwan in intensifying its effort to attract more overseas Chinese students to the island for education. To those policymakers, the expansion of education of overseas Chinese would help contain the Chinese Communist penetration in Southeast Asia and push Taipei to shift its focus from using Taiwan as a beachhead for military attacks on the Communist-controlled mainland to building the island as an anticommunist cultural bastion.

Washington's deep involvement in the expansion of education for overseas Chinese in Taiwan began with Vice President Richard Nixon's visit to the island in November 1953. Only months in the White House, President Eisenhower asked Nixon to take an official trip to South and Southeast Asia to remedy what he believed to be Truman's neglect of the region. Such a trip gained importance as the Korean War came to a stop and Beijing intensified its effort to expand Communist China's interaction with newly independent nations in Southeast Asia. Nixon set four major goals for his Asian visit: reassuring American friends and allies, explaining American policies, having a firsthand look at the situation in Indochina, and assessing Asian attitudes toward rising Red China. Deeply concerned with the lack of understanding and even suspicion of the United States prevailing in those young nations, Nixon decided to maximize his direct interactions with students, laborers, businessmen, intellectuals, politicians, military men, and farmers. Through these direct and broad contacts with local people, Nixon found out that Communist China's influence "was already spreading throughout the area" and that Beijing was successful in attracting many young overseas Chinese students to receive college education in mainland China, with about one thousand students from Indonesia each year.[73]

Once he arrived in Taipei, Nixon took every opportunity to question various groups as well as individuals about the situation and recommend that a program be instituted in Taiwan to meet the challenge.[74] Nixon's strenuous effort to push for the expansion of education for overseas Chinese was best illustrated by his speech delivered at the groundbreaking ceremony for Tunghai University in Taichung on November 11, 1953. Speaking in front of a large group of high-ranking government officials, educators, and local dignitaries, Nixon praised the military and economic strength gained by Taiwan in the past three years with assistance from the United

States. However, he warned his audience that it was still possible to lose the fight against Communism despite all the strength in all these fields because thousands and thousands of young students had gone from Southeast Asia to Beijing and other cities on the mainland for education. He emphasized that the future of Southeast Asia depended very much on the training of local leaders. It would be devastating for Southeast Asia if a large number of young students were allowed to go to mainland China. Having noticed that only a small number of overseas Chinese students attended schools in Taiwan, Nixon called upon the Nationalist leaders to take steps to attract more young overseas Chinese to Taiwan and promised more American financial support for that effort. He made it clear that he wanted to see the island become not only "a bastion of military and economic strength for free China," but also "a bastion of cultural strength, of spiritual strength, and a sample for all people to see."[75]

Although military bastion was mentioned in his widely publicized speech, Nixon, like many other American officials who visited Taiwan before and after him, set very clear limits for the use of such a bastion. During his seven-hour meeting with Jiang Jieshi, Nixon, while refraining from telling him outright that "his chances of reuniting China under his rule were virtually nonexistent," did make it clear that "American military power would not be committed to support any invasion he might launch."[76] If the U.S. government must tell the Nationalist leaders that "they can't go back to the mainland," what should be done with Taiwan? Nixon offered an answer to his own rhetoric question at a National Security Council meeting on December 2, 1953. He believed that it was still important to "retain Formosa as the receptacle of overseas Chinese culture and as a symbol."[77]

Expanding American aid to education for overseas Chinese in Taiwan was anything but Nixon's spontaneous personal response to the situation in Southeast Asia. On November 6, 1953, about a week before Nixon's cultural bastion speech, the National Security Council (NSC) issued a Statement of Policy, NSC 142/6, clearly listing U.S. objectives and courses of action with respect to Taiwan and the Nationalist government. Most of the objectives, especially the first one, were aimed at strengthening the political, military, and economic positions of the Nationalist government so that Washington could keep its commitment to the "maintenance of the security of Formosa, independent of communism, as an essential element within the U.S. Far East defense position." The eighth objective, reflecting Eisenhower administration's attention to Southeast Asia after the Korean War came to a stop, was relatively new. It called for increased "support for the Chinese National Government by all non-Communist Chinese groups outside mainland China and Formosa, especially the overseas Chinese of Southeast Asia." In order to achieve the last objective, the course of action prescribed by the NSC included encouraging the Nationalist government to establish closer contact with overseas Chinese communities and "take steps to win their sympathy and their support." While making efforts to show continuing friendship to the Nationalist government, the NSC directed American officials to avoid giving "any implication of U.S. obligation to underwrite the [Nationalist] Government or to guarantee its return to power on the mainland."[78] The NSC's opposition to overthrowing the Chinese Communist regime with U.S. military forces was emphasized in another statement of policy, NSC 166/1, approved by President Eisenhower on the same day.[79]

Winning support from overseas Chinese communities and even offering education for overseas Chinese students were nothing new for the Nationalists. The Nationalist revolution led by Sun Yat-sen, the founder of the Nationalist Party, depended very much on support from overseas Chinese communities since the very beginning. As soon as the Nationalist government fled to Taiwan, Jiang Jieshi began to pay even closer attention to overseas Chinese. To him, the Nationalist Party's retake of mainland China depended on three major forces: overseas Chinese, the military and people in Taiwan, and anticommunist forces on the mainland. He was confident that "with the three forces joined together, the victory of the anti-Communist war is certain."[80] Following Jiang's instruction, the MOE issued a guideline in 1950 allowing overseas Chinese students to enter colleges and universities on the island without taking an entrance examination. More special regulations were adopted in the following years to encourage overseas Chinese students to return to Taiwan for education and to provide special treatment in visa applications and college admission. In October 1952 the Nationalist Party held the First Conference on Overseas Chinese Affairs and Jiang required all officials and overseas Chinese representatives at the meeting to pay immediate and most serious attention to youth education. He emphasized that in order to support anticommunist national policy, all overseas Chinese needed to have wisdom and skills so that they could fight for the survival of the nation. Cheng Yan-fen (Zheng Yanfen), chair of the Overseas Chinese Affairs Commission (OCAC), echoed Jiang by stressing that "the focus of our work is developing overseas Chinese education."[81]

Although some practical measures were taken to attract overseas Chinese students to Taiwan for education since 1952, the results did not meet expectations. The National Taiwan University and other provincial colleges were open to overseas Chinese students despite the high demand for enrollment among local people. In addition to low tuition and inexpensive dormitory spaces, scholarships were provided to needy students to cover maintenance costs. The average time needed to obtain an entry permit was reduced from eight months to eight weeks by 1953. Despite all these efforts, only 1,145 students entered higher education institutions in Taiwan between 1950 and 1953, including 242 admitted to military colleges and academies. The vast majority of these students, 1,008 in total, came from Hong Kong and Macau. Only 137 arrived from Southeast Asia, while 826 came to Taiwan in 1953. In sharp contrast, about ten thousand overseas Chinese students went to mainland China during the same period. Both the Nationalist government and the American embassy in Taipei believed that such a situation could not be changed with the "present limited facilities and lack of funds for more financial aid to students who might wish to come here."[82]

Given this situation, Nixon's call for sharper focus on education for overseas Chinese understandably aroused immediate and positive response from officials in both governments. On November 20, Chen Cheng called a meeting attended by the ministers of foreign affairs and education, the American ambassador, and the director of the FOA mission in Taipei. The top Chinese officials and American diplomats at the meeting all agreed to work together to expand education for overseas Chinese in Taiwan. Cheng Yan-fen forwarded the commission's proposal to Yeh Kung-chao, the minister of foreign affairs, on December 14, 1953, seeking his help in obtaining financial assistance from the U.S. government for the implementation.[83] After informal discussions among themselves, American diplomats and officials at the embassy, the USIS, and the FOA all agreed to push for further action. Karl Rankin sent a letter to Chen Cheng on November 24, 1954, suggesting the formation of a working group composed of appropriate Chinese officials to further explore the subject. He informed the premier that "we shall all be happy to consult with the group."[84] After a discussion on the subject at Chen's residence on January 20, 1954, Rankin designated H. Emmett Brown and Dorothy Whipple, the cultural attaché at the American embassy, as American representatives at the working group.[85] After

Cheng Tien-fong; Cheng Yan-fen; Wong Peng (Wang Peng), secretary of the CUSA; and Teng Chuan-kai (Deng Chuankai), director of the department of education of Taiwan Province, were appointed by Chen Cheng as the Chinese representatives, the joint working group was formed.

While the American diplomats and Chinese officials worked diligently to get the ball rolling, the Office of Intelligence Research of the State Department conducted a thorough investigation on the subject. On January 4, 1954, the office submitted a special report, *The Problem of Education of Overseas Chinese*, providing badly needed information and analysis on the subject. The report emphasized that the ten to twelve million Chinese residents in various countries in the Far East represented an "important and as yet uncommitted element in the East-West struggle." Both the Chinese Communist regime and the Nationalist government, the report showed, had launched programs to compete for "their minds, loyalty and energies." However, it recognized that the Chinese Communist regime had been more successful, since at least ten thousand overseas Chinese students traveled to mainland China for middle school and university education in 1953 and an additional twelve thousand students went between 1949 and 1952, with the vast majority of them, about fourteen thousand, coming from Indonesia. In sharp contrast, only 1,199 overseas Chinese students went to Taiwan by the end of 1953, with 935 from Hong Kong and Macau. It credited Beijing's success to its greater influence on secondary education in Southeast Asian countries, more generous monetary inducement offered to students, and greater physical facilities in advanced education. It also identified the major causes for fewer overseas Chinese students in Taiwan. The first was the shortage of educational facilities in Taiwan, which were already stretched to the limit when the eight higher-education institutions enrolled about 9,800 students in fall 1952. The second was the lack of promotion from the Nationalist government, especially before 1952, as well as financial assistance for overseas Chinese students after that. The third was the requirement for two guarantors in student visa applications, presenting "a serious psychological barrier to many overseas Chinese students."[86]

The information and analysis of the report became immediately useful when discussions between the American and Chinese officials started in Taipei. Chaired by Cheng Tien-fong, the working group met three times in February 1954. It had heated discussions on the proposals presented by the MOE and the OCAC. While taking issue with almost all the key features of the expansion program proposed by the Nationalist government, the opposition of American representatives was focused on two areas. One was the activities proposed by the OCAC that included providing textbooks for overseas Chinese schools in Southeast Asian nations, training teachers for those schools, sending teachers and cultural workers to those countries, subsidizing or assisting anticommunist newspapers there, and more. American members worried that those activities would not be acceptable to the host countries and that the million dollars requested for those projects would be wasted. Thus, they insisted that the U.S. government have no part in this kind of operation, at least overtly.[87]

The other was the MOE's plan to build a separate university and middle school to accommodate 5,050 and 2,700 overseas Chinese students respectively. The MOE requested $10 million up front for facilities as well as equipment and $30 million for a trust fund that would generate enough return to cover the $2 million annual maintenance cost.[88] The American members believed that this plan would not help significantly increase the admission of overseas Chinese students to colleges and schools in Taiwan in the coming 1954–1955 academic year. More important, overseas Chinese students attending these separate institutions would have "little opportunity to come in contact with the people in free China and find out the extent of their mutuality of interests," defeating "one aspect of the purpose of the program."[89]

Having voiced their objections to the Chinese proposals, the American representatives presented their recommendations to the working group. Instead of building new separate educational institutions and utilizing only one university for overseas Chinese education, they proposed adding classrooms, dormitories, and other physical facilities in all existing colleges and some middle schools. With such a moderate program, they called for only nine million NTC, equivalent to about $580,000, to be drawn from counterpart funds for the first year. However, based on careful study, they set a clear and ambitious goal for academic year 1954–1955. They proposed to offer grants to a thousand overseas Chinese students, rather than five hundred as originally proposed by the Nationalist government, with eight hundred from Hong Kong and Macau and two hundred from Southeast Asian nations. They also recommended that grants be offered to three hundred middle school students.[90] Without counting students attending military colleges and academies, this total would far exceed the number of overseas Chinese students admitted to colleges and schools in Taiwan in the previous four years.[91]

With backing from the American embassy and the FOA mission in Taipei, the recommendations made by American representatives were approved by the working group and forwarded to Chen Cheng on March 2 for discussion and decision by senior officials.[92] Such a meeting was held in Xingzhengyuan on April 22, and four resolutions were reached based on the working group's recommendation. First, it approved that the expansion of education for overseas Chinese would begin in summer 1954 with the expectation of admitting one thousand college students and three hundred middle school students through adding classes in existing colleges and schools. Construction and equipment expenses, totaling 8.67 million NTC, would be drawn from counterpart American aid, while maintenance expenses, 2,176,800 NTC in total, would be shouldered by the Nationalist government. Second, it accepted in principle the recommendation to establish a new middle school with a college preparation class for overseas Chinese students the next year. The working group was instructed to come up with a detailed plan for final approval. Third, recognizing that it was impractical to establish a separate university for overseas Chinese, it considered adding a college of business administration to the National Taiwan University and overseas Chinese teacher-training classes at the Taiwan Teachers College if needed in the future. The working group was directed to discuss and report on the subject. The last, while agreeing to leave activities in Southeast Asian nations for further discussion, instructed the OCAC to draft a plan to subsidize textbooks for overseas Chinese schools, with funding coming from the Nationalist government.[93]

As soon as the decisions were made, the Chinese and American officials took steps to implement them. Charged by Premier Chen to obtain American aid for the program, Wong Peng sent a letter to J. I. Brent, director of the FOA mission in Taipei, claiming that Nixon had promised additional funding for the expansion of education for overseas Chinese during his visit. Wong requested that the 8.67 million NTC in American assistance for the program be listed as "special projects" and covered by "a special extra appropriation."[94] It is obvious that the Nationalist government wanted to use the expansion of education for overseas Chinese students as an opportunity to obtain more financial assistance from the U.S. government. Agreeing that part of the overseas Chinese education program did go beyond the scope of the FOA China Aid Program's stated objectives, Brent immediately forwarded Wong's inquiry to headquarters in Washington for clarification.[95] Having received no clear instruction on the matter from Washington for weeks, Brent sent a cablegram requesting "soonest FOA/Washington approval" of 8.67 million NTC in fiscal year 1954 for the construction of classrooms and dormitories for 1,300 overseas Chinese students.[96] Upon receiving Brent's letter and cablegram about the same time, Harold Stassen, the FOA director, approved the request on May 21, marking the official beginning of American aid for the expansion of education for overseas Chinese students in Taiwan.[97] However, Stassen sent another letter to Taipei a couple of weeks later, clearly informing the embassy and FOA mission that "no FOA funds outside of regular economic aid for Taiwan are currently available or anticipated to become available for expansion of educational facilities in Taiwan for overseas Chinese." Thus, he requested that the mission in Taipei and the Nationalist government "take this factor into consideration" in preparing future budgets for the program.[98]

Despite the efforts made by American as well as Chinese officials, construction of the new facilities was delayed. The first two dormitory and classroom buildings financed by the FOA for the expansion of education for overseas Chinese at the National Taiwan University were not completed until February 1955. The new dormitory was capable of accommodating 550 students. Although designed to house overseas Chinese students from Southeast Asian countries, about 130 local mainland and Taiwanese students were taken in to provide an opportunity for residents to know and learn from each other. The new classroom building provided spaces for 800 students. The new buildings effectively alleviated the pain caused by the shortage of housing and instructional facilities. Even Ambassador Rankin was aware that many overseas Chinese students came to Taiwan in fall 1954 "were crowded, fifty to a hundred, into one room in the already inadequate dormitories." He hoped that the original resentment among overseas Chinese students would wear off with these new buildings as evidence that "the Chinese and American governments are making an effort to look after them."[99]

A special ceremony was held at the National Taiwan University on February 13, 1955, to celebrate the opening of the two new buildings as well as a fishery laboratory and law library also financed by the FOA. Many high-ranking Chinese officials and top American diplomats attended the ceremony. Vice President Chen Cheng and Ambassador Rankin gave speeches at the event. It was Rankin who made clear the significance of the new buildings and expansion of education for overseas Chinese. He pointed out that the new facilities meant "for the first time more young men from overseas Chinese communities can come to Free China for an education in Chinese—their mother tongue—in the sure knowledge that they will learn the true values of life, learn to penetrate the disguises of communist philosophy and see the false premises on which it is erected, and return to their homes abroad as militant ambassadors on the cause of freedom." He emphasized that schools and universities had become very important places as "the world is plunged into a battle for the minds of men and women—for in them are fought today the battles of tomorrow." He asserted that "if there were enough students attending enough universities in the free world, there would be no battles of tomorrow."[100]

Although the number of overseas Chinese students enrolled at colleges and schools in Taiwan in academic year of 1954–1955 did not quite meet the target, Washington continued to expand its support for the program because of its strategic significance. As early as December 1954, Stassen instructed the FOA mission in Taipei to proceed with the planning for FY1955 American aid to the overseas Chinese education program "as rapidly as possible." He added, "It is our conviction that further action should be taken this fiscal year to attract overseas Chinese to higher educational institutions in Formosa, as the most practical way to counteract the tendency of overseas Chinese to go to Communist China for educational purposes."[101] After months of discussion, the FOA approved the plan presented by its mission in Taipei for FY1955. In addition to 10,810,000 NTC for the building program, the OCAC was authorized to use up to US$80,000 and 500,000 NTC to cover recruitment costs and living expenses for overseas Chinese students.[102] In early 1955 the FOA mission in Taipei decided to subsidize an overseas student newspaper to enrich and improve their educational experiences in Taiwan. After a few meetings with students and faculty representatives at the National Taiwan University, the mission selected *Sea Breeze* (*Haifeng*), a monthly newspaper published by the Sea Breeze Literacy Society organized by students from Hong Kong and Macau. It agreed to subsidize the publication at $330, half of the cost, for each issue with the understanding that the newspaper would expand from four to eight pages and solicit articles from students coming from Southeast Asia countries.[103]

Although several U.S. government agencies and their offices in Taipei worked together closely to start American aid to education for overseas Chinese in Taiwan, serious disagreements began to emerge on how to evaluate and expand the program. First of all, the FOA and its successor, the International Cooperation Administration (ICA) mission in Taipei believed that the United States should aid education for overseas Chinese students at the senior high school level, while the embassy and USIS insisted that only college-level education for overseas Chinese students be supported. The embassy countered that there was adequate opportunity for middle school students in Southeast Asian nations to get an education locally and that drawing them away from their home community violated the State Department's policy of assimilation. Second, the FOA/ICA mission, while putting greater emphasis on attracting students from Southeast Asian countries, recognized the importance of offering education to students from Hong Kong and Macau. However, the embassy did not want to see much American aid go to those students. It believed that it was pointless to support educating those students because they would not go back to mainland China and the two cities could be taken over by the Communists any time. Last, although both the FOA/ICA mission and the embassy wanted to see overseas Chinese students return to their home countries after receiving education in Taiwan, they disagreed on whether any of them should be allowed to have extended stay after graduation. The embassy would consider it a complete failure if some overseas Chinese students did not return home after graduation. The FOA/ICA mission recognized the fact that a large number of overseas Chinese students did not want to return to their home countries and would not see it as a complete failure if a large minority decided to remain in Taiwan. Unable to resolve their differences, the ICA mission and the embassy in Taipei agreed to involve ICA headquarters and the Department of State for solutions.[104]

Neither the ICA headquarters nor the Department of State issued a clear policy directive on those disagreements immediately. Instead, they decided to wait for the report from Payne Templeton, the Overseas Chinese educationist assigned to the educational section of the ICA mission in Taipei. He was sent to Southeast Asian countries to study "various phases of the problem of overseas Chinese education," beginning on January 29, 1956. In a cablegram sent to the ICA mission in Taipei, ICA Acting Director Dennis A. Fitzgerald made it clear that the State Department, USIS, and ICA wanted to emphasize the danger of the generalization of education for overseas Chinese and the necessity of assessing the situation on a country-by-country basis. He pointed out that the success of Templeton's trip depended on his contribution to the mission's understanding of the situation and provision of guidance on recommendations for the future development of overseas Chinese education in Taiwan.[105] Well aware of expectations, Templeton set out to "extend our understanding of the general situation facing the overseas Chinese in Southeastern Asian countries" and "find more exact information concerning the Chinese Schools and the possibilities of greater recruitment to Taiwan."[106]

After meeting with American officials in ICA missions, American embassies and consulates, USIS posts, and representatives of the Asian Foundation in Singapore, the Malayan Federation, Indonesia, Burma, Thailand, Cambodia, and Vietnam, Templeton completed a detailed report in mid-March. In addition to providing country-by-country data on overseas Chinese education, Templeton presented his findings and a long list of recommendations. His first recommendation was to amend the present policy so that secondary school students could receive American support. Such an expansion, he insisted, was needed because "any competition with the Communists for students in Burma, Cambodia, and Thailand "must take place largely on the secondary school level, since there are no Chinese senior middle schools to prepare students for college." He also recommended that needy Hong Kong and Macao students be included in receiving American aid for transportation and living expenses. He argued that it was necessary and important to recruit students from Hong Kong and Macao because "without the possibility of going to Taiwan there is too much chance that many more students than now would go to Mainland China." He did see the need for overseas Chinese students to return to their home countries and proposed that it "may be necessary for American personnel to require periodic reports from the responsible Chinese officials concerning the return home after graduation."[107]

The Templeton report received immediate attention, strong support, and quick approval from almost all the U.S. government agencies involved in the program. Emboldened by Templeton's findings and conclusions, the ICA mission in Taipei began to plan the limited use of money available in the current fiscal year to aid Taiwan secondary school expansion for overseas Chinese education even before he could officially submit his report.[108] Once Templeton's report was received, the Department of State, ICA, and USIS quickly issued a joint instruction, approving in principle the limited secondary school program.[109] Only days later, five officials, one from the USIS and two each from the embassy as well as the ICA mission in Taipei held a group discussion on Templeton's report and reached agreements on all three major issues. They agreed that "senior middle school students should be included in the Overseas Chinese Education Program" and that at least six hundred students at that level should be admitted in fall 1956. They shared Templeton's view that junior middle school students could be admitted under special circumstances. They also agreed that it was impossible to force overseas Chinese students to go back to their home countries after graduation despite the obvious need for their return. What they could do was to "impress the Chinese officials the desirability of encouraging such return." As for the large number of students from Hong Kong in the program, they all accepted that it did not handicap the overall objective of preventing as many students as possible from going to the mainland.[110] In their formal statement attached to the Templeton report disseminated among ICA missions in Southeast Asian countries, the embassy and the USIS formally declared that they were in agreement with most of his recommendations. "It is in the interests of denying Chinese students to the Mainland," they emphasized, that they changed their positions.[111]

Backed by Templeton's comprehensive report and support from the embassy and the USIS, the ICA took immediate steps to expand its aid to education for overseas Chinese. By early May 1956, the education section of ICA mission in Taipei had convinced the MOE to organize a joint committee on guidance and send it to various colleges involved in overseas Chinese education. Its visits drew much attention to the problems in guidance and counseling services for overseas Chinese students. A specialist was recruited from the United States and sent to Taipei to address those problems. The ICA mission also worked closely with the OCAC in preparing publicity materials targeting prospective students in Southeast Asia countries. Their joint effort resulted in the publication of a combined catalogue for collegiate institutions in Taiwan and a pictorial booklet. They also planned to cooperate with OCAC in making a film on educational opportunities on the island so that they could be sent to any Southeast Asian countries that were willing to accept it.[112] Later in the year, the ICA mission extended the existing policy and practices in planning the Overseas Chinese Education Program for FY1957 by admitting overseas Chinese students to secondary schools in Taiwan, training teachers for Chinese schools overseas, subsidizing the Chung Hwa Correspondence School operated by the OCAC for overseas Chinese students, and publishing textbooks for overseas Chinese schools and other propaganda materials.[113] The State

Department and ICA headquarters quickly approved the plan. The only restriction was to limit American support for the publication and supply of textbooks to Cambodia as an emergency measure.[114]

With the increase of American aid and involvement, the overseas Chinese education program kept growing in 1957 and 1958. In 1957, 3,200 overseas Chinese students went to Taiwan for education. By fall 1958, there were about 7,000 overseas Chinese students in Taiwan, 5,000 attending colleges and 2,000 going to senior middle school. With $190,688 and 15 million NTC from the U.S. government, the OCAC alone was able to provide living allowance for 4,109 overseas Chinese students, pay medical expenses for 446, and cover travel expenses for 1,727. With additional scholarships, free books, and other assistance offered by the MOE and other nongovernmental agencies, most overseas Chinese students enjoyed free secondary as well as higher education in Taiwan. Such a sharp increase of overseas Chinese students could be best seen at the National Taiwan University. Between 1950 and 1953, the University admitted only 159 overseas Chinese students. With the influx of American aid, the National Taiwan University enrolled 2,477 overseas Chinese students between 1954 and 1957. In fall 1958, among 7,000 students attending the university, 1,900, over 27 percent, were from overseas.[115] As the institution with the largest enrollment of overseas Chinese students, National Taiwan University received the most funding, more than NTC67 million, from the U.S. government, allowing it to expand its facilities and improve its equipment.[116]

The sharp increase in overseas Chinese students in Taiwan between 1954 and 1958, while giving satisfaction to many American government officials, caused increasing concern at the same time. The State Department and the ICA constantly instructed posts in Southeast Asia to review and evaluate the progress as well as effectiveness of the overseas Chinese education program. On July 2, 1958, Secretary Dulles sent instructions to eleven embassies in Southeast Asia to "furnish the latest figures they be able to obtain on the movement of students during the latter half of 1957 and 1958." Having recognized the impressive increase in overseas Chinese students going to Taiwan since 1950, he pointed out that there was "a limit to the number that can be accommodated." He even wondered whether the point had been reached when the number of new students might have to be determined by the number of graduates who could vacate slots for them. He asked the embassy in Taipei to "bear this point in mind in future reporting on the subjects." From the consulate general in Hong Kong, he demanded figures on overseas Chinese students who went to mainland China. And he requested that all posts report on the effect of the apparent shift in Chinese Communist policy that discouraged overseas Chinese students from going to the mainland and on the impact of the exodus of several hundred Chinese students who had become disillusioned with conditions in Communist China.[117]

The reports coming back from the posts, especially those from the embassy in Taipei, proved that Dulles's concerns were not unfounded. In an update sent to the State Department in January 1959, the embassy reported that although overseas Chinese students in Taiwan totaled 6,977, an impressive new high, in January 1959, the new students admitted in academic year 1958–1959 drastically decreased to 1,601, only about half of the number of new students enrolled in January 1958. More alarmingly, the decrease was seen in all countries and regions without exception. The greatest proportional decreases in new students took place in South Vietnam, Thailand, the Philippines, and Cambodia. The decrease, according to the embassy, was caused by three factors. One was the tighter visa restrictions imposed by Southeast Asian countries, making it difficult if not impossible for many students to go to Taiwan. Among 869 students accepted by colleges and schools in Taiwan, only 343 were allowed to leave Indonesia.[118] Another was the stricter admission standard adopted by colleges and universities in Taiwan, reflecting the Nationalist government's new emphasis on quality over quantity. Among 4,000 plus overseas Chinese students who applied for colleges and schools in Taiwan in 1958, only 2,848 were accepted, fewer than the number of students actually enrolled the year before.[119] Applicants in Hong Kong reached 1,659 the same year, the highest number since 1950. However, only 729 were accepted, the lowest since 1954 both in number and percentage.[120] The last was the Second Taiwan Strait Crisis, which broke out in August 1958 when Communist forces started shelling Jinmen (Quemoy) and Mazu (Matsu), the two offshore islands controlled by Nationalist forces. The military actions in the Taiwan Strait intensified the concern about the security and future of Taiwan, keeping some students from coming to the island.

Faced with this new situation, the embassy started to contemplate major changes in American aid to education for overseas Chinese in Taiwan. Before it formally presented its recommendations to Washington, the embassy sent inquiries first to American embassies in Southeast Asia nations and the consulate general in Hong Kong for their comments. Most posts shared the same belief that "a levelling off or decrease in the number of overseas Chinese students coming to Taiwan would be unlikely to result in increasing number of students going to the Communist mainland or a notable enhancement in Communist influence among the overseas Chinese or others in Southeast Asia." It was after receiving this assuring assessment that Ambassador Everett F. Drumright forwarded the embassy's six-point recommendation to the Department of State on August 5, 1959. He suggested that further construction and purchases of new equipment for the overseas Chinese education program be halted, that support for maintenance of new college students be sharply curtailed, that no further new high school students be supported, that ICA subsidies for recruitment, publication, films, and similar materials be suspended, and that the funds saved from those expenditures be used to finance small groups of education officials, teachers, and students from Southeast Asian countries for short-term visits to the ROC. He added that greater emphasis should be placed on treating the education of overseas Chinese as part of the total educational program in Taiwan.[121]

Besides its concurrence with Ambassador Drumright's recommendation, the ICA mission in Taipei started to plan the reduction of American aid to overseas Chinese education program in mid-July. In a report sent to ICA headquarters in September, the mission pointed out that changes had become necessary because of the successful completion of certain phases of the program and political as well as economic conditions prevailing in Southeast Asian nations. With an anticipated smaller number of overseas Chinese students coming to Taiwan in 1960, about 1,700 rather than 2,500, and sufficient dormitories, classrooms, laboratories, and libraries built in the previous years, it planned to stop adding new faculties after all the construction projects were completed in 1960, gradually reduce and eventually discontinue the admission of high school students, and deemphasize the recruitment of overseas Chinese students. It stopped financial support for recruiting those students; reduced the budget for facility construction from NTC27 million for 1959, which was already a couple of million less than 1958; slotted only NTC5.6 million for 1960 to complete unfinished construction projects; and set no budget for 1961. The total American aid to overseas Chinese education from counterpart funds would be cut from NTC48 million in 1959 to NTC28 million in 1960. While recognizing that there was still a need to develop better programs of guidance, leadership training, curricular activities, and tutorial services for the overseas students who were already in Taiwan, the mission was ready to shift "the programs initiated in the overseas education project to education in general and applying to all students on the island."[122]

Given the importance of the overseas Chinese education program, Washington sought more detailed assessment to make sure that the reduction of American aid would not be unbearable for Taipei or impede the struggle against Communist China. Immediately after receiving the embassy's recommendation for the revision of overseas Chinese educational program, the State Department requested an analysis of the probable reaction from the Nationalist government to the proposed revisions and the extent to which it would be willing and financially able to go ahead with the programs on its own.[123] The embassy's assessment was comprehensive and nuanced. While recognizing that it would be unlikely for the Nationalist government to maintain the size of the current overseas Chinese educational program in the face of the certain reduction of American aid, it assured that with the reduced amount of aid, the U.S. government would still be able to support five hundred new college students each year and maintain two thousand overseas students in Taiwan in total. This would help provide for those overseas Chinese who had no other educational outlet except for the Communist mainland. Most important, the embassy emphasized that it "does not believe it is advisable to consider the overseas Chinese educational program primarily in the light of a contest with Peiping for students," given the available evidence that most overseas Chinese students did not want to go to Communist China and the Communist regime did not want them because they were regarded as troublemakers. Because Communist penetration and influence were no longer a problem, the embassy insisted that the overseas Chinse education program "should be subordinated to the broader aim of encouraging the overseas Chinese to identify themselves with their countries of residence."[124]

The recommendations from the embassy and the ICA mission in Taipei received approval from Washington. American aid to building construction and equipment purchase was stopped in 1961 and 1962 respectively. Funding for overseas Chinese students' transportation, living expenses, and extracurricular activities was reduced in 1961 and terminated in 1965 as the U.S. government halted economic and technical assistance to Taiwan. Between 1954 and 1965, Washington provided more than NTC311 million and more than $1 million to support the overseas Chinese education program in Taiwan. Totaling more than $21 million, this was twice the amount provided for the emergency aid program to Chinese students in the United States and no doubt the largest American aid to an educational program in a foreign country. It was with such generous aid, counting for about 90 percent of the funding for the program during the period, that the Nationalist government was able to attract and support more than twenty thousand overseas Chinese students for education in Taiwan.[125] In sharp contrast to the steady growth of the number of overseas Chinese students going to Taiwan since the mid-1950s, fewer students went to Communist China from overseas, and more than twelve thousand overseas Chinese students fled the mainland in 1962 because of the deterioration of political and economic conditions.[126] Based on the sharp decline of the number of Chinese students going to Communist China from Singapore, Hong Kong, and Southeast Asia countries, Reuters concluded in a report published on February 6, 1961, that Beijing's plan to attract more foreign and overseas Chinese students had failed.[127]

The reduction and eventual termination of American aid only drove the Nationalist government to intensify its own effort at attracting overseas Chinese students to Taiwan for education. Beginning in 1962, the Nationalist government allocated more funds to the program, although it required overseas Chinese students to pay for their own transportation, fees, books, housing; allowed private colleges to admit students from overseas; and offered specially designed vocational and technical education for those students to increase the appeal of education in Taiwan.[128] As a result, only 1961 and 1962 saw a minor reduction, about four hundred, of new overseas Chinese students entering colleges in Taiwan. The enrollment of new overseas Chinese college students returned to more than eighteen hundred in 1963, the highest level reached in 1959 and 1960. The number went beyond two thousand for the first time in 1967 and kept growing in the following decade. According to a survey conducted by the OCAC in 1971, more than fifteen thousand overseas Chinese students graduated from colleges in Taiwan. While 14 percent of the graduates pursued further education in the United States and other countries, the vast majority of them, more than 11,500, went back to their countries of residence. The educational experience in Taiwan not only helped the returnees make great contributions to their local economic and cultural development but also solidified their identification with the Nationalist government in Taiwan and strengthened the anticommunist forces in overseas Chinese communities. Qian Zhongjie, a manager at the Nanfeng Textile factory in Hong

Kong and a returnee from Taiwan, organized many workers to stay away from riots as well as strikes instigated by Chinese Communists in the city in 1967. More than thirty overseas Chinese graduates studying at Waterloo University, Canada, went across the country urging the government not to recognize the People's Republic of China or allow it to enter the United Nations.[129]

The reduction and termination of American aid to education for overseas Chinese in Taiwan was anything but the end of the expansion of bilateral cultural exchange. Actually, cultural and educational exchanges between the United States and Taiwan kept growing throughout the remaining years of the Cold War, with strong support from both Taipei and Washington. Through their collaboration on the reactivation of the Fulbright Program in 1957, the implementation of Taiwan's National Long-Term Science Development Plan beginning in 1959, and the support for science education in Taiwan and student exchange, hundreds of professors, teachers, scholars, scientists, educational leaders and thousands of students from both sides were able to participate in various exchange programs.[130] By the end of the 1960s, the number of Taiwanese students in the United States and the number of American students going to Taiwan far exceeded the number of the students involved in the Sino-American educational exchange in the previous century. The close cultural relations built between the United States and Taiwan in the 1950s and the 1960s not only strengthened their military and political alliance but also modernized Taiwan's education as well as science, turning the island into a bastion to contain Chinese Communist ideological and cultural expansion.

CHAPTER V

Faking the Exchange

Having terminated all cultural ties with the United States, Beijing suddenly issued official invitations to a large number of American journalists for a monthlong visit to mainland China in August 1956. Although Washington managed to persuade the first group of invited reporters and their employers to abide by existing travel restrictions and turn down the invitations, three American journalists openly defied the travel ban and entered Communist China in December. Under heavy pressure from journalists and news organizations, the State Department gave up its plan to punish the travel-ban breakers and allowed twenty-plus news companies to send representatives to mainland China in the summer of 1957. However, Beijing, on the grounds that no reciprocity was guaranteed by Washington, refused to grant visas to any of those American reporters, even though many had received its invitation the year before and all had obtained proper authorization from the U.S. government. The State Department's promise to review visa applications from Chinese reporters for admission to the United States was not enough to convince Beijing to change its position. By allowing no Chinese reporters to apply for admission to the United States and approving no visa applications from American correspondents, Beijing not only made the exchange of journalists impossible but also shut the door to any cultural interactions sanctioned by both governments.

Neither Beijing nor Washington was really interested in restoring cultural relations, including the exchange of journalists, in the mid-1950s. When Beijing packaged the restoration of cultural relations in its agenda for the ambassadorial talks in Geneva and sent invitations to some small groups of carefully chosen Americans, it continued to cleanse American cultural influence in China. Its real goal for the new moves was to build an international united front with the American people and isolate the U.S. government through intensifying the contradictions between Americans and their leaders and thus force Washington to enter negotiations on substantive matters in Geneva, weakening its position at home and abroad. The visit of the three American reporters allowed Beijing not only to claim a small victory in intensifying the confrontation between the American journalists and the U.S. government but also to institutionalize the mechanisms designed to manage the experience and shape the views of American visitors. In order to ease pressure from journalists and news organizations, Washington made a limited concession by allowing some American reporters to visit the PRC. However, it did not change its overall policy toward Beijing or lift the travel ban on all other Americans. With no intention to restore bilateral cultural ties, the maneuvers made by both sides on the exchange of journalists became just another battle on the cultural front in the Sino-American Cold War.

Issuing Invitations

The need for cultural contact with American people became more urgent when the military actions taken by the PLA in the Taiwan Strait in late 1954 and early 1955 backfired. Pressed by his sense of mission to liberate Taiwan and concerned with the formation of a formal military alliance between Washington and Taipei, Mao Zedong ordered the massive shelling of Jinmen and attacks on a number of islands along the east coast in September 1954. Mao did take extreme caution to avoid direct military confrontation with the United States by giving numerous orders to PLA officers not to engage American military forces along China's east coast. He even postponed the attack on the Yijiangshan Islands from late 1954 to early 1955 to allow American forces to complete their military exercises in that area.[1] However, the Communist military actions pushed a reluctant Washington to sign the Sino-American Mutual Defense Treaty with the

Nationalist government in December 1954.[2] After the PLA occupation of Yijiangshan, the U.S. Senate quickly rectified the Treaty and passed the Formosa Resolution, authorizing the president to use force to defend the Republic of China and its possessions in the Taiwan Straits. In March, Secretary of State John Foster Dulles openly stated that Washington was seriously considering nuclear strikes when the PRC attacked Taiwan. Faced with such strong reaction from Washington, Beijing had little choice but go back to the negotiation table to find a way to "liberate" Taiwan without having a war with the United States. Zhou Enlai issued a statement at the Bandung Conference on April 23, 1955, that "China is friendly with the American people" and that "the Chinese people did not want to fight the United States." He made it clear that "the Chinese government is willing to sit down and negotiate with the U.S. government to alleviate the tense situation in the Far East, especially the tense situation in the Taiwan area."[3] Mao said the same thing to Ali Sastroamidjojo, the Indonesian prime minister, in May 1955 that all problems, including the Taiwan issue, could be resolved through negotiation.[4]

In addition to public appeals, Beijing tried to reestablish contacts with selected Americans so that it could use them to push Washington to the negotiation table and with luck resolve the Taiwan issue. In January 1955, Beijing invited their relatives to visit American soldiers who were captured during the Korean War and chose to go to mainland China rather than return to their homeland. A few months later, a couple of members in the Organization of Mothers with Sons Lost in Korea also received similar invitations from the Communist regime. In July 1955, Beijing invited Robert Breen, the codirector of *Porgy and Bess*, to bring the opera, which had just toured the major capitals of Europe, to the PRC. In return, a Peking opera troupe would be sent to the United States to repeat what Mei Lanfang, one of the best-known Peking opera singers in China, had done in 1930.[5] However, no Americans were able to make these trips to the PRC because of the strict travel ban imposed by Washington. Since Beijing's early effort to directly interact with American citizens had all failed, Wang Bingnan made cultural exchange one of his top priorities when Beijing and Washington started ambassadorial talks in Geneva in August 1955. He shared with U. Alexis Johnson Beijing's desire for foreign visitors and reiterated the proposal for exchange of people between the two nations at a rare dinner hosted by the latter on August 22. However, instead of a positive response, Johnson took the opportunity to make it clear that "no possibility even considering American visitors until all Americans now detained [in the PRC are] released." He also pointed out that the secrecy and hypersensitivity to criticism prevalent among Communist countries remained as "major barriers to fruitful interchange of persons and ideas."[6]

Immediately after the agreement reached by both sides on the repatriation of nationals was announced in September 1955, Beijing urged Washington to enter the second round of ambassadorial talks so that other important issues such as Taiwan, trade, ministerial-level meetings, and cultural exchange could be discussed and acted upon. When Washington refused to expand the scope of the negotiation before all American citizens imprisoned in Communist China were released, Beijing decided to take bolder actions in cultural exchange. This time it turned to American journalists because many of them had worked in China before 1949 and were eager to have the opportunity to report on China under Communist rule.[7] The initial proposal was presented by the Information Division (Xinwen Si), newly morphed from the Intelligence Division (Qingbao Si), of the Ministry of Foreign Affairs (MFA) to Zhou Enlai in January 1956.[8] The Office of Policy Research presented a similar recommendation to MFA leadership five months later. Recognizing the difficulty of normalizing Sino-American relations in the near future, it pointed out that it would be more practical to gradually "open up channels, increase influence, and make progress in various fields" through nongovernmental contacts and cultural exchange. Better results could be received, it believed, if an appropriate number of American journalists were allowed to do firsthand reporting in China at a time when "we need to exert pressure and influence on Sino-American relations."[9]

The proposals from the Information Division and the Office of Policy Research reflected the strategic thinking of Mao and Zhou at the time. Mao made it clear at the Politburo meeting held on July 7, 1954, that the PRC "should cooperate with all those who want peace so as to isolate the warmongers, that is, the American government." He also asserted that there were "contradictions within the United States" and that things "can also be done even in such a country like the United States." What Mao wanted to do was to take advantage of the division among the Americans and isolate the U.S. government. Once it was isolated, he believed, Americans would be further divided.[10] Mao's ideas, drawn from the Chinese Communists' long "united front" practice, were turned into a two-pronged strategy and methodically implemented by Beijing. One part of the strategy was to improve PRC's relations with noncommunist countries. Mao met and talked with Jawaharlal Nehru, the Indian prime minister, four times in October 1955 and told him that the PRC needed friends desperately since it had to face a powerful opponent, the United States.[11] The other part was to engage directly with the American people to intensify and exploit the contradictions between them and their government. At a meeting held to prepare for the visit of Nehru, Zhou stressed that while building friendly relations with peaceful nations like India and working directly with the governments and peoples of status quo nations like Great Britain and France, the PRC should focus most of its effort on the American people. Having cut off all ties with the United States and focused on "cleaning house" since 1949, Zhou announced at the meeting that "the house has been cleaned in the past few years and is now ready to invite some guests." The goal, Zhou emphasized, was to "isolate the United States."[12]

The Information Division sprang into action as soon as Zhou Enlai approved the proposals.[13] It gathered information on a selected group of American journalists who had applied to visit China as well as the news agencies with which they were affiliated. Having carefully reviewed and evaluated the vitae, influence, recent speeches and publications, and political positions of those American journalists, in July 1956 the Information Division called a meeting with officials from the Association of Journalists, Ministries of Investigation and Public Security, the Guidance Committee for International Activities of Chinese Communist Party Central Committee (Zhongyang Guoji Huodong Zhidao Weiyuanhui), and the Division of American and Australian Affairs of the MFA to discuss inviting American journalists. Officials worked out a reception plan, including approval guidelines, reception standard, and preparation for hosting American journalists, at the meeting and submitted it to Zhou Enlai for approval.[14] With a quick nod from Zhou, the Information Division took immediate action to prepare for the invitation and reception of a large number of American journalists.

Although a sharp break from Beijing's ban on American journalists since 1949, inviting American reporters to visit Communist-controlled areas was nothing new to CCP leaders. As soon as Edgar Snow, an American reporter who was also teaching part-time at Yenching University, had sought Song Qingling's help for a visit to Communist-controlled Northern Shanxi, the CCP quickly sent him an invitation and smuggled him into its base area in summer 1936.[15] Right after Snow, Agnes Smedley, a left-wing American reporter who had published *China's Red Army Marches* in 1933, based on information from a couple of Red Army commanders, paid her first visit to Yanan in January 1937. Mao welcomed her and gave permission for her to write a biography of Zhu De.[16] In April 1937, Helen Foster Snow, Edgar Snow's wife, went to Yanan with special approval from Mao. She interviewed Mao and numerous other Communist leaders gathering materials for her own book.[17] A year later, Anna Louis Strong, another American journalist, visited the Eighth Route Army Headquarters in Shanxi and met with Zhu De, Peng Dehuai, He Long, Liu Bocheng, and Lin Biao.[18]

In addition to individual American journalists who followed Snow's footsteps, the Communist leaders invited and hosted groups of American reporters later in the war. The largest group of foreign as well as Chinese reporters arrived in Yanan in May 1944. Five out of six foreign reporters in the group were either Americans or working for American news organizations. Israel Epstein was there for the *New York Times* and *Time* and *Life* magazines, Harrison Forman for the *New York Herald-Tribune* and the UPI, Gunther Stein for the *Christian Science Monitor* and Associated Press, Father Cormac Shanahan for American Catholic publications, and Maurice Votaw for the *Baltimore Sun* and Reuters. All Americans were given opportunities to meet or interview Mao Zedong, Zhu De, Zhou Enlai, Lin Biao, and many other top Communist leaders.[19] In September of the same year, Brooks Atkinson of the *New York Times* and Theodore White of *Time* and *Life* also made their trips to Yanan.[20] The visits of these journalists and their mostly positive reporting helped CCP break the isolation imposed by the Nationalist government and win sympathy and support from many Chinese as well as foreigners.

It was in their interactions with these American journalists during those tumultuous years that CCP leaders developed a system of arranging tightly controlled visits for foreign reporters. Prior to Snow's arrival, the standing members of the CCPCC Politburo, including Mao Zedong, Zhang Wentian, Bo Gu, and Yang Shangkun, held a special meeting and had a lengthy discussion on how to prepare for Snow's interviews. Zhou Enlai, accompanied by Ye Jianying and Li Kenong met with Snow at Baijiaping, a small village near the border, on July 9, 1936. At the end of their two-day meeting Zhou worked out an itinerary for Snow "containing items covering a trip of ninety-two days."[21] When Snow arrived in Baoan three days later, he was welcomed by most of the CCPCC and Politburo members. In the following three months, Snow had dozens of lengthy interviews with Mao.

In order to make sure that Snow got all the information, Mao provided his own notes. Snow later admitted that Mao "was not giving me just dead facts to which I had to bring life, but a nearly finished piece of self-analysis and explanation of a generation of revolutionists."[22] Similar arrangements were made for all other American journalists in the following years. When Epstein, Forman, and Votaw followed Mao's advice and went to the frontline to see the Eighth Route Army in action, several Communist officials and two interpreters accompanied them.[23] Those officials and interpreters not only secured the safety of all the Americans and provided logistical services for them, but also made sure that the reporters met only the people they were allowed to meet and see the things that they were supposed to see.[24] Journalists who had interviewed Mao and other Communist leaders usually sent their related reports to the interviewees for clearance. Theodore White did not publish his interview with Mao because it was "so edited as to be useless for publication."[25]

Such kind of control over foreign visitors was further tightened and institutionalized when the American journalists were invited to visit the PRC in 1956. Now in power, the Communist government was able to decide who should be invited, in what way they should be admitted, how long they could stay, where they should go, what they could see, whom they were allowed to meet, and what they would hear from the people who met with them. Beijing's decision to pick American journalists rather than simply granting visas to any applicants not only allowed it to choose visitors more friendly to the PRC but also made those invitees feel like special guests, and thus less likely to write something to embarrass their host. Although the guidelines set by the Information Division stated that journalists with diverse political positions should be invited, no hard-core conservative reporters with strong critical attitude toward the PRC were included. Since most American journalists who had visited Communist-controlled areas in the 1930s and the 1940s had written positive articles and books afterward, they were favored by the MFA and counted for about half of the invitees. Those who had not been to China before were chosen mostly because of their positive views or remarks. On top of the invitee list was Cyrus Sulzberger of the *New York Times*. The Information Division recommended that extra effort be made to get him to China because of his friendly reports on the PRC and his high status as a journalist in the United States. William Worthy of the *Baltimore Afro-American* was ranked number ten on the list. He was included mostly because he was a Black journalist working for a Black magazine. Having sent visa applications to Beijing several times and visited the Soviet Union in 1954, he was lumped with Snow, Strong, and Forman as friendly reporters.[26]

In order to exert effective control over the American journalists after their arrival, a special leading group (*lingdao xiaozu*) with officials from the Guidance Committee on International Activities of the CCPCC, the Journalist Association, the Ministries of Foreign Affairs, Investigation, and Public Security was set up with the Information Division as the convener. Within the Information Division, a new office, the Office for the Reception of American Journalists (Jiedai Meiguo Jizhe Bangongshi), was established and charged with management of the project. More than a dozen interpreters chosen from the MFA, the Foreign Language Press, the China International Travel Agency, and other government offices and institutions were assigned to the office. They gathered for a week to familiarize themselves with information about the visiting journalists as well as related MFA policies and guidelines in late July.[27] Similar offices were set up and trainings conducted in Shanghai, Guangzhou, and other major cities the American journalists would visit. Gong Peng even went to Shanghai herself to ensure proper preparation. Detailed information and answers to major sensitive questions that might be asked by the American visitors were compiled by the Information Division and distributed to all government offices that they might visit.[28]

Once thorough preparations had been made, the MFA sent telegrams to eighteen American journalists on August 5 informing them that their visa applications were accepted and they were approved for a monthlong visit to China beginning on August 20.[29] The invited journalists were instructed to pick up their visas either at the PRC embassy in Moscow or at Shenzhen (Sumchon) across the river from Hong Kong between August 20 and 30. Except for one freelance reporter, the rest of the journalists were employed by fifteen different newspapers and magazines. While three of them, Cyrus Sulzberger, Henry Lieberman, and Tillman Durdin, worked for the *New York Times*, the others represented fourteen different newspapers, news agencies, magazines, and radio-TV networks, including the AP, the *Christian Science Monitor*, the National Broadcasting Company (NBC), the Columbia Broadcasting System (CBS), *Life* and *Time*, *U.S. News and World Report*, *BusinessWeek*, *The Nation*, the *Baltimore Afro-American*, McGraw-Hill Publishing, UPI, the *New York Post*, the International News Service, and the *Chicago Daily News*.[30]

The invitation of such an unprecedentedly large number of American journalists all at once was designed to mobilize as many reporters and news organizations as possible to maximize pressure on the U.S. government. Beijing's plan worked fairly well, since almost all the journalists and their employers expressed clear intentions to accept the invitation. Many immediately sent their requests to the State Department for approval for their journey to the PRC.[31] Beijing expected the response, since many of the invited journalists had worked in China before 1949 and were eager to go back to a country that had been closed to Americans for almost a decade, and most of the news agencies had repeatedly sent requests for permission to enter Communist China in previous years. According to MFA records, a total of sixty-five American journalists from twenty-seven news organizations applied eighty-five times for visas from the beginning of 1950 to April 1956. The majority of the applications came in recent years, with sixteen in 1954, thirty-five in 1955, and twenty-two in the first four months of 1956. The general manager of the *New York Times* had even written to Zhou Enlai requesting a visa for Henry Lieberman to visit China.[32] Now, with the surprise invitations from Beijing, the invited reporters and their employers did everything they could to make sure that this once-a-lifetime opportunity would not slip away.

Maintaining the Travel Ban

The request from the reporters for government approval for their visit to the PRC challenged the travel ban imposed by Washington. Cyrus Sulzberger raised the issue directly to President Dwight Eisenhower on the morning of August 6. Unable to get a positive response from the president, Sulzberger went to the State Department for clarification on the same day. He told Robert Murphy, the deputy assistant secretary of state for political affairs, that since he and two other colleagues at the *New York Times* had received invitations from Beijing he wanted to find out the Department's "real" attitude on the question of American correspondents' visit to the PRC. Dissatisfied with Murphy's reiteration of existing policy, Sulzberger further inquired what would happen if one or more journalists accepted Beijing's invitation and made a trip to the PRC despite the travel ban. Murphy warned that those who dared to break the ban could lose their passports. Obviously unhappy with the State Department's attitude, Sulzberger complained that the American journalists were put in a difficult position "because there is undoubtedly a most interesting story to be obtained." Feeling certain that the same question would be raised to the State Department spokesman and even John Foster Dulles himself, Murphy sent a summary of his meeting to William J. Sebald, the deputy assistant secretary of state for Far Eastern affairs, recommending that an "immediate study should be given to this question so that there will be no doubt about the Department's attitude."[33]

Lincoln White, the State Department press officer, had already faced tough questions on the matter from journalists on the same day. What he did was to tell the reporters again that no passports would be issued to Americans to travel to areas controlled by governments with which the United States did not have diplomatic relations. He branded Beijing's invitation to American journalists as propaganda and pointed out that it continued to hold a number of American citizens despite its promise made the previous September for their release.[34] Although American journalists never liked travel restrictions on Communist countries, the travel ban on Communist China did not cause any problems for the State Department in previous years since it was the Chinese Communist regime that had thrown all American reporters out of that country in 1949 and ignored their repeated visa applications afterward. Once Beijing reversed its position and granted visas to a large number of American reporters, the State Department's travel ban immediately became the only barrier for their entry into the Communist country and an open target for criticism. A spokesman for NBC stated right after the press briefing on August 6 that an effort was made by news organizations to reach an agreement on a common approach. Believing that sending correspondents to Communist China did not express approval of the regime but simply a "proper and important move to keep the American public informed," he revealed dissatisfaction over State Department policy.[35]

The strong resentment and criticism from journalists and news organizations forced the State Department to take further steps to demonstrate its determination to maintain the existing travel ban on China. On August 7, it issued a formal news release for the press on the subject. Before the release went public, Dulles called President Eisenhower to seek his advice. Eisenhower made it clear that he was not happy with the situation, one in which "you are damned if you do and damned if you don't." Known as a strong advocate for cultural exchange and people diplomacy,

Eisenhower asked Dulles to include a key point in the statement that "it is our policy to open up exchanges, etc. but Red China has not made it possible for self-respecting countries to do it, etc."[36] The State Department then emphasized in its press release that the United States "welcomes the free exchange of information as between different countries irrespective of political and social differences," and that "the Chinese Communist regime has created a special impediment" by taking American citizens into captivity, holding them as political hostages, and breaking its promise made at Geneva on September 10, 1955. "So long as these conditions continue," the State Department declared, "it is not considered to be in the best interests of the United States that Americans should accept the Chinese Communist invitation to travel in Communist China."[37] John Reap, the State Department spokesman, also called attention to the criminal statute that provided a maximum of five years in prison and a $2,000 fine for violating restrictions on a passport. He reminded journalists that the Treasury Department's regulation prohibited any monetary transactions with Communist China. Any violation of this regulation could be punished with a fine of $10,000 or imprisonment up to ten years for each transaction.[38]

The State Department's reaffirmation of its travel ban on China aroused stronger criticism and protests from leading news organizations with reporters who had received invitation from Beijing. On August 7, Arthur Hays Sulzberger, president and publisher of the *New York Times*; Frank Starzel, general manager of AP; Frank Bartholomew, president of UPI; Herbert Brucker, editor of the *Hartford Courant* and chairman of the Freedom of Information Committee of the American Society of Newspaper Editors; Erwin Canham, editor of the *Christian Science Monitor*; and representatives of CBS and NBC sent protest letters or telegrams to the State Department.[39] Canham urged the State Department to give "careful reconsideration" to its policy. He insisted that "It is urgent to give the American people . . . every bit of accurate information we can about events inside Communist China," adding, "Whatever the motives of the Peiping government . . . we have the right to have confidence in the integrity and experience of the correspondents invited." He warned that "We must not erect our own bamboo curtain and place ourselves in an intolerable and inconsistent position before the world." The *New York Times* published an editorial on August 8, declaring that "this newspaper would be glad to be represented in China as it is and has been Russia."[40]

Some American journalists waiting in Hong Kong for their entrance to mainland China took the protest one step further. They tried to circumvent the State Department's travel ban by forwarding messages to Beijing seeking its reaction to their proposal for visiting the PRC without using passport or receiving permission from the State Department.[41] Such arrangements were nothing new to the Communist regime, since it had issued entrance visas on a separate piece of paper (*lingzhi qianzheng*) to journalists and other visitors from various capitalist countries in the past so that they could claim that they had not used their passports in the PRC. The Information Division had prepared to do the same for the American reporters when they entered China. However, it refused to accept the proposal from the American journalists in early and mid-August and agreed only to extend the deadline for their entry. Its purpose, as clearly stated in a report presented to the MFA on August 31, was to extend and intensify the confrontation between the American journalists as well as news organizations and the State Department. The Information Division's decision was based on its observation and evaluation of the increasingly strong criticism and protest from the American news organizations right after the invitations to American journalists were issued. It expected that Washington would be forced to change its position under heavy pressure from the media.[42]

Neither the State Department's repeated reaffirmation of its travel ban nor Beijing's initial rejection to the proposal from American journalists could stop American news organizations from finding ways to get their reporters into Communist China. On August 14, the AP sent John Hightower, its correspondent covering the State Department, to meet with Carl W. McCardle, the assistant secretary of public affairs, to inform him of the decision made by AP officials. Their decision was to instruct John Roderick, the AP's correspondent in Hong Kong, to deposit his passport for safekeeping there and accept the invitation from the Chinese Communist government for a one-month visit to Red China. AP would also order Roderick not to use any U.S. currency or disclose any opinion about U.S. policy while he was in mainland China. They defended their decision by pointing out that "the AP's interests were not similar to those of the State Department." Alarmed by the AP's decision, McCardle immediately pointed out that if the AP went against State Department policy and sent Roderick into Red China, other correspondents in Hong Kong would quickly follow and "the line will be broken." The chances of "getting our prisoners back," he warned, "will be lessened." Although Hightower agreed to pass McCardle's reasoning to AP officials, he warned that the actions might have already been taken.[43]

The AP's decision immediately sent the State Department into crisis-management mode. A special staff meeting was held the next day. On August 16, acting secretary of state Herbert Hoover Jr. instructed staff to "prepare an analysis of the problem of passports for newsmen wishing to visit Communist China." He emphasized that the analysis should "cover the rights of the government and the individuals."[44] In a report sent to Hoover by the Division of Far Eastern Affairs the next day, Sebald recognized that Beijing's move to grant visas to eighteen American correspondents and radio commentators had aroused "tremendous interest in press and radio circles." He also confessed that editorial comments had been "almost unanimously hostile to the Department's decision to disapprove such travel" and the press had "generally disregarded or disagreed with the Department's statement of August 7." He believed that if AP was "successful in getting their man in, other organizations may rapidly follow suit and we would be faced with the collapse of our policy." Once correspondents were allowed to enter Communist China, it would be difficult for the State Department, he pointed out, to "bar other Americans with equally valid reasons for wishing to make the trip." Thus, Sebald recommended that as pressure from the press had grown to such a point that the State Department should be prepared to enforce sanctions "against any individual who proceeds to Communist China in contravention of our policy."[45]

With consensus reached among top officials in the State Department, Acting Secretary Hoover and his aides met with Frank Starzel, general manager of the AP, on August 17. They tried to persuade him to reverse AP's decision to send Roderick to the PRC. Having little sympathy toward the State Department's position, Starzel reluctantly agreed only to refrain from sending Roderick to China if the policy expressed in the Department's press release on August 7 could have specific and public approval from President Eisenhower himself. He recognized that "no employer of American correspondents would likely defy the explicitly expressed position of the president on this matter." Unable to persuade Starzel to change his position, the State Department was forced to seek unequivocal and open support from President Eisenhower. On August 18, Eisenhower approved a brief statement that "the President has authorized the Department to make clear the President's full concurrence in the policy statement issued by the State Department on August 7, 1956 regarding travel to Communist China." This statement was included in another press release issued by the State Department on August 20, the first day when the invited American journalists were allowed to enter the PRC for their visits.[46]

Before President Eisenhower's support for the State Department policy was made public, several American journalists had already gathered in Hong Kong, getting ready to enter the PRC. The UPI told Robert Miller to go ahead with the visit to Red China if he wanted to. However, he was instructed not to use his passport in China, take American money with him, or make any statements on U.S. policy. NBC made it clear that James Robinson was going to Red China on his own. NBC was not sending him, but it was not objecting to his visit either. John Roderick was also in Hong Kong even though the AP announced that it was still awaiting further development and the final decision was not yet reached. The *New York Times* reported that these journalists planned to use British pounds in the PRC to avoid being prosecuted under the Trading with the Enemy Act. They had also decided that they would not submit their passports to the Communist government or surrender them to the American Consulate General in Hong Kong. Deeply concerned with their imminent travel to the PRC, Everett Drumright, the American consul general in Hong Kong, followed State Department instructions and tried to stop them. He told Roderick that any attempt to enter Communist China would be considered disloyalty. Undeterred by the warning from Drumright, Roderick rebutted that "the Bill of Rights in the Constitution supported freedom of press without political interference."[47]

President Eisenhower's support for the State Department's travel ban on August 20 was so clear and strong that all news agencies decided to reverse their position on sending reporters to the PRC, though not without reluctance or regrets. As promised, Starzel announced on August 20 that the AP "accepts President Eisenhower's expressed view" and instructed Roderick to decline Beijing's invitation. At the same time, he expressed regret that "existing circumstances compel us to forego an opportunity to report to the people of the world on the situation existing in the vast country which no American reporter has been able to visit for approximately eight years." Bartholomew ordered Miller not to make the trip to China even though he believed that "the American public should be given access to the reports of American newsmen in Red China." With three reporters on Beijing's invitee list, the *New York Times* also decided, in view of the government's position, to advise them that the invitation from Beijing "should not be accepted."[48] However, the nation's leading newspaper published an editorial the next day emphasizing that there were different opinions among individual Americans "as to whether the State Department does right in suppressing the gathering of news and as to whether the President does right sustaining it in that position." The editors insisted that there was a "serious constitutional question involved as to whether the State Department has the right to deny the public the right to read about certain subjects and listen to discussions about them."[49] Herbert Brucker went even further accusing the State Department of "erecting an Iron Curtain of our own."[50] After receiving their employers' instructions, all American reporters who had been invited by Beijing for a monthlong visit in August reluctantly turned down the invitation.

Although no American journalists accepted the invitation or entered the PRC before August 30, the initial deadline set by the MFA, the Information Division still claimed that Beijing had "won a gigantic victory in propaganda" in the first phase of the struggle in inviting American journalists for a visit to the PRC. By forcing the U.S. government to enforce the travel ban, Beijing, it asserted, not only demonstrated that it had nothing to hide and took a position promoting cultural exchange, freedom of press, and friendship with the American people but also exposed the true nature of U.S. government policy and helped the world media recognize that it was the United States rather than socialist countries that had erected the "iron curtain." It concluded that because of U.S. government actions "the vast majority of the American news agencies have formed a united front with us and the hostile policy of U.S. government toward our country has become increasingly isolated."[51] The Information Division's assessment rather accurately reflected the response from American News organizations. In his letter to Dulles, Starzel pointed out that the Chinese Communist government "is directing an effective propaganda campaign with the peoples in Southeast Asia as a result of U.S. correspondents declining invitation to visit the China Mainland in the deference to the position taken by the U.S. government." He recognized that nothing could be done to counteract the "effects of the action." However, he did strongly recommend that the State Department thoroughly review its policy and announce its position only after "fullest sort of consultation with the organizations most directly concerned" if another opportunity arose in the future.[52]

Hosting the Ban Breakers

Although the Information Division of MFA believed that Beijing had already scored a major victory, it recognized that an even bigger victory could be won with a visit by American reporters to the PRC.[53] The sharp complaints of American news agencies and strong interest displayed by journalists in visiting China made the MFA believe that it still had a chance to achieve the original goal. Thus, it extended the deadline set for the American reporters to enter the PRC and issued invitations to more than a dozen additional American journalists on September 4, 1956.[54] If the former was intended to give the American journalists more time to fight the State Department, the latter was designed to "intensify the contradiction between the American media and the American government."[55] It also kept the Office for the Reception of American Journalists in the Information Division up and running so that its staff could continue to collect information and train interpreters assigned to the project.

At the same time, Beijing launched a new offensive to push for cultural exchange at the Sino-American Ambassadorial Talks in Geneva. On September 22, Wang Bingnan introduced a draft announcement at his meeting with U. Alexis Johnson, proposing that both sides "adopt measures respectively on their own initiative to eliminate existing barriers interfering with freedom of mutual contacts and cultural exchange between [the] peoples of their two countries." Wang cited Washington's ban on American journalists' visit to the PRC as one piece of evidence for its obstruction to bilateral cultural exchange. Johnson repudiated Wang's accusation on the spot by pointing to Beijing's treatment of Americans, including diplomats in China, since the Communists took over the mainland, its failure to implement the Agreed Announcement made public a year ago, and its refusal to renunciate the use of force in the Taiwan area. He reemphasized that those blocks had to be removed before any attempt could be made to improve the relations between the two countries.[56] Unable to receive any positive response from Washington, the MFA and the Chinese delegation released the Chinese proposal for cultural exchange in Beijing and Geneva simultaneously on October 16. Taking advantage of the opportunity, Beijing attacked Washington in a separate statement that the "American side has refused to discuss the Chinese proposal for the promotion of mutual contacts and cultural exchange between their peoples on pretexts that no agreement has yet been reached" on several other issues.[57]

Johnson knew at the very beginning that Wang's proposal was "part of a continuing pattern of attempting to build up a record of 'sweet responsibleness.'"[58] However, he might not be aware that Beijing, while publicly proposing cultural exchange with the United States, launched a nationwide movement in the mid-1950s to further destroy American cultural and intellectual influence in China as represented by John Dewey and Hu Shi. Dewey was the most influential American scholar in China whose philosophical and educational theories had shaped to a large extent Chinese educational and intellectual developments since the late 1910s. Hu, Dewey's student at Columbia University, was one of China's most influential intellectuals in the twentieth century. In a letter to more than twenty top Chinese communist leaders on October 16, 1954, Mao told them that it was time to start the struggle against Hu Shi faction's bourgeois idealism, which had dominated ancient literature research for over three decades.[59] The Propaganda Department of the CCPCC immediately implemented Mao's instruction by organizing a meeting for writers and decided to expand the discussion to other areas including philosophy, history, education, and linguistics. Mao approved such an expansion and instructed it to replace discussion with denunciation.[60] Following Mao's call, Wang Huanxun, like thousands of Chinese intellectuals who publicly denounced Hu, published a pamphlet in 1956 attacking Hu Shi's thinking on education. He asserted that since Hu, like Dewey, tried to train students for a so-called democratic society, his purpose of education was to produce "obedient subjects as well as servants for the reactionary ruling class and compradors and lackeys" for the American imperialists.[61]

Beijing's extension of the invitation to more American reporters and public promotion for cultural exchange with the United States were anything but a true reflection of its actual attitude toward American culture and ideals. However, its shrewd posturing not only kept pressure on the U.S. government but also reaped a surprising result when three American reporters ignored the travel ban and entered Red China in December 1956. Having not been included among the first group of journalists invited by the MFA, Edmund Stevens and Phillip Harrington, a reporter and a photographer for *Look* magazine, sent their visa applications to Beijing on August 29. Happy to receive the new applications from them, the MFA forwarded invitations to both on September 4. Following the established guidelines, the Information Division had scrutinized their backgrounds and the magazine's political position. It was satisfied to find out that *Look*, as a pictorial biweekly magazine published by Cowles Newspapers in Iowa, had a circulation over two million, and as a competitor to *Life* magazine *Look* supported moderate Republicans in the election of 1948. Through the Chinese embassy in Moscow it also came to know that Stevens, who had been stationed there for many years, was capable and well respected. More important, his reports on the Soviet Union and other socialist countries were generally objective. Harrington also passed scrutiny because, while known for numerous cover photos, he had not published any distorting or slandering pictures in his eight years at *Look*.[62]

William Worthy was the other American reporter who entered the PRC in December 1956. Although he was among the first group of American reporters invited by the MFA in early August, he did not receive the telegram because he was visiting Africa at the time. Having settled in as a Nieman Fellow at Harvard University in the fall semester, Worthy sent a letter to the Information Division expressing his desire to be the first American reporter visiting the PRC during the winter break. He told the Chinese that being the first would be a major "scoop" not just for him personally but for "the prestige of the Negro press." He explained that Black reporters were "rarely at the points of major international news" because the Black press did not "have sufficient financial resources to keep a corps of correspondents stationed permanently abroad."[63] The Information Division had no problem reissuing an invitation since it had known that Worthy was a talented and hardworking reporter who had visited the Soviet Union and openly opposed U.S. interventions in Asia and Africa. It was also aware that he had applied repeatedly for a visa to visit the PRC since 1953 and made it clear in his 1955 application letter that he would sue the Department of State in federal court if it refused to issue him a passport. However, the Information Division did have some concerns in making him the first American journalist to visit the PRC because he was not influential as a journalist and the newspaper that he worked for was little known with a limited readership. In the end, the Information Division sent him another invitation on December 15 without guaranteeing that he would be the first American reporter to visit mainland China since the beginning of the Korean War.⁶⁴

Determined to be first, Worthy flew to Hong Kong as soon as Beijing's invitation arrived in Boston and crossed the bridge to Shenzhen on December 24.⁶⁵ Although Stevens and Harrington had arrived in Beijing on December 22, two days ahead of Worthy, they intentionally kept a low profile until their activities in the city were picked up by a Reuters reporter on December 26. By that time, Worthy's arrival in Beijing had already been widely reported, and the media and the public regarded him as the first American journalist in the PRC after the Communists came to power. While Stevens and Harrington received PRC visas on a separate piece of paper at the Chinese embassies in Moscow and Stockholm respectively, Worthy got his visa in the same format after crossing the bridge to Shenzhen. This kind of visa became a standard practice based on the clear stipulation in Article Four of the Temporary Guidelines for Issuing Entrance and Transit Visas to Foreigners by Embassies and Consulates issued by the MFA in October 1955. It was granted to all visitors from capitalist countries that did not have diplomatic relations with Beijing to demonstrate the invalidity of the passports issued by the governments of those countries in the PRC. The French, German, and Japanese reporters who had visited the PRC before the Americans received the same kind of visas.⁶⁶ The Media Division intentionally hid this information from the American journalists in mid-August in order to keep them fighting the Department of State as long and hard as possible.

The MFA viewed the arrival of the three American reporters in late December 1956 as a huge success. The Information Division claimed that the visit of the three American journalists was "doubtlessly a heavy blow to the American government's stubborn ban on journalists' traveling to China and its consistent information isolation policy against our country." Now, with the first group of American reporters in the country, it shifted its focus to shaping their experiences in the country so that they would file favorable reports on China. It believed that if their reports could contain "a slight element of objectivity" they would have an extremely positive impact.⁶⁷ Any positive, even neutral, reports would be, to the Chinese officials, a slap in the face for Washington. In order to leave positive impressions on the American visitors and make it more difficult for them to say anything negative about the PRC, Chinese officials applied hospitality techniques, set strict restrictions on access, imposed close surveillance, and engaged in pointed exchanges with the visitors.

The existing mechanisms designed to regulate and influence foreign reporters made it relatively easy for Beijing to manage the first group of American journalists visiting the PRC. Like all other foreign reporters, especially those from capitalist countries, the three American journalists had to register at the MFA right after their arrival in Beijing before they could do any real reporting. They were clearly told that all their interviews and travel plans had to be approved and arranged by the MFA. They were also made aware that the MFA had the authority to repeal the registration of any foreign reporters at any time if they violated the PRC's laws or published "distorted" reports.[68] While they were waiting for their registration to be approved and between their formal interviews, the Information Division arranged sightseeing for them. Accompanied by English interpreters from China International Travel Agency, they toured numerous well-known sites such as the Forbidden City, Summer Palace, Great Wall, Jing Hill, and Zhongshan Park. Besides Rongbaozhai and other well-known antique stores, they were also taken to movies, Peking opera shows, and dances.[69]

While giving the American reporters VIP treatment as tourists, the Information Division approved only part of their ambitious interview plans.[70] Following Chinese regulations, all American reporters handed in lists of places and institutions that they wanted to visit and the people to interview. Worthy, like Stevens and Harrington, asked to visit factories, schools, hospitals, and courts. However, he made it clear to Information Division officials that no visits or meetings should interfere with interviews with American prisoners, Mao Zedong, or Zhou Enlai, who were on the top of his list.[71] Given the significance of the visits of the first group of American journalists, the Chinese officials allowed all three the opportunity to interview Premier Zhou Enlai but did not arrange any meetings with Mao. Like other foreign journalists, the Americans had to spend most of their time in Beijing with a short side trip to Shanghai. Having already hosted some visitors including reporters from other capitalist countries, the Information Division had a number of carefully selected people for them to meet and sites for them to visit in those cities. For example, some famous Chinese novelists and poets, including Guo Xiaochuan, Feng Yidai, Xie Bingxin, and Xiao Qian, invited Stevens and Harrington for a dinner on January 18, 1957. Guo was then the deputy secretary of the Communist

Party Committee at the National Association of Writers, which managed and paid all professional writers in the country, while Feng was the editor of the English version of *Chinese Literature* (*Zhongguo Wenxue*). Feng brought copies of the current issue to the American reporters as a gift.[72]

Beijing's control over the experiences of the American reporters also depended very much on the various sites that it had carefully chosen and closely managed. Over the years, the Chinese Communist regime had identified and built a number of so-called model units, including factories, shops, schools, universities, kindergartens, villages, hospitals, and neighborhoods, for foreigners to visit. These sites were chosen not only because of their advanced equipment or outstanding performances but also because of their political trustworthiness and specially trained workers, peasants, students, cadres, and managers. The regime was confident that few if any in those sites would dare utter any "inappropriate" words about their unit or the country in front of foreign visitors. Since the American reporters could make only vague requests on what kind of places that they wanted to visit, they usually had to go to the sites picked by their host. For example, all three American reporters were taken to visit the Shijingshan Iron and Steel Factory and the Beijing First Textile Factory. The former was the largest and most advanced iron and steel factory in central China at that time. More important, the Communists had taken it over in late 1948, and its workers, technicians, and engineers went through political education by the end of 1950, becoming staunch supporters of the new regime.[73] The latter was the most modern textile factory in China, built in 1954, with spinning machines imported from East Germany. Its workers were mostly young women with various levels of education, and some even joined the Communist Party. Obviously, the Information Division wanted to impress the American visitors with the PRC's industrial achievements through these two model factories.

In addition to showing off these well-established model units, Beijing allowed all three American reporters to meet a couple of American prisoners in a jail in Shanghai, an item on top of their agendas. The last-minute decision was made partly as a reward to their open defiance of the State Department's travel ban and partly as a step to further increase pressure on Washington.[74] Since no foreign journalists had been allowed inside the jail in Shanghai or met with the Americans imprisoned there, the Ministry of Public Security had to send two express telegrams to the Bureau of Public Security in Shanghai on January 7 and 10 respectively, transmitting strict guidelines for the planned visits and interviews. Upon receiving the telegrams, the Shanghai Bureau conducted a rehearsal on January 14. Clear instructions were given to Stevens and Harrington before their interviews with Reverend Paul Mackensen and Father Fulgence Gross on January 15. The same was done for Worthy the next day, since he was unable to arrive as scheduled the day before. Prohibited from asking questions about their cases, the American reporters could only inquire about the prisoners' lives in prison. Since no pictures with the American prisoners were allowed inside the jail, the reporters had to take photos in front of the jail gate as proof of their visits. Shanghai Bureau officials watched closely over the meetings and reported that the American prisoners gave good answers to all the questions from the visitors. However, they concluded that the report filed by Stevens and Harrington right after the visit was "not entirely truthful."[75]

Another useful tool at Beijing's disposal in controlling and influencing the American reporters were the interpreters the MFA assigned to accompany the visitors. Mostly from the China International Travel Agency, they, under the guidance of the Information Division, had carefully studied background information on the visiting journalists and methodically prepared answers to all possible questions that they might ask. In addition to providing translation service, the interpreters kept close eyes on the American reporters and constantly reported their observations to their supervisors. It was through their reports that the Information Division was able to get to know more about American reporters and assess the effectiveness of its hospitality techniques as well as access control. The American journalists, the interpreters observed, were impressed by the PRC's economic achievements and by Chinese traditional music, dances, paintings, and handicrafts. They also reported that the American visitors were unfriendly and even hostile to the PRC and the Soviet Union. When an official from the Information Division stated that the American people wanted to have friendly relations with the Chinese people, Harrington corrected him by pointing out that "not all the American people think that way." Worthy clearly expressed that he resented the suppression of the Hungarian people by the Soviet army in 1956. When he was asked to pay 120 percent in tariff on a parcel from Hong Kong, he decried the "robber's behavior."[76]

As instructed by the Information Division, the interpreters sometimes also got into heated exchanges with American reporters in order to correct their "misunderstandings" or "misperceptions." Having viewed editorial cartoons supporting the Egyptian fight against the British and French invasion at Peking University, Harrington stated that the Americans were not happy with the British and French invasion of Egypt either. When the accompanying interpreter tried to correct him and asserted that only the American people were not happy, Harrington emphasized that both the American people and the government were not happy, which the newspapers in the PRC had not reported. Unwilling to accept the point, the interpreter responded that he had not seen any denunciations from the U.S. government. After hearing Harrington's defense that the U.S. government was at least neutral on that matter, the interpreter followed with another sharp question: If your government was not happy, why didn't it support Egypt? Unable or willing to speak for Washington, Harrington ended the exchange without answering the question.[77]

Having visited the Soviet Union and other Communist countries before, all three American reporters were well aware of Beijing's attempt to influence them and made great efforts to resist or evade the tight restrictions imposed on them. Stevens always asked the host to explain all programed activities and took notes when he and Harrington were discussing scheduling with Chinese officials. He did not like most of the "official" arrangements and tried to reject as many as possible. Having accepted the Chinese arrangement and spent a day visiting the Hongxing Advanced Agricultural Production Cooperative near Shanghai, Stevens and Harrington were not happy with it because the cooperative was too close to the city and its leaders were impeccably prepared for them. They insisted on taking a short car trip to Suzhou and Wuxi, two smaller cities in adjacent Jiangsu Province, so that they could see real countryside, albeit more prosperous than most other rural districts in the PRC at the time. On their way, they stopped four times to ask the peasants who were building roads or digging a canal what they thought about the agricultural cooperatives. Quite a number of pictures taken by Harrington during that short side trip appeared in their report published in March 1957.[78]

With the combination of tight access control and hospitality techniques, Beijing was able to achieve at least part of its goal in hosting the three American reporters. Based on what they had seen in various sites and heard from the interviewees selected by their hosts, all three American journalists were favorably impressed by some aspects of life in the PRC. Stevens and Harrington told their hosts that Beijing was full of vigor and color, and

Suzhou had more commercial goods than Moscow. They were impressed not only by the size and equipment of the Number 1 Textile Factory in Beijing but also by the healthy children in its nursery and kindergarten who had received vaccines for tuberculosis and smallpox.[79] The same observations were shared with American readers in their formal publication, too. Stevens reported that the Chinese people were friendlier, the officials more relaxed and agreeable, the streets cleaner, shops better stocked, and the hotels more comfortable in comparison to Russia. Based on those observations, Stevens concluded that the Communist regime was firmly in the saddle and there to stay, China not a Russian satellite, the opposition either liquidated or won over, the living standard raising, and American influence not obliterated.[80] Harrington's photographs published with Steven's article in *Look* magazine showed Chinese children being well cared for, women pursuing engineering education, and farmers working hard.[81] Sharing a similar impression, Worthy let his hosts know that the city of Shanghai had greater vitality than Moscow. If freedom from racial discrimination were the only consideration in the pursuit of human happiness, the PRC in 1957, Worthy wrote in one of his reports published during his visit, "could be a mecca for half the population of Mississippi and all the residents of Harlem."[82]

As experienced independent investigators, the American reporters were able to see through at least part of the facade presented to them. Having thumbed through *Chinese Literature*, Harrington told the Chinese writers at the meeting that the journal had too much propaganda, with all the writings focusing on agricultural cooperatives. He even advised the Chinese writers that if they wrote something about him and Stevens they should not depict the American journalists as workers under oppression because both he and Stevens worked happily and lived with joy. Stevens and Harrington also let their host know that they doubted the Chinese intellectuals had freedom of "independent thinking" and that they were deeply concerned about the ideological conformity and suspected the accuracy of the growth rate of the population.[83] In an article published in *Look* magazine in April 1957, Stevens reported that much of the Chinese Communist system "is hateful: the arbitrariness and brutality of the police-state methods; the mental conformity (which is the only way to escape 'reeducation'—brainwashing); the monotony of dress, of slogans, of conversation; the oppressive, puritanical morality that extolls toil and frowns frivolity; the conditions of well-fed slavery under which most industrial workers are forced to live; the lying propaganda of the outside world."[84] The editors further proved the last point by exposing Zhou's false accusation that Washington had violated the agreement reached at Geneva by detaining a large number of Chinese in the United States and releasing only one Chinese prisoner. Citing a statement issued by the State Department, the editors informed readers that among the thirty-four Chinese detained in the United States ten were released, two went to Taiwan according to their own choice, one returned to mainland China, and the rest chose to complete their sentence in the United States. Thus, they concluded that "Chou Enlai is not to be believed—on this subject or on any other."[85]

Although more sensitive and subtle as an African American, Worthy made a conscientious effort to maintain his objectivity and critical thinking as a journalist. While praising the absence of racial discrimination in the PRC, he lamented that the revolution in China got rid of Jiang Jieshi and semicolonialism "only to usher in the Communists," who had embedded "dictatorship in its official ideology." He shared with his readers that he had heard an instructor lecturing budding technicians at Qinghua University that democracy without bounds or limits as known in the West would sabotage and decrease production while bringing no benefits to the workers themselves.[86] Having included Zhou Enlai's accusation of the United States for its so-called violation of the Geneva Agreement, almost verbatim, in his report on January 19, 1957, Worthy went back to the same issue in another article published in March with verification and exposure. He pointed out that all Chinese prisoners in American jails were there on murder and narcotics charges, that no government was eager to repatriate killers and dope peddlers, and that Beijing's mechanical championship of those prisoners was to "conceal their real demands under the camouflage of demanding a humanitarian exchange of prisoners." Worthy also criticized Beijing for ignoring his major requests: an interview with Mao, a trip to Fujian Province, observation of a union meeting, a chat with Song Qingling, delivery of a New Year's Day message from Mao to the American people, a visit to a Chinese home, a meeting with Chinese journalists, and a tape-recorded question-and-answer session with three or four English-speaking intellectuals. He concluded that either by learning from the Russians or by devising their own security techniques, "the Chinese have their country now so rigged that only authorized news gets out."[87]

Making an Exception

The defiant visit of the three American journalists to the PRC received immediate and strong reaction from the Department of State. Ralph N. Clough, deputy director of the Office of Chinese Affairs, pointed out in a memorandum to Assistant Secretary of State for Far Eastern Affairs Walter Robertson that if no punitive actions were taken against Worthy, "the ban on travel to the China mainland will collapse rapidly, as he will be followed by a stream of other correspondents and probably also missionaries, scholars and others." Thus, he recommended that the State Department instruct the consulate in Hong Kong and the embassy in Moscow to pick up Worthy's passport and limit its use to his return to the United States only. He also proposed that the department send a request to the Department of Treasury to block Worth's bank accounts and discuss with the legal office the advisability of further legal action against him.[88] Accepting all of Clough's proposals, the State Department issued a public statement on December 28, announcing that the three reporters' passports would be revoked after their return to the United States and their cases would be referred to the Treasury Department in view of the relevant provisions of the Trading with the Enemy Act.[89] Robertson called separate meetings with Garner Cowles, the publisher of *Look* magazine, and Cliff Mackey, editor of the *Baltimore Afro-American*, right after New Year's Day. He managed to persuade Cowles to instruct Stevens and Harrington to leave China as soon as possible. Although Mackey, who had his lawyer by his side and continued to challenge the travel restriction, reluctantly agreed to do the same, no evidence could be found that he ever sent such a telegram to Beijing.[90] Actually, Worthy left China in early February, far exceeding the originally planned one-month stay.

Despite the strong call for severe punishment from some officials for the three journalists, the State Department was forced to soften its position on the matter. In addition to continued defiance from the journalists and strong opposition from many news organizations, disagreement within the department and concern for the weak legal footing made such punishment difficult if not impossible. Some State Department officials acknowledged at the very beginning that if the U.S. government took any harsh action against the three reporters it would make propaganda fodder for the Communists.[91] Walter McConaughy, director of the Office of Chinese Affairs, confessed that "the decision to seek to restrict the passports was taken with some reluctance in view of the legal uncertainty."[92] The lack of a solid legal ground for harsh punishments was soon laid bare in a legal opinion issued by the Overseas Press Club on January 10, 1957. Written by Morris L. Earnest, an authority on civil rights legislation, the opinion asserted that the U.S. government's attempt to punish the three reporters who had gone to Communist China was unconstitutional and an open violation of freedom of press and movement. Revocation of passports without notice or hearing, Ernest further pointed out, violated constitutional requirements for due process of law.[93] It was largely because of these legal difficulties that the State Department was unable to send clear instructions to the American embassy in Moscow on what concrete action it should take against the three reporters before their arrival from Communist China.[94] Believing that "no useful purpose would be served," the Passport Office even recommended reversing the previous instructions on Stevens's and Harrington's passports, since the Chinese Communist regime did not endorse them and Harrington's passport had expired on February 4, 1957.[95] By mid-February, the State Department had abandoned any attempt on court action against the three journalists and sought to "hold the line by voluntary action of the press, plus limited administrative action where necessary."[96]

Although unable to punish the three defiant reporters, the State Department continued to defend the travel ban by expanding its attacks on Beijing. When answering a question at his press conference on February 5, 1957, Dulles claimed that the Chinese Communist regime had for some time been trying to get American reporters, preferably those picked by it, to come into Communist China, and it had repeatedly tried to use the illegal detention of Americans in Communist China as pressure to accomplish its ends in that respect. He insisted that if "we allow that to happen in one case, then I think that the safety of all Americans throughout the world is lowered by several degrees."[97] However, that kind of defense was not well received among journalists or news organizations. On February 7, *Editor & Publisher* published an editorial accusing the State Department of creating a "confusion" in its ban on visits to Communist China by the American journalists. The editorial pointed out that the State Department had been forbidding American reporters from going to Red China because it did not recognize the Communist regime and could not guarantee the protection of U.S citizens in that country. Now, Dulles suddenly gave a different justification for its policy. The editors not only had serious doubts concerning

Dulles's charges, but they also believed that even if it were true that Beijing had linked the entry of American reporters to the release of prisoners, the State Department should stand on its principle that "the travel of American newsmen has no relation to diplomatic negotiations."[98] On February 16, James Russell Wiggins, executive editor of the *Washington Post* and the *Times Herald*, told the audience at a civil liberties conference in New York City that the U.S. government had become "so all pervasive" that it was now limiting "the right of citizens to know not only about Government itself but about other matters." He demanded that the right of newsmen to travel in China "should be immediately acknowledged" and "the use of press travel restrictions as a diplomatic weapon should be disavowed."[99]

Having failed to silence or even weaken strong protests from journalists or harsh criticism from news organizations, the Eisenhower administration was forced to take extra steps to save the travel ban. Agreeing with most of his aides that "we had not yet articulated properly the policies under which we were operating in this area, i.e., the relationship with Communist China in terms of admission of U.S. citizens, and that we therefore had not had any success in selling the policy," Dulles gathered senior officials of the State Department on February 12 to prepare for a meeting with representatives from various news organizations. He viewed the planned meeting as a testing ground and wanted to present "our policy with the greatest force" to these "high-minded, public-spirited and interested people" and "see whether it would stand up."[100] In order to help Dulles give the most powerful articulation of the State Department's policy, the Division of Far East Affairs prepared a paper listing eleven talking points that could be used to support the policy on travel to Communist China.[101] President Eisenhower also request a clearer articulation of policy on the matter. He called Dulles on February 13, saying that after talking to some of his friends about Beijing's various "evil deeds," including its attempt to "use 10 Americans as hostage to gain political ends," the group "felt that the full story had never been adequately told to the American people, and that if it were, they would understand why we did not issue passports to China and discouraged travel to Communist China." Having heard Dulles's plan for the meeting with news organization leaders, Eisenhower suggested that both he and Dulles discuss the issue again at their next news conferences.[102]

As planned, Dulles met with Robert Hurleigh, president of the American Association of Radio and Television Correspondents; William Dwight, president of the Newspaper Publisher Association; Jenkin Jones, president of the American Society of Newspaper Editors; and Henry Luce, editor of Time-Life-Fortune, an elected representative for weeklies, on February 18. He first recognized that the State Department had perhaps not put forward as convincing a case as it should have, partly because not all the information could be made public and partly because it had not taken all the elements into consideration. Then he defended the State Department's refusal to lift the ban on travel to Communist China by listing points in the talking paper. He stressed that the existing travel ban must continue because the United States was in a state of near-war with Communist China because of the Korean hostilities, that Beijing continued to violate the Korean armistice, and that lifting the travel ban would make it difficult to maintain morale in anticommunist countries in the Pacific and Southeast Asia while making it easy for Beijing to penetrate those countries through cultural exchange. He emphasized that one of the main goals of the travel ban was to continue the isolation of the PRC. Despite his long list of justifications, Dulles was unable to convince most of the attendees. Jones made it clear that reporters resented being made an instrument of foreign policy. Dwight stressed that an informed U.S. public was the strongest weapon against Communist China and the American public had real confidence only in American reporters. Although speaking in a more moderate tone, Luce sided with Jones and Dwight. Unable to consult with other association members on the issue, Hurleigh expressed his personal support for the State Department.[103] That was the only positive response that Dulles received at the meeting.

As it became clear that his argument was not enough to sell the State Department's position to the leaders of media organizations, Dulles was forced to consider a minor revision of the existing travel policy to reduce some of the public pressure. He told his top aides that "we should not hold to this and any other policy which was not understood and not supported by the American people."[104] Thus, when at a dinner on March 3 Frank Bartholomew, president of UPI, suggested that an arrangement be made to allow one or possibly three reporters agreed upon by all the news agencies to go to Communist China on a reporting mission, Dulles gave him a rather positive response. Believing that such a framework could be free of the difficulties that might be caused by any general relaxation of restrictions, he invited Bartholomew to explore it further.[105]

Bartholomew soon sent Dulles a letter, formally presenting his proposal on sending journalists to the PRC. According to his plan, the three major wire services—AP, UPI, and the International News Service—should be allowed to send one high-level correspondent apiece to Communist China for a period not exceeding two months. They would not file their reports until they left the PRC. Dulles called a meeting on March 27 to discuss whether he should approve Bartholomew's plan. During the deliberation, Dulles, while insisting that no significant change in overall China policy should be made, speculated that Beijing might well not accept such kind of offer from Washington. He told the officials at the meeting that he would actually like to see rejection from Beijing because it "would be beneficial to us."[106] Soon after the meeting, Dulles sent a reply to Bartholomew reaffirmed that he was willing to "consider such a plan if the news media could agree upon one person or not more than a very limited number to be sent to Communist China on a reporting mission." He also assigned Andrew Berding, the assistant secretary of public affairs, to continue the discussion with Bartholomew.[107]

Dulles's willingness to consider the proposal to send a small number of reporters to Communist China soon became well publicized.[108] However, it could not prevent protests against the travel ban. On April 1, the Writers Guild of America sent a telegram to Senator Theodore Francis Green, chairman of the Senate Foreign Relations Committee, demanding the removal of the passport restriction imposed by the State Department. Calling the restriction an act of censorship, the Guild pointed out that a "veil is thrown over China—not by others but by our own government" and that the travel ban "hampers the flow of facts" and "undermines our advocacy of worldwide freedom of information."[109] About the same time, the Gallup Poll conducted a survey revealing that 65 percent of Americans were in favor of the U.S. government's allowing American reporters to go to Communist China.[110] Upon hearing the State Department's willingness to permit a small pool of reporters to go to Red China, Senators Michael Mansfield of Montana and Estes Kefauver of Tennessee demanded on April 24 that the travel ban be repealed completely and American reporters be allowed to be stationed there permanently.[111] On July 11, the American Newspaper Guild adopted a resolution at its annual convention demanding that Dulles rescind the State Department's ban against American reporters traveling in Communist China. Representing more than 29,000 members, the Guild insisted that the travel ban was an "offensive intrusion against people's right to know in a democracy such as ours and an unwarranted hindrance of newsmen in the pursuit of their duty to keep our people informed."[112]

Faced with growing pressure, Dulles intensified his effort to get the State Department out of a difficult situation without fundamentally changing U.S. policy toward the PRC. On the one hand, he defended the State Department's position toward Communist China and vowed "continuance of our present policies" in public speeches.[113] On the other hand, he held another meeting with the leaders of media organizations on July 18, trying to finalize the plan that would allow a small number of American reporters to visit Communist China. It was at this meeting that Dulles announced that ten to fifteen, rather than three, reporters would be allowed to visit Red China if the press were willing to select them. However, the enlargement of the pool failed to change the minds of leaders from various news organizations at the meeting. Dwight; Wiggins; Theodore Koop, president of the Radio-TV Directors Association; and the representative for the American Society of Newspaper Editors were all on record as opposing any limitation set by the government. They insisted that American correspondents had the right to go anywhere and that they could not let the government decide how many newspapermen were adequate to cover the news. Even Hurleigh made it clear that his organization was also opposed in principle to the limitation set by the State Department. Unable to sell the existing plan to media leaders, Dulles agreed with the attendees that Berding would conduct a survey of American news organizations and ask each of them whether it wished to send a full-time American reporter to Communist China on a regular basis for six months or more. The State Department would make its policy decision after the facts on this matter were gathered.[114]

Besides domestic pressure, what happened in the PRC in summer 1957 added importance and urgency to the matter. One was the beginning of the Anti-Rightist movement in China. In order to prevent Hungarian-type political upheavals from happening in the PRC, Mao Zedong started a rectification movement in spring 1957. He spearheaded the movement with the Hundred Flower campaign to encourage people to criticize the Communist Party and government. However, criticism from intellectuals soon became too fierce for Mao and other Communist leaders to bear. Having warned the CCP of the attacks from many intellectuals in his article "Things Are Changing" in mid-May, Mao approved the editorial "What

Was This for?" in *People's Daily* on June 8, 1957, officially launching the anti-rightist movement.[115] The criticism offered by many intellectuals suddenly became evidence for their "anti-Party" and "anti-people" crimes. Both the Hundred-Flower and the Anti-Rightist movements had aroused strong attention and interest in the State Department. Dulles even quoted Ge Peiqi, a professor at the Renmin University, in his speech. Citing Ge's statement that to "overthrow you cannot be called unpatriotic, because you Communists no longer serve the people" as an example, he asserted that "Communism is repugnant to the Chinese people" and that "international communism's rule of strict conformity is, in China as elsewhere, a passing and not a perpetual phase."[116] However, when some of the leaders of minority political parties in Communist China started to recant publicly, State Department officials like Robertson began to wonder whether the "rightist" critics would be removed from office and punished.[117] Dulles now saw the advantage in having American reporters in China observing and reporting on what he hoped would be the end of Communist rule.

Another was Mao Zedong's reaffirmation of his determination not to establish diplomatic relations with the United States in the near future despite a series of diplomatic gestures pushing for cultural exchange. Via a highly sensitive source, the State Department became aware of Mao's speech delivered on January 27, 1957, that it would be better to delay establishment of diplomatic relations with the United States until the third five-year plan period, 1962–1967. The purpose of such a delay, according to Mao, was to "deprive as much of the United States' political capital as possible and place it in a position of unreasonableness and isolation."[118] Based on this and other information received earlier, the State Department concluded that "the Chinese Communists do not expect any early progress in the direction of formal relations with the United States and are willing to bide their time."[119] Thus, it strongly believed that Beijing would maintain a hardline policy toward the United States and that its promotion for cultural exchange was merely a tactic to instigate and intensify the confrontation between the American people and their government. Such a belief not only further strengthened its determination to do the same in return but also made it less concerned about its permission for a small group of reporters to visit the PRC.

Still another was the visit of a group of young Americans to Communist China in August 1957. Taking advantage of the Sixth World Youth and Student Festival held in Moscow, Beijing first invited fifteen American attendees to visit the PRC after the festival with all expenses covered. When more Americans showed their interest in visiting the PRC, it extended the invitation to all American attendees, who would pay the travel fare departing from Beijing while their host would take care of all other expenses. Seeing it as another attempt made by Beijing to attack existing U.S. policy, Christian A. Herter, acting secretary of state, sent a letter through the American embassy in Moscow to each young American telling them that by "traveling to Communist China at this time you will, in the considered view of your Government, be acting as a willing tool of Communist propaganda intended, whenever possible, to subvert the foreign policy and the best interests of the United States, of which you are a citizen." He warned them that if they violated the travel restriction, their passports would be taken away when they got home and their willful violation of passport restriction would be duly considered when they applied for passports in the future.[120] Despite his warning, forty-two young Americans accepted Beijing's invitation and arrived in Beijing on August 23. Although Shalby Tucker, one of the students, was deported back to Moscow on August 31 because he had refused to show his passport to Chinese officials, they were still the largest group of Americans to visit mainland China since 1949.[121]

The American youth delegation's visit to the PRC further exposed the vulnerability of the travel ban and pushed the State Department to act with greater speed as well as flexibility on the number of journalists to be allowed to go to Communist China. When the American youths embarked on their long journey to Beijing, the State Department completed the survey. It found out that twenty-four news organizations currently with reporters overseas were willing to have a correspondent stationed in the PRC for six months or longer, and eleven organizations wanted to send representatives on a more temporary basis. Loftus Becker, legal advisor to the secretary of state, believed that "the twenty-four full-time resident American correspondents will be able, adequately, to satisfy the demand for on-the-spot reporting from Communist China" and that the number was not unreasonably in excess of the fifteen that Dulles had been ready to clear at an earlier date. Furthermore, he felt that it would be "grossly unfair" to continue the ban for the professional journalists who had followed the rule while a large number of American youths were traveling to the PRC, some of whom would file news reports and photos as amateur correspondents from China. Thus, he recommended that Dulles approve the press release he drafted so that the twenty-four organizations could be informed as soon as possible.[122] Dulles gave his approval, and a press release was issued on August 22, one day before the American youth delegation's arrival in Beijing. While stressing the experimental nature of the project, the State Department told the public that in addition to allowing the reporters chosen by twenty-four news organizations to go to Communist China, it had asked the Treasury Department to issue licenses under the Trading with the Enemy Act to make it possible for them to carry out their functions.[123]

By allowing twenty-four American reporters to visit Communist China in summer 1957, Dulles not only satisfied most news organizations' demand and relieved much of the pressure on the State Department but also launched a counterattack on Beijing by tweaking rules and requirements. Its news release issued on August 22 made it clear that the reporters would be permitted to stay in Communist China for six months rather than the one month allowed by Beijing, that they would make additional information available to the American people "respecting current conditions within China," that their visit "does not change the basic policy toward communism in China," and that "the United States will not accord reciprocal visas to Chinese bearing passports issued by the Chinese Communist Regime."[124] These arrangements were designed to weaken Chinese government control over the visiting American reporters and intensify the confrontation between them.

Fighting Over Reciprocity

As expected, Beijing's response to State Department's new move was swift and combative. In a long "Commentary" published on August 26, 1957, *People's Daily* denounced Washington's approval for twenty-four American reporters to visit the PRC as "a clumsy deception" and attacked all the major points made by the State Department in its recent news release and news conference. It pointed out that Washington's new move was merely a tactic to relieve the "tremendous pressure exerted on it from within and outside the country" and "shift the responsibility [for obstructing mutual visits] to the Chinese government." Taking issue with the statement made by Lincoln White, who showed interest in the so-called anti-Party and antisocialist activities of the rightists in the PRC, it accused Washington of using "American correspondents as its tools to collect intelligence and carry out activities on its behalf." At the same time, it characterized Washington's decision not to grant visas to Chinese reporters as "a typical expression of an imperialist government's attitude, ignoring equality and reciprocity, interfering in the internal affairs of other countries, and attempting to impose its will on other people." Thus, *People's Daily* declared that the "unilateral declaration of U.S. State Department included in its press release is completely unacceptable to the Chinese people."[125]

Chinese Communist leaders and diplomats continued the attack on the State Department's rejection of reciprocity in the following months. When a member of the American youth group asked whether the twenty-four American reporters would be allowed to enter China at their meeting with Zhou Enlai on September 7, Zhou, instead of giving a direct answer to the question, provided a long statement on the principle of reciprocity. He insisted that the PRC had taken the initiative to invite a large number of American journalists to visit China the previous year with an expectation that it would lead to a reciprocal response from the American government and people. He regretted that Beijing's effort had failed. While Chinese reporters could not go to the United States, American journalists were not allowed to come to China. Although the State Department had recently permitted some reporters to visit the PRC, Zhou continued, it not only forced them to collect information from a hostile position but also denied the opportunity for Chinese reporters to visit the United States. As a result, it was Washington that killed the exchange program by making reciprocity impossible.[126] Obviously, Zhou was trying not only to defend Beijing's new demand for reciprocity but also to continue instigating confrontation between the American people and their government by putting the blame again on Washington.

Besides reiterating all the major points made by Zhou, Wang Bingnan proposed another agreed announcement on cultural exchange at the ambassadorial talks in Geneva on September 12. After attacking Washington's position on the exchange of journalists, especially its refusal to accord reciprocal visas to Chinese reporters, Wang presented Johnson with another announcement stating that both Beijing and Washington would "agree to give permission, on an equal and reciprocal basis, for correspondents of the other side to enter their respective countries for news coverage in order to promote the mutual understanding" between the two peoples. Johnson hit back immediately by reminding Wang that he had stressed the PRC's position that it was not seeking reciprocity for admission of correspondents the previous year. Johnson emphasized that existing U.S. laws and regulations made it impossible to assure reciprocity, since Communists were not allowed to enter the country. He also found it astounding that Wang now characterized the entry of American correspondents as undisguised interference in China's internal affairs when many of them were the same men who had earlier received an invitation from Beijing. He told Wang that it was entirely Beijing's own choice if it now wanted to exclude American reporters. However, Johnson assured Wang that if any journalist from Communist China desired to enter the United States he was entirely free to apply at any U.S. foreign service post for a visa and "it will be considered on its merits just the same as any other visa application." In the end, Johnson rejected Wang's proposal for an agreed announcement on cultural exchange.[127]

Beijing was not alone in uttering strong criticism against Washington's rejection of reciprocity on the exchange of reporters. The *New York Times* published an editorial on August 27 openly criticizing Dulles for not granting reciprocal visas to Chinese reporters. It reminded Dulles that the United States had nothing to be afraid of and instead that it had "the right to be proud of our institutions, inherited from many lands, notably from Great Britain, of our freedom, of our hopes." Thus, it believed, Dulles was wrong in delaying and limiting American reporters from going to Communist China and "still wrong in refusing reciprocal visas to the Chinese reporters." It insisted that it would be best "to have no curtain at all against any law-abiding foreigners who come here on temporary visas to look us over."[128] On the same day, a reporter asked Dulles why the issue of reciprocity was included in the State Department release at his press conference. Dulles was forced to defend the department's position by emphasizing that the existing law required a finding by the attorney general in order to permit any Communist to enter the United States. He was not sure whether the attorney general was willing or able to make such findings given the current relations between the two nations and the lack of necessary facilities. At the same time, he took half a step back and recognized that the U.S. government had never laid down any absolute rule that no Chinese Communist could come to this country and promised that if any application was made "it will be considered under the law."[129]

While Beijing and Washington were bickering about the issue of reciprocity, a large number of American reporters from the twenty-four publishing and news gathering companies quickly gathered in Tokyo and Hong

Kong preparing for their trip to China. On August 23, several of them sent telegrams to the MFA applying for visas. After a brief delay, John Roderick and five other reporters became the first to receive passport validations from U.S. Consulate in Hong Kong for travel to Communist China on August 25.[130] By the beginning of September, fifteen American reporters were in Hong Kong with their passports validated and waiting for their China trip to begin. However, they got no response from Beijing about their visa applications even though many of them had received invitation from the MFA a year ago and Gong Peng had recently promised to issue visas to American journalists as soon as they received the necessary approval from the State Department.[131] As a result, no American reporters with State Department authorization were able to visit the PRC in 1957.

Beijing's refusal to issue visas to any American reporters in 1957 was anything but a simple reaction to Washington's rejection of reciprocity, as it publicly claimed.[132] Instead, the lack of reciprocity was just a convenient excuse for Beijing to keep a large number of American journalists out of the PRC when their visits were no longer perceived beneficial. Beijing never had a plan to send Chinese visitors to the United States when it invited Americans to visit the PRC in 1955 or 1956. That was why Beijing did not ask for reciprocity when it invited eighteen American reporters for a monthlong visit to the PRC in August 1956 or when it issued visas to more than forty American youths in August 1957. Beijing began to contemplate the issue only after the State Department openly rejected reciprocity. It was in early September when the CCPCC Department of Propaganda conducted political review of four journalists for possible assignments in the United States.[133] However, the number was far smaller than the American journalists invited by Beijing the year before, and more important, none of them ever sent their visa applications to Washington. Wang Bingnan attempted to exonerate Beijing by claiming that the PRC government had never prohibited Chinese correspondents from going to the United States and claimed at his meeting with Johnson on October 10 that the Chinese reporters made their own decisions on this matter. Although Johnson failed to point out that the Chinese journalists were state employees under Communist rule and their jobs, especially overseas posts, had to be assigned by the government, he sharply responded that if what Wang stated was true then Washington should not be blamed for the lack of reciprocity, since no Chinese reporters wanted to apply for a visa to visit the United States.[134]

Beijing's decision to reject the American journalists in 1957 was shaped by its foreign as well as domestic policy needs. Deeply concerned with Washington's move toward a "two China" policy and inspired by the more favorable conditions for Communist countries in 1957, Beijing took a tougher stance toward the United States. In order to break the "two China" conspiracy plotted by Washington, Beijing made it loud and clear that it would not recognize any country that tried to have diplomatic relations with both the PRC and the Republic of China. Mao told Czechoslovakian visitors in March 1957 that Beijing was not afraid of nonrecognition and that it would be better if the United States recognized the PRC later. In this way, the PRC would have more time to do a more thorough house cleaning. If it had an embassy in China, Washington, Mao asserted, would carry out various sabotage activities from it. The main task at the present time, Mao declared, was to fight against the major Western countries rather than establish diplomatic relations with them. Beijing, Mao confessed, stayed in the ambassadorial talks only because it wanted to see Washington break off the engagement so that it could blame the Americans for their bad behavior.[135] Therefore, Washington's open refusal to guarantee the admission of an equal number of Chinese journalists gave Beijing an opportunity to reject the American reporters and launch a fierce attack on the U.S. government. To Mao, socialist countries had gained an overwhelming upper hand over capitalist countries in the world in 1957 when Great Britain and France were forced to stop fighting in Egypt under Moscow's strong opposition and the Soviet Union launched a satellite before the United States did.[136] Seeing the arrival of another turning point in human history, Beijing wanted to ride the tide by heightening its struggle against the United States. Rejecting American reporters was an integral part of it.

The lack of complete control over the visitors also contributed to Beijing's refusal to admit any American journalists in 1957. Beijing was willing to invite about two dozen American reporters and host three of them in 1956 mostly because it carefully picked them, granted a brief stay, and put them under tight control once they arrived. American reporters who applied for admission visas in 1957 were unacceptable because most of them were selected by their employers and approved by the State Department for a six-month stay in China. It would be difficult if not impossible for Beijing to have as much control and influence if they all came at the same time and were allowed an extended stay. By this time, Beijing had permitted only a handful of reporters from capitalist countries to cover special events for a short period in the PRC.

At the height of the Anti-Rightist movement, Beijing had even less confidence in the loyalty of Chinese intellectuals, especially journalists, who would inevitably come into close contact with the American reporters if they were allowed to visit the PRC. Encouraged by Mao, many journalists, like other intellectuals, offered strong criticism of the Communist regime and its leaders during the Hundred Flower campaign. At a forum organized by the National News Association on May 16, 1957, more than two hundred editors, reporters, professors, and chairmen of journalism departments from Beijing, Shanghai, Shanxi, and Liaoning complained that newspapers had become an instrument for class struggle led by the Communist Party, that journalists were not allowed independent thinking or writing their own news reports, and that freedom of press was overwhelmed by bureaucratism, sectionalism, and subjectivism.[137] *Wenhuibao*, a newspaper founded during the war against Japan in Shanghai, and the *Guangming Daily*, a newspaper run by the Democratic League in Beijing, carried a large amount of criticism from intellectuals in May. That made them top targets once the Anti-Rightist movement started in June 1957.[138] Mao warned in an internal instruction that a large number of intellectuals who had recently joined the CCP refused the Party's leadership and appreciated bourgeois liberalism.[139] In order to crush the so-called rightists, Mao wrote an editorial for the *People's Daily* and had it published on July 1, calling on all people to criticize the bourgeois orientation of *Wenhuibao*. In addition to Pu Xixiu, the publisher of *Wenhuibao*, Mao specifically named and viciously attacked the *Guangming Daily* and its publisher, Zhang Bojun, as well as its chief editor, Chu Anping.[140] Two months later, *People's Daily* published a long article by Li Zhang, who asserted that the bourgeois concept of freedom of press was brought in from the United States and used to resist the political and ideological leadership of the CCP.[141] Thus, it was only natural for Beijing to reject a large number of American reporters in 1957 when it was fighting with all its might against rightist journalists and freedom of the press in China.

American reporters and news organizations did become more critical toward their government when Beijing refused to issue visas to American journalists. However, the State Department was able to alleviate confrontation with the media. At a press conference held in Hong Kong on

September 10, Herter told the American reporters that whether they could enter Red China completely depended on the Chinese Communist government. He further explained that the United States had recognized the Soviet Union many years ago and allowed its reporters to be admitted to the United States as government officials. Since Communist China did not have diplomatic relations with the United States, the PRC reporters' applications for visas had to be considered on individual basis.[142] Having agreed to consider visa applications from PRC reporters on individual basis, Dulles instructed State Department officials to study related articles of immigration law carefully and get ready to review those applications. However, no Chinese journalists, who were all government employees, applied for visas to visit the United States in 1957 or the whole decade after that. With no entrance admission granted to any American journalists with State Department authorization despite their constant applications, the exchange of journalists between the two nations remained a mere mirage.

CHAPTER VI

Setting a New Pattern

Beijing's refusal to admit American reporters and send any Chinese journalists across the Pacific clearly demonstrated its commitment to keeping the PRC's door closed to regular cultural interactions with the United States, especially those sanctioned by Washington. However, that position did not prevent Beijing from inviting and hosting some carefully selected private American citizens for short visits or extended stay in the 1950s and the 1960s. Americans who went to the PRC during these two decades could be divided into three large categories. The first were either the CCP's old friends or members of the Communist Party of the United States of America (CPUSA) who had been persecuted during the anticommunist hysteria. They were granted extended or permanent stays in the PRC and integrated into the CCP's propaganda apparatus. The second included those who possessed particular skills needed by the PRC. Mostly experts in English language, they also had extended stays in China for their employment in various state-run institutions. The last comprised those Americans coming from diverse backgrounds such as journalists, writers, artists, students, doctors, prisoners of war, CPUSA members, and civil rights leaders and other progressive activists. Carefully chosen for their friendly attitude and their ability to influence American public opinion, they were invited for short visits. These direct interactions between the PRC government and individual Americans not only kept the

Sino-American cultural relations alive during the Cold War years but also brought fundamental changes to them.

Before the Communists came to power in 1949, most Americans, like many other Westerners, went to China as advisors and teachers with a broadly shared mission to change it.[1] Once Mao declared the United States the chief enemy of the Chinese revolution and American cultural activities in China an aggression, advice and teachings from the Americans were no longer needed or acceptable in the "new China." The need to confront the United States in "hot" as well as cold wars and the strong belief in the universal applicability of the Chinese revolutionary model and superiority of the Chinese socialist system made it necessary for Beijing to establish and maintain direct interactions with some carefully picked U.S. citizens. The goal was to turn them into students of the Chinese revolution who would help disseminate information for the PRC, isolate the U.S. government, and eventually defeat American imperialism. With the sophisticated mechanisms developed since the Yanan years and perfected during the Cold War, the CCP was effective in fitting American comrades and experts into its propaganda machine and turning most short-term visitors into enthusiastic carriers and disseminators of its messages. It was through its direct interactions with those individual American citizens that Beijing managed to play its new role as the teacher in the Sino-American cultural interactions and to exert considerable influence on the American people while keeping American ideals and values away from the Chinese people.

Making Mouthpieces

As Mao clearly indicated in his conversation with Mikoyan in early 1949, Beijing welcomed foreign comrades and friends to China when the newly established PRC shut its door to capitalist countries, especially the United States. While welcoming thousands of Soviet advisors and experts, the CCP also invited some CPUSA members and sympathizers, especially those who had worked well with Chinese Communist leaders in the past. With shared ideological ground or work experiences or both, these American comrades were not only allowed extended or permanent stays in the PRC but also were assigned the most important jobs by their host. As a result, they became an important and integral part of the CCP's international propaganda machine.

In order to create a positive image for the PRC in the world, Zhou Enlai approached Song Qingling, vice chairman of the PRC and widow of Sun Yat-sen, in 1950, asking her to publish an English-language magazine as she had done during the war against Japan. Song agreed and sent an invitation to Israel Epstein, the wartime editor and translator of Mao's article "On the Protracted War." Having worked for UPI in the 1930s, Epstein went to live in the United States after World War II and published his book *The Unfinished Revolution in China* in 1947.[2] Partly because of his activities in China, he was accused of spying for the Soviet Union in the early 1950s. Happy to receive Song's invitation, he returned to China with his wife, Elsie Fairfax-Cholmeley, in the summer of 1951. He first served as an adviser for *People's China* (*Renmin Zhongguo*), the PRC's first international propaganda publication and forerunner of the *Peking Review*. Then he joined Song in starting *China Reconstructs* (*Zhongguo Jianshe*), a new magazine catering to readers in capitalist countries. After serving as its executive editor for a few years, he became its editor-in-chief and held that position until his retirement in 1985. It was under his leadership that the magazine became one of the PRC's most prominent international propaganda venues. Besides his work at *China Reconstructs*, he was also involved in the translation of the *Selected Works of Mao Zedong* (*Mao Zedong Xuanji*). In recognition of his contribution and loyalty, Epstein received PRC citizenship in 1957 and joined the CCP in 1964.[3] Despite his citizenship, the Ministry of Foreign Affairs (MFA) still listed him as an American reporter for the *National Guardian*, a left-wing newspaper in New York, in the 1960s.[4]

Having enjoyed close working relations with the CPUSA since the 1920s, the CCP also took in quite a number of its members and sympathizers in the late 1950s and early 1960s. Manya Reiss, one of the founding members of the CPUSA, arrived in China to work at the Xinhua News Agency in 1957. She died of cancer in 1962 and was buried in Babaoshan Revolutionary Cemetery, the resting place of high-ranking government officials and revolutionary heroes in Beijing, hailed as a comrade by the PRC government. Zhou Enlai, Chen Yi, and Lu Dingyi all went to see her in the hospital. *People's Daily* reported on her death and the memorial service for her on March 7 and 10 respectively. Wu Lengxi, director of the New China News Agency, and Sidney Rittenberg, an American comrade who stayed in China working for the CCP after World War II, delivered eulogies. They both recognized her contribution to the world Communist movement and praised her as a resolute fighter against modern revisionism and monopolistic capitalism, turning her funeral into another propaganda campaign against the CCP's enemies.[5]

Following in the footsteps of Reiss, Frank Coe and Solomon Adler, both underground Communist sympathizers, arrived in China in 1958 and 1962 respectively. As well-established economists, Coe was a former senior official in the Department of Treasury and secretary of the International Monetary Fund, and Adler was the senior economist in the Treasury. They were forced to leave the United States because they were suspected by the FBI as members of a Soviet espionage ring. They were welcomed in the PRC not only because of the persecution they underwent but also because of their direct and indirect ties with the CCP. However, neither of them was given a position in his field consummate with his expertise and experiences. The fact that in 1957 Adler had published a well-received book, *The Chinese Economy*, did not help.[6] Like most Americans in the PRC in the 1950s and 1960s, they were used as English-language experts. Together with Epstein and Rittenberg, they were both assigned to the elite group charged with the responsibility for translating and polishing the fourth volume of the *Selected Works of Mao Zedong*, the top priority for the PRC's international propaganda during this period.[7] Although Wu Xueqian, the vice chairman of the CPPCC, praised the "extraordinary contribution" made by Adler in the translation work at his memorial service, historian Anne-Marie Brady rightly called it "a waste of energy for two such high-flying academics."[8]

The most distinguished figure among the American comrades in the PRC was Anna Louise Strong, who arrived in Beijing in fall 1958. She had earned the deep trust of the CCP leaders because of her lasting connections with them since the 1920s and her effective dissemination of their messages during and after World War II. Her friendship with top Communist leaders such as Mao Zedong, Liu Shaoqi, Zhu De, Zhou Enlai, Peng Dehuai, and Lu Dingyi was greatly deepened during her extended stay in Yanan in 1946, when she dined, danced, played cards, and watched shows with them.[9] It was in one of her interviews with Mao in August 1946 that the Communist leader made the famous statement that the atomic bombs possessed by the United States and the American reactionaries were merely "paper tigers."[10] Before her departure, Mao not only gave her some important documents to be shared with Communist Parties in other countries but also asked her to tell the American people that the CCP must win and that American imperialism and Jiang Jieshi (Chiang Kai-shek) "can be defeated."[11] Strong lived up to Mao's trust by publishing several books and delivering numerous speeches to systematically introduce Mao Zedong Thought, the CCP, and its history, leaders, and strategy to the Americans.[12] Based predominantly either on interviews with Chinese Communist leaders or on documents provided by them without independent verification or critical analysis of their contents, all her publications and speeches cast Mao and his comrades in extremely positive light.[13]

The Chinese Communist leaders liked her work so much that they kept inviting her back to China in the late 1940s and after. However, her return trip was delayed by her involvement in the U.S. general election in 1948, her arrest in the Soviet Union in 1949, and the State Department's refusal to renew her passport since 1950. As her age grew and health deteriorated, Strong's desire for one last long trip became increasingly strong. With all her good feelings for the Soviet Union evaporated, she sent an inquiry in mid-1955 to Chen Hansheng, an adviser at the MFA and associated editor of *China Reconstructs*, who had transmitted several invitations to her in the past. Chen quickly sent her another invitation for a visit to or an extended stay in the PRC as the guest of the National Association of Writers and the Chinese People's Association of Cultural Relations with Foreign Nations (CPACRFN).[14] As soon as she finally got her passport after the Supreme Court ruled on the case of *Rockwell Kent v. John F. Dulles* in June 1958 that the right to travel was an inherent element of liberty that cannot be denied to U.S. citizens, Strong left for the Peace Conference at Stockholm.[15] She met some of her old Chinese friends at the conference who not only reaffirmed their welcome to her but also issued an invitation to Emily Pierson, her friend and companion. After a short stay in the Soviet Union, Strong and Pierson arrived in Beijing on September 22, 1958.

Obviously happy with the return of Strong, Chinese Communist leaders gave her the warmest welcome and the most preferential treatment. Tang Mingzhao, a senior official in the CCP Liaison Department, and Chu Bosheng, the deputy secretary general of the CPACRFN, met Strong at the airport and escorted her and her friend directly to the Peking Hotel, the best in the city. Zhou Enlai gave her a welcome reception and dinner two days after her arrival in Beijing. Peng Dehuai, the minister of defense and her old friend, gave a detailed briefing on the military situation in Jinmen and Mazu before the reception. Lu Dingyi, her interpreter in Yanan and now director of the CCPCC Propaganda Department, came to the dinner.[16] About a week later Strong was invited to participate in the National

Day celebration on top of the Tiananmen, the first American given such an honor. After watching fireworks in the evening, Mao Zedong, Zhu De, Liu Shaoqi, Zhou Enlai, and many other leaders walked up to greet Strong. Having asked about her health, Mao, according to *People's Daily*, told Strong that "we should unite and fight together."[17] She was one of two Americans invited to the New Year's party for top leaders on December 31, 1958. Marshall He Long, the vice premier, danced with her before midnight, and Zhou Enlai invited her for the first dance of 1959.[18] Beginning in 1959, Zhou Enlai, Chen Yi, Deng Yingchao, Zhou's wife, and other officials always remembered to celebrate her birthday every year. In 1965, Mao and Zhou gave her two birthday parties separately for her eightieth birthday. Since Mao was in Shanghai at the time, she and more than thirty of her friends were flown from Beijing to the eastern metropolis for the occasion.[19]

When it became clear that Strong did not want to go back to the United States, Zhou told her that she was welcome to stay and work in the PRC as long as she wanted. Tired of living in a hotel, she was given an apartment in the Committee of the Chinese People Defending World Peace (CCPDWP) compound located on Taijichang Avenue, only a few blocks from Tiananmen Square. Formerly the Italian embassy, the compound was used by the CCPDWP to house prominent foreigners who were working for the PRC government or staying in Beijing as its distinguished guests. Located on the first floor of an old European-style building, her new apartment comprised a large living room, a study, a bedroom, and a dining room. It was well furnished with luxurious pieces taken from old imperial residences. She was assigned a full-time housekeeper and shared a cook with a few other families in the compound. Most important, all these accommodations were free for Strong, making it the most comfortable living arrangement that she had ever had. She could not help but tell one of her friends that life in Beijing "is nearly as perfect as human beings can make it."[20] Fully enjoying the lifestyle she had been seeking all her life, she "found herself growing younger, healthier, and better tempered" five years after moving to the PRC.[21]

Eager to see Strong pick up her writing, her hosts started to provide her information immediately after her arrival. Besides Peng Dehuai's briefing on the military situation, Lu Dingyi went to Strong's hotel room the next day after Zhou's welcome reception and spent the whole afternoon and evening explaining political developments in the PRC. Lu told Strong that her book *The Stalin Era* had been translated into Chinese and sold more than 110,000 copies in China. He highly praised her book for its fair assessments and analysis. Like Mao, she continued to recognize Stalin as a great Communist leader who had made some minor mistakes.[22] Lu also let Strong know that the CCPCC had made the people's communes the centerpiece of its domestic policy since mid-1957, and 75 percent of peasants had joined the communes by September 1958.[23] Having sensed her concerns over the rapid development of the people's communes based on her experience in the Soviet Union, her host immediately made an arrangement for her to visit the Evergreen People's Commune near Beijing and other famous communes in Henan, Jiangsu, and Guangdong provinces. After returning to Beijing, Strong quickly finished a book, *The Rise of the Chinese People's Commune*. It was published in March 1959 by the New World Press, a Chinese foreign-language publisher established in 1950 as part of Beijing's international propaganda apparatus.[24]

Printed within sixteen days, Strong's book became part of Beijing's response to recent attacks from John Foster Dulles and negative reports by American media. In a speech delivered in Seattle on November 13, 1958, Dulles accused the PRC of "feverishly imposing upon the 650 million people of Chinese mainland a backward system of mass slavery which is labeled the 'commune' system." He denounced the Chinese Communist regime for using communes as an instrument in confiscating the property of the Chinese peasants, degrading the dignity of human individual, destroying the family, plowing the graves of ancestors, and obliterating traditional Chinese culture and values. He also pointed out that the "hate America" campaign carried out throughout mainland China was designed to divert hatred among the Chinese people on the communes.[25] Strong believed that the misinformation on the people's commune was spread by Dulles for the purpose of attacking China and "portraying the Chinese people as lawless and sub-human creatures who might with clear conscience be atom-bombed from the world in the next Taiwan Strait war." Thus, she solicited comments from commune members on some specific points made by Dulles in his speech during her visit to the Evergreen Commune and quoted many in her book. In order to prove that Chinese peasants were not just material units valued only as laborers for the state, Strong told her readers that Evergreen Commune members wrote more than 200,000 poems and included quite a few.[26] She emphasized that she had not yet "found in China even that form of coercion which every small town in

America uses ruthlessly, the truant officer compelling attendance at the primary school." Strong concluded that the people's communes "have given China an economic mechanism that incites every township and county to get irrigation, roads, water-power, steel and modern industry by local initiative, as fast as the local people can do the work."[27]

Strong also wrote three more books to defend Beijing's policy toward Tibet and attack Washington's position on the issue and its involvement in Indochina within a couple of years. In *Tibetan Interviews* (figure 6.1), Strong denounced the Tibetan rebels for violating the agreement signed by the Dalai Lama and the central government in 1950. She also ridiculed Secretary of State Christian Chester for going "all out in a moral crusade for 'the indomitable spirit of man,' which in this case to mean the serf-owners' insistence on keeping their serfs." She concluded that for most Tibetans quelling the rebellion opened the door to reform and to a new Tibet that should be truly a "Greater Tibet," not through extension of territory but

Figure 6.1 Anna Louise Strong interviewing two Tibetan college students in her apartment for her book *Tibetan Interviews*.
Source: Anna Louise Strong, *Tibetan Interviews* (Beijing: New World Press, 1959).

by the expansion of production and a prosperous life for all.[28] After a brief trip organized by the MFA to Tibet in August 1959, Strong published *When Serfs Stood Up in Tibet* in mid-1960. As part of Beijing's effort to repudiate attacks from the United States and other Western nations, Strong's book praised the reform centered on the abolition of the serf system and lauded the development of the remote region of China as "building paradise" on the roof of the world.[29]

As Washington deepened its involvement in Southeast Asia, Strong took a trip carefully arranged by Beijing and Hanoi to North Vietnam as well as Laos in 1961. After her three-week visit, Strong completed another book, *Cash and Violence in Laos and Viet Nam*. It was in this book that Strong began to call the United States an imperialist country and denounced its expansion into Laos, Cambodia, and South Vietnam with the power of financial and military aid. She attacked Washington for forcing the new governments established after the Geneva Conference to "break their pledged neutrality and bend them into a military base against China and North Viet Nam."[30] Strong also boldly predicted that if American imperialism persisted in conducting a war in Vietnam, "its defeat will be worse than in the Korean War." While denouncing U.S. intervention in Southeast Asia, she praised China for its influence in the area over centuries and asserted that "it will get further with gifts of rice-transplanters and textile factories than Washington with bombs."[31]

While enjoying her high productivity, Strong lost much of the ability to have her books accepted for publication in the United States. As an established writer, Strong was able to publish all but one of her previous thirty or so books in the United States by mainstream publishers including Henry Holt and Company, Macmillan, Doubleday, Viking Press, the University of Chicago Press, and Little, Brown. The only exception was *Dawn Over China*, which was published by the People's Publishing House in Bombay, India, in 1948.[32] In sharp contrast, Strong managed to have only *Cash and Violence in Laos and Viet Nam* published by a little-known left-wing press in New York. The other three were all published by the New World Press in Beijing with limited availability in the United States through China Books & Periodicals, a company established by Henry H. Noyes in 1960 to sell printed materials from the PRC as an agent of Beijing's International Bookstore (Guoji Shudian). Strong's inability to have most of her new China books or articles published in the United States was largely the result of their lack of investigative quality and close resemblance to Communist government propaganda. Carey McWilliams, editor of *The Nation*, told her that her articles needed to contain a "critical awareness . . . toward the subject matter" and to be on guard even against her own enthusiasm. James Aronson, a friend and executive editor of the *National Guardian*, also let her know that her stories, although "honestly felt and in many cases movingly reported, still lacked a sense of journalistic detachment and attribution which is essential for the American readers today."[33]

Although frustrated and unhappy with the rejections, Strong generally agreed with the editors' assessments of her writings done in the PRC and even identified the major causes for her problem. In a letter sent to Liao Chengzhi in November 1962, she confessed that what she had written so far could not convince "any honest opponent, or even a careful expert," let alone herself. Strong acknowledged that she had many holes in her recent writings and had "papered them to make a good case." She was worried that if she wrote a book on the border clash between the PRC and India "the holes would become too big and would ruin my reputation and my case." The root cause of the problem, she pointed out, was "in China's present propaganda that you demand that no picture of actual hard struggle be shown." She tried to prove her point by pointing out that she could not do a good article on the reduction of mortality or crime in China's cities in comparison with an American city because "you permit no admission that anyone in China ever dies or commits crime." She also complained that she could not show China's "struggle for grain and a sound agriculture, because I am not allowed to admit that anyone in these three years ever starved to death." At the end of her letter, she let Liao know that "it is worth doing" a book that "can make a real contribution to the future." However, she emphasized that "just to copy *Hsinhua* (New China News Agency) is not enough."[34] Receiving no reply from Liao and seeing no changes in PRC's propaganda system, Strong wrote no further books after 1962.

Just like all other writers and journalists in the PRC, Strong had to follow the CCP's strict guidelines on propaganda and subject her writings to tough censorship. As a member of CPUSA who had lived in the Soviet Union for about three decades, Strong was no stranger to Communist censorship. Thus, she not only practiced self-censoring in all her writings in the PRC but also asked for a reliable official with whom she could consult on any materials to be sent abroad for publication. To meet her request,

Zhou Enlai assigned Tang Mingzhao to look over substantive matters while Wang Chuliang kept an eye on the language. They worked together to ensure that Strong made no mistakes. In addition to this special "consultation" arrangement, Strong had to go through the regular review process for all her books conducted by the New World Press editors. She usually accepted all the editorial changes made by the press because she knew she was not really in a position to make a hard bargain. Once she cried nonstop for many hours and stayed in bed for nine days after arguing with the New World Press editors over a term used in *When Serfs Stood Up in Tibet*. However, in the end she had to give up what she believed an accurate term and accept a compromise proposed by a friend so that her book could be published.[35]

Somewhat disappointed with Strong's inability to have her writings published in the United States, Chinese leaders worked with her to remedy the situation. When Strong raised the issue at a dinner with Zhou Enlai in August 1962, Zhou suggested that she write a monthly general letter to those who sought information about the PRC. Strong heartily embraced Zhou's idea, and her first *Letter from China* was published on September 17, 1962. Titled "On Harvest Moon, U-2, Peace," her letter began with the news that good crops were reaped in northern as well as many parts of southern China. Her goal was to assure readers that grain "is now in fair supply in all areas of China." In her discussion on a U-2 spy plane recently shot down by the PRC, she pointed out that the U.S. military directed the Nationalist spying operation as part of President Kennedy's plan to step up tensions and look for war.[36] Three more letters focusing on Sino-Indian border clashes and Sino-Soviet ideological debate were sent out in the following months. While some of her friends mimeographed the letters for discussion groups in the United States, newspapers in Indonesia, Ghana, Australia, and New Zealand published some of them.[37]

Strong's timely and favorable report on China's domestic conditions, lucid discussion of Beijing's foreign policy positions, and sharp attack on Washington made her Chinese hosts quickly see the advantage and usefulness of her letters as a "nonofficial" propaganda venue. Beginning in January 1963, the letters were nicely printed on thin, high-quality paper on both sides from edge to edge to accommodate as much content as possible. Tang Mingzhao and Wang Chuliang stepped up their involvement by suggesting topics for her letters and providing comments for revision of her drafts. At Zhou's urging, writing the letters became a regular "job" for Strong until the end of 1969, months before she passed away in Beijing. Fulfilling her promise made at the very beginning, she published sixty-nine letters in the last seven years of her life. To help reduce her workload, Elsie Fairfax-Cholmeley was assigned as assistant editor for the enterprise. Strong drew most of the contents for her letters from interviews with and speeches by top CCP leaders, news reports and editorials from state media, and personal observations and experiences. From time to time, she also solicited writings from other foreigners, especially Americans working in the PRC, including Israel Epstein, Sidney Rittenberg, Talitha Gerlach, Gerald Tannebaum, Joan Hinton, Shirley Wood, George Hatem (Ma Haide), and Rewi Alley.

In addition to persistent praise for the people's communes, strenuous coverups of the disasters caused by the Great Leap Forward, and sharp attacks on Soviet revisionism, Strong's letters focused on Beijing's policy toward the United States in 1964 and 1965 as Washington escalated its war effort in Vietnam and on the Great Proletarian Cultural Revolution (GPCR) launched by Mao in 1966. Citing numerous statements made by Mao Zedong, Zhou Enlai, Chen Yi, Lin Biao, and Luo Ruiqing, Strong set out to repudiate the two contradictory campaigns in the United States, with one attempting to assure the American people that China would never come into the war and the other accusing Beijing of being bellicose. She reiterated the four points made by Zhou during a recent interview that China, while not provoking a war with the United States, would support any country that was fighting against imperialist aggression headed by the United States, be prepared to annihilate all American forces if they dared invade the PRC, and not be limited by any boundaries once the war broke out.[38] Writing about the GPCR only weeks after it was officially launched, Strong vehemently rejected a *New York Times* report that Communist China was in the grip of a nationwide political purge, that the removal of Peng Zhen, the Communist Party chief of Beijing, was essentially the outcome of a power struggle among potential heirs of Mao, and that Lin Biao appeared to be the leading victor who had consolidated his success and increased his prestige. Instead she gave her readers the standard Maoist definition that the GPCR was a life and death struggle that would decide whether "the Chinese people will be able to consolidate socialism and drive through to communism or whether the 'bourgeois remnants,' acting through culture and education especially on the young generation, will eventually restore capitalism."[39]

Unlike her earlier personal newsletter *Today*, which was edited by Strong alone and financed with subscription fees in the early 1950s while she was in the United States, *Letters from China* was a de facto official publication, with the PRC government involved not only in planning and editing but also in printing and mailing. According to Strong, it cost twelve cents to print a copy and fifty-four cents to airmail it, totaling "about one pound sterling for ten airmailed issues." Since it was against U.S. law to send money to the PRC, Strong told her readers in the United States not to subscribe her letter. Instead, they could consider the letters as a gift from her to "educate my country."[40] By the mid-1960s, more than forty thousand copies of each issue were printed and mailed to the United States and many other countries. Based on the expense figures provided by Strong, *Letters from China* easily cost Beijing about one hundred thousand U.S. dollars each year. With all expenses paid by her host and her close parroting of the Communist propaganda in all her writings, Strong became a quintessential employee of the PRC government.

Top Chinese Communist leaders, including Mao, deeply appreciated her work. When he held a big party for her eightieth birthday in Shanghai on November 24, 1965, Mao specifically congratulated her on the success of *Letters from China* and told her that "we couldn't do our job without you." He also instructed Kang Sheng, one of his most trusted associates at the time, to make the necessary arrangements so that it could be translated into other languages.[41] Saddened by her death in March 1970, Mao Zedong, Lin Biao, Zhou Enlai, and many other leaders sent wreaths to her memorial service. Guo Moruo addressed her as "Comrade Strong" eight times in his eulogy delivered on April 2, 1970. He praised her for reporting "with her elegant pen to readers throughout the world China's brilliant achievements in socialist revolution and socialist construction" and for propagating "the fact that invincible Mao Tsetung Thought has gone deep into the hearts of the people."[42] It was because of the special treatment received by Strong from CCP leaders and her willingness to parrot their propaganda that led Alan Winnington, a British Communist who also worked in China after 1949 as a journalist, and her biographers to reach the same conclusion that Strong was the trusted mouthpiece of the Chinese Communist regime in the 1950s and 1960s.[43]

Influencing the Influencers

Besides American comrades who were granted extended or permanent stays in the PRC, Beijing also invited a much larger number of Americans for short visits. Coming from diverse backgrounds, they were invited because Beijing believed that they had the ability or at least the potential to influence U.S. public opinion, political organizations or movements, and government policy. Their visits to the PRC gave Chinese Communist leaders opportunities to shape their views toward China and turn them into messengers or influencers for Beijing. A visit to China during those years, as Anne-Marie Brady accurately observed, "was not meant to be an exchange of ideas: the visitors' role was to learn and admire, and if possible write favorable reports which could be used in China and the West."[44] Beijing was able to achieve its goal in most cases because of its careful selection of the visitors and its skillful use of the sophisticated mechanisms specially developed to create a controlled reality and experiences for them.

The first American visitors arrived in China in late 1949, only weeks after the PRC was founded. Taking advantage of the Women's International Democratic Federation Conference held in Moscow, Beijing invited all the delegates, including a couple of African American activists, to attend the Conference of Asian Women in China. One was Ida Jackson, a Black Brooklyn-based American Labor Party activist and a tough community organizer. The other was Eslanda Robeson, a Black anthropologist and wife of the actor and singer Paul Robeson. Eslanda Robeson was especially welcomed in China because her husband was well known in mainland China for his strong support for the Chinese in their war against Japan and the establishment of the PRC.[45] Before her trip to Beijing, Robeson read Mao's "The Chinese Revolution and the Chinese Communist Party" very carefully and took detailed notes.[46] After the conference, she was invited to visit Nanjing as well as Shanghai. In a speech delivered at the Shanghai Railway Station on December 21, 1949, she praised the Chinese music, plays, and movies, calling them "of the people, by the people, and for the people." Inspired by the Communist victory in China, she told her audience that the Black artists and writers in the United States had the obligation to report, explain, persuade, and convince their countrymen that Blacks were not inferior simply because their skin color was different. During her stay in Shanghai she met and dined with Song Qingling a few times. Deeply impressed by her conversations with Song, Robeson published an article after returning to the United States calling Song a revolutionary leader in a revolutionary new world who stood as a "magnificent example of courage, warm humanity, and common sense." Thus, she concluded that Soong was definitely "World Woman Number One."[47]

Although Beijing was unable to recruit any Americans from the United States for cultural interactions in 1955, it managed to have Aubrey Pankey, an African American singer residing in Czechoslovakia, perform in the PRC at the end of the year. Accompanied by Kathryn Weatherly, his wife, and Marie Knotkova, a Czech pianist, Pankey arrived in China on November 8 and gave several concerts in Beijing and Shanghai, becoming the first American singer to perform in the PRC since 1949 (figure 6.2).[48] Pankey was invited not only because of his repeated requests and the Czech government's strong endorsement, but also because of his reputation as "Robeson Number Two" (*dier Luoboxun*) and the potential publicity generated by his visit.[49] As a common practice in the PRC, the Art Group of the CCP Shanghai Municipal Committee worked out a comprehensive reception plan. The plan provided detailed background information of the visitors, shared the guidelines set by the CCPCC, laid out the organizational structure for the reception, listed all the sites to be visited by the guests, specified the publicity actions to be taken, and specified housing and transportation arrangements. While taking every opportunity to show the great successes achieved by Shanghai, the hosts obviously did not tell the visitors that many things were still rationed in the PRC. As a result, Weatherly and Krotkova were surprised to see their host provide ration coupons for the cloth and silk they bought in stores.[50] In addition to reports carried by *People's Daily*, Beijing broadcast the news on the radio so that it could be received and publicized abroad.[51] Pankey's wife sent photos to the United States of them with Chen Yi, the vice premier and the mayor of Shanghai who came to the first concert with his deputies. The picture appeared in the *Pittsburgh Courier* on January 7, 1956, with a short report recognizing Pankey as the first American artist to visit the PRC and sharing his impression: "Audiences very receptive . . . high enthusiasm for Negro spirituals . . . fabulous hospitality."[52]

The arrival of the American Youth Delegation in Beijing in late August 1957 brought the largest group of visitors from the United States. Headed by a preselected core of pro-Communist leaders, the forty or so young Americans came at Beijing's invitation as part of its effort to subvert

Figure 6.2 Program for Aubrey Pankey's concert in Shanghai, December 1955.
Source: Shanghai Municipal Archives, Shanghai, China.

Washington's travel ban against the PRC and isolate the U.S. government from the American people. In order to better coordinate the reception of the American youths, a special group led by Liu Xiyuan, a member of the Secretariat of the Communist Youth League Central Committee, was established. Charged by Zhou Enlai to sway progressive members in the delegation, it assigned two officials from the Communist Youth League Central Committee and eight interpreters to accompany the delegation during its visit. The group sent thousands of Chinese students to greet the American visitors in major cities, placed the visitors in the best hotels, and offered them gourmet food. It also extended their visas so that they could be part of the National Day celebration on October 1. On that day, those who had accepted the extension were put on the terrace right below the Tiananmen, with other dignitaries to view the parade and given the opportunity to meet Mao. This arrangement allowed Beijing not only to further demonstrate its hospitality but also to show off the support the American people gave the PRC.[53]

The visit of the American youths offered Beijing a rare opportunity to articulate its positions on various issues and intensify young Americans' doubts about and criticism of their own government. At his meeting with the American youth delegation on September 7, Zhou not only defended Beijing's insistence on reciprocity in the exchange of journalists but also explained why Beijing refused to denounce the use of force in Taiwan, decried Washington's military threat, and reissued the invitation for relatives of American prisoners in the PRC to visit them. Zhou repeatedly told the visitors how much the PRC wanted to establish normal diplomatic and trade relations with the United States and blame Washington for the hostility between the two nations.[54] Mao made a similarly grand gesture when he greeted those young Americans at the National Day celebration. Mao hoped that the Chinese and American peoples could exchange friendly visits in peace.[55] However, it was difficult if not impossible for the young Americans to know whether the Chinese leaders meant what they said and whether what they said was consistent with their policy toward the United States.

While displaying hospitality to the young American visitors, Beijing exerted extremely tight control over their activities and experiences in China. To accommodate their request for a visit to the Number One Middle School in Hanyang County near Wuhan, where more than thirty students had been expelled and three educators executed after a student protest in mid-June, a special tour was methodically arranged for them. Under instruction from the CCP Hubei Provincial Committee, local officials ordered a thorough cleaning of the whole town and removed posters announcing the execution of the three educators. The school issued strict orders that no students or teachers take the initiative in approaching the American visitors, all conversations go through the interpreters, and all answers to questions on the Hanyang Incident strictly follow the published official statements. Although a meeting was arranged with the newly appointed school principal, the visitors were not allowed to talk with student organizers or family members of those who had been executed. After a heated debate over whether the incident was a suppression of student movement, the visitors were taken to a banquet. They used the new dinnerware specifically bought for them and enjoyed rare delicacies prepared by a famous chef specially hired for the occasion.[56] However, despite their importance, neither the Hanyang Incident nor the Anti-Rightist movement was mentioned in *Inside the Red China*, the first documentary on the PRC made by Robert Cohen, a member of the American youth delegation.[57]

Having not issued any visas to American journalists for a year, Beijing suddenly gave a quick approval to John Strohm, the representative of *Reader's Digest* and the Newspaper Enterprise Association. He got the nod from Beijing most likely because of his related experience in the past and his bold initiative in the moment. As a seasoned American journalist, Strohm had worked in China as a freelance reporter for about a year in 1937 and visited the Soviet Union after that. Unwilling to follow the same path taken by his peers who had sent their visa applications to the MFA and been ignored, Strohm took, in his editor's words, an audacious approach. He sent a telegram directly to Mao in summer 1958, telling the Chinese leader that he would like to see the progress of China's farm program.[58] Although Strohm did not know Mao personally, he was fully aware that the CCPCC chairman had the final say on Beijing's policy toward the United States and was devoted to the promotion of the people's commune, a new agrarian institution that would extend Communist control to the rural areas and allow China to sprint into communism (*paobu jinru gongchan zhuyi*).[59] Despite serious doubts and criticisms from the Soviet leaders, Mao was excited by this grand experiment and eager to let the people of the world, especially the Americans, see this historical event as it was unfolding.[60] In addition to his perfectly timed proposal, Strohm, as the president of

Agricultural Publishers, Inc. and the editor of the *Ford Almanac*, catering mostly to American farmers, seemed at least on the paper to be a perfect fit for the task.[61]

As the first American who entered the PRC with official approvals from both governments, Strohm traveled 7,500 miles in three weeks with all arrangements made by his host, who most likely recognized him as a writer rather than a reporter. His report, published in *Reader's Digest* in January 1959, did provide some insightful observations on the rapid rise of the people's communes in Communist China. He informed his readers that there was an unprecedented drive to form communes of some two thousand families each in China's rural areas. Each commune, designed to fit into the Communist monolith as a cell, consolidated all farming, trading, industry, schools, and militia in the area. He observed that China's warp-speed movement toward a form of Communism made Russia look as if she were standing still. To him, the Chinese style of Communism was a different brand, but "no less Red, and potentially, more virulent."[62] However, most of his attention was attracted by "a hate-America campaign that extended from Mao's headquarters in Peiping to the most remote peasant village." Visiting the PRC at the height of the second Taiwan Strait Crisis, Strohm saw with his own eyes millions of Chinese demonstrating in streets, hundreds of thousands of posters carrying hate-America messages being pasted to walls of homes, factories, hospitals, and schools, with his country being portrayed as "a blood-fanged wolf, a ruthless and ravaging soldier or a dollar-bloated Uncle Sam." He even had a rifle shoved in his stomach by a militiaman in a factory in Nanjing to dramatize the Chinese worker's anger toward American imperialism. He did try to defend his country by telling his hosts that the United States had never started a war with China and had no reason to start one now. However, they would come back and remind him of what had happened in Korea. Strohm knew that no further discussion would be possible or necessary, since most Chinese were made to believe that the United States started the Korean War and that Chinese volunteers won it.[63]

While doubting that the Chinese Communist leaders really wanted a war with the United States, Strohm clearly identified the real goal of Beijing's hate-America campaign and its connection with the people's commune movement after his three-week visit. He sharply pointed out in his report that the Communist leaders were willing to risk the war in order to "achieve their aim of driving a backward people toward seemingly impossible social and industrial goals." He told his readers that in factories, on trains or farms, and in the streets, loudspeakers constantly blared that the United States was talking peace while plotting war. Thus, the Chinese all vowed to "work harder to produce more food, more goods, to stop the American attack." He found a specific and clear-cut example of Beijing's using hatred to prod the labor force when the chairman of a collective in northern China told him that peasants were so angry with the American aggressors that they worked fifteen days and nights to overfulfill the farming plan.[64] His assessment was close to the interpretations advanced by leading scholars decades later about the period.[65]

The most impressive part of Strohm's report was his sharp analysis of what made the hate-America campaign as well as the people's commune movement possible in Communist China. Although he shared the belief that China throughout its history was a nation of individuals who owed their first and undying loyalty to their immediate family, he came to disagree with those old China hands who insisted that the Chinese would never be regimented. After his three-week tour, he believed that they had been regimented and "compressed into a monolith which overpowers every human soul." The Communist regime succeeded because those who refused to go along with it were shot and the rest were systematically remolded. With active resistance eliminated, Mao, he observed, was substituting molding for murder, making remolding the most dramatic single enterprise in Red China. While all private businesses had been swallowed up by it, hundreds of thousands, if not millions, of government officials, writers, artists, and businessmen had been sent to farms or construction projects to "work the conservative ideas out of their systems." He believed that Mao's goal was a body of citizens who "accept the Red book from cover to cover: to think otherwise—out loud—is treason." Thus, he concluded that "no human beings have ever been held in more complete mental and physical bondage than the subjects of Mao Zedong," and that nowhere has human intelligence been brainwashed into a more violent fury against American leaders.[66]

Beijing's harsh response to Strohm's "unfriendly" responses during his visit and critical report afterward was immediate and long-lasting. Deeply disappointed by the unsympathetic views revealed during his visit, Chinese Communist leaders not only denied him an interview with Zhou Enlai, a privilege bestowed on the three American journalists who had visited the PRC in 1956, but also became more adamant in keeping all mainstream American journalists out of mainland China. They made that position clear by ignoring visa applications from W. Averell Harriman, the former governor of New York and a reporter employed by the North American Newspaper Alliance, and Vincent Sheean, a veteran freelance writer working for the Westinghouse Broadcasting Company, in spring 1959.[67] Such a rejection was a surprise to American media, including the *New York Times*, which believed that "the refusal of a visa by the Chinese would probably cause Mao Tse-tung's government more embarrassment than it would be worth."[68] However, the decision was made by CCP leaders as a key component of their recently adopted strategy aimed at resolving the Taiwan issue and as an expression of resentment toward the mainstream American journalists. At a meeting with the Chilean journalist delegation in June 1964, Mao told the visitors that Beijing rejected Washington's proposal for sending journalists to the PRC and starting trade between the two nations because "we believe that before the major problem is resolved, these small and particular problems may not be resolved in a hurry."[69] At another meeting with a large group of Japanese youths on November 25, 1965, Mao made it clear that he would welcome American students to visit China because they were demonstrating in the streets against Washington's war policy and starting a revolution in the United States. However, he emphasized that "we don't welcome their journalists, or don't welcome the majority of them, only welcome particular individuals."[70]

As Beijing's relations with Moscow quickly deteriorated, the CCP invited James Jackson, the CPUSA secretary for international affairs, to visit the PRC in spring 1959. Seeing it as a good opportunity to influence another major Communist Party in the world, top CCP leaders including Mao Zedong, Liu Shaoqi, and Deng Xiaoping all met with him. In his meeting with Jackson, Liu tried to beef up the CPUSA's confidence in confronting the strongest imperialist power in the world and persuade American comrades to join the CCP in fighting the revisionists in the international Communist movement. He told Jackson that based on the CCP's experience, dogmatists and revisionists within Communist parties should be treated differently. While the former should be criticized and helped as comrades, the latter should be denounced ruthlessly and expelled from the Party, since they were no longer comrades but bourgeois surrogates.[71] Mao and Deng had a talk with Jackson on Mao's train in Zhengzhou, Henan Province, on March 4, 1959. Mao was very happy to meet with Jackson and told him that "we welcome American comrades visiting us more frequently." Having shared his views on the world situation, Mao emphasized that the imperialists were having a hard time because ten important events had taken place in the past fourteen months that were all damaging to the imperialists. When Jackson told his hosts that he often studied Mao's works and hoped to learn some lessons from them, Mao, after showing a bit modesty, affirmed that the Chinese experiences could be somewhat helpful and might be used as a reference by the American comrades. He emphasized that although American imperialism looked very strong, "it is also weak" and "it is afraid of you."[72] However, neither Jackson nor the CPUSA took the CCP's advice. They soon chose to side with Moscow when the CCP decided to break away from the Communist movement led by the Soviet Union in the early 1960s.

To show off the achievements of the Great Leap Forward and remedy the negative impact caused by Strohm, Beijing invited and hosted quite a number of other American visitors in 1959. One was Frank Pestana, a lawyer in Los Angeles, secret member of the CPUSA with broad connections with local elites, and frequent reader of *China Reconstructs* and the *Peking Review*. The Chinese leaders considered him a friend who could offer inside information on the United States and help them improve their work on the Americans. Since he was the guest of the CCPDWP and his tour included Shanghai, the Peace Committee's Shanghai Branch worked out a detailed plan for his reception. Following instructions from headquarters, the local branch set out to show him China's achievements in all areas and the power of the Chinese people so that he could "learn from our work experiences" and be more courageous and confident in his fight in the United States. Since Pestana's visit was secret, his local hosts also made sure that he would not be seen by other guests from Western capitalist countries in his hotel or during his tour of the city.[73] His local hosts took him to many sites open to foreign visitors, including the Children's Palace, Workers' Cultural Palace, Shanghai Export Merchandise Exhibit, Fangua Neighborhood, Ganxuan New Village, Industrial Art Research Institute, Jade Buddha Temple, and the Grand World (Dashijie). He was also allowed to attend a court trial in Changning District and participate in the discussion on social reform and urban planning. He exalted that only socialist countries had children's palaces and that Chinese court trials were superior to those of capitalist countries. However, he believed that it took too long, more than a year, for the case to go to trial. He refused to accept any justification from the host because if this was allowed, he insisted, someone could be kept in jail for ten years and die there. His hosts were happy to hear his praises, but not so much his "advice."[74]

The Chinese leaders did show great interest in getting more information on the United States in general and the CPUSA in particular. As requested, Pestana spent a whole morning on July 8 talking about the situation in the United States. He told his hosts that the American industrial workers did not listen to the CPUSA, some progressives did not want to cooperate with the CPUSA, and many CPUSA members quit after the Twentieth Congress of the Soviet Communist Party. He also noted that the CPUSA leaders were paying close attention to theoretic study and intensifying Marxist and Leninist education among its members. The current task for the CPUSA, Pestana revealed, was to improve unity, expel revisionists and rightists, win over unemployed workers, and fight for peace. He believed that nothing was more important than Sino-Soviet unity and that with the rapid growth of the PRC a united China and the Soviet Union could beat the United States. He even predicted that "the United States could not survive if it does not change its system in 10 years."[75]

Impressed by what he saw during his visit, Pestana gave many talks on Communist China after his return to the United States. One of them, "Six Weeks in Communist China," was delivered at the Leboro Theater in Santa Barbara, California, on May 4, 1961. That address was later used by the House Subcommittee on Internal Security as evidence to prove his trip to the PRC and his general purpose were to "influence the public within the United States with respect to the political or public interests and policies of the Communist regime." While refusing to answer most of the questions posed by the committee at a hearing held on August 5, 1963, Pestana rebutted his interrogators by sharply pointing out that "the public of the United States is as competent to judge information as you, and perhaps much better," and that they "have a right to listen, to judge, and do not need you or this committee to tell them what they shall hear or what they shall not hear."[76]

Beside Pestana, Beijing invited and hosted some other new as well as old friends in 1959. Hershel D. Meyer and his wife, Dora Teytelboym, an American couple who claimed to be CPUSA members, were Beijing's new friends. Meyer was a doctor and the author of the book *The Last Illusion: American Plan for World Dominance*, which had been translated into Russian as well as Chinese.[77] Teytelboym was a well-known poet who had recently published *Little Rock*, a Yiddish narrative focusing on the fight against racial segregation in southern schools. They attracted Beijing's attention not only because they had published books and poems exposing the dark side of the United States but also because they planned to write a new book on China and the Soviet Union.[78] The old friends included Maud Russell and Ida Pruitt. Russell worked for the YWCA in China from 1917 to 1943 and served as executive director of the Committee for a Democratic Far East Policy from 1946 to 1952 in New York. As soon as the committee was dismantled, she started to publish a newsletter, *Far East Reporter*, and drive across the country each year since 1953 giving talks on China, opposing American involvement in the Korean War, and promoting the recognition of the PRC.[79] Pruitt was sent by the Rockefeller Foundation to China to establish the Department of Medical Social Work at the PUMC hospital in 1920 and served as its chief until 1939. As one of the key players in the organization of the Chinese Industrial Cooperative in the war against Japan, she returned to the United States in 1939 to serve as its chief American spokesperson and fundraiser.[80] They all received warm and methodically planned receptions in China. Although Meyer's book never came out, Russell completed a booklet, *New People in New China: Some Personal Glimpses of People in China*, and had it published after her return to the United States.[81]

Still committed to showing off the success of the Great Leap Forward and attacking the United States, Beijing kept inviting American influencers for short visit in 1960. Emily Pierson, a doctor and strong opponent of U.S. war policy; Martha Dodd, a writer whose recent book *The Search Light* exposed the deprivation of academic freedom in the United States; and Alfred Stern, the millionaire husband of Dodd, were some of them. Of course, the most prominent visitor was Edgar Snow, an old friend of many top CCP leaders who had introduced Mao and his revolution to the American readers with his book *Red Star Over China*. Busy working on his autobiography, Snow turned down Beijing's initial invitation in summer 1957. Once his book was completed and published, he sent letters to Beijing for a visa and sought financial support in England for his trip.[82] Uncertain about Snow's political position in the Cold War and extremely cautious after the disappointing interaction with Strohm, the Chinese Communist leaders solicited Strong's assessment of Snow. Strong gave her support because "he can write and get an audience." However, she also warned the Chinese officials that Snow had developed a strong inclination toward

Gandhi as well as Tito and a disquieting tendency to quote historical figures verbatim about things not meant for the public. For the same reason, she asked them not to tell Snow how much she got for free, fearing that he might make it a story and publicize it.[83]

While the Chinese leaders were still deliberating his application for a visit, Snow published an article, "Recognition of the People's Republic of China," in July 1959. His article analyzed the failure of American policy toward the PRC and recommended the recognition of Beijing as an alternative.[84] This article proved not only his pro-PRC stance but also his ability to have his writings published in mainstream American media. Thus, when he explored the possibility of a visit to the PRC again while passing through Hong Kong in fall 1959, Mao Zedong, Zhou Enlai, Peng Zhen, and Lu Dingyi were briefed by Kang Sheng, a Politburo member who was in charge of cultural affairs and education, on Snow's request at a meeting in Hangzhou on December 17, 1959.[85] After careful evaluation, the decision was made and another invitation was extended to Snow in mid-1960 after he returned to Europe.

Beijing's approval for Snow's visit to the PRC, while causing some concern for State Department officials, offered them an opportunity to raise the issue of sending more American reporters to Communist China. With Beijing's invitation in hand, Snow started immediately to look for a sponsor for his trip so that he did not have to violate the travel ban or become a state guest of the Communist regime. His first appeal to the *Saturday Evening Post*, his former employer, was unsuccessful because the editors did not like his approach in China reporting.[86] He then turned to *Look* magazine, which had sent two correspondents to the PRC in 1956 and still attempted to get more of its reporters there. Having learned that Snow was able to get a visa to the PRC, Cowles, chief editor of *Look*, quickly agreed to list him as its representative. However, the State Department was reluctant to validate Snow's passport for his China trip. A State Department spokesman openly stated that when the program was instituted the department wanted objective reporting and that the reporter chosen by Cowles could not be objective in its opinion. Cowles persisted, and the State Department finally gave in, since it had promised to let news agencies select their own representatives.[87] Having validated Snow's passport for his travel to the PRC, the State Department instructed Jacob D. Beam, U.S. Ambassador to Poland, to let Wang Bingnan know that it was happy to see Beijing have "abandoned its previous position on need to [a] signed agreement between two sides by issuing visa to correspondent Edgar Snow." Well prepared for Washington's move, Wang rebutted that Snow was a "writer," not a "correspondent."[88] In another word, there was no change in Beijing's position on the exchange of correspondents.

Arriving in Beijing in late June 1960, Snow was given greater access than other mainstream American reporters who went before him but not as pampered as Strong. He was greeted at the airport by a small group of his old friends—Rewi Alley, Israel Epstein, and George Hatem, all working in Beijing as senior foreign experts and Ji Chaoding, Tang Mingzhao, and Huang Hua, all senior government officials now. He was left in a small suite in Xinqiao, a new hotel specially built to house foreign visitors. Unlike all other influencers visiting the PRC, Snow had to pay for his room and meals at the hotel. The room cost him 24 Chinese yuan a day, equivalent to about $10 at the time.[89] Having heard that Snow could afford only sixteen-cent meals provided for hotel staff, Zhou Enlai called a special meeting on August 2 discussing the reception for Snow. Zhou instructed that Snow be paid 5,000 to 10,000 yuan for the film and photo negatives that he had taken during his visit to Yanan in the 1930s. Huang Hua and Gong Peng were ordered to discuss the matter with Snow, leaving the specific amount to be determined by him. Zhou also instructed that Snow be allowed to systematically take photos and make a film.[90] Having contemplated selling the first movie footage ever taken of Mao, Zhou, and others to finance a trip to the PRC in the 1950s, Snow accepted payment from the Chinese for the films and photo negatives. However, he returned 8,000 yuan to the Revolutionary Museum in Beijing through Rewi Alley before he departed the PRC from Kunming, Yunnan Province, at the end of his visit.[91]

In order to show his hospitality and shape Snow's experience in China, Zhou had several meetings and meals with Snow during his visit. At the beginning of his first interview with Snow on August 30, 1960, Zhou reminded him that he was in China as a writer or historian, not as a "correspondent." Zhou's explanation was that no American "correspondents" could be admitted into China because the issue had "become a question integrally related to negotiations over the major problems created by an American policy which had established a protectorate over Taiwan." Until Washington was ready to recognize the fact that Taiwan belonged to China, Zhou declared, "American correspondents could not be welcomed by China."[92] Zhou's statement clearly demonstrated that by this time Beijing had shifted its basis for the rejection of American correspondents from the lack of reciprocity to Taiwan and other related issues. When they met again on October 18, Zhou reiterated the two major conditions for the improvement of Sino-American relations. One was that the United States and PRC should agree to settle all the problems between the two sides through peaceful negotiations rather than resorting to the use or threat of force. The other was that the United States should withdraw all its armed forces from Taiwan and the Taiwan Strait.[93] These two points, as Huang Hua pointed out, not only constituted the core of Beijing's policy toward the United States throughout the 1960s but also provided the framework for the normalization of Sino-American relations in the 1970s.[94]

The highlight of Snow's visit to the PRC was his meetings with Mao in Beijing. After their brief chat at the top of Tiananmen on October 1, Mao had a long meeting and dinner with Snow on October 22. Having read the transcript of Snow's conversation with Zhou, Mao praised him for his suggestion that Beijing's propaganda be more considerate about the feelings of the American middle class and petty bourgeoisie who did not always agree with U.S. government policy. As a remedy, Mao believed that a special research institute or a group should be established to study the United States.[95] Like Zhou, Mao blamed the United States for the Taiwan problem and emphasized that he was prepared to struggle with Washington over Taiwan for two more decades. When Snow asked how many years it would take China to catch up with the United States in terms of personal income, Mao showed much restraint by replying that he was not quite sure whether half a century would be enough.[96] Mao's new estimate was much longer than the seven, ten, or fifteen years he had boldly predicted just a couple of years earlier.[97] Although Snow did not ask Mao the cause for the inconsistency, he did complain that he was not allowed to visit any PLA units. Mao responded by issuing an order on the spot giving him the permission to visit some military units and take pictures as he wanted. After visiting the Engineering College of Armored Forces and the 196th Infantry Division, Snow went back to see Mao for another time on October 27. Mao answered more questions and allowed Snow to make a five-minute film of their meeting.[98] It was with such special treatment that Snow was able to bring back home not only about half a million words of notes, interviews, and diary entries, but also four thousand feet of movie film and fifty-odd rolls of Kodachrome film when he completed his trip in mid-November.[99]

After his visit, Snow tried to disseminate what he had seen and heard in the PRC through various mainstream venues in the United States. His "Report from Red China" appeared in *Look* magazine on January 31, 1961, providing a detailed account of his long interviews with Zhou Enlai. Only half of a page was devoted to his conversation with Mao because the Communist leader wished to keep the talk off the record. Snow not only faithfully presented the Chinese Communist leaders' ideas about peace but also related their attacks on U.S. foreign policy, including Truman's failure to heed Beijing's warning at the beginning of the Korean War and the American military occupation of Taiwan.[100] Although *Look* editors agreed that much of what Mao and Zhou said could be labeled "Red Chinese Propaganda," they printed the interviews anyway because they believed that "it is vitally important for the American people and its government to know as much as possible about these men and their attitudes."[101] In order to make up the lack of critical analysis in Snow's report, *Look* also published a short comment written by A. Doak Barnett, a leading Chinese specialist, in the same issue. Barnett pointed out that Beijing's peaceful coexistence was only one option, which did not exclude armed revolution. He also defended Washington's presence in and policy toward Taiwan.[102] However, the editors decided not to publish Snow's two other reports on China because they were "too skeptical about many of the facts and figures, and too concerned about the obvious slant."[103]

Snow managed to present a more comprehensive observation of the PRC in his book *The Other Side of the River: Red China Today*, which was published by Random House in 1962. With eighty chapters and eight hundred–plus pages, Snow attempted to address a wide range of questions that the Americans had at the time. Approaching the subject from a "long perspective," Snow fully recognized the progress made by the PRC and justified the centralized control while offering some minor criticism on the lack of transparency, honesty, freedom, and the development of personal cult.[104] Although angry with the criticism from and rejection by the *Look* editors, Snow did try to get more data from his friends in the PRC for his book. In a letter to Israel Epstein, Snow begged for more facts, even a single national figure on crop output, steel, industry growth, so that he could include them in his book before it went to the printer.[105] Unfortunately, no facts or figures came from Epstein because Beijing had imposed tight control over the information desired by Snow.

Driven by his belief in the significance of the message from the CCP leaders, Snow had a brief reunion with his family in Switzerland, then flew to New York City for a meeting with Dean Rusk, who had just been nominated by President-elect John F. Kennedy as secretary of state. Coming in late, Rusk ate through the meeting and ended the conversation right after his breakfast. Despite Rusk's lack of attention to the message carried by Snow, the State Department took advantage of his recent visit to the PRC to put more pressure on Beijing. It instructed Beam to tell Wang Bingnan that the most productive first steps to improve the bilateral relations were for Beijing to release the Americans imprisoned in China and admit American newsmen. Since Snow was allowed to enter China with the validated passport, he told Wang that the U.S. government would be pleased to see Beijing admit any or all of the remaining newsmen who were eligible to receive the same validation for their passports in the same fashion. Beam also invited Wang to provide a list of Chinese correspondents who desired entry into the United States and assured him that the State Department would take under immediate consideration the issuance of visas to those individuals once they applied. Wang was let know that an arrangement could be worked out so that the number of Chinese correspondents admitted to the United States would be equal to the number of American newsmen admitted to Communist China.[106] However, the State Department's new effort was ignored since Beijing was determined not to make any deals with Washington on trade or cultural exchange before the Taiwan issue was resolved.[107]

Generally happy with Snow's writings about the PRC after his 1960 visit, Zhou granted him another interview while visiting Africa in December 1963 and quickly approved his request for another visit in 1964. Snow managed to get his trip to PRC authorized by the State Department after a special visit to Washington, DC. However, he was unable to get approval for his wife since the general travel ban on the PRC remained unchanged.[108] Snow arrived in Beijing in late October 1964, right after the PRC successfully tested its first atomic bomb. At their first meeting on October 31, Zhou gave Snow a dozen photos of the nuclear test and told him to publish them after his return to Switzerland.[109] It is obvious that Zhou wanted to show off the PRC's newly gained nuclear power to the Western world through Snow. When they met again on December 16, Zhou repeated the two preconditions for any improvement in Sino-American relations.[110]

Before Snow's departure, Mao had a conversation with him dealing with nuclear war, Sino-American relations, a UN seat for the PRC, and China's domestic issues. Mao took the opportunity to clarify and even modify what he had said about atomic bombs and nuclear war before. He came to recognize that atomic bombs did kill people and that he would prefer to fight a traditional war rather than a nuclear one. Mao impressed Snow most with a statement that PLA troops would not intervene in the Vietnam War.[111]

Snow was able to spread the messages from Mao and Zhou in several European countries after he left China in February 1965. However, his effort to do the same in the United States did not go as well as he had hoped. All major American newspapers and magazines refused to publish his interviews with the Communist leaders under his term. When the *Washington Post* did publish the interviews, it cut much of the content and rewrote what did appear in the newspaper, making Snow furious over the so-called misrepresentation. His plan to publish his most recent interviews with Mao and Zhou in a small book by the end of 1965 with Macmillan did not work out because the company wanted to have a long authoritative account of the Chinese Communist revolution.[112] What he did accomplish was a documentary film, *One Fourth of Humanity: The China Story*, at the end of 1967. The *New York Times* review was at most mixed, with strong criticism of its lack of hard probing, making him Mao's friendly visitor rather than an inquiring reporter.[113]

Snow failed to meet the Macmillan editor's demand partly because of the tighter control imposed by the Communist government during his visit to the PRC in 1964 and partly because of the chaos caused by the GPCR soon after that. In order to better cope with the increasingly large number of foreign journalists visiting the PRC, the Information Division of the MFA held a weeklong meeting on the reception and the management of foreign reporters in July 1964.[114] Deputy directors of provincial-level MFA offices and their section chiefs in charge of foreign reporters were required to attend. The meeting focused on the model units' sharing experiences on how to improve the reception and management of foreign reporters. In his keynote speech, Qin Jialin, deputy director of the Information Division, emphasized that in order to do a better job in receiving and managing foreign reporters a grassroots unit should have a strong reception group, a well-established reception standard and protocol, a set of briefing materials on various subjects, a number of carefully selected model subunits, trusted individuals, families of well-behaved commune members and workers ready to be visited by foreign reporters, and experience in successfully receiving foreign reporters and propagating government policies.[115] Ironically, although Snow was officially invited as a writer, he was still listed in one of the meeting documents as the only American reporter approved for a visit later in the year.[116] When Snow arrived in China in late October, all the measures on tighter control over foreign reporters had been implemented by provinces and cities. As a result, Snow was allowed to visit fewer places and given similar briefings no matter where he went. When the GPCR began and turned China upside down, Snow lamented that while there was so much going on in the PRC there was too little reliable information. He had no choice but gave up his book project.[117] Thus, Beijing's tighter control over the reception of foreign visitors became a double-edged sword. While increasing the CCP's power in shaping American visitors' experience in the PRC, it inadvertently reduced their ability and effectiveness as influencers in the United States.

Employing the Experts

As relations between Beijing and Moscow deteriorated and all Russian experts, including college teachers, were withdrawn from China in July 1960, the PRC hired more English-language experts and teachers to help it restore English education in China, expand trade with Western countries, and compete with the Soviet Union in English-speaking nations in Africa and Asia. Although English used to be the predominant foreign language taught in almost all Chinese schools and colleges before 1949, English education was almost banned after the establishment of the PRC as it leaned to the Russian side. Beijing began to intensify its propaganda in English and rebuild English education programs in the country in the late 1950s and early 1960s. In March 1962, Zhou Enlai approved a report from the Beijing Foreign Language Institute proposing to strengthen the teaching of five foreign languages, with special emphasis on English.[118] Following Zhou's instruction, in July 1962 the Ministry of Education (MOE) mandated that foreign languages, mostly English, be taught at senior grades at elementary schools. In another order issued the next year, the MOE required all colleges and schools to intensify their effort at training English teachers, discovering talents in the English language, and gradually increasing the number of English classes.[119] Because of Beijing's increasing needs for experts with English as their native tongue to help it train those teachers and work in its international propaganda apparatus, the PRC government not only recruited teachers and experts from Great Britain but also hired quite a number of Americans, mostly from outside the United States.

The first American experts hired by Beijing in the 1960s were from a group of former Korean War POWs who had chosen to stay in the PRC and graduated from Chinese universities. Having accepted the propaganda from their captors that the PRC was a society where "there is no contradiction between what is preached and what is practiced, a society there is freedom for our ideas," twenty-one young Americans, instead of returning to the United States, entered mainland China in February 1954.[120] After receiving political education in Taiyuan, Shanxi Province, for about eight months, they were tested on what they had learned and on their aptitude for further education. One of them died of disease, while eleven low scorers were either sent to a farm in Henan Province or assigned to work in a papermaking factory in Jinan, Shandong Province. The rest were enrolled in a two-year program at Renmin University in Beijing to study Chinese language, history, and politics. After completing their program, this first group of Americans attending a university in the PRC received new assignments depending on their performance. Those who had done well in the two-year program were allowed to continue their education at elite colleges in Beijing and Wuhan. Those who did not do as well in their studies were sent to do manual labor, with two in the papermaking factory in Jinan and two in an auto repair factory in Wuhan. Like all other Chinese students, the Americans who went to college had to take courses on Marxism, Leninism, and Maoism in addition to the regular courses in their fields, mostly Chinese language and literature.[121] Finally, five of those who continued their college graduation managed to graduate. With two leaving China after graduation, the rest—Clarence Adams, William White, and Morris Wills—were hired by the Foreign Language Press in Beijing as translators and editors in 1961 or 1962.[122]

They arrived at the Foreign Language Press in time to fill some of the vacancies left by older experts who had to leave the PRC because they had been sent by Communist parties that sided with Moscow after the Sino-Soviet split. Like all other experts, each of them signed a two-year contract that could be renewed if things worked out all right for both sides. Adams entered the children's book section in 1961, translating and editing books for children and working-class readers. He enjoyed his work because those small books, while they always contained a Communist message, "helped the peasants and workers learn to read."[123] Wills was assigned to the magazine sections working on *China Pictorial* (*Zhongguo Huabao*). He did not like some of the Chinese content and its ridiculous English translation. He complained that he had to translate "Lei Feng's Diary" three times because the press kept changing the content of the "Diary" to make it more glorious each time. At the end, Lei Feng, according to Wills, was turned into "an absolute believer in Mao" who studied Mao's works every day and taught others Mao's writings. By including the new nationwide Learning from Lei Feng Movement in its English publications, Beijing wanted to make him an example to be followed not only by the Chinese but also by people in other countries. However, Wills did not believe that such a "hero" ever existed and observed that the campaign failed sooner than expected.[124]

Besides their regular translation and polishing responsibilities, the American experts at the Foreign Language Press also participated in political activities like their Chinese coworkers. As Wills reported, CCP leadership often staged big demonstrations when a crisis occurred in the world to publicize Chinese feelings, or more accurately the feelings of Mao and the top Chinese leaders. The government organized all demonstrations, instructing work units to send a certain number of their people to participate. One of the major demonstrations that Wills took part in was during the Cuban Missile Crisis. He recalled that great demonstrations went for more than a week nonstop and observed that the protests were outwardly directed against the United States, but in reality they were aimed at the Russians who had backed down in the confrontation with the Americans.[125] Adams did something extraordinary beyond his regular participation in political activities at his workplace in 1965. Having read the news about the U.S. escalation of the war in Vietnam, he wanted to let African American soldiers know what other young Black Americans, including himself, had experienced in Korea a little over a decade earlier. He went to the Vietnam National Liberation Front Office in Beijing in August and offered to make a tape about his experience in Korea. The tape was soon aired through Radio Hanoi and broadcast to the American soldiers on the frontlines over loudspeakers. After telling his listeners how his all-Black regiment was sacrificed to save white units, he asked the Black soldiers "what kind of freedom do you have at home, sitting in the back of the bus, being barred from restaurants, stores, and certain neighborhoods, and being denied the right to vote?" He ended his broadcast by urging them to "go home and fight for equality in America."[126] Partly because of the PRC government's tighter control over foreigners in China and partly because of improving conditions for African Americans in the United States, Wills and White returned to their homeland with their families in 1965. Adams did the same right before the GPCR got officially started in 1966.

Although the employment of the former Korean War POWs was helpful, it was not nearly enough to meet the PRC's needs for English-language experts, especially at colleges. Having failed to lure Robert Friend, an American instructor who had taught English in Mexico and Guinea, to take a teaching position at a Chinese college after giving him a tour of a few cities in 1963, the PRC government was able to hire several American instructors, including Vicki Garvin and David and Nancy Dall Milton, in 1964.[127] The Miltons were assigned to teach English at Beijing Foreign Language Institute. Unlike their countrymen who were in China before the Communists took power, Nancy Milton pointed out that Americans, including herself and her husband, who went to the PRC in the 1950s and 1960s were there "as learners more than teachers." They wanted to "witness and study the accomplishment of the revolution, hoping to learn a few lessons which could be applied at home."[128] Garvin took a similar position at the Shanghai Foreign Language Institute (SFLI). She got the position mostly because of her experience as a tutor for Chinese staff members at the PRC embassy in Accra and an English instructor at the Institute of Foreign Languages in Ghana in 1963. Garvin received assistance for her application from her new Chinese friends, including Huang Hua, the PRC ambassador to Ghana. She was a good match for the position at SFLI not only because she was a native speaker with a master's degree and teaching experience, but also because she was a radical African American union organizer with a working-class background and had been persecuted during the McCarthy era.[129]

By joining the faculty at SFLI in fall 1964, Garvin became the first African American to have the opportunity to teach at a Chinese college and one of the few Americans who were offered teaching positions in the PRC in the 1950s and 1960s. Working in a completely different environment all by herself, she followed a path sharply different from her predecessors in similar positions before 1949. Unlike hundreds if not thousands of American missionaries and educators who had established missionary schools as well as colleges, transformed the Chinese educational system, and transplanted American curriculum, ideals, and values in China before the Communists took power, Garvin made conscientious efforts to thoroughly integrate herself into life at SFLI and methodically implement the educational principles established by Mao Zedong. She did all this not only because of necessity, since she was paid by the Communist government, but also because she and her hosts shared views on the superiority of the socialist system in China, the decadent nature of capitalist America, and the termination of the capitalist system in the United States as the only solution to racial discrimination and oppression.

Having lived and worked in Nigeria and Ghana for several years, Garvin was quick to adapt to the new political environment in the PRC. Her past experiences and her radical political stance landed her the honor to speak as the representative for all new foreign instructors at the SFLI's opening ceremony for the 1964–1965 academic year in September. Reflecting her conscientious adaptation, she changed the opening of her speech by first addressing the secretary of the Communist Party instead of the president of the institute as she had originally drafted. This simple change clearly revealed that only days after her arrival in China, Garvin had already learned that the party secretary was ranked higher and had greater power than the president at a Chinese college. Having expressed appreciation for the cordial reception, courtesy, and cooperation extended to the new foreign instructors, Garvin, on behalf of the newcomers, pledged their "maximum efforts and energy" to the implementation of their assignments "in the Chinese educational programme which has been developed by Chairman Mao." She also let her audience know that she expected her experience at the Institute "will be two-sided: receiving as well as giving, learning as well as teaching." While looking forward to a "mutually beneficial stay" in China, Garvin demonstrated what she could do as a Black instructor in class by devoting 85 percent of her first speech to the African American fight for voting rights in the United States. She informed her audience that a "significant section of the youth, black Americans in particular, are actively participating in and leading a major national militant and direct-action struggle for the democratic rights of the Negro minority."[130]

Garvin's strong pledge and obvious expertise in race and other issues in the United States attracted the attention of the SFLI leadership. She was assigned to teach the highest-level students, a teachers' training class in

1964–1965 and a senior class in 1965–1966, although she herself believed that she was not well prepared for the teaching position because of her lack of pedagogical training in English instruction.[131] Weeks later, the English Department chair asked her to include in her teaching schedules a series of lectures on various aspects of life in the United States. She was happy to receive such a request because this gave her, in her own words, "an opportunity to discharge what I consider my responsibility:" facilitating "communication among peoples."[132] As the SFLI leadership had expected, Garvin chose to focus her lectures on African American history, a subject that had never been covered at Chinese schools and colleges before. Her first lecture, "The Negro Liberation Movement and the 1964 Election," was delivered in early November 1964, days before the general election took place in the United States. Two more lectures, "The Other Side of the United States: Increasing Poverty Amidst Plenty" and "The Negro Liberation Movement," were delivered in January 1965. After that, she delved into various specific topics on African American history in half a dozen or so additional lectures.[133] By covering such a wide range of topics, Garvin was able to provide her students a comprehensive and an in-depth historical overview of the African American sufferings as well as their struggle for freedom and equality.

Focusing mostly on the African American struggle for equal rights and the "dark side" of the United States, Garvin's lectures shared some common themes. The first was singing high praises for Mao Zedong and the socialist system in China. In her first lectures she credited "the example of China, the guidance of Chairman Mao and the correct policy consistently pursued by the Communist Party of China" for the "victorious struggles against colonialism and neo-colonialism" waged by the liberation movements and peoples in other countries. She also thanked the Chinese Communist leaders for "singling out U.S. imperialism as the main enemy of the world, and in relentlessly exposing its true aims and character," making it possible that "today a truly broad united front is in motion against the common enemy."[134]

The second theme was informing Chinese students of the miserable lives led by the African Americans and their strenuous struggle for equal rights. In addition to her speech at the opening ceremony, Garvin devoted two of her first lectures on the African American liberation movement. She told her students that African Americans, about one-tenth of the American population, were "super-exploited & segregated," and "still living a semi-colonial life, fighting for those rights of citizenship which were incorporated in the Constitution years ago." She characterized the Civil Rights Act of 1964 as a "pathetic compromise of the Negros' original demands, limited in scope & coverage, & relying for the most part on good will & pursuance for enforcement."[135] Garvin also asserted that African Americans "out of historical circumstances have been cast into the role of natural revolutionaries" and that they were tightening another noose "around the U.S. imperialism inside its own fortress."[136]

The third theme was exposing the hypocritical and vicious nature of the United States as the leading capitalist power. She told her students that the Republican and Democratic parties, as instruments of the bourgeoisie, "are identical in basic outlook and are as one on strategy, i.e. the preservation of capitalism." Their only points of difference, she pointed out, "lie in tactics." Thus, neither the Democratic nor the Republican parties, she insisted, "have any intention of solving the Negro problem, administrating justice to the American working class."[137] Based on Michael Harrington's new book *The Other America: The Poverty of the United States*, Garvin revealed that agricultural workers in the United States were truly the "have-nots" who worked and lived "under inhuman conditions, unorganized and without a voice to champion their needs." The unskilled, the uneducated, and the minorities, she asserted, were the "rejects" of the U.S. economy, who never had any prospect of realizing their "American Dream."[138]

The last was showing her support for the use of violence in fighting for civil rights and overthrowing the capitalist system in the United States. In her lecture on African American liberation movement, Garvin asserted that so-called mainstream African American organizations, including the National Association for the Advancement of Colored People (NAACP) and the Urban League, were "moulded to delude the Negro masses and divert and dilute their struggle." She even criticized Martin Luther King Jr. for insisting that African Americans must "suffer in order to defeat violence by peaceful manner." To Garvin, the right direction of the African American liberation movement was represented by Robert Williams, who advocated and practiced armed self-defense in the 1950s and 1960s.[139] She actually went one step further than Williams by agreeing with Mao that "the Negro freedom movement is, in the last analysis, a class struggle."[140] Thus, she believed that "the concrete tactics of Negro violent revolution, which will inevitably be part of the whole of the U.S. proletarian revolution, will have to be developed and rounded out in practical struggles."[141]

Like all other teachers in China, Garvin adapted her teaching "to the Party's instructions that students must strive to become ideologically sound and professionally competent, placing politics in the forefront, to develop into worthy successors to the revolution, and to master language as a weapon in the class struggle, nationally and internationally."[142] In order to achieve those goals, Garvin adopted a heuristic method in her classroom instruction from the very beginning. Her choice actually fit well with Beijing's recent effort to promote the same teaching method nationwide.[143] However, Garvin soon realized that her students, especially those in teachers' training class, had trouble in adapting to such an active learning mode. Blaming this weakness on the "previous deficiencies on teaching methods, especially that of learning by rote," she tried to address the problem by asking students to make "an intensive, critical study of data from a variety of sources (books, magazines, newspapers) on the Negro question, to encourage initiative, independence and creativity." One concrete step taken by her was to have all the students develop an outline on "The Role of Fascist Racist Organizations in Suppressing Negroes" to improve their critical thinking and writing abilities.[144] Another was to ask the whole class to work together in preparing a comprehensive survey on "The History of the Negro in the U.S." Each student got a special topic and conducted research on it for a term paper. Then, all the papers were put together to form a cohesive text after classwide discussion and revision. The text was first delivered as a lecture to all fourth-year students as well as Chinese educators attending a conference at SFLI in May 1965 and then kept as a textbook to be used by subsequent classes.[145]

In addition to fulfilling her teaching obligations at SFLI, Garvin gave numerous speeches at many SFLI as well as citywide meetings and rallies. Her participation was needed because it was important and glorifying for the Communist regime to have an African American woman on the stage to show her admiration for the great leader Chairman Mao and expose the vicious nature of imperialist America on behalf of the American people. Her most important speech was delivered at the million-man rally held at the People's Square, Shanghai, to support Mao's statement issued after the assassination of Martin Luther King on April 18, 1968. On behalf of "the revolutionary black people of the United States and their likeminded white allies," Garvin expressed "deep love and respect for, and sincere appreciation to Chairman Mao, the world's revolutionary leader, for his recent statement of encouragement and firm support of the

Afro-American struggle against violent suppression." She completely agreed with Mao that the racial question was in essence a class question and that the unity of the people in the world was not one of race but one of comrades and friends. She reported that "the slogan, 'Black Power,' has already become a battle cry and the truth that 'political power grows out of the barrel of a gun' is being grasped by an ever-increasing number of revolutionaries who recognize that the entire existing social system of monopoly capitalism and imperialism in the U.S. must be changed if full and genuine liberation is to be won."[146] This speech was so important to Garvin that she listed it in her résumé years later as one of her two major achievements in China.[147] She even wrote a short article on the experience for *New China*, a journal published by the U.S.-China People's Friendship Association (USCPFA).[148]

Garvin's teaching assignment at SFLI came to an end when it was forced to suspend all regular classroom instruction to allow students and the faculty to devote all their time and energy to the GPCR. When all other foreign instructors at the SFLI went back to their homeland, Garvin was asked to stay. She was assigned to teach English classes to workers at the Peace Hotel where she had been staying since her arrival in the city and to some technicians who were to be sent to work in African countries.[149] Benefiting again from her working-class background, she was able to actively participate in the Cultural Revolution at the SFLI. Unlike most Chinese faculty members, who were attacked by the Red Guards, she was asked by the students to accompany them to Beijing and joined rallies held at Tiananmen Square, where Mao received students and showed his support for their rebellion. Through her close ties with the Red Guards, she was invited to give a speech at the rally to celebrate the merger of various student organizations in 1967. Later she was transferred to Beijing to work as a polisher for the *Peking Review*, an English magazine published by the Foreign Language Press. Many years later, she thanked Huang Hua for her transfer to Beijing, which not only extended her stay in China but also helped her reunite with her new husband, Leibel Bergman.[150]

Garvin's work at the SFLI as well as the *Peking Review* and her active participation in various political movements on the "right" side won her high praises and appreciation. When she decided to return to the United States, like most other foreign friends and experts in China in the height of the GPCR, the Foreign Language Publication Administration approved her request for a brief visit to Xian, Taiyuan, and Dazhai in July 1970.

According to the administration's report to the State Council, Garvin fought against imperialism and revisionism resolutely, had correct understanding of the reactionary nature of imperialism, supported the Vietnamese fight against the United States, actively studied Marxism, Leninism, and Mao Zedong Thought, loved Chairman Mao, regarded her meetings with Mao as the happiest moments in her life, had a friendly attitude toward the PRC, and appreciated the Cultural Revolution. That was an extremely high evaluation for a foreign expert in China. Thus, she was approved for a special ten-day tour, with transportation and lodging paid by the *Peking Review*.[151] Garvin impressed her local hosts with many specific questions about the Chinese revolution, such as how they fought in the enemy-controlled territories, unite the people, and win support from the bourgeoisie and landlords in the war against Japan. In the end, she vowed to utilize the Chinese experiences in the revolutionary struggle in the United States. However, when her host emphasized that the success of the Chinese revolution depended on seizing power through armed struggle, she insisted that the top priority was to establish a united front because it was still impractical to ask American workers to pick up weapons and start armed struggle now.[152]

Like many other American experts and influencers, Garvin devoted much of her time and energy to giving public lectures on the PRC after her return to the United States. While working full-time educational jobs in the New York City area, Garvin actively involved herself in the USCPFA and made a special effort to focus the association's activities on workers and minorities to "expand their horizon."[153] Based mostly on the information that she had gathered from the Chinese government, state media, and conversations with students, collogues, and officials, her lectures on China were well organized, covering a wide range of topics, and were filled with high praise for the PRC. She even went back to China in 1974 to update her information on the GPCR. However, she finally stopped giving lectures on China after her 1978 trip partly because the Chinese themselves began to denounce the disastrous GPCR and partly because she finally got some less distorted information about life in the PRC. It was during that trip that she found out that the information received from her students and colleagues during her extended stay as well as her previous visit to the PRC was anything but accurate because they dared not tell her what they had suffered or how much they had lost of their foreign-language skills during the GPCR.[154] Her experience clearly showed how effective the PRC government was, with its unprecedentedly complete control over the Chinese society, in preventing foreigners, especially Americans, from knowing the real lives led by ordinary Chinese people. By hosting Vicki Garvin and other American comrades, influencers, and experts in the 1950s and 1960s, Beijing managed to establish and maintain a new type of cultural ties with selected groups of individual Americans aimed at projecting a positive image of the PRC and attacking the U.S. government and its policies.

CHAPTER 7

Forging the Black Blade

The establishment of new Sino-American state-to-people interactions in the 1950s and 1960s culminated in the formation of an alliance between Beijing and several radical African American leaders. Having hosted W. E. B. Du Bois and his wife, Shirley Graham Du Bois, in 1959 and 1962, Beijing invited Robert Williams and Mabel Williams to visit the PRC in 1963 as well as 1964 and granted them and their two sons an extended stay in 1966. Top Chinese Communist leaders demonstrated their affection and support for the African American visitors by having many well-publicized meetings with them, putting them atop the Tiananmen for the National Day celebration; giving them opportunities to deliver speeches at universities and mass rallies; having their books, articles, and poems published in China; and sending their newsletters, documentary films, and other propaganda materials back to the United States for dissemination. More important, Mao issued two public statements to support the African American struggle in 1963 and 1968 respectively, making him the most outspoken national leader of the African American struggle. Inspired by Mao's powerful statements and impressed by the PRC's achievements, Williams agreed with Mao that the African American struggle was an integral part of the world revolution and recognized Mao as the leader of oppressed people everywhere, including African Americans. His constant denunciation of the decadent, hypocritical nature of the American capitalist system and strong belief in and staunch support for the Chinese revolution made him a powerful ally in the world revolution led by Mao in the 1960s.

The building of the alliance with radical African American leaders was part of Beijing's effort to establish itself as the new leader for the world revolution and weaken the U.S. government from within in the late 1950s and early 1960s. The Communist government was happy to hear the powerful calls Du Bois issued to African countries during his visit in 1959 urging them to turn to China and learn from the Chinese. However, his refusal to apply Mao's revolutionary theory in the United States forced CCP leaders to look for a better match. Robert Williams caught their attention because of his unique experience as a leading advocate and practitioner of armed self-defense and his repeated appeal for support for the American civil rights movement. By issuing a strong supporting statement under Williams's request, Mao not only won an admirer and ally but also redefined the nature of the American civil rights movement and reset the ultimate goal for it. It was through his close interactions with the Chinese Communists that Williams morphed into an ardent advocate of armed Black revolution as well as a fervent disseminator of Mao Zedong Thought. Inspired by Mao and Williams, several African American organizations were established to carry out armed struggle in the United States, making guerrilla warfare an increasing concern for some American policymakers in the 1960s. While the PRC's interaction with Robert Williams and other African American activists was clearly aimed at exporting Chinese-style revolution to the United States, its effort, unlike that in some Asian and African countries with generous military, economic, financial support, focused mostly on providing theoretical guidance and tactical advice, keeping it in the realm of broadly defined cultural interaction.

Making the Initial Push

Not long after the Ministry of Foreign Affairs (MFA) issued its invitation to a large number of American journalists in August 1956, Guo Moruo (Kuo Mu-Jo), director of the Chinese Academy of Science (CAS), sent letters to many American scholars, scientists, and officials soliciting their attendance at the celebration of the 250th birthday of Benjamin Franklin in Beijing scheduled for December the same year.[1] In addition to the conference, the invitees were asked to stay in China for a month to deliver lectures and tour the country. All traveling expenses, Guo made it clear, would be covered by the Chinese organizers.[2] W. E. B. Du Bois, the best-known African American scholar, leader, and activist, was among the invitees.[3] This was not the first time the PRC government had communicated with Du Bois or invited him for a visit. Guo had sent Du Bois telegrams in 1951 and 1952 to celebrate his birthday and recognize his "contribution to science and literature" as well as his "undaunted spirit in the struggle for peace and human progress."[4] Du Bois earned Beijing's recognition because of his strong opposition to American involvement in the Korean War and his open support of Beijing's accusation that the United States had used biological weapons in Korea and China. When Beijing was putting together the Peace Conference of the Asian and Pacific Regions in Beijing in 1952, Liu Ningyi, secretary general of the Preparatory Committee, sought not only his attendance but also his help in organizing a "broad American delegation" and "informing regularly progress of preparation work."[5] Unable to attend the 1952 Peace Conference because the Department of State refused to issue him a passport, Du Bois continued to participate in the activities organized by the China Welfare Appeal Inc., providing various assistance to the PRC during the Korean War. Although happy to be invited by Beijing again in 1956, he still could not get a passport and had to turn down the Chinese invitation one more time. In his letter to Guo, Du Bois shared his unfortunate situation and made it clear that "there is no place in the world which I am so anxious to visit as China."[6]

Despite these setbacks, Beijing maintained communication with Du Bois and kept alive the effort to bring the Black leader to the PRC. As he had promised in his letters to Chinese leaders, Du Bios continued to fight for his right for international travel. On February 22, 1957, his eighty-ninth birthday, he wrote a letter to John Foster Dulles appealing his case directly. He told Dulles that he had been refused the right to travel internationally three times since 1952 with no specific charges and that it was unjust and illegal for the U.S. government to do so. He asked for permission to visit Ghana to participate in the celebration of its independence.[7] Later that year, William Peterson, a close friend of Du Bois and a member of the Communist Party of the United States of America (CPUSA), wrote to Chen Hansheng, a renowned scholar and an advisor of the MFA, proposing that the CAS grant Du Bois honorary membership to celebrate his ninetieth birthday. Peterson emphasized that no scientific institutions in the United States would give Du Bois such an honor and that the leading African

American scholar was proscribed by his own government. Although the CAS did include the Division of Philosophy and Social Science, it had never designated any honorary fellows. After receiving advice from the MFA, the CAS sent a telegram to Du Bois, celebrating his birthday while keeping silent on the matter of the honorary fellowship.[8] In this way, Beijing was able to show its respect for the most prominent African American scholar and maintain contact with him without forcing the CAS to create an honorary membership.

Du Bois, like Anna Louise Strong and other American leftists, was finally able to resume his international travel after the Supreme Court issued its ruling on the case of *Kent v. Dulles* in mid-June 1958. Compelled by the Supreme Court ruling, the State Department issued new passports to Du Bois and his wife on June 30.[9] Wasting no time, the couple started to plan their trip to Europe. Having set Great Britain as their first destination, Du Bois wrote letters to Guo Moruo and Song Qingling separately on July 6, inquiring after an opportunity to visit China. Du Bios thanked Guo for his birthday greetings and let him know that they would be delighted to go to China even though they might not have the resources to make such a trip.[10] Du Bois was more explicit with Song and told her that they hoped to see China before returning to the United States and that "the expense may prevent" their trip to her country. He lamented that he was unable to accept Guo's generous invitation two years ago, with all expenses covered by the Chinese government.[11] Both Guo and Song gave positive responses to Du Bois and reissued their invitation to him for a visit to the PRC. Happy to hear the good news, Du Bois decided to go to China after visiting the Soviet Union, even though his passport was clearly marked with a notice that travel to China was prohibited and that he might be charged and imprisoned for "trading with the enemy."[12]

Du Bois was willing to take the risk partly because he wanted to have a close look at the country he had visited more than two decades earlier, partly because he desired to have his book *John Brown* published in the PRC.[13] Coming out originally in 1909, the biography of the best-known American abolitionist was largely ignored by white historians as well as so-called mainstream readers in the United States. The year 1959 was the centennial anniversary of John Brown's raid on the federal arsenal at Harpers Ferry, Virginia. Du Bois believed that what he had written fifty years earlier was still relevant and useful at the end of the 1950s, when both the civil rights struggle in the United States and the national independence movement in Africa were on the rise. Thus, he wanted to reintroduce his book to more people in the world by having it translated into Chinese and published in the most populous nation in 1959. He was encouraged by the Chinese treatment of his and Shirley Graham's writings in previous years. In 1950, a publisher in China had translated and published Shirley Graham's *Paul Robeson* under the Chinese title *Heiren Geshou Luoboxun* (The Black Singer Robeson). Right before Christmas 1955, Talitha Gerlach, a good friend of the Du Boises working for the Chinese Welfare Institute in Shanghai, told them that she had found Du Bois's autobiography *In Battle for Peace* still selling in her city and Beijing. She was wondering whether any of the Chinese translations had reached them.[14]

Arriving in Beijing on February 13, 1959, Shirley Graham and W. E. B. Du Bios were greeted by Ding Xilin, the deputy chairman of the Chinese People's Association for Cultural Relations with Foreign Nations (CPACRFN), Bao Erhan, the deputy chairman of the Committee of the Chinese People Defending World Peace (CCPDWP), and other Chinese officials.[15] While they waited for their luggage at the airport, a Chinese official asked whether they wanted to keep their visit secret. Both the hosts and the visitors were aware of Washington's strict travel ban on the PRC, and many Americans had gotten in and out of the Communist country without any publicity. James Jackson was in China about the same time, and his visit was kept in complete secrecy.[16] Du Bois, according to his wife, "scorned such behavior" and told the Chinese official without hesitation that they would like the whole world to know about their activities in China. As soon as Du Bois made his intention clear, a group of reporters was let in to take photos and interview the visitors.[17] A short report on their arrival appeared with a photo in *People's Daily* the next day. This publicity turned the visit of the Du Boises into another open challenge to the State Department's travel ban and its policy toward the PRC.[18]

Unlike his previous trip to China, which went without any government attention or intervention, this visit was fully sponsored and controlled by Beijing. During his weeklong stay in China in 1936, Du Bois visited the University of Shanghai and had a meeting with a few prominent Chinese businessmen and publishers in the city.[19] Both activities were arranged by Herman C. E. Liu, president of the University of Shanghai, a private college established by the American Baptist Missionary Union and the Southern Baptist Convention in the early 1900s. Chih Meng, associate director of the China Institute in America (CIIA), introduced Liu to Du Bois.[20]

When Du Bois toured Beijing, he paid seventy cents out of pocket to have four men carry him on their shoulders to the top of the Great Wall.[21] Du Bois's longer visit in 1959 was a completely different experience. Shortly after receiving the invitation from Guo Moruo, Du Bois got the necessary travel funds from the PRC chargé d'affaires in London.[22] The PRC government not only covered all the travel costs for the couple but also picked up the tab for all expenses once they landed in Beijing. Their Chinese hosts made sure that they were put in the best hotels wherever they went and traveled first class, accompanied by high-ranking officials and a designated interpreter. Du Bois was also assigned a nurse who stayed with him throughout his visit in China, providing personalized medical care. Although Du Bois was reluctant to be given such special treatment, he enjoyed the services paid for by the Communist government.[23]

As sponsor and facilitator, Beijing had its own goals to achieve with Du Bois's visit. In 1956 Du Bois was invited to take part in Beijing's effort to break the cultural isolation and intensify the confrontation between the American people and their government. After the Afro-Asian People's Solidarity Conference was held in Cairo in 1957, the second Taiwan Strait Crisis occurred in 1958, and the Cuban revolution succeeded at the beginning of 1959, Beijing expanded its expectations for interaction with the visiting African American activists. The Chinese Communist leaders now wanted to use the unparalleled reputation Du Bois enjoyed among Africans and African Americans to strengthen China's position among the newly independent nations in Africa and Asia, intensify its attack on the United States over Taiwan, and spread armed revolution to North America. It was to achieve all these goals that Beijing warmly received the Du Boises, publicized their activities in China, offered them various opportunities for public speeches, took them to carefully chosen sites around the nation, provided advice for the African American struggle for equal rights, and made the initial push for a Cuban-style armed revolution in the United States.

Fully aware that each day spent by the Du Boises in China was an embarrassment for Washington, Beijing did everything it could to publicize their activities in the country. Although many activities looked ceremonial in form, the PRC government used all of them to achieve its political and strategic goals. Four days after their arrival, the CPACRFN and the CCPDWP held a big banquet to formally welcome the Du Boises. In his welcome speech, Ding Xilin fully recognized the great contributions made by Du Bois to world peace, the fight against racial discrimination, and the progressive cause of human beings. Having expressed the highest respect of the Chinese people for Du Bois, Ding extended special thanks to their deep friendship while denouncing the American occupation of Taiwan. Ding also thanked Shirley Graham, who had removed the national flag of the Republic of China at the Pan-African People's Conference, held in Accra, Ghana, in December 1958. Her action, Ding asserted, smashed Washington's "two-China" conspiracy and provided great encouragement for the Chinese people. W. E. B. Du Bois told his Chinese hosts that two decades after his first short visit to China he came to understand how important the existence of the new PRC was to not only the Chinese people but also the whole world. After Lao She performed a short piece of Peking opera, Li Dequan, the minister of public health, sang "Socialism Is Good" and "Our Friends All Over the World." Affected by the electrifying atmosphere, the Du Boises joined with a song popular among peace activists, "Aren't Gonna Study War No More."[24]

Du Bois's ninety-first birthday gave Beijing the best opportunity to show its respect and appreciation for him. On February 22, Premier Zhou Enlai threw a birthday party for Du Bois. Chen Yi, the vice premier in charge of foreign affairs, attended, as did Guo Moruo, Ding Xilin, Tang Mingzhao, and Shen Jian, the director of American and Australian Affairs at the Ministry of Foreign Affairs. *People's Daily* carried a brief but impressive report on the front page accompanied with a picture the next day, showing Zhou shaking hands with Du Bois.[25] *People's Daily* also published a special essay written by Mao Dun, one of the most famous Chinese writers, and a long interview with the Du Boises the same day, praising the couple's contributions to the world peace movement and their support for the PRC during the Korean War.[26]

Beijing turned February 23, W. E. B. Du Bois's birthday, into "a national celebration."[27] The celebration began with a lecture delivered by Du Bois to more than a thousand students and faculty members at Peking University.[28] Having been told that the lecture would be broadcast to the world, he focused his talk on Africa. Du Bois advised Africans to turn away from the West, including the United States, and "face the rising sun," the new PRC. China, as he emphasized, had "arisen to her feet and leapt forward" after long centuries of hard struggle. He urged Africa to do the same: "arise, and stand straight, speak and think!" He warned Africa that "America bargains for your soul" and that African Americans could not lead Africa since most of them were still second-class citizens themselves, "liable to insult and discrimination at any time." Thus, he exhorted Africans to come to China to look around and asked the Chinese to "see what you can teach by pointing."[29] After his speech, students sang and danced to celebrate his birthday. Beijing liked what Du Bois said in the lecture so much that it translated the speech into Chinese and published it in *People's Daily* the next day.[30] The climax of the birthday celebration was a big official party held in the top-floor ballroom of the Peking Hotel. Attended by more than a hundred top government officials, including Chen Yi, and prominent scholars and artists, the party gave Beijing another opportunity to express its appreciation for Du Bois and attack the United States. As the official host, Guo Moruo praised Du Bois for fighting American imperialism, the number one enemy of peace-loving people in the world, in the past decades. Mao Zedong sent a message, and Zhou Enlai presented a bowl of longevity peaches as well as a birthday cake for the occasion.[31] A detailed report on the celebration appeared in *People's Daily* the next day with a photo.

While *People's Daily* carried frequent and detailed reports on their activities in China, the Du Boises, as expected by their hosts, shared their experiences and views with international readers. Not long after his birthday celebration, W. E. B. Du Bois published a short essay, "Our Visit to China," in *China Pictorial*. In the essay, he explained that he visited the PRC because although "our people have gained important victories in our fight for equality in the last two centuries," "their battle is not yet won." The cause of the "Negro Problem," he argued, was the rise of "colonial imperialism which sought to reduce most of the world's workers to serfs of Western Europe and North America." The "fatal threat" to this colonial imperialist system, he asserted, was socialism as practiced in the Soviet Union and China. However, most African Americans, he lamented, did not realize this fact. He blamed this lack of knowledge and understanding on the travel ban imposed by Washington and the "fantastic tales of the failure of Socialism and the impossibility of Communism" filling American periodicals and books. He declared that he and his wife came to China to learn the facts so that they would be able to tell African Americans "the truth about Communism."[32] Shirley Graham sent an article to the *Pittsburgh Courier* about the same time, telling her readers that the Chinese people "are happy and excited about what they are doing."[33]

While doing everything possible to befriend Du Bois and show its appreciation for his support for the PRC, Beijing attempted to push him to become a leader of an armed revolution in the United States. Mao himself made the initial effort at his meeting with Du Bois in Wuhan, Hubei Province, on March 13 (figure 7.1). Mao told Anna Louise Strong, who was also invited to the meeting, that Du Bois was a new friend and had the first right of talking and asking questions. Mao revealed that he had listened to the speech delivered by Du Bois at Peking University about a month ago and acknowledged that Du Bois spoke with authority based on the knowledge and experience accumulated through his lifelong struggle. When the conversation moved on to world events, Mao talked about how China shelled the Nationalist troops in Jinmen and forced the United States to stop at the brink of war. As a leader of the peace movement, Du Bois interrupted Mao and asked about the sufferings that the people in Taiwan and African Americans in the United States would have in a war. He did not hide his fear that the African Americans would be exterminated, since many of his Black friends had already been killed. Mao replied calmly that

Figure 7.1 Mao Zedong meeting with W. E. B. Du Bois, Shirley Graham Du Bois, and Anna Louise Strong in Wuhan, Hubei Province, on March 14, 1959.
Source: Schlesinger Library, Harvard Radcliffe Institute, Cambridge, Massachusetts.

he had lost six family members, including his son, who was killed in an American air raid during the Korean War. Having assured Du Bois that wars could not kill all the Communists, Mao praised the Cuban revolutionaries by pointing out that Cuba was a very small nation with only six million people, "one third as many as the Negro population in the United States." More important, the Cubans, Mao especially stressed, "did not worry about A-Bombs and H-Bombs even though the nation was in close proximity to the United States, right under it." By his making demographic and geographical connections, it is clear that Mao wanted to see African Americans learn from the Cubans and take similar actions in the United States.[34]

Having addressed the population imbalance between white and Black Americans, Mao took on the psychological hurdle that African Americans had to overcome before they could start an armed revolution. He shared with Du Bois that the Chinese people had feared and admired American imperialism in the past. He believed that these sentiments were diseases that affected not only landlords, the bourgeoisie, and Nationalists but also some working-class people, though to a lesser extent. Mao proudly announced that "in the past nine years we have been able to change this mentality." The same worship of power, he asserted, affected other people, including African Americans. However, Du Bois disagreed and insisted that working-class people in the United States were not affected by fear or admiration as much as by low income. The disagreement led the two into a discussion on whether the economic factor was more powerful than superstition. Mao used many concrete examples, including personal ones, to show the power of social custom and explained why working people often sided against their own interests. Unable to convince Du Bois, Mao had to reiterate his own belief that "one should not fear war or imperialists" and that he, already sixty-six at the time, still thought it possible that he might "live to see the end of imperialism."[35] Mao's meeting with Du Bois appeared on the front page of *People's Daily* the next day. Although two photos were published, the report itself was extremely brief, keeping silent on the content of the conversation among the parties.[36]

Mao's initial effort to nudge African Americans toward armed revolution marked a significant change of Beijing's handling of the so-called color problem in the United States. Although the PRC government had paid close attention to racial discrimination suffered by African Americans since its founding, it confined its action to the exposure of racial problems in

Chinese media. Its main purpose was to reveal the hypocritical nature of American democracy and make the Chinese people despise and hate the United States. Generally, it deferred to the Communist Party of the Soviet Union (CPSU) and CPUSA in providing guidance to African Americans in their struggle for equality and justice. On October 2, 1957, *People's Daily* reported that the CPUSA had issued a statement on the Little Rock incident, demanding that the Justice Department take every step to protect Blacks and make sure that they could fully enjoy all the rights of citizens.[37] Mao's encouragement for African Americans to accept his revolutionary ideology and start a Cuban-style armed rebellion in the United States indicated that Beijing had begun to abandon its decades-long deference and offer direct advice to Black activists. Such a dramatic change reflected Beijing's new needs to cope with its deteriorated relations with the United States as well as the Soviet Union. The shelling of Jinmen and Mazu, begun on August 23, 1958, led Washington to reinforce the Seventh Fleet, resupply the Nationalist forces stationed in those islands, provide more advanced weaponry, and strengthen the defense of Taiwan. Unable to gain an upper hand in the military confrontation in the Taiwan Strait, Mao turned to the African Americans and pushed them to start a revolution that would greatly weaken Washington's position.

An armed revolution in the United States would also help challenge the peaceful coexistence advocated by Moscow since the mid-1950s and establish China as a model and leader for the world revolution. Most Communist leaders in the world followed the Soviet Union and adopted a new position centered on peaceful coexistence, peaceful competition, and peaceful transition, for which reason Harry Pollitt, chairman of the British Communist Party, proposed removing the first two paragraphs of Mao's article "Issues on War and Strategy" in March 1954 before the English edition of the second volume of *The Selected Works of Mao Zedong* was published in Great Britain. The first paragraph clearly stated that the "central task and the supreme form of the revolution is to take over the government with arms and resolve all the problems through wars." First published in 1938, Mao's article asserted that this "Marxist and Leninist revolutionary principle is universally correct." Pollitt was concerned about Mao's writing because it seriously deviated from the program published by the British Communist Party in 1951, which had clearly stated that given the changed international situation, the method used by the Soviet Union to take over the national government was no longer applicable in Great

Britain. He also emphasized that keeping those two paragraphs would create tremendous difficulty for Communists in the United States. Under Mao's direct instruction, the CCP Department of Propaganda rejected Pollitt's proposal and reemphasized that what Mao stated in those two paragraphs was the Marxist universal truth and should not be removed. The department proposed that either only those volumes of Mao's selected works allowed in the United States be published there or that all the volumes be published there after removing the legally banned articles as well as speeches. It also demanded that Mao approve the table of contents before the U.S. edition was published.[38]

While deeply impressed by Mao and the progress achieved by the Chinese people under his leadership, Du Bois stuck with his own view on the role of violence in the worldwide liberation and revolution. In his speech delivered at Peking University, he emphasized that the "essence of the revolution in the Soviet Union and China and in all the 'iron curtain' nations, is not the violence that accompanied the change—no more than starvation at Valley Forge was the essence of the American Revolution against Britain." He insisted that "the real revolution is the acceptance on the part of the nation of the fact that hereafter the main object of the nation is the welfare of the mass of the people and not of a lucky few."[39] Thus, violence, to Du Bois, was just a by-product, not essential to the success of a revolution. Based on that belief, Du Bois kept silent on a Cuban-style revolution in the United States after his meeting with Mao. About a month after his trip to China, Du Bois published an article titled "The Vast Miracle of China Today" in the *National Guardian* as a report on his visit to the PRC. In his coverage of the four-hour long conversation with Mao, he only revealed Mao's reiteration that war was a "paper tiger" and that China did not fear it. To him, the Chinese success was made possible because Mao, Zhou, and a half dozen others "undertook to lead the nation by example," "by infinite patience," and by making a nation believe that the people "composed the real nation."[40] His explanation was anything but in line with Mao's model of the Chinese revolution, seizing power through armed revolution and laying siege to the cities from the countryside. Bill V. Mullen and Cathryn Watson were accurate when they pointed out that Du Bois's essay "is also significant for what it doesn't include." Du Bios not only ignored China's food shortage and political repression, which his hosts effectively kept from him, but also remained silent on Mao's call for an African American armed revolution.[41]

If the "breathless and sweeping travelogue of China's Communist successes" presented in his essay demonstrated Beijing's effectiveness in reshaping Du Bois's view, the absence of a positive response to Mao's call for an armed revolution in the United States reflected his commitment to nonviolence.[42] Although Du Bois regarded war as a necessary step toward progress when he was young and frustrated by the "paradox of eternal and world-wide war and the coming of the Prince of Peace," he still believed that the remedy would be "education for all children and education all together, so as to let them grow up knowing each other human." Even when he recognized that the South had refused to follow that path as late as 1957, he kept rejecting violence. "If we cannot civilize the South, or will not even try," Du Bois believed, "we continue in contradiction and riddle."[43] He actually reaffirmed his conviction when he applied for admission to the CPUSA in October 1961. Having recounted his search for the best political solutions to social problems over the past decades, he told Gus Hall, the chairman of the CPUSA, that "Communism—the effort to give all men what they need and ask of each the best they can contribute—is the only way of life." However, Communism, to him, "is a difficult and hard end to reach." He believed that the path for the CPUSA was clear: "It will provide the United States with a real Third Party and thus restore democracy to this country." While fully recognizing the different paths taken by the Soviet Union and other European nations, he did not mention the Chinese model that Mao advocated.[44] It is obvious that although Du Bois accepted Communism and even agreed that racial problems could not be resolved until the capitalist system came to an end, he, like the CPUSA, still refused to see armed revolution as an option to achieve that goal and remained in line with the peaceful transition and peaceful coexistence the CPSU and CPUSA advocated.

The lack of positive response from Du Bois did not stop Beijing from continuing its work on him even after he left China. One of the ways was to have his books published in China and offer criticism on them at the same time. In addition to *John Brown*, the PRC published the Chinese translation of *The Souls of Black Folk* later in 1959. Du Bois saluted its first readers in Asian and Communist countries in a new foreword written for the Chinese translation. While recognizing that he was not a socialist and knew little about Communism when he wrote the book over half a century earlier, he believed that he understood human suffering, and his book expressed their sorrow as well as his own. Thus, he hoped that the book would win

Figure 7.2 W. E. B. Du Bois and Shirley Graham Du Bois joining Chinese leaders in reviewing the National Day parade on top of the Tiananmen on October 1, 1962. Deng Xiaoping stands next to W. E. B. Du Bois.
Source: Schlesinger Library, Harvard Radcliffe Institute, Cambridge, Massachusetts.

sympathy from Chinese readers.[45] The translator praised the author's vivid description of the poverty and oppression suffered by African Americans after the Civil War, commended his open opposition to Booker T. Washington's capitulationism, and regarded his book as the declaration of a rising new trend in the Black Liberation movement. However, the translator also criticized some views in the book, including his emphasis on overcoming racial bias and bringing liberation for Blacks through education and building a small Black agricultural economy.[46] Identical criticisms were made by Huang Xinxi in his review of the book published in *People's Daily* on May 19, 1959, weeks after Du Bois went back to Moscow to receive the Lenin Peace Medal.[47]

Beijing's hospitality left such a deep impression on the couple that when Du Bois needed a place to recuperate from major surgery in fall 1962 they chose China. Although some Chinese diplomats were not happy with his close relations with the Soviet Union and his lack of strong support for the Chinese revolutionary model, Beijing still invited him back for another visit in September. Now a citizen of Ghana and chief editor of the *Encyclopedia Africana*, Du Bois enjoyed a reputation and influence among young

African nations that still made him valuable to Beijing as its competition and confrontation with the Soviet Union in Africa increasingly intensified in the early 1960s. He and his wife arrived in Beijing on September 29, two days before the PRC's National Day celebration. Zhou and his wife held a welcome banquet for the Du Boises the next day to demonstrate Beijing's respect.[48] On October 1, Du Bois was invited to join Mao and other top Chinese leaders in reviewing the National Day parade atop the Tiananmen (figure 7.2). Standing next to Deng Xiaoping, Zhou Enlai, and Mao Zedong, he and his wife were the first Americans to be given such an honor. Again, a photo showing them with Chinese leaders on Tiananmen and a report with their names listed appeared in *People's Daily* the next day.[49] However, after the celebration, Du Bois was taken to a remote site to recover. After returning to Ghana, he was too weak to handle his job as editor or participate in other political or social activities. It was only natural for Beijing to look for younger African American activists who could step in and provide leadership closer to its desires and needs.

Building an Alliance

Robert F. Williams, a middle-aged African American activist known for his advocacy and practice of armed self-defense, caught Beijing's attention in the late 1950s and presented himself as a potential ally in spring 1963. Having worked in factories in Detroit and served in the U.S. Army in World War II, Williams returned to Monroe, North Carolina, his hometown, and became president of the Union County NAACP chapter in 1951. He was known for organizing a Black armed guard in Monroe and defending the Black community with arms against violent attacks from local Ku Klux Klan members. He was removed from NAACP position in 1959 because he publicly stated that he would meet violence with violence when the local court acquitted two white men of raping a pregnant Black woman. Williams and his family fled to Cuba after North Carolina charged him with the kidnapping of a white couple in the middle of a confrontation between armed African Americans and Klan members in April 1961. He remained active in Cuba, publishing *The Crusader*, his personal newsletter, and hosting Radio Free Dixie with backing from Fidel Castro.[50] While maintaining close ties with other civil rights activists and his followers in the United States, Williams intensified his effort to seek international support for the African American fight against racial discrimination. He had observed that "because of the international situation, the Federal Government does not want racial incidents which draw the attention of the world to the situation in the South." Therefore, international publicity and support for African American self-defense, as he concluded in his 1962 book *Negroes with Guns*, would surely arouse so much attention that "the Federal Government will be more willing to enforce law and order if the local authorities don't."[51] Based on this belief, Williams sent telegrams to several national leaders, including the CCP chairman, the presidents of Indonesia and Ghana, and the king of Cambodia on May 7, 1963, asking them to add their voices to "that of the shocked humanity in protest against the savage oppression of the Americans of African descent in racist Birmingham, Alabama, USA."[52] Specifically, he wanted to hear their support for the African American March on Washington planned for late August.

Williams's request came at a time when Beijing faced unprecedented challenges brought by the split of the international Communist movement and the signing of the Treaty Banning Nuclear Weapon Tests in Atmosphere, in Outer Space, and Under Water by the Soviet Union, the United States, and Great Britain. After years of behind-closed-doors debate, the CPSU and CCP made their fight over the direction and leadership of the international Communist movement open in mid-1963. On July 20, the CCPCC published its reply to the March 30 letter from the CPSU in *People's Daily*, publicly denouncing the peaceful coexistence, peaceful competition, and peaceful transition Moscow advocated as a betrayal of Marxist and Leninist revolutionary theory. The core of the general line of the international Communist movement, the CCP insisted, was to establish a broad united front against the imperialists led by the United States and carry the proletarian world revolution to the end.[53] With the split between Moscow and Beijing becoming public, most Communist parties in other countries, including the CPUSA, chose to side with the CPSU. As a result, Beijing could no longer allow the CPUSA to steer the revolution in the United States under the guidance of Moscow if it wanted to lead Maoist-style world revolution.

The increasing confrontation with Moscow made the Tripartite Treaty more threatening to Beijing and resulted in the CCP leaders' strong denunciation. As soon as the treaty was initialed in Moscow on July 25, Mao met with Liu Shaoqi, Zhou Enlai, and Deng Xiaoping and published a stern statement in *People's Daily* on July 31.[54] The statement pointed out that the treaty was merely a hoax, aimed at strengthening the nuclear monopoly enjoyed by the three powers and straitjacketing those countries that loved peace but faced nuclear threat. Thus, it proposed to have a meeting of government leaders of all nations in the world to comprehensively, thoroughly, completely, and resolutely prohibit and destroy all nuclear weapons.[55] A few days later *People's Daily* published an editorial and a long news report on the treaty. The former accused Moscow of collaborating with the United States and betraying the peoples of the Soviet Union as well as China.[56] The latter used John F. Kennedy's own words to reveal the real intent of the treaty, which, the editors asserted, was to cope with the potential threat posed by the PRC.[57]

Williams's request for help offered a great opportunity for Beijing to build an alliance with African American civil rights fighters and establish itself as the true leader of the world revolution. After a careful study of Williams's background and the rapid development of the civil rights movement in the United States, Zhou sent a report to Mao on August 3, 1963, recommending that the chairman issue a public statement in support of the African American struggle. Mao agreed and instructed Pu Shouchang, one of Zhou's secretaries, to draft a statement for him based on the report.[58] After making some editorial changes, Mao approved Pu's draft.[59] The statement, with some polishing done by Frank Coe and Sidney Rittenberg, was first read at Mao's meeting with a group of visitors from four African countries on August 8 and then published by *People's Daily* the next day.[60] Mao made it clear at the very beginning that his statement was issued at the request of Robert Williams, a Black leader in exile in Cuba. Having provided a brief account of the sufferings endured by African Americans and their increasingly strong resistance, Mao asserted that the rapid development of the Black struggle reflected the increasing intensity of the class as well as national struggle within the United States. To counter fascist suppression from the U.S. government, Mao called upon all the workers, farmers, revolutionary intellectuals, bourgeoisie, and other liberals among people of all colors in the world to support the African American struggle against racial discrimination. He emphasized that "the struggle of races, after all, is the struggle of classes." Having pointed out that the white oppressors were a minority, no more than 10 percent of the world population, Mao assured that with support from more than 90 percent of the people in the world Black Americans would win their just struggle. "The evil colonial and imperialist systems that have risen and prospered with the enslavement and sale of the blacks," Mao declared, "will inevitably end with the complete emancipation of the black race."[61]

Mao's statement was unique in its format and important in its content in many ways. It was the first time Mao issued such an important statement in his own name without mentioning the PRC government or the CCP. He did it partly because he was no longer the legal head of the state and partly because he wanted to establish himself as a great leader of the world revolution.[62] Second, he openly recognized that his statement was made at the request of an individual African American activist, Robert F. Williams. This unprecedented act not only helped justify Mao's intervention in the domestic struggle in the United States but also identified Williams as a Black leader, which would help enhance his position among the African Americans fighting for freedom and equal rights. Third, Mao took the opportunity to present his own definition of the nature and goal of the African American struggle without consulting or even meeting with those who were waging it. In this way, Mao put himself in a leadership position and set the direction for the African American struggle. Last, by linking African Americans with the 90-plus percent of the world population, Mao addressed the concern of W. E. B. Du Bois and many other Black leaders about the viability of a revolution waged by a minority ethnic group in the United States. As the only leader who responded to Robert Williams's requests, Mao succeeded to a certain degree in intensifying domestic strife within the United States, establishing himself as a true follower of Marxist and Leninist revolutionary theory, and building himself up as a leader of world revolution.

Once Mao's statement was issued, Beijing did not lose any time in contacting Williams and made every effort to turn him into an active ally. On August 10, Shen Jian, the Chinese ambassador to Cuba, invited Williams to the PRC embassy so that a copy of Mao's statement could be presented to him. Williams was happily surprised, since Mao Zedong was the last among the world leaders who was expected to make such a strong statement to support the African American struggle in the United States. He thanked Mao and Chinese people for their resolute support and told Ambassador Shen that African Americans were happy to hear Mao's statement and would become more confident because they now knew that the majority of the people in the world were on their side. While giving highest praises to Mao's statement, Williams denounced the jingoism demonstrated by "some people," clearly referring to the leaders of the CPSU and CPUSA, who wanted African Americans to give up their fight and wait patiently. He declared that African Americans were the oppressed and had the right to fight for their liberation.[63]

Williams's clear and positive response to Mao's statement not only proved that he had the potential to become a good ally in Beijing's fight for the leadership of the international Communist movement, but it also made collaboration between the two sides relatively easy. On August 11, Beijing held a rally with more than ten thousand attendees, including Zhou Enlai; Chen Yi; Luo Ruiqing, the newly appointed chief of staff of the PLA; and Beijing's friends from about a dozen African, Asian, and Latin American nations. The rally was designed to show international support for the African American fight against racial discrimination and form a new alliance led by the PRC to oppose the peaceful coexistence the Soviet Union advocated. Unable to attend the rally in person, Williams sent a brief statement via telegram to Beijing, expressing his gratitude to the support given by Mao and the Chinese people. He also emphasized that African Americans and the peoples of Latin America, Africa, and Asia shared a common enemy, the racist and reactionary Americans and their imperialist government. He called upon them to unite and fight this barbarian enemy.[64] His telegram, when read at the rally, received thunderous applause from the audience. Guo Moruo opened the rally by accusing American imperialism of being the enemy of all oppressed nations and peoples in the world. Some so-called Marxists and Leninists, he asserted, betrayed oppressed nations and peoples by luring them to peacefully coexist with the imperialists and reactionaries.[65] Liu Ningyi called the African American fight for equality "the revolutionary struggle taking place within the heart of American imperialism." Thus, their fight, Liu stated, was essential in the common struggle waged by the world's people against the imperialists led by the United States.[66] Anna Louise Strong, who was vacationing in Beidaihe at the time, sent a taped speech to the rally, calling the African American struggle the spark for an American revolution.[67] Frank Coe pointed out in his speech that racial discrimination was part of the core of the American monopolistic capitalism. To remove the fatal evil, Coe insisted, American monopolistic capitalism must be destroyed at home as well as abroad.[68]

Beijing continued to build its alliance with Williams by publishing his writings in *People's Daily* after the August 11 rally. In his long article originally published on August 14 in Cuba, Williams asserted that the great liberation promised by Abraham Lincoln's Emancipation Proclamation was never completed and credited Mao for declaring freedom and equal rights for African Americans a century later. Thus, he believed that Mao's statement marked the beginning of a new era in the four-century-long African American struggle for civil rights. He claimed that more African Americans accepted the philosophy of self-defense and violent resistance against reactionary forces as well as racial oppression. He rejected the "fake Marxists" who forced Black Americans to be patient and go to the courts and polls to seek liberation. He insisted that African Americans had the right to use any means to wipe out barbaric and violent policies. He believed that Mao's statement was the second Emancipation Proclamation, which would make vicious imperialists and racial oppressors tremble with fear, and, at the same time, "spur our people to fight more bravely and resolutely."[69] On August 29 *People's Daily* published a statement issued by Robert Williams via his Radio Free Dixie on the eve of the historic March on Washington. He stressed that the dignity of Black people required self-defense, and self-defense required counterattack. He asked Black men, women, and children to become soldiers and patriots in the cause of liberation.[70]

When Mao's supporting statement reached Accra, W. E. B. Du Bois was already too ill to make any public response. Shirley Graham met with the New Chinese News Agency reporter on August 20, giving her and her husband's thanks to Mao. Having recognized that never had a leader of a great country issued such kind of statement before, she believed that most people in the world would answer Mao's call and ring the death knell for all types of imperialism.[71] However, Du Bois passed away on August 27. The next day more than 200,000 African Americans participating in the March on Washington showed their respect and sorrow with one minute of silence. Chinese leaders, including Mao Zedong, Zhou Enlai, Song Qingling, and Chen Yi, sent their condolences to Shirley Graham.[72] With the death of Du Bois, Robert Williams was destined to rise as the most prominent figure in African American interaction with the PRC in the following years.

At his meeting with Williams on August 10, Ambassador Shen also passed another message from Mao, inviting him for a visit to China. Williams was somewhat surprised since he had not asked for such a visit in his letter to Mao, and the country he wanted to see most was Ghana. He had talked about a visit to the newly independent African nation with a

Ghanaian diplomat in Havana and sent a letter to A. K. Barden, chairman director of the Bureau of African Affairs in Accra, expressing his interest.[73] While still waiting for a positive reply from Accra, Mao's invitation arrived, and Williams accepted it on the spot. Robert and Mable Williams arrived in Beijing on September 25, 1963, as guests of the CCPDWP. Guo Moruo greeted the couple at the Beijing airport, a treatment no other American visitors, including Strong and Du Bois, had ever received. He told Williams that his name was known to many people, including children in China.[74] Unlike Du Bois, Williams was treated as a renowned African American leader since the moment of his arrival. He and his wife were greeted at the airport by not only a large number of Chinese officials, the Cuban ambassador, and almost every American working in Beijing at the time, but also an honor guard, a treatment usually reserved for a visiting head of state. The Chinese told him that this was a rare occasion for them because "it was the first time an Afro-American leader from the United States southland had visited liberated China."[75]

Taking advantage of Williams's presence in Beijing, the Chinese leaders invited him and his wife to all major National Day celebration activities and used the occasion to strengthen his leadership status and offer encouragement. The couple was invited to attend the National Day reception held by Premier Zhou Enlai on the evening of September 30.[76] Because of the presence of Williamses at the event, Mao added another line in the toast section of Zhou's speech to include "the great unity of the comrades and people of Europe, North America, and Australia."[77] Up to this time, Zhou's toast was limited to the unity of the comrades and people of Africa, Asia, and Latin America. He never mentioned Europe or North America, mostly because the Soviet Union, according to the division of labor established by Stalin during Liu Shaoqi's visit to Moscow in 1949, was responsible for guiding the revolutionary movements in those regions. Although Mao began to oppose the division of labor between the two Communist powers during Khrushchev's visit to China in 1958, it was Mao's recent statement supporting African American fight against racial discrimination and Williams's visit to the PRC that clearly demonstrated Beijing's determination to establish itself as a leader in the revolutionary movements in Europe as well as the United States. Like the Du Boises, Williams and his wife reviewed the National Day parade on the Tiananmen with Mao, Zhou, and other top Chinese leaders on October 1. In addition to these traditional events, the Williamses were also given the honor of meeting separately with Mao Zedong, Liu Shaoqi, and Zhu De on the same day. Among all the foreign dignitaries attending the National Day celebration, Mao met only two couples. The other was Tanzan Ishibashi, the former prime minister of Japan and incumbent president of the Japanese Liberal Democratic Party, and his wife. Two pictures of the Williamses' meeting with the top Chinese leaders appeared in the second page of *People's Daily* on October 2.[78]

In addition to the photos designed to help strengthen Williams's position as an African American leader, Beijing offered encouragement and advice on revolution in the United States. At his meeting with Williams before the National Day parade, Mao began their conversation by asking Williams the development of the Black Liberation movement and his view about its future. When Williams predicted a long and difficult fight, Mao commented that the Black leader was still young and advised that he be patient because anyone who was impatient was not waging a revolutionary struggle, only reacting from emotion. Mao emphasized that it was not enough merely lashing out at injustice and oppression. A true revolutionary program, Mao concluded, must be planned and sustained, since its aim was to change society permanently.[79] Mao's straightforward advice clearly showed that he had strong confidence in Williams's commitment to revolution in the United States and treated him as its top leader. The same message was sent when Beijing arranged the translation of *Negroes with Guns* into Chinese in the summer of 1963. The translator praised Robert Williams for leading Blacks to pick up guns and defend themselves against racist attacks and persecution. The translator agreed with Williams that violence was needed to end racial oppression and was confident that the Black brothers, together with all other oppressed and exploited laboring masses, would become the real masters of the United States. In order to highlight Williams's main argument on armed self-defense, the translator deleted the original "Editor's Note" as well as the "Epilogue" by Marc Schleifer and moved the three articles by Martin Luther King and Truman Nelson from the front of the book to the back.[80] The cover was also changed by adorning it with a drawing of a Black worker with a rifle in his hands.

With Williams in Beijing, the Chinese leaders organized another big rally on October 10. Since a similar rally had been held just two months ago, this one was clearly designed to impress Williams and tell him how the African American fight against racial discrimination should be defined as well as carried out. He Long, vice chairman of the Military Committee of the CCPCC, attended the rally with more than ten thousand people.[81] Guo Moruo started the program by recognizing that the massive struggle waged by Blacks against racial discrimination had reached an unprecedented level since April and praising Williams as a brave African American fighter and leader. He quoted Williams extensively to prove that violence was needed in order to end racial oppression and credited the armed struggle led by Williams for revitalizing the self-defense tradition of the United States and turning a new page in the liberation of African Americans. He also quoted Mao, emphasizing that national struggle was class struggle and that the evil colonial and imperialist system would end with the complete liberation of the Black race. He pledged that the 650 million Chinese would support the revolutionary struggle of their Black American brothers and the American people until they won their final victory.[82]

Delivering his first major public speech in China right after Guo, Robert Williams echoed his hosts' major points. He thanked Mao for China's support for the African American struggle to civilize the racist jungle in the so-called free world and praised the PRC's great revolutionary achievements. He let the audience know that it was in China that for the first time in his life he felt that he was considered a human being. Then he pointed out that the American imperialism was racist imperialism and that the United States was attempting to establish a new world order based on Birmingham-style injustice. Thus, he believed that those who talked about peaceful coexistence with these barbaric beasts could never really put the highest interests of the human race on top. The only place where Williams showed any deviation from Mao's view was about the nature of racial discrimination in the United States. He could accept that racism was a product of capitalist exploitation. However, he insisted that racism had become part of the American way of life and the number of the white Americans who could be considered brothers and allies of Black people was very small.[83] Although the deviation would remain a concern for Beijing, it was not big enough to prevent the Chinese leaders from working with the young and outspoken African American leader.

After the rally in Beijing, Williams and his wife were given a nationwide tour, including a number of major cities and the base area established by the Soviet Republic of China under Mao's leadership in Jiangxi Province. Before they left Beijing, the CCPDWP had not only made a detailed travel and reception plan but also set two goals for the tour. One was to help Williams realize that the African American fight was after all class struggle and one kind of racism should not be replaced with another. In order to improve his understanding of Mao's statement and solve the line problem (*luxian wenti*) of the African American struggle, the hosts included the history of the Chinese revolution and visits to minority nationality regions in the tour. The CPCDWP believed that the second area was more important since it was Williams's first visit to China.[84]

Following clear instructions from Beijing, local hosts in the cities and provinces visited by Williams and his wife did their best to achieve those goals. When the Williamses arrived in Shanghai on October 18, Ke Qingshi, the city mayor, held a big welcoming rally and invited Williams to deliver a speech.[85] In addition to Ke's long conversation at the welcome banquet, other officials gave a detailed historical account of Shanghai workers' long revolutionary struggle and helped him make right connections with Mao's August 8 statement during his visit. Local officials reported that Williams, recognized at the farewell banquet that "blacks are the lowest class in the United States and that the black struggle is class struggle." At the same time, they arranged for Williams to see an exhibit on supporting African American struggle, visit several modern factories, go to a church, and shop in the markets. When they found out that Williams was not impressed with a truck repair shop, they took him to a big chemical factory and a watch factory, the biggest and most modern enterprises in China. These activities, they believed, helped him have a correct understanding of China's industrial development, economic recovery, and religious life. In the summary of their reception of the Black leader, the local hosts concluded that Williams was resolute in fighting against imperialism and friendly to China. However, they also believed that he still had a few shortcomings: lack of a good understanding of China as well as the nature of the African American struggle, influence by narrow racist sentiments, inadequate desire to learn from the Chinese revolutionary experience, and unfamiliarity with social etiquette.[86]

Before his departure from China, Williams was given the opportunity to meet with Zhou Enlai, who also left deep impression on him. Like Mao, Williams noticed, Zhou expressed interest in race issues in the United States and asked the guest what China could do to support the Black people of America. Williams told Zhou that the Black Liberation movement might need material assistance in the future. At present, Williams believed that the moral support from the Chinese was more than enough. To him, the strong support demonstrated by the Chinese formed a sharp contrast to the Soviet leaders who not only capitulated in the Cuban missile crisis but also denounced wars of national liberation. Thus, Williams was convinced through his first visit to China that Beijing was a real ally for African Americans.[87]

Exporting the Revolution

Williams's visit to the PRC in 1963 marked not only the consolidation of the alliance between Beijing and radical Black activists but also the beginning of his transformation from a local practitioner of armed self-defense to a prominent advocate for Black revolution in the United States. As soon as he returned to Cuba, Williams started to fervently promote armed Black revolution through the publication of long and substantive articles in his newsletters as well as communications and meetings with other civil rights activists. While generally happy with Williams's actions after his first China trip, Beijing kept pushing him to engage in armed struggle and violent revolution along the line set by Mao. The effort made by Beijing came in many forms, such as holding numerous mass rallies in major cities in the PRC to support African American struggle; inviting Williams for an additional visit to and extended stay in the PRC; exporting Mao's writings, especially *Quotations from Chairman Mao*, to the United States; and printing Williams's newsletters in China. It was through its carefully planned actions that Beijing was able to help Williams strengthen his leadership position in the Black revolution, disseminate Mao's revolutionary ideology among African Americans, create genuine fear of guerrilla warfare among policymakers in Washington, and consolidate Mao's role as the leader of the world revolution.

The rise of Williams as a fervent advocate for an alliance with the PRC and an armed revolution in the United States can be clearly seen from his writings published in his newsletter, *The Crusader*, after his visit to the PRC. Williams launched the newsletter in 1959 to "serve as a vehicle of communication for the militant and radical forces." Before his China trip, *The Crusader* was just "a local NAACP publication," carrying mostly news about those involved in Monroe Branch and his Radio Free Dixie program.[88] The newsletter grew into a more substantial periodical after

Williams's visit to the PRC, with longer essays promoting armed Black revolution and with new concepts, terms, strategies, and tactics borrowed mostly from the Chinese Communists, especially Mao. In the February 1964 issue Williams gave his first account of his China trip under the title "China: New Hope of Oppressed Humanity." He told his readers that contrary to what reactionaries would like people to believe, "China is far from being isolated and it now playing a major role in the international liberation struggle." As one of the most dynamic countries in the world today, China, he predicted, "in a short time is destined to become leader of the truly free world." He also shared with readers that the Chinese people "whole-heartedly support Afroamericans who struggle against Jim Crow and racial oppression in the so-called free world of the racist USA." Thus, African Americans were "extremely fortunate to have such honest, sincere, and militant people as our allies."[89]

In the same issue, Williams also published "Revolution Without Violence?," laying out, for the first time, the necessity and strategy of a new revolution to be made by African Americans. As an oppressed and dehumanized people, African Americans, Williams wrote, should see the fact borne out in history that "oppressors never voluntar[il]y relinquish their tyrannical grip on the oppressed" and that the oppressed "must break the strangle hold of their oppressor" by themselves. He went on to show that nonviolent resistance was not working, racial integration impossible, and revolution inevitable. He advised his readers that "let us not be so naïve as to believe that we can conduct a revolution without violence." The new concept of revolution, he elaborated, "is lightening campaign conducted in highly sensitive urban communities with the paralysis reaching the small communities and spreading to the farm areas." He even outlined the strategies for urban guerrilla warfare: sporadic rioting and massive sniping during the day, organized fighting and unlimited terror against the oppressor and his forces at night. He was confident that such a campaign "will bring about an end to oppression and social injustice in the USA in less than 90 days." His confidence was built largely on his recent visit to China, which made him believe that the world "has changed and the favor of the situation has shifted to the side of the Afroamericans." Thus, he concluded that "we can win because our struggle is just and our friends are many."[90]

More provocative essays written by Williams promoting war and revolution continued to appear in subsequent issues of *The Crusader*. In "Psychological Warfare," published in the March–April issue, Williams stressed that "Afroamerican Freedom Fighters must coordinate street action with psychological warfare" and "must be able, willing and ready to strike the oppressor in his Achilles heel." In order to win the fight for freedom, the African Americans, he wrote, must bring job discrimination, discrimination in housing, police brutality, court frame-ups, and racist violence to the attention of the entire world.[91] Williams defended armed Black revolution in another essay, "USA: The Potential of a Minority Revolution." Published in the next issue, it pointed out that revolution "is necessitated by abusive and reactionary power" that "perpetuates itself through the medium of violence." It reminded the readers that the evil force of Nazism "was not crushed by nonviolence and love but a fighting spirit, backed up by force and violence." Thus, to "limit the Afroamerican struggle to the narrow confines of non-violence, while the white oppressor class wages a violent struggle to maintain the status quo," Williams insisted, "is to invoke the principle of Jim Crow and its racial inequality." He also believed that "a minority revolution has as much, or more, chance of succeeding in the racist USA as any place in the world." He even offered advice on how to make gasoline firebombs and where to buy hand grenades, bazookas, light mortars, rocket launchers, machine guns, and ammunition. Instead of using these weapons just for self-defense, he asked African Americans to aim them at the racist police and use them to bring destruction and create panic. He predicted that "1964 is going to be a violent one, the storm will reach hurricane proportion by 1965 and the eye of the hurricane will hover over America by 1966."[92]

Williams's call for violent revolution aroused great attention among many African Americans and gained enthusiastic following from some of them. Maxwell C. Stanford, a young Black student at Central State University in Ohio who cofounded the Revolutionary Action Movement (RAM), believed that Williams's essay "Revolution Without Violence?" "changed the direction of the black liberation movement." Formed mostly by young Black students in response to Williams's call for armed defense issued in 1961, RAM remained fluid and small, focusing mostly on publishing various journals and working with other African American organizations such as the Congress of Racial Equality (CORE) and the Student Nonviolent Coordinating Committee (SNCC) until spring 1964. The publication of the February 1964 issue of *The Crusader* and the meeting between Robert Williams and RAM leaders including Maxwell Stanford and Ernest Allen in Cuba right after, injected fresh energy into the movement. Inspired to apply the theories and strategies Williams prescribed, Stanford organized the first Afro-American Student Conference on Black Nationalism at Fisk University in Nashville, Tennessee, in early May. The participants agreed that Black Nationalists were the vanguard of Black revolution in America and assigned themselves the task to draft a thirteen-point program to carry it out. Their program sought to establish a permanent underground secretariat to implement the plan, unite with the African, Asian, and Latin American revolution, and build revolutionary centers in the United States. They also designated Robert Williams as their leader in exile.[93] This conference, as Stanford pointed out, allowed Black activists from the North and South to discuss Black Nationalism for the first time since the founding of the SNCC in 1960 and served as the "ideological catalyst that eventually shifted the Civil Rights Movement into the Black Power movement."[94]

As Black Nationalist sentiment rose among many African American activists and the staff of the SNCC in Mississippi was ready to move into armed self-defense in the winter of 1963 and 1964, the need for a centralized organization to coordinate the new movement became apparent. Stanford called a meeting of Black Liberation Front cadres, including James and Grace Boggs, in Detroit. After some discussion, RAM was given responsibility and a twelve-point program was adopted. The development of a Rifle Club, Underground Vanguard, Liberation Army, and nation within the nation were included in the program. Robert Williams was elected the international chairman of the movement, while Malcolm X served as its spokesman. As a result, RAM finally became a national organization with a well-structured leadership and clear action plan for Black revolution.[95]

The strong push for armed self-defense and revolution from Williams and other radical African American leaders also began to show clear impact on protests taking place in many cities in summer 1964. After a young Black student was killed by a white off-duty police officer in New York City on July 18, about eight thousand Blacks in Harlem went to the streets and confronted police for many days. When some Black leaders tried to persuade the protesters to follow the nonviolent tradition, their proposal was rejected in favor of guerrilla warfare. Instead of passively taking attacks from police, the protesters fought back with bricks, glass bottles, and even Molotov cocktails.[96] *People's Daily* carried detailed reports on the protest almost daily. Beijing was happy to recognize that the ongoing protest was drastically different from demonstrations in the past as African Americans now started to use violence to counter the brutal suppression.[97] Williams issued a statement in Havana on July 23 asking people around the world to lend their moral as well as material support for the African American struggle.[98] RAM members in the United States sprang immediately into revolutionary action, building secret political cells in different areas of the country. Their goal was to transform the civil rights movement into a Black Nationalist revolution.[99]

Largely because of the critical development of the African American struggle in several major cities in summer 1964 and the need to demonstrate the PRC's status as world revolutionary leader at the fifteenth National Day celebration, Beijing invited Williams for another visit in September 1964 (figure 7.3). As it had done for his first visit a year earlier, the CCP-DWP, the official host for Williams and his family, worked out a detailed plan for their reception. CCPDWP officials recognized that Williams had showed sincere friendliness to China, praised Chairman Mao as the contemporary revolutionary leader who had spoken out for Blacks, and regarded the PRC as the center and hope for oppressed people. The main goal for the visit, they spelled out, was to spur further development of the African American struggle through demonstrating China's support, raise Williams's political consciousness, and enhance his reputation and influence

Figure 7.3 Robert Williams, Mabel Williams, and their two sons arriving in Beijing on September 23, 1964. They were greeted by Chinese leaders and American friends working in Beijing.
Source: Robert F. Williams Papers, HS 1092, Bentley Historical Library, University of Michigan, Ann Arbor.

in the Black movement. Political consciousness as known in the PRC at the time referred to following Mao's teachings in carrying out class struggle at home and supporting armed revolution abroad. They also proposed that the reception for the Williams family be warm and positive, meeting as many of their requests as possible and giving them relatively high status. In order to show the Chinese hospitality, they even included two hundred yuan in pocket money and a one-hundred-yuan gift for the family in the plan.[100]

The CCPDWP reception plan was approved and implemented. On September 30, Williams was invited to the National Day state banquet and met with Mao Zedong again.[101] The photo showing Mao shaking hands with Williams at the meeting appeared on the cover of the October special edition of *The Crusader*. The next day he joined the Chinese leaders and a few foreign dignitaries atop Tiananmen to review the National Day parade for the second time. As in the previous year, he was recognized as a famous African American leader. His name as well as pictures of him in the reviewing party appeared on the front page of *People's Daily* the next day.[102] In order to maintain and strengthen his status as an African American leader in the eyes of his hosts, Williams told the Chinese officials at the welcome banquet held on September 24 that the RAM was the most militant Black organization in the United States and he was its "chairman in exile." He provided more information about RAM when he had a longer conversation with Vice Premier Deng Zihui on September 30. He told Deng that RAM fought imperialism as well as racism at home, supported the PRC abroad, and followed the Chinese path in its own fight. He also informed Deng that the RAM, as the center of the African American struggle, had many peripheral Black organizations and requested all RAM members to study Mao's writings.[103]

As planned, the CCPDWP did everything it could to satisfy the requests from Williams and his family during their monthlong stay. One of the first things that Williams asked immediately after his arrival was to have his two sons, who were accompanying him, stay in Beijing for schooling.[104] Williams and his wife wanted their sons to have as much education as possible, and they believed that schools in China were as good as those anywhere in the world. Having faced increasing frustration and even hostility in Cuba, Williams was looking for a safe place for his children so that he could leave that country when it became necessary.[105] With special arrangements made by Chinese officials, Williams's two sons were admitted to the Middle School Affiliated to Peking University (Beida Fuzhong), one of the best middle schools in the country. This allowed the Williamses to leave their sons in China for school when they returned to Cuba late in October.

Another request made by Williams was to visit some minority nationality communities, more factories, and the city of Guangzhou. In order to meet these requests, CPC arranged visits to the College of Nationalities in Beijing and sent him and his family to Mongol and Korean ethnic communities in Inner Mongolia and Jilin. It was through these visits that Williams concluded that racial problems had been completely resolved in China.[106] Having visited the Military Museum and watched militiamen practicing shooting at the College of Physical Education in Beijing, Williams asked to observe the exercises of the PLA. As soon as he returned from his trip to the Northeast region, he was accompanied by Suo Libo, deputy chief of staff of the Beijing Military District, to a military exercise. Before the event, he told his host that this would be the most important program of his China visit. After reviewing the exercise, Williams praised the high quality of the training and the lightness of Chinese weapons. He inquired about the role of political commissars in the Chinese military and declared that the African Americans were sure to win because they had such a powerful military force on their side.[107]

There was one thing that Williams was unable to get it done completely in the way as he wished. Right after his arrival in Beijing, Williams let his host know that he wanted to make a documentary film about his visit to China and proposed to have it done with an American crew led by William Worthy. Beijing had already received several requests from Worthy for another visit to China. However, it had ignored his requests because of his complex connections (*guanxi fuza*).[108] Responding to Williams's plea, a CCPDWP official told him that it would be inconvenient for Beijing to invite Worthy at this time because it involved the bigger issue of the exchange of journalists between the two nations. But Williams was informed that the CCPDWP could make a documentary film on his visit to China with a Chinese crew. Williams accepted the Chinese arrangement and suggested that a copy of the film be forwarded to Worthy, who should have ways to show it on some television programs in the United States. He also proposed that the documentary focus on the great achievements made by the Chinese in heavy industry and the people's commune, with coverage of militiamen, especially female ones; religious activities; the daily life of the Chinese people; the statement issued by Mao Zedong to support African American struggle against racial discrimination; and the actions taken by the PRC to provide such a support.[109] The main purpose of the documentary, in Williams's words, was to boost the African American struggle and strengthen ties with the Chinese people. As requested by Williams, the documentary film, *Robert Williams in China*, was made in 16mm format so that it could be easily shown to the public. Once the production was completed, Williams wrote to many universities and public libraries in the United States, offering them the film without charge.[110] After receiving an import permit from the federal government, Howard University got its copy from Williams in December 1967.[111] The film was also shown on the campus of the University of North Carolina and in classes at George Peabody College for Teachers in Nashville, Tennessee.[112]

Similar effort was made by Beijing in Williams's extended stay in China beginning in 1966. As his relations with officials there deteriorated, Williams began to find a way to leave Cuba. Believing that he had learned a great deal during his exile, Williams wanted to return to the United States so that he could apply his knowledge at home and observe the Black Liberation movement firsthand. However, he soon changed his mind because the condition was still not ripe for his return to his homeland. After his attempts to relocate to Ghana, Canada, and other countries failed, Williams turned to Beijing. The Chinese ambassador in Havana told him he could visit the PRC whenever he wished and stay as long as he liked.[113] Williams accepted Beijing's offer and left Cuba with the help of the North Vietnamese government.

Williams and his wife arrived in Beijing just in time to participate in the celebration of the seventeenth anniversary of the PRC. In addition to inviting him to join Chinese leaders reviewing the National Day parade on top of Tiananmen, as had been done in the past, Beijing bestowed a greater honor on him this time by asking him to deliver a speech in front of one and a half of million Chinese with Mao standing by his side. While denouncing the American imperialists as warmongers, robbers, and cold-blooded murderers, Williams praised Mao as the greatest leader of world revolution, to which U.S. civil rights movement belonged. He saluted the glorious Chinese brothers and the mighty Chinese People's Republic on behalf of "all revolutionary American people," especially "the brutally oppressed and victimized Afro-American freedom fighters." The salute to the PRC, Williams emphasized, was only a way to "pay tribute to its great architect, liberator, helmsman, and universal leader and teacher, whose thought is transforming the whole world." He asserted that on this great National Day revolutionaries throughout the world realized more than ever how much "we are indebted to the architect of people's warfare, the immortal leader and teacher, Chairman Mao Tse-tung."[114] By praising Mao with "five greats," Williams not only recognized Mao as a universal revolutionary leader but also outdid Lin Biao, who had capped Mao with "four greats": great teacher, great leader, great commander, and great helmsman. Beijing published his speech and picture in *People's Daily* on October 2. *The Crusader* carried both items as well as detailed instructions on how to make black powder cocktails in its October issue.[115]

Another honor was bestowed on Williams on the National Day when Mao presented him an autographed copy of *Quotations from Chairman Mao*.[116] As one of the few foreigners who had received the *Little Red Book* from Mao himself, Williams not only carefully studied the book but also quoted Mao frequently in his own writings and printed many sections directly selected from the *Little Red Book* in *The Crusader*. Most of the quotations reprinted in *The Crusader* were about revolutionary theory and guerrilla warfare tactics. For example, at the top of page 10 of the January 1967 issue, a sentence from Mao's *Little Red Book* appeared in boldface: "We should support whatever the enemy opposes and oppose whatever the enemy supports."[117] In the July 1967 issue, five sentences selected from the *Quotations from Chairman Mao*, all about guerrilla warfare, were printed in boldface in one special section. One of them read: "The enemy advances, we retreat; the enemy camps, we harass; the enemy tires, we attack; the enemy retreats, we pursue."[118] Williams kept doing this until the last issue of *The Crusader*, published in China in the summer of 1969.[119] His action was not only in line with the new standard practice in all publications in China at the time but also met expectations from Beijing that he should take steps to help spread Mao Zedong Thought among the American people.

In addition to publicizing Mao's writings in his newsletter, Williams used his distribution channel to send copies of *Quotations from Chairman Mao* to Black as well as white activists in the United States. At the end of 1966, he sent fifty copies of *The Crusader* and a New Year's card to Duane Price, a college student and antiwar activist in Salt Lake City, Utah. What really made Price excited was the copy of the *Little Red Book* that came with *The Crusader*. After reading the book, Price wrote a sketch on Mao and had it published in *The Utah Free Press*. He even sent a copy of his essay to Mao and asked to have it published in the *Peking Review*.[120] About two months later, Price happily informed Williams that he had helped organize an antiwar demonstration and a teach-in on the University of Utah campus. He and his collaborators managed to sell a hundred copies of *Quotations from Chairman Mao* at the teach-in.[121] One Sister Mary also received a "special gift" from Williams with *The Crusader*. She wrote back and told him that her family cherished the "best seller." She also told him that Black militants everywhere waited for his periodical and that his messages "give guidance, inspiration, ideas, and bridge the physical gap between you and the movement here; also unify organizations and individuals here."[122]

As the best-known early Black organizer of armed self-defense movement in the 1950s and the most recognized representative of African American struggle in the PRC, Williams rose as one of the most prominent Black leaders and had profound influence on the Black Power and Black Nationalist movements in the 1960s. Inspired by the armed self-defense led by Williams and his book *Negroes with Guns*, Huey Newton and Bobby Seale named their new organization established in October 1966 the Black Panther Party for Self-Defense and organized patrols to follow police around with loaded guns. With limited resources at its inception, the Black Panther Party raised funds for their guns by buying *Quotations from Chairman Mao* in bulk from China Books & Periodicals in San Francisco and selling them to students at University of California at Berkeley at a three-times markup. In Seale's words, they would "sell the books, make the money, buy the guns, and go on the streets with the guns."[123] Following the example set by Williams, Black Panther Party members carried Mao's *Little Red Book* all the time and studied it diligently.

With the help from Williams and other African American activists, Beijing's effort to spread Mao Zedong Thought across the Pacific made great headway since the publication of the English version of the *Little Red Book* in fall 1966. By early 1967, it had become, as Henry Noyes, the owner of China Books & Periodicals, observed, "a status symbol for anybody opposing bureaucratic authority." Noyes's store sold out its first order of one thousand *Quotations from Chairman Mao* within two days in spring 1967 and the next 25,000 were gone within a month. By the end of 1968, his store had distributed 250,000 copies, and in the following fifteen years it sold more than one million copies of the *Little Red Book*.[124] The opportunities created by the *Little Red Book* frenzy also caught the attention of American mainstream publishers. In February 1967, Bantam Books published the first complete and unexpurgated version of the *Quotations*. Demand for the book was so great that a second printing came out in March. In his introduction written for the Bantam volume, A. Doak Barnett, the foremost China expert in the United States, pointed out that how to cope with China "will be one of the most difficult problems for U.S. foreign policy." In order to deal with China successfully, the Americans, he argued, must clearly improve their understanding of the forces now at work in China. Thus, he concluded that "the non-Communist world cannot afford to ignore Mao's writings on subjects such as class struggle, the 'mass line,' and 'people's war,' in this volume."[125] The Peabody International Center published a version with a slightly different title, *Mao Tse-tung's Quotations: The Red Guards' Handbook*, with an introduction by Stewart Fraser in April. Fraser even sent an order form to Williams in Beijing.[126]

The influence and prestige of Robert Williams continued to grow while he was in exile. In the wake of the most violent riot/rebellion in Detroit in 1967, a few hundred African American activists and leaders met in that city in March 1968 and established the Republic of New Africa (RNA). The participants not only drafted a constitution for the Republic and signed a Declaration of Independence, but also elected many leaders from various Black organizations as officials for the RNA's provisional government. Williams received nominations for many positions and was eventually chosen as the president of the RNA.[127] As the first separate nation built by African Americans within the United States, the founders of the RNA designated five Southern states—Alabama, Georgia, Louisiana, Mississippi, and South Carolina—as its territory. While deeply rooted in the long history of the Black Nationalist tradition, the RNA bore clear resemblance to the Soviet Republic of China established by Mao and his followers in the early 1930s. Although the RNA was founded without Williams on the scene, his influence was clearly felt in many ways during the convention and his guidance was sought immediately after it. A small delegation, including Milton Henry (Gaidi Obadele), the first vice president; Richard Henry (Imari Obadele), the minister of information; and Mae Mallory, Williams's former colleague, who had fought with him in Monroe, went to Tanzania in June 1968 to meet with him. Williams confirmed his acceptance of the RNA presidency and proposed some diplomatic initiatives for the new government at the meeting. After the meeting, senior RNA officials made great effort to achieve the diplomatic goals Williams set and sent him detailed reports to keep him informed of their progress.[128]

Williams's activities as a fervent advocate of armed revolution, close ally of the PRC, and prominent leader in the Black Nationalist movement aroused serious concern and fear in Washington. Testifying before the House Appropriation Subcommittee on February 16, 1967, J. Edgar Hoover, director of the FBI, identified the RAM as "a highly secretive all negro, Marxist-Leninist, Chinese Communist-oriented organization" "dedicated to the overthrow of the capitalist system in the United States, with violence if necessary."[129] In May 1968, the House Committee on Un-American Activities published a report, *Guerrilla Warfare Advocates in the United States*, warning Congress and the American public that "there are mixed Communists and black nationalist elements in this country which are planning and organizing guerrilla-type operations against the United States." The committee asserted that guerrilla warfare, which seemed absurd a few years ago, "may not be so farfetched today." Having traced the root of modern guerrilla warfare to the Communists, especially Mao, who had most clearly articulated its nature, goal, strategy, and tactics, the report named RAM as the most dangerous organization because it "identifies itself with the Chinese model of revolutionary warfare." The committee quickly tied RAM to Robert Williams by pointing out that although Max Stanford had founded it, "it takes its lead from Robert Williams, who now lives in Beijing." As RAM's mentor and leader, Williams, the committee emphasized, promoted a new type of guerrilla warfare. Unlike Mao, Che Guevara, and other Communist leaders who had conceived of guerrilla warfare primarily as a rural operation, Williams kept his focus on urban areas and advanced a new concept with sharp emphasis on huddling "as close to the enemy as possible so as to neutralize his modern and fierce weapons." Later in the report, the committee also noted the establishment of the RNA and the election of Williams as its president in March 1968.[130]

The assassination of Martin Luther King on April 4, 1968, pushed the African American fight against racial discrimination to new heights. Upon hearing the tragic news, thousands of African Americans went immediately into the streets to protest in more than a hundred cities across the country. Devastating riots broke out in major urban centers including Washington, Chicago, Baltimore, and Detroit. Stokely Carmichael, the African American militant activist who played a leading role in the protest in Washington, called upon Black men to go home, get guns, and come back out to the street to "make the white racist Americans understand that Negroes have the necessary force to set right the outrages which have been made against Negroes in the United States."[131] The unprecedented nationwide protests forced the federal and state governments to send in thousands of national guardsmen and army units to restore and maintain order. The United States was at the brink of a civil war.

The explosive situation also presented Mao Zedong another opportunity to show his support and leadership. Mao issued his second statement to support the African American struggle against violence on April 16, 1968, without waiting for any requests from Black activists this time. He opened his statement by pointing out that although Martin Luther King was a believer in nonviolence, the American imperialists had not tolerated him. Instead, he was bloodily suppressed by them with the use of reactionary violence. Mao believed that the assassination had taught the Black people a deep lesson and started a new storm of violent struggle. The unprecedented number of protests in hundred plus cities, Mao asserted, demonstrated that extremely powerful revolutionary forces existed among the twenty-plus-million African Americans. He reemphasized that racism was the by-product of colonialism and that the contradiction between the African Americans and the ruling group of the United States was one of class. Thus, African Americans could win their complete liberation, Mao concluded, only with the overthrow of the monopolistic capitalist class. He again called up on the workers, farmers, revolutionary intellectuals of all countries in the world to give their strong support to the African American struggle and launch persistent and fierce attacks on the American imperialists and their lackeys. He was confident that the world revolution had entered a great new era and that the complete collapse of the colonialism, imperialism, and all exploiting systems was just around the corner.[132]

To help spread Mao's newest message among African Americans, *People's Daily* immediately interviewed Robert Williams as well as Shirley Graham Du Bois in Beijing and published their responses to Mao's statement. Williams thanked Mao for issuing another statement to support the African American struggle against violence. However, with many direct quotations from Mao's statement, Williams's response was merely a repetition of all the major points made by the Chinese leader. He agreed with Mao that the complete collapse of colonialism and imperialism was imminent, that the common enemies of the Chinese and African Americans were all paper tigers, and that all reactionaries would be defeated. What was missing in his statement was his usual fervent call for violent revolution or armed self-defense. In sharp contrast, Shirley Graham Du Bois gave a more pointed response for the occasion by pointing out that the assassination of Martin Luther King told Black Americans that freedom could not be won with nonviolence and that they must pick up guns and fight.[133] Williams's pro forma response clearly reflected his recent decision to return to the United States to fight the legal charges against him in court. As part of his preparation for his return to the United States, he had started to raise bail money for the upcoming legal procedures and to tone down his rhetoric on armed revolution to keep his case as simple as possible. During his visit to Tanzania, he not only met with top RNA officials, but also applied for a passport at the U.S. embassy in Dar Es Salaam. Although Williams was still not quite sure about the prospect of his return to his homeland, his new focus on fighting legal battles in court marked the beginning of the end of the revolutionary alliance between him and the PRC.

CHAPTER VIII

Lowering the Sword

After unexpected detention in London, Robert Williams finally returned to the United States in September 1969, ending his three-year extended stay in the PRC. Instead of leading a Black armed revolution as many had expected, Williams quickly resigned his position as RNA president and devoted himself to fighting legal charges against him and disseminating information on the PRC. By acquiescing to Williams's new endeavors, Beijing signaled its intention to stop supporting armed revolution in the United States and seek ways to reduce tension in its relations with Washington. Richard Nixon, who started his political career as a red hunter, had also made great effort to establish contacts with the PRC after entering the White House. Although the resurrected ambassadorial talks in Warsaw were short-lived, Beijing and Washington kept sending signals to each other through other venues. By inviting and hosting the U.S. Table Tennis Team (USTTT) in April 1971, Beijing made it clear that it was finally ready to allow more Americans, including President Nixon, to visit the PRC. Once the Chinese ping-pong players toured the United States soon after Nixon's historical trip to the PRC in 1972, the first bilateral cultural exchange since 1949 was finally completed. Following the footsteps of those ping-pong players, an increasingly large number of journalists, athletes, scientists, doctors, scholars, artists, and politicians crisscrossed the Pacific, rebuilding cultural ties between the two nations. However, with the Taiwan issue unresolved and the normalization of diplomatic relations lagging, cultural exchange programs were kept unofficial in nature, small in scale, short in duration, and limited in subject fields until 1979.

Williams's decision to shift his focus from promoting armed Black revolution to fighting the legal charges against him in court represented his abandonment of Mao's revolutionary theory and return to a long-held belief that armed self-defense or revolution was necessary only when nonviolent actions could not bring justice or equality to African Americans. That reversion was largely based on his assessment of the political conditions in the United States as well as the PRC in the late 1960s. CCP leaders tolerated Williams's backpedaling because they themselves were forced to improve their relations with the United States so that they would not have to fight two superpowers at the same time. As Williams and other militant African American leaders went back to nonviolence, a major hurdle was removed in the normalization of U.S.-China relations in the late 1960s and early 1970s. However, the reestablishment of cultural ties between the two nations was out of expediency rather than based on shared ideas, values, and world outlook. As a result, Beijing kept exerting tight control on cultural exchange with the United States and used exchange programs as an instrument to influence American views as well as policy toward the PRC while keeping American ideals and values as far away as possible. When Beijing's effort met strong resistance from the U.S. government and organizations involved in cultural exchange, the Sino-American confrontation on the cultural front persisted, even though with lower intensity.

Morphing into a Messenger

While enjoying the hospitality offered by Beijing, Robert Williams began to contemplate his return to the United States in summer 1967, merely a year after settling down in Beijing.[1] Williams publicly announced his plan to end his exile, at least on the surface, as a response to a call from Max Stanford, the national chairman of the Revolutionary Action Movement (RAM), for an emergency meeting of Black leaders. Stanford wrote to Williams on July 5, 1967, informing him that sixteen people had been arrested on the accusation of plotting the assassination of moderate Black leaders including Roy Wilkins, executive director of NAACP, and Whitney Young, executive director of the National Urban League, two weeks earlier.

He felt that "it is very important that we meet to discuss this matter and the subject of our people's survival before our common enemy begins to assassinate our leaders, saying that we assassinated one another." Therefore, he called leaders from all major Black organizations, including Wilkins, Young, Martin Luther King, Stokely Carmichael, and Williams, for a Black Unity Conference to discuss the formation of a National African American United Liberation Front.[2] Only days after receiving the letter, Williams started to prepare for his return to his homeland. Still under a kidnaping charge from the state of North Carolina, Williams wrote to the Union County Superior Court on July 28, announcing his plan for an early return to Monroe and seeking information on the charges against him as well as the amount of bail bond required by the court.[3]

At the same time, William communicated with his close friends and issued public statements about his plan to return to the United States, seeking their understanding and support. In order to make sure that he would not be put in jail right after his return, he devoted much of his communications to raising a substantial amount to cover the bail. Besides his comrades and followers in the United States, Williams turned to his Japanese activist friends for financial support.[4] In his public statement issued on August 17, Williams emphasized that he went into exile because "no black man can expect legal justice in America's kangaroo-type racist court." His return, he believed, would expose racist America's concept of justice for Black people before the entire world, and he wanted to "disillusion people who still have illusions about American democracy and justice." He intended to organize an international movement for his defense and invite ten thousand people to his Union County trial so that he could "use his trial as part of a seminar on the study of legalized, white supremacy lynching in America."[5] He told Mae Mallory that given the existing conditions this was "the only positive contribution" that he could make at the time.[6]

While preparing for the worst, Williams was encouraged not only by the fact that all the other African American activists involved in the same case were able to shed the charges against them but also by the strong support received for his court battle against the U.S. Post Office. On September 19, Williams sent a formal letter to Lawrence O'Brien, the postmaster general, challenging the Post Office's ban on *The Crusader*.[7] On the same day, Williams also informed the American Civil Liberties Union (ACLU) in New York City of the Post Office ban and asked it to take any action necessary "in defense of Constitutional and international postal and literacy rights."[8] The ACLU immediately agreed to represent him and sue the U.S. Postal Service in court if necessary.[9] While authorizing the ACLU to undertake the lawsuit, Williams wrote to many supporters asking them to send protest letters to the Post Office.[10] Under pressure from the ACLU and Williams's supporters, Timothy May, the Post Office general counsel, was forced to explain to Williams that the Post Office had refused to carry the May 1967 issue of *The Crusader* only because it "advocates violence by Negroes in our cities," and "encourages Negro servicemen in Vietnam to sabotage operations in the field and in their units," including murdering "their Caucasian fellow servicemen."[11] May's explanation failed to stop Williams or his lawyers from filing their lawsuit. Melvin Wulf, the general counsel of ACLU, made it clear that he was willing to go to U.S. Supreme Court, if necessary, to get unimpeded mail distribution of *The Crusader* and to secure Williams's right to return to the country.[12] Although a favorable decision from U.S. District Court was not made until June 17, 1970, the effective work done by ACLU lawyers and strong support from many American citizens and organizations gave Williams greater confidence to face the kidnapping charges against him in the United States.[13]

In addition to the urgent request from Stanford, other new developments in the PRC as well as the United States made Williams feel his return necessary and possible. The chaos caused by the Cultural Revolution in the PRC and his disagreements on some major issues with Chinese leaders had turned his stay in the PRC into a less attractive option. Although Williams deeply appreciated Mao's strong support for the African American struggle and enthusiastically borrowed Chinese guerrilla warfare strategies and tactics, he never agreed with Mao that the African American fight against racial discrimination could be categorized as simply class struggle. He insisted that he had seen with his own eyes how vicious the working-class white Americans were toward African Americans. In the last issue of *The Crusader* published before his departure from China, Williams continued to accuse some "super duper 'revolutionaries' and Uncle Tom 'communists'" for "disseminating the thought of the C.I.A." and inducing "further division by focusing unwarranted attention on an exaggerated class structure." He emphasized that there were no "black imperialists or monopoly capitalists in America."[14] Thus, he did not share Mao's confidence that the American masses would soon "wake up to the folly of capitalism and create a Socialist state."[15] He even told V. Khanna, a visiting Indian diplomat, that class struggle was "sociologically blind" and offered nothing to American Blacks. Although he had never expressed these opinions to Chinese officials, the ideological gap, he claimed, was an "open secret."[16]

Despite his reciprocal support for the Cultural Revolution led by Mao in its early stage, Williams and his family, just like many other Chinese as well as American families in China, suffered from the chaos caused by extreme emphasis on class struggle. Most Chinese high-ranking officials, including Liu Shaoqi and Deng Xiaoping, suddenly became enemies of the revolution and were removed from office. Some Americans, including Bob Winter, Israel Epstein, and Sidney Rittenberg, were accused of spying for the United States and put in jail without due legal processes in early 1968.[17] Frustrated by the disorder, Williams frequently complained to his friends that everything moved slowly and that it was hard to get things done in China. Since most educators were persecuted and all colleges were shut down, his two sons, Robert Williams Jr. and John Williams, nineteen and seventeen respectively in 1968, could not get any formal education at school or attend college. As a result, Mabel Williams had to give English, algebra, and other lessons to them at home. Despite her efforts, her two teenage sons, as she had observed, became restless.[18] This kind of situation was not acceptable to Robert or Mabel Williams, who had sought as much schooling as possible for themselves and brought their sons to China in 1964 for a better education.[19] Unwilling to see her sons waste their time in the PRC, Mabel discussed joining forces with David and Nancy Milton in demanding the right to leave the PRC in summer 1968.[20] The two sons were excited when Robert telegrammed Mabel in June 1968, asking her to go to Dar es Salaam immediately to apply for her passport at the American embassy there for their return to the United States.[21]

At the same time, conditions in the United States favored Williams's return. Having signed the Civil Rights Act of 1964 and the Voting Right Act of 1965, President Lyndon Johnson issued an executive order to establish the National Advisory Commission on Civil Disorders in the wake of 1967 urban riots. The commission concluded in its report in 1968 that among the top causes for the disorders were pervasive discrimination and segregation in employment, education, and housing. It recommended that actions be taken to expand opportunities for ghetto residents to participate in the formulation of public policy, recruit more African Americans into the regular police force, and ensure fair promotion for Black officers.[22] It was in this historical context that Johnson appointed Walter Washington the commissioner of Washington, DC, in 1967, making him the first Black mayor of a major city in the United States since 1871. In the same year, Carl Stokes and Richard Hatcher were elected mayor of Cleveland, Ohio, and Gary, Indiana, respectively, becoming the first Black mayors there. This kind of slow but steady improvement for African Americans convinced Williams that it was safe for him to return to the United States and to fight for equal rights for African Americans without an armed revolution.[23]

The softening of Washington's position also made Williams's return to the United States relatively easy. When Williams applied for a passport for his trip back to the United States in Dar es Salaam in the summer of 1968, the FBI was alarmed at the prospects of his assuming a prominent leadership role among African Americans. However, instead of doing everything possible to keep him out of the country as it had done in the past, it sent out repeated instructions to all FBI offices throughout the nation to make sure that neither Mabel Williams nor her two children were arrested or detained when entering the United States.[24] Without any opposition from the FBI, the State Department approved Williams's passport application after a lengthy interview at the American embassy in Dar es Salaam on August 8, 1968.[25] With Mabel Williams also receiving her passport a month after her husband, the Williamses and their two children returned to Tanzania in May 1969 to prepare for their trip back to the United States.[26] In order to make sure that he could bring his household items and documentary films back to the United States, Williams sent a telegram directly to President Nixon on June 28, 1969. Following instructions from the State Department, the American embassy assured Williams that his application for a license to ship his household goods to the United States would receive full and fair consideration in accordance with existing regulation and policies.[27] In addition to relaying the State Department's message, Dwight Burgess, the consul at the American embassy, also wrote in his letter that "to the best of our knowledge, your charge of intimidation and harassment are completely unfounded."[28] Although this comment on Williams's case was not part of the State Department instruction, it must have been encouraging for Williams before he embarked on his homebound journey.

As part of his preparation for his return to the United States, Williams started to tone down his rhetoric on armed revolution after the summer of 1967. After Mao issued another statement to denounce the assassination of Martin Luther King in April 1968, Williams gave an interview to show his support for Mao Zedong but without mentioning armed revolution or guerrilla warfare. His silence on this principal issue received no criticism from CCP leaders who had minced no words in denouncing the nonviolent movement led by Martin Luther King Jr. since the 1950s. Instead, Williams and his family continued to enjoy their VIP treatment, and Beijing even helped him and Mabel travel to Tanzania to apply for and receive their passports for their journey back to the United States. On May 1, 1969, Williams was invited to celebrate International Labor Day at Tiananmen Square. He took the advantage of the event to have both Mao and Lin Biao autograph his copy of *Quotations from Chairman Mao*. Zhou Enlai had a meeting with him and his wife the evening before their departure for the United States (figure 8.1). Having expressed his concern for Williams's safety in the United States, Zhou asked Williams to work for better understanding between the Chinese and American peoples after returning home.[29]

Beijing's acquiescence of Williams's abandonment of armed revolution and Zhou's request for Williams to help improve the American understanding of the PRC revealed CCP leaders' rethinking of their role in the

Figure 8.1 Zhou Enlai meeting with Robert and Mabel Williams before their return to the United States in May 1969.
Source: Robert F. Williams Papers, HS 1094, Bentley Historical Library, University of Michigan, Ann Arbor.

world revolution and their relations with the United States. Mao opposed calling Beijing the center of the world revolution in January 1968, and an order was issued under his instruction on May 18 prohibiting the use of the term in all newspapers, magazines, internal documents, and speeches, especially at meetings with foreign guests.[30] About ten days later, Mao, after reading the Ministry of Foreign Affairs (MFA)'s proposal to strengthen the dissemination of Mao's thought and support for the struggle of the revolutionary masses in Western Europe and North America, instructed officials not to impose their views on other peoples or publicize the people's movements in foreign countries at China's instigation. Mao's instruction was again printed and circulated on June 8, 1968.[31] At a meeting on the Sino-Soviet border clashes on March 22, 1969, Mao recognized that in foreign relations "we are now isolated" and thus proposed that "we need to relax a little."[32] He made that point clear again when he met with the foreign ambassadors in Beijing on top of the Tiananmen on May 1, 1969. He told them that China wanted to improve and develop relations with all countries in the world. Soon after, Beijing began to send ambassadors to foreign countries to restore the function of Chinese embassies that had been interrupted by the Cultural Revolution.[33] Therefore, Williams's decision to return to the United States and shift his focus to legal battles in court fit well with Beijing's changing needs.

With the help of his lawyers and intervention from the State Department, Williams finally landed at the Detroit airport on a special Trans World Airline flight on September 12, 1969.[34] He chose Detroit as his port of entry partly because he could receive political and financial support from the RNA headquarters located there, and partly because he had more confidence on the court system in the state of Michigan, which had led the nation in civil rights reforms in the 1950s and 1960s.[35] As expected, federal agents immediately arrested Williams and took him to the federal court downtown. After a hearing lasted for only seven minutes, he was released by the judge on $1,000 bail and then escorted by an African American deputy sheriff to the Wayne County court nearby, where he was released on a personal recognizance bond of $10,000 with a court hearing scheduled for November 12.[36] Having completed the legal procedures, he met with journalists and about a hundred followers in a nearby motel owned by African Americans. Williams vehemently denied the kidnapping charges against him and vowed to put up a tough fight if the courts decided to return him to North Carolina because people there, he asserted, "are still uncivilized." However, Williams remained vague about the role that he might play in America's Black revolution and was silent on armed revolution or the RNA's commitment to a program of violence. What Williams pledged to do was to "serve the cause of justice and freedom—to help black people in whatever way possible."[37]

The "vagueness" of Williams's role and position quickly evaporated after he and his family settled down in the Detroit area. Although Williams attended a few RNA meetings immediately after his return, he talked only about raising funds for his legal battle and kept silent when some key issues, including the training of RNA forces in the swamps and the purchase of five thousand guns and dynamite, were discussed.[38] After those brief engagements, Williams stayed away from all RNA's activities and refused to receive the records of and briefings on RNA. Then he resigned as its president. In a public announcement on December 3, 1969, Williams made it clear that his resignation was caused by his deep involvement in extradition proceedings, his need for broader support for his legal battles, and his belief in integration rather than separatism in bringing about an ideal society.[39] In private communications with his friends and supporters, Williams tried to alleviate the shock caused by his departure by emphasizing that his decision "did not come about so much from doctrine as it did from the fact that I am busy with my extradition fight."[40]

Besides the publicly announced justifications, other factors also contributed to his quick resignation. One of them was the intensification of infighting among RNA leaders. On October 12, 1969, John Taylor (Mweusi Chui), minister of defense, removed Richard Henry from the chain of command of the Department of Defense and the Black Legion. Richard Henry responded with a long letter asking Taylor to withdraw his order and informing him that RNA citizens in the Midwest region, including officers of the Black Legion and the Ministry of Defense, had been directed not to promulgate his order until further notice.[41] Frustrated and angered by Richard Henry's defiance, his brother Milton Henry first issued an order on behalf of Williams on November 12 to cancel an RNA convention that Henry had scheduled for Thanksgiving weekend without consulting any of his superiors. Days later he issued another executive order to suspend Richard Henry as regional vice president for the Midwest region and as minister of the interior.[42] The intense infighting and the split of the RNA made resignation the preferred choice for Williams. He had already told his close friends before his departure from the PRC that he would "keep out of the internal struggle" and avoid fighting for "leadership the way many others are doing."[43] Another factor was the increasingly more difficult situation he faced at the time. Besides the extradition warrant issued by the governor of Michigan, Williams was also subpoenaed by the Senate Internal Security Subcommittee to appear in its hearings soon after his return. Leaving the RNA allowed him not only to concentrate on the tough legal fight but also to be cooperative with the Senate investigating committee without damaging the RNA, since he did not have much information on its operations.[44]

Free from the infighting as well as the controversial activities of the RNA, Williams devoted most of his time and energy to legal battles against extradition and to his new role as a speaker on China-related issues. Assisted by his capable lawyers, Williams managed to keep himself from being extradited to North Carolina until December 1975. When he finally was forced to return to North Carolina to face the trial, the state dropped all charges against him on January 16, 1976, because its major witness was too physically weak to testify in court.[45] Williams's effort to exonerate himself through legal battles eventually paid off. While going through all the court procedures, Williams, taking advantage of the increasing public interest in the PRC, established himself as an unofficial messenger for Beijing by giving interviews to newspapers, appearing on TV and radio programs, showing documentary films made by the PRC, publishing newspaper articles, meeting with federal government officials, and presenting lectures at schools, colleges, and various civil organizations across the country. Since he had shifted his focus to court battles and resigned from the RNA presidency, China was no longer presented as the strongest supporter for the armed Black revolution in the United States, aimed at destroying its capitalist system. Instead, he tried to make Americans believe that the Chinese were friendly and hardworking people who were building a selfless society and seeking mutual understanding and respect.

Williams started to disseminate information on China long before he returned to the United States. At the request of Moses Newson, executive editor of the *Baltimore Afro-American*, Williams published an article there on April 12, 1969 with the title "Black Militant in Red China Sizes Up 'Cultural Revolution.'"[46] Having received a U.S. government license, Williams sent two documentary films made by the Central Newsreel and Documentary Film Studio of the PRC to WBTV in Charlotte, North Carolina, through the post office while still in Tanzania.[47] One film was on

CCP's recent Ninth National Congress, and the other, titled *Anti China Atrocities of the New Tsars*, provided historical background on and a detailed account of the Sino-Soviet border clashes that took place in March 1969. The TV station managed to have parts of the two films shown on CBS and other mainstream networks.[48] While refusing to give interviews to any journalists in Dar es Salaam, Williams did have a phone conversation with Harry Thayer, deputy director of the State Department's Office of Asian Communist Affairs, for over two hours. It was during this phone conversation that Williams revealed his last meeting with Zhou Enlai the evening before his departure.[49]

Williams's effort to disseminate information on China intensified after he settled down in Detroit. Besides the brief meeting with journalists only hours after his landing there, Williams gave a two-hour long interview to reporters from the *New York Times* and the *Washington Post* two days later. Both newspapers published detailed reports on Williams and his experience in China.[50] At the invitation of Harrison Salisbury, assistant managing editor of the *New York Times*, Williams wrote an article, "On the Platform with Mao Tse-tung," published on February 19, 1971. Williams told his readers that China impressed him "as a variety of worlds with variety of people bound by profound human qualities, some of which the Western world must cultivate if it is to survive." While creating "great wonders of the world," the Chinese people, Williams continued, wanted to know conditions as well as attitudes in the United States and asked when the "American people could be counted on to force U.S. leaders to adopt a more peaceful and sane foreign policy." He concluded that "China is not a fearful dragon of plunder requiring isolation and quarantine," but a plodding dragon making her way toward the top of humanity. Thus, he emphasized that the Chinese, who were manifesting the "greatest human qualities," deserved "understanding and recognition."[51] At the same time, Williams continued to make the documentary films available to colleges and universities. He even signed a contract to have a professional promote the films and handle their reproduction, rental, and sales in the United States.[52]

Williams also managed to stay in the spotlight through delivering numerous lectures and talks on the PRC. His early lectures were given mostly to local schools, colleges, and civil societies because he had to obtain permission from the county court judge for any out-of-state travel. His impressive speeches at the University of Michigan in February 1970 won him a one-year appointment as a consultant at the Center for the Chinese

Studies on a fellowship provided by the Ford Foundation.[53] As his appeals for his case became routine, he was able to gain the necessary approvals for his frequent out-of-state trips, making it possible for him to deliver lectures throughout the country. In his speech at Rutgers University in April 1970, Williams, appearing in his Mao suit, told the audience that the Chinese society was clean and wholesome and that the Chinese people "live unmolested and without fear, free from drug abuse." A local reporter also noticed that "the rhetoric of violence was totally absent" from his talk. Instead, Williams called upon African Americans to learn from the Chinese to "put collective good above individual good" and change themselves before they tried to change the system. He asserted that "as a matter of peaceful coexistence, a matter of survival, Western people must respect China."[54] These lectures helped Williams win broader support for his legal battle—and considerable income. For example, he received a $600 honorarium for his talk at the Rutgers University in addition to the coverage of his travel and lodging expenses. After his speech, Gwendolyn Hall, an assistant professor of history, sent letters to James Brickley, the lieutenant governor of Michigan, urging a review and reversal of Governor William Milliken's decision to extradite Williams.[55]

While busy with public speaking obligations, Williams kept his communications with the U.S. government, especially the State Department, open. Deeply impressed and intrigued by Williams's meeting with Zhou before his departure from China, Paul H. Kreisberg, director of the Office of Asian Communist Affairs, wrote to Williams in December 1969 requesting a meeting so that he could hear about Williams's experiences in China and Beijing's attitude toward the United States. He informed Williams that Secretary of State William Rogers "has indicated on several occasions that the United States seeks to improve understanding and reduce tensions between people of China and the United States."[56] While it is uncertain when or whether the meeting between the two took place, Williams did have a four-hour in-person meeting with Thayer on January 12, 1970. Williams took the opportunity to volunteer his insights into Chinese attitudes and his recommendations on how to "facilitate more profitable dealings with them." Williams recommended that the United States stop pushing its status as the great "Pacific power, dismantle American bases on the China periphery, offer conciliatory gestures specifically in trade and travel, and reduce "the public references to our connection with Taiwan." Williams's recommendations and insights made Thayer believed that he "looks at Sino-U.S. relations from Chinese viewpoint" and that he "does represent a possible channel that we should, with caution, exploit as opportunities arise."[57] Although Washington never used Williams as an official channel to engage the Chinese leaders, he kept playing the role as a tireless and imposing messenger for the PRC throughout the rapprochement.

Entertaining More Guests

As Robert Williams and his family settled down in Detroit, both Washington and Beijing worked hard to find ways to reduce tension between the two nations so that they could better cope with the increasing threat from the Soviet Union. In addition to restarting the ambassadorial talks in Warsaw and employing foreign leaders as intermediaries, Beijing and Washington took steps to reestablish cultural contacts between the two peoples as part of their effort to normalize the U.S.-China relations. As soon as Washington repealed its travel ban on China, Mao decided to invite the USTTT for a visit in April 1971. In the following months, Beijing granted more visas to an unprecedentedly large number of American visitors and welcomed many scientists, journalists, scholars, students, and doctors from the United States. Through hosting these American visitors with diverse backgrounds, Beijing signaled that it was ready to open China's doors to American guests even though the Taiwan issue was not yet resolved and the nation was still in the middle of "cleansing." This reversal was mostly driven by Beijing's desperate need to reduce the tension in its relations with the United States so that it would not have to fight two superpowers in a major war that CCP leaders perceived to be imminent.

The 1960s witnessed the escalation of confrontation between the PRC and the Soviet Union. When the Chinese Communist leaders publicized the fight between Beijing and Moscow over many issues in early 1960, Khrushchev recalled all 1,500 Soviet experts from China, ending 343 contracts and supplementary contracts and stopping 257 projects on scientific and technical cooperation, including research on and production of nuclear weapons.[58] As Beijing intensified its attack on the Soviet revisionism, Moscow countered with help from other Communist parties in the world, which not only led to the formal split of the Communist camp but also further isolated the PRC. While fighting over the direction and leadership of the international Communist movement, Moscow increased its forces along the Sino-Soviet border, turning an ideological feud into a military showdown. After signing the Treaty of Friendship, Cooperation and Mutual Assistance with Mongolia in January 1966, Moscow sent mechanized troops to its neighbor immediately. The massive Russian military presence along China's long northern frontier, with stretch of it less than four hundred miles from Beijing, led to more than four thousand clashes with Chinese forces. The bloody battles between the Chinese and Soviet soldiers on Zhenbao Island in Heilongjiang Province in March 1969, the annihilation of a Chinese platoon by Soviet troops in the Tielieketi region in Xinjiang on August 13, and the well-publicized Soviet contemplation of a strike on Chinese nuclear facilities later that year made top CCP leaders, especially Mao, believe that a war with the Soviet Union, now their greatest enemy, was imminent.[59]

CCP leaders responded to the Soviet threat with military preparation and foreign policy adjustment. Right after the battles on Zhenbao Island, Mao asked Chen Yi and three other marshals to research the international situation. After many intense discussions, they presented two reports to Mao through Zhou in July and September respectively. In their first report, which was printed and circulated among CCPCC leaders, the marshals pointed out that the Soviet Union treated the PRC as its archenemy and thus posed a greater threat to China's security than the United States. Their second report was completed after the Soviet attack in Xinjiang and the issuance of an order by CCPCC to troops and civilians along the northern border to prepare for war. Alerted by the Soviet military deployment along the Chinese border and encouraged by Nixon's early signals at improving the Sino-American relations, they recommended flexibility in tactics and the resumption of the ambassadorial talks if Washington requested it. Chen Yi went even further, proposing to reinitiate the request for high-level talks with no preconditions.[60] Mao's approval in late 1969 and early 1970 of the resumption of the ambassadorial talks and the reception of an American representative in Beijing largely mirrored the proposals from the marshals, especially Chen Yi.[61] Afraid of a sudden Soviet attack on Beijing on October 1, Mao issued an order on September 19 instructing all provincial leaders and army officers not to come to the capital for the celebration of the twentieth anniversary of the CCP's victory in the civil war. Although no Soviet attack took place on the National Day and Moscow agreed to start talks on border issues with Beijing, Mao still sent most senior leaders out of Beijing in mid-October to keep them safe from a Soviet invasion. When Lin Biao issued an order on October 17 to put all military forces on alert without seeking Mao's approval, Mao suppressed his anger and let the war preparations go ahead.[62]

The aggravating threat from the Soviet Union was also felt by President Nixon, who had worked to improve relations with Beijing since his first day in office. In his inaugural address on January 20, 1969, Nixon stated that "We seek an open world—open to ideas, open to exchange of goods and people—a world in which no people, great or small, will live in angry isolation."[63] A few days later, he instructed Henry Kissinger, his advisor for National Security Affairs, to "give every encouragement to the attitude that the administration was exploring possibilities of rapprochement with the Chinese."[64] Following Nixon's order, on February 5 Kissinger asked the secretary of state, secretary of defense, and director of the Central Intelligence Agency to prepare a study on U.S. policy toward China. They were specifically instructed to include "alternative views and interpretations of the issues involved."[65] On September 15, Nixon met with Walter Stoessel, the American ambassador to Poland, in the White House, asking him to find a way to pass a message to the Chinese chargé at Warsaw. Stoessel and his aide managed to chase down a couple of Chinese diplomats in late November and passed Nixon's message to Lei Yang in early December.[66] With a quick and positive response from Beijing, the ambassadorial talks resumed on January 20, 1970. Stoessel informed Wang Bingnan, his Chinese counterpart, at the 135th meeting that Washington was considering sending a representative to Beijing for direct discussions on any subjects agreed upon by both sides.[67] Wang, with Mao's approval, responded at the 136th meeting on February 20 that Beijing was willing to receive a ministerial representative or a presidential envoy from the United States.[68]

Despite the early agreement reached at Warsaw, Beijing and Washington quickly lost their only official channel for communication when the ambassadorial talks were interrupted again by the American invasion of Cambodia at the end of April. Mao approved postponing the 137th meeting in Warsaw three days before he publicly denounced the American escalation of the war.[69] Despite the postponement, Beijing continued its effort to improve relations with the United States. Extremely isolated, Mao turned to his old friend Edgar Snow for help. Having ignored Snow's requests for another visit to China, mostly because of his criticism of the cult of personality surrounding Mao, the Chinese government urged him and his wife to visit China as soon as possible.⁷⁰ As usual, the MFA kept a close eye on Snow and was not happy when he held on to his belief that "absolute power leads to absolute corruption" and insisted on paying at least the basic cost of his travel.⁷¹ However, the MFA justified its reception of Snow by emphasizing its significance in propagating the success of the Cultural Revolution, winning over the American people, establishing a broader united front, and opposing and isolating American imperialism. The MFA also reminded all the officials involved in his reception that since Snow understood some Chinese, they should not conduct any "private talks" in front of him or show him any big-character posters (*dazibao*) unsuitable for foreigners to see.⁷²

Despite his poor health and the heated struggle within the CCP at the time, Zhou met with Snow many times and made sure that his visit would be fully utilized. At his first meeting with Snow, Zhou asked many detailed questions about the United States. When Snow inquired about the possibility of the two countries' taking a new step forward in their relations, Zhou confessed that he and his colleagues were trying to find an answer to that question and that Snow's visit was part of the effort. After sending Snow and his wife to observe two operations with acupuncture anesthesia at the Fandi (Anti-Imperialism) Hospital, formally the Union Hospital, in Beijing, Zhou invited them to view the National Day parade on top of the Tiananmen on October 1.⁷³ During the celebration, Mao asked Zhou to move Snow to his side, and the two talked in the middle of the rostrum for about forty minutes. The photo of Mao and Snow on the Tiananmen was published in the front page of *People's Daily* on December 25 (figure 8.2). As Mao told Huang Hua, who was asked by Zhou to host Snow, the meeting was part of the signal "meant to test the intentions of the U.S."⁷⁴

Mao sent clearer and more substantive signals at his meeting with Snow on December 18. At Mao's request, the focus of their conversation was on the "international situation."⁷⁵ After defending the practice of the cult of personality in China by likening it to the popular support received by politicians in the United States, Mao quickly turned to the topic of Nixon and uttered his preference for Nixon's rise to power. He specifically told Snow that if Nixon "wants to come to Beijing, you can pass a message to him that he can secretly, not publicly, come here in an airplane." He also wanted Nixon to know that it would be all right whether their talk was a success

Figure 8.2 Mao Zedong chatting with Edgar Snow on the Tiananmen on October 1, 1970. Ji Chaozhu, who returned to China from the United States in 1950, was standing behind them serving as their interpreter. The photo was published by *People's Daily* on December 25, 1970, signaling Beijing's intention to reduce tension in its relations with the United States.
Source: Xinhuashe (New China News Agency), Beijing, China.

or not. Mao even directed the MFA, in Snow's presence, to change its policy so that Americans from the left, middle, and right could all visit China. He explained that Nixon should be allowed to come to China even though he represented the monopolistic capitalists because problems between the two countries could be solved only with the conservatives. In order to make it easy for Nixon, Mao barely mentioned Taiwan and blamed Truman and Eisenhower for the Taiwan problem.[76] Mao's message revealed his strong desire to meet with Nixon and reduce tensions in Sino-American relations through direct negotiations at the highest level. In order to prepare Chinese officials and people for the dramatic changes in its policy toward the United States, the CCPCC widely disseminated the transcripts of Mao's conversation with Snow.[77]

Despite Beijing's thoughtful arrangements and high expectations, Snow was not that effective as a messenger. He did publish a few reports on his trip in newspapers and magazines in Europe while he was in China. However, Mao's invitation to Nixon was not made publicly known until the end of April 1971, when Snow's "A Conversation with Mao Tse-tung" appeared in *Life*.[78] By that time, Zhou had already sent oral as well as written messages to Nixon through Pakistani President Yahya Khan informing him of the Chinese leaders' decision to receive a special representative of Nixon or Nixon himself in Beijing for high-level discussions.[79] Snow's efficiency as a messenger was undermined by Beijing as well as himself. The famous photo of Mao and Snow atop Tiananmen was not that special since many similar pictures of Mao and other American visitors, including Du Bois, Williams, and Strong, had been published throughout the 1960s. Snow was also forced to extend his stay in China for weeks after his last interview with Mao to wait for the transcripts of his conversations with Mao and Zhou to be reviewed and approved for publication. Eventually, he had to leave China in early February without Zhou's material, which had to be forwarded to his home in Switzerland later. In order to guarantee the accuracy of his report on Mao's statements, Snow insisted that no changes be made without his approval. This not only led to rejection by the *New York Times* but also made it difficult for him to negotiate with other publishers, further delaying the publication of his conversation with Mao in the United States.[80]

Encouraged by the positive response from Beijing, Nixon and his administration quickly took additional measures to improve the relations between the two nations. The State Department relaxed its travel restriction on the PRC in July 1969 for scholars, students, scientists, physicians, and journalists. In 1970, the State Department validated 270 passports for U.S. citizens who desired to go to the PRC, and the number went up to a thousand by early 1971.[81] In his *Annual Foreign Policy Report* issued on February 25, 1971, Nixon promised that he would carefully examine what further steps that the United States "might take to create broader opportunities for contacts between the Chinese and American peoples."[82] A few weeks later, he ordered that all travel restrictions on China be removed.[83] As a result, the road to the PRC was cleared for all U.S. citizens, at least from the American side.

Although secret as well as open invitations to Nixon were issued, Beijing was slow to open the door to other Americans. Among 830-plus Americans who had applied, only very few received visas to enter mainland China.[84] Snow was able to go to the PRC mostly because of his direct plea to Mao. With Mao's direct intervention, Snow was invited as a "friendly person" (*youhao renshi*) instead of as a journalist or writer because Beijing wanted to avoid the appearance of accepting the new State Department policy on travel restriction.[85] Even Yang Zhenning, the famous Nobel Prize laureate, was not allowed to visit his parents in Shanghai. The only special treatment that he received was an arrangement made with Zhou's approval for his parents to go to Hong Kong so that they could meet there.[86] When the MFA, following Mao's instruction, finally worked out a plan to invite some thirty Americans to visit China in 1971, it made sure that most of them were friendly progressives and reputable centrists, including just a few helpful rightists. Mao approved the plan and emphasized that no invitations should be given to anyone who had not applied for a visa to China.[87] The MFA, still in shambles because of the Cultural Revolution, was slow in implementing its own plan.

It was the visit of the USTTT that finally swung the door to the PRC open to a large number of American visitors. However, the visit of the American ping-pong players was anything but "meticulously planned" or "vintage Chou En-lai," as Kissinger asserted in his memoir.[88] In reality, Zhou had trouble getting Chinese players to participate in the Thirty-First World Table Tennis Championships tournament in Nagoya, Japan, in early 1971. Besides strong opposition from the CCP's ultraleftist leaders and Beijing's ally, Cambodia, most players believed that the Chinese team should not go to the tournament based on political considerations. Zhou had to hold a long meeting with the team to persuade the officials and players to go to the event.[89] Chinese participation was finalized with the strong support of Mao, who also reviewed and approved the plan submitted by the Chinese team. According to that plan, Chinese players and officials would not initiate conversation with the Americans. However, Chinese players were allowed to shake hands with American players at the matches. In his farewell meeting with the team, Zhou did not even mention the Americans. He asked the team only to avoid being imposing in conducting propaganda to foreigners and to discuss whether they should always hold a copy of *Quotations from Chairman Mao* while in Japan.[90] It was based on Zhou's advice that the Chinese players and officials did not hold the *Little Red Book* in their hands at all times, making it easier for them to interact with foreign players.

Once in Japan, Chinese players and officials strictly followed the rules and did not initiate contacts with the Americans. However, they did engage in conversation after the American players greeted them. On March 30, Song Zhong, the head of the Chinese delegation, had two short conversations with Graham Steenhoven, his American counterpart. Steenhoven told Song that the U.S. government had just repealed the travel ban on the PRC and expressed his regret that the American ping-pong players had missed the Twenty-Sixth World Table Tennis Championships held in China in 1961 because of that ban. He hoped that the USTTT could have the opportunity to compete in the PRC in the future. The Chinese team officials, under direct orders from Mao, not only reported their activities in Japan several times a day but also concluded after deep analysis that the USTTT truly wanted to visit China. They sent their assessment to Beijing and sought clear instructions on the matter.[91] The initial response from the MFA and the Chinese National Sports Commission (CNSC) was negative because they believed that it was politically disadvantageous to let the American ping-pong players visit China before American leftists and other influential figures did. Fully aware of the ministry's existing plan and Mao's approval of it, Zhou concurred with the report on April 4 and forwarded it to Mao. However, he did request that the Chinese officials in Japan get an address for the American delegation and inform the Americans of the PRC's clear position on Taiwan.[92] It was obvious that Zhou wanted to have the opportunity to invite the American team later and at the same time protect himself by demonstrating his consistent position on Taiwan.

The report from the MFA and the CNSC presented a thorny problem even for Mao. He kept the report on his desk for two days and finally signed off on it on the evening of April 6. During those two days he paid close attention to the tournament and ordered the Chinese delegation to increase its reporting from three times to five times a day. He was especially impressed by the latest reports on the interaction between Chinese player Zhuang Zedong and American athlete Glenn Cowen. Zhuang not only responded to Cowen's greeting after he got on the Chinese team's bus on April 4 but also presented a small gift to Cowen, who returned with a T-shirt the next day. Mao praised Zhuang for his diplomatic skills in handling the situation. Having taken his sleeping medicine late in the evening on April 6, Mao suddenly instructed Wu Xujun, his head nurse, to inform the MFA to invite the USTTT to visit China. After clear and repeated confirmations from Mao, Wu passed his order to the MFA at the midnight.

The MFA first forwarded Mao's order to Zhou and then immediately instructed the Chinese delegation in Nagoya to invite the American team to visit China.[93] It was Mao's last-minute reversal of his own decision that made it possible for the USTTT to become the first large group of Americans to pay a legal visit to the PRC since 1949.

Once the invitation was issued, Zhou worked hard to make sure that the American visitors were warmly received, even though that inevitably clashed with the predominant anti-American sentiment throughout the nation at the time. Before the Americans crossed the Luohu Bridge between Hong Kong and Shenzhen on April 10, 1971, Zhou asked the leading official of the Chinese People's Association for Friendship with Foreign Nations (CPAFFN) to have dinner with the American guests. Later that day, Zhou ordered the necessary arrangements to be made so that the American visitors could watch *The Red Detachment of Women*, a popular modern ballet in China during the Cultural Revolution. On the second day, he told Ding Xiling, who was hosting the exhibit competitions between the Chinese and American teams, that the audience must be informed that they should clap during the event and the Chinese team should not win all the games. As a result, the first exhibition matches ended with the Chinese team winning four games out of seven, demonstrating the spirit of "friendship first and competition second." He also reviewed and approved the public announcements prepared by the TV and radio stations before their live broadcasts, making sure that they were warm and positive.[94] It was under Zhou's clear and detailed instructions that the American team were warmly welcomed not only in exhibit matches but also in their visits to Qinghua University, the industrial museum, a people's commune, the Summer Palace, Tiananmen Square, and the Great Wall, setting an example for hosting American guests and sending out an assuring message to future American visitors.

The apex of USTTT's visit to China was its meeting with Zhou on April 14. Although the conversation was relatively short, Zhou managed to send clear signals to American officials and people. First, Zhou greeted the American guests as friends of the Chinese people with a short quotation from Confucius. Then he assured them that their visit was just a beginning and that more Americans would have opportunities to come to China. When Cowen inquired his view toward American hippies and their movement, Zhou skillfully demonstrated his grandfatherly tolerance by characterizing the movement as a truth-seeking effort and expressing his support for them. At the end, Zhou pointed out that the Chinese and the American peoples used to have frequent exchanges in the past. Without elaborating on what or who was responsible for the long interruption in recent decades, Zhou praised the American ping-pong players for "opening the door for the friendly exchange between the two nations."[95] Through this brief meeting, Zhou made it clear that Beijing was ready to open China's door to more Americans with diverse backgrounds.

Actually, Beijing started doing so by admitting a small group of American journalists with the USTTT on April 10. Although their visas allowed them to cover only the exhibition tour of the USTTT, they became the first group of American journalists to visit the PRC since the late 1950s. The three American journalists who went with the USTTT included John Roderick of AP and John Rich and Jack Reynolds of NBC. Rich was the Far East Division chief and Reynolds the head of news satellite broadcasts in Saigon and Tokyo. Rich had applied for a visa to enter China every three months for the previous nine years.[96] Assisted by two Japanese technicians, they became the first American TV crew to visit the PRC. Zhou quickly sought out Roderick at the beginning of the meeting with the USTTT and acknowledged him as an old acquaintance. Recognizing that many American reporters wanted to come to China, Zhou told Roderick that they should be able to come in groups. At the end of the meeting, Zhou turned to Roderick again and praised him for opening the door.[97] Although flattering and friendly, Zhou's compliment was misplaced, since the door was actually opened by Beijing.

Following the American ping-pong players and journalists, a slew of Americans with diverse backgrounds were invited to visit the PRC, far exceeding the number originally planned by the MFA. Inspired by the USTTT's visit to China, Arthur W. Galston and Ethan Signer, two well-known biologists from Yale University and the Massachusetts Institute of Technology respectively, sent their visa applications to the Chinese embassy in Ottawa and received approvals from Beijing while visiting North Vietnam. They immediately left Hanoi for Guangzhou and arrived in Beijing on May 13. Zhou met with them on May 19 and told them that they were especially welcome in China because of their strong opposition to the American war in Indochina.[98] Zhou also tried to quash the fear that Americans had for the PRC by reminding them that the Pacific, while a small pond for the Americans, was still a huge ocean for the Chinese to cross.[99] Zhou emphasized that China, as a weak nation, "had no desire to become a superpower or send soldiers abroad." The two scientists passed these messages to the American public through a report published by the *New York Times* only days after their meeting.[100] As the first American scientists visiting China since 1949, Galston and Signer played a key role in promoting the exchange of scientists by giving high praise to the reception received in China and helping the Federation of American Scientists organize its first delegation to visit the PRC the following year.[101]

Following the MFA's plan, more American journalists were invited to visit China in summer 1971. Seymour Topping, assistant managing editor of the *New York Times*, and James Reston, its famous columnist, received their visas at the same time in May. Topping entered China on May 20 and Reston went later in July to extend the paper's coverage of China as long as possible. Right before his departure from China, Topping and his wife, Audrey Ronning, a photojournalist and daughter of the retired Canadian diplomat Chester Ronning, flew back from Guangzhou to Beijing for a dinner meeting with Zhou. After waiting in their hotel for three days, Topping joined William Atwood, president and publisher of the *Daily News*, and Robert Keatley, chief State Department correspondent of the *Wall Street Journal*, all of whom had worked in China before 1949, for dinner with Zhou in the Great Hall of the People. Zhou, after apologizing for recalling Topping from Guangzhou, praised the *New York Times* for its recent publication of the Pentagon Papers despite strenuous opposition from the U.S. government. He claimed that the publication was "not only in the interest of the United States, but of the whole world."[102]

Again Zhou took the opportunity of his dinner meeting with influential American journalists to send important messages on some major issues. In response to a comment made by Topping on the importance of China in the world, Zhou emphasized that China "is comparatively important, not so very important." He also pledged that "China will never become a superpower" because a superpower had to strive for hegemony and compete with other superpowers, which would bring about opposition from the people.[103] Obviously Zhou was trying to tell his guests and the American public that the PRC was not an enemy of or even a competitor with the United States. When Atwood asked what the U.S. government could do to remove Taiwan as a barrier to improving relations with the PRC over the next six months, Zhou refused to accept a time limit or speak for Washington. However, he did tell Atwood that the PRC wanted the United States to stop its interference in Chinese domestic politics, withdraw all its military forces from Taiwan and the Taiwan Strait, and respect the sovereignty, independence, and territorial integrity of the PRC. Once this issue was resolved, Zhou asserted, Beijing would establish diplomatic relations with the United States.[104] Similar messages were also conveyed during his long interview with Reston in early August. Zhou emphasized that China was not a major nuclear power yet and promised that it would conduct limited tests only when necessary.[105] The *New York Times* published a transcript of Reston's recorded interview with Zhou in toto under the premier's request and authorization.[106]

Zhou never hid Beijing's purpose for inviting American visitors, especially reporters, and most of the Americans willingly cooperated in accepting the arrangements made by their hosts and publicizing the messages from the Chinese. Zhou told Topping and other American journalists that how soon he could visit the United States depended on the efforts of both sides, but especially on them in mobilizing public opinion.[107] Topping, like those who went to China before and after him, let their hosts decide how long they should stay, whom they could see, where they could go, and what they should do in China. For example, Topping and his peers at the dinner with Zhou agreed to allow Ma, an MFA official, to check direct quotes in their dispatches against the Chinese transcript prepared by the secretary at the table. Topping went to the MFA with his dispatch at 1:00 a.m., hoping that he could get it cleared on the spot. However, Ma told him that his copy would not be cleared until next afternoon. Topping had to wait for another day until all the dispatches were cleared even though the Chinese required no corrections.[108] It is obvious that the procedure that had been followed by Snow and Strong since the 1930s remained in place for the visiting American journalists in the 1970s.

Besides scientists and journalists, many friendly Americans, including young China scholars, the Progressive Labor Party leaders, and African American civil rights activists, were invited to visit the PRC. About the same time when Topping started his return trip, the Committee of Concerned Asian Scholars (CCAS) delegation entered the PRC. The delegation was made of nine graduate students doing research on China in Hong Kong and four brought their wives with them. They applied for visas right after the USTTT went to the PRC as members of CCAS without consulting headquarters. Their applications were approved in early June mostly because of the well-known position of the CCAS against the Vietnam War and U.S. support for the Nationalist regime in Taiwan. They were able to start their trip on short notice partly because all the applicants were already in Hong Kong and partly because all the expenses for their month-long visit were fully covered by their host, the Chinese People's Association of Cultural Relations with Foreign Nations (CPACRFN).[109] Although unhappy with their "self-arranged" visit to the North Vietnamese embassy in Beijing, Zhou still met with them on July 19. He made it clear that the PRC, while interested in normalizing its relations with the United States, believed that the withdrawal of American forces from Indochina was more important. However, he insisted at the same time that there were no preconditions set for Nixon's visit to the PRC, which had been announced just a few days earlier. With clearance from the MFA, the CCAS released the content of Zhou's talk to the media and the public the next day, sending Zhou's messages to Hanoi and Washington.[110]

Shortly after the CCAS delegation returned to Hong Kong, another group of seventeen Americans, mostly youths, started a longer visit to the PRC. They were led by Carmelita Hinton, mother of Joan Hinton, who had been working in the PRC with her husband before the CCP came to power. Arriving in Beijing in late September, they were invited to participate in the traditional National Day celebration and join with many other American visitors and permanent residents in meeting with Zhou Enlai on October 5. Having visited her daughter for over half a year from 1962 to 1963, Carmelita Hinton had won the trust of Beijing.[111] Thus, her group was given more freedom in designing its own itinerary. The members worked out an arrangement with their host that allowed them to work one month in Dazhai, a model village in Shanxi, hike for a month with some young Chinese, and engage in various other activities in the Beijing area for another month. Since there were four African Americans in the group, their unusually long stay also gave the host the opportunity to gather more information on African American organizations and explain why Nixon was invited to visit China and why Mao was always right.[112] Just as they were doing at home, the CCP had to justify its foreign policy change and at the same time maintain Mao's infallibility among his American followers.

A number of well-known African American civil rights leaders were also invited to the PRC before its National Day. William Leo Epton Jr., a Progressive Labor Party leader and civil rights activist, was one of them. Like many other American visitors, he was sent to visit Yanan right after his arrival. He told his host that he was greatly inspired after walking through the long river of the Chinese revolution and that he would share what he had seen to the American people. He also vowed that African Americans would listen to Chairman Mao to avoid various mistakes. However, his hosts did not push him toward armed revolution as they had done to many other African American activists in the past.[113] Hosea Williams, a close friend of Martin Luther King Jr. and leader of the Southern Christian Leadership Conference, had a similar experience. Although Beijing regarded the Southern Christian Leadership Conference as a right-wing organization known for its commitment to nonviolence, it still invited him because he wanted to learn about the origins of the Chinese revolution, land reform, the educational revolution, and interpersonal relations among the Chinese people. In its reception plan submitted to the MFA, the CCP-DWP proposed to show China's support for Williams's fight against racial discrimination, saying that when he talked about his nonviolence principle he should be informed of Beijing's position without imposing it on him. Since the CCPCC approved his visit, the CCPDWP recommended that all expenses incurred after his arrival in China be covered. However, it suggested that his request to present a gift to Chairman Mao in person should be turned down gently and his desire to establish formal relations with a Chinese organization, if he proposed to do so, should be rejected too.[114]

Huey Newton's visit to China in 1971 gave Beijing another opportunity to demonstrate clearly that it had stopped pushing for armed revolution in the United States. As the founder of the Black Panther Party and strong advocate of armed struggle, Newton was invited to visit China in 1970. Unable to make the trip that year, Newton, accompanied by Elaine Brown, finally went to Beijing in late September 1971. Newton and Brown were given the honor of meeting with Zhou Enlai and participating in the National Day celebration in Beijing. However, unlike Du Bois or Williams, Newton did not meet with Mao, the highest honor bestowed on foreign visitors. Unaware of the deep political crisis the CCP was facing at the time, Newton spent ten days in the country marveling at the classless society.[115] Although Newton refused to reveal details about his meeting with Zhou, he did declare immediately after his return to San Francisco on October 8 that the Black Panther Party would enter electoral politics. He openly told the media that his decision was inspired by China's entry into the United Nations.[116] Newton's announcement sent another clear message for Beijing that the PRC was no longer an inspiration or driving force for armed revolution in the United States.

Of course, Beijing's hosting of American guests culminated with the visit of President Nixon in February 1972. He arrived in China not only with many government officials, including Henry Kissinger and William Rogers, but also with eighty-seven reporters, the largest group of American visitors received by the PRC since its founding.[117] Just hours after arriving at Diaoyutai State Guest Houses, Nixon and Kissinger were called for a meeting with Mao at his residence. Having given a brief review of the U.S.-China relations, Mao made a rare self-criticism, recognizing that he was wrong in the past ten-plus years when he rejected the American proposal for exchange visits of people by insisting that there would be no solution to small issues without first resolving the big ones. He told Nixon that "you are right, and thus [we] played ping-pong."[118] Although Mao also recognized that he knew very little about the United States and asked Nixon to send some instructors, especially history and geography instructors, to China, the Politburo did not include cultural exchange in its eight-point principles adopted to guide China's negotiation with the United States.[119] It was because of the strong request from the American officials and, more important, Mao's praise for the interaction of the ping-pong players that Chinese officials agreed to turn their one brief and noncommittal sentence on cultural exchange into a paragraph in the communiqué.[120] As a result, the two sides, after listing their different positions on numerous issues in the joint communiqué issued in Shanghai on February 27, 1972, agreed that it "is desirable to broaden the understanding between the two peoples," recognized that "people-to-people contacts and exchanges would be mutually beneficial" in the fields of science, technology, culture, sports, and journalism, and vowed that "each side undertakes to facilitate the further development of such contacts and exchanges."[121] Finally, both governments were ready to resume their role as facilitators for cultural exchange between the two nations.

Establishing New Exchanges

Given the deep differences on many major issues, the agreement reached by Beijing and Washington on contacts and exchanges became the highlight of Nixon's visit to China. In his address at the welcome ceremony in Washington, DC, on February 28, Nixon acknowledged that he did not bring back any agreements that would guarantee peace. However, he emphasized that he did reestablish communication with the PRC and made some necessary and important beginnings. The first thing he mentioned was "the agreements to expand cultural, educational, and journalistic contacts between the Chinese and the American people."[122] In order to implement that agreement, Nixon immediately instructed the National Security Council to conduct a study on "the ways in which the U.S.-PRC exchange in the fields such as science, technology, culture, sports, and journalism, agreed on the joint United States-PRC Communique, can be facilitated."[123]

The return visit of the Chinese ping-pong players provided an opportunity for both Beijing and Washington to demonstrate their commitment to establishing cultural ties between the two nations. Although Zhou made sure that the Chinese National Table Tennis Team (CNTTT) received the invitation to visit the United States from Steenhoven at their meeting in April 1971, he waited until early January 1972 to ask Ron Ziegler, the White House press secretary, who was in Beijing preparing for Nixon's visit to the PRC, to inform the USTTA that the Chinese team was ready to pay its return visit in the spring.[124] Mao's mention of the exchange of the ping-pong players in his meeting with Nixon further illustrated the importance of the CNTTT's visit.[125] Within a couple of weeks after his return from the PRC, Kissinger met with officials from the National Committee on United States-China Relations (NCUSCR) to check whether enough funds were raised to cover the CNTTT's visit. Both Nixon and Kissinger assigned aides to work with U.S. Table Tennis Association and the NCUSCR in planning the itinerary for the Chinese team. It was the White House's direct involvement that thawed the attempt from the right-wing organizations to invite the Taiwan Table Tennis Team for a visit at the same time and forced the State Department to provide security service for the Chinese team.[126]

With careful planning and preparation under close supervision from both governments, the Chinese ping-pong players finally set feet on American soil on April 12, 1972. Zhou reviewed and approved the report from the MFA and the CNSC on the CNTTT's visit to the United States as well as Canada after adding a few famous players to the team.[127] As the first group of PRC visitors since 1949, the Chinese players toured Detroit, Ann Arbor, Williamsburg, Washington, New York City, Memphis, and Los Angeles. Wherever they went they visited schools and colleges and had friendly matches with local students. They were also invited to meet with President Nixon at the White House on April 18. Nixon welcomed the

Chinese players and pointed out in his remarks that "the big winner, because of this people-to-people contact that you are initiating between our two peoples, will be friendship between the people of the United States and the people of the People's Republic of China" (figure 8.3).[128] Nixon was unaware that Mao's direct intervention had saved his meeting with the Chinese team at the last minute. After the U.S. bombing of Hanoi and Haiphong on April 16, Zhou had called an emergency meeting before dawn on April 18 and reported to Mao the attendees' proposal to cancel the CNTTT's meeting with Nixon in the White House on that day. Mao immediately met with Zhou and ordered the Chinese team to stick to its original itinerary. Mao pointed out that the CNTTT's visit to the United States was unofficial and that it would leave a bad impression on the American people if the Chinese team refused to meet with Nixon after the American athletes had met with the Chinese leaders during their visit the year before. Following Mao's decision, the Chinese players went on to meet with Nixon and tour the White House as planned.[129]

Figure 8.3 President Richard Nixon greeting members of the Chinese National Table Tennis Team on the lawn of the White House, Washington, DC, on April 18, 1972. *Source*: U.S. News & World Report magazine photograph collection, Prints and Photographs Division, Library of Congress, Washington, DC, https://www.loc.gov/item/2015647169/.

Once the door for cultural exchange was reopened, more than ten thousand American and seven hundred Chinese scientists, scholars, journalists, athletes, doctors, artists, students crisscrossed the Pacific between 1971 and 1979, becoming pioneers of new cultural interactions between the two nations. Although Beijing insisted that all the exchange programs had to be implemented by the nongovernmental organizations because there were no diplomatic relations between the two countries, the exchanges were actually coordinated and controlled by the government. Since the government-coordinated exchanges were generally reciprocal, the number of Americans and Chinese involved in those exchanges was relatively small. Most Americans went to China through direct negotiation with PRC agencies or American organizations with friendly relations with the PRC, which had little concern for reciprocity. Since Washington did not have any meaningful control over cultural exchange once the travel ban against the PRC was lifted, Beijing imposed most of the restrictions on the exchanges. It was at Beijing's insistence that all the exchange programs remained "unofficial" in nature, focused mostly on science and technology, and lasted for about a month. As in the previous decades, the visits of the Americans were carefully planned and closely supervised, and the Chinese leaders were more interested in showing off their achievements and sending their messages than in American culture per se.

Beijing's position on U.S.-China cultural relations was shaped by its conflicting needs in the 1970s. On the one hand, the Chinese Communist leaders wanted to expand direct contact with the American people to win their support for the normalization of the diplomatic relations between the two nations and a satisfactory solution to the Taiwan issue. On the other hand, they still held on to Mao's revolutionary ideology and were committed to maintaining the CCP's absolute control over the state, society, and culture. Thus, they entered cultural contacts and exchange with the United States not because they really appreciated American ideals and values but because they had to work with the Americans to cope with the imminent threat of war with the Soviet Union. Thus, it was only natural for them to do everything possible to limit cultural exchanges so that they could prevent the influx of bourgeois ideas and practices and maintain their tight control over ideology and culture at home. As a result, the Sino-American cultural contacts and exchanges in the 1970s were anything but a simple restoration of the old cultural ties built before 1949 or a product shaped by the U.S.-Soviet, U.S.-Taiwan, and U.S.-Hong Kong cultural interactions in the 1950s and the 1960s.[130]

All cultural exchanges between the two nations before 1979 were unofficial, at least in name, as Beijing demanded. Although it was Mao who made the final decision to invite the American ping-pong players to visit China and all the expenses incurred during their visit were covered by the PRC government, the formal invitation to the USTTT was issued by the Chinese Table Tennis Association, a so-called nongovernmental organization. Following this precedent, all American science, educational, technological, medicine, athletic, and art delegations were invited and hosted by the CAS, the China Association for Science and Technology (CAST), the CPAFFN, and other national institutions or organizations with nongovernmental facades. It was never a secret in China that all these institutions and organizations were part of the state apparatus, fully funded and staffed by the government. Thus, Beijing's insistence on the nongovernmental nature of all the Sino-American cultural exchanges was meant to demonstrate its nonrecognition of the U.S. government while Washington maintained diplomatic ties with Taiwan. The same principle was followed when Chinese delegations were sent to the United States. The CNTTT was hosted jointly by the USTTA and the NCUSCR. It was the NCUSCR that raised all the funds and organized most of the activities for the CNTTT delegation.[131] The first Chinese physicians' delegation was invited and hosted by the Institute of Medicine and the American Medical Association for its visit in October 1972.[132] Similarly, the first Chinese delegation of scientists was, at Beijing's request, the guest of the CSCPRC and the Federation of American Scientists.[133]

Beijing's desire to keep cultural exchange unofficial and conduct early programs through nongovernmental entities was well received among American scholarly and civil societies. After all, it was the American scholars and scientists who started to push for exchange with the PRC in 1964 and established the Committee on Scholarly Communications with Mainland China in 1966 with funding from Carnegie Corporation of New York. Sponsored by the National Academy of Science (NAS), the Social Science Research Council (SSRC), and the American Council of Learned Societies, the Committee believed that scholarly communication would help men and nations better understand each other and live in peace.[134] Encouraged by recent signals from both Beijing and Washington, the committee, now officially the Committee on Scholarly Communications with the People's Republic of China (CSCPRC), wrote to President Nixon in January 1971 to endorse his effort to establish cultural contacts with the PRC. At the same time, it sent a message to Guo Moruo, inviting Chinese scientists to participate in academic exchange in the United States in 1972.[135] As soon as the USTTT received an invitation to visit China, Steenhoven sought private financial support to cover the team's travel to the PRC and the reception of the CNTTT in the future. The quick commitment from the NCUSCR allowed him to issue a formal invitation to the CNTTT at the meeting with Zhou.[136] Soon after the reception of the CNTTT, the NCUSCR and the CSCPRC sent a joint position paper to the White House and the Department of State. While urging steps to be taken to prepare for cultural and educational exchanges, they insisted that the contents and formats of these exchanges should be determined by private institutions. They also proposed that at least two national organizations be designated to serve as intermediaries between American and Chinese participants.[137]

The White House welcomed the proposal. In his reply to Alexander Eckstein, chairman of the NCUSCR, Kissinger not only agreed with NCUSCR's position and recommendation but also promised that he would make his staff members involved in cultural exchange with the PRC to get familiar with Eckstein's thinking. He told Eckstein that the Chinese leaders knew the NCUSCR and CSCPRC because the former played a key role in the reception of the CNTTT and the latter in hosting the Chinese medical delegation. He hoped that these two organizations would keep close contact with his staff members in the future cultural exchange with the PRC.[138] Kissinger's hope came true as the NCUSCR and the CSCPRC, while remaining independent in choosing exchange projects and selecting participants, did cooperate with the U.S. government and often shared their plans and expressed their concerns over exchange projects to Chinese officials through American diplomats.[139] By the end of 1978, the CSCPRC alone organized and received more than seventy American as well as Chinese scholarly exchange delegations, becoming a major player in the reestablishment of cultural ties between the two nations.[140]

Although much of the legwork, especially on the American side, was done by nongovernmental organizations, the governments played a key role in coordinating and even controlling, particularly on the Chinese side, over almost all aspects of the exchange in the 1970s. In order to maintain the momentum of cultural exchange, the U.S. government presented its proposal for cultural exchange in 1973 to the Chinese government through the Paris channel in November 1972. During Kissinger's visit to China in February 1973, diplomats from both sides held a special meeting on the subject, agreed on a near-term exchange program, and worked out a framework for cultural exchange in the future.[141] Based on the agreement, State Department officials met with their Chinese counterparts in Beijing each year to discuss an overall exchange "package" that included the proposal from CSCPRC, NCUSCR, and other organizations. Once the overall package was agreed upon, the participating organizations would negotiate all the details by themselves for its implementation. While the CSCPRC was designated to implement exchange programs in science, technology, and various academic areas, the NCUSCR was selected to administer professional, political, educational, and cultural exchanges.[142]

Despite its active promotion of cultural exchange with the PRC through diplomatic effort, Washington had little influence on the organization and implementation of specific exchange programs.[143] The CSCPRC and NCUSRC had to work out the details of each exchange program with their Chinese counterparts, the CAST and CAS for the former and the CPAFFN for the latter. In its first meeting with CAST and CAS officials in mid-1973, the CSCPRC proposed twelve exchange programs. The Chinese accepted nine groups of visitors in plant science, seismology, pharmacology, malacology, archaeology, anthropology, child psychology, and linguistics. These subject areas were carefully chosen by the CSCPRC not only because they reflected the interests of the participating organizations, but also because Americans potentially could learn a great deal from the Chinese. Another group of scholars in population studies, including contraceptive technology, was added later because Zhou showed clear interest in that area at the meeting. The three groups of visitors turned down by the Chinese were in other social sciences, and the explanation given by Zhou was that all Chinese social scientists were still going through "a period of self-criticism."[144] Probably for the same reason, among the ten Chinese delegations sent to the United States in 1974, nine were in the fields of science, technology, agriculture, and commerce, with the tenth in martial arts.[145]

As it had done in the past, Beijing used cultural exchange programs to show off its achievements and elaborate its position on Taiwan and other issues. Just as with the CNTTT's visit to the United States in 1972, Zhou personally reviewed the thirteen members of the first medical delegation, making sure that they were able to share China's successes in traditional medicine, including acupuncture anesthesia and the national healthcare system. Wu Weiran, director of the Surgery Department of Union Hospital, was designated as the head of the delegation. He was chosen not only because he had been Zhou's personal physician since 1955, but also because he had successfully removed James Reston's appendix during his visit to China in 1971. Zhou met with all the delegation members before their departure, reminding them to be neither humble nor arrogant while dealing with the Americans. As prepared, the delegation showed an acupuncture film and presented mannequins with acupuncture points as gift to many medical institutions, including the National Institute of Health.[146] In order to demonstrate its sovereignty over Taiwan, Beijing added several new items to the program two weeks before the Chinese performing arts troupe's scheduled visit to the United States in late March 1975. One of them was a popular new song, "The People of Taiwan Are Our Brothers," which vowed "we must liberate Taiwan." Viewing it as a potential embarrassment to local hosts across the country and a direct challenge to U.S. government policy, the State Department and the NCUSRC opposed the program change.[147] Believing that the liberation of Taiwan and the unification of the nation were the domestic issues of the Chinese people, Beijing refused to withdraw the song from the program as Washington requested. Blaming Washington for its retreat from the Shanghai Communiqué, Beijing accepted the decision made by the NCUSRC on March 27 to indefinitely postpone the troupe's visit.[148]

The mechanisms developed in the 1950s and 1960s for hosting American visitors were reinforced in the 1970s, making it easy for Beijing to control the experience of American visitors and turn their visits into propaganda opportunities. After the carefully arranged visit to the Eighth Route Army Office, a store, and a textile factory in Xian on September 21, 1971, Hosea Williams was deeply moved and impressed. He told his hosts that the PLA was truly a people's army and the Chinese Communist government was truly a government of the people, by the people, and for the people. He even assured his hosts that the Chinese store had more stuff than an American store and that only a few officials and capitalists could afford air travel in the United States, while in the PRC the broad masses were all able to do it.[149] Obviously, much of the information provided to him as well as other American visitors, especially those related to the material life in the PRC, was anything but accurate. Because of the short supply of all consumer goods, most things in China were rationed at the time and government-issued coupons were needed to buy rice, flour, cooking oil, meat, sugar, eggs, matches, coal, cloth, watches, bicycles, radios, and many other goods. Weeks before Nixon's visit to China in February 1972, residents in Shanghai and Beijing received special training and were given "correct answers" to various questions that American reporters might ask. When American reporters went to a supermarket in Shanghai, selected customers were let in and allowed to buy things without using coupons. However, once the Americans left, those customers had to return all the things they had "bought."[150]

While the mechanism used by Beijing to generate positive images of the PRC was effective with most American visitors in the 1970s, it failed to convince all of them, especially those who had studied China and knew the Chinese language. Jonathan Mirsky, a Chinese language and history instructor at Dartmouth College, visited the PRC in 1972 as a member of the second CCAS delegation. Following the itinerary, the delegation met with a worker's family in Guangzhou the day after they entered the PRC. The family of five, Mirsky recalled, lived in a brightly painted apartment with three rooms plus kitchen, bathroom, and toilet. They also had a radio, television, and several shining bicycles. As young scholars and students with enquiring minds, they asked the hosts why the windows were barred and the bicycles all had built-in locks if there was no crime in China, as they had been told. The answers to the two questions were the same: the flats were built in 1949, when there were crimes, and the bicycles were pre-liberation models from when there was bike stealing. The American visitors were impressed with the family and their prosperous life. However, Mirsky woke up early the next morning and wandered back to the flats the delegation had visited the day before. He saw his former host feeding his baby from a bottle in front of the building. The man invited Mirsky into the family's real home, which was shabby and poorly painted, with only two rooms. Sharing a kitchen and bathroom with many other families, they did not have a television, and their only well-used bicycle was locked. The man also told Mirsky that the building was constructed in 1962 and the window bars and bicycle locks were needed because there were many thieves. After this, Mirsky was "suspicious of every venue, every briefing, and every account of how everything should be understood." He turned, in his own words, from a Mao fan into a counterrevolutionary in forty-eight hours.[151]

Keeping American social scientists out of the Sino-American scholarly exchange was an essential part of Beijing's effort to project a positive image for the PRC while minimizing the influence of American ideas and values. However, restrictions on social scientists received strong pushback from the Americans since the very beginning. When the NAS sent its first delegation to the PRC in 1973, the group included several social scientists such as Eleanor Sheldon, a well-known sociologist and president of the SSRC; Albert Feuerwerker, a historian of the modern Chinese economy; and Ezra F. Vogel, another sociologist. Zhou told them again that the lingering disruption of the Cultural Revolution made it impossible for the American social scientists to investigate Chinese society. Sheldon and the CSCPRC were unwilling to accept this, because they knew that the American social scientists wanted more than anyone else to be allowed into China after being cut off from the country for over two decades. Thus, the CSCPRC insisted that all American exchange delegations sent to the PRC have two Sinologists as their "scholarly escorts" if Sinologists were not allowed to form their own delegation to visit China. Beijing could not reject the CSCPRC's initiative outright since both sides had agreed that each had the right to choose its own participants in exchange. When Beijing tried to deny the admission of Frederick Mote, a historian at Princeton University, because of his early service for the Office of Strategic Services during World War II, the CSCPRC dug in and told the Chinese that the whole delegation would not go if Mote were not allowed to go with it. Eventually Beijing gave in, and social scientists and humanities scholars went to the PRC as scholarly escorts in the following years.[152]

Although Beijing could not keep all American social scientists or humanists from bilateral exchange, it continued to make every effort to limit their inquiries. When the first NAS delegation arrived in China, there were no social scientists in the local welcoming committee. After Vogel complained about it, a social scientist was included in the welcoming committee in the next city. But the Chinese scholar was so afraid of making an error that every time Vogel asked questions he quickly changed the subject to talk about the weather or the scenery.[153] Unhappy with the packed itinerary and watchful eyes of the guides accompanying the delegation all the time, he tried to have unsupervised interaction with local people by walking the streets early in the morning before the official schedule began. However, he was disheartened to see people so petrified when he tried to stop them for a brief conversation or ask for directions that they all evaded him and quickly walked away. Despite his knowledge of the PRC gained through interviews with many Chinese refugees in Hong Kong before his trip, he still had not expected the ordinary people in mainland China to be so frightened of talking with foreigners.[154]

Andrew Nathan, a political scientist teaching at Columbia University, had a more depressing experience. As a member of the New York Faculty Study Tour, Nathan entered China in mid-July 1973, only a month after Vogel's departure from the PRC. While unhappy with the guides from the national and local offices of the China International Travel Service who smothered the members with a protocol that "bore a faint edge of hostility," he soon learned that the local people also watched them closely. When the delegation was touring downtown Hangzhou, he took a couple of photos of some big-character posters. Some local people reported his behavior to the hotel where he stayed, and the guides criticized him sharply, ordering him to hand in his film. After hard negotiation he was allowed to finish the roll and then turn the film in for development so that the photos with big-character posters could be identified and destroyed. When no photos of a big-character poster were found after the roll was finished and developed the next day, the Chinese guides called Nathan a cheat and angrily demanded his immediate departure. He was eventually allowed to stay when the delegation leader strongly defended him. At the end of his trip, Nathan concluded that the "photo incident suggests how the society as a unit keeps its eye on us" and "nobody will talk freely."[155]

Beijing's restriction on the PRC's cultural interactions with the United States before the normalization of diplomatic relations was also clearly demonstrated in its refusal to send Chinese students to American colleges and recruit Americans to teach in China. While unable to have extended stays in the PRC for research for themselves, many American visitors urged their Chinese hosts to send students to the United States for education during their visits to the PRC. The CCAS delegation not only invited Chinese students to come to the United States in 1971 but also sent letters to CCAS headquarters asking it to get necessary resources ready for hosting Chinese scholars and students.[156] John King Fairbank proposed in his meeting with Zhou Enlai in June 1972 that China sent students to the United States to study English. As the leading Chinese historian, he knew well not to ask his host to send students to the United States to study history or any other subjects in the humanities or social sciences. American officials also conveyed Columbia University's plan to accept Chinese students for language education and Chinese scholars for scientific collaboration at meeting with their Chinese counterparts in February 1973. Again, those two areas were chosen to minimize resistance from the Chinese officials. However, Chinese officials rejected the proposals, pointing out the lack of diplomatic relations between the PRC and the United States. With many Taiwanese students as well as teachers in the United States and a Nationalist embassy in Washington, it would be awkward and embarrassing for PRC students and scholars if they were sent to the United States, the officials claimed.[157] When the Ministry of Education and Ministry of Foreign Affairs planned to run fifteen classes to train foreign-language teachers in 1978, they decided to invite forty-five instructors from Great Britain, France, Canada, Japan, West Germany, Australia, New Zealand, Syria, and Mexico. Given the fact that a number of American instructors were hired to teach English at Chinese colleges in the 1960s, their absence in Beijing's new program was no doubt intentional.[158]

Some changes began to take place only after Mao died in 1976 and Deng Xiaoping returned to power again in mid-1977. Determined to end the chaos caused by the GPCR and save the national economy from a complete collapse, Deng managed to shift the CCP's focus from class struggle to reaching the two goals set by Zhou Enlai in his report at the First Plenary of the Fourth National People's Congress in January 1975. Having overseen the drafting of Zhou's report, Deng devoted most of his energy to building an independent and relatively comprehensive industrial system by 1990 and modernize China's agriculture, industry, national defense, and science and technology by the end of the century.[159] Believing that the Four Modernizations had to start with education and science, he first pushed for a college admission reform by including an entrance examination in the admission process and allowing recent high school graduates to attend college in 1977. Once the first class of students selected through entrance examinations entered colleges and universities in spring 1978, Deng started to expand China's higher education by sending students and scholars to foreign countries. He told top education officials at a meeting in June 1978 that he supported to have thousands and tens of thousands of students sent abroad, with the vast majority of them studying natural science.[160] When Frank Price, the science advisor for President Jimmy Carter and former director of the CSCPRC, raised the issue of student exchange again during his visit in July, Deng immediately agreed and informed him that

Beijing would like to send more than five hundred students and scholars to the United States the following year. Deng made it clear that China was willing to learn from the United States because American science and technology were more advanced in many areas than other countries.[161]

With the strong push from Deng, Beijing took immediate steps to send a large number of students to the United States. In October, the Chinese educational delegation led by Zhou Peiyuan, president of Peking University, visited the United States and met with the American team led by Richard Adkinson, director of the National Science Foundation. According to the agreement reached by both sides, China would send five hundred to seven hundred students and scholars to the United States in the academic year of 1978–1979 while the United States would support sixty students and scholars go to the PRC during the same period with the understanding that other American students could go to China under separate arrangements. While Beijing committed to funding Chinese students and scholars, they would be eligible for American institutional scholarships.[162]

Following the agreement, the first group of fifty researchers and teachers was selected from the CAS and Qinghua, Peking, Nankai, and other universities for the exchange program. Averaging about forty years old, all the members were specialists in natural science, engineering, and medicine. Under direct orders from Deng, this group, plus two students of Zhou Peiyuan's who had received scholarships from American universities, left Beijing on December 26, 1978. Vice Premier Fang Yi met with them before their departure and Leonard Woodcock, the director of U.S. Liaison Office in Beijing, saw them off at the airport. They arrived in Washington, DC, on December 27, days before the establishment of Sino-American diplomatic relations and a month before Deng's visit to the United States. As planned, they went to the airport to greet Deng and participated in other welcome activities organized by the U.S. government. Deng and his wife met with them at the newly opened Chinese embassy. After Deng left for Atlanta to continue his visit, the fifty Chinese students spent three months improving their English at Georgetown University and American University before they went on to other universities across the country for study and research in their own specific fields.[163] The educational exchange between the United States and mainland China was finally restarted.

The normalization of the diplomatic relations between the two countries and Deng's visit to the United States in 1979 lay the foundation for the expansion of cultural exchange. On January 31, Deng and Carter signed two agreements on cultural relation and on science as well as technology collaboration. Other Chinese and American officials signed three additional agreements on high-energy physics, consular services, and education. According to the five-year science and technology agreement, both sides would collaborate in agriculture, energy, space, health, environment, machinery, management, education, personnel exchange, and other fields. In order to help the implementation of the agreement, a U.S.–PRC Joint Commission on Scientific and Technological Cooperation was established. As agreed, the commission met in the two countries alternately each year.[164] The implementation of these agreements ushered in a new era in bilateral science collaboration and cultural exchange. By the end of 1979, there were more than a thousand Chinese students and scholars in the United States, with about a hundred American students and scholars in China.[165]

The rapid expansion of cultural and educational exchange between the two nations in the late 1970s was made possible not only because of the strong push from many people on both sides of the Pacific, but also because of the staunch support from Deng Xiaoping. He repeatedly told the media and the public during his visit that he came to the United States to learn from the American people, who had created the advanced industrial civilization. He emphasized that learning from the Americans was completely "in keeping with the interest of the Chinese people."[166] He even accepted an honorary doctoral degree from Temple University in Philadelphia, making himself part of the Sino-American cultural and educational interaction. During his visit to Atlanta, Deng laid a wreath at Martin Luther King's tomb and met with his family. Through such a special arrangement, Deng reaffirmed Beijing's position that the CCP had abandoned its support for armed revolution and now preferred peaceful reform, as King had advocated in the 1950s and the 1960s.[167]

However, Deng's support for cultural and educational exchange did not prevent him from keeping his commitment to the CCP's cause or ideology. Deng often reminded the Americans as well as the Chinese that the PRC and the United States had different social systems and ideologies. He insisted that the Chinese Communist system had worked pretty well in the previous thirty years except for the distraction and interruption caused by the Cultural Revolution. Thus, he told Robert Novak, the well-known American columnist who was visiting the PRC in November 1978, that the major obstacles to China's Four Modernizations were the lack of technology and high-quality management. Confident of the learning ability of China's people, he believed that such a problem could be solved by sending more of them abroad for education and training. If it was done right, Deng asserted, "our current system, after some necessary reform, will be more efficient in doing things than your system."[168] He made his point more clearly at the CCPCC's conference a couple of weeks later. While promoting the "emancipation of minds" (*jiefang sixiang*), he pointed out that there would be no new China without Chairman Mao and there would be no modern CCP without Mao Zedong Thought. Therefore, he emphasized that "Mao Zedong Thought will always be the most valuable spiritual treasure for our whole Party, whole Army, and the whole nation comprised of various nationalities."[169] Thus, under Deng's leadership, China's reform focused mostly if not solely on the economy, and its opening was limited largely to science and technology. For Deng and his comrades, learning science and technology from the United States was the most efficient way for the PRC to catch up with and surpass the capitalist stronghold, prove the superiority of China's socialist system, and, most important, keep the CCP in power.

Epilogue

Beyond Rattling

With the normalization of Sino-American diplomatic relations and Deng Xiaoping's visit to the United States in early 1979, U.S.-China cultural interactions expanded dramatically in the 1980s and remained at a high level even after a major setback in 1989. As in previous years, the government continued to play a prominent role in planning, coordinating, and sponsoring exchanges in education, science, technology, arts, sports, and the like. The deep involvement of the government, while contributing tremendously to the sharp growth of cultural exchange between the two nations, made it convenient for both Beijing and Washington to use those exchange programs as an instrument to achieve their strategic goals. Driven by its need for the Four Modernizations, Beijing actively promoted and participated in various exchange programs in science and technology. However, at the same time, CCP leaders continued to reject or restrict exchange programs in social sciences and humanities deemed detrimental to the CCP's political and ideological control over the Chinese people. While enthusiastically supported exchange in science and technology, Washington insisted on broadening cultural interactions between the two countries so that American ideals and values could also be shared with the Chinese people. The bloody crackdown on student protesters in Tiananmen Square in 1989 brought Beijing and Washington into open confrontation over human rights, which led to the suspension of a number of exchange programs. Although U.S.-China relations, including cultural exchange, gradually returned to normal in the 1990s, both Beijing and Washington staunchly committed to their own ideas and values, making fierce confrontation on the cultural front a constant phenomenon in U.S.-China relations well into the twenty-first century.

As soon as diplomatic relations between the two nations were normalized, the PRC government took immediate steps to rebuild old cultural ties and establish new ones. Following the same format used in selecting the first group of fifty students, Beijing sent more than eight hundred government-sponsored students to the United States and approved more than five hundred self-sponsored students to pursue higher education in America in 1979. The number of Chinese students going to the United States increased sharply in the following years. By 1984, about 20,000 Chinese students, 12,500 of them government-sponsored and 7,500 or so self-sponsored, were studying in the United States, equaling the total number of Chinese students educated in America in the century before 1949.[1] The number of Chinese students admitted to American colleges and universities in 1988 rose to 25,000. Meanwhile, the Ministry of Culture extended an invitation to the Boston Symphony Orchestra for a visit to Beijing and Shanghai in March 1979. Deng helped the orchestra raise money for its first trip to China by publicly announcing the invitation during his visit to the United States. With generous donations from various businesses, the Boston Symphony Orchestra arrived in Beijing as planned, and Deng attended its first concert with Song Qingling on March 17. Deng and Song met with conductor Seiji Ozawa as well as other leading members of the orchestra during the intermission. Deng welcomed the musicians and pointed out that their visit illustrated the increasing interactions between the Chinese and American peoples.[2] About the same time, the China Film and Exhibition Corporation bought *Futureworld* from American International Pictures and screened it in four thousand Chinese theaters, making it the first American movie shown to the general public since the early 1950s.[3] China Central Television purchased *The Man from Atlantis*, a thirteen-episode science fiction TV series produced by the Solow Production Company, in late 1979 and aired it in early 1980, adding a new genre to the Sino-American cultural exchange.[4]

The U.S. government was also anxious in playing an active role in cultural exchange with the PRC. On May 2, 1979, Michel Oksenberg, senior staff member of the National Security Council in charge of Chinese affairs, chaired a meeting to discuss the implementation of cultural agreements with China. The meeting, as Oksenberg claimed, brought together for the first time those agencies involved in cultural exchange with the PRC, including the United States International Communications Agency (USICA); the Department of Health, Education, and Welfare; the National Endowment for the Humanities; the National Endowment for the Arts; the Department of Interior; the Library of Congress; and the Smithsonian Institution. After some discussion, the group decided to invite Huang Zhen, the minister of culture, to lead an interdepartmental Chinese cultural delegation to visit Washington. The USICA was designated to serve as host and charged to develop, through interagency consultation, an inventory of exchange programs within a month so that they could be proposed to the Chinese delegation.[5] Although Huang, near the end of his tenure at the Ministry of Culture, was unable to visit the United States in 1979, Vice President Walter Mondale went to China in August and signed an implementation agreement with Deng in Beijing to expand exchanges in art, culture, education, sports, broadcasting, library materials, social sciences, and book translation and publication in 1980–1981.[6] During his visit, Mondale delivered a speech at Peking University to a mixed audience of students, professors, and researchers on August 27. His speech was broadcast by Chinese Central Television later in the evening, and the full text of it was published in *People's Daily* the next day.[7] Mondale became the first U.S. government official to communicate directly with the Chinese masses since 1949.

Although both Beijing and Washington were active in promoting cultural exchange between the two nations, they approached it with different strategies and goals. For the Chinese Communist leaders, the expansion of cultural relations with the United States was essential not only for strengthening the new diplomatic ties between the two nations as part of their effort to resist the Soviet threat but also for the realization of the Four Modernizations. Deng wanted to expand the PRC's engagement with the United States in science, technology, and education as much as possible so that the Chinese economy and society could grow and prosper. In order to shift people's attention from class struggle to economic growth, he advocated "thought liberation" for a short period of time and stopped the publication of *Quotations from Chairman Mao* in early 1979.[8] However, his ultimate goal remained unchanged: proving the superiority of the socialist system and strengthening the CCP's rule in China. In his speech at a

CCPCC conference in March 1979, Deng emphasized that the premise of the Four Modernizations in China was to stand fast on four basic principles: adherence to the socialist road; proletarian dictatorship; the leadership of the CCP; and Marxism, Leninism, and Mao Zedong Thought. He also stressed that the unequivocal conclusion reached by the Chinese people since the May 4th Movement was that only socialism could save China.[9] He later pointed out that the core of the "four adherences" was adherence to the CCP's leadership, because without the CCP there would be no contemporary China.[10] As soon as he had consolidated his leadership position within the CCP, Deng launched a national campaign against bourgeois liberalism in 1979, leading to the closing of the Democracy Wall in Beijing, the arrest of many democracy movement activists, the denunciation of pro-democracy writers and artists, the ban of their publications and artwork as evidence of so-called bourgeois spiritual pollution, and bloody suppression of the student protesters in Tiananmen Square.[11] Believing that Hu Yaobang and Zhao Ziyang were too soft in handling student protesters, Deng removed the two top CCP leaders from their offices in 1987 and 1989 respectively.

Like Mao, Deng and his successors saw American ideas and values as implacable enemies of the CCP. Since they had to keep China's door open to American science and technology, they did everything possible to minimize the influence of American ideas and values while engaging in cultural exchange with the United States. In addition to the rigorous political review process in the selection of candidates for cultural and educational exchange with the United States, the PRC government, like the Qing court, made the calculated decision to choose mostly scholars and graduate students for those programs. It hoped that these middle-aged scholars and mature graduate students with solid political as well as family backgrounds could withstand bourgeois ideological and cultural "corrosion." It also made sure that most if not all the state-sponsored scholars and students entered only fields that could make direct contributions to the Four Modernizations. Among the state-sponsored scholars and students who did research and degree programs in the United States from 1980 and 1984, about 30 percent were in the field of engineering, 25 percent in physical science, 10 percent in health science, and 9 percent in life science. In sharp contrast, none of them did American studies, and only about 2 percent were in the humanities.[12]

Beijing's effort to set strict ideological restrictions on bilateral cultural exchanges was in direct opposition to American beliefs and practices. At the meeting chaired by Oksenberg on May 2, 1979, officials clearly identified the dissemination of American values in China as one of the major goals of U.S.-China cultural exchange.[13] This was nothing new, for the U.S. government had been disseminating American ideals and values in China since the early twentieth century. It just became more urgent and important when the PRC government tried covertly as well as overtly to circumvent and even reject the American effort. In his speech delivered at Peking University in August 1979, Mondale reminded his audience that it was at this university where the May 4th movement began, "launching an era of unprecedented intellectual ferment" and inaugurating "an effort to modernize Chinese culture and society." He passed a message from President Carter to the audience that "our politics are rooted in our values" and "we cherish our fundamental beliefs in human rights and compassion and social justice." With these values institutionalized by the American democratic system, Mondale proudly shared with his audience that "the opportunities available to our citizens are incomparable," that "our debates are vigorous and open," and that "the differences we air among ourselves—whether on strategic nuclear policy or on energy—are signs of our society's enduring strength."[14] It was clear that Washington wanted to see not only a strong China but also a different China through cultural exchange between the two nations.

However, the pleas from U.S. officials were either ignored or pushed back by Chinese Communist leaders. When Deng met Mondale the next day, he mentioned only the $2 billion credit from the Export-Import Bank of the United States that Mondale had announced in his speech.[15] Actually, earlier that year, Deng had already told a group of American congressmen that he would not talk about human rights with President Carter during his visit to the United States. If Carter insisted on it, he would remind the president of the American imperialist invasion of China and U.S. assistance to Jiang Jieshi in killing Chinese people.[16] As a result, human rights issues never came up at their meetings during Deng's visit. Only weeks after Mondale's visit, Wei Jingsheng, one of the democracy movement activists and the author of "The Fifth Modernization: Democracy and Others," was tried and sentenced to fifteen years in jail, another clear demonstration of Beijing's position on political reform in China. When the issue did pop up during former President Carter's visit to China in 1987, Deng told him that China would never copy the American system even though it was considered the most democratic in the world because it would cause chaos and leave no energy for construction.[17] Deng further elaborated his point when he met with President George H. W. Bush in February 1989. Deng asserted that stability was most important to China, and nothing could be done without it. Drawing lessons from the Cultural Revolution, he emphasized that if demonstration was allowed in China there would be demonstrations every day, making economic development impossible. He thus concluded that China could not adopt the Western system and that civil war would be inevitable if a billion people were allowed to have multiparty campaign and election.[18]

The opposing views and goals on cultural exchange were not only expressed by top government officials in their public speeches as well as closed-door meetings but also reflected in the implementation of various exchange programs. As soon as the agreement on normalization of diplomatic relations between the two nations was reached, Beijing stopped jamming the VOA's signal, making it easily available to Chinese listeners. However, in its order issued on January 5, 1979, the CCP Propaganda Department made it clear that only listening to the VOA's English instruction program and requesting English textbooks from the VOA's office in Hong Kong were permitted.[19] The VOA was allowed to open its bureau in Beijing in 1981, and regular exchanges with Radio Peking were established after six Chinese broadcasters visited the United States in 1982. But the MFA refused to reissue the official accreditation to Maxwell Ruston as the VOA's resident reporter in China because he was the first foreign journalist who reported on student protests in Shanghai in December 1986. Although the VOA was accused of helping spread the protest movement to other cities in China with its broadcasts, the MFA, not ready to cut ties with the VOA yet, asked it to nominate someone else.[20]

While Beijing was trying to set strict restrictions on cultural exchange, Washington made great effort to disseminate American ideas and values through all the exchange programs. Eager to send American scholars and students to the PRC as soon as possible, Washington restored the Fulbright Program in 1979 by dispatching four English professors to train a selected group of college English instructors at Peking University. In addition to regular content for an English teaching program, the visiting professors provided information on American history, literature, and culture to their students as enrichment and background. In 1980, about a dozen Fulbright professors were sent to China teaching American history, literature, economics, law, journalism, and English in three different cities. By 1988, the total of Fulbright professors sent to China reached 170, with forty-four in American literature, thirty-five in economics, twenty-eight in U.S. history, and twenty in law. Only thirteen of them, less than 8 percent of the total, were in the field of linguistics. "The history of the China Fulbright program," as Guangqiu Xu accurately observed, "depicts a clear intention to disseminate American ideas in the politically sensitive disciplines of social sciences and humanities."[21] Besides sending many professors in social sciences and humanities to the PRC, Washington began to include three Chinese graduate students in the Fulbright program in 1981 and kept increasing their number in the following years. In 1987, the number of Chinese graduate students participating in the Fulbright exchange rose to seventeen, while the number of Chinese scholars fell to thirteen, clearly demonstrating the American interest in training and influencing Chinese youths.[22]

The strong positions taken by Beijing and Washington on the content of cultural exchange inevitably led to frequent confrontations between the two sides. One of the early clashes erupted during the first official American art exhibit in China in fall 1981. As part of the cultural exchange agreement signed by Mondale and Deng in 1980, the Museum of Fine Arts Boston (MFAB) was selected to exhibit American paintings at the National Art Gallery in Beijing on September 1, 1981. However, the opening of the exhibit was delayed by about an hour because Chinese officials demanded the removal of thirteen abstract works from the seventy masterpieces carefully chosen by professionals at the MFAB. The Americans, led by Charles Wick, director of the USICA, and Jan Fontein, director of the MFAB, refused to accept the request and threatened to cancel the exhibition if the thirteen paintings were deleted. The Chinese relented, and the exhibit was opened with Huang Zhen, commissioner for external cultural relations, and Warren Burger, U.S. Supreme Court chief justice, cutting the ribbons and delivering pointed remarks. Huang, while recognizing that most of the paintings on display were "realistic and excellent from which we can learn a great deal," told the audience that the rest, a few in number, should be "looked upon objectively by the viewers as another artistic trend and school in painting of present-day American society." His unsubtle statement clearly indicated that those abstract paintings were not welcome in

China. Justice Burger responded sharply by going astray from his prewritten remarks. He rebutted that the art selected for this exhibit from one of the great museums in America "represents something really more than art." 'It represents," he pointed out, "an expression of the American spirit of freedom in which each person may paint, or write, or do whatever he wants, or whatever she wants, as long as it does not violate the constitution."[23] The fierce exchange between Huang and Burger epitomized the root cause of the confrontation on U.S.-China cultural exchange. When *People's Daily* reported the event the next day, it published only the key statements made by Huang without even mentioning Burger's remarks.[24]

Beijing's retreat on its censorship on American contents was rare especially when it dealt with individual U.S. citizens or organizations. Steve Mosher, a doctoral student from Stanford, was the first American who was allowed to do anthropological fieldwork in rural China with President Carter's intervention. Taking advantage of his ex-wife's family ties in a village in Guangdong Province, he studied abortion in rural China and published an article in Taiwan, revealing that many Chinese women were forced into abortion seven, eight, and even nine months in their pregnancy. The Chinese police arrested him on charges of smuggling and forced him out of China. The anthropology faculty at Stanford University, with seven members either absent or excusing themselves, voted to dismiss him from the doctoral program for his "unprofessional conduct." One professor explained the decision in a written statement that the inconsiderate action taken by the anthropologist to further the welfare of the study population "may foreclose the opportunity of other researchers to carry out research in the same area, and harm the populations that the anthropologist would like to assist."[25] The Stanford anthropology faculty's fear of collateral damage was not ill founded. Beijing soon banned Americans from social-science field studies in China. The CSCPRC had to argue for the importance of Americans' studying Chinese society in situ for many years before it could reach a compromise that opened Zouping County in Shandong Province to American scholars. With special funding from Mellon Foundation, CSCPRC was able to support a multidisciplinary research team for long-term survey work in Zouping beginning in 1988. Part of the work done by researchers involved in the Shandong Field Research Project between 1988 and 1993 was showcased in an edited volume published by Harvard University Press in 1998.[26]

The confrontation of values and ideas escalated to a major crisis when CCP leaders ordered a bloody crackdown on peaceful student protesters in Tiananmen Square in June 1989. Washington's denunciation of and sanctions on the massacre seriously strained U.S.-China diplomatic relations and brought huge setbacks in cultural and educational exchange. Treating the student democracy movement as an organized effort instigated by the U.S. government to overthrow the CCP's rule in China, Beijing first started jamming VOA broadcasts on May 21, the day after martial law was imposed on the city. Then it expelled two American reporters, VOA bureau chief Alan W. Pessin and API's John Pomfret, on June 12, 1989.[27] Pessin was charged with "writing stories to distort facts, spread rumor, stir up turmoil, and incite counter-revolutionary rebellion."[28] A few weeks later, Mark Hopkins, another VOA reporter, was also accused of spreading "rumors and false propaganda" and ordered to leave China.[29] On the same day, *People's Daily* published an article attacking the VOA for its zealous support for the "anti-Party and anti-Socialist violent rebellion" and its resurrection of the old dream of "peaceful evolution" (*heping yanbian*) in the PRC initiated by Dean Acheson and reinforced by John Foster Dulles.[30] In July, Beijing suspended the Fulbright program, forcing U.S. Information Agency to assign its twenty-four American professors to teach in other countries.[31]

The American response to the tragic event on June 4 was just as swift. For their safety, the CSCPRC office in Beijing managed to get all American scholars and students under CSCPRC auspices back to the United States by mid-June. While the NAS, the home institution for the CSCPRC, suspended all cooperation with China, U.S. government agencies and other funders of the CSCPRC curtailed their support for various programs.[32] Only hours after the Tiananmen massacre, President George H. W. Bush ordered Attorney General Richard L. Thornburgh to defer enforcing the departure of Chinese nationals for a year so that Chinese students and scholars, especially those who were sponsored by the Chinese government, would not be forced to return to China. On April 11, 1990, President Bush issued an executive order to waive the two-year home residency rule and allowed the Chinese students to seek employment in the United States.[33] In May 1992, Congress passed the Chinese Students Protection Act, which consolidated the policy measures included in Bush's executive order and established permanent residency for Chinese nationals who were in the

United States from June 5, 1989, to April 11, 1990.[34] By the mid-1990s, more than 54,000 Chinese, mostly students and scholars, chose to stay in the United States permanently so that they did not have to face possible persecution in the PRC.

Although Deng saw the student protest in Tiananmen Square as a smokeless world war or a new Cold War launched by the United States to defeat socialism, he and his successors stuck with their restricted opening and lopsided reform so that they could continue to receive American technology and capital, which were essential to maintain the CCP's rule and build a socialist society with Chinese characteristics.[35] As in the past, they turned to educational and cultural exchanges to repair seriously damaged U.S.-China relations. In December 1989, the PRC government informed the U.S. embassy in Beijing that a new VOA chief reporter could return to China and discussion on the resumption of the Fulbright Scholarship Program could be started, too.[36] The CSCPRC office in Beijing, closed with the departure of Perry Link, its director, right after June 4 crackdown, was allowed to reopen with John Olsen as the new director.[37] At the same time, the Chinese government continued to send an increasingly large number of scholars to the United States. It did sharply reduce the number of government-sponsored students to American colleges and universities after 1989. However, the drastic increase of self-sponsored students, including undergraduate students, easily made up the loss. Mostly because of the influx of self-sponsored students, the number of Chinese students in the United States grew from 25,170 in 1988 to 46,858 in 1998, 81,127 in 2008, and 363,341 in 2018, making them the largest foreign student body since 2009.[38]

While repairing its diplomatic and cultural relations with the United States, Beijing continued and intensified its effort to restrict and resist the dissemination of American ideas and values. With the rapid growth of China's economic as well as military power, Deng's tactic of "keeping a low profile" (*taoguang yanghui*) was gradually abandoned by his successors, making confrontation on the cultural front more frequent and acute. When the Fulbright program was restored in 1990, China sent only two graduate students to the United States that year and kept the number largely unchanged in the following years. At the same time, the number of scholars was increased to ten or more each year because the PRC government believed that those middle-aged men and women could see all kinds of problems in American society and do a better job in defending national interest.³⁹ While allowing the VOA to send its reporters back to China in 1990, Beijing continued to jam its broadcasts despite repeated attempts made by the Bush and Clinton administrations to negotiate for its stop.⁴⁰ In response to harsh American criticism on China's human rights problems presented in the State Department's annual *Country Reports on Human Rights Practices*, Beijing started to publish its annual rebuttal, *Human Rights Record of the United States*, in 1999. It attacked Washington for not saying "a single word about the human rights problems in the United States" while criticizing China for "committing widespread and well documented human rights abuses." Drawing mostly from American media publications, the Chinese report listed American human rights problems in six areas, including prevalent violent crimes, low voter turnout in elections, increasing poverty as well as homelessness, continuous racial discrimination, inadequate protection for women and children, and disregard of international human rights pacts.⁴¹

Shocked by the bloody crackdown in Tiananmen Square in 1989 and encouraged by the collapse of the Soviet Union in the following years, American policymakers focused more on China's human rights and put greater resources in the dissemination of American ideas and values in China. After years of negotiation, the Peace Corps, a U.S. government agency established in 1961 to improve America's global image through providing international developmental assistance to developing countries, was able to send its first group of eighteen American volunteers to Sichuan Province to teach English at small rural colleges in 1993.⁴² With the successful two-year experiment of the first group, the Peace Corps began to send more volunteers to Sichuan, Gansu, and Guizhou provinces and the city of Chongqing yearly in 1995 under a slightly different Chinese name, the Sino-American Friendship Volunteers Program. In 2002, the cohort grew to more than eighty volunteers who worked in the fields of education and environmental protection as requested by the Chinese government.⁴³ While cutting the budget for the VOA, Congress passed the International Broadcasting Act in 1994, authorizing the "creation of a new broadcasting service to the people of the People's Republic of China and other countries of Asia which lack adequate sources of free information." That service, which was later named Radio Free Asia, was charged with promoting democratic values and human rights.⁴⁴ Focusing mostly on local news, it began its broadcast with a half-hour news program in Mandarin on September 29, 1996, with Cantonese, Uyghur, and Tibetan added later. With ten of eleven programs in those four languages, the PRC was indisputably the most important target for Radio Free Asia.

The rehabilitation of U.S-China cultural relations climaxed with the establishment of the U.S.-China High-Level Consultation on People-to-People Exchange that coordinated and organized exchanges in education, science, technology, sports, women, health, and youth in the early 2010s.[45] However, the new mechanism did not prevent Beijing and Washington from fighting each other on the cultural front. Actually, in 2009, the same year when Liu Yandong, the vice premier of the PRC, proposed the high-level coordination during her visit to the United States, Beijing banned YouTube, Twitter, and Facebook in China as part of its effort to tighten its control over the internet and prevent the so-called color revolution from taking place in the PRC. By forcing Google to leave mainland China in 2010, Beijing managed to expel all major U.S. social media platforms and put the country under self-imposed virtual isolation with the help of the "Great Firewall."

Beijing's effort to stop what it called Western hostile cultural penetration was greatly intensified after Xi Jinping rose to the top of the CCP leadership in 2012. As a response to investigative reports on the massive wealth accumulated by family members and relatives of top Chinese leader Wen Jiabo and Xi Jinping by the *Wall Street Journal* and the *New York Times* in 2012, Beijing immediately blocked access to their websites and expelled a *New York Times* reporter by refusing to renew his visa in January 2014.[46] More important, the CCPCC issued a strict instruction in 2013, prohibiting the advocacy of Western democracy, universal values, civil society, neoliberalism, Western views on journalism, historical nihilism, and questioning the reform and opening.[47] Following the order, universities encouraged students to report on their teachers who violated the "seven prohibitions" in their classroom instruction or private conversations. At the same time, Chinese universities and colleges established numerous schools of Marxism (Makesi Zhuyi Xueyuan), bringing their total from about a hundred in 2012 to more than 1,440 in 2021. With strong support from the CCP Department of Propaganda and the Ministry of Education, the doctoral and master's programs in Marxist theory offered by those schools increased sharply since 2016, exceeding graduate programs in any other fields by 2021.[48]

Alarmed by the tightening of state control over the Chinese media and their more aggressive use in spreading pro-Beijing propaganda in the United

States, Washington began in February 2020 to treat five Chinese state-run media entities with U.S. operations, including the Xinhua News Agency, China Global Television Network, China Radio International, China Daily Distribution Corp., and Hai Tian Development U.S.A., as foreign embassies and required them to register their employees and U.S. properties to the State Department.[49] At the end of the year, President Donald Trump signed the National Defense Authorization Act for Fiscal Year 2021, withholding federal research funding to colleges and universities hosting Confucius Institutes, language centers that had sprung up on college campuses with instructors, textbooks, and funding from the PRC government since 2004.[50] As a result, the number of Confucius Institutes in the United States dropped from more than 110 at its peak to fewer than twenty in mid-2022.[51]

In addition to the new restriction imposed on Chinese state-run media companies and educational centers in the United States, the Trump administration took steps to stop some exchange programs with the PRC. The Peace Corps terminated its China program and withdrew all the American volunteers in June 2020. Senator Marco Rubio justified his demand to end the program in the PRC by pointing out that it was no longer a developing nation and thus did not need the Peace Corps' assistance. However, the hostile position he and Senator Rick Scott shared, as Peter Hessler observed, "reflected their deep disappointment and frustration over American cultural interactions with the PRC." Scott asserted that the American volunteers in the PRC "don't coordinate anything with the State Department, they don't promote American values, they don't promote capitalism."[52] As his response to Beijing's imposition of a new National Security Law that denied Hong Kong's autonomy and freedom, President Trump also canceled the Fulbright Program with China as well as Hong Kong in July with an executive order.[53] Pan Gongyu, a columnist for the online leftist news website *Observer* (Guanchazhe), celebrated the termination of the Peace Corps program in a familiar tone and style. He told his readers in his commentary that the Peace Corps was just an instrument for exporting American cultural values, and the withdrawal of the American volunteers marked a serious setback for the United States on the ideological front in the PRC. Pan concluded by mimicking Mao's 1949 essay, "Farewell, Leighton Stuart!" "The Peace Corps has departed," he wrote, "and the U.S.-Trade Agreement is here, very good, very good. Both events are worth celebrating."[54]

The antagonistic actions taken by both governments and the bellicose statements made by political leaders as well as public opinion influencers in recent years clearly demonstrated that the reestablishment and expansion of bilateral exchange programs after the normalization of diplomatic relations between the PRC and the United States didn't stop either side from confronting each other on the cultural front. The expansion of the U.S.-China cultural exchange after 1979 was made necessary and possible mostly by the shared security threat from the Soviet Union, Beijing's desperate need to bring about the Four Modernizations, and Washington's confidence in the democratization of Chinese society through its opening to and interaction with Western countries, especially the United States. However, such an expansion took place only in limited areas with strict restrictions imposed by Beijing. Severe clashes over those restrictions remained constant and became intensified when the shared security concern was alleviated with the collapse of the Soviet Union, Beijing's assertiveness grew with the rapid growth of its economic and military power, and more Americans doubted the effectiveness of heavily restricted cultural exchange in the democratization of China. The American devotion to upholding and spreading their ideals as well as values embodied in democratic capitalism, and the CCP's determination to repel the so-called American cultural aggression and spiritual pollution as part of its effort to perpetuate its absolute rule in China not only turned the two sides into mortal enemies in the wake of World War II, but also kept them as fierce ideological and political foes after the normalization of diplomatic relations between the two nations. As a result, the sustained fighting on the cultural front became the most striking hallmark of U.S.-China relations since the 1940s.

Acknowledgments

"It took ten years to whet a sword."

This was how Jia Dao, a well-known Chinese poet, opened his four-line poem "The Swordsman" (Jianke) twelve centuries ago. With the increasing popularity of the poem, that line quickly morphed into a proverb widely used by the Chinese to describe an extremely long and arduous undertaking. When I finally finished the writing of this book after working on it for over a decade and tried to find a succinct way to summarize my experience, this proverb immediately jumped to mind. It's fitting not only because my book project has taken just as long, if not longer, to complete, but because the subject of the book is also about the making of swords, albeit a different kind. While uncertain whether the swordsman in Jia's poem received any assistance from others in whetting his blade, I know clearly that I owe a great deal to a lot of people and institutions who have helped me in all these years for the completion of this book.

First of all, I want to thank Kent State University, my home institution, for its strong support that has made the completion of this time- and resource-consuming project possible. Numerous grants from the University Research Council have allowed me to travel to various archives and libraries, pay for some data collection expenses, and present results of my research at national as well as international conferences. I have also benefited from the Faculty Professional Improvement Leaves and the Faculty Professional Development Time Releases that have relieved me from my teaching responsibilities, permitting me to devote more time and energy to my research and writing. The Interlibrary Loan Office of the Kent State University Library has done an amazing job in locating numerous primary and secondary sources, including some of the rarest ones in the country, for me despite all the logistic difficulties caused by the COVID-19 pandemic.

Many capable staff members at various archives and libraries have provided me professional assistance that has made my research efficient and fruitful. I want to thank those who have helped me during my research at a number of institutions in the United States, including the National Archives in College Park, Maryland; the Richard Nixon Presidential Library and Museum, Yorba Linda, California; the Bentley Library, University of Michigan, Ann Arbor; the Schlesinger Library, Radcliff Institute for Advanced Studies, Harvard University, Cambridge, Massachusetts; the Yale University Library Manuscript Collections and the Divinity Library Special Collections, Yale University, New Haven, Connecticut; and the Schomburg Center for Research in Black Culture, New York Public Library, and the Tamiment Library, New York University, New York City. I also want to thank those who have given me generous assistance during my visit to several institutions in the People's Republic of China and Taiwan, including the Ministry of Foreign Affairs Archives and the Beijing Municipal Archives in Beijing, the Shanghai Municipal Archives in Shanghai, the Shanxi Provincial Archives in Xian, the Hubei Provincial Archives in Wuhan, the National Archives Administration under the National Development Council and the Academia Historica, both in Taipei, Taiwan.

I greatly appreciate the comments and advice from many scholars who have reviewed my papers and have come to my conference presentations. In the past decade, different parts of my research on the subject have been published in peer reviewed journals and presented at professional conferences. The candid comments from anonymous reviewers, usually three or more for each article, have made the final version of my papers much better. The questions as well as insights from the audiences at my conference panels helped me sharpen my arguments and widen my scope, which in turn made the integration of those papers into this book much smoother. Special thanks go to the four anonymous book reviewers, two for the initial proposal and two for the completed manuscript, for their generous encouragement and constructive recommendations that are invaluable for the improvement and completion of this book. I also want to thank Thomas

Christensen, Mark Bradley, and Rosemary Foote for including this book in the Nancy B. Tucker and Warren I. Cohen Book Series on American–East Asian Relations. The pioneering and exemplary work done by Nancy Tucker and Warren Cohen on U.S.-China cultural relations inspired me to keep laboring on this book until its completion.

A few chapters of this book have drawn from my two previously published papers after various degrees of revision. I am grateful to the Massachusetts Institute of Technology Press for allowing me to use my article published in the summer 2018 issue of the *Journal of the Cold War Studies* in chapters 5, 7, and 8 of this book. I am also grateful to Springer for giving me the permission to include part of my paper from issue number 1 of the 2016 volume of the *Frontier of History in China* in chapters 1 and 3 of this book. I want to express my deep appreciation to the Bentley Historical Library of University of Michigan and the Schlesinger Library, Radcliff Institute for Advanced Studies at Harvard University, for granting me the permission to use several photos from the Robert Williams Papers and the Shirley Graham Du Bois Papers respectively in my book.

It has been such a great pleasure to work with Stephen Wesley, my editor at Columbia University Press, who handled the whole publication process with unmatched professionalism, efficiency, and compassion. His patience and understanding have made this challenging task an enjoyable experience.

Last but not least, my heartfelt thanks go to my wife Liu Yang and my son Ran. They have not only tolerated my absences and absentmindedness for many years but also adapted their schedules whenever possible to accompany me to my conferences and research sites at home and abroad, making this project a truly shared journey for the whole family. The completion of this book is only possible because of their unfailing love and support.

Notes

Introduction: Beating Plowshares into Swords

1. Ikira Iriye, "Culture and Power: International Relations as Intercultural Relations," *Diplomatic History* 3, no. 2 (Spring 1979): 115.
2. Nathan Glazer, "American Values & American Foreign Policy," *Commentary* 62, no. 1 (July 1, 1976): 32.
3. For detailed discussion on U.S.-China cultural and educational relations before 1949, see Hongshan Li, *U.S.-China Educational Exchange: State, Society, and Intercultural Relations, 1905–1950* (New Brunswick, NJ: Rutgers University Press, 2008).
4. John Haddad, *America's First Adventures in China: Trade, Treaties, Opium, and Salvation*, (Philadelphia: Temple University Press, 2013), 1–13.
5. "Zhongyang Zhengzhiju Guanyu Xianzheng Wenti De Zhishi" (Directive from the Politburo of the Central Committee on Constitutional Government), March 1, 1944; "Yanan Xieding Caoan" (Draft of the Yanan Agreement), November 10, 1944, in *Zhonggong Zhongyang Wenjian Xuanji* (Selected Documents of the Chinese Communist Party Central Committee), 25 vols., ed. Zhongyang Danganguan (Beijing: Zhonggong Zhongyang Dangxiao Chubanshe, 1989), 14:178–79, 393–94.
6. Haddad, *America's First Adventure in China*; Li, *U.S.-China Educational Exchange*; Jessie Gregory Lutz, *China and the Christian Colleges, 1850–1950* (Ithaca, NY: Cornell University Press, 1971); Mary Brown Bullock, *The Oil Prince's Legacy: Rockefeller Philanthropy in China* (Palo Alto, CA: Stanford University

Press, 2011); Yunxiang Gao, *Arise, Africa! Roar, China!: Black and Chinese Citizens of the World in the Twentieth Century* (Chapel Hill: University of North Carolina Press, 2021); Wilma Fairbank, *America's Cultural Experiment in China, 1942–1949* (Washington, DC: U.S. Government Printing Office, 1976); Shuhua Fan, *The Harvard-Yenching Institute and Cultural Engineering: Remaking the Humanities in China, 1924–1951* (Lanham, MD: Lexington Books, 2014); Iris Chang, *Thread of the Silkworm* (New York: Basic Books, 1995).

7. C. Martin Wilbur, "Sino-American Relations in Scholarship as Viewed from the United States," in *U.S.-ROC Relations: From the White Paper to Taiwan Relations Act*, ed. Cecilia S. T. Chang (New York: Institute of Asian Studies, St. John's University, 1984), 89–145; Zhang Pengyuan, "Cong Taiwan Kan ZhongMei Jin Sanshi Nian Zhi Xueshu Jiaoliu" (An Examination of Sino-American Academic Exchange in the Past Thirty Years from Taiwan's Perspective), *Hanxue Yanjiu* Sinology Research) 2, no. 1 (June 1984): 23–56; Zhao Qina, "Meiguo Zhengfu Zai Taiwan De Jiaoyu Yu Wenhua Jiaoliu Huodong (Yijiuwuyi Zhi Yijiuqiling Nian)" (The U.S. Government's Educational and Cultural Exchange Activities in Taiwan from 1951 to 1970), *OuMei Yanjiu* (Research on Europe and America) 31, no. 1 (March 2001): 79–127.

8. Warren Cohen, "While China Faced East: Chinese-American Cultural Relations, 1949–1971," in *Educational Exchanges: Essays on Sino-American Experience*, ed. Joyce K. Kallgren and Denis Fred Simon (Berkeley: Institute of East Asian Studies University of California, Berkeley, 1987), 44–57; Nancy Bernkopf Tucker, *Taiwan, Hong Kong, and the United States, 1945–1992: Uncertain Friendship* (New York: Twayne Publishers, 1994), 79–93.

9. Paul Hollander, *Political Pilgrims: Travel of Western Intellectuals to the Soviet Union, China, and Cuba, 1928–1978* (New York: Oxford University Press, 1981); Anne-Marie Brady, *Making the Foreign Serve China: Managing Foreigners in the People's Republic* (Lanham, MD: Rowman & Littlefield, 2003); Beverley Hooper, *Foreigners Under Mao: Western Lives in China, 1949–1976* (Hong Kong: Hong Kong University Press, 2016).

10. Allen S. Whiting, *China Crosses the Yalu: The Decision to Enter the Korean War* (Stanford, CA: Stanford University Press, 1960); Jian Chen, *China's Road to the Korean War: The Making of the Sino-American Confrontation* (New York: Columbia University Press, 1994); Chen Jian, *Mao's China and the Cold War* (Chapel Hill: University of North Carolina Press, 2010); William Stueck, *The Korean War: An International History* (Princeton, NJ: Princeton University Press, 1995); Qiang Zhai, *China and the Vietnam Wars, 1950–1975* (Chapel Hill: University of North Carolina Press, 2000); Shuguang Zhang, *Economic Cold War: America's Embargo Against China and the Sino-Soviet Alliance, 1949–1963* (Stanford, CA: Stanford University Press, 2002); Tao Wenzhao, *ZhongMei Guanxi Shi, 1949–2000* (A History of China-U.S. Relations, 1949–2000)

(Shanghai: Shanghai Renmin Chubanshe, 2004); Robert S. Ross and Jiang Changbin, eds., *Re-examining the Cold War: U.S.-China Diplomacy, 1954–1973* (Cambridge, MA: Harvard University Press, 2001); Niu Jun, *Lengzhan Shiqi De Zhongguo Zhanlue Jueci* (China's Strategic Decisions in the Cold War) (Beijing: Shijie Zhishi Chubanshe, 2019).

11. Walter Hixson, *Parting the Curtain: Propaganda, Culture, and the Cold War, 1945–1961* (New York: St. Martin's Press, 1997); Christopher Mayhew, *A War of Words: A Cold War Witness* (London: I. B. Tauris, 1998); Frances Stonor Saunders, *The Cultural Cold War: The CIA and the World of Arts and Letters* (New York: New Press, 1999); Scott Lucas, *Freedom's War: The U.S. Crusade Against the Soviet Union 1945–56* (Manchester: Manchester University Press, 1999); Richard M. Fried, *The Russians Are Coming! The Russians Are Coming! Pageantry and Patriotism in Cold-War America* (New York: Oxford University Press, 1998); Yale Richmond, *Cultural Exchange and the Cold War: Raising the Iron Curtain* (University Park: Pennsylvania State University Press, 2003); Yale Richmond, *Practice Public Diplomacy: A Cold War Odyssey* (New York: Berghahn Books, 2008).

12. Simei Qing, *From Allies to Enemies: Visions of Modernity, Identity, and U.S.-China Diplomacy, 1945–1960* (Cambridge, MA: Harvard University Press, 2007); Robeson Taj Frazier, *The East Is Black: Cold War China in the Black Radical Imagination* (Durham, NC: Duke University Press, 2015); Fabio Lanza, *The End of Concern: Maoist China, Activism, and Asian Studies* (Durham, NC: Duke University Press, 2017).

1. Drawing the Sword

1. David Holm, *Art and Ideology in Revolutionary China* (Oxford: Clarendon Press, 1991), 17–18.
2. Gong Li, *Mao Zedong Yu Meiguo* (Mao Zedong and the United States) (Beijing: Shijie Zhishi Chubanshe, 1999), 7.
3. Zhonggong Zhongyang Wenxian Yanjiushi, ed., *Mao Zedong Nianpu, 1893–1949* (Chronicles of Mao Zedong, 1893–1949) (Beijing: Zhongyang Wenxian Chubanshe, 2013), 2:532, 544, 555–56.
4. Mao Zedong, "Jianzu He Shengchang Shi Baowei Jiefangqu De Liangjian Dashi" (Rent Reduction and Production are the Two Major Tasks for the Liberated Areas), November 7, 1945, in *Mao Zedong Xuanji* (Selected Works of Mao Zedong) (Beijing: Renmin Chubanshe, 1969), 1068–69.
5. Mao Zedong, "Yu Meiguo Jizhe Anna Luyisi Sitelang De Tanhua" (A Conversation with American Journalist Anna Louise Strong), August 1946, in *Mao Zedong Xuanji*, 1091.

6. Mao Zedong, "Meiguo Tiaojie Zhenxiang He Zhongguo Neizhan Qiantu: He Meiguo Jizhe Sidier De Tanhua" (The Truth of American "Mediation" and the Future of China's Civil War: A Conversation with American Journalist Steele), September 29, 1946, in *Mao Zedong Xuanji*, 1098.
7. Mao Zedong, "Yingjie Zhongguo Geming De Xin Gaochao" (Welcoming the New High Tide of the Chinese Revolution), February 1, 1947, in *Mao Zedong Xuanji*, 1107–13.
8. Mao Zedong, "Quanshijie Geming Liliang Tuanjie Qilai, Fandui Diguo Zhuyi De Qinglue" (All the Revolutionary Forces in the Whole World Unite to Fight Imperialist Aggression), November 1948, in *Mao Zedong Xuanji*, 1250.
9. "Zhonggong Zhongyang Guanyu Duidai ZaiHua Waiguo Qiaomin Zhengce De Zhishi" (Instruction from the Chinese Communist Party Central Committee on the Policy Toward Foreign Residents in China), February 7, 1948, in *Jiandang Yilai Zhongyao Wenxian Xuanbian* (Selected Important Documents Since the Founding of the Party), ed. Zhonggong Zhongyang Wenxian Yanjiushi (Beijing: Zhongyang Wenxian Chubanshe, 2011), 25:88–89.
10. "Zhonggong Zhongyang Guanyu Xin Jiefang Chengshi Zhong Zhongwai Baokan Tongxunshe Chuli Banfa De Jueding" (The Chinese Communist Party Central Committee's Decision on the Handling of Chinese and Foreign Newspapers, Magazines, and Presses in the Newly Liberated Cities), November 8, 1948, in *Jiandang Yilai Zhongyao Wenxian Xuanbian*, 25:630–34.
11. Gao Hua, *Hong Taiyang Shi Zenyang Shengqi De: Yanan Zhengfeng Yundong De Lailong Qumai* (How Did the Red Sun Rise: A History of the Yanan Rectification Movement) (Hong Kong: Hong Kong Chinese University Press, 2000), 372–74.
12. "Zhongyang Guanyu Waijiao Gongzuo De Zhishi" (Instruction from the Central Committee on Diplomatic Work), August 18, 1944, in *Zhonggong Zhongyang Wenjian* Xuanji (Selected Documents of the Chinese Communist Party Central Committee), ed. Zhongyang Danganguan (Beijing: Zhonggong Zhongyang Dangxiao Chubanshe, 1989), 14:314–18.
13. "Zhongyang Guanyu Meiguo DuiHua Zhengce De Biandong He Wodang Duice De Zhishi" (An Instruction from the Central Committee on the Change of U.S. Policy Toward China and the Countermeasures of Our Party), December 19, 1945, in *Zhonggong Zhongyang Wenjian Xuanji*, 15: 494–95.
14. Mao Zedong, "Muqian Xingshi He Dang Zai Yijiusijiu Nian De Renwu" (The Current Situation and the Party's Tasks in 1949), January 8, 1949, in Mao Zedong, *Mao Zedong Wenji* (Collection of Mao Zedong's Writings) (Beijing: Renmin Chubanshe, 1996), 5:235–36n6.
15. Mao, "Muqian Xingshi He Dang Zai Yijiusijiu Nian De Renwu," 5:231–36.
16. "Zhonggong Zhongyang Dui Chuli Diguo Zhuyi Tongxunshe Dianxun Banfa De Guiding" (The Chinese Communist Party Central Committee's

Regulation on the Methods in Handling the Dispatches from the Imperialist News Presses), January 18, 1949, in *Dang De Xuanchuan Gongzuo Wenjian Xuanbian* (Selected Documents on the Party's Propaganda Work), ed. Zhongyang Xuanchubu Bangongting (Beijing: Zhonggong Zhongyang Dangxiao Chubanshe, 1994), 1: 2–3.

17. Zhonggong Zhongyang Wenxian Yanjiusishi, ed., *Mao Zedong Nianpu, 1949–1976* (Chronicles of Mao Zedong, 1949–1976) (Beijing: Zhongyang Wenxian Chubanshe, 2013), 1:441.
18. "Zhongyang Guanyu Waijiao Gongzuo De Zhishi" (Instruction from the Central Committee on Diplomatic Work), January 19, 1949, in *Zhonggong Zhongyang Wenjian Xuanji*, 18:44–45.
19. Shi Zhe, *Wo De Yisheng: Shi Zhe Zishu* (My Life: A Self-Narrative) (Beijing: Renmin Chubanshe, 2001), 275–76.
20. "Zhongyang Guanyu Waijiao Gongzuo De Zhishi," 18:45–49.
21. "Zhonggong Zhongyang Dui Beiping Shi Baozhi, Zazhi, Tongxunshe Dengji Zanxing Banfa De Pishi" (The Chinese Communist Party Central Committee's Comment on Temporary Procedures for the Registration of Newspapers, Magazines, and Presses in Beijing), in *Dang De Xuanchuan Gongzuo Wenxian Xuanbian*, 1:9–10.
22. Mao Zedong, "Zai Zhongguo Gongchandang Diqijie Zhongyang Weiyuanhui Dierci Quanti Huiyi Shang De Baogao" (Speech at the Second Plenary of the Seventh National Congress of the Chinese Communist Party), March 5, 1949, in *Mao Zedong Xuanji*, 1314–29.
23. Mao Zedong, "'Zhengzhi Zhoubao' Fakan Liyou (The Reason for the Inauguration of *Political Weekly*), December 5, 1925, in *Mao Zedong Wenji*, 1:21–23.
24. Mao Zedong, "Zhongguo Gongchandang Hongjun Disijun Dijiuci Daibiao Dahui Jueyian" (Resolution of the Ninth Chinese Communist Party Convention of the Fourth Army of the Red Army), December 1929, in *Mao Zedong Wenji*, 1:78–117.
25. For detailed information on the CCP's fight on the cultural front during the War against Japan and China's Civil War, see Peng Yaxin, ed., *Zhonggong Zhongyang Nanfangju: Wenhua Gongzuo* (Cultural Work of the Southern Bureau of the Chinese Communist Party Central Committee) (Beijing: Zhonggong Dangshi Chubanshe, 2009).
26. Mao Zedong, "Jinkuai Pairen Dao Shanghai Dengdi Banbao" (Sending People to Shanghai and Other Places to Publish Newspapers as Soon as Possible), September 14, 1945, in *Mao Zedong Wenji*, 4:23.
27. Mao, "Resolution of the Ninth Chinese Communist Party Convention," 1:78–88.
28. Mao Zedong, "Fandui Ziyou Zhuyi" (Fighting Against Liberalism), September 7, 1937, in *Mao Zedong Xuanji*, 769–86.

29. Mao Zedong, "Zhengdun Dang De Zuofeng" (Rectifying the Work Style of the Party), February 1, 1942, in *Mao Zedong Xuanji*, 330–32; Mao Zedong, "Guanyu Zhengdun Sanfeng" (On Rectification of Three Work Styles), April 20, 1942, in *Mao Zedong Wenji*, 2:411–23.
30. Mao Zedong, "Zai Yenan Wenyi Zuotanhui Shang De Jianghua" (Speech at the Art Forum in Yanan), May 1942, in *Mao Zedong Xuanji*, 804–5.
31. "Zhongyang Zongxuewei Guanyu Xuexi Mao Zedong 'Zai Yenan Wenyi Zuotanhui Shang De Jianghua' De Taongzhi" (The Circular from the Supreme Committee on Study of the Central Committee on the Study of Mao Zedong's Speech at the Art Forum in Yanan), October 20, 1943; "Zhongyang Xuanchuanbu Guanyu Zhixing Dang De Wenyi Zhengce De Jueding" (Decision of the Propaganda Department of the Central Committee on the Implementation of the Party's Policy on Art), November 7, 1943, in *Zhonggong Zhongyang Wenjian Xuanji*, 14:102, 107–10.
32. Wang Jiaxiang, "Zhongguo Gongchandang Yu Zhongguo Minzu Jiefang De Daolu: Jinian Gongchandang Ershier Zhounian Yu Kangzhan Liu Zhounian" (The Chinese Communist Party and the Road of the Chinese National Liberation: Celebrating the Twenty-Second Anniversary of the Communist Party and the Sixth Anniversary of the War Against Japan), July 5, 1943, in *Zhonggong Zhongyang Wenjian Xuanji*, 14:477–79.
33. "Zhongguo Gongchandang Dangzhang" (Constitution of the Chinese Communist Party), June 11, 1945, in *Zhonggong Zhongyang Wenjian Xuanji*, 15:115.
34. Gao, *Hong Taiyang Shi Ruhe Shengqi De*, 299–439.
35. Mao Zedong, "Huijian Zhongwai Jizhe Xibei Canguantuan De Jianghua" (Speech at the Meeting with Chinese and Foreign Reporters Visiting the Northwest), June 12, 1944, in *Mao Zedong Wenji*, 3:167–71.
36. Theodore White, *In Search of History: A Personal Adventure* (New York: Warner Books, 1978), 247–59.
37. "Mei Jizhe Feibang Beiping Renmin—Renmin You Quanli Geiyu Youli Dafu" (American Reporters Slander the Beiping People: The Beiping People Have the Right to Give Them a Forceful Reply), *People's Daily*, February 12, 1949.
38. "Sipo Meidi Jizhe Zuilian Ba Tamen Zhuchu Jiefangqu—Beiping Renmin Jixu Kangyi Mei Jizhe Feibang" (Exposing the True Color of the American Imperialist Reporters and Expel Them from the Liberated Area: The Beiping People Continue to Protest Slander by the American Reporters), *People's Daily*, February 14, 1949.
39. "Beiping Junguanhui Fachu Tongling—Tingzhi Waiguo Tongxunshe Ji Jizhe Huodong" (The Beiping Military Control Commission Issues an Order: Stopping the Activities of Foreign News Agencies and Reporters), *People's Daily*, March 1, 1949.

40. Liu Shaoqi, "Daibiao Zhonggong Zhongyang Gei Liangong (Bu) Zhongyang Sidalin De Baogao" (A Report on Behalf of the Chinese Communist Party Central Committee to the Soviet Communist Party [Bolshevik] Central Committee and Stalin), July 4, 1949, in Zhongyang Wenxian Yanjiushi, ed., *Jianguo Yilai Liu Shaoqi Wengao* (Writings of Liu Shaoqi Since the Founding of the People's Republic of China) (Beijing: Zhongyang Wenxian Chubanshe, 2005), 1:21.
41. "Ping Junguanhui Fachu Mingling—Tingzhi Mei Xinwenchu Huodong" (The Beiping Military Control Commission Issues Order—Stop the Activities of the United States Information Service), *People's Daily*, July 20, 1949; "Beiping, Tianjin, Hankou, and Nanjing—Tingzhi Mei Xinwenchu Feifa Huodong" (Beijing, Tianjin, Hankou, and Nanjing—Stop the Illegal Activities of the U.S. Information Service), *People's Daily*, July 27, 1949.
42. Dean Acheson, "Letter of Transmittal," July 30, 1949, in U.S. Department of State, *United States Relations with China: With Special Reference to the Period 1944–1949* (Washington, DC: U.S. Government Printing House, 1949), iii.
43. Mao Zedong, "Wei Shenme Yao Taolun Baipi Shu" (Why the White Paper Should Be Discussed), August 28, 1949, in *Mao Zedong Xunji*, 1391.
44. Grace Boynton Diary, December 20 and 23, 1948, quoted in Philip West, *Yenching University and Sino-Western Relations, 1916–1952* (Cambridge, MA: Harvard University Press, 1976), 195–96.
45. Minutes of Meeting: United Board for Christian Higher Education in China Yenching Interim Committee, March 11, 1949, Archives of the United Board for Christian Higher Education in Asia, RG 11, Series IV, Reel 301, Divinity School Library, Yale University, New Haven, Connecticut (hereafter cited as UBCHEA.)
46. "Most Staff Remaining at Posts on Campus," *Yenching News*, vol. xxvii, no. 2, June 1949, 3; Minutes of Meeting: United Board for Christian Higher Education in China Yenching Interim Committee, May 9, 1949, UBCHEA, Reel 301.
47. Wang Licheng, *Meiguo Wenhua Shentou Yu Jindai Zhongguo Jiaoyu: Hujiang Daxue De Lishi* (American Cultural Penetration and Modern Chinese Education: The History of Shanghai University) (Shanghai: Fudan University Press, 2000), 395–99.
48. "Zhongguo Renmin Jiefangjun Di Shisan Bingtuan Zhengzhi Bu Bugao" (A Public Announcement Issued by the Department of Political Affairs, the Thirteenth Corps of the People's Liberation Army), December 18, 1948, in *Qinghua Daxue Shiliao Xuanbian* (The Selected Historical Records of Qinghua University), ed. Qinghua Daxue Xiaoshi Yanjiushi (Beijing: Qinghua Daxue Chubanshe, 1994), 4:xxxiv.

49. Mao Zedong, "Diudiao Huanxiang, Zhunbei Douzheng" (Throw Away the Fantasy and Prepare to Fight), August 14, 1949, in *Mao Zedong Xuanji*, 1372–79.
50. Mao Zedong, "'Youyi,' Haishi Qinglue" ("Friendship" or Aggression?), August 30, 1949, in *Mao Zedong Xuanji*, 1394–97.
51. Mao Zedong, "Diudiao Huanxiang," in *Mao Zedong Xuanji*, 1372–79.
52. "Zhongguo Zhengzhi Xieshang Huiyi Gongtong Gangling" (The Common Program of the Chinese People's Political Consultative Conference), September 29, 1949, in *Zhonghua Renmin Gongheguo Zhongyao Jiaoyu Wenxian, 1949–1997* (Important Documents on Education in the People's Republic of China, 1949–1997), ed. He Dongchang (Changsha: Hainan Chubanshe, 1998), 1:1.
53. Guo Moruo, "Guanyu Wenhua Jiaoyu Gongzuo De Baogao" (Report on Cultural and Educational Work), June 17, 1950, in *Zhonghua Renmin Gongheguo Zhongyao Jiaoyu Wenxian*, 1:29.
54. "Yenching Opens with Fall Enrollment of 900; Academic and Religious Freedom are Unimpaired," *Yenching News* 28, no. 1 (1949): 1.
55. "Staff Member Describes Government Study 'Camp,'" *Yenching News* 28, no. 1 (1949): 1.
56. "Zhonggong Zhongyang Guanyu Zhongyang Renmin Zhengfu Chengli Hou Dang De Wenhua Jiaoyu Gongzuo Wenti De Zhishi" (Instructions from the Chinese Communist Party Central Committee on the Cultural and Educational Work After the Establishment of the Central People's Government), December 5, 1949, in *Zhonghua Renmin Gongheguo Zhongyao Jiaoyu Wenxian*, 1:2.
57. "Ma Xulun Buzhang Zai Diyici Quanguo Jiaoyu Gongzuo Huiyi Shang De Kaimuci" (Opening Remarks of Minister Ma Xulun at the First National Work Meeting on Education), December 23, 1949, in *Zhonghua Renmin Gongheguo Zhongyao Jiaoyu Wenxian*, 1:6–7.
58. "Jiaoyubu Guanyu Diyici Quanguo Jiaoyu Gongzuo Huiyi De Baogao" (Report from the Ministry of Education on the First National Work Meeting on Education), January 6, 1950, in *Zhonghua Renmin Gongheguo Zhongyao Jiaoyu Wenxian*, 1:10–11.
59. They included *Gaodeng Xuexiao Zanxing Guicheng* (Temporary Regulations for Higher Education Institutions), *Sili Gaodeng Xuexiao Guanli Zanxing Banfa* (Temporary Regulations for Private Higher Education Institutions), and *Zhengwu Yuan Guanyu Gaodeng Xuexiao Lingdao Guanxi Wenti De Jueding* (Resolution of the Executive Council on the Administrative Relations for Higher Education Institutions). "Diyici Quanguo Gaodeng Jiaoyu Huiyi De Baogao" (Report on the First National Conference on Higher Education),

July 17, 1950, in *Zhonghua Renmin Gongheguo Zhongyao Jiaoyu Wenxian*, 1:41–43.
60. "Zhengwuyuan Guanyu Gaodeng Xuexiao Lingdao Guanxi Wenti De Jueding," July 28, 1950; "Gaodeng Xuexiao Zanxing Guiding," July 28, 1950, in *Zhonghua Renmin Gongheguo Zhongyao Jiaoyu Wenxian*, 1:44–45, 41–43.
61. "Sili Gaodeng Xuexiao Guanli Zanxing Banfa" (Temporary Regulations on the Management of Private Higher Education Institutions), July 27, 1950, in *Zhonghua Renmin Gongheguo Zhongyao Jiaoyu Wenxian*, 1:47–48.
62. Mao Zedong, "Bu Yao Simian Chuji" (Don't Strike in All Four Directions), in *Mao Zedong Wenxuan*, 5:21–24.
63. "Zhonggong Zhongyang Guanyu Tianzhu Jiao, Jidu Jiao Wenti De Zhishi" (Instruction from the Chinese Communist Party Central Committee on Catholic and Protestant Churches), August 19, 1950, in *Jianguo Yilai Zhongyao Wenxian Xuanbian*, 1:408–12.
64. "Ma Xulun Buzhang Fabiao Shumian Tanhua Shuoming Zhengfu Jieban Fuda Jingguo" (Minister of Education Ma Xulun's Written Statement on the Government's Taking Over Fujen University), *Guangming Daily*, October 13, 1950.
65. Zhou Enlai's comments on Ma Xulun's "Report on the Handling of the Private School Furen University in Beijing," September 6, 1950, *Zhou Enlai Nianpu* (Chronicles of Zhou Enlai), ed. Zhonggong Zhongyang Wenxian Yanjiushi (Beijing: Zhongyang Wenxian Chubanshe, 1997), 1:76.
66. *Zhou Enlai Nianpu*, 1:84–85.
67. Mao Zedong, "Bu Yao Simian Chuji," 5:21–24.
68. "Jiaoyu Bu Guanyu Diyici Quanguo Jiaoyu Gongzuo Huiyi De Baogao" (Report from the Ministry of Education on the First National Working Meeting on Education), in *Zhonghua Renmin Gongheguo Zhongyao Jiaoyu Wenxian*, 1:10–11.
69. "Yenching Maintains Academic Standards as Enrollment Reaches New Height," *Yenching News* 29, no. 1 (1950): 2.
70. "Yenching Still Very Much Alive; Life Marked by Austerity and Earnestness"; "Western Professor Sees Continued Place for Yenching for Decade or Longer," *Yenching News* 29, no. 1 (1950): 1, 3.
71. Liu, "Daibiao Zhonggong Zhongyang Gei Liangong (Bu) Zhongyang Sidalin De Baogao," 1:21.
72. For more detailed discussion on the termination of the Fulbright Program, see Wilma Fairbank, *American Cultural Experiment in China, 1942–1949* (Washington, DC: U.S. Government Printing Office, 1976), 153–209; Hongshan Li, *U.S.-China Educational Exchange: State, Society, and Intercultural Relations, 1905–1950* (New Brunswick, NJ: Rutgers University Press, 2008), 162–64.

73. Letter from U.S. Embassy in Nanking to the Department of State, September 30, 1948, Department of State, *Correspondence, Memorandums, and Reports of the Chinese and Korean Assistance Branch*, Box 4, National Archives, RG 59, College Park, Maryland (hereafter cited as CMR).
74. Letter from Han to Presidents of American Colleges and Universities, September 13, 1948, CMR Box 4.
75. Letter from Chin to Meng, December 15, 1949, CMR Box 4.
76. Memo from Allen to the Under Secretary, February 24, 1949, CMR Box 4.
77. Memo from Johnstone, March 10, 1950, CMR Box 7; U.S. Department of State, *The Program of Emergency Aid to Chinese Students, 1949–1955* (Washington, DC: U.S. Government Printing Office, 1956), 4.
78. Letter from Smith to Meng, December 3, 1948; Estimated Financial Needs of Chinese Students in the United States, December 30, 1948, included as Appendix I in Meng to the Secretary of State, January 10, 1949, CMR Box 4.
79. Letter from Stone to Luce, April 9, 1948, CMR Box 4.
80. Memo of Conversation, January 10, 1949, CMR Box 4.
81. Meng to the Secretary of State, January 10, 1949, CMR Box 4.
82. Letter from Colligan to Cleveland, January 14, 1949, CMR Box 4.
83. Letter from Koo to Hoffman, February 12, 1949; Letter from Hoffman to Webb, March 23, 1949, CMR Box 4.
84. Memorandum from Allen to the Under Secretary, February 28, 1949; Recommendations of the United States Advisory Commission on Educational Exchange, February 28, 1949, CMR Box 4.
85. Memorandum from Johnstone to Allen, February 28, 1949, CMR Box 4.
86. Memorandum from Johnstone to Allen, March 7, 1949, CMR Box 4.
87. Recommendations of the Advisory Commission on Educational Exchange.
88. Rules Announced for Chinese Student Emergency Aid Program, April 7, 1949, CMR, Box 24.
89. U.S. Department of State and Economic Cooperation Administration, "For the Press," March 30, 1949, CMR, Box 24.
90. Rules Announced for Chinese Student Emergency Aid Grants.
91. Memorandum from Johnstone to Allen, March 7, 1949, CMR, Box 4.
92. Memorandum from Colligan to Johnstone, September 20 and 22, 1949, CMR, Box 4.
93. Letter from Allen to Hoffman, May 28, 1949, CMR, Box 4.
94. Letter from Hoffman to Allen, June 9, 1949; Memo from Fisher to Russell, July 27, 1951, CMR, Box 4.
95. Emergency Aid to Chinese Students Status of Program, May 19, 1949, CMR, Box 4.
96. Memorandum from Colligan to Johnstone, September 22, 1949, CMR, Box 4.

97. Memo from Johnstone, March 10, 1950, CMR, Box 7.
98. Fairbank, *America's Cultural Experiment in China*, 106–9.
99. Memorandum from Sargeant to the Under Secretary, October 24, 1949, CMR, Box 16.
100. Memo from Caldwell to Cook, July 11, 1949, CMR, Box 4.
101. Memo from Colligan to Connors, November 29, 1951, CMR, Box 21.
102. "Public Law 327, 81st Congress," Department of State, *The Program of Emergency Aid to Chinese Students*, 25.
103. Letter from Allen to Lucas, June 16, 1949, Department of State Press Release, CMR, Box 4.
104. "China Bills, Laws and Policies," *CQ Almanac, 1949*, 5th ed., 05-375–05-382, (Washington, DC: Congressional Quarterly, 1950), http://library.cqpress.com/cqalmanac/cqal49-1400096.
105. U.S. Congress, *Relief of Chinese Students*, July 14, 1949, House Report 1039, 81st Cong., 1st Sess., 2.
106. "Aid for Chinese Students: House Votes $4,000,000 to Help 4,000 Stranded in U.S.," *New York Times*, August 2, 1949.
107. Memorandum from Fisher to Caldwell, September 29, 1949, CMR, Box 13.
108. Memorandum from Sargeant to Free et al., October 6, 1949, CMR, Box 4.
109. Memorandum from Johnstone to Merchant, December 16, 1949, CMR, Box 13.
110. Memorandum from Caldwell to Colligan, October 12, 1949, CMR, Box 13.
111. Memorandum from Caldwell to Colligan, October 12, 1949, CMR, Box 13
112. Memorandum from Grondahl to Sargeant, October 14, 1949, CMR, Box 13.
113. Memorandum from Caldwell to Colligan, October 14, 1949, CMR, Box 13.
114. Memorandum from Grondahl to Sargeant, October 14, 1949, CMR, Box 13.
115. Memorandum from Cook to Sargeant, January 11, 1950, CMR, Box 13.
116. Memorandum from Johnstone to Merchant, November 30, 1949, CMR, Box 16.
117. Federal Bureau of Investigation Report 100–96007, November 8, 1949, CMR, Box 2.
118. Peng Yaxin, *Zhonggong Zhongyang Nanfangju: Wenhua Gongzuo* (South Bureau of the Chinese Communist Party Central Committee: Its Work on Culture) (Beijing: Zhonggong Dangshi Chubanshe, 2009), 340.
119. Peng, *Zhonggong Zhongyang Nanfangju*, 312–16.
120. Chen Yiming and Chen Xiuxia, "Qingxi Zuguo, Qingxi Renmin" (Loving Motherland, Loving People), in *Jianguo Chuqi Liuxuesheng Guiguo Jishi* (Records of the Students Returned from Overseas in the Early Period of the Nation), ed. Quanguo Zhengxie (Beijing: Zhongguo Wenshi Chubanshe, 1999), 15–27.
121. Chen and Chen, "Qingxi Zuguo," 28–29.

122. "The 'Paper Tiger' Cannot Stand One Blow," *People's Daily*, July 26, 1950.
123. Memorandum from Fisher to Caldwell, August 18, 1950, CMR, Box 13.
124. Memorandum from Johnstone Jr. to Hulten, October 12, 1950, CMR, Box 13.
125. China Institute in America, Annual Report of the Director, 1950, CMR, Box 20.
126. China Institute in America, Annual Report of the Director, 1950; Annual Report of the Director, 1951; Annual Report of the Director, January 1952–August 1953, CMR, Box 20.
127. Clarence Linton and Samuel Kung, "Exploratory Study of Chinese Students," October 15, 1953, CMR, Box 2.
128. Dean Acheson, "United States Policy Toward Asia," March 15, 1950; *Department of State Bulletin*, March 27, 1950, 467–72.
129. Memorandum from Byers to Fisher, et al., April 4, 1950, CMR, Box 4.
130. Letter from McFall to Lawton, May 29, 1950, CMR, Box 4.
131. Report to Congress on the Chinese Students Emergency Aid Program (Final Draft), n.d., 1955, Department of State Press Release, CMR, Box 4.
132. *United States Statutes at Large*, 81st Cong., 2nd Sess., 64:202.

2. Cutting All Ties

1. Jin Chongji, *Zhou Enlai Zhuan* (Biography of Zhou Enlai) (Beijing: Zhongyang Wenxian Chubanshe, 1998), 1020–21.
2. Iris Chang, *Thread of the Silkworm* (New York: Basic Books, 1995), 149–75.
3. "U.S. Seizes Four Chinese in Jet Document Case," *New York Times*, September 21, 1950; Zhu Jiping, *Genxi Zhonghua: Zhuming Guiguo Kexuejia Caifeng* (Rooted in China: Reports on Famous Returned Scientists) (Hefei: Anhui Jiaoyu Chubanshe, 1997), 335–36.
4. Although no banned documents or equipment were found in the luggage of those three scholars, Zhao had sent some bigger parts for an accelerator back to China separately and put some blueprints and small parts such as vacuum tubes in the luggage of Bao Wenkui, another Chinese student on the same ship. Bao Wenkui, "'Weierxun Zongtonghao' Youlun Shang De Zhenshi Gushi" (The True Story on Board Ocean Liner SS *President Wilson*), in *1950 Niandai Guiguo LiuMei Kexuejia Fangtanlu* (Interviews with Scientists Returned from the United States in the 1950s), ed. Hou Xianglin et al. (Changsha: Hunan Jiaoyu Chubanshe, 2013), 37–40.
5. Materials Related to the Return of Qian Xuesen, A Chinese Scientist in the United States, Ministry of Foreign Affairs Archives, 111-00081-03, Beijing, China (hereafter cited as MFAA).

6. Materials Related to the Return of Qian Xuesen, MFAA.
7. "Huiguo Liuxuesheng 183 Ren Dian Lianheguo Yaoqiu Zhicai Meidi" (183 Returned Students Telegraphed the United Nations Demanding Sanctions on the American Imperialists), *Guangming Daily*, October 18, 1950.
8. Jin, *Zhou Enlai Zhuan*, 1021.
9. Zhou Enlai, "Kangmei Yuanchao, Baowei Heping" (Resist America—Aid Korea, Defend Peace), in *Zhou Enlai Waijiao Wenxuan* (Selected Diplomatic Essays of Zhou Enlai), ed. Zhonghua Renmin Gongheguo Waijiaobu (Beijing: Zhongyang Wenxian Chubanshe, 1990), 30–33.
10. Mao Zedong, "Zai Zhongyang Guanyu Muqian Shishi Xuanchuan Zhishi Gao Shang Jiaxie De Yiduan Hua" (A Paragraph Added to the Draft of the Instruction from the Chinese Communist Party Central Committee on Current Affairs Propaganda), October 1950, in *Jianguo Yilai Mao Zedong Wengao* (Mao Zedong's Writings Since the Founding of the Nation), ed. Zhonggong Zhongyang Wenxian Yanjiushi (Beijing: Zhongyang Wenxian Chubanshe, 1998), 1:616; *Zhou Enlai Nianpu* (Chronicles of Zhou Enlai) (Beijing: Zhongyang Wenxian Chubanshe, 2007), 1: 89.
11. "Zhonggong Zhongyang Guanyu Zai Quanguo Jinxing Shishi Xuanchuan De Zhishi" (Directive from the Chinese Communist Party Central Committee on Carrying Out Nationwide Propaganda on Current Affairs), October 26, 1950, in *Jiangguo Yilai Zhongyao Wenxian Xuanbian* (Selected Important Records Since the Founding of the People's Republic of China), ed. Zhonggong Zhongyang Wenxian Yanjiushi (Beijing: Zhongyang Wenxian Chubanshe, 1992), 1:436–40.
12. "Zhonggong Zhongyang Guanyu Zai Quanguo Jinxing Shishi Xuanchuan De Zhishi," 436–40; Jin, *Zhou Enlai Zhuan*, 1022.
13. "Beida Jiaoshi Sanbai Qishiliu Ren Shangshu Mao Zhuxi Chi Meidi Zuixing" (376 Peking University Teachers Wrote to Chairman Mao to Denounce the Crimes Committed by American Imperialists), *Guangming Daily*, November 4, 1950.
14. "Wei Fankang Meidi Qinglue Gonggu Renmin Shengli Er Douzheng" (Fighting to Resist American Imperialist Aggression and Consolidate People's Victory), *Guangming Daily*, November 4, 1950.
15. "Shanghai Dianyingjie Zhigong Juxing Zuotan Jianjue Jujue Fangying Meipian" (Shanghai Film Industry Workers Hold a Forum: Resolutely Refuse to Show American Movies), *Guangming Daily*, November 25, 1950.
16. "Gedi Xiangji Jujue Fangying" (Various Cities Refused to Show), *Guangming Daily*, January 3, 1951.
17. "Jing Yingyuanye Jihui Fabiao Shengming Jue Yi Xingdong Xiangying Lianhe Xuanyan" (The Cinema Industry in Beijing Held a Meeting and

Issued a Statement Pledging to Answer the Joint Declaration with Concrete Action), *Guangming Daily*, November 12, 1950.
18. "Zhongguo Renmin Dianying Shiye Yinian Lai Huo Guanghui Chengjiu" (Chinese People's Movie Industry Made Brilliant Achievements in the Past Year), *Guangming Daily*, January 3, 1951.
19. "Beida Quanxiao Jiaozhi Yuangong Haozhao: Jujue Shouting 'Meiguo Zhi Ying' " (All Faculty and Staff Members of the Peking University Issuing a Call: Refuse to Listen to Voice of America), *Guangming Daily*, November 4, 1950.
20. "Fuda Jiaoyuan Juxing Zuotanhui" (Fujen University Faculty Holding a Forum), *Guangming Daily*, November 24, 1950.
21. "Furen Daxue Jiaozhi Yuangong Fabiao Xuanyan: Zhuzhang Qudi Shouting 'Meiguo Zhi Ying' " (Fujen University Faculty and Staff Issuing a Statement: Urging to Ban Listening to VOA), *Guangming Daily*, November 26, 1950.
22. Letter from Lu to McMullen, October 28, 1950, quoted in Philip West, *Yenching University and Sino-Western Relations* (Cambridge, MA: Harvard University Press, 1976), 201.
23. "Zhonggong Beijing Shiwei Guanyu KangMei YuanChao Yundong Xiang Zhongyang Bing Huabeiju De Baogao" (A Report from the Chinese Communist Party Beijing Committee on the Resist America, Aid Korea Movement to the Central Committee and the North China Bureau), November 5, 1950, File 1-5-38; "Zhonggong Beijing Shiwei Guanyu KangMei YuanChao Yundong Xiang Mao Zhuxi, Zhongyang Bing Huabeiju De Dierci Baogao" (Second Report from the Chinese Communist Party Committee of Beijing City to Chairman Mao, the Central Committee, and the North China Bureau on the Resist America, Aid Korea Movement), November 12, 1950, File 1-5-549, Municipal Archives of Beijing.
24. Warren R. Austin, "U.S. Appeals to Chinese Communists to Stop Aggression in Korea," Department of State, *Department of State Bulletin*, December 11, 1950, 929–36.
25. Letter from William Fenn to Warren Austin, Archives of the United Board for Christian Higher Education in Asia, December 8, 1950, Reel 71, Divinity School Library, Yale University, New Haven, Connecticut (hereafter cited as UBCHEA).
26. "Beiman Deng Bage Jiaohui Zhongxue Lianhe Kangyi Aositin Yanshuo" (Eight Missionary Middle Schools, Including Bridgman, Joined to Protest Austin's Speech), *Guangming Daily*, December 11, 1950.
27. "Meidi Zai Zhongguo Ban Xuexiao Zhengshi Weile Wenhua Qinglue" (The American Imperialists Established Schools in China for Cultural Aggression), *Guangming Daily*, December 11, 1950.

28. Mao Zedong, "Dui Wu Yaozong Deng De Zhongguo Jidu Jiaohui Sanzi Xuanyan De Piyu" (Comments on the Chinese Christian Church's Three-Self Declaration Drafted by Wu Yaozong et al.), July 19, 1950, in *Jianguo Yilai Mao Zedong Wengao*, 1:438.
29. Mao Zedong, "Guangyu Guangbo Wu Yaozong Wenzhang Gei Hu Qiaomu De Xin" (Letter to Hu Qiaomu on Broadcasting Wu Yaozong's Article), October 21, 1950, in *Jianguo Yilai Mao Zedong Wengao*, 1:581.
30. "Quanguo Gedi Jidutu Erwan Yu Ren Zai Gexin Xuanyan Shang Qianming" (Over Twenty Thousand Christians Throughout the Nation Have Signed the Reform Declaration), *Guangming Daily*, December 13, 1950.
31. "Kuoda Zongjiaojie De Fandi Aiguo Yundong" (Expanding the Patriotic Anti-Imperialism Movement in Religious Circles), *Guangming Daily*, December 20, 1950.
32. Wei Zichu, "Meidi Zai Zhongguo De Zongjiao Wenhua Qinglue" (American Imperialist Religious and Cultural Aggression in China), *Guangming Daily*, December 25, 1950.
33. Memorandum of Telephone Conversation by the Deputy Director of the Office of Chinese Affairs, June 29, 1950, *Foreign Relations of the United States*, 1950, (Washington, DC: U.S. Government Printing Office, 1976), 6:640 (hereafter cited as FRUS).
34. Memorandum by the Deputy Director of the Office of Chinese Affairs to the Assistant Secretary of State for Far Eastern Affairs, November 28, 1950, FRUS, 6:664–65.
35. The Joint Chiefs of Staff to the Secretary of Defense, December 13, 1950, FRUS, 6:680–81.
36. Memorandum of Conversation, December 14, 1950, FRUS, 6:681.
37. Letter from Fenn to Dean Rusk, December 28, 1950, UBCHEA, Reel 71.
38. Letter from Rusk to Fenn, January 10, 1951, UBCHEA, Reel 71.
39. "Zhengwuyuan Banbu Mingling: Guanzhi Meiguo Zai Wo Jingnei Caichan Dongjie Wo Jingnei Suoyou Yinhang Yiqie Meiguo Cunkuan" (The Executive Council Issues Order to Control American Assets Within Our Borders and Freeze All American Deposits in All Banks Within Our Borders), *Guangming Daily*, December 29, 1950.
40. *Zhou Enlai Nianpu*, 1:109–10.
41. Guo Moruo, "Guanyu Chuli Jieshou Meiguo Jingtie De Wenhua Jiaoyu Jiuji Jiguan Ji Zongjiao tuanti Fangzhen De Baogao" (Report on the Policy Toward Taking Over American Subsidized Cultural, Educational, Relief Institutions and Religious Organizations), *People's Daily*, December 30, 1950.
42. "Suqing Meidi Wenhua Qinglue De Yingxiang: Zhengwu Huiyi Jueding Chuli Fangzheng" (Eradicating the Influence of the American Imperialist

Cultural Aggression: The Executive Council Meeting Decides the Handling Policy), *Guangming Daily*, December 30, 1950.

43. "Jieshou Waiguo Jingtie Ji Waizi Jingying Zhi Wenhua Jiaoyu Jiuji Jiguan Ji Zongjiao Tuanti Dengji Tiaoli" (Decree on the Registration of Foreign-Subsidized and Foreign-Managed Cultural, Educational, and Relief Institutions and Religious Organizations), *Guangming Daily*, December 30, 1950.

44. "Yanda Yu Beiman Deng Ba Zhongxue Fabiao Xuanyan Yonghu Zhengwuyuan Guanyu Suqing Meidi Wenhua Qinglue De Jueding" (Yenching University and Eight Middle Schools Including Bridgman School for Girls Issuing Statements to Support the Executive Council's Decision to Eradicate American Imperialist Cultural Aggression), *Guangming Daily*, January 3, 1951.

45. "Shida Deng Xiao Yizhi Biaoshi Yonghu" (The Normal University and Other Institutions Show Unanimous Support), *Guangming Daily*, December 31, 1950.

46. "Suqing Meidi Zai Zhongguo De Jingji He Wenhua Qinglüe De Yingxiang" (Exterminating the Influence of American Imperialist Economic and Cultural Aggression in China), *People's Daily*, December 30, 1950.

47. "Jiaoyu Ying Jiaqiang Wei Guofang Jianshe Fuwu" (Education Should Strengthen Its Service for National Defense Construction), *Guangming Daily*, January 5, 1951.

48. "Jiaoyubu Guanyu Chuli Jieshou Meiguo Jingtie De Jiaohui Xuexiao Ji Qita Jiaoyu Jiguan De Zhishi" (Directive from the Ministry of Education on Taking Over American-Subsidized Missionary Schools and Other Educational Institutions), January 11, 1951, in *Zhonghua Renmin Gongheguo Zhongyao Jiaoyu Wenxian*, 1:75–76.

49. "Jieshou Waiguo Jingtie Ji Waizi Jingying Zhi Wenhua Jiaoyu Jiuji Jiguan Ji Zongjiao Tuanti Dengji Shishi Banfa" (Implementation Methods for the Registration of Foreign-Subsidized and Foreign-Managed Cultural, Educational, and Relief Institutions, and Religious Organization), January 14, 1951, in *Zhonghua Renmin Gongheguo Zhongyao Jiaoyu Wenxian*, 1:76–77.

50. "Yanjiu Chuli Jieshou Waiguo Jingtie Gaodeng Xuexiao Wenti Zhongyang Jiaoyubu Zhaokai Huiyi" (The Ministry of Education of the Central Government Holds a Meeting to Study Taking Over Foreign-Subsidized Higher Learning Institutions), *Guangming Daily*, January 25, 1951.

51. "Jianjue Suqing Meiguo Wenhua Qinglue Yingxiang, Fazhan Xin Minzhu Zhuyi Jiaoyu" (Resolutely Eradicate the Influence of American Cultural Aggression and Develop the New Democratic Education), *People's Daily*, January 26, 1951.

52. William P. Fenn, *Ever New Horizon: The Story of the United Board for Christian Higher Education in Asia, 1922–1975* (North Newton, KS: Mennonite Press, 1980), 64–65.
53. "Liyou Yanda Deng Xiao Zao Jianjue Jujue: Meidi You Yi Yinmou Pochan" (Yanching and Other Universities Resolutely Rejected the Lure: Another American Imperialists' Intrigue Fell Through), *Guangming Daily*, January 25, 1951.
54. "Zhongyang Renmin Zhengfu Weishengbu Zuo Jieshou Xiehe Yixueyuan" (The Ministry of Health of the Central People's Government Took Over the Union Medical College Yesterday), *Guangming Daily*, January 21, 1951.
55. About the founding of the Peking Union Medical College, its close ties with the Rockefeller Foundation, its rise as the leader in the field, and its role in the Korean War, see Mary Brown Bullock, *The Oil Prince's Legacy: Rockefeller Philanthropy in China* (Washington, DC: Woodrow Wilson Center Press, 2011), 47–116.
56. "Chedi Suqing Meidi Wenhua Qinglue Yingxiang: Jiaoyubu Zuo Jieshou Yanjing Daxue" (Completely Eradicate American Imperialist Cultural Aggression Influence: The Ministry of Education Takes Over Yenching University Yesterday); "Yanda Huidao Le Renmin Zuguo De Huaibao" (Yenching University Has Returned to the Arms of the People's Motherland), *Guangming Daily*, February 13, 1951.
57. "Jiaoyubu Guanyu 1951 Nian Chuli Jieshou Meiguo Jingtie De Xuexiao De Zongjie Baogao" (Summary Report of the Ministry of Education on Taking Over American-Subsidized Schools in 1951), December 26, 1951, in *Zhonghua Renmin Gongheguo Zhongyao Jiaoyu Wenxian*, 1:133–35.
58. "Zhongyang Weishengbu Zhaokai Huabeiqu Chuli Jieshou Meiguo Jingtie De Yiyuan Huiyi" (The Health Ministry of the Central Government Holds a Meeting to Take Over American-Subsidized Hospitals in Northern China), *Guangming Daily*, February 25, 1951.
59. "Chuli Jieshou Meiguo Jingtie De Jidujiao Tuanti Huiyi Bimu: Tongguo Chuli Banfa Ji Lianhe Xuanyan" (Meeting on Taking Over American-Subsidized Christian Organizations Closes: Approving the Handling Measures and Joint Declaration), *Guangming Daily*, April 22, 1951.
60. "Zhengwuyuan Zhaoji Quanguo Jiuji Fuli Jie Daibiao Kaihui Chuli Jieshou Meiguo Jingtie Jiuji Jiguan" (The Executive Council Called the Meeting of Representatives from National Relief and Welfare Circles to Handle Taking Over American-Subsidized Relief and Welfare Institutions), *Guangming Daily*, April 28, 1951.
61. "Chuli Jieshou Meiguo Jingtie Jiuji Jiguan Huiyi Bimu" (Meeting on Taking Over American-Subsidized Relief Institutions Closes), *Guangming Daily*, May 5, 1951.

62. "Yanda Huidao Le Renmin Zuguo De Huaibao."
63. "Meidi Zenyang Zai Yanda Jinxing Wenhua Qinglue" (How the American Imperialists Carried out Cultural Aggression at Yenching University), *Guangming Daily*, January 29, 1951.
64. Lu Zhiwei, "Yanjing Daxue Shoudao De Mei Diguo Zhuyi Wenhua Qinglue" (The American Imperialist Cultural Aggression Suffered by Yenching University), *Guangming Daily*, January 22, 1951.
65. "Xianqi Quanxiaoxing De Fandi Aiguo Sixiang Jiaoyu Yundong" (Launching a University-Wide Anti-Imperialist and Patriotic Thought Education Movement), *Guangming Daily*, March 7, 1951; "Yanda Zhankai Aiguo Sixiang Jiaoyu Yundong, Quanxiao Shisheng Chenzhong Juxing Kongsu Dahui" (Yenching University Launches Patriotic Thought Education Movement and All Teachers and Students Sorrowfully Hold Denunciation Meeting), *Guangming Daily*, March 12, 1951.
66. About the resistance to the college and department reorganization proposed at the First National Conference on Higher Education held in June 1950, see Yu Fengzheng, *Gaizao* (Reform) (Zhengzhou: Henan Renmin Chubanshe, 2001), 126–38; Qian Junrui, "Gaodeng Jiaoyu Gaige De Guanjian" (The Key to Higher Education Reform), *Guangming Daily*, November 2, 1951.
67. Ma Xulun, "Zhongyang Jiaoyubu Ma Xulun Buzhang Fabiao Tanhua" (A Speech by Ma Xulun, the Minister of Education of the Central Government), *Guangming Daily*, October 3, 1951.
68. "Zhongyang Renmin Zhengfu Zhengwuyuan Guanyu Gaige Xuezhi De Jueding" (The Resolution by the Executive Council of the Central Government on the Educational System Reform), *People's Daily*, October 3, 1951.
69. "Chedi Suqing OuMei Zichan Jieji Sixiang Yishi De Canyu: JingJin Gaoxiao Jiaoshi Zhankai Gaizao Sixiang Xuexi Yundong" (Thoroughly Eradicating the Remnant Euro-American Bourgeois Ideology: College Faculty Members in Beijing and Tianjing Start a Study Movement to Reform Their Thoughts), *Guangming Daily*, October 23, 1951.
70. Mao Zedong, "Zai Ma Yinchu Guanyu Beijing Daxue Jiaoyuan Zhengzhi Xuexi Wenti Gei Zhou Enlai De Xin Shang De Piyu" (Comments on the Letter from Ma Yinchu to Zhou Enlai About the Political Studies for Peking University Faculty), September 11, 1951, in *Jianguo Yilai Mao Zedong Wengao*, 2:448.
71. Zhou Enlai, "Guanyu Zhishi Fenzi De Gaizao Wenti" (On the Reform of the Intellectuals), September 29, 1951, in *Zhonghua Renmin Gongheguo Zhongyao Jiaoyu Wenxian*, 1:119–22.
72. Jiang Yinen, "Nuli Gaizao Sixiang, Zuo Yige Xin Zhongguo De Renmin Jiaoshi" (Strive for Thought Reform and Become a Teacher Working for the People in the New China), *People's Daily*, November 13, 1951.

73. Mao Zedong, "Zai Quanguo Zhengxie Yijie Sanci Huiyi Shang De Jianghua" (Speech at the Third Meeting of the First National Political Consultative Conference), October 23, 1951, in *Mao Zedong Wenji* (The Writings of Mao Zedong) (Beijing: Renmin Chubanshe, 1999), 6:183–84.
74. Mao Zedong, "Zhongyang Yinfa Guanyu Zai Xuexiao Jinxing Sixiang Gaizao He Zuzhi Qingli Gongzuo De Zhishi De Tongzhi" (Circular from the Central Committee on Printing and Issuing the Directive on Thought Reform and Organizational Cleansing in Schools), November 30, 1951, in *Jianguo Yilai Mao Zedong Wengao*, 2:526–27.
75. "Zhonggong Zhongyang Guanyu Zai Xuexiao Zhong Jinxing Sixiang Gaizao He Zuzhi Chuli Gongzuo De Zhishi" (Directive from the Chinese Communist Party Central Committee on Thought Reform and Organizational Cleansing in Schools), November 1951, in *Zhonghua Renmin Gongheguo Zhongyao Jiaoyu Wenxian*, 1:132.
76. Deng Jiadong, "Women Yao Pipan Guoqu 'Xiehe' De Yiqie" (We Should Denounce Every Aspect of the Old Peking Union Medical College), *Guangming Daily*, November 17, 1951.
77. Xu Yingkui, "Wo Juexin Zhanduan Yu 'Jiu Xiehe' Yiqie Sixiang Shang De Lianxi" (I Am Determined to Cut All the Ideological Ties with the Old Peking Union Medical College), *Guangming Daily*, January 16, 1952.
78. This method was widely used during the rectification movement in Yanan in 1942. Aimed at eliminating "liberalism" (*ziyou zhuyi*) among officials and intellectuals, the CCP required all participants to conduct thorough self-examination and self-criticism. The process was called "taking off pants" (*tuo kuzi*) and "cutting off the tail" (*ge weiba*). Gao Hua, *Hong Taiyang Shi Zenyang Shengqi De: Yanan Zhengfeng Yundong De Lailong Qumai* (How Did the Red Sun Rise: A History of the Yanan Rectification Movement) (Hong Kong: Hong Kong Chinese University Press, 2000), 423–27.
79. "Yanda Jiaoshi Pubian 'Xiashui Xizao' Qingxi Wudu" (Yenching University Faculty Members Universally "Take Bath" to Clean the Pollution and Poison), *Guangming Daily*, March 4, 1952.
80. "Huadong Gaodeng Xuexiao Yuanxi Yi Shidang Tiaozheng" (Appropriate Reorganization of Colleges and Departments in Higher Education Institutions Has Been Completed in East China), *Guangming Daily*, November 15, 1951.
81. Ma Xulun, "Guanyu Quanguo Gongxue Yuan Tiaozheng Fangan De Baogao" (A Report on the Reorganization Plan of Engineering Schools in the Nation), November 30, 1951, in *Zhonghua Renmin Gongheguo Zhongyao Jiaoyu Wenxian*, 1:131.
82. "Furen Daxue Bingru Beijing Shifan Daxue" (Fujen University Merges with Beijing Normal University), *Guangming Daily*, June 12, 1952.

83. Chen Yuan, "Relie Yonghu Yuanxi Tiaozheng" (Warmly Support the Reorganization of Colleges and Departments), *Guangming Daily*, June 12, 1952.
84. "Xiang Mao Zhuxi Baozheng Zuohao Yuanxi Tiaozheng Gongzuo" (Pledging to Chairman Mao to Successfully Implement the College Reorganization), *Guangming Daily*, July 2, 1952.
85. "Gaodeng Jiaoyubu Guanyu 1953 Nian Gaodeng Xuexiao Yuanxi Tiaozheng Gongzuo De Zongjie Baogao" (Summary Report from the Ministry of Higher Education on the College and Department Reorganization in Higher Education Institutions in 1953), January 15, 1954, in *Zhonghua Renmin Gongheguo Zhongyao Jiaoyu Wenxian*, 1:281–84.
86. The PUMC was allowed to maintain its structure and curriculum mostly because its highly skilled experts won the respect of top CCP leaders. Instead of breaking up the college, they put it under the military control and borrowed its medical staff to establish the General Hospital of the People's Liberation Army, which provided top-notch medical care for the military as well as civilian leaders.
87. Jiang Nanxiang, "Dang De Lingdao Shi Shengli Wancheng Jiaoyu Gaige De Guangjian—Zai Qinghua Daxue Jiaozhi Yuangong Ji Xuesheng Daibiao De Huanyinghui Shang De Jianghua" (The Party's Leadership Is the Key to the Successful Completion of the Educational Reform: A Speech at the Welcome Meeting of the Faculty, Staff, and Student Representatives at Qinghua University), December 31, 1952, *Jiang Nanxiang Wenji* (Collection of Writings by Jiang Nanxiang), ed. Zhongguo Gaodeng Jiaoyu Xuehui and Qinghua Daxue (Beijing: Qinghua Daxue Chubanshe, 1998), 1:432–33.
88. Jiang Nanxiang, "Xiang Qinghua Daxue Quanti Jiaoshi Dang, Tuanyuan De Jianghua" (A Speech Given to All the Party and Youth League Members in the Faculty at Qinghua University), March 2, 1953, in *Jiang Nanxiang Wenji*, 1:446–47.
89. Memorandum from Fisher to Colligan, November 17, 1950; Memorandum from Cook to Fisher, November 29, 1950, CMR, Box 4.
90. Memorandum from Fisher to Russell, July 27, 1951, CMR, Box 4.
91. Ten Chinese students sent a letter to the State Department urging the adoption of the new regulation regarding Chinese students so that they could support themselves during their extended stay in the United States and return to China at a time of their own choice. CMR, Box 4.
92. Memorandum from Fisher to Russell, July 27, 1951, CMR, Box 4.
93. "Title 8—Aliens and Nationality," *Federal Register*, April 13, 1951, 16, 72:3250.
94. Meredith Oyen, *The Diplomacy of Migration: Transnational Lives and the Making of U.S.-Chinese Relations in the Cold War* (Ithaca, NY: Cornell University Press, 2015), 4–5.

95. Memorandum for the File, June 12, 1951, CMR, Box 21.
96. Letter from Habberton to All District Directors, October 9, 1951, CMR, Box 16.
97. He Guozhu, "Gei Lianheguo Mishuzhang Xie Gongkaixin" (Writing the Open Letter to the United Nations' Secretary General), in Hou Xianglin et al., *1950 Niandai Guiguo LiuMei Kexuejia Fangtanlu*, 288–314.
98. Li Hengde, "Fuze Bianji 'LiuMei Kexie Tongxun' " (In Charge of Editing the Newsletter for the Chinese Science and Technology Workers in the United States), in Hou et al., *1950 Niandai Guiguo LiuMei Kexuejia Fangtanlu*, 194–225.
99. When the ship docked in Los Angeles on August 11, Luo Peilin, who received emergency aid from the California Institute of Technology, joined the group. Memorandum from Jenkins to Christie, September 29, 1950, CMR, Box 7.
100. "Report on 135 Chinese Students Serviced by Orientation and Service Center, San Francisco, August 1 1950 to September 29, 1950," enclosure in Memorandum from Jenkins to Christie, September 29, 1950.
101. "Deng Jiaxian," in *Liangdan Yixing Yuanxun* (The Two Bombs and One Satellite Heroes), ed. Song Jian (Beijing: Qinghua Daxue Chubanshe, 2001), 1:258–303.
102. Ji Chaozhu, *The Man on Mao's Right: From Harvard Yard to Tiananmen Square—My Life Inside China's Foreign Ministry* (New York: Random House, 2008).
103. "Liuxue Meiguo Xuesheng Wang Liangneng Jiu Bei Meiguo Zhengfu Kouliu De Jiuming Zhongguo Xuesheng Shi Zhi Zhou Enlai Zongli De Han" (Letter from Wang Liangneng to Prime Minister Zhou Enlai on Nine Chinese Students Detained by the United States Government), October 30, 1951, 111-00102-09(1), MFAA.
104. "Minutes of the Third Meeting Between Wang Bingnan and Johnson on Chinese and American Nationals and the Return of Chinese Students," June 15, 1954, in *Zhonghua Renmin Gongheguo Waijiao Dangan Xuanbian* (Selected Diplomatic Archives of the People's Republic of China), ed. Zhonghua Renmin Gongheguo Waijiaobu Danganguan (Beijing: Shijie Zhishi Chubanshe, 2007), 391–93.
105. Li, "Fuze Bianji 'LiuMei Kexie Tongxun,' " 206.
106. Draft Memorandum from Clubb to Johnstone, October 26, 1950, CMR, Box 7.
107. "Title 8—Aliens and Nationality."
108. Memorandum from Fisher to Russell, July 27, 1951, CMR, Box 4.
109. Ninkun Wu, *A Single Tear: A Family's Persecution, Love, and Endurance in Communist China* (Boston: Little, Brown, 1993), 4–6.

110. Wu, *A Single Tear*, 25–72; "Tsung-Dao Lee: Biographical," Nobel Prize in Physics, 1957, https://www.nobelprize.org/prizes/physics/1957/lee/biographical/.
111. Li, "Fuze Bianji 'LiuMei Kexie Tongxun,'" 209–13.

3. Fighting Over the Stranded

1. Mao Zedong had begun to recognize that the CPVA was incapable of completely destroying a regiment of the American army by mid-1951. Thus, he was forced to abandon his early ambitious plan aimed at wiping out several American divisions in a major campaign. On May 26, 1951, he instructed Peng Dehuai, the commander of the CPVA, to seek the destruction of one or two American battalions by each Chinese army in small-scale battles instead. Mao Zedong, "Dui MeiYing Jun Muqian Zhi Shiyi Yu Da Xiao Jianmiezhan" (It's Suitable to Engage the American and British Forces Currently Only in Small-Scale Annihilation Battles), in *Mao Zedong Wenji*, (Collection of Mao Zedong's Writings) (Beijing: Renmin Chubanshe, 1996), 6: 172–73.
2. *Mao Zedong Nianpu, 1949–1976* (Chronicles of Mao Zedong, 1949–1976) (Beijing: Zhongyang Wenxian Chubanshe, 2013), 2:262–63.
3. Mao Zedong, "Tong Yiqie Yuanyi Heping De Guojia Tuanjie Hezuo" (Unite and Cooperate with All the Nations That Want Peace), July 7, 1957, in *Mao Zedong Wenji*, 6:333–34.
4. Yafeng Xia, *Negotiating with the Enemy: U.S.-China Talks during the Cold War* (Bloomington: Indiana University Press, 2006); Wenzhao Tao, *ZhongMei Guangxi Shi, 1949–2000* (A History of China-U.S. Relations, 1949–2000) (Shanghai: Shanghai Renmin Chubanshe, 2004), 2:181–209.
5. "Zhongguo Zhengfu Tongyi Pai Quanquan Daibiao Chuxi Rineiwa Huiyi De Xinwengao" (News Release on the Chinese Government's Agreement to Send a Plenipotentiary Representative to Attend the Geneva Conference), March 4, 1954; "Zhonghua Renmin Gongheguo Canjia Rineiwa Huiyi Daibiaotuan Mingdan" (The List of the People's Republic of China Delegation Attending the Geneva Conference), n.d., Zhonghua Renmin Gongheguo Waijiaobu Danganguan, ed., *Zhonghua Renmin Gongheguo Waijiao Dangan Xuanbian* (Selected Diplomatic Archives of the People's Republic of China) (Beijing: Shijie Zhishi Chubanshe, 2007), 11, 15.
6. Wang Bingnan, *ZhongMei Huitan Jiunian Huigu* (Memoir of the Nine-Year Sino-American Talk) (Beijing: Shijie Zhishi Chubanshe, 1985), 18.
7. The Under Secretary of State to the Department of State, May 6, 1954, *Foreign Relations of the United States, 1952–1954*, 14:414–15 (hereafter cited as FRUS).

8. The Secretary of State to the United States Delegation at the Geneva Conference, May 13, 1954, FRUS, 1952–1954, 14: 416–17.
9. The Secretary of State to the United States Delegation at the Geneva Conference, May 13, 1954, FRUS, 1952–1954, 14:416–47.
10. The Under Secretary of State to the Department of State, May 17, 1954, FRUS, 1952–1954, 14:417–18.
11. The Under Secretary of State to the Department of State, May 18, 1954, FRUS, 1952–1954, 14:421.
12. "Huan Xiang Yu Duweilian Guanyu ZhongMei Liangguo Qiaomin Huiguo Wenti De Tanhua Jilu" (The Transcript of the Conversation Between Huan Xiang and Trevelyan on the Repatriation of Chinese and American Nationals), May 19, 1954, in *Zhonghua Renmin Gongheguo Waijiao Dangan Xuanbian*, 379.
13. Wang, *ZhongMei Huitan Jiunian Huigu*, 23–24.
14. Wang, *ZhongMei Huitan Jiunian Huigu*, 30.
15. "Huang Hua Guanyu Meiguo Zhengfu Wuli Kouya Zhongguo Qiaomin He Liuxuesheng Wenti Dui Jizhe Fabiao Tanhua" (Huanghua Talks to Journalists About the United States Unjustified Detention of Chinese Nationals and Students), in *Zhonghua Renmin Gongheguo Waijiao Dangan Xuanbian*, 380–81.
16. Wang, *ZhongMei Huitan Jiunian Huigu*, 24.
17. "Huan Xiang Yu Duweilian Guanyu ZhongMei Liangguo Qiaomin Huiguo Wenti De Tanhua Jilu" (The Transcript of the Conversation Between Huan Xiang and Trevelyan on the Repatriation of Chinese and American Nationals), May 27, 1954, in *Zhonghua Renmin Gongheguo Waijiao Dangan Xuanbian*, 381–82.
18. The Under Secretary of State (Smith) to the Department of State, May 27, 1954, FRUS, 1952–1954, 14:434–36.
19. "Discussions Concerning Americans Detained in Communist China, Statement of May 29," *Department of State Bulletin*, June 21, 1954, 949–50.
20. The Under Secretary of State (Smith) to the Department of State, May 27, 1954.
21. The Secretary of State to the United States Delegation at the Geneva Conference, May 28, 1954, FRUS, 1952–1954, 14:436–37.
22. The Under Secretary of State (Smith) to the Department of State, May 28, 1954, FRUS, 1952–1954, 14:437.
23. The Under Secretary of State (Smith) to the Department of State, May 30, 1954, FRUS, 1952–1954, 14: 438–40.
24. Memorandum by the Deputy Assistant Secretary of State for Far Eastern Affairs (Drumright) to the Secretary of State, May 31, 1954, FRUS, 1952–1954, 14:438–40.

25. Extract from the Diary of James C. Hagerty, Press Secretary to the President, June 3, 1954, FRUS, 1952–1954, 14:442.
26. Telegram from the Secretary of State to the United States Delegation at the Geneva Conference, June 3, 1954, FRUS, 1952–1954, 14:443.
27. "Zhou Enlai Guanyu Meiguo Yaoqiu Zhongguo Shifang Zai Hua Fanzui Qiaomin Shi Zhi Mao Zedong, Liu Shaoqi Bing Zhongyang De Dianbao" (Telegram from Zhou Enlai to Mao Zedong, Liu Shaoqi, and the Central Committee on American Request to Release Convicted Nationals in China), June 3, 1954, in *Zhonghua Renmin Gongheguo Waijiao Dangan Xuanbian*, 383.
28. "Zhonggong Zhongyang Dui Zhou Enlai 6 Yue 3 Ri Guanyu Meiqiao Wenti Dian De Fudian" (Reply from the Chinese Communist Party Central Committee to the June 3 Telegram from Zhou Enlai on American Nationals), June 3, 1954, in *Zhonghua Renmin Gongheguo Waijiao Dangan Xuanbian*, 384.
29. "Wang Bingnan Yu Meifang Daibiao Yuehanxun Guanyu ZhongMei Liangguo Qiaomin Ji Liuxuesheng Huiguo Wenti Diyici Huiwu Tanhua Jilu" (The Transcript of the First Meeting Between Wang Bingnan and American Representative Johnson on the Repatriation of Chinese and American Nationals and Students), June 5, 1954, in *Zhonghua Renmin Gongheguo Waijiao Dangan Xuanbian*, 384–86; The Under Secretary of State (Smith) to the Department of State, June 5, 1954, FRUS, 1952–1954, 14:462–63.
30. The Under Secretary of State (Smith) to the Department of State, June 7, 1954, FRUS, 1952–1954, 14:463–64.
31. "Discussions Concerning Americans Detained in Communist China, Statement of June 5," *Department of State Bulletin*, June 21, 1954, 950.
32. "Wang Bingnan Yu Meifang Daibiao Yuehanxun Guanyu ZhongMei Liangguo Qiaomin Ji Liuxuesheng Huiguo Wenti Dierci Huiwu Tanhua Jilu" (Transcript of the Second Meeting Between Wang Bingnan and American Representative Johnson on the Repatriation of Chinese and American Nationals and Students), June 10, 1954, in *Zhonghua Renmin Gongheguo Waijiao Dangan Xuanbian*, 387–90; The Under Secretary of State (Smith) to the Department of State, June 10, 1954, FRUS, 1952–1954, 14:464–66.
33. The Under Secretary of State (Smith) to the Department of State, June 12, 1954, FRUS, 1952–1954, 14:466–67.
34. "Wang Bingnan Yu Meifang Daibiao Yuehanxun Guanyu ZhongMei Liangguo Qiaomin Ji Liuxuesheng Huiguo Wenti Disanci Huiwu Tanhua Jilu" (Transcript of the Third Meeting Between Wang Bingnan and American Representative Johnson on the Repatriation of Chinese and American Nationals and Students), June 10, 1954, in *Zhonghua Renmin Gongheguo Waijiao Dangan Xuanbian*, 390–96; The Under Secretary of State (Smith) to the Department of State, June 15, 1954, FRUS, 1952–1954, 14:468–71.

35. The Under Secretary of State (Smith) to the Department of State, June 16, 1954, FRUS, 1952–1954, 14:471–72.
36. This was the first time that the attorney general confirmed that the number of the Chinese students whose departure had been banned by the U.S. government was 124. Memorandum of Telephone Conversation, June 17, 1954, FRUS, 1952–1954, 14:474.
37. The Secretary of State to the United States Delegation at the Geneva Conference, June 17, 1954, FRUS, 1952–1954, 14:475.
38. The Under Secretary of State (Smith) to the Department of State, June 19, 1954, FRUS, 1952–1954, 14:476.
39. The Head of the United States Delegation at the Geneva Conference (Johnson) to the Department of State, June 21, 1954, FRUS, 1952–1954, 14:477n3.
40. "Wang Bingnan Yu Meifang Daibiao Yuehanxun Guanyu ZhongMei Liangguo Qiaomin Ji Liuxuesheng Huiguo Wenti Disici Huiwu Tanhua Jilu" (Transcript of the Fourth Meeting Between Wang Bingnan and American Representative Johnson on the Repatriation of Chinese and American Nationals and Students), June 10, 1954, in *Zhonghua Renmin Gongheguo Dangan Xuanbian*, 397–401; The Head of the United States Delegation at the Geneva Conference (Johnson) to the Department of State, June 21, 1954, FRUS, 1952–1954, 14:477–79.
41. The Head of the United States Delegation at the Geneva Conference (Johnson) to the Department of State, June 21 and June 22, 1954, FRUS, 1952–1954, 14:666–67, 478–80.
42. The Secretary of State to the United States Delegation at the Geneva Conference, July 1, 1954, FRUS, 1952–1954, 14:666–67, 489.
43. The Under Secretary of State (Smith) to the Department of State, July 21, 1954, FRUS, 1952–1954, 14:501.
44. The Head of the United States Delegation at the Geneva Conference (Johnson) to the Department of State, July 22, 1954, FRUS, 1952–1954, 14:501–3.
45. The Consul General of Geneva (Gowen) to the Department of State, September 29, 1954, FRUS, 1952–1954, 14:666–67n5.
46. Li Hengde, "Buqu De Douzheng Zihao De Shengli" (The Unyielding Fight and the Proud Triumph); "Zhongguo Liuxuesheng 1954 Nian Zhi Meiguo Zongtong Aisenhaoweier De Liangfeng Gongkai Xin" (Two Open Letters from Chinese Students to United States President Eisenhower in 1954), August 5, 1954, in *Jianguo Chuqi Liuxuesheng Guiguo Jishi* (Records of the Students Returned from Overseas in the Early Period of the Nation), ed. Quanguo Zhengxie (Beijing: Zhongguo Wenshi Chubanshe, 1999), 59–61, 479–480.
47. "Zhongguo Liuxuesheng 1954 Nian Zhi Meiguo Zongtong Aisenhaoweier De Liangfeng Gongkai Xin", September 2, 1954, in *Jianguo Chuqi Liuxuesheng Guiguo Jishi*, 481–83.

48. "Zhongguo Liuxuesheng 1954 Nian Zhi Lianheguo Mishuzhang Hamasheerde De Gongkaixin" (Open Letter from Chinese Students in the United States to Secretary General of the United Nations Hammarskjöld in 1954), December 16, 1954, in *Jianguo Chuqi Liuxuesheng Guiguo Jishi*, 484–87.
49. "5,000 Students 'Retained,'" Associated Press, May 26, 1954, Waijiaobu, *Diaocha Ji Zuzhi LiuMei Xuesheng Fanhui Dalu* (Investigate and Prevent Chinese Students in the United States from Returning to the Mainland), vol. 1, A303000000B/0043/451.5/0030-0031, National Archives Administration, National Development Council, Taipei, Taiwan (hereafter cited as NAA); "100 Barred," United Press International, May 26, 1954.
50. "Transcript of President Eisenhower's Press Conference on Foreign and Home Affairs," *New York Times*, August 12, 1954.
51. "Chinese Students Seek Exchange for U.S. Airmen," *New York Times*, December 18, 1954.
52. Memorandum from the Secretary of State to the President, April 1, 1955, FRUS, 1955–1957, 2:442–43.
53. "For the Press," April 2, 1955, *Department of State Bulletin*, April 11, 1955, 627. Two slightly different numbers were cited in the memorandum from Dulles to Eisenhower and the State Department press release. However, fifty-six was the number used in all official statements issued to the public.
54. "Chinese Students Free to Go Home as U.S. Ends Curb," *New York Times*, April 3. 1955.
55. Telegram from the Consul General at Geneva (Gowen) to the Secretary of State, April 8, 1955, FRUS, 1955–1957, 2:467–70.
56. Telegram from the Consul General at Geneva (Gowen) to the Secretary of State, May 30, 1955, FRUS, 1955–1957, 2:583–85.
57. "U.S. Urges Peiping to Free 52 Others," *New York Times*, May 31, 1955.
58. Memorandum from the Acting Assistant Secretary of State for Far Eastern Affairs (Sebald) to the Secretary of State, June 10, 1955, FRUS, 1955–1957, 2:590n3.
59. Memorandum of a Conversation Between the President and the Secretary of State, June 10, 1955, FRUS, 1955–1957, 2:588–89.
60. Memorandum of a Conversation Between the President and the Secretary of State, June 10, 1955, FRUS, 1955–1957, 2:589n5.
61. Telegram from the Consul General at Geneva (Gowen) to the Secretary of State, May 30, 1955, FRUS, 1955–1957, 2:583n2.
62. "Waijiaobu Shoudian" (Telegram Received by the Ministry of Foreign Affairs), September 13, 1955, *Diaocha Ji Zuzhi LiuMei Xuesheng Fan Feiqu*, vol. 1, NAA.
63. "Qian Xuesen Zhi Chen Shutong Xin" (Letter from Qian Xuesen to Chen Shutong), June 15, 1955, *Guanyu Woguo LiuMei Kexuejia Qian Xuesen Huiguo*

De Youguan Cailiao (Related Documents on the Return of Qian Xuesen, One of Our Scientists in the United States), 111-00081-03(1), Ministry of Foreign Affairs Archives, Beijing, China (hereafter cited as MFAA).
64. Iris Chang, *Thread of the Silkworm* (New York: Basic Books, 1995), 173–77.
65. "For the Press," April 2, 1955, *Department of State Bulletin*, April 11, 1955, 627.
66. Procedure for Issuance of Travel Grants to Chinese Nationals under P.L. 535, March 11, 1955, CMR, Box 4.
67. Chinese students and scholars were required to submit applications for travel grants since many had graduated long before and had worked for quite some time. They had to prove that they were still in financial difficulty and needed U.S. government support for their trips back to China. Chiang Li-Chin (Jiang Lijing), Chiao Jui-Shen (Jiao Ruishen), Chow Tung-whei (Zhou Tonghui), Ho Kuo-Chu (He Guozhu), Ho Ping-Lum (He Binglin), Hsieh Chia-Lin (Xie Jialin), Hsu Shun-Sheng (Xu Shunsheng), Lee Teh-Hsun (Li Deshun), Li Cheng-Wu (Li Zhengwu), Lin Cheng-Sen (Lin Zhengxian), Sha Yi-hsien (Sha Yixian), Shih Chang-Hsu (Shi Changxu), and Tung Shih-Pai (Tong Shibai) were among those Chinese students who returned to China in 1955 with travel grants from the State Department. They all became prominent scientists and scholars in the PRC. Memorandum from Nelson to Riley, May 27, 1955, CMR, Box 4.
68. Memorandum from Ripley to Riley, July 8, 1955, CMR, Box 4.
69. Zhou Enlai, "Zhongguo Yuan Jiu Taiwan Diqu Wenti Tong Meiguo Jinxing Tanpan" (China Is Willing to Negotiate with the United States Over Issues on Taiwan), in *Zhou Enlai Waijiao Wenxuan* (Selected Works of Zhou Enlai on Diplomacy) (Beijing: Zhongyang Wenxian Chubanshe, 1990), 134.
70. Telegram from the Secretary of State to the Embassy in Italy, July 7, 1955, FRUS, 1955–1957, 2:637–39.
71. "Editorial Note," FRUS, 1955–1957, 2:678.
72. Zhou Enlai, "Muqian Guoji Xingshi He Zhongguo Waijiao Zhengce" (Current International Situation and China's Foreign Policy), in *Zhongmei Guanxi Ziliao Huibian* (Collection of Records on Sino-American Relations), ed. Shijie Zhishi Chubanshe (Beijing: Shijie Zhishi Chubanshe, 1957), 2: 2287–89.
73. Gordon H. Chang, *Friends and Enemies: The United States, China, and the Soviet Union, 1948–1972* (Stanford, CA: Stanford University Press, 1990), 156.
74. Wang Bingnan fully recognized that there was a big gap on the agenda and goal for the ambassadorial talks between Beijing and Washington. In order to get the talks started, Beijing agreed to discuss the repatriation of civilians first and then cover other substantive matters. Wang, *ZhongMei Huitan Jiunian Huigu*, 47.
75. "Meiguo Kouliu Zhongguo Xuesheng He ZhongMei Qiaomin Wenti" (Issues of Chinese Students Detained by the United States and Chinese

and American Nationals), May 26–October 23, 1954, 111-00054-01(1), MFAA.

76. "Bei Mei Kouliu Wo Liuxuesheng Shi Jiqi Duice Xiang Bu Lingdao De Baogao" (A Report to the Leadership of the Ministry on the Chinese Students Detained by the United States and the Proposed Response), April 26, 1954, 111-00239-04(1), MFAA.

77. Telegram from the Consul General at Geneva (Gowen) to the Department of State, May 30, 1955, FRUS, 1955–1957, 2:583–85.

78. Telegram from the Consul General at Geneva (Gowen) to the Department of State, June 23, 1955, FRUS, 1955–1957, 2:613–15.

79. "Yijiuwusi Nian Rineiwa Huiyi Hou Wo LiuMei Xuesheng Huiguo Qingkuang" (Information on the Return of Our Students from the United States Since the 1954 Geneva Conference), July 10, 1955, 111-00123-16(1), FMAA.

80. "Zhou Enlai Zongli Jiu Zhongguo Zai Mei Qiaomin He Liuxuesheng Wenti Yu Yindu Zhuhua Dashi Laijiawen Tanhua Jiyao" (Record of the Conversation Between Premier Zhou Enlai and the Indian Ambassador to China Raghavan on Chinese Nationals and Students in the United States), July 7, 1955, 105-00061-02(1), FMAA.

81. "Zhou Enlai Zongli Jiu Zhongguo Meiguo Guanxi Ji Zai Mei Qiaomin He Liuxuesheng Deng Wenti Zhi Meinong Dian" (Telegram from Premier Zhou Enlai to Menon on the Sino-American Relations and the Chinese Nationals and Students in the United States), July 14, 1955, 105-00061-03(1), FMAA.

82. Memorandum of a Conversation, July 6, 1955, FRUS, 1955–1957, 2:632–33.

83. "Baogao" (Report), July 29, 1955, in *Guanyu Wo LiuMei Kexuejia Qian Xuesen Huiguo De Youguan Cailiao*, 46–50, 111-00081-03, FMAA.

84. "Guanyu ZhongMei Dashiji Daibiao Zai Rineiwa Huitan De Zhishi" (Instructions on the Sino-American Ambassadorial Level Representative Talks in Geneva), July 30, 1955, 111-00009-01(1), FMAA.

85. Telegram from Ambassador U Alexis Johnson to the Department of State, August 2, 1955, FRUS, 1955–1957, 2:8–10.

86. "Qiaqing Meifang Shefa Zuzhi LiuMei Xuesheng Fan Dalu You" (Request for the American Side to Take Steps to Prevent Students in the United States from Returning to the Mainland), March 3, 1956, *Diaocha Ji Zuzhi LiuMei Xuesheng Fanhui Dalu*, vol. 1, NAA.

87. Jiaoyubu, "Mei Zhengfu Zhunxu LiMei Ji Ziqing LiMei Zhongguo Liuxuesheng Ziliao Biao" (List of Chinese Students in the United States Who Were Permitted by the American Government to Depart the Country and Who Chose to Leave the Country on Their Own), May 10, 1956, *Diaocha Ji Zuzhi LiuMei Xuesheng Fanhui Dalu*, vol. 1, NAA.

88. Telegram from Ambassador U Alexis Johnson to the Department of State, August 4, 1955, FRUS, 1955–1957, 3:14–15; Telegram from the Secretary of State to Ambassador U Alexis Johnson, at Geneva, August 5, 1955, FRUS, 1955–1957, 3:17–18.
89. "ZhongMei Dashiji Huitan Disanci Huiyi Zhong Guanyu Huxiang Pairen Shicha Wenti De Fudian Ji Xiangguan Fayan Gao (Dui Meifang Zai Disanci Huiyi Zhong Fanyan De Pinglun, Guanyu Qian Xuesen De Lizi)" (The Reply to and Related Statements on the Issue of Sending Investigative Representative to Each Other's Country as Discussed at the Third Meeting of the Sino-American Ambassadorial Talks: Comments on the American Statement at the Third Meeting, The Case of Qian Xuesen), August 7, 1955, 111-00015-07(1), FMAA.
90. Telegram from Ambassador U Alexis Johnson to the Department of State, August 8, 1955, FRUS, 1955–1957, 3:19–20.
91. Telegram from Ambassador U Alexis Johnson to the Department of State, August 8, 1955, FRUS, 1955–1957, 3:11–12.
92. Telegram from Ambassador U Alexis Johnson to the Department of State, August 12, 1955, FRUS, 1955–1957, 3:33–34.
93. Telegram from Ambassador U Alexis Johnson to the Department of State, August 13, 1955, FRUS, 1955–1957, 3:35.
94. Telegram from Secretary of State to Ambassador U Alexis Johnson, at Geneva, August 14, 1955, FRUS, 1955–1957, 3:38–39.
95. Agreed Announcement of the Ambassadors of the United States of America and the People's Republic of China, September 10, 1955, FRUS, 1955–1957, 3:85–86.
96. Ambassadorial Talks at Geneva: Discussions Between the United States and the Chinese Communists, August 1, 1955–October 18, 1956, n.d., Office of East Asian Affairs, Central Files, 1947–1964, RG 59, Box 18, National Archives, College Park, Maryland (hereafter cited as OEAA).
97. While the Indian government claimed that ninety Chinese students received assistance from its embassy in the United States, Beijing was certain about only eighty-seven of them. "LiuMei Xuesheng Huiguo Renshu Qingkuangbiao" (Table of the Number of Students Returned from the United States), March 11, 1960, FMAA, 111-00313-05(1).
98. Ambassadorial Talks at Geneva, n.d., OEAA.
99. "Zhu Jinshan Zonglingshiguan Kuaiyou Dai Dian" (Express Mail from the Consulate General in San Francisco), February 4, 1956, *Diaocha Ji Zuzhi Liu-Mei Xuesheng Fanhui Dalu*, vol. 2, NAA.
100. Wang, *ZhongMei Huitan Jiunian Huigu*, 47–55.
101. Ambassadorial Talks at Geneva: Discussions Between the United States and the Chinese Communists, August 1, 1955–October 18, 1956, n.d., OEAA.

The last thirteen Americans detained in China were not released until after President Richard Nixon's first visit to China in 1972.

102. "LiuMei Xuesheng You Shenme Huiguo Ziyou?" (What Freedom Did Students in the United States Have in Returning to Their Country?), *People's Daily*, August 24, 1955.
103. "Woguo LiuMei Xuesheng Jiashu De Laixin" (Letters from the Relatives of Our Students in the United States), *People's Daily*, December 31, 1955.
104. "Yingdang Rang Zai Meiguo De Zhongguo Liuxuesheng Liji Huiguo" (Chinese Students in the United States Should Be Allowed to Return to Their Country Immediately), *People's Daily*, December 31, 1955.
105. Jin, *Zhou Enlai Zhuan*, 1092.
106. "Guanyu Zhengqu LiuMei Xuesheng Huiguo De Jixiang Juti Banfa" (Several Concrete Measures to Get Chinese Student Return from the United States), January 18, 1956, 111-00239-02(1), FMAA.
107. "Guanyu Zhengqu Zai Ziben Zhuyi Guojia Liuxuesheng Huiguo De Fangzhen Renwu Cuoshi Deng Yijian Gei Zhou Enlai Zongli De Baogao" (Report to Premier Zhou Enlai on the Proposed Principles, Tasks, and Measures to Get Back the Students Still in Capitalist Countries), January 27, 1956, 111-00239-05(1), FMAA.
108. Bureaus of Civil Affairs, Public Security, and Education of Hubei Province, "Guanyu Dui Woguo Zai Ziben Zhuyi Guojia Liuxuesheng Jinxing Dengji Gongzuo De Lianhe Tongzhi" (Joint Circular on the Registration of Students in the Capitalist Nations), April 10, 1956, SZ118-2-171, Hubei Provincial Archives, Wuhan, Hubei Province, China (hereafter cited as HPA).
109. "Guanyu Zhengqu Shangzai Ziben Zhuyi Guojia De Liuxuesheng Huiguo Gongzuo Zhong De Jige Wenti" (On Several Issues in Winning the Return of Chinese Students Who Are Still in Capitalist Countries), June 26, 1956, SZ118-2-171, HPA.
110. "Wang Ren Deng Huiguo Liuxuesheng De Gongkaixin" (The Public Letter Written by Wang Ren and Other Students Returned from the United States), July 11, 1955, 111-00234-06, MFAA.
111. Ministries of Higher Education, Interior, and Public Security, "Guanyu Zhengqu Haizai Ziben Zhuyi Guojia Liuxuesheng Huiguo Xiayibu Gongzuo Bushu Wenti De Lianhe Tongzhi" (Joint Circular on the Next Step of Winning the Students Still in the Capitalist Countries), September 8, 1956, SZ118-2-171, HPA.
112. "Beijingshi Guanyu Zhengqu Haizai Ziben Zhuyi Guojia Liuxuesheng Guiguo Gongzuo Jinxing Qingkuang He Jinhou Gongzuo De Yijian" (The Progress and Future Plan of Beijing City on Getting Students in Capitalist Countries Back to the Country), February 6, 1958, 2-10-219, BMA.

113. "LiuMei Xusheng Huiguo Renshu" (The Number of Students Returned from the United States), March 11, 1960, 111-00313-05, MFAA.
114. Wang, *ZhongMei Huitan Jiunian Huigu*, 55–56.
115. Chinese National Association of Science and Technology, "Guanyu Jiang Zhengqu Haizai Ziben Zhuyi Guojia Liuxuesheng Huiguo Gongzuo Huagui Ge Shengshi Zhijie Guanli De Tongzhi" (Circular on Shifting Management Responsibility Over Getting Chinese Students Back from the Capitalist Countries to Provinces and Municipalities), December 6, 1958, SZ124-2-0026-1, HPA.
116. Advice to Chou Wen-te, March 7, 1956; Letter from V. T. Chou to Nagoski, February 22, 1957; Memorandum for the File: Visit of Dr. Victor Chou to the Dept, August 21, 1957; Bureau of Far Eastern Affairs/Office of Chinese Affairs, Decimal Files, 1954–1957, Box 22, RG 59, National Archives, College Park, Maryland.
117. "A Letter to the President of the United States," September 9, 1955, *Diaocha Ji Zuzhi LiuMei Xuesheng Fanhui Dalu*, vol. 1, NAA.
118. "Jiujinshan Zong Lingshiguan Zhi Wajiaobu Kuaiyou" (Express Mail from the Consulate General in San Francisco to the Ministry of Foreign Affairs), September 9, 1955, *Diaocha Ji Zuzhi LiuMei Xuesheng Fanhui Dalu*, vol. 1, NAA.
119. "Red Pen Poison: How Red China Follows Soviet Letter Barrage," *Houston Press*, June 8, 1956.
120. Jack Lotte, "Refugees," International News Service, October 18, 1956.
121. Chen Tushou, *Guguo Renmin Yousuo Si: 1949 Nian Hou Zhishi Fenzi Sixiang Gaizao Ceying* (Some of the People's Thoughts in My Homeland: Profiles of Intellectuals in the Thought Reform After 1949) (Beijing: Sanlian Shudian, 2013), 152–75; Fu Ying, "Xiang Zhenli Touxiang" (Surrender to the Truth), *Wenhui Bao*, May 4, 1958.
122. Xu Zhangben was released from jail only in 1975 and exonerated from all the charges in 1979. Wang Mingzhen, "Jiang Qing Rang Women Dun Wunian Dalao" (Jiang Qing Put Us in Jail for Five Years), in *1950 Niandai Guiguo LiuMei Kexuejia Fangtanlu* (Interviews with Scientists Returned from the United States in the 1950s), ed. Wang Delu (Changsha: Hunan Jiaoyu Chubanshe, 2013), 242–43.

4. Building a Cultural Bastion

1. "United States Policy Toward Formosa: Statement by President Truman," January 5, 1950, *Department of State Bulletin*, January 16, 1950, 79.

2. "Extemporaneous Remarks by Secretary Acheson," January 5, 1950, *Department of State Bulletin*, January 16, 1950, 81.
3. The Secretary of State to the American Embassy in Taipei, February 8, 1950, U.S. Department of State, *Foreign Relations of the United States* (Washington, DC: U.S. Government Printing Office, 1950), 6:306–7 (hereafter cited as FRUS).
4. The Chargé in China (Strong) to the Secretary of State, February 10, 1950, FRUS, 1950, 6:307–8.
5. The action was taken under the request from the British government to prevent those heavy weapons from falling into the hands of communist forces, which might then use them in attacking Hong Kong in the future. Dean Acheson urged the Department of Defense to "take steps to prevent the transfer of such items to the Chinese Government from its stocks." The Secretary of State to the Secretary of Defense (Johnson), March 7, 1950, FRUS, 1950, 6:316–17.
6. Memorandum of Conversation, by Mr. John Foster Dulles, Consultant to the Secretary of State, May 25, 1950, FRUS, 1950, 6:343–44.
7. Letter from C. C. Chang to Raymond T. Moyer, April 13, 1950, RG 469, Records of U.S. Foreign Assistance Agencies, 1948–1961, Office of Far Eastern Operations, China Subject File, 1948–1957, Box 45, National Archives, College Park, Maryland (hereafter cited as CSF).
8. The Acting Secretary of State to the Embassy in Taipei, May 19 and May 26, 1950, FRUS, 1950, 6:342–46.
9. Memorandum by the Deputy Special Assistant for Intelligence (House) to Mr. W. Park Armstrong, Special assistant to the Secretary of State for Intelligence and Research, May 31, 1950, FRUS, 1950, 6:347–49.
10. "U.S. Air and Sea Forces Ordered into Supporting Action: Statement by President Truman," June 27, 1950, *Department of State Bulletin*, July 3, 1950, 5.
11. "U.S. Air and Sea Forces Ordered into Supporting Action: Statement by President Truman," June 27, 1950, *Department of State Bulletin*, July 3, 1950, 5.
12. The Secretary of State to the American Embassy in Taipei, June 27, 1950, FRUS, 1950, 7:188.
13. The Chargé in China (Strong) to the Secretary of State, June 29, 1950, FRUS, 1950, 7:225.
14. The Secretary of Defense (Johnson) to the Secretary of State, July 19, 1950, FRUS, 1950, 6:382–83.
15. Memorandum by the Joint Chiefs of Staff to the Secretary of Defense (Johnson), July 27, 1950, FRUS, 1950, 6:391–94.
16. NSC 37/10: Immediate United States Course of Action with Respect to Formosa, August 3, 1950, FRUS, 1950, 6:413–14.

17. Extracts of a Memorandum of Conversation, by Mr. W. Averell Harriman, Special Assistant to the President, with General MacArthur in Tokyo on August 6 and 8, 1950, FRUS, 1950, 6:427–30.
18. "'Meiyuan Peihe Shengchan Jianshe Zhi Yanjiu' Caoan" (Draft for "A Study of the Use of American Aid in Production and Reconstruction"), in *Taiwan Guangfu Hou Meiyuan Shiliao* (Documentary Collection on U.S. Aid to R.O.C., 1948–1965), ed. Anne H. Chou (Taipei: Academia Historica Republic of China, 1995), 1:34–35.
19. James Yen's vacancy was filled by T. H. Chien (Qian Tianhe), another mainland Chinese official. Huang Junjie, *Nongfuhui Yu Taiwan Jingyan* (Joint Commission of Rural Reconstruction and the Taiwan Experiences) (Taipei: Sanmin Shuju, 1991), 318.
20. Letter from James T. Ivy to John B. Nason, August 4, 1951, CSF, Box 45.
21. Memorandum from John B. Nason to Harlan Cleveland, August 11, 1950, CSF, Box 45.
22. Zhang Xianqiu, *Nongfuhui Huiyi Lu* (A Memoir of JCRR) (Taipei: Xingzhengyuan Nongye Weiyuanhui, 1990), 6–7.
23. Parts 3 and 4 provided support for the "on-the-job training" in the United States and Japan. The proposed budget for the whole program was about $800,000. Memorandum from Owen L. Dawson to the Joint Commission on Rural Reconstruction, September 15, 1950, CSF, Box 45.
24. Notes on Conversation Regarding Progress for Students from Formosa, October 11, 1950, CSF, Box 45.
25. Letter from R. Allen Griffin to William C. Johnstone, Jr., October 20, 1950, CSF, Box 45.
26. Letter from William C. Johnstone Jr. to R. Allen Griffin, November 3, 1950, CSF, Box 45.
27. Memorandum from Frank L. Turner to Shannon McCune, November 27, 1950, CSF, Box 45.
28. Telegram from the ECA Administrator to the American Embassy in Taipei, December 6, 1950, CSF, Box 45.
29. Memorandum from John F. Embree to Shannon McCune, December 18, 1950, CSF, Box 45.
30. Memorandum from Shannon McCune to John F. Embree, December 21, 1950, CSF, Box 45.
31. Minutes of the 1st Meeting of the Committee on ECA/JCRR Scholarships, December 20, 1950, CSF, Box 45.
32. Minutes of the 2nd Meeting of the Committee on ECA/JCRR Scholarships, January 15, 1951, CSF, Box 45.
33. Memorandum Dictated by Telephone by Mr. Hummel, Department of State, January 18, 1951, CSF, Box 45.

34. Letter from Livingston T. Merchant to Shannon McCume, February 2, 1951, CSF, Box 45.
35. Memorandum from the Working Committee on Scholarships to the ECA/JCRR Scholarship Committee, n.d., CSF, Box 45.
36. Scholarship Students under ECA/JCRR Scholarship Program, n.d., CSF, Box 45.
37. Cablegram from Hubert G. Schenck to Mutual Security Agency Headquarters, January 7, 1952, CSF, Box 45.
38. Mutual Security Agency Headquarters to American Embassy in Taipei, January 17, 1952, CSF, Box 45.
39. Cablegram from Hubert G. Schenck to Mutual Security Agency Headquarters, February 19, March 10, 1952, CSF, Box 45.
40. Lee Teng-hui won another opportunity to further his education at Cornell University in 1965 and earned his doctorate in 1968. Lee's educational experience in the United States helped him rise fast in the Nationalist government, becoming mayor of Taipei in 1978, governor of Taiwan Province in 1981, and vice president in 1984. When Chiang Ching-kuo died in 1988, Lee succeeded him as the president of the Republic of China and held that position until 2000.
41. Letter from John Earl Baker to Frank L. Turner, November 23, 1951, CSF, Box 45.
42. *Cosin Commentator* 1, October 24, 1951, CSF, Box 46.
43. "Meiyuan Jishu Xiezhu Jihua Jiantao Baogao" (Reports on the Review of American Aid Technical Assistance Programs), January 1959, in Chou, *Taiwan Guangfu Hou Meiyuan Shiliao*, 3:296–302.
44. Letter from G. St. Louis to W. A. Rex, Jr., April 1, 1953, CSF, Box 46.
45. Letter from Karl L. Rankin to the Department of State, November 4, 1953, CSF, Box 46.
46. Cablegram from Hubert Schenck to MSA Headquarters, February 9, 1952, CSF, Box 46.
47. Letter from Clarence R. Decker to Tien-fong Cheng, July 9, 1952, CSF, Box 46.
48. Letter from Tien-fong Cheng to Clarence R. Decker, July 19, 1952, CSF, Box 46.
49. Letter from Kuo-chen Wu to Wayne O. Reed and J. Russell Andrus, August 25, 1952, CSF, Box 46.
50. USOE recommended Louisiana State University, the University of Missouri, the University of Nebraska, and Pennsylvania State College. Cablegram from MSA Headquarters to Mission in Taipei, August 28, 1952, CSF, Box 46.
51. Report on a Survey of the Need on Formosa for a Program of Vocational Teacher Education in Agriculture and Industrial Education, December 8,

1952; Cablegram from Hubert Schenck to MSA Headquarters, December 10, 1952, CSF, Box 46.
52. Memorandum from J. Russell Andrus to Laura Hughes, October 14, 1953, CSF, Box 46.
53. Introduction, September 1952, CSF, Box 46.
54. Letter from C. L. Terrel to Clayton Lane, October 3, 1952, CSF, Box 46.
55. Letter from J. Russell Andrus to E. C. Watson, September 10, 1952, CSF, Box 46.
56. Letter from H. Emmett Brown to J. Russell Andrus, October 17, 1952, CSF, Box 46.
57. Letter from A. A. Potter to J. Russell Andrus, October 26, 1952, CSF, Box 46.
58. Letter from United States Information Service Office in Taipei to United States Information Service Headquarters in Washington, January 10, 1955, CSF, Box 46.
59. Letter from H. Emmett Brown to J. Russell Andrus, February 2, 1953, CSF, Box 46.
60. Cablegram from Stassen to Foreign Operations Administration Mission in Taipei, May 1, 1954; Cablegram from Brent to Foreign Operations Administration in Washington, May 7, 1954, CSF, Box 46.
61. H. Emmett Brown, "FOA Assisted Educational Programs in Free China: A Summary of Two and Half Years of Cooperation Action," April 21, 1955, CSF, Box 46.
62. "FOA Assisted Educational Programs in Free China."
63. Zhao Jichang, *Meiyuan De Yunyong* (The Use of American Aid) (Taipei: Lianjing Chuban Shiye Gongsi, 1985), 189–95.
64. "FOA Assisted Educational Programs in Free China"; Zhao, *Meiyuan De Yunyong*, 195–96.
65. Introduction, September 1952, CSF, Box 46.
66. Conference on Industrial Training Program, October 20, 1952, enclosure in Letter from H. Emmett Brown to J. Russell Andrus, October 22, 1952, CSF, Box 46.
67. MSA/CM Staff Critique of Dr. Givens' Draft Statement of Education Policy, enclosure in Letter from Hubert G. Schenck to Samuel P. Hayes, Jr., April 30, 1953, CSF, Box 46.
68. Sino-American Conference on Vocational-Industrial Education, March 3, 1953, CSF, Box 46.
69. Letter from R. Allen Griffin to Raymond T. Moyer, May 8, 1951, CSF, Box 45.
70. American Embassy in Taipei to the Department of State, July 22, 1953; Memorandum, July 3, 1953, enclosure, CSF, Box 46.

71. Letter from Raymond Moyer to Jiang Menglin, October 27, 1953, CSF, Box 46.
72. Letter from Russell Andrus to Emmett Brown, Nov. 13, 1953, CSF, Box 46.
73. Richard Nixon, *The Memoirs of Richard Nixon* (New York: Grosset & Dunlap, 1978), 119–37.
74. Letter from American Embassy in Taipei to the Secretary of State, April 12, 1954, CSF, Box 46.
75. Richard Nixon, "Free China—Also a Bastion of Cultural Strength," in *U.S. Vice President Nixon's Visit to Free China: A Collection of Mr. Nixon's Speeches and Remarks on Free China*, ed. Hangzhong Wang (Taipei: China Cultural Publishing Foundation, 1953), 12.
76. Nixon, *Memoirs of Richard Nixon*, 126.
77. Memorandum of Discussion at the 177th Meeting of the National Security Council, December 23, 1953, FRUS, 1952–54, 14:349.
78. Statement of Policy by the National Security Council, November 6, 1953, FRUS, 1952–54, 14:307–9.
79. Statement of Policy by the National Security Council, 14:280–82.
80. Quoted from He Jiefu, *Xingzhengyuan Fudao Qiaosheng Huiguo Shengxue Zhi Zhengce Yanjiu* (A Study of the Executive Council's Policy on Advising Overseas Chinese Students Returning to China for Education) (Taipei: National Chengchi University Press, 1975), 245n9.
81. Zhu Jingxian, *Huaqiao Jiaoyu* (The Overseas Chinese Education) (Taipei: Zhonghua Shuju, 1973), 42–43.
82. "Cheng Tien-fang Zhi Ye Kung-chao Han" (Letter from Cheng Tien-fang to Ye Kung-chao), March 2, 1954, Waijiaobu Dangan (Ministry of Foreign Affairs Archives), 020-19908-0005, Dongnanya Qiaojiao Jihua (Plan for Overseas Chinese Education in Southeast Asia), Guoshiguan (Academia Historica), Taipei, Taiwan (hereafter cited as DQJ); American Embassy in Taipei to the Department of State, April 12, 1954, CSF, Box 46.
83. "Cheng Yanfen Zhi Ye Kungchao Han" (Letter from Cheng Yanfen to Ye Kungchao), December 14, 1953, DQJ.
84. Letter from Karl L. Rankin to Chen Cheng, November 24, 1953, DQJ.
85. Letter from Karl L. Rankin to Chen Cheng, January 21, 1954, DQJ.
86. Frank L. Turner, Chief of China Division, Office of Far East, FOA, wrote on the margin of the cover of the report: "Great stuff! This is important to keep on to. We may need it any moment because of Nixon's interest." Office of Intelligence Research, Department of State, Intelligence Report No. 6506: The Problem of Education of Overseas Chinese, January 4, 1954, CSF, Box 46.
87. "Cheng Tien-fang Zhi Ye Kung-chao Han" (Letter from Cheng Tien-fang to Ye Kung-chao), March 2, 1954, DQJ; Letter from American Embassy to the Department of State, April 20, 1954, CSF, Box 46.

88. "Cheng Tien-fang Zhi Ye Kung-chao Han"; Letter from American Embassy to the Department of State.
89. Letter from American Embassy in Taipei to the Department of State, April 12, 1954, CSF, Box 46.
90. "Cheng Tien-fang Zhi Ye Kung-chao Han."
91. Office of Intelligence Research, Department of State, Intelligence Report No. 6506: The Problem of Education of Overseas Chinese, January 4, 1954, CSF, Box 46; "Xingzhengyuan Mishuchu Zhi Waijiaobu Han" (Letter from the Secretariat of the Executive Council to the Ministry of Foreign Affairs), April 26, 1954, DQJ.
92. "Xingzhengyuan Mishuchu Zhi Waijiaobu Han."
93. "Xingzhengyuan Mishuchu Zhi Waijiaobu Han."
94. Letter from Martin Wong to J. I. Brent, April 28, 1954, CSF, Box 100.
95. Letter from J. I. Brent to Frank L. Turner, May 6, 1954, CSF, Box 100.
96. Cablegram from J. I. Brent to Foreign Operations Administration in Washington, May 19, CSF, Box 100.
97. Cablegram from Stassen to J. I. Brent, May 21, 1954, CSF, Box 100.
98. Airgram from Stassen to Joint-Embassy/MSM/C, June 11, 1954, CSF, Box 100.
99. Letter from K. L. Ranking to the Secretary of State Department, February 23, 1955, CSF, Box 100.
100. Ambassador Rankin's Speech at the Dedication Ceremony, February 13, 1955, enclosure in Letter from K. L. Ranking to the Secretary of State Department, February 23, 1955, CSF, Box 100.
101. Stassen to FOA Mission in Taipei, December 22, 1954, CSF, Box 100.
102. Letter from H. Emmitt Brown to Charles Hendershot, October 3, 1955, CSF, Box 100.
103. Memorandum from S. I. Nadler to the USIS, n.d., CSF, Box 100.
104. Memorandum from Donald E. Webster to the Department of State, November 9, 1955; Airgram from Brent to International Cooperation Administration, December 5, 1955, CSF, Box 100.
105. Cablegram from Fitzgerald to ICA Mission in Taipei, January 31, 1956, CSF, Box 224.
106. Report on the Visit of Mr. Payne Templeton in February 1956 to the Southeast Asian Countries, April 20, 1956, CSF, Box 224.
107. Report on the Visit of Mr. Payne Templeton in February 1956 to the Southeast Asian Countries.
108. Cablegram from Brent to ICA/W, March 19, 1956, CSF, Box 224.
109. Cablegram from Hollister to ICA Mission in Taipei, April 3, 1956, CSF, Box 224.
110. Meeting Minutes, April 13, 1956, CSF, Box 100.

111. Embassy-USIS Supplement to ICA Report on Overseas Chinese Education, enclosure in Report on the Visit of Mr. Payne Templeton in February 1956 to the Southeast Asian Countries, April 20, 1956, CSF, Box 224.
112. Letter from H. Emmett Brown to Clarence Hendershot, May 3, 1956, CSF, Box 224.
113. Airgram from Brent to International Cooperation Administration, November 23, 1956, CSF, Box 224.
114. Cablegram from Hollister to ICA Mission in Taipei, June 19, 1957, CSF, Box 224.
115. Letter from David L. Osborn to the Department of State, September 3, 1958; Chen Ch'ing-wen, "Report on Educational Program for Overseas Chinese Students," December 3, 1959, enclosure in Richard M. McCarthy to the Department of State, December 30, 1959, CSF, Box 224.
116. For each overseas Chinese student enrolled, a college would receive NTC12,000 to NTC22,000 American aid depending on the subject field. This gave incentive to colleges and universities to increase enrollment of overseas Chinese students for more cash funding. Zhao, *Meiyuan De Yunyong*, 203–6.
117. Memorandum from Dulles to Bangkok, etc., July 2, 1958, CSF, Box 224.
118. Letter from David L. Osborn to the Department of State, January 23, 1959, CSF, Box 224.
119. Memorandum from Haraldson to ICA Washington, September 29, 1958, CSF, Box 224.
120. Memorandum from Harald W. Jacobson to the Department of State, January 15, 1959, CSF, Box 224.
121. Memorandum from N. T. Noyer to D. A. FitzGerald, August 6, 1959; Memorandum from Everett F. Drumright to the Department of State, August 5, 1959, CSF, Box 224.
122. Memorandum from N. T. Noyer to D. A. FitzGerald; Airgram from James to ICA Washington, September 1, 1959, CSF, Box 224.
123. Memorandum from Dillon to American Embassy in Taipei, September 8, 1959, CSF, Box 224.
124. Memorandum from Alexander L. Peaslee to the Department of State, November 2, 1959, CSF, Box 224.
125. Zhang Xizhe, *Zhonghua Minguo De Qiaosheng Jiaoyu* (Education for Overseas Chinese Students in the Republic of China) (Taipei: Zhongzheng Shuju, 1991), 9–11; He Jiefu, "Xingzhengyuan Fudao Qiaosheng Huiguo Shengxue Zhengce Zhi Yanjiu" (A Study of the Executive Council's Policy on Helping Overseas Chinese Return for Education) (MA thesis, National Chengchi University, Taiwan, 1975), 71–72; Xia Chenghua, "Yijiusijiu Nian Yilai De Zhonghua Minguo Qiaosheng Jiaoyu Huigu" (The Recollection of the

Republic of China's Education for Overseas Chinese Since 1949), *Yanxi Zixun* (Information on Research and Learning) 23, no. 2 (April 2006): 27.

126. Theodore H. E. Chen, "Government Encouragement and Control of International Education in Communist China," in *Government Policy and International Education*, ed., Steward Fraser (New York: John Wiley & Son, 1965), 124.

127. *Zhongyang Ribao* (Central Daily), a newspaper run by the Central Committee of the Nationalist Party, carried the piece on February 7, 1961. Zhang, *Zhonghua Minguo De Qiaosheng Jiaoyu*, 8.

128. Qiaowu Weiyuanhui Yanjiu Fazhan Kaohechu, *Qiaosheng Huiguo Shengxue Jianjie* (Brief Introduction to Returning to the Country for Education for Overseas Chinese Students) (Taipei: Zhongzheng Shuju, 1972), 32–43.

129. Zhang, *Zhonghua Minguo De Qiaosheng Jiaoyu*, 24–33.

130. For statistics of participants in various educational and cultural exchanges between the United States and Taiwan from the 1950s to the 1970s, see Qina Zhao, "Meiguo Zhengfu Zai Taiwan De Jiaoyu Yu Wenhua Jiaoliu Huodong (Yijiuwuyi Zhi Yijiuqiling Nian)" (The U.S. Government's Educational and Cultural Exchange Activities in Taiwan from 1951 to 1970), *OuMei Yanjiu* (Research on Europe and America) 31, no. 1 (March 2001): 79–124; and Pengyuan Zhang, "Cong Taiwan Kan ZhongMei Jin Sanshi Nian Zhi Xueshu Jiaoliu" (An Examination of Sino-American Academic Exchange in the Past Thirty Years from Taiwan's Perspective), *Hanxue Yanjiu* (Research on Sinology) 2, no. 1 (June 1984): 23–55.

5. Faking the Exchange

1. Zhonggong Zhongyang Wenxian Yanjiushi, ed., *Mao Zedong Nianpu, 1949–1976* (Chronicles of Mao Zedong, 1949–1976) (Beijing: Zhongyang Wenxian Chubanshe, 2013), 2:244, 260–61, 320–21.

2. Despite its commitment to helping Jiang Jieshi (Chiang Kai-shek) defend Taiwan, Washington repeatedly asserted its position that the United States would not support any attempt by the Nationalist regime to retake the mainland by force. Warren I. Cohen, *America's Response to China* (New York: Columbia University Press, 2000), 184–85.

3. Zhonggong Zhongyang Wenxian Yanjiushi, ed., *Zhou Enlai Nianpu* (Chronicles of Zhou Enlai) (Beijing: Zhongyang Wenxian Chubanshe, 2007), 1:470.

4. Mao Zedong, "Heping Wei Shang" (Peace Is the Top Priority), May 26, 1955, in *Mao Zedong Waijiao Wenxuan* (Selected Works of Mao Zedong on Diplomacy), ed. Zhonghua Renmin Gongheguo Waijiaobu (Beijing: Shijie Zhishi Chubanshe, 1994), 211.

5. List of Chinese Communist Efforts to Induce Americans to Travel to Communist China, enclosure in Memorandum from McConaughy to Robertson, February 12, 1957, Bureau of Far Eastern Affairs/Office of Chinese Affairs Files, 1954–1957 (hereafter cited as OCA), National Archives, College Park, Maryland, Box 22.
6. Telegram from Ambassador U. Alexis Johnson to the Department of State, August 23, 1955, in *Foreign Relations of the United States* (hereafter cited as FRUS), 1955–1957 (Washington, DC: U.S. Government Printing Office, 1957), 3:59; Wang Bingnan, *ZhongMei Huitan Jiunian Huigu* (Memoir of the Nine-Year Sino-American Talks) (Beijing: Shijie Zhishi Chubanshe, 1985), 58–60.
7. Some paragraphs in this chapter are taken with modification and revision from Hongshan Li, "Building a Black Bridge: China's Interactions with African-American Activists in the Cold War," *Journal of Cold War Studies* 20, no. 3 (Summer 2018): 114–52.
8. The Intelligence Division (Qingbao Si) was renamed the Information Division (Xinwen Si) in July 1955. It continued to supervise visiting foreign journalists, a responsibility assumed by the MFA in 1952. Between 1949 and 1952, foreign journalists in the PRC were under the supervision of the International News Bureau (Guoji Xinwenju) of the National News Administration (Guojia Xinwen Zongshu). Zhou Qingan and Wang Di, "Cong Waijiao Dangan Kan Zhongguo Zhengzhi Chuanbo Qibu: 1956–1957 Zhongguo Zhengfu Dui Waiguo Jizhe Guanli Zhidu Shi Chutan" (An Examination on the Beginning of China's Political Communication Based on the Diplomatic Archives: A Preliminary History of the Management System Established by the Chinese Government for Foreign Journalists), *Xiandai Chuanbo* (Contemporary Communications) 34, no. 6 (2014): 29–30.
9. Quoted in Zhang Jingjing, "Zhongguo Ruhe Xiang Meiguo Jizhe Caifang Kaijin" (How China Lifted the Ban on Interviews by American Journalists), in *Dangan Jiemi Waijiao Fengyun* (Exposing Secrecy in Diplomatic History Through the Archives), ed. Zhu Jihua (Shanghai: Xuelin Chubanshe, 2015), 173–74.
10. Mao Zedong, "Tong Yiqie Yuanyi Heping De Guojia Hezuo" (Cooperate with All Nations That Want Peace), July 7, 1954, in *Mao Zedong Wenji* (Writings of Mao Zedong), ed. Zhonggong Zhongyang Wenxian Yanjiushi (Beijing: Renmin Chubanshe, 1993), 6:333–34.
11. Mao Zedong, "Tong Yindu Zongli Nihelu De Sici Tanhua" (Four Conversations with Indian Prime Minister Nehru), October 26, 1954, in *Mao Zedong Wenji*, 6:371.
12. *Zhou Enlai Nianpu*, 1:419–20.

13. Waijiaobu, "Pizhun Meiguo Jizhe Laihua" (Approval for the Visit of American Journalists), January 30, 1956, Ministry of Foreign Affairs Archives (MFAA), Beijing, China.
14. "Gong Peng Zhi Waijiaobu Dangwei Xin" (Letter from Gong Peng to the Party Committee of the Ministry of Foreign Affairs), July 17, 1956, File No. 116-00197-03(1), MFAA.
15. Yu Qi, "Changzheng Duiwai Xuanchuan De 'Sange Diyi' " (The Three Firsts in International Propaganda on the Long March), *Jundui Zhenggong Lilun Yanjiu* (Theoretical Studies of the People's Liberation Army Political Work) 17, no. 4 (August 2016): 51–52.
16. Agnes Smedley's book *The Great Road: The Life and Times of Chu Teh* was finally published in unfinished form by Monthly Review Press in 1956, a few years after the author had passed away.
17. Nym Wales, *Inside Red China* (New York: Doubleday, Doran & Co., 1939); Jiang Jiannong and Wang Benquan, *Sinuo Yu Zhongguo* (Snow and China) (Haerbing: Heilongjiang Renmin Chubanshe, 1993), 144–48.
18. Tracy B. Strong and Helene Keyssar, *Right in Her Soul: The Life of Anna Louise Strong* (New York: Random House, 1983), 177–79.
19. Paul French, *Through the Looking Glass: China's Foreign Journalists from Opium to Mao* (Hong Kong: Hong Kong University Press, 2009), 243–46; Zhang Wei, "Kangzhan Shiqi De Guomin Dang Duiwai Xuanchuan Ji Meiguo Jizhe Qun" (The Nationalist Government Foreign Propaganda and the American Journalists in the War Against Japan), *Hangzhou Shifan Daxue Xuebao (Shehui Kexue Ban)* (Journal of Hangzhou Normal University, Social Science Edition) 5 (September 2008): 39.
20. Theodore White, *In Search of History: A Personal Adventure* (New York: Warner Books, 1978), 239–81.
21. Edgar Snow, *Red Star Over China* (New York: Random House, 1938), 42–44.
22. Edgar Snow, *Journey to the Beginning* (New York: Random House, 1958), 150–63; Yu Qi, "Changzheng Duiwai Xuanchuan De 'Sange Diyi,' " 51–52.
23. The two interpreters were Ke Bainian and Ling Qing. They later became the directors of the Division and the Section of American and Australian Affairs respectively after the establishment of the PRC. "Zhongwai Jizhe Guancha Tuan 1944 Nian Fangwen Yanan" (Observation Group of Chinese and Foreign Journalists Visiting Yanan in 1944), *Renmin Zhengxie Bao* (The Newspaper of the People's Political Consultative Conference), November 28, 2013.
24. For a detailed and in-depth analysis on the American reporters visiting Yanan in 1944, see Morrell Heald and Lawrence S. Kaplan, *Culture and Diplomacy: The American Experience* (Westport, CT: Greenwood Press, 1977), 188–214.

25. White, *In Search of History*, 250.
26. "Gong Peng Zhi Waijiaobu Dangwei Xin," MFAA.
27. "Gong Peng Zhi Waijiaobu Dangwei Xin," MFAA; Zhang Jingjing, "Chongpo Meiguo Jinling, Tamen LaiHua Caifang Le Sha?" (Breaking U.S. Ban: What Did They See in China?), *Jiefang Ribao* (Liberation Daily), February 6, 2015.
28. Zhang, "Zhongguo Ruhe Xiang Meiguo Jizhe Caifang Kaijin," 175.
29. Xinwen Si, "Meiguo Jizhe Fanghua Xiaojie" (A Brief Summary of the Visits of the American Journalists), August 31, 1956, MFAA.
30. Anthony Lewis, "Peiping Lifts Ban on U.S. News Men," *New York Times*, August 6, 1956; "U.S. Firm in Ban on Red China Trip: State Department Refuses News Men Visas Despite Number of Protests," *New York Times*, August 7, 1956.
31. Not all the media companies were eager to send their invited reporters to Communist China. Howard Flieger, the directing editor of the world staff of the *U.S. News and World Report*, immediately rejected Beijing's offer "in view of the fact that the United States, as a member of the United Nations, is still in the state of war with the Red Communist China." Lewis, "Peiping Lifts Ban on U.S News Men."
32. "Gong Peng to the Party Committee of the Ministry of Foreign Affairs," July 17, 1956, MFAA; Zhang, "Zhongguo Ruhe Xiang Meiguo Jizhe Caifang Kaijin," 173.
33. Memo from Murphy to Sebald, August 6, 1956, OCA, Box 22.
34. Red China Bid to News Correspondents Called Propaganda, Wireless File no. 188, August 6, 1956, OCA, Box 22.
35. Lewis, "Peiping Lifts Ban on U.S. News Men."
36. Memorandum of a Telephone Conversation Between the President and the Secretary of State, August 7, 1956, FRUS, 1955–1957, 3:417–18.
37. Department of State for the Press, August 7, 1956, OCA, Box 22.
38. "U.S. Firm in Ban on Red China Trip."
39. "U.S. Press Protests on China Ban Rise," *New York Times*, August 8, 1958.
40. "U.S. Firm in Ban on Red China Trip."
41. "Special to *The New York Times*," *New York Times*, August 8, 1956.
42. Xinwen Si, "Meiguo Jizhe Fanghua Xiaojie," MFAA.
43. For the Secretary, August 14, 1956, OCA, Box 22.
44. The Acting Secretary, August 16, 1956, OCA, Box 22.
45. Memorandum from Sebald to the Acting Secretary, August 17, 1956, OCA, Box 22.
46. Telegram from the Acting Secretary of State to the Consulate General at Hong Kong, August 20, FRUS, 1955–1957, 3:421.

47. Greg MacGregore, "4 U.S. Newsmen Waited in China: Red Agent Says They Plan to Visit Despite the Objection of State Department," *New York Times*, August 19, 1956.
48. Dana Adams Schmidt, "Eisenhower Backs China Travel Ban," *New York Times*, August 21, 1956.
49. "Reporting Red China," *New York Times*, August 21, 1956.
50. Schmidt, "Eisenhower Backs China Travel Ban."
51. Xinwen Si, "Meiguo Jizhe Fanghua Xiaojie," MFAA.
52. Letter from Frank Starzel to John Foster Dulles, December 29, 1956, OCA, Box 22.
53. Xinwen Si, "Meiguo Jizhe Fanghua Xiaojie," MFAA.
54. Zhang, "Zhongguo Ruhe Xiang Meiguo Jizhe Caifang Kaijin," 175.
55. Xinwen Si, "Meiguo Jizhe Fanghua Xiaojie," MFAA.
56. Telegram from Ambassador U. Alexis Johnson to the Department of State, September 22, 1956, FRUS, 1955–1957, 3:431–32.
57. Telegram from Ambassador U. Alexis Johnson to the Department of State, October 18, 1956, FRUS, 1955–1957, 3:439n4.
58. Telegram from Ambassador U. Alexis Johnson to the Department of State, September 22, 1956, FRUS, 1955–1957, 3:432n5.
59. Mao Zedong, "Guanyu Honglou Meng Yanjiu Wenti De Xin" (A Letter on Research on *The Dream of the Red Chamber*), October 16, 1954, in *Mao Zedong Wenji*, 6:352–53. Both John Dewey and Hu Shi had already been sharply criticized during the thought-reform movement in 1951 and 1952.
60. *Mao Zedong Nianpu*, 3:309–10, 316–17.
61. Wang Huanxun, *Hu Shi Jiaoyu Sixiang Pipan Yinlun* (An Introduction to the Denunciation of Hu Shi's Educational Thoughts) (Wuhan: Hubei Renmin Chubanshe, 1956), 12.
62. Zhang, "Zhongguo Ruhe Xiang Meiguo Jizhe Caifang Kaijin," 175–76.
63. "Meiguo 'Meiguo Feizhouren Bao' He Gelunbiya Guangbo Gongsi Jizhe Wosai Fanghua" (American "Afro-American" and CBS Reporter Worthy Visits China), November 27, 1956, MFAA.
64. Zhang, "Zhongguo Ruhe Xiang Meiguo Jizhe Caifang Kaijin," 176.
65. "A U.S. Reporter Enters Red China: Crosses Border in Defiance of Washington Ban," *New York Times*, December 24, 1956.
66. Zhang, "Zhongguo Ruhe Xiang Meiguo Jizhe Caifang Kaijin," 176–77.
67. Zhongguo Guoji Lüxingshe, "Jiedai Meiguo Jizhe Fanghua Gongzuo Xiaojie" (A Brief Summary of the Reception of the American Journalists in Visits to China), February 6, 1957, MFAA.
68. Xinwen Zongshu, "Xinwen Zongshu Zhuanfa 'Waijiaobu Banfa Waiguo Jizhe Dengji Zheng Zanxing Tiaoli' " (The Administration of Information

Transmitting the Temporary Regulation Issued by the Ministry of Foreign Affairs on the Registration of Foreign Journalists), n.d., Beijing Municipal Archives, 008-002-00032, Beijing, China.
69. Zhongguo Guoji Lüxingshe, "Jiedai Meiguo Jizhe Fanghua Gongzuo Xiaojie," MFAA; Zhang, "Zhongguo Ruhe Xiang Meiguo Jizhe Caifang Kaijin," 178.
70. Zhang, "Zhongguo Ruhe Xiang Meiguo Jizhe Caifang Kaijin," 177.
71. William Worthy, "Reporting in Communist China," Look, March 25, 1957, 9.
72. Zhang, "Zhongguo Ruhe Xiang Meiguo Jizhe Caifang Kaijin," 179.
73. Li Yang, "Chujin Da Gongchang—1949 Nian Qianhou Zhonggong Dui Shijingshan Gangtie Chang De Jieguan Yu Gaizao" (First Entrance Into Big Factories: The Chinese Communist Party's Taking Over and Reformation of the Shijingshan Steel and Iron Factory Around 1949), Yanyuan Shixue (Yanyuan Historical Studies) 9 (September 2014): 142–68.
74. Worthy, "Reporting in Communist China," 10.
75. Zhongguo Guoji Lüxingshe, "Jiedai Meiguo Jizhe Fanghua Gongzuo Xiaojie," MFAA; Zhang, "Zhongguo Ruhe Xiang Meiguo Jizhe Caifang Kaijin," 181.
76. Zhongguo Guoji Lüxingshe, "Jiedai Meiguo Jizhe Fanghua Gongzuo Xiaojie," MFAA.
77. Zhongguo Guoji Lüxingshe, "Jiedai Meiguo Jizhe Fanghua Gongzuo Xiaojie," MFAA.
78. Edmund Stevens and Philip Harrington, "Inside Red China," Look, April 16, 1957, 43, 50.
79. Zhang, "Zhongguo Ruhe Xiang Meiguo Jizhe Caifang Kaijin," 181.
80. Stevens and Harrington, "Inside Red China," 33–37.
81. Stevens and Harrington, "Inside Red China," 33–46.
82. William Worthy, "Worthy Looks at 'Color' in China," Baltimore Afro-American, January 29, 1957.
83. Zhang, "Zhongguo Ruhe Xiang Meiguo Jizhe Caifang Kaijin," 179.
84. Stevens and Harrison, "Inside Red China," Look, April 16, 1957, 37–52.
85. "Chou Talks to Look . . . and the U.S. Talks Back," Look, April 17, 1957, 52.
86. Worthy, "Worthy Looks at 'Color' in China."
87. Worthy, "Reporting in Communist China," 9–11.
88. Memorandum from Ralph Clough to Walter Robertson, December 26, 1956, OCA, Box 22.
89. "Newsmen in China Penalized by U.S.," New York Times, December 29, 1956.
90. Memorandum of Conversation Between E. Youde and Ralph Clough, January 2, 1957, OCA, Box 22.
91. "Red China," December 28, 1956, news report in file, OCA, Box 22.

92. Letter from the Director of the Office of Chinese Affairs (McConaughy) to Ambassador U. Alexis Johnson in Geneva, February 11, 1957, FRUS, 1955–1957, 3:473–74.
93. "Curb on Newsmen Is Called Invalid: Morris Ernest Attacks U.S. Stand on 3 in Red China," *New York Times*, January 11, 1957.
94. "Newsmen," Associated Press, January 24, 1957, OCA, Box 22.
95. Memorandum from Frances Knight to McLeod, February 8, 1957, OCA, Box 22.
96. Letter from the Director of the Office of Chinese Affairs (McConaughy) to Ambassador U. Alexis Johnson in Geneva, February 11, 1957, FRUS, 1955–1957, 3:473–76.
97. "Secretary Dulles' News Conference of February 5," *Department of State Bulletin*, February 25, 1957, 301.
98. "Writer Refuses to Yield Passport," *New York Times*, February 8, 1957.
99. "Curb on Newsmen Scored by Editor: Wiggins Says U.S. Reporters Should Be Permitted to Travel in China," *New York Times*, February 17, 1957.
100. Memorandum of a Conversation, Department of State Washington, February 12, 1957, FRUS, 1955–1957, 3:477–78.
101. Memorandum from Walter Robertson to the Secretary, n.d., OCA, Box 22.
102. Memorandum of a Telephone Conversation Between the President and the Secretary of State, Washington, February 13, 1957, FRUS, 1955–1957, 3:478–79.
103. Memorandum of a Conversation, Washington, February 18, 1957, FRUS, 1955–1957, 3:481–87.
104. Memorandum of a Conversation, Department of State, Washington, February 12, 1957, FRUS, 1955–1957, 3:477.
105. Memorandum of a Conversation Between the Secretary of State and Frank Bartholomew, Head of United Press, Washington, March 3, 1957, FRUS, 1955–1957, 3:478–79.
106. Memorandum of a Conversation, Department of State, Washington, March 27, 1957, FRUS, 1955–1957, 3:513–14.
107. Memorandum from William Sebald to Berding, April 4, 1957, OCA, Box 23.
108. Russell Baker, "Special Report," *New York Times*, May 15, 1957.
109. Thomas M. Fryor, "Writers Protest China Travel Ban: Film Guild Asks End of State Department Restriction in Note to Senate Group," *New York Times*, April 2, 1957.
110. Recent Public Opinion Polls on U.S. Relations with Red China, April 3, 1957, OCA, Box 23.
111. "2 Senators Oppose Red China News Ban," *New York Times*, April 25, 1957.
112. "Convention Demands Dulles Rescind Barrier to Travel in Communist China," *New York Times*, July 11, 1957.

113. John Foster Dulles, "Our Policies Toward Communist China," June 28, 1957, *Department of State Bulletin*, July 15, 1957, 91–95.
114. Memorandum of a Conversation, Department of State, Washington, July 18, 1957, FRUS, 1955–1957, 3:574–77.
115. *Mao Zedong Nianpu*, 3:154–56; "Zheshi Wei Sheme" (What Was This For?), *People's Daily*, June 8, 1957.
116. Dulles, "Our Policies Toward Communist China," 95. The statement appeared first in *People's Daily* on May 31, 1957, and then in the *New York Times* on June 22, 1957. "Zhongguo Renmin Daxue Jixu Juxing Zuotanhui Jiaoshimen Cong Butong Guandian Tichu Wenti" (Renmin University Continues to Hold Forums: Instructors Raise Questions from Different Perspectives), *People's Daily*, May 31, 1957; Greg MacGregor, "Peiping Organ Publishes Letters of Critics Scoring Red 'Perfidy,'" *New York Times*, June 22, 1957.
117. Memorandum from Assistant Secretary of State for Far Eastern Affairs (Robertson) to the Secretary of State, July 18, 1957, FRUS, 1955–1957, 3:577–78.
118. Mao Zedong, "Zhongmei Guanxi He ZhongSu Guanxi" (Sino-American Relations and Sino-Soviet Relations), January 27, 1957, in *Mao Zedong Waijiao Wenxuan*, 280–81.
119. Telegram from Ambassador U. Alexis Johnson to the Department of State, August 8, 1957, FRUS, 1955–1957, 3:579–80.
120. "Americans' Trip to Communist China Called Violation of U.S. Policy," August 13, 1957, *Department of State Bulletin*, September 2, 1957, 392–93.
121. Song Chundan et al., "1957 Nian Meiguo Qingnian Fanghua Zhi Lü: Bingfeng Shiqi De Qingnian Waijiao" (The American Youths' Trip to China in 1957: Youth Diplomacy During the Frozen Era), *Zhongguo Xinwen Zhoukan* (China News Weekly), July 3, 2017.
122. Memorandum From the Legal Advisor (Becker) to the Secretary of State, August 15, 1957, FRUS, 1955–1957, 3:581–83.
123. "Twenty-Four U.S. Newsmen May Visit Red China," August 22, 1957, *Department of State Bulletin*, September 9, 1957, 420–21.
124. "Twenty-Four U.S. Newsmen May Visit Red China," 420–21.
125. "Meiguo Guowuyuan De Yige Zhuolie Pianju" (A Clumsy Deception of the U.S. State Department), *People's Daily*, August 26, 1957.
126. Zhou Enlai, "Tong Meiguo Qingnian Daibiaotuan De Tanhua" (A Conversation with the American Youth Delegation), September 7, 1957, in *Zhou Enlai Waijiao Wenxuan* (Selected Works of Zhou Enlai on Diplomacy), ed. Zhonghua Renmin Gongheguo Waijiaobu (Beijing: Zhongyang Wenxian Chubanshe, 1990), 240–41.
127. Telegram from Ambassador U. Johnson to the Department of State, September 12, 1957, FRUS, 1955–1957, 3: 601–3.

128. "Let's Have No Curtain Here," *New York Times*, August 27, 1957.
129. "Secretary Dulles' News Conference of August 27," August 27, 1957, *Department of State Bulletin*, September 16, 1957, 460.
130. Greg MacGregor, "U.S. Acts to Speed China Reporters: The Consulate in Hong Kong Carries Out Validation of Newsmen's Passports," *New York Times*, August 25, 1957; "Zai Xianggang De Yipi Mei Jizhe Zheng Zhunbei Xingzhuang" (A Group of American Reporters Is Packing for Travel), *Cankao Xiaoxi* (Reference News), August 25, 1957.
131. "Zai Xianggang Dengdai Qianlai Woguo De Mei Jizhe Yiyou Shiwu Ren" (The American Reporters in Hong Kong Waiting to Enter Our Country Now Reach Fifteen), *Cankao Xiaoxi*, September 3, 1957.
132. Cohen, *America's Response to China*, 185; Wenzhao Tao, *ZhongMei Guanxi Shi, 1949–2000* (A History of China-U.S. Relations, 1949–2000) (Shanghai: Shanghai Renmin Chubanshe, 2004), 2:207–8.
133. The four Chinese journalists who went through the review conducted by the CCP Department Propaganda were Peng Di from the New China News Agency, Chen Long from the *Dagong Bao*, Wu Wenshou from the *People's Daily*, and Yang Zhaoling from the Central People's Radio. Zhang, "Zhongguo Ruhe Xiang Meiguo Jizhe Caifang Kaijin," 184–85.
134. Telegram from Ambassador U. Alexis Johnson to the Department of State, October 10, 1957, FRUS, 1955–1957, 3:630.
135. Mao Zedong, "Zhongguo Waijiao Fangmian De Mouxie Zhengce Wenti" (Some Issues in Chinese Foreign Policy), March 22, 1957, in *Mao Zedong Waijiao Wenxuan*, 286–88.
136. Mao Zedong, "Guoji Xingshi Daole Yige Xinde Zhuanzhedian" (The International Situation Has Reached a New Turning Point), November 18, 1957, in *Mao Zedong Waijiao Wenxuan*, 291–300.
137. "Beijing Xinwen Jie 'Ming' Qilai Le" (The Journalistic Circle in Beijing Is Speaking Out), *People's Daily*, May 17, 1957.
138. Cai Mingze, "Xinwenjie De Fan Youpai Douzheng" (The Anti-Rightist Struggle in Media Circles), *Xinwen Yu Chuanbo Yanjiu* (The Study of Journalism and Communications) 2 (1993): 163–78.
139. Mao Zedong, "Shiqing Zhengzai Qi Bianhua" (Things Are Changing Now), May 15, 1957, in *Mao Zedong Xuanji*, 5: 424.
140. Mao Zedong, "Wenhuibao De Zichan Jieji Fangxiang Yingdang Pipan" (The Bourgeois Orientation of the Wenhuibao Must Be Criticized), July 1, 1957, in *Mao Zedong Xuanji*, 5:434–39.
141. Li Zhang, "Women He Xinwenjie De Youpai Fenzi Zhenglun Shenme?" (What Are We Debating with the Rightists in News Media?), *People's Daily*, September 27, 1957.

142. "Hetuo Shuo Mei Jizhe Nengfou Rujing Wanquan Qüjüe Yü Woguo" (Herter Said the Admission of the American Reporters Depends Completely on Our Country), *Cankao Xiaoxi*, September 14, 1957.

6. Setting a New Pattern

1. Jonathan Spence, *To Change China: Western Advisers in China, 1620–1960* (New York: Penguin Books, 1980).
2. Israel Epstein, *The Unfinished Revolution in China* (Boston: Little, Brown, 1947).
3. Hou Ruili, "Aipositan: Yi Chizi Zhi Xin Jianzheng Zhongguo" (Epstein: Witnessing China with a Loyal Son's Heart), *Jinri Zhongguo* (China Today), May 21, 2021.
4. "Waijiaobu Xinwensi Waiguo Jizhe Jiedai Guanli Gongzuo Huiyi Wenjian" (Documents for the Meeting on the Reception and Management of Foreign Reporters Organized by the Information Division of the Ministry of Foreign Affairs), n.d., Shanxi Provincial Office of Foreign Affairs File, 196-1-191, Shanxi Provincial Archives, Xian, China. (Hereafter cited as SPA.)
5. "Xinhuashe Zhuanjia Lü Si Shishi" (Xinhua News Agency Expert Reiss Passed Away), *People's Daily*, March 7, 1962; "Xinhuashe Zhuanjia Lü Si Tongzhi Zhuidaohui Zai Jing Juxing" (Memorial Service for Xinhua News Agency Expert and Comrade Reiss Is Held Here in Beijing), *People's Daily*, March 10, 1962.
6. Solomon Adler, *The Chinese Economy* (London: Routledge & Paul, 1957).
7. Sidney Rittenberg and Amanda Bennett, *The Man Who Stayed Behind* (New York: Simon & Schuster, 1993), 251–53.
8. "Aidele Daonianhui Zai Jing Juxing" (Adler's Memorial Service Is Held in Beijing), *People's Daily*, September 3, 1994; Anne-Marie Brady, *Making the Foreign Serve China: Managing Foreigners in the People's Republic* (Lanham, MD: Rowman & Littlefield, 2003), 135.
9. Anna Louise Strong, *Tomorrow's China* (New York: Committee for a Democratic Far Eastern Policy, 1948), 15–16.
10. Mao Zedong, "He Meiguo Jizhe Anna Luyisi Sitelong De Tanhua" (A Conversation with American Reporter Anna Louise Strong), August 1946, in *Mao Zedong Xuanji* (The Selected Works of Mao Zedong) (Beijing: Renmin Chubanshe, 1969), 1090–91.
11. Tracy B. Strong and Helene Keyssar, *Right in Her Soul: The Life of Anna Louise Strong* (New York: Random House, 1983), 215–30.

12. Strong published four books between 1947 and 1949: *The Thought of Mao Zedong* (New York: Amerasia, 1947); *Dawn Over China* (Bombay: People's Publishing House, 1948); *Tomorrow's China*; and *The Chinese Conquer China* (Garden City, NY: Doubleday, 1949).
13. Strong, *The Thought of Mao Zedong* and *Tomorrow's China*.
14. Strong and Keyssar, *Right in Her Soul*, 282–85.
15. Strong and Keyssar, *Right in Her Soul*, 284–86; Kent v. Dulles, 357 U.S. 116 (1958), Justia U.S. Supreme Court, https://supreme.justia.com/cases/federal/us/357/116/#129.
16. Strong and Keyssar, *Right in Her Soul*, 291–93.
17. "Tongkan Jieri Yanhuo Tongxiang Heping Youyi" (Watching Festival Fireworks and Enjoying Peace and Friendship Together), *People's Daily*, October 2, 1958; Strong and Keyssar, *Right in Her Soul*, 293.
18. Yang Lin, "Anna Louyisi Sitelang Liuci Zhongguo Xing: Zhao Fengfeng Fangtan Lu" (Anna Louise Strong's Six Visits to China: An Interview with Zhao Fengfeng), *Bainian Chao* 1 (2015): 47; Strong and Keyssar, *Right in Her Soul*, 294.
19. Zhonggong Zhongyang Wenxian Yanjiushi, ed., *Mao Zedong Nianpu, 1949-1976* (Chronicles of Mao Zedong, 1949–1976) (Beijing: Zhongyang Wenxian Chubanshe, 2013), 5:542–43; Aibositan and Qiu Moli, "Huiyi Anna Louyisi Sitelang" (Remembering Anna Louise Strong), *Jinri Zhongguo* 3 (1980): 22; Yang Lin, "Anna Louyisi Sitelang Liuci Zhongguo Xing," 47.
20. Strong and Keyssar, *Right in Her Soul*, 295–303.
21. "Letter Number 10," July 26, 1963, Anna Louise Strong, *Letters from China* (Beijing: New World Press, 1963), 120–22.
22. Anna Luisi Sitelang, *Sidalin Shidai* (The Stalin Era), trans. Shi Ren (Beijing: Shijie Zhishi Chubanshe, 1959), 1.
23. Strong and Keyssar, *Right in Her Soul*, 294.
24. Anna Louise Strong, *The Rise of the Chinese People's Communes* (Beijing: New World Press, 1959), 1–3.
25. John Foster Dulles, "Progress and Human Dignity," November 13, 1958, *Department of State Bulletin*, December 1, 1959, 866–68.
26. Strong, *The Rise of the Chinese People's Communes*, 68–80.
27. Strong, *The Rise of the Chinese People's Communes*, 1–8.
28. Anna Louise Strong, *Tibetan Interviews* (Beijing: New World Press, 1959), 1–9.
29. Anna Louise Strong, *When Serfs Stood up in Tibet* (Beijing: New World Press, 1960), 289–94.
30. Anna Louise Strong, *Cash and Violence in Laos and Viet Nam* (New York: Mainstream Publishing, 1962), 13–22.
31. Strong, *Cash and Violence*, 125–27.

32. Strong and Keyssar, *Right in Her Soul*, 377–78.
33. Strong and Keyssar, *Right in Her Soul*, 306–14.
34. "Letter from Anna Louise Strong to Liao Cheng-chih," November 3, 1962, quoted in Strong and Keyssar, *Right in Her Soul*, 318.
35. Strong and Keyssar, *Right in Her Soul*, 309.
36. "Letter One," September 17, 1962, Strong, *Letters from China*, 1:1–6.
37. "Letter Seven," April 12, 1963, Strong, *Letters from China*, 1:76.
38. "When and How Will China Go to War," April 1966, Strong, *Supplement to Letters from China*, April 25, 1966, 38:1–4.
39. Strong, *Letters from China*, June 30, 1966, 40:1; "Purge Is Reaching China's Provinces," *New York Times*, June 11, 1966.
40. "Letter Seven," April 12, 1963, Strong, *Letters from China*, 1:76–77.
41. Strong and Keyssar, *Right in Her Soul*, 317–22.
42. "Address by Kuo Mo-jo at the Meeting to Pay Last Respects to Anna Louise Strong," April 2, 1970, Strong, *Letters from China*, April 17, 1970, 70:2.
43. Alan Winnington, *Breakfast with Mao: Memoirs of a Foreign Correspondent* (London: Lawrence and Wishart, 1986), 209.
44. Brady, *Making the Foreign Serve China*, 94.
45. Gao Yunxiang, *Arise, Africa! Roar, China!: Black and Chinese Citizens of the World in the Twentieth Century* (Chapel Hill: University of North Carolina Press, 2021), 79–91.
46. Barbara Ransby, *Eslanda: The Large and Unconventional Life of Mrs. Paul Robeson* (New Haven, CT: Yale University Press, 2013), 197–98.
47. Eslanda Robeson, "World Woman Number One," *New World Review* 19, no. 5 (July 1951): 20–27.
48. "Mei Gechangjia He Jie Gangqinjia Dao Jing" (American Singer and Czech Pianist Arrive in Beijing), *People's Daily*, November 9, 1955; "Mei Heiren Gechangjia He Jie Gangqinjia Juxing Shouci Yingyuehui" (Black American Singer and Czech Pianist Give First Concert), *People's Daily*, November 20, 1955.
49. "Jiedai Meiguo Henren Gechangjia Ji Jieke Nü Gangqinjia Gongzuo Jihua (Caoan)" (Reception Plan for the Black American Singer and the Female Czech Pianist [Draft]), n.d., 1C37-2-1, SMA.
50. Shanghai Wenyizu Waibin Jiedai Bangongshi, "Waibin Qingkuang Jianbao" (Brief Report on Foreign Guests), 56, December 15, 1955, 1C37-2-1, SMA.
51. Based on the PRC's radio broadcast, the UPI sent a short dispatch on November 10, 1955, that Pankey and his wife arrived in Beijing. "Arrive in Tokyo," *Tonawanda News*, November 10, 1955.
52. "Pankey in New China," *Pittsburgh Courier*, January 7, 1956.
53. Song Chundan et al., "1957 Nian Meiguo Qingnian Fanghua Zhi Lü: Bingfeng Shiqi De Qingnian Waijiao" (The American Youths' Trip to China in

1957: Youth Diplomacy During the Freezing Era), *Zhongguo Xinwen Zhoukan,* July 3, 2017, http://www.zgxwzk.chinanews.com.cn/2/2017-07-03/3537.shtml.

54. Zhou Enlai, "Tong Meiguo Qingnian Daibiaotuan De Tanhua" (Conversation with the American Youth Delegation), September 7, 1957, in *Zhou Enlai Waijiao Wenxuan* (Selected Diplomatic Essays of Zhou Enlai), ed. Zhonghua Renmin Gongheguo Waijiaobu (Beijing: Zhongyang Wenxian Chubanshe, 1990), 239–52.

55. "Guoqing Zhiye Zai Tiananmen Chenglou Shang Mao Zhuxi Huijian Geguo Guibin" (On the Evening of National Day Chairman Mao Meets with Distinguished Guests from Various Nations), *People's Daily,* October 2, 1957.

56. Song Chundan et al., "1957 Nian Meiguo Qingnian Fanghua Zhi Lü."

57. Robert Cohen, *Inside Red China,* 1957.

58. John Strohm, "How They Hate Us in Red China," *Reader's Digest,* January 1959, 30.

59. Meng Ranwen, "Diyige Renmin Gongshe: 'Mao Zedong Kandao Jianzhang Ruhuo Zhibao' " (The First People's Commune: Mao Zedong Treats the Commune Bylaws as A Treasure Once Has His Eyes on It), Dahe Wang-Dahe Bao, August 14, 2009, http://news.sina.com.cn/c/sd/2009-08-14/141218436048_2.shtml.

60. Chen Jian, *Mao's China and the Cold War* (Chapel Hill: University of North Carolina Press, 2010), 77–78.

61. Strohm, "How They Hate Us in Red China," 31.

62. Strohm, "How They Hate Us in Red China," 34.

63. Strohm, "How They Hate Us in Red China," 31–33.

64. Strohm, "How They Hate Us in Red China," 31–32.

65. Chen, *Mao's China and the Cold War,* 77.

66. Strohm, "How They Hate Us in Red China," 30–34.

67. "Sheean Lacks Visa: Seeks Peiping's Permission for Trip Approved by U.S.," *New York Times,* May 21, 1959.

68. William J. Jordan, "Chinese News Curtain Shows Signs of Rising: Passports to Harriman and Sheean Could Lead to Wider Opening," *New York Times,* May 24, 1959.

69. Mao Zedong, "Zhichi Bei Yapo Renmin Fandui Diguo Zhuyi De Zhanzheng" (Support the Oppressed Peoples' War Against Imperialism), in *Mao Zedong Waijiao Wenxuan,* 533.

70. Mao Zedong, "Yaoba Meiguo Diguo Zhuyi Fenzi He Meiguo Renmin Huafen Qingchu" (Clearly Differentiate the American Imperialists from the American People), November 25, 1965, in *Mao Zedong Waijiao Wenxuan,* 574–76.

71. Zhonggong Zhongyang Wenxian Yanjiushi, ed., *Liu Shaoqi Nianpu* (Chronicles of Liu Shaoqi) (Beijing: Zhongyang Wenxian Chubanshe, 1995), 2:232–33.
72. *Mao Zedong Nianpu*, 3:621–22.
73. Shanghaishi Heda Fenhui Waibin Jiedai Bangongshi, "Jiedai Meiguo Heping Daibiao Beisitanna Jihua (Caoan)" (Reception Plan for American Peace Delegate Pestana [Draft]), July 2, 1959, C36-2-84, SMA.
74. Shanghaishi Heda Fenhui Jiedai Waibin Bangongshi, "Waibin Qingkuang Jianbao: Meiguo Heping Daibiao Beisitanna" (Brief Report on Foreign Guests: American Peace Delegate Pestana), July 10, 1959, C36-2-84, SMA.
75. Shanghaishi Heda Fenhui Jiedai Waibin Bangongshi, "Waibin Qingkuang Jianbao: Meiguo Heping Daibiao Beisitanna," SMA.
76. U.S. Congress House Committee on Un-American Activities, *Violations of State Department Travel Regulations and Pro-Castro Propaganda Activities in the United States: Hearings Before the Committee on Un-American Activities House of Representatives*, 88th Cong., 1st Sess. (Washington, DC: U.S. Government Printing Office, 1965), 582–83.
77. Hexieer Maiye, *Zuihou De Huanxiang* (The Last Illusions), trans. Wu Pengwu (Beijing: Shijie Zhishi Chubanshe, 1955).
78. They told their Chinese hosts that Khrushchev and other Soviet leaders met with them during their visit to the Soviet Union, and Teytelboym's poem was going to be translated into Russian. Shanghaishi Heda Fenhui Waibin Jiedai Bangongshi, "Jiedai Meiguo Zuojia Maiye Fufu Jihua (Caoan)" (Reception Plan for American Writer Meyer and His Wife [Draft]), July 12, 1959; Shanghaishi Heda Fenhui Jiedai Waibin Bangongshi, "Waibin Qingkuang Jianbao: Meiguo Zuojia Maiye Fufu" (Brief Report on Foreign Guests: American Writer Meyer and His Wife), July 16, 20, C36-2-83, SMA.
79. Shanghaishi Difangzhi Bangongshi, *Shanghai Waishizhi* (The History of Shanghai Foreign Affairs), http://www.shtong.gov.cn/dfz_web/DFZ/DulanMu?idnode=69969&tableName=userobject1a&id=-1.
80. Robert D. McFadden, "Ida Pruitt, 96, Who Fostered Friendship with the Chinese," *New York Times*, August 11, 1985.
81. Maud Russel, *New People in New China: Some Personal Glimpses of People in China* (New York: Far East Reporter, 1959).
82. John Maxwell Hamilton, *Edgar Snow: A Biography* (Bloomington: Indiana University Press, 1988), 221.
83. Strong and Keyssar, *Right in Her Soul*, 304.
84. Edgar Snow, "Recognition of the People's Republic of China," *Annals of the American Academy of Political and Social Science* 324 (July 1959): 75–88.
85. *Mao Zedong Nianpu*, 4:247–48.
86. Hamilton, *Edgar Snow*, 222.

87. "A Report from Red China," *Look*, January 31, 1960, 85; Hamilton, *Edgar Snow*, 222; "Snow Job," *Time*, July 25, 1960, 60.
88. Telegram from the Embassy in Poland to the Department of State, July 15, 1960, *Foreign Relations of the United States, 1958–1960* (Washington, DC: U.S. Department of State, 1960), 14: 694–95 (hereafter cited as FRUS).
89. Edgar Snow, *Red China Today* (New York: Vintage Books, 1971), 47–51. The exchange rate was US$1 for 2.44 yuan of renminbi. Zhou Enlai was paid about 400 yuan a month.
90. "Sinuo Sanci Fanghua Neimu" (Inside Stories of Snow's Three Visits to China), *Qilu Wanbao*, December 23, 2004.
91. Jiang, *Sinuo Yu Zhongguo*, 228; Hamilton, *Edgar Snow*, 252.
92. Edgar Snow, "Red China's Leaders Talk Peace—On Their Own Terms," *Look*, January 31, 1961, 86; Snow, *Red China Today*, 105–6.
93. *Zhou Enlai Nianpu*, 2:358–59; Snow, *Red China Today*, 114–19.
94. Huang Hua, *Huang Hua Memoirs* (Beijing: Foreign Language Press, 2008), 210.
95. Following Mao's instruction, the MOE established two American history research groups at Wuhan and Nankai Universities in 1964. They were designated to study the American labor movement and the African American liberation movement. Seriously interrupted by the Cultural Revolution, the group at Nankai University managed to publish only a short history of African American liberation after the Cultural Revolution. Department of History, *Meiguo Heiren Jiefang Yundong Jianshi* (A Brief History of Black American Liberation Movement) (Beijing: Renmin Chubanshe, 1977).
96. *Mao Zedong Nianpu*, 4:464–68.
97. Cong Jin, *Quzhe Fazhan De Suiyue: 1945–1989 Nian De Zhongguo* (The Years of Tortuous Development: China, 1945–1989) (Zhengzhou: Henan Renmin Chubanshe, 1989), 185–87.
98. *Mao Zedong Nianpu*, 4:470–71.
99. Hamilton, *Edgar Snow*, 225–27.
100. Snow, "Red China's Leaders Talk Peace—On Their Own Terms," 86–98.
101. "A Report from Red China," *Look*, January 31, 1961, 85.
102. A. Doak Barnett, "What Chou En-lai's Words Mean to Us," *Look*, January 31, 1961, 105.
103. Hamilton, *Edgar Snow*, 239.
104. Edgar Snow, *The Other Side of the River: Red China Today* (New York: Random House, 1962).
105. Hamilton, *Edgar Snow*, 239.
106. Telegram from the Department of State to the Embassy in Poland, March 4, 1961, FRUS, 1961–1963, 12: 23–24.
107. Gong Li, *Mao Zedong Yu Meiguo* (Mao Zedong and the United States) (Beijing: Shijie Zhishi Chubanshe, 1999), 132.

108. Hamilton, *Edgar Snow*, 252–54.
109. *Zhou Enlai Nianpu*, 2:688.
110. *Zhou Enlai Nianpu*, 2:693–94.
111. *Mao Zedong Nianpu*, 5:464–66.
112. Hamilton, *Edgar Snow*, 258–59.
113. Harry Gilroy, "Snow's Red China," *New York Times*, October 3, 1968.
114. "Waijiaobu Xinwensi Waiguo Jizhe Jiedai Guanli Gongzuo Huiyi Wenjian" (Documents for the Meeting on the Reception and Management of Foreign Reporters Organized by the Information Division of the MOE), n.d., 196-1-191, SPA.
115. "Jiaqiang Duiwai Xuanchuan Jinyibu Tigao Jiedai Guanli Waiguo Jizhe Gongzuo Shuiping" (Strengthening International Propaganda and Further Improving the Reception and Management of Foreign Reporters), n.d., 196-1-191, SPA.
116. "Waijiaobu Xinwensi Waiguo Jizhe Jiedai Guanli Gongzuo Huiyi Wenjian," 196-1-191.
117. Hamilton, *Edgar Snow*, 259.
118. *Zhou Enlai Nianpu*, 2:465.
119. "Zhonghua Renmin Gongheguo Jiaoyu Dashiji" (Chronicles of Education of the People's Republic of China), in *Makesi Zhuyi Yu Zhongguo Jiaoyu* (Marxism and Chinese Education) (Wuhan: Hubei Jiaoyu Chubanshe, 1994), 1749–89.
120. "Ershisanming Meiguo Zhanfu He Yiming Yingguo Zhanfu Fenbie Fabiao Shengming Shuoming Buyuan Qianfan De Yuanyin" (Twenty-Three American POWs and One British POW Issued Separate Statements Explaining the Reasons for Their Rejection of Repatriation), *People's Daily*, September 25, 1953. Two American POWS changed their minds and left the group during the ninety-day "cooling" period.
121. Clarence Adams, Della Adams, and Lewis H. Carlson, *An American Dream: The Life of an African American Soldier and POW Who Spent Twelve Years in Communist China* (Amherst: University of Massachusetts Press, 2007), 76–77.
122. Adams, *An American Dream*, 94–95; Morris R. Wills, *Turncoat: An American's 12 Years in Communist China* (Englewood Cliffs, NJ: Prentice-Hall, 1966), 124–25.
123. Adams, *An American Dream*, 94.
124. Wills, *Turncoat*, 128.
125. Wills, *Turncoat*, 129–30.
126. Adams, *An American Dream*, 102–4.
127. Zhonghua Renmin Gongheguo Duiwai Wenhua Lianluo Weiyuanhui, "Jiedai Meiguoren Luobote Feilande Gongzuo Jihua" (Reception Plan for American Robert Friend), August 2, 1963, 196-1-170, SPA.

128. David Milton and Nancy Dall Milton, *The Wind Will Not Subside: Years in Revolutionary China—1964–1969* (New York: Pantheon Books, 1976), 8.
129. Vicki Garvin, "Letter from Vicki Garvin to Huang Hua," August 1992, Box 2, Vicki Garvin Papers, Schomburg Center for Research in Black Culture, New York Public Library, New York (hereafter cited as VGP); Daro F. Gore, "From Communist Politics to Black Power: The Visionary Politics and Transnational Solidarity of Victoria 'Vicki' Ama Garvin," in *Want to Start a Revolution? Radical Women in the Black Freedom Struggle*, ed. Daro F. Gore et al. (New York: New York University Press, 2009), 71–94.
130. Vicki Garvin, "Vicki Garvin in China," September 1964, VGP, Box 2.
131. Students in the teachers' training class were selected from newly graduated seniors at the SFLI. After receiving another year of special training, they were assigned teaching positions at colleges and schools. At least fifteen of them remained at SFLI as teachers. Vicki Garvin, "Education B: Shanghai Foreign Language Institute," n.d., VGP, Box 2.
132. Garvin, "Vicki Garvin in China," September 1964, VGP, Box 2.
133. The lectures on African American history delivered by Vicki Garvin in her first academic year at SFLI included "The Negro Liberation Movement and the 1964 Election," n.d., 1964; "The Other Side of the United States: Increasing Poverty Amidst Plenty," January 12, 1965; "The Negro Liberation Movement," n.d.; "Nineteen Century Negro Struggles for Freedom," June 21, 1965; "Outstanding Negro Leaders in the 19th & 20th Centuries," n.d., 1965; "Major Aims and Demands of Negro Freedom Movement in the 20th Century," n.d., 1965; "Racial Discrimination in the United States," n.d., 1965; "Struggle for Civil Rights in Mississippi," n.d., 1965; "Ideology and Tactics of the Main Organizations Fighting for Negro Rights in the 20th Century," n.d., 1965; "Role of the Federal Government Vis-à-Vis the Negro Freedom Struggle in the 20th Century," n.d., 1965; and "Negro-White Unity in the Struggle for Negro Rights," n.d., 1965. The drafts of these lectures can be found in VGP, Box 2.
134. Garvin, "The Negro Liberation Movement."
135. Garvin, "The Negro Liberation Movement and the 1964 Election."
136. Garvin, "The Negro Liberation Movement."
137. Garvin, "The Negro Liberation Movement and the 1964 Election."
138. Garvin, "The Other Side of the United States."
139. Garvin, "The Negro Liberation Movement."
140. Garvin, "Major Aims and Demands of Negro Freedom Movement in the 20th Century."
141. Garvin, "Nineteen Century Negro Struggles for Freedom."
142. Vicki Garvin, "Summary of Teaching in China," 1966, VGP, Box 2.

143. "Peiyang Shengdong Huobo De Zhudong De Xuexi Kongqi" (Nurturing Lively and Active Learning Atmosphere), editorial, *People's Daily*, April 11, 1964.
144. Vicki Garvin, "Outline of the Role of Fascist Racist Organizations in Suppressing Negroes," n.d. VGP, Box 2; Garvin, "Summary of Teaching in China."
145. Vicki Garvin, "Comments @ Students' Lecture," May 1965; "Summary of Teaching in China"; "Shanghai Foreign Language Institute," n.d. VGP, Box 3.
146. Vicki Garvin, "Speech of Vicki Garvin, A Black American," April 1968, VGP, Box 2.
147. The other achievement was her introduction of African American history to Chinese college students. Vicki Garvin, "Personal History," n.d., VGP, Box 1.
148. Vicki Garvin, "China and Back Americans: A Demonstration in Shanghai Connects the Chinese People with the Black Liberation Struggle in the United States," *New China* 1, no. 3 (Fall 1975): 23.
149. Garvin, "Shanghai Foreign Language Institute."
150. Vicki Garvin, "Speech Delivered at Sara Laurence College," April 6, 1992, Box 1; "Personal History," n.d., VGP, Box 4; Vicki Garvin, Letter to Huang Hua, August 1992, VGP, Box 2.
151. Zhongguo Renmin Jiefangjun Waiwen Chuban Faxing Shiye Guanliju Junguan Xiaozu, "Qing Shenpi Meiji Zhuanjia Jiaerwen Qu Xian Canguan Fangwen De Baogao" (Request for the Approval of American Expert Garvin's Visit to Xian), July 24, 1970, 196-1-423, SPA.
152. Shanxi Sheng Geweihui Waishizu, *Waishi Gongzuo* (Foreign Affairs Work) 30, August 1, 1970, 196-1-423, SPA.
153. Vicki Garvin, "USCPFA," n.d., 1976, VGP, Box 2.
154. Vicki Garvin, "Shanghai Foreign Language Institute," n.d., VGP, Box 3.

7. Forging the Black Blade

1. Some of the paragraphs in this chapter are drawn after revision from Hongshan Li, "Building a Black Bridge: China's Interactions with African-American Activists in the Cold War," *Journal of Cold War Studies* 20, no. 3 (Summer 2018): 114–52.
2. According to the information received by the State Department, Beijing tried more than a dozen times to invite large groups of Americans to visit China in 1955 and 1956. List of Chinese Communist Effort to Induce Americans to Travel to Communist China, n.d., Bureau of Far Eastern Affairs/Office of

Chinese Affairs Files, 1954–1957 (hereafter cited as OCA), National Archives, College Park, Maryland, Box 23.
3. Telegram from Kuo Mu-Jo to W. E. B. Du Bois, October 12, 1956; Letter from Kuo Mu-Jo to W. E. B. Du Bois, October 18, 1956, W. E. B. Du Bois Papers (MS 312), Special Collections and University Archives, University of Massachusetts Amherst Libraries (hereafter cited as DBP).
4. Telegram from Kuo Mu-Jo to W. E. B. Du Bois, February 23, 1951; Telegram from Kuo Mu-Jo to W. E. B. Du Bois, June 9, 1952, DBP.
5. Telegram from Liu Ningyi to W. E. B. Du Bois, August 9, 1952, DBP.
6. Letter from W. E. B. Du Bois to Kuo Mo Jo, November 4, 1956, DBP.
7. Letter from W. E. B. Du Bois to John Foster Dulles, February 22, 1957, DBP.
8. "Wei Meiguo Heiren Lishi Xuejia Duboyisi Jiushi Danchen Shi" (On the Ninetieth Birthday of American Black Historian Du Bois), December 10, 1957, File No. 111-00292-01, Ministry of Foreign Affairs Archives, Beijing, China (hereafter cited as MFAA).
9. U.S. Department of State, W. E. B. Du Bois Passport (No. 1101544), June 30, 1958, DBP.
10. Letter from W. E. B. Du Bois to Kuo Mo Jo, July 6, 1958, DBP.
11. Letter from W. E. B. Du Bois to Madame Soong, July 6, 1958, DBP.
12. W. E. B. Du Bois, *The Autobiography of W. E. B. Du Bois: A Soliloquy on Viewing My Life from the Last Decade of Its First Century* (New York: Oxford University Press, 2007), 28.
13. Du Bois, *Autobiography*, 28; "Letter from W. E. B. Du Bois to George B. Murphy," December 26, 1958, in *The Correspondence of W. E. B. Du Bois*, 3 vols., ed. Herbert Aptheker (Amherst: University of Massachusetts Press, 1978), 3:433.
14. Letter from Talitha Gerlach to Shirley and W. E. B. Du Bois, November 15, 1955, DBP.
15. "Duboyisi Boshi He Furen Daojing" (Du Bois and His Wife Arrive in Beijing), *People's Daily*, February 14, 1959.
16. Public mention of his activities in China appeared only decades later in Zhonggong Zhongyang Wenxian Yanjiushi, ed., *Mao Zedong Nianpu, 1949–1976* (Chronicles of Mao Zedong, 1949–1976) (Beijing: Zhongyang Wenxian Chubanshe, 2013) and *Liu Shaoqi Nianpu* (Chronicles of Liu Shaoqi) (Beijing: Zhongyang Wenxian Chubanshe, 1995).
17. Shirley Graham Du Bois, *His Day Is Marching On: A Memoir of W. E. B. Du Bois* (Philadelphia: J. B. Lippincott, 1971), 277.
18. The Chinese government did make sure that no visa or border entrance/exit record was left in the Du Boises' passports. W. E. B. Du Bois Passport; U.S. Department of State, Shirley Graham Du Bois Passport (No. 1103545), June 30, 1958, Shirley Graham Du Bois Papers, Box 4, Schlesinger Library,

Radcliff Institute for Advanced Studies, Harvard University, Cambridge, Massachusetts.
19. Letter from Poeliu Dai to W. E. B. Du Bois, November 27, 1936; Letter from Herman C. E. Liu to W. E. B. Du Bois, December 2, 1936, DBP.
20. Letter from Chih Meng to W. E. B. Du Bois, September 10, 1936, DBP.
21. Du Bois, *Autobiography*, 26–27.
22. Letter from William Peterson to Chen Hansheng, November 11, 1957, included in "Meiguo Heiren Xuezhe Duboyisi Fanghua Ji Qizi LaiHua Xuexi Deng Wenti" (Issues on the Visit of Du Bois, an African American Scholar, and His Wife's Study in China), File No. 111-00292-01(1), MFAA.
23. Shirley Graham Du Bois included detailed descriptions about the exceptional receptions that she and her husband were given in China in *His Day Is Marching On*, 276–95.
24. "Huanying Duboyisi Boshi He Furen" (Welcome Dr. Du Bois and His Wife), *People's Daily*, February 18, 1959.
25. "Zhou Zongli Jiejian Duboyisi Boshi" (Premier Zhou Receives Dr. Du Bois), *People's Daily*, February 23, 1959.
26. Mao Dun, "Yuan Yueyuan Renshou, Guangming De Geng Guangming, Buxiu De Yongyuan Buxiu!" (Wish Full Moon and Longevity, the Bright Become Brighter, the Immortal Become Forever Immortal!); Yu Minsheng, "Guanghui De Shiye, Heping De Zhanshi: Duboyisi Fufu Fangwenji" (The Shining Cause and the Warriors for Peace: Interview with the Du Boises), *People's Daily*, February 23, 1959.
27. Du Bois, *Autobiography*, 262.
28. Students from the Peking Foreign Language Institute and the Institute of International Relations were also among the audience. "Shoudu Renshi Jubei Wei Duboyisi Zhushou" (People in the Capital Raise Their Glasses to Celebrate Du Bois's Birthday), *People's Daily*, February 24, 1959.
29. Du Bois, *Autobiography*, 264.
30. "Duboyisi Xiang Feizhou Renmin Fachu Zhaohuan: Feizhou, Zhan Qilai! Mian Xiang Shengqi De Taiyang!" (Du Bois Calls on the African People: Africa, Rise! Face the Rising Sun!), *People's Daily*, February 24, 1959.
31. "Jiushi Gaoling You Fendou Heping Zhanshi Yong Qingchun" (Still Fighting at the High Age of 90 and Forever Young as a Peace Fighter), *People's Daily*, February 24, 1959.
32. W. E. B. Du Bois, "Our Visit to China," *China Pictorial*, March 20, 1959, 6–7.
33. Du Bois, *His Day Is Marching On*, 278.
34. Tracy B. Strong and Helene Keyssar, "Anna Louise Strong: Three Interviews with Chairman Mao Zedong," *China Quarterly* 103 (September 1985): 494–95; *Mao Zedong Nianpu*, 3:631–32.

35. Anna Louise Strong kept detailed notes of the conversation, which was published in 1985. Strong and Keyssar, "Anna Louise Strong," 495–97.
36. "Mao Zhuxi Jiejian Duboyisi He Sitelang" (Chairman Mao Receives Du Bois and Strong), *People's Daily*, March 14, 1959. A documentary was also made by the Chinese government on W. E. B. Du Bois's visit to China. Although extensive footage showed Mao's meeting with the Du Boises, no substantive matters were revealed in the narration.
37. "Meigong Jiu Xiaoshicheng Shijian Fabiao Shengming, Yaoqiu Zhengfu Baohu Heiren Quanli" (U.S. Communist Party Issues a Statement on the Little Rock Incident: Demanding That the Government Protect the Rights of Blacks), *People's Daily*, October 2, 1957.
38. *Mao Zedong Nianpu*, 2:268–69.
39. Bill V. Mullen and Cathryn Watson, eds., *W. E. B. Du Bois on Asia: Crossing the World Color Line* (Jackson: University Press of Mississippi, 2005), 200.
40. W. E. B. Du Bois, "The Vast Miracle of China Today: A Report on a Ten-Week Visit to the People's Republic of China," *National Guardian*, June 8, 1959; Mullen and Watson, *Du Bois on Asia*, 190–95.
41. Mullen and Watson, *Du Bois on Asia*, 173.
42. Mullen and Watson, *Du Bois on Asia*, 172.
43. W. E. B. Du Bois, "Will the Great Gandhi Live Again?" *National Guardian*, February 11, 1957; Mullen and Watson, *Du Bois on Asia*, 171.
44. Letter from W. E. B. Du Bois to Gus Hall, October 1, 1961, Jack and Esther Cooper Jackson Papers, Tamiment Library, New York University, Box 5.
45. Wei Ai Bo Duboyisi, "Zhong Yi Ben Xu" (Foreword to the Chinese Translation), in Wei Ai Bo Duboyisi, *Heiren De Linghun* (*The Souls of Black Folk*), trans. Wei Qun (Beijing: Renmin Wenxue Chubanshe, 1959,) 1.
46. "Yi Hou Ji" (Notes on the Translation), in Duboyisi, *Heiren De Linghun*, 231–35.
47. Huang Xinxi, "Heiren De Xinsheng: Du *Heiren De Linghun*" (The Voice from the Heart of Black People: Reading *The Souls of Black Folk*), *People's Daily*, May 19, 1959.
48. Du Bois, *His Day Is Marching On*, 350–51; Gerald Horne, *Black & Red: W. E. B. Du Bois and the Afro-American Response to the Cold War, 1944–1963* (Albany: State University of New York Press, 1985), 325.
49. "Shoudu Longzhong Jinian Jianguo Shisan Zhounian" (The Capital Solemnly Celebrates the Thirteenth Anniversary of the Founding of the Nation), *People's Daily*, October 2, 1962.
50. About Robert Williams's activities as a civil rights leader in the United States as well as Cuba, see Timothy Tyson, *Radio Free Dixie: Robert F. Williams & the Roots of Black Power* (Chapel Hill: University of North Carolina Press, 1999).

51. Robert Williams, *Negro with Gun* (Chicago: Third World Press, 1962), 41.
52. Telegram from Williams to Mao, May 7, 1963, in *The Black Power Movement: The Papers of Robert F. Williams* (Bethesda, MD: University Publications of America, 2001), Reel 1 (hereafter referred to as PRW).
53. "Guanyu Guoji Gongchan Zhuyi Yundong Zongluxian De Jianyi: Zhongguo Gongchandang Zhongyang Weiyunhui Dui Sulian Gongcahndang Zhongyang Weiyunhui Yijiuliusan Nian San Yue Sanshi Ri Laixin De Fuxin" (A Proposition on the General Line of the International Communist Movement: The Reply of the CCPCC to the Letter from the Central Committee of the Communist Party of the Soviet Union Dated March 30, 1963), *People's Daily*, July 20, 1963.
54. *Mao Zedong Nianpu*, 5:243–44.
55. "Zhongguo Zhengfu Zhuzhang Quanmian, Chedi, Ganjing, Jianjue Di Jingzhi He Xiaohui Hewuqi, Changyi Zhaokai Shijie Geguo Zhengfu Shounao Huiyi De Shengming" (Chinese Government Statement Proposing to Comprehensively, Thoroughly, Completely, and Resolutely Prohibit and Destroy Nuclear Weapons, and Calling for a Meeting of Government Leaders of All Nations in the World), *People's Daily*, July 31, 1963.
56. "Zheshi Dui Sulian Renmin De Beipan!" (This Is a Betrayal of the Soviet People!), *People's Daily*, August 3, 1963.
57. "Chumai Zhongguo Yinmou De Jinyibu Baolu: Kennidi Daopo Sanguo Tiaoyue Zhuyao Shi Hehuo Duifu Zhongguo" (The Further Revelation of the Selling-Out of China: Kennedy Confesses the Tripartite Treaty a Conspiration Against China), *People's Daily*, August 3, 1963.
58. Pu Shouchang graduated from University of Michigan in 1942 and received a doctoral degree from Harvard University in 1946. He joined the Communist Party in 1944 while studying in the United States. He stayed in the United States after graduation to be in charge of the work on Chinese students. He was also involved in translating Mao Zedong's writings into English at the same time. Pu returned to China in 1949 and served as the secretary to the premier of the State Council between 1954 and 1965. "Pu Shouchang," Waijiaobu (Ministry of Foreign Affairs), http://www.fmprc.gov.cn/web/ziliao_674904/wjrw_674925/lrfbzjbzzl_674933/t9085.shtml.
59. *Mao Zedong Nianpu*, 5:248.
60. Sidney Rittenberg and Amanda Bennett, *The Man Who Stayed Behind* (New York: Simon & Schuster, 1993), 269–71; "Mao Zhuxi Jiejian Feizhou Pengyou Fabiao Zhichi Meiguo Heiren Douzheng De Shengming" (Chairman Mao Receives African Friends and Issues a Statement to Support African American Struggle), *People's Daily*, August 9, 1963.
61. *Mao Zedong Nianpu*, 5:247–49; Mao Zedong, "Zhichi Meiguo Heiren Fandui Zhongzu Qishi Douzheng De Shengming" (A Statement to Support the

African American Struggle Against Racial Discrimination), *People's Daily*, August 9, 1963.
62. Mao Zedong served as the president of the PRC between 1954 and 1959. Liu Shaoqi was elected president at the second National People's Congress in April 1959.
63. "Luobote Weilian Ganxie Mao Zhuxi Zhichi Meiguo Heiren Douzheng" (Robert Williams Thanks Mao for His Support for the Struggle of Black Americans), *People's Daily*, August 12, 1963; Robert Carl Cohen, *Black Crusader: A Biography of Robert Franklin Williams* (New York: Lyle Stuart, 1972), 250–51.
64. "Rang Women Tuanjie Yizhi Tong Mei Diguo Zhuyi Douzheng" (Let's Unite and Fight Against American Imperialism), *People's Daily*, August 13, 1963.
65. "Shoudu Shengda Jihui Zhichi Meiguo Heiren Fandui Zhongzu Qishi De Yingyong Douzheng" (A Grand Rally Held in the Capital to Support American Blacks in Their Heroic Fight Against Racial Discrimination), *People's Daily*, August 13, 1963.
66. "Meiguo Heiren Kaishi Le Zhengqu Jiefang De Weida Geming Douzheng" (American Blacks Start Their Great Revolutionary Struggle for Liberation), *People's Daily*, August 13, 1963.
67. "Shoudu Shengda Jihui Zhichi Meiguo Heiren Fandui Zhongzu Qishi De Yingyong Douzheng."
68. "Meiguo Heiren Douzheng Shi Dui Longduan Ziben Zhuyi De Weixie" (The Struggle of the American Blacks Is a Threat to Monopolistic Capitalism), *People's Daily*, August 13, 1963.
69. "Mao Zhuxi Shengming Ba Meiguo Heiren Douzheng Tidao Yingyou Guoji Diwei" (Chairman Mao's Statement Elevates the African American Struggle to Its Deserving International Status), *People's Daily*, August 27, 1963.
70. "Haozhao Meiguo Renmin Zhankai Jianjue Douzheng Fandui Zhongzu Qishi" (Calling on the American People to Start a Resolute Fight Against Racial Discrimination), *People's Daily*, August 29, 1963.
71. "Quan Shijie Renmin Relie Huanying Mao Zhuxi Shengming" (The People of the Whole World Warmly Welcome Chairman Mao's Statement), *People's Daily*, August 20, 1963.
72. "Mao Zhuxi Dianyan Duboyisi Boshi Shishi" (Chairman Mao Sends Condolences on the Passing of Du Bois), *People's Daily*, August 30, 1963.
73. Letter from Williams to Barden, January 16, 1963, PRW, Reel 1.
74. "Meiguo Heiren Lingxiu Luobote Weilian Fufu Daojing" (Black American Leader Robert Williamses Arrive in Beijing), *People's Daily*, September 26, 1963.
75. Robert Williams, "China: New World Awakening," n.d., PRW, Reel 7.

76. "Zhou Enlai Zongli Juxing Shengda Guoqing Zhaodaihui" (Premier Zhou Enlai Holds Grand National Day Reception), *People's Daily*, October 1, 1963.
77. *Mao Zedong Nianpu*, 5:266.
78. "Mao Zhuxi, Liu Zhuxi, Zhu Weiyuanzhang Fenbie Jiejian Weilian Fufu He Shiqiao Fufu" (Chairman Mao, Chainman Liu, and Chairman Zhu Separately Receive the Williamses and the Tanzans), *People's Daily*, October 2, 1963.
79. Cohen, *Black Crusader*, 256–57.
80. "Yizhe De Hua" (Words from the Translator), in Luobote Weilian, *Daiqian De Heiren* (Negroes with Guns), trans. Lu Ren (Beijing: Shijie Zhishi Chubanshe, 1963), 1–2.
81. "Fandui Mei Diguo Zhuyi Zhichi Meiguo Heiren Zhengyi Douzheng" (Opposing American Imperialism and Supporting the Just Struggle of African Americans), *People's Daily*, October 11, 1963.
82. "Guo Moruo De Jianghua" (The Speech of Guo Moruo), *People's Daily*, October 11, 1963.
83. "Luobote Weilian De Jianghua" (The Speech of Robert Williams), *People's Daily*, October 11, 1963.
84. "Meiguo Heiren Lingxiu Luobote Weilian Jiedai Gongzuo Xiaojie Taolun Zhaiyao" (The Excerpts of the Discussion on the Summary of the Reception of the Black American Leader Robert Williams), n.d., File No. C36-2-175–95, Shanghai Municipal Archives, Shanghai, China (hereafter cited as SMA).
85. "Jianjue Fandui Meidi, Zhichi Meiguo Heiren Zhengyi Douzheng" (Resolutely Oppose American Imperialism, Support African Americans' Just Struggle), *Jiefang Ribao*, October 19, 1963.
86. "Meiguo Heiren Lingxiu Luobote Weilian Jiedai Gongzuo Xiaojie Taolun Zhaiyao."
87. Cohen, *Black Crusader*, 265.
88. Robert Williams, "The Ramparts We Watch," *The Crusader*, July–August 1963, 4.
89. Robert Williams, "China: New Hope of Oppressed Humanity," *The Crusader*, February 1964, 6–7.
90. Robert Williams, "Revolution Without Violence?" *The Crusader*, February 1964, 1–5.
91. Robert Williams, "Psychological Warfare," *The Crusader*, March–April 1964, 1–3.
92. Robert Williams, "USA: The Potential of a Minority Revolution," *The Crusader*, May–June 1964, 1–7.
93. Maxwell C. Stanford, "Revolutionary Action Movement (RAM): A Case Study of an Urban Revolutionary Movement in Western Capitalist Society," MA thesis, Atlanta University, May 1985, 74–76.

94. Akbar Muhammad Ahmad, "The Revolutionary Action Movement," in *Black Power in the Belly of the Beast*, ed. Judson L. Jeffries (Urbana: University of Illinois Press, 2006), 263.
95. Stanford, "Revolutionary Action Movement," 74–100; Ahmad, "The Revolutionary Action Movement," 265–67.
96. Fred C. Shapiro and James W. Sullivan, *Race Riots, New York, 1964* (New York: Crowell, 1964), 74.
97. "Meiguo Heiren Zheng Zai Juexing Zhong" (African Americans Are Awakening), *People's Daily*, July 25, 1964; "Meiguo Heiren Yong Baoli Ziwei Fankang Baoli Zhengya" (African Americans Resist Violent Suppression with Violent Self-Defense), *People's Daily*, August 1, 1964.
98. "Meiguo Heiren Zheng Zai Juexing Zhong."
99. Ahmad, "The Revolutionary Action Movement," 267.
100. CCPDWP, "Jiedai Meiguo Heiren Lingxiu Luobote Weilian Quanjia De Jihua (Caoan)" (Reception Plan for the Black American Leader Robert Williams and His Whole Family [Draft]), n.d., C36-2-215, MSA.
101. CCPDWP, "Waibing Qingkuang Huibao" (Reports on Foreign Guests), October 2, 1964, C36–2-215, MSA.
102. "Shoudu Qishiwan Ren Longzhong Juxing Guoqing Shengdian" (Seven Hundred Thousand People Held Grand National Day Ceremony in the Capital), *People's Daily*, October 2.
103. CCPDWP, "Waibing Qingkuang Huibao" (Reports on Foreign Guests), September 26; October 2, 1964, C36–2-215, MSA.
104. CCPDWP, "Waibing Qingkuang Huibao" (Reports on Foreign Guests), September 25, 1964, C36–2-215, MSA.
105. Cohen, *Black Crusader*, 280.
106. CCPDWP, "Waibing Qingkuang Huibao" (Reports on Foreign Guests), October 4, 1964, C36–2-215, MSA.
107. CCPDWP, "Waibing Qingkuang Huibao" (Reports on Foreign Guests), October 17, 1964, C36–2-215, MSA.
108. CCPDWP, "Waibing Qingkuang Huibao" (Reports on Foreign Guests), September 29, 1964, C36–2-215, MSA.
109. CCPDWP, "Waibing Qingkuang Huibao" (Reports on Foreign Guests), October 5, 1964, C36–2-215, MSA.
110. Letter from Williams to New York Public Library, September 22, 1967, PRW, Reel 3.
111. Letter from Reason to Williams, November 15, 1967, PRW, Reel 3.
112. Letter from Fraser to Williams, April 16, 1968, PRW, Reel 3.
113. Cohen, *Black Crusader*, 298–312.
114. "Speech of Robert Williams," October 1, 1966, *The Crusader*, October 1966, 2; "Weida De Mao Zedong Sixiang Zheng Gaizao Zhe Shijie" (The Great

Mao Zedong Thought Is Changing the World), *People's Daily*, October 2, 1966.

115. Robert Williams, "China's 17th Anniversary: Afro-Americans Represented," *The Crusader*, October 1966, 1–3.

116. Robert Williams, "On the Platform with Mao Tse-tung: China Through the Eyes of a Black American Dissident," *New York Times*, February 20, 1971.

117. *The Crusader*, January 1967, 10.

118. *The Crusader*, July 1967, 3.

119. *The Crusader*, Summer 1969, 5.

120. Letter from Duane Price to Robert Williams, February 12, 1967, PRW, Reel 2.

121. Letter from Duane Price to Robert Williams, April 19, 1967, PRW, Reel 2.

122. Letter from Sister Mary to Brother Rob and Sister Mabel, March 28, 1967, PRW, Reel 2.

123. Bobby Seale, *Seize the Time: The Story of the Black Panther Party and Huey P. Newton* (New York: Random House, 1970), 79–83.

124. Henry Noyes, *China Born: Adventures of a Maverick Bookman* (San Francisco: China Books & Periodicals, 1989), 82.

125. A. Doak Barnett, "Introduction," in *Quotations from Chairman Mao Tse-tung* (New York: Bantam Books, 1967), v.

126. Letter from Fraser to Williams, May 15, 1967, PRW, Reel 2.

127. Christian Davenport, *How Social Movements Die: Repression and Demobilization of the Republic of New Africa* (New York: Cambridge University Press, 2016), 162–71; Edward Eugene Onaci, "Self Determination Means Determining Self: Lifestyle Politics and the New Republic of Africa, 1968–1989," PhD diss., University of Illinois at Urbana-Champaign, 2012, 43.

128. Letter from Brother Imari Obadele to Robert Williams, August 9, 1968, PRW, Reel 22; November 22, 1968, PRW, Reel 4.

129. "Hoover Links Carmichael to Negro Leftist Group: Tells Congress Black Power Advocate Has Ties with Revolutionary Group," *New York Times*, May 17, 1967.

130. Committee on Un-American Activities, *Guerrilla Warfare Advocates in the United States*, May 8, 1968, U.S. House of Representatives, 90th Congress, 2nd session (Washington, DC: U.S. Government Printing Office, 1968), 1–25.

131. "Fauntroy, Carmichael Reactions to Slaying," *Washington Evening Star*, April 5, 1968; Miriam Ottenberg, "Test of New Riot Law Seen; Carmichael's Role Assessed," *Washington Evening Star*, April 7, 1968.

132. " Zhongguo Gongchandang Zhongyang Weiyuanhui Zhuxi Mao Zedong Tongzhi Zhichi Meiguo Heiren Kangbao Douzheng De Shengming" (Statement Issued by the Chairman of the CCPCC Comrade Mao Zedong to Support the African-American Struggle Against Violence), *People's Daily*, April 17, 1968, 1.

133. "Mao Zhuxi Shengming Youli Guwu Meiguo Heiren Douzheng" (Chairman Mao's Statement Greatly Inspires Black Americans in Their Struggle), *People's Daily*, April 18, 1968.

8. Lowering the Sword

1. Some of the paragraphs in this section are drawn after revision from Hongshan Li, "Building a Black Bridge: China's Interactions with African-American Activists in the Cold War," *Journal of Cold War Studies* 20, no. 3 (Summer 2018): 114–52.
2. Letter from Stanford to Williams, July 5, 1967, in *The Black Power Movement: The Papers of Robert F. Williams* (Bethesda, MD: University Publications of America, 2001), Reel 3 (hereafter referred to as PRW).
3. Letter from Williams to Clerk of Union County Superior Court, PRW, Reel 3.
4. Letter from Williams to Kochiyama, August 10, 1967; Letter from Williams to Malbury, September 15, 1967, PRW, Reel 3; Robert Williams, "Why I Propose to Return to Racist America," *The Crusader*, December 1967, 1–7.
5. Robert Williams, "Press Release," August 14, 1967, PRW, Reel 25; Jean Vincent, "Williams' Return to Expose US Racist Justice," Agence France-Presse, August 17, 1967, PRW, Reel 17.
6. Letter from Williams to Mallory, September 15, 1967, PRW, Reel 3.
7. Letter from Williams to O'Brien, September 19, 1967, PRW, Reel 3.
8. Letter from Williams to American Civil Liberties Union, September 19, 1967, PRW, Reel 3.
9. Telegram from Wulf to Williams, September 21, 1967; Letter from Wulf to Williams, October 24, 1967; Letter from Wulf to Williams, April 25, 1968, PRW, Reel 3.
10. Letter from Williams to Gordon, October 8, 1967, PRW, Reel 3.
11. Letter from May to Williams, October 9, 1967, PRW, Reel 3.
12. Letter from Lynn to Williams, November 17, 1967, PRW, Reel 3.
13. ACLU sent Williams a letter informing him of the victory in mid-1970. Letter from Sanford Jay Jones to Robert Williams, June 26, 1970, Robert Williams Papers, Box 7, Bentley Library, University of Michigan, Ann Arbor (hereafter cited as RWP).
14. Robert Williams, "My Bag's Up Tight, Cool It!," *The Crusader*, Summer 1969, 4.
15. Robert Carl Cohen, *Black Crusader: A Biography of Robert Franklin Williams* (New York: Lyle Stuart, 1972), 264.

16. Telegram from American Consul in Hong Kong to Secretary of State, May 13, 1968, RWP, Box 1.
17. Sidney Rittenberg and Amanda Bennett, *The Man Who Stayed Behind* (New York: Simon & Schuster, 1993), 165.
18. Mabel Williams, *Diary*, June 8, 16, 1968, PRW, Reel 22.
19. Timothy Tyson, *Radio Free Dixie: Robert F. Williams & the Roots of Black Power* (Chapel Hill: University of North Carolina Press, 1999), 72; CCPDWP, "Waibin Qingkuang Huibao" (Reports on Foreign Guests), September 25, 1964, C36-2-215, Shanghai Municipal Archives, Shanghai, China (hereafter cited as SMA).
20. David and Nancy Milton arrived in China to teach English at the Beijing Foreign Language Institute with their three children in 1964. They fought and managed to send their oldest son back to the United States in summer 1968 and the other two sons in summer 1969. They themselves returned home in late November 1969. David Milton and Nancy Dall Milton, *The Wind Will Not Subside: Years in Revolutionary China—1964–1969* (New York: Pantheon Books, 1976), 349–50, 358.
21. Mabel Williams, *Diary*, June 19 and June 30, 1968, PRW, Reel 22.
22. The National Advisory Commission on Civil Disorder, *Report of the National Advisory Commission on Civil Disorder* (Washington, DC: U.S. Government Printing Office, 1968), 1, 91, 150–55.
23. Robert Williams, "On the Platform with Mao Tse-tung: China Through the Eyes of a Black American Dissident," *New York Times*, February 19, 1971; U.S. Congress, Senate Committee on the Judiciary, Subcommittee to Investigate the Administration of the Internal Security Act and Other Internal Security Laws, *Testimony of Robert F. Williams* (Washington, DC: U.S. Government Printing Office, 1971), 38.
24. Airtel from Director of FBI to SACs, September 24, 1968; Memorandum from SAC Richmond to FBI Director, November 7, 1968, PRW, Reel 17.
25. Memorandum from SAC, WFC to FBI Director, September 11, 1968, PRW, Reel 22.
26. In order to make his international travel safe and smooth, Williams also applied and received the Alien Travel Document from the Ministry of Foreign Affairs. Listing his profession as writer, he applied for his visas to Tanzania with this document. MFA, People's Republic of China Alien Travel Document, No. 000944, May 6, 1969, PRW, Reel 22.
27. Telegram from Secretary of State to American Embassy in Dar es Salaam, July 8, 1969, RWP, Box 11.
28. The U.S. embassy had already sent necessary forms to Williams on July 1 so that he could apply for permission to import household items and films from Communist China. Letter from Dwight Burgess, American Consul at Dar

es Salaam, to Robert Williams, July 10, 1969; Letter from Charles Behrens, American Vice Consul at Dar es Salaam, to Robert Williams, July 1, 1969, PRW, Reel 4.

29. Robert Williams, "On the Platform with Mao Tse-tung," *New York Times*, February 19, 1970.
30. Zhonggong Zhongyang Wenxian Yanjiushi, ed., *Mao Zedong Nianpu, 1949–1976* (Chronicles of Mao Zedong, 1949–1976) (Beijing: Zhongyang Wenxian Chubanshe, 2013), 6:164.
31. *Mao Zedong Nianpu*, 6:167–68.
32. *Mao Zedong Nianpu*, 6:237.
33. *Mao Zedong Nianpu*, 6:249.
34. "T.W.A. Faces Suit on Williams Trip: A.C.L.U. Considers Action on Behalf of Militant," *New York Times*, September 11, 1969; Thomas A. Johnson, "Williams Seized on Return to U.S.," *New York Times*, September 13, 1968.
35. Edward Onaci, *Free the Land: The Republic of New Afrika and the Pursuit of a Black Nation-State* (Chapel Hill: University of North Carolina Press, 2020), 31–34.
36. William Allen, "Williams' Detroit Hearing Nov. 12," *Daily World*, September 17, 1969.
37. Johnson, "William Seized on Return to U.S."
38. Christian Davenport, *How Social Movements Die: Repression and Demobilization of the Republic of New Africa* (New York: Cambridge University Press, 2016), 250.
39. "'New Africa' President Quits Post," *Washington Post*, December 4, 1969.
40. Letter from Robert Williams to Bill, December 19, 1969, PRW, Reel 4.
41. Letter from Imari Obadele to Mweusi Chui, October 13, 1969, PRW, Reel 4.
42. Order: Cancelling Thanksgiving Convention, November 12, 1969; Executive Order, November 22, 1969, PRW, Reel 4.
43. Letter from Robert Williams to Robert Cohen, April 26, 1969, PRW, Reel 22.
44. Davenport, *How Social Movements Die*, 250–51.
45. United Press International, "Charges Dropped Against Williams," *Morning Star* (Wilmington, NC), January 17, 1976.
46. Moses Newson to Robert Williams, January 20, 1969, PRW, Reel 4; Robert Williams, "Black Militant in Red China Sizes Up 'Cultural Revolution,'" *The Afro-American*, April 12, 1969.
47. Telegram from American Embassy in Dar es Salaam to the Secretary of State, July 10, 1969, RWP, Box 11.
48. Letter from Clyde McLean to Arlene Posner, February 2, 1971, PRW, Reel 4.

49. Memorandum of Conversation, January 12, 1970, RWP, Box 11.
50. Thomas Johnson, "Militant Hopeful on Racial Justice: Williams Finds U.S. Today Yields Chance for Change," *New York Times*, September 15, 1969; Robert Maynard, "Williams Says Duty Calls Him Back," *Washington Post*, September 15, 1969.
51. Williams, "On the Platform with Mao Tse-tung," *New York Times*, February 19, 1970.
52. Contract Between Robert Williams and Mark Scher, May 16, 1971, PRW, Reel 4.
53. Letter from Allen Whiting to Robert Williams, February 11, 1970; Letter from Robert Williams to Allen Whiting, February 13, 1970, PRW, Reel 4.
54. Jim Robbins, "Williams Talks on China," *The Rutgers Daily TARGUM*, April 30, 1971; "Butter—Not Bullets—Can Make It in Asia for U.S.," *New Brunswick Home News*, May 1, 1971.
55. Letter from Gwendolyn Hall to James Brickley, June 11, August 10, 1971, PRW, Reel 4.
56. Letter from Paul Kreisberg to Robert Williams, December 22, 1969, PRW, Reel 4.
57. Memorandum of Conversation, January 12, 1970, RWP, Box 11.
58. John Gittings, *Survey of the Sino-Soviet Dispute* (New York: Oxford University Press, 1968), 139.
59. For detailed discussion on Sino-Soviet border clashes, see Li Danhui, "The Breakdown of State Relations," in *A Short History of Sino-Soviet Relations, 1917–1991*, ed. Zhihua Shen (New York: Palgrave Macmillan, 2020), 310–17; Chen Jian and Yang Kuisong, "Chinese Politics and the Collapse of the Sino-Soviet Alliance," in *Brothers in Arms: The Rise and Fall of the Sino-Soviet Alliance, 1945–1963*, ed. Odd Arne Westad (Washington, DC: Woodrow Wilson Center Press, 1998), 246–94.
60. Huang Hua, *Huang Hua Memoirs* (Beijing: Foreign Language Press, 2006), 220–21; Xiong Xianghui, "Dakai ZhongMei Guanxi De Qianzou: 1969 Nian Siwei Laoshuai Dui Guoji Xingshi De Yanpan He Jianyi De Qianqian Houhou" (The Prelude to the Opening of the Sino-American Relations: The Research and Recommendation on International Relations by Four Senior Marshals in 1969), in *Zhonggong Dangshi Ziliao* (Historical Materials of the Chinese Communist Party), ed. Zhonggong Zhongyang Dangshi Ziliao Zhengji Weiyuanhui (Beijing: Zhonggong Dangshi Ziliao Chubanshe, 1992), 42:56–96.
61. *Mao Zedong Nianpu*, 6:275, 281.
62. *Mao Zedong Nianpu*, 6:267–72.
63. Richard Nixon, "Inaugural Address," January 20, 1969, American Presidency Project, University of California, Santa Barbara, https://www.presi

dency.ucsb.edu/documents/inaugural-address-1. This address attracted Mao's attention, and he ordered it to be translated and published in the *People's Daily*. "Yipian Juemiao De Fanmian Jiaocai: Meidi Xin Toumu Nikesong De 'Jiuzhi Yanshuo' " (A Perfect Negative Example: The Inaugural Speech of the New American Imperialist Chieftain), *People's Daily*, January 28, 1969.

64. Richard Nixon, *The Memoirs of Richard Nixon* (New York: Grosset & Dunlap, 1978), 545.
65. National Security Study Memorandum 14, February 5, 1969, National Security Council Institutional Files, Box H-207, Richard Nixon Presidential Library and Museum, Yorba Linda, California.
66. Jun Niu, *Lengzhan Shiqi De Zhongguo Zhanlue Juece* (China's Strategic Decisions in the Cold War) (Beijing: Shijie Zhishi Chubanshe, 2019), 379–81.
67. Telegram from Embassy in Poland to the Department of State, January 20, 1970, *Foreign Relations of the United States, 1969–1976* (Washington, DC: U.S. Department of State, 2006), 17:167–70 (hereafter cited as FRUS).
68. *Mao Zedong Nianpu*, 6:281.
69. *Mao Zedong Nianpu*, 6:299–300.
70. John Maxwell Hamilton, *Edgar Snow: A Biography* (Bloomington: Indiana University Press, 1988), 266; Zhu Hong, *Huang Zhen Zhuan* (Biography of Huang Zhen) (Beijing: Renmin Ribao Chubanshe), 308–9.
71. "Sinuo Jiedai Xiaozu (1)" (Snow Reception Group, 1), August 16, 1970, 196-1-423, Shanxi Provincial Archives, Xian, China (hereafter cited as SPA).
72. Zhonghua Renmin Gongheguo Waijiaobu, "Sinuo Qu Xian Yanan Diqu Caifang De Tongzhi" (Circular on Snow's Visit to Xian and Yanan), September 16, 1970, 196-1-423, SPA.
73. Zhonggong Zhongyang Wenxian Yanjiushi, ed., *Zhou Enlai Nianpu* (Chronicles of Zhou Enlai) (Beijing: Zhongyang Wenxian Chubanshe, 2007), 3:393, 397.
74. Huang, *Huang Hua Memoirs*, 215; Hamilton, *Edgar Snow*, 267–68.
75. Mao Zedong, "Guanyu Tongyi Huijian Meiguo Zuojia Sinuo De Piyu" (Comment on the Approval of the Meeting with American Writer Snow), October 1970, in *Jianguo Yilai Mao Zedong Wengao* (Mao Zedong's Writings Since the Founding of the Nation), ed. Zhonggong Zhongyang Wenxian Yanjiushi (Beijing: Zhongyang Wenxian Chubanshe, 1998), 13:150.
76. Mao Zedong, "Huijian Sinuo De Tanhua Jiyao" (Transcript of the Conversation with Snow), December 18, 1970, *Jianguo Yilai Mao Zedong Wengao*, 13:163–82; Edgar Snow, "A Conversation with Mao Tse-tung," *Life*, April 30, 1971, 49.
77. *Mao Zedong Nianpu*, 6:361.
78. Snow, "A Conversation with Mao Tse-tung."

79. Pakistani President Yahya Khan visited Beijing in November 1970 and met with Mao and Zhou. He passed Nixon's oral message to Zhou at their first meeting on November 10 and received Zhou's oral message at their last meeting on November 14. *Zhou Enlai Nianpu*, 3:409–10; Record of Discussion Between the President's Advisor for National Security (Kissinger) and the Pakistani Ambassador to the United States (Hilaly), December 16, 1971, FRUS, 1969–1976, 17:251–52; Message from Premier of the People's Republic of China Chou En-lai to President Nixon, April 21, 1971, FRUS, 1969–1976, 17:300–301; Henry Kissinger, *White House Years* (Boston: Little, Brown, 1979), 713–14.
80. Hamilton, *Edgar Snow*, 273–74.
81. "Department Lists Steps Taken on Contacts with Mainland China," March 15, 1971, *Department of State Bulletin*, April 12, 1971, 510.
82. Richard Nixon, "Annual Foreign Policy Report," *Department of State Bulletin*, March 22, 1971, 321.
83. "Department Lists Steps Taken on Contacts with Mainland China," 510.
84. Mao Zedong, "Zai Waijiaobu Guanyu Meiguoren Laihua Wenti Qingshi Baogao Shang De Piyu" (Comments Made on the Report from the Ministry of Foreign Affairs on the Issue of Americans Coming to China), February 1971, *Jianguo Yilai Mao Zedong Wengao*, 13:211.
85. Zhonghua Renmin Gongheguo Waijiaobu, "Sinuo Qu Xian Yanan Diqu Caifang De Tongzhi"; "Women De Weida Lingxiu Mao Zhuxi He Tade Qinmi Zhanyou Lin Fuzhuxi Tong Shoudu Junmin Gongqing Zhonghua Renmin Gongheguo Chengli Ershiyi Zhounian" (Our Great Leader Chairman Mao and His Close Comrade Vice Chairman Lin Celebrate the Twenty-First Anniversary of the People's Republic of China with Soldiers and Civilians in the Capital), *People's Daily*, October 2, 1970; Mao Zedong, "Guanyu Tongyi Huijian Meiguo Zuojia Sinuo De Piyu," 13:150.
86. *Zhou Enlai Nianpu*, 3:416.
87. Mao Zedong, "Zai Waijiaobu Guanyu Meiguoren Laihua Wenti Qingshi Baogao Shang De Piyu."
88. Kissinger, *White House Years*, 709–11.
89. *Zhou Enlai Nianpu*, 3:442; Qian Jiang, *Ping Pong Waijiao Shimo* (History of Ping Pong Diplomacy) (Beijing: Dongfang Chubanshe, 1987), 68–73.
90. *Zhou Enlai Nianpu*, 3:443–44; Qian, *Ping Pong Waijiao Shimo*, 76.
91. Qian, *Ping Pong Waijiao Shimo*, 88–93.
92. Cheng Yuanxing, *Xin Zhongguo Waijiao Douzheng Zhuiyi: Linghui Mao Zedong De Xiongcai Dalue* (Recollections of New China's Diplomatic Struggle:

Understanding Mao Zedong's Tremendous Talents) (Beijing: Zhongyang Wenxian Chubanshe, 2011), 122–23.
93. *Zhou Enlai Nianpu*, 3:449; Lin Ke and Wu Xujun, et al., *Lishi De Chengshi: Mao Zedong Shenbian Gongzuo Renyuan De Zhengyan* (Historical Honesty: The Testimonies of Mao's Staff Members) (Hong Kong: Liwen Chubanshe, 1995), 126; Cheng, *Xin Zhongguo Waijiao Douzheng Zhuiyi*, 123–24.
94. Qian, *Ping Pong Waijiao Shimo*, 152–58.
95. Zhou Enlai, "Tong Meiguo Pingpongqiu Daibiaotuan De Tanhua" (Conversation with the United States Table Tennis Delegation), April 14, 1971, in *Zhou Enlai Waijiao Wenxuan* (Selected Works of Zhou Enlai on Diplomacy), ed. Zhonghua Renmin Gongheguo Waijiaobu (Beijing: Zhongyang Wenxian Chubanshe, 1990), 469–75.
96. Benjamin Welles, "U.S. Officials View Chinese Action as a Move to Ease Isolation," *New York Times*, April 11, 1971.
97. Zhou, "Tong Meiguo Pingpongqiu Daibiaotuan De Tanhua," in *Zhou Enlai Waijiao Wenxuan*, 469–75.
98. Arthur W. Galston, "An American Biologist in China," n.d., Arthur William Galston Papers, Box, 14, Yale University Library Manuscript Collections, Yale University, New Haven, Connecticut.
99. Huang Renguo, *Jiaoyu Yu Zhengzhi, Jingji De Sanxiang Hudong* (The Three-Dimensional Interaction Among Education, Politics, and Economy) (Beijing: Shijie Zhishi Chubanshe, 2010), 84–86; *Zhou Enlai Nianpu*, 3:457.
100. Seymour Topping, "U.S. Biologists in China Tell of Scientific Gains," *New York Times*, May 24, 1971.
101. Kathlin Smith, "The Role of Scientists in Normalizing the U.S.-China Relations, 1965–1979," *Annals of the New York Academy of Science* 866, no. 1(December 1998): 121.
102. Seymour Topping, *Journey Between Two Chinas* (New York: Harper & Row, 1972), 394–95.
103. *Zhou Enlai Nianpu*, 3:464; Topping, *Journey Between Two Chinas*, 396.
104. Zhou Enlai, "Taiwan Huigui Zuguo, ZhongMei Guanxi Hui Genghao" (Taiwan's Reunion with the Motherland Will Further Improve U.S.-China Relations), *Zhou Enlai Waijiao Wenxuan*, 476–80; Topping, *Journey Between Two Chinas*, 396–400.
105. *Zhou Enlai Nianpu*, 3:473.
106. "Official Transcript of Wide-Ranging Interview with Premier Zhou: Effort by the Two Sides in Korea to Achieve Reunification Was Proposed by Zhou," *New York Times*, August 10, 1971.
107. Topping, *Journey Between Two Chinas*, 401.
108. Topping, *Journey Between Two Chinas*, 402.

109. "9 U.S. Students Cross Into China: 4 Wives Also in the Group—Visit to Last 4 weeks," *New York Times*, June 24, 1971; Committee of Concerned Asian Scholars, *China! Inside the People's Republic* (New York: Bantam Books, 1972), 6–9; Fabio Lanza, *The End of Concern: Maoist China, Activism, and Asian Studies* (Durham, NC: Duke University Press, 2017), 109–11.
110. "Zhou Emphasizes U.S. War Pullout: He Tells American Students Step Must Precede Move to Improve Relations," *New York Times*, July 21, 1971.
111. "Zhonggong Guoying Caotan Nongchang Dangwei Guanyu Meiguoren Xingdun Furen Jiedai Gongzuo Baogao" (Summary Report by the CCP Caotan State Farm Committee on the Reception of American Madame Hinton), June 10, 1963, 196-1-170, SPA.
112. "Jiedai Meiguo Xindun Furen He Qingnian Daibiaotuan Jianbao" (Brief Reports on the Reception of Madame Hinton from the United States and the Youth Delegation Led by Her), October 2, 1971; "Waibin Jiedai Jianxun" (Brief News on the Reception of Foreign Guests), no. 51, October 8, 1971; "Waibin Huodong Jianbao" (Brief Reports on the Activities of Foreign Guests), November 3, 1971, 196-1-466, SPA.
113. "Mei Heqiya Weiliansi Fanghua Canguan Huodong Xiaojie" (Brief Summary of Hosea Williams's Activities in His Visit to China), in *Waishi Gongzuo Qingkuan Fanying* (Reports on Foreign Affairs Work Situation) 126, October 15, 1971, 196-1-466, SPA.
114. "Zhong Heweihui He Zi 035 Hao" (CCPDWP No. 035), September 18, 1971; "Guanyu Jiedai Meiguo Hexiya Weiliansi Fufu Fanghua Jihua" (The Reception Plan for Hosea Williams's Visit to China), September 21, 1971, 196-1-468, SPA.
115. Elaine Brown, *A Taste of Power: A Black Woman's Story* (New York: Pantheon Books, 1992), 78–81.
116. Robin D. G. Kelley and Betsy Esch, "Black Like Mao: *Red China and Black Revolution*," *Souls* 1, no. 4 (1999): 6–41; "Black Panther Leader Huey Newton Speaks of His Meeting with Chou En-lai," https://www.youtube.com/watch?v=Djf23DyJQss.
117. Tsan-kuo Chang, *The Press and China Policy: The Illusion of Sino-American Relations 1950–1984* (Norwood, NJ: Ablex, 1993), 73.
118. Mao Zedong, "Xianzai Bu Cunzai ZhongMei Liangguo Dazhang De Wenti" (The Issue of War Between China and the United States Does Not Exist), in *Mao Zedong Waijiao Wenxuan* (Selected Works of Mao Zedong on Diplomacy), ed. Zhonghua Renmin Gongheguo Waijiaobu (Beijing: Shijie Zhishi Chubanshe, 1994), 595.
119. *Zhou Enlai Nianpu*, 3:427.
120. Kissinger, *White House Years*, 1080.

121. "Text of Joint Communique, Issued at Shanghai, February 27," *Department of State Bulletin*, March 20, 1972, 435–38.
122. "Remarks by President Nixon," February 28, 1972, *Department of State Bulletin*, March 20, 1972, 434.
123. National Security Study Memorandum, 148, March 9, 1972, National Security Council Institutional Files.
124. *Zhou Enlai Nianpu*, 3:506.
125. Mao Zedong, "Xianzai Bu Cunzai ZhongMei Liangguo Dazhang De Wenti," 595.
126. Xu Guoqi, *Olympic Dreams: China and Sports, 1895–2008* (Cambridge, MA: Harvard University Press, 2008), 152–55.
127. *Zhou Enlai Nianpu*, 3:515–16.
128. "Remarks by President Nixon," April 18, 1972, *Department of State Bulletin*, May 15, 1972, 698.
129. *Zhou Enlai Nianpu*, 3:520. In sharp contrast, four of the six American interpreters accompanying the CNTTT in its tour of the United States boycotted the meeting with Nixon on that day. Perry Link, "Dawn in China," in *My First Trip to China*, ed. Kin-ming Liu (Hong Kong: East Slope Publishing Limited, 2012), 50.
130. Mary Brown Bullock, "Scholarly Exchange and American China Studies," in *American Studies of Contemporary China*, ed. David Shambaugh (Washington, DC: Woodrow Wilson Center Press, 1993), 282–84.
131. Ruth Eckstein, "Ping Pong Diplomacy: A View from the Behind the Scenes," *Journal of American-East Asian Relations* 2, no. 3 (Fall 1993): 327–42.
132. National Research Council, *Annual National Report*, 1973–1974, 51.
133. Qi Qiao, "1972 Nian Zhongguo Kexuejia Daibiaotuan Fang OuMei Zhilü" (The Chinese Scientist Delegation's Visit to Europe and America in 1972), *Zhishi Fenzi* (The Intellectual), http://k.sina.com.cn/article_5705191799 _1540e51770190139je.html.
134. Smith, "The Role of Scientists in Normalizing U.S.-China Relations," 1:115–18; Pete Millwood, "An 'Exceedingly Delicate Undertaking': Sino-American Science Diplomacy, 1966–1978," *Journal of Contemporary History* 56, no. 1 (2021): 170.
135. Smith, "The Role of Scientists in Normalizing U.S.-China Relations," 1:121–22.
136. Xu Guoqi, *Olympic Dreams*, 148–50.
137. Memorandum for Henry Kissinger from John Holdridge, August 29, 1972, Nixon Presidential Materials Project, White House Central Files, Subject Files, FO Box 5, Richard Nixon Presidential Library and Museum, Yorba Linda, California (hereafter cited as RNPLM).

138. Letter from Henry Kissinger to Alexander Eckstein, September 6, 1972, RNPLM, FO Box 5.
139. Mary Brown Bullock, "Mission Accomplished: The Influence of CSCPRC on Educational Relations with China," in *Bridging Minds Across the Pacific: U.S.-China Educational Exchanges, 1978–2003*, ed. Cheng Li (Lanham, MD: Lexington Books, 2005), 62.
140. Bullock, "Mission Accomplished," 51–53.
141. Memorandum of Conversation, Chang Wen-chin and Alfred Jenkins, February 17, 1973, National Security Council Files, Henry A. Kissinger Files, Country Files—Far East, RNPLM, Box 86.
142. Smith, "The Role of Scientists in Normalizing U.S.-China Relations," 1:124.
143. Bullock, "Scholarly Exchange and American China Studies," 287.
144. Harrison Brown, "Scholarly Exchange with the People's Republic of China," *Science* 183, no. 4120 (January 11, 1974): 52–53.
145. Memorandum of Conversation, Lin P'ing and Hummel, November 11, 1973, National Security Council Files, Henry A. Kissinger Files, Country Files—Far East, RNPLM, Box 86.
146. Su Jingjing and Zhang Daqing, "Xin Zhongguo Shouci FuMei Yixue Daibiaotuan Zhi Tanjiu" (Exploration of New China's First Medical Delegation's Visit to the United States), *Zhongguo Kejishi Zazhi* (Journal of Chinese History of Science and Technology) 32, no. 3 (2011): 395–405.
147. Douglas P. Murray, "Exchange with the People's Republic of China: Symbols and Substance," *Annals*, AAPSS 424, March 1976, 38.
148. "Meifang Wuli Quxiao Woguo Yishutuan FangMei Yanchu" (The American Side Unreasonably Canceled the Visit of Our Performing Arts Troupe to the United States), *People's Daily*, March 3, 1975.
149. "Zhong Heweihui He Zi 035 Hao," September 18, 1971; "Guanyu Jiedai Meiguo Hexiya Weiliansi Fufu Fanghua Jihua."
150. Luo Weiguo, "Yi Nikesong Zongtong Yixing Fanghu" (Remembering the Visit of President Nixon and His Entourage to Shanghai), *Shiji* (Century) 2 (2012): 12–14.
151. Jonathan Mirsky, "From Mao Fan to Counter-Revolutionary in 48 Hours," in *My First Trip to China*, 24–28.
152. Millwood, "An 'Exceedingly Delicate Undertaking,'" 1:175–76.
153. Ezra F. Vogel, "China Before the Deng Transformation," in *My First Trip to China*, 190–92.
154. Vogel, "China Before the Deng Transformation," 192–93.
155. Andrew Nathan, "Nan De Hu Tu," in *My First Trip to China*, 197–206.
156. Lanza, *The End of Concern*, 113.
157. Memorandum of Conversation, Chang Wen-chin and Alfred Jenkins, February 17, 1973, National Security Council Files, Henry A. Kissinger Files,

Country Files—Far East, RNPLM, Box 86; Murray, "Exchange with the People's Republic of China," 39.
158. Jiaoyubu Waijiaobu, "Guanyu Yaoqing Waiguo Yuyan Xuezhe, Jiaoshi Lai-Hua Gongzuo De Qingshi" (A Request for Inviting Foreign Language Experts and Instructors to Work Temporarily in China), December 19, 1977, SZ142-4-455, Hubei Provincial Archives, Wuhan, Hubei Province, China (HPA).
159. Zhonggong Zhongyang Wenxian Yanjiushi, ed., *Deng Xiaoping Nianpu* (Chronicles of Deng Xiaoping) (Beijing: Zhongyang Wenxian Chubanshe, 2004), 1:5.
160. *Deng Xiaoping Nianpu*, 1:331.
161. *Deng Xiaoping Nianpu*, 1:339–40; Bullock, "Mission Accomplished," 54–55.
162. Bullock, "Mission Accomplished," 55; Smith, "The Role of Scientists in Normalizing U.S.-China Relations" 1:128–29.
163. Liu Baicheng, "Sishinian Qian Women 50 Ren FuMei Liuxue" (Forty Years Ago 50 of Us Went to Study in the United States), *Zhongguo Jingji Zhoukan* (Chinese Economic Weekly) 41 (2018), http://www.ceweekly.cn/2018/1022/237904.shtml.
164. "Deng Fuzongli He Kate Zongtong Qianshu ZhongMei Keji Xieding He Wenhua Xieding Bing Fabiao Jianghua" (Vice Premier Deng and President Carter Signed the Agreement on Science and Technology and the Agreement on Culture, and Gave Speeches), *People's Daily*, February 2, 1979; Smith, "The Role of Scientists in Normalizing U.S.-China Relations," 1:129.
165. David Lampton, *A Relationship Restored: Trends in U.S.-China Educational Exchange, 1979–1984* (Washington, DC: National Academy Press, 1986), 32, 54.
166. *Deng Xiaoping Nianpu*, 1:480.
167. *Deng Xiaoping Nianpu*, 1:483, 485.
168. *Deng Xiaoping Nianpu*, 1:438.
169. Deng Xiaoping, "Jiefang Sixiang, Shishi Qiushi, Tuanjie Yizhi Xiangqiankan" (Emancipate Minds, Seek Truth from Facts, Look Forward in Solidarity), December 13, 1978, in *Deng Xiaoping Wenxuan* (Selected Writings of Deng Xiaoping), ed. Zhonggong Zhongyang Wenxian Bianji Weiyuanhui (Beijing: Renmin Chubanshe, 1983), 138–39.

Epilogue: Beyond Rattling

1. David A. Lampton, ed., *A Relationship Restored: Trends in U.S.-China Educational Exchanges, 1978–1984* (Washington, DC: National Academy Press, 1988), 32.
2. Harold C. Schonberger, "Boston Symphony Off on China Tour Today," *New York Times*, March 12, 1979; "Deng Xiaoping Fuzongli Song Qingling

Fuweiyuanzhang Chuxi Xinshang Boshidun Jiaoxiang Yuetuan Yanchu" (Vice Premier Deng Xiaoping and Vice Chairwoman Song Qingling Attend and Enjoy the Boston Symphony Orchestra's Performance), *People's Daily*, March 18, 1979.

3. "China Buys Rights to a U.S. Film," *New York Times*, January 7, 1979; Barbara Bry, "American International Epic: Chinese Book U.S. Film 'Futureworld,'" *Los Angeles Times*, January 5, 1979.

4. "China Buys 'Atlantis' TV Show," *Tuscaloosa News*, October 3, 1979; Zhongyang Dianshitai, ed., *Zhongyang Dianshitai De Diyi Yu Bianqian* (China Central Television's Firsts and Changes) (Beijing: Dongfang Chubanshe, 2003), 125.

5. Summary of a Policy Review Committee Meeting, May 2, 1979, *Foreign Relations of the United States, 1977–1980* (Washington, DC: U.S. Department of State, 1980), xiii:867–68 (hereafter cited as FRUS).

6. "ZhongMei Wenhua He Shuili Fadian Liangge Xieyi ZaiJing Qianding" (The Sino-American Agreements on Culture and Hydroelectricity Are Signed in Beijing), *People's Daily*, August 29, 1979.

7. "Meiguo Fuzongtong Mengdaier Zai Beijing Daxue De Yanjiang" (Speech by U.S. Vice President Mondale at Peking University), *People's Daily*, August 28, 1979.

8. "Zhongyang Xuanchuanbu Guanyu Tingzhi Faxing Mao Zhuxi Yülu De Tongzhi" (Instruction from the Central Propaganda Department on Stopping the Publication of *Quotations from Chairman Mao*), *Dang De Xuanchuan Gongzuo Wenjian Xuanbian* (Selected Documents on the Party's Propaganda Work), ed. Zhonggong Zhongyang Bangongting (Beijing: Zhonggong Zhongyang Dangxiao Chubanshe, 1994), 2:679.

9. Deng Xiaoping, "Jianchi Sixiang Jiben Yuanze" (Adhering to Four Basic Principles), March 30, 1979, in *Deng Xiaoping Wenxuan* (Selected Writings of Deng Xiaoping), ed. Zhonggong Zhongyang Wenxian Bianji Weiyuanhui (Beijing: Renmin Chubanshe, 1983), 2:166–67; *Deng Xiaoping Nianpu*, 1:501–3.

10. Deng Xiaoping, "Muqian De Xingshi He Renwu" (The Current Situation and Tasks), January 16, 1980, in *Deng Xiaoping Wenxuan*, 2:266.

11. At his meeting with editorial writers from the United States and Canada on June 5, 1980, Deng Xiaoping told the visitors that "we closed off the 'Xidan Wall' because it had sabotaged our stable and united political situation." *Deng Xiaoping Nianpu*, 1:645.

12. Lampton, *A Relationship Restored*, 37–40.

13. Summary of a Policy Review Committee Meeting, May 2, 1979, FRUS, 1977–1980, xiii:867–68.

14. Remarks of Vice President Walter F. Mondale, Peking University, August 27, 1979, Walter F. Mondale Papers, Minnesota Historical Society, St. Paul,

Minnesota, http://www2.mnhs.org/library/findaids/00697/pdfa/00697-000 66-2.pdf.
15. Memorandum of Conversation, August 28, 1979, Walter F. Mondale Papers, http://www2.mnhs.org/library/findaids/00697/pdfa/00697-00104.pdf.
16. *Deng Xiaoping Nianpu*, 2:929.
17. Deng Xiaoping, "Meiyou Anding De Zhengzhi Huanjing Shenmeshi Ye Ganbucheng" (Nothing Can Be Done Without a Stable Political Environment), in *Deng Xiaping Wenxuan*, 3:244.
18. Deng Xiaoping, "Yadao Yiqie De Shi Wending" (Stability Trumps Everything Else), in *Deng Xiaping Wenxuan*, 3:284–85.
19. "Zhongyang Xuanchuanbu Guanyu Shouting 'Meiguo Zhi Ying' Huayu Guangbo Zhong Yingyu Jiaoxue Jiemu Ji Shifo Keyi Xiang 'Meiguo Zhi Ying' Zhu Xianggang Banshi Jigou Hansuo Yingyu Jiaocai Deng Wenti De Tongzhi" (A Circular from the Central Propaganda Department on the Listening to the English Instruction Program of the Voice of America and the Permission to Request English Textbooks from the Voice of America's Office in Hong Kong by Mail and Other Issues), in *Dang De Xuanchuan Gongzuo Wenjian Xuanbian*, 2:667.
20. "China Bars Return of VOA Correspondent," UPI, August 17, 1988.
21. Guangqiu Xu, "The Ideological and Political Impact of U.S. Fulbrighters on Chinese Students: 1979–1989," *Asian Affairs: An American Review* 26, no. 3 (Fall 1999): 141–44.
22. Tan Youzhi, *Meiguo DuiHua Gonggong Waijiao Zhanlue* (The Strategy of the United States Public Diplomacy Toward China) (Beijing: Shishi Chubanshe, 2011), 195–96.
23. Paul Loong, "China Objects to Modern Art," UPI, September 1, 1981, https://www.upi.com/Archives/1981/09/01/Chinese-object-to-modern-art/5262368164800/.
24. "Boshidun Bowuguan Meiguo Minghua Yuanzuo Zhanlan ZaiJing Kaimu" (The Exhibit of Boston Museum's Famous Original American Paintings Opens in Beijing), *People's Daily*, September 1, 1981.
25. Wallace Turner, "Stanford Ousts Ph.D. Candidate Over His Use of Data on China," *New York Times*, February 26, 1983.
26. Mary Brown Bullock, "Mission Accomplished: The Influence of CSCPRC on Educational Relations with China," in *Bridging Minds Across the Pacific: U.S.-China Educational Exchanges, 1978–2003*, ed. Cheng Li (Lanham, MD: Lexington Books, 2005), 57–58; Andrew G. Walder, ed., *Zouping in Transition: The Process of Reform in Rural China* (Cambridge, MA: Harvard University Press, 1998).
27. Jim Mann, "Voice of America Directs to Restive Chinese," *Los Angeles Times*, January 15, 1990.

28. "Jieyan Qijian Weifan Wo Falü He Faling Mei Liangming Jizhe Bei Xianqi Chujing" (Having Violated Our Laws and Orders, Two American Reporters Are Ordered to Depart with a Time Limit), *People's Daily*, June 14, 1989.
29. Mark Fineman, "China Orders 7th Reporter to Leave: 2nd Voice of America Journalist Expelled; U.S. Protests," *Los Angeles Times*, July 9, 1989.
30. Wu Ge, "Meiguo Zhi Ying De Biaoyan Yu 'Heping Yanbian' Celue" (The Behavior of the VOA and the Strategy of "Peaceful Evolution"), *People's Daily*, July 8, 1989.
31. "China Suspends U.S. Fulbright Scholar Exchange," *Los Angeles Times*, August 17, 1989; Tan, *Meiguo DuiHua Gonggong Waijiao Zhanlue*, 196–97.
32. Bullock, "Mission Accomplished," 60–61.
33. George H. W. Bush, Executive Order 12711: Policy Implementation with Respect to Nationals of the People's Republic of China, April 11, 1990, American Presidency Project, University Santa Barbara, https://www.presidency.ucsb.edu/documents/executive-order-12711-policy-implementation-with-respect-nationals-the-peoples-republic.
34. Public Law 102–404, October 9, 1992, 106 Stat, 1969–1971.
35. Deng Xiaoping, "Women You Xinxin Ba Zhongguo De Shiqing Zuo De Genghao" (We Have Confidence to Make China Better), September 16, 1989, *Deng Xiaoping Wenxuan*, 3:325–26; Deng Xiaoping, "Jianchi Shehui Zhuyi, Fangzhi Heping Yanbian" (Adhering to Socialism and Preventing Peaceful Evolution), November 23, 1989, *Deng Xiaoping Wenxuan*, 3:344.
36. "Secret Scowcroft-Eagleburger Visit to China: Press Briefing by President's Press Secretary (Fitzwater)," December 19, 1989, in *American Foreign Policy Current Documents, 1989*, ed. Nancy Golden (Washington, DC: U.S. Government Printing Office, 1990), 529; Tao Wenzhao, *Zhongmei Guanxishi* (History of Sino-American Relations) (Shanghai: Shanghai Renmin Chubanshe, 2004), 3:211.
37. Bullock, "Mission Accomplished," 60.
38. Cheng Li, "Reforming and Opening-Up, 1979–2016," in *Finding Firmer Ground: The Role of Higher Education in U.S.-China Relations*, ed. Yawei Liu and Michael Cerny, (Atlanta: Carter Center, 2022), 38–40.
39. Tan, *Meiguo DuiHua Gonggong Waijiao Zhanlue*, 197–98.
40. Jim Mann, "After 5 Years of Political Wrangling, Radio Free Asia Becomes a Reality," *Los Angeles Times*, September 30, 1996.
41. "Meiguo De Renquan Jilu" (The Human Rights Record of the United States), *Guangming Daily*, March 2, 1999.
42. Matt Forney, "U.S. Peace Corps Arrives in China," UPI, July 16, 1993.
43. "Peace Corps Returns to China," July 21, 2004, Peace Corps, https://www.peacecorps.gov/news/library/peace-corps-returns-to-china/.
44. U.S. Congress, The International Broadcasting Act of 1994, April 30, 1994, Public Law 103–236, United States Statute at Large, 108: 432–33.

45. The first meeting of the U.S.-China High-Level Consultation on People-to-People Exchange was held in Beijing in May 2010, chaired by Liu and Secretary of State Hilary Clinton. Six more annual meetings were held alternately in Beijing and Washington until 2016. "ZhongMei Renwen Jiaoliu Gaoceng Cuoshang Jizhi Chengli Bing Zhaokai Diyici Huiyi" (The Mechanism of Sino-American High-Level Consultation on People-to-People Exchange Establishes and Holds Its First Meeting), May 25, 2010, Zhonghua Renmin Gongheguo Zhongyang Zhengfu, http://www.gov.cn/ldhd/2010-05/25/content_1613568.htm; U.S. Department of State, "U.S.-China Consultation on People-to-People Exchange," June 7, 2016, https://2009-2017.state.gov/r/pa/prs/ps/2016/06/258141.htm.

46. Keith Bradsher, "China Blocks Web Access to Times After Article," *New York Times*, October 25, 2012; William Wan, "China Forces New York Times Reporter to Leave Country," *Washington Post*, January 30, 2014.

47. Stanley Lubman, "Document Number 9: The Party Attacks Western Democratic Ideals," *Wall Street Journal*, August 27, 2013.

48. "Jiaoyubu: Quanguo Gaoxiao Makesi Zhuyi Xueyuan Zengzhi 1440 Yu Jia" (The Ministry of Education: The Number of School of Marxism at Higher Learning Institutions in the Nation Has Increased to Over 1,400), *Beijing Shangbao*, March 17, 2022, https://baijiahao.baidu.com/s?id=1727513359026785901&wfr=spider&for=pc.

49. Jonathan Landay, "U.S. Imposes New Rules on State-Owned Chinese Media Over Propaganda Concerns," Reuters, February 19, 2020, https://www.reuters.com/article/us-usa-china-media/u-s-imposes-new-rules-on-state-owned-chinese-media-over-propaganda-concerns-idUSKBN20C2G1.

50. Jennifer Pignolet, "University of Akron to Close Its Confucius Institute to Comply with Federal Grant Restrictions," *Akron Beacon Journal*, November 8, 2021.

51. Lin Yang, "Controversial Confucius Institutes Returning to U.S. Schools Under New Name," VOA, June 27, 2022, https://www.voanews.com/a/controversial-confucius-institutes-returning-to-u-s-schools-under-new-name/6635906.html.

52. Peter Hessler, "Broken Bonds," *The New Yorker*, March 16, 2020, 69–85.

53. Elizabeth Redden, "Trump Targets Fulbright in China, Hong Kong," *Inside Higher Ed*, July 14, 2020, https://www.insidehighered.com/news/2020/07/16/trump-targets-fulbright-china-hong-kong?v2.

54. Pan Gongyu, "Meiguo ZaiHua 'Hepingdui,' Zouhao, Busong" (Farewell, Peace Corps in China, We Won't See You Off), *Guanchazhe* (Observer), January 20, 2020, https://www.guancha.cn/pangongyu/2020_01_20_532304_3.shtml.

Bibliography

Primary Sources

Archival Documents

Academia Historica, Taipei, Taiwan
    Ministry of Foreign Affairs Archives, Dongnanya Qiaojiao Jihua (Plan for Overseas Chinese Education in Southeast Asia) (DQJ)
Beijing Municipal Archives, Beijing, China
    Declassified Chinese Communist Party and Government Records
Bentley Library, University of Michigan, Ann Arbor, Michigan
    Robert Williams Papers (RWP)
Divinity Library Special Collections, Yale University, New Haven, Connecticut
    Archives of the United Board of Christian Higher Education in Asia (UBCHEA)
Hubei Provincial Archives, Wuhan, Hubei Province, China (HPA)
    Declassified Chinese Communist Party and Government Records
Ministry of Foreign Affairs Archives, Beijing, China (MFAA)
    Declassified Diplomatic Records from 1949 to 1960
Minnesota Historical Society, St. Paul, Minnesota
    Walter F. Mondale Papers
National Archives, College Park, Maryland
    Record Group 59: Records of Department of State

Bureau of Far Eastern Affairs/Office of Chinese Affairs Files, 1954–1957 (OCA)
Correspondence, Memorandums, and Reports of the Chinese and Korean Assistance Branch, 1948–55 (CMR)
Office of East Asian Affairs, Central Files, 1947–1964 (OEAA)
Record Group 469: Records of the U.S. Foreign Assistance Agencies, 1948-1961
Office of Far Eastern Operations, China Subject File, 1948–1957 (CSF)
National Archives Administration, National Development Council, Taipei, Taiwan
Ministry of Foreign Affairs Documents (NAA)
Richard Nixon Presidential Library and Museum, Yorba Linda, California
National Security Council Institutional Files
Schlesinger Library, Radcliff Institute for Advanced Studies, Harvard University, Cambridge, Massachusetts
Shirley Graham Du Bois Papers
Schomburg Center for Research in Black Culture, New York Public Library, New York
Vicki Garvin Papers (VGP)
Shanghai Municipal Archives, Shanghai, China (SMA)
Declassified Chinese Communist Party and Government Records
Shanxi Provincial Archives, Xian, China (SPA)
Shanxi Provincial Office of Foreign Affairs File
Special Collections and University Archives, University of Massachusetts Amherst Libraries
W. E. B. Du Bois Papers (DBP)
Tamiment Library, New York University, New York
Jack and Esther Cooper Jackson Papers
Yale University Library Manuscript Collections, Yale University, New Haven, Connecticut
Arthur William Galston Papers

Published Document Collections

The Black Power Movement: The Papers of Robert F. Williams. Bethesda, MD: University Publications of America, 2001 (PRW).
Chou, Anne H., ed. *Taiwan Guangfu Hou Meiyuan Shiliao* (Documentary Collection on U.S. Aid to the R.O.C., 1948–1965), 3 vols. Taipei: Academia Historica Republic of China, 1995.
Golden, Nancy, ed. *American Foreign Policy Current Documents, 1989*. Washington, DC: U.S. Government Printing Office, 1990.

National Advisory Commission on Civil Disorder. *Report of the National Advisory Commission on Civil Disorder.* Washington, DC: U.S. Government Printing Office, 1968.

U.S. Department of State. *Department of State Bulletin.*

———. *Foreign Relations of the United States.*

———. *Program of Emergency Aid to Chinese Students, 1949–1955.* Washington, DC: U.S. Government Printing Office, 1956.

U.S. House of Representatives. *Relief of Chinese Students,* July 14, 1949, House Report 1039, 81st Congress, 1st Sess. Washington, DC: U.S. Government Printing Office, 1950.

U.S. House of Representatives, Committee on Un-American Activities. *Guerrilla Warfare Advocates in the United States,* May 8, 1968, U.S. House of Representatives, 90th Congress, 2nd session. Washington, DC: U.S. Government Printing Office, 1968.

———. *Violations of State Department Travel Regulations and Pro-Castro Propaganda Activities in the United States: Hearings Before the Committee on Un-American Activities House of Representatives,* 88th Cong., 1st Sess. Washington, DC: U.S. Government Printing Office, 1965.

U.S. Senate. *A Compilation of the Laws, Treaties, and Regulations and Rulings of the Treasury Department Relating to the Exclusion of Chinese,* Senate Document, No 291, 57th Congress, 1st sess. Washington, DC: U.S. Government Printing Office, 1902.

U.S. Senate, Committee on the Judiciary. *Testimony of Robert F. Williams: Hearings Before the Subcommittee to Investigate the Administration of the Internal Security Act and Other Internal Security Laws,* 91st Congress, 1st sess. Washington, DC: U.S. Government Printing Office, 1971.

United States Statutes at Large, 81st Congress, Sess. 2, vol. 64.

Zhonggong Zhongyang Bangongting, ed. *Dang De Xuanchuan Gongzuo Wenjian Xuanbian* (Selected Documents on the Party's Propaganda Work). 4 vols. Beijing: Zhonggong Zhongyang Dangxiao Chubanshe, 1994.

Zhonggong Zhongyang Wenxian Bianji Weiyuanhui, ed. *Deng Xiaoping Wenxuan, Yijiuqiwu—Yijiubaer* (Selected Writings of Deng Xiaoping, 1975–1982). Beijing: Renmin Chubanshe, 1983.

Zhonggong Zhongyang Wenxian Yanjiushi, ed. *Deng Xiaoping Nianpu* (Chronicles of Deng Xiaoping). 2 vols. Beijing: Zhongyang Wenxian Chubanshe, 2004.

———. *Jianguo Yilai Liu Shaoqi Wengao* (Writings of Liu Shaoqi Since the Founding of the Nation). 4 vols. Beijing: Zhongyang Wenxian Chubanshe, 2005.

———. *Jianguo Yilai Mao Zedong Wengao* (Mao Zedong's Writings Since the Founding of the Nation). 13 vols. Beijing: Zhongyang Wenxian Chubanshe, 1998.

———. *Jianguo Yilai Zhongyao Wenxian Xuanbian* (Selected Important Records Since the Founding of the Nation). 14 vols. Beijing: Zhongyang Wenxian Chubanshe, 1992.

———. *Liu Shaoqi Nianpu* (Chronicles of Liu Shaoqi). 2 vols. Beijing: Zhongyang Wenxian Chubanshe, 1995.

———. *Mao Zedong Nianpu, 1893–1949* (Chronicles of Mao Zedong, 1893–1949). 3 vols. Beijing: Zhongyang Wenxian Chubanshe, 2013.

———. *Mao Zedong Nianpu, 1949–1976* (Chronicles of Mao Zedong, 1949–1976). 6 vols. Beijing: Zhongyang Wenxian Chubanshe, 2013.

———. *Mao Zedong Wenji* (Writings of Mao Zedong). 8 vols. Beijing: Renmin Chubanshe, 1993.

———. *Zhou Enlai Nianpu* (Chronicles of Zhou Enlai). 3 vols. Beijing: Zhongyang Wenxian Chubanshe, 2007.

Zhongguo Gaodeng Jiaoyu Xuehui, Qinghua Daxue, ed. *Jiang Nanxiang Wenji* (Collection of Writings by Jiang Nanxiang). 2 vols. Beijing: Qinghua Daxue Chubanshe, 1998.

Zhonghua Renmin Gongheguo Waijiaobu, ed. *Mao Zedong Waijiao Wenxuan* (Selected Works of Mao Zedong on Diplomacy). Beijing: Shijie Zhishi Chubanshe, 1994.

———. *Zhou Enlai Waijiao Wenxuan* (Selected Works of Zhou Enlai on Diplomacy). Beijing: Zhongyang Wenxian Chubanshe, 1990.

Zhonghua Renmin Gongheguo Waijiaobu Danganguan, ed. *Zhonghua Renmin Gongheguo Waijiao Dangan Xuanbian* (Selected Diplomatic Archives of the People's Republic of China). Beijing: Shijie Zhishi Chubanshe, 2007.

Zhongyang Danganguan, ed. *Zhonggong Zhongyang Wenjian Xuanji* (Selected Documents of the Chinese Communist Party Central Committee). 25 vols. Beijing: Zhonggong Zhongyang Dangxiao Chubanshe, 1989.

Books and Articles

Adams, Clarence, Della Adams, and Lewis H. Carlson. *An American Dream: The Life of an African American Soldier and POW Who Spent Twelve Years in Communist China*. Amherst: University of Massachusetts Press, 2007.

Adler, Solomon. *The Chinese Economy*. London: Routledge & Paul, 1957.

Aptheker, Herbert, ed., *The Correspondence of W. E. B. Du Bois*. 3 vols. Amherst: University of Massachusetts Press, 1978.

Brady, Anne-Marie. *Making the Foreign Serve China: Managing Foreigners in the People's Republic*. Lanham, MD: Rowman & Littlefield, 2003.

Brown, Elaine. *A Taste of Power: A Black Woman's Story*. New York: Pantheon Books, 1992.

Brown, Harrison. "Scholarly Exchange with the People's Republic of China." *Science* 183, no. 4120 (January 11, 1974): 52–54.
Bullock, Mary Brown. "Mission Accomplished: The Influence of CSCPRC on Educational Relations with China." In *Bridging Minds Across the Pacific: U.S.-China Educational Exchanges, 1978–2003*, ed. Cheng Li, 49–68. Lanham, MD: Lexington Books, 2005.
——. *The Oil Prince's Legacy: Rockefeller Philanthropy in China*. Washington, DC: Woodrow Wilson Center Press, 2011.
——. "Scholarly Exchange and American China Studies." In *American Studies of Contemporary China*, ed. David Shambaugh, 281–300. Washington, DC: Woodrow Wilson Center Press, 1993.
Chang, Gordon H. *Friends and Enemies: The United States, China, and the Soviet Union, 1948–1972*. Stanford, CA: Stanford University Press, 1990.
Chang, Iris. *Thread of the Silkworm*. New York: Basic Books, 1995.
Chang, Tsan-kuo. *The Press and China Policy: The Illusion of Sino-American Relations, 1950–1984*. Norwood, NJ: Ablex, 1993.
Chen, Jian. *China's Road to the Korean War: The Making of the Sino-American Confrontation*. New York: Columbia University Press, 1994.
——. *Mao's China and the Cold War*. Chapel Hill: University of North Carolina Press, 2001.
Chen, Jian, and Kuisong Yang. "Chinese Politics and the Collapse of the Sino-Soviet Alliance." In *Brothers in Arms: The Rise of Fall of the Sino-Soviet Alliance, 1945–1963*, 246–294. Washington, DC: Woodrow Wilson Center Press, 1998.
Chen Tushou. *Guguo Renmin Yousuo Si: 1949 Nian Hou Zhishi Fenzi Sixiang Gaizao Ceying* (Some of the People's Thoughts in My Homeland: Profiles of Intellectuals in Thought Reform After 1949). Beijing: Sanlian Shudian, 2013.
Cheng Yuanxing. *Xin Zhongguo Waijiao Douzheng Zhuiyi: Linghui Mao Zedong De Xiongcai Dalue* (Recollections on New China's Diplomatic Struggle: Understanding Mao Zedong's Tremendous Talents). Beijing: Zhongyang Wenxian Chubanshe, 2011.
Cohen, Robert Carl. *Black Crusader: A Biography of Robert Franklin Williams*. New York: Lyle Stuart, 1972.
Cohen, Warren I. *America's Response to China: A History of Sino-American Relations*. 4th ed. New York: Columbia University Press, 2000.
——. "While China Faced East: Chinese-American Cultural Relations, 1949–1971." In *Educational Exchanges: Essays on Sino-American Experience*, ed. Joyce K. Kallgren and Denis Fred Simon, 44–57. Berkeley: Institute of East Asian Studies University of California, Berkeley, 1987.
Committee of Concerned Asian Scholars. *China! Inside the People's Republic*. New York: Bantam Books, 1972.

Cong Jin. *Quzhe Fazhan De Suiyue: 1945–1989 Nian De Zhongguo* (The Years of Tortuous Development: China, 1945–1989). Zhengzhou: Henan Renmin Chubanshe, 1989.

Cook, Alexander C. ed. *Mao's Little Red Book: A Global History*. New York: Cambridge University Press, 2014.

Davenport, Christian. *How Social Movements Die: Repression and Demobilization of the Republic of New Africa*. New York: Cambridge University Press, 2016.

Du Bois, Shirley Graham. *His Day Is Marching On: A Memoir of W. E. B. Du Bois*. Philadelphia: J. B. Lippincott, 1971.

Du Bois, W. E. B. *The Autobiography of W. E. B. Du Bois: A Soliloquy on Viewing My Life from the Last Decade of Its First Century*. New York: Oxford University Press, 2007.

———. "Our Visit to China," *China Pictorial*, March 20, 1959, 6–7.

Eckstein, Ruth. "Ping Pong Diplomacy: A View from the Behind the Scenes." *Journal of American-East Asian Relations* 2, no. 3 (Fall 1993): 327–42.

Epstein, Israel. *The Unfinished Revolution in China*. Boston: Little, Brown, 1947.

Fairbank, Wilma. *American Cultural Experiment in China, 1942–1949*. Washington, DC: U.S. Government Printing Office, 1976.

Fan, Shuhua. *The Harvard-Yenching Institute and Cultural Engineering: Remaking the Humanities in China, 1924–1951*. Lanham, MD: Lexington Books, 2014.

Fenn, William P. *Ever New Horizon: The Story of the United Board for Christian Higher Education in Asia, 1922–1975*. North Newton, KS: Mennonite Press, 1980.

Fraser, Steward, ed. *Government Policy and International Education*. New York: John Wiley & Sons, 1965.

Frazier, Robeson Taj. *The East Is Black: Cold War China in the Black Radical Imagination*. Durham, NC: Duke University Press, 2015.

French, Paul. *Through the Looking Glass: China's Foreign Journalists from Opium War to Mao*. Hong Kong: Hong Kong University Press, 2009.

Fried, Richard M. *The Russians Are Coming! The Russians Are Coming! Pageantry and Patriotism in Cold-War America*. New York: Oxford University Press, 1998.

Fu Ying. "Xiang Zhenli Touxiang" (Surrender to the Truth). *Wenhui Bao*, May 4, 1958.

Gao Hua. *Hong Taiyang Shi Zenyang Shengqi De: Yanan Zhengfeng Yundong De Lailong Qumai* (How Did the Red Sun Rise: A History of the Yanan Rectification Movement). Hong Kong: Hong Kong Chinese University Press, 2000.

Gao, Yunxiang. *Arise, Africa! Roar, China!: Black and Chinese Citizens of the World in the Twentieth Century*. Chapel Hill: University of North Carolina Press, 2021.

Gittings, John. *Survey of the Sino-Soviet Dispute*. New York: Oxford University Press, 1968.

Glazer, Nathan. "American Values & American Foreign Policy." *Commentary* 62, no. 1 (July 1, 1976): 32–36.

Gong Li. *Mao Zedong Yu Meiguo* (Mao Zedong and the United States). Beijing: Shijie Zhishi Chubanshe, 1999.

Gore, Daro F. "From Communist Politics to Black Power: The Visionary Politics and Transnational Solidarity of Victoria 'Vicki' Ama Garvin." In *Want to Start a Revolution? Radical Women in the Black Freedom Struggle*, ed. Daro F. Gore et al., 71–94. New York: New York University Press, 2009.

Haddad, John R. *America's First Adventure in China: Trade, Treaties, Opium, and Salvation*. Philadelphia: Temple University Press, 2013.

Hamilton, John Maxwell. *Edgar Snow: A Biography*. Bloomington: Indiana University Press, 1988.

He Guozhu. "Gei Lianheguo Mishuzhang Xie Gongkaixin" (Writing the Open Letter to the United Nations' Secretary General). In *1950 Niandai Guiguo LiuMei Kexuejia Fangtanlu* (Interviews with Scientists Returned from the United States in the 1950s), ed. Hou Xianglin et al., 288–314. Changsha: Hunan Jiaoyu Chubanshe, 2013.

Heald, Morrell, and Lawrence S. Kaplan. *Culture and Diplomacy: The American Experience*. Westport, CT: Greenwood Press, 1977.

He Dongchang, ed. *Zhonghua Renmin Gongheguo Zhongyao Jiaoyu Wenxian, 1949–1997* (Important Documents on Education in the People's Republic of China, 1949–1997). 3 vols. Changsha: Hainan Chubanshe, 1998.

He Jiefu. "Xingzhengyuan Fudao Qiaosheng Huiguo Shengxue Zhengce Zhi Yanjiu" (A Study of the Executive Council's Policy on Helping Overseas Chinese Return for Education). PhD diss., National Chengchi University, Taiwan, 1975.

Hessler, Peter. "Broken Bonds." *The New Yorker*, March 16, 2020, 69–85.

Hixson, Walter. *Parting the Curtain: Propaganda, Culture, and the Cold War, 1945–1961*. New York: St. Martin's Press, 1997.

Hollander, Paul. *Political Pilgrims: Travel of Western Intellectuals to the Soviet Union, China, and Cuba, 1928–1978*. New York: Oxford University Press, 1981.

Holm, David. *Art and Ideology in Revolutionary China*. Oxford: Clarendon Press, 1991.

Hooper, Beverley. *Foreigners Under Mao: Western Lives in China, 1949–1976*. Hong Kong: Hong Kong University Press, 2016.

Horne, Gerald. *Black & Red: W. E. B. Du Bois and the Afro-American Response to the Cold War, 1944–1963*. Albany: State University of New York Press, 1985.

Hou Xianglin et al. *1950 Niandai Guiguo LiuMei Kexuejia Fangtanlu* (Interviews with Scientists Returned from the United States in the 1950s). Changsha: Hunan Jiaoyu Chubanshe, 2013.

Huang, Hua. *Huang Hua Memoirs*. Beijing: Foreign Language Press, 2008.

Huang Junjie. *Nongfuhui Yu Taiwan Jingyan* (The Joint Commission of Rural Reconstruction and the Taiwan Experiences). Taipei: Sanmin Shuju, 1991.

Huang Renguo. *Jiaoyu Yu Zhengzhi, Jingji De Sanxiang Hudong* (The Three-Dimensional Interaction Among Education, Politics, and Economy). Beijing: Shijie Zhishi Chubanshe, 2010.

Iriye, Akira. "Culture and Power: International Relations as Intercultural Relations." *Diplomatic History* 3, no. 2 (Spring 1979): 115–28.

Jeffries, Judson L. ed. *Black Power in the Belly of the Beast*. Urbana: University of Illinois Press, 2006.

Ji, Chaozhu. *The Man on Mao's Right: From Harvard Yard to Tiananmen Square: My Life Inside China's Foreign Ministry*. New York: Random House, 2008.

Jiang Jiannong and Benquan Wang. *Sinuo Yu Zhongguo* (Snow and China). Haerbing: Heilongjiang Renmin Chubanshe, 1993.

Jin Chongji. *Zhou Enlai Zhuan* (The Biography of Zhou Enlai). Beijing: Zhongyang Wenxian Chubanshe, 1998.

Kelley, Robin D. G., and Betsy Esch. "Black Like Mao: *Red China and Black Revolution*." *Souls* 1, no. 4 (1999): 6–41.

King, Marjorie. *China's American Daughter: Ida Pruitt (1888–1985)*. Hong Kong: The Chinese University Press, 2006.

Kissinger, Henry. *White House Years*. Boston: Little, Brown, 1979.

Lampton, David. *A Relationship Restored: Trends in U.S.-China Educational Exchange, 1979–1984*. Washington, DC: National Academy Press, 1986.

Lanza, Fabio. *The End of Concern: Maoist China, Activism, and Asian Studies*. Durham, NC: Duke University Press, 2017.

Li, Cheng, ed. *Bridging Minds Across the Pacific: U.S.-China Educational Exchanges, 1978–2003*. Lanham, MD: Lexington Books, 2005.

———. "Reforming and Opening-Up, 1979–2016." In *Finding Firmer Ground: The Role of Higher Education in U.S.-China Relations*, ed. Yawei Liu and Michael Cerny, 37–47. Atlanta, GA: Carter Center, 2022.

Li, Danhui. "The Collapse of Party Relations and the Deterioration of State Relations, October 1961–July 1964." In *A Short History of Sino-Soviet Relations, 1917–1991*, ed. Zhihua Shen, ed., 247–66. New York: Palgrave Macmillan, 2020.

Li Hengde. "Buqu De Douzheng Zihao De Shengli" (The Unyielding Fight and the Proud Triumph). In *Jianguo Chuqi Liuxuesheng Guiguo Jishi* (Records of the Students Returned from Overseas in the Early Period of Nations), ed. Quanguo Zhengxie, 32–92. Beijing: Zhongguo Wenshi Chubanshe, 1999.

———. "Fuze Bianji 'LiuMei Kexie Tongxun' " (In Charge of Editing the Newsletter for Chinese Science and Technology Workers in the United States). In *1950 Niandai Guiguo LiuMei Kexuejia Fangtanlu* (Interviews with Scientists Returned from the United States in the 1950s), ed. Hou Xianglin et al., 194–225. Changsha: Hunan Jiaoyu Chubanshe, 2013.

Li, Hongshan. "Building a Black Bridge: China's Interactions with African-American Activists in the Cold War." *Journal of Cold War Studies* 20, no. 3 (Summer 2018): 114–52.

———. *U.S.-China Educational Exchange: State, Society, and Intercultural Relations, 1905–1950*. New Brunswick, NJ: Rutgers University Press, 2008.

———. "The Hidden Helping Hand: The U.S. Government's Assistance to Chinese Returnees, 1949–1955." *Frontiers of History in China* 11, no. 1 (2016): 95–134.

Lin Ke et al. *Lishi De Chengshi: Mao Zedong Shenbian Gongzuo Renyuan De Zhengyan* (Historical Honesty: The Testimonies of Mao's Staff Members). Hong Kong: Liwen Chubanshe, 1995.

Liu, Kin-ming, ed. *My First Trip to China*. Hong Kong: East Slope Publishing Limited, 2012.

Lucas, Scott. *Freedom's War: The U.S. Crusade Against the Soviet Union 1945–56*. Manchester: Manchester University Press, 1999.

Lutz, Jessie Gregory. *China and the Christian Colleges, 1850–1950*. Ithaca, NY: Cornell University Press, 1971.

Maiye Herxieer. *Zuihou De Huanxiang* (The Last Illusions). Trans. Wu Pengwu. Beijing: Shijie Zhishi Chubanshe, 1955.

Mao Zedong. *Mao Zedong Xuanji* (Selected Works of Mao Zedong). Beijing: Renmin Chubanshe, 1969.

———. *Mao Zedong Xuanji* (Selected Works of Mao Zedong). 5 vols. Beijing: Renmin Chubanshe, 1977.

Mayhew, Christopher. *A War of Words: A Cold War Witness*. London: I. B. Tauris, 1998.

Millwood, Pete. "An 'Exceedingly Delicate Undertaking': Sino-American Science Diplomacy, 1966–1978." *Journal of Contemporary History* 56, no. 1 (2021): 166–90.

Milton, David, and Nancy Dall Milton. *The Wind Will Not Subside: Years in Revolutionary China—1964–1969*. New York: Pantheon Books, 1976.

Mirsky, Jonathan. "From Mao Fan to Counter-Revolutionary in 48 Hours." In Liu, *My First Trip to China*, 24–28.

Mullen, Bill V., and Cathryn Watson, eds. *W. E. B. Du Bois on Asia: Crossing the World Color Line*. Jackson: University Press of Mississippi, 2005.

Murray, Douglas P. "Exchange with the People's Republic of China: Symbols and Substance." *Annals* 424 (March 1976): 29–42.

Nathan, Andrew. "Nan De Hu Tu." In Liu, *My First Trip to China*, 197–206.

Niu Jun. *Lengzhan Shiqi De Zhongguo Zhanlue Juece* (China's Strategic Decisions in the Cold War). Beijing: Shijie Zhishi Chubanshe, 2019.

Nixon, Richard. *The Memoirs of Richard Nixon*. New York: Grosset & Dunlap, 1978.

Noyes, Henry. *China Born: Adventures of a Maverick Bookman.* San Francisco: China Books & Periodicals, 1989.

Onaci, Edward. *Free the Land: The Republic of New Afrika and the Pursuit of a Black Nation-State.* Chapel Hill: University of North Carolina Press, 2020.

———. "Self Determination Means Determining Self: Lifestyle Politics and the New Republic of Africa, 1968–1989." PhD diss., University of Illinois at Urbana-Champaign, 2012.

Oyen, Meredith. *The Diplomacy of Migration: Transnational Lives and the Making of U.S.-Chinese Relations in the Cold War.* Ithaca, NY: Cornell University Press, 2015.

Peng Yaxin. *Zhonggong Zhongyang Nanfangju De Wenhua Gongzuo* (The Cultural Work of the Southern Bureau of the Chinese Communist Party Central Committee). Beijing: Zhonggong Dangshi Chubanshe, 2009.

Qian Jiang. *Ping Pong Waijiao Shimo* (The History of Ping Pong Diplomacy). Beijing: Dongfang Chubanshe, 1987.

Qing, Simei. *From Allies to Enemies: Visions of Modernity, Identity, and U.S.-China Diplomacy, 1945–1960.* Cambridge, MA: Harvard University Press, 2007.

Qinghua Daxue Xiaoshi Yanjiushi. *Qinghua Daxue Shiliao Xuanbian* (Selected Historical Records of the Qinghua University). 4 vols. Beijing: Qinghua Daxue Chubanshe, 1994.

Quanguo Zhengxie, ed. *Jianguo Chuqi Liuxuesheng Guiguo Jishi* (The Records of the Students Returned from Overseas in the Early Period of the Nation). Beijing: Zhongguo Wenshi Chubanshe, 1999.

Ransby, Barbara. *Eslanda: The Large and Unconventional Life of Mrs. Paul Robeson.* New Haven, CT: Yale University Press, 2013.

Richmond, Yale. *Cultural Exchange and the Cold War: Raising the Iron Curtain.* University Park: Pennsylvania State University Press, 2003.

———. *Practice Public Diplomacy: A Cold War Odyssey.* New York: Berghahn Books, 2008.

Rittenberg, Sidney, and Amanda Bennett. *The Man Who Stayed Behind.* New York: Simon & Schuster, 1993.

Robeson, Eslanda. "World Woman Number One." *New World Review* 19, no. 5 (July 1951): 20–27.

Ross, Robert S., and Jiang Changbin, ed. *Re-examining the Cold War: U.S.-China Diplomacy, 1954–1973.* Cambridge, MA: Harvard University Press, 2001.

Russel, Maud. *New People in New China: Some Personal Glimpses of People in China.* New York: Far East Reporter, 1959.

Saunders, Stonor. *The Cultural Cold War: The CIA and the World of Arts and Letters.* New York: New Press, 1999.

Seale, Bobby. *Seize the Time: The Story of the Black Panther Party and Huey P. Newton.* New York: Random House, 1970.

Shapiro, Fred C., and James W. Sullivan. *Race Riots, New York, 1964.* New York: Crowell, 1964.

Shi Zhe. *Wo De Yisheng: Shi Zhe Zishu* (My Life: A Self-Narrative). Beijing: Renmin Chubanshe, 2001.

Smith, Kathlin. "The Role of Scientists in Normalizing the U.S.-China Relations, 1965–1979." *Annals of the New York Academy of Science* 866, no. 1 (December 1998): 114–36.

Snow, Edgar. "A Conversation with Mao Tse-tung." *Life*, April 30, 1971, 48–50.

———. *Journey to the Beginning.* New York: Random House, 1958.

———. *The Other Side of the River: Red China Today.* New York: Random House, 1962.

———. "Recognition of the People's Republic of China." *Annals of the American Academy of Political and Social Science* 324 (July 1959): 75–88.

———. *Red China Today.* New York: Vintage Books, 1971.

———. "Red China's Leaders Talk Peace-On Their Own Terms." *Look*, January 31, 1961, 86–98.

———. *Red Star Over China.* New York: Random House, 1938.

Song Jian. *Liangdan Yixing Yuanxun* (The Two Bombs and One Satellite Heroes). 2 vols. Beijing: Qinghua Daxue Chubanshe, 2001.

Spence, Jonathan. *To Change China: Western Advisers in China, 1620–1960.* New York: Penguin Books, 1980.

Stanford, Maxwell C. "Revolutionary Action Movement (RAM): A Case Study of an Urban Revolutionary Movement in Western Capitalist Society." MA thesis, Atlanta University, May 1985.

Strohm, John. "How They Hate Us in Red China." *Reader's Digest*, January 1959, 30–39.

Strong, Anna Louise. *Cash and Violence in Laos and Viet Nam.* New York: Mainstream Publishing, 1962.

———. *Letters from China.* Beijing: New World Press, 1963.

———. *The Rise of the Chinese People's Communes.* Beijing: New World Press, 1959.

———. *Sidalin Shidai* (The Stalin Era). Trans. Shi Ren. Beijing: Shijie Zhishi Chuban She, 1959.

———. *The Thought of Mao Zedong.* New York: Amerasia, 1947.

———. *Tibetan Interviews.* Beijing: New World Press, 1959.

———. *Tomorrow's China.* New York: Committee for a Democratic Far Eastern Policy, 1948.

———. *When Serfs Stood up in Tibet.* Beijing: New World Press, 1960.

Strong, Tracy B., and Helene Keyssar. "Anna Louise Strong: Three Interviews with Chairman Mao Zedong." *China Quarterly*, no. 103 (September 1985): 489–509.

———. *Right in Her Soul: The Life of Anna Louise Strong.* New York: Random House, 1983.

Stueck, William. *The Korean War: An International History*. Princeton, NJ: Princeton University Press, 1995.
Su Jingjing and Daqing Zhang. "Xin Zhongguo Shouci FuMei Yixue Daibiaotuan Zhi Tanjiu" (Exploration of China's First Medical Delegation's Visit to the United States). *Zhongguo Kejishi Zazhi* (Journal of Chinese History of Science and Technology) 32, no. 3 (2011): 395–405.
Tao Wenzhao. *ZhongMei Guanxi Shi, 1949–2000* (A History of China-U.S. Relations, 1949–2000). 3 vols. Shanghai: Shanghai Renmin Chubanshe, 2004.
Topping, Seymour. *Journey Between Two Chinas*. New York: Harper & Row, 1972.
Tucker, Nancy Bernkopf. *Taiwan, Hong Kong, and the United States, 1945–1992: Uncertain Friendship*. New York: Twayne Publishers, 1994.
Tyson, Timothy. *Radio Free Dixie: Robert F. Williams & the Roots of Black Power*. Chapel Hill: University of North Carolina Press, 1999.
Vogel, Ezra F. "China Before the Deng Transformation." In Liu, *My First Trip to China*, 190–92.
Wales, Nym. *Inside Red China*. New York: Doubleday, Doran & Co., 1939.
Wang Bingnan. *ZhongMei Huitan Jiunian Huigu* (Memoir of the Nine-Year Sino-American Talks). Beijing: Shijie Zhishi Chubanshe, 1985.
Wang Delu, ed. *1950 Niandai Guiguo LiuMei Kexuejia Fangtanlu* (Interviews with Scientists Returned from the United States in the 1950s). Changsha: Hunan Jiaoyu Chubanshe, 2013.
Wang Huanxun. *Hu Shi Jiaoyu Sixiang Pipan Yinlun* (An Introduction to the Denunciation of Hu Shi's Educational Thoughts). Wuhan: Hubei Renmin Chubanshe, 1956.
Wang Licheng. *Meiguo Wenhua Shentou Yu Jindai Zhongguo Jiaoyu: Hujiang Daxue De Lishi* (American Cultural Penetration and Modern Chinese Education: The History of Shanghai University). Shanghai: Fudan University Press, 2000.
West, Philip. *Yenching University and Sino-Western Relations*. Cambridge, MA: Harvard University Press, 1976.
Westad, Odd Arne, ed. *Brothers in Arms: The Rise and Fall of the Sino-Soviet Alliance, 1945–1963*. Washington, DC: Woodrow Wilson Center Press, 1998.
White, Theodore. *In Search of History: A Personal Adventure*. New York: Warner Books, 1978.
Whiting, Allen S. *China Crosses the Yalu: The Decision to Enter the Korean War*. Redwood City, CA: Stanford University Press, 1960.
Wilbur, C. Martin. "Sino-American Relations in Scholarship as Viewed from the United States." In *U.S.-ROC Relations: From the White Paper to Taiwan Relations Act*, ed. Cecilia S. T. Chang, 89–145. New York: Institute of Asian Studies, St. John's University, 1984.
Williams, Robert. *Negroes with Guns*. New York: Marzani & Munsell, 1962.

Wills, Morris R. *Turncoat: An American's 12 Years in Communist China.* Englewood Cliffs, NJ: Prentice-Hall, 1966.

Winnington, Alan. *Breakfast with Mao: Memoirs of a Foreign Correspondent.* London: Lawrence and Wishart, 1986.

Wu, Ningkun. *A Single Tear: A Family's Persecution, Love, and Endurance in Communist China.* Boston: Little, Brown, 1993.

Xia Chenghua. "Yijiusijiu Nian Yilai De Zhonghua Minguo Qiaosheng Jiaoyu Huigu." (Recollections of the Republic of China's Education for Overseas Chinese Since 1949) *Yanxi Zixun* (Information on Research and Learning) 23, no. 2 (April 2006): 23–33.

Xia, Yafeng. *Negotiating with the Enemy: U.S.-China Talks During the Cold War.* Bloomington: Indiana University Press, 2006.

Xiong Xianghui. "Dakai ZhongMei Guanxi De Qianzou: 1969 Nian Siwei Laoshuai Dui Guoji Xingshi De Yanpan He Jianyi De Qianqian Houhou" (The Prelude to the Opening of the Sino-American Relations: Research and Recommendations on International Relations by Four Senior Marshals in 1969). In Zhonggong Zhongyang Dangshi Ziliao Zhengji Weiyuanhui, *Zhonggong Dangshi Ziliao* (Historical Materials of the Chinese Communist Party), 42:56–96. Beijing: Zhonggong Dangshi Ziliao Chubanshe, 1992.

Xu, Guangqiu. "The Ideological and Political Impact of U.S. Fulbrighters on Chinese Students: 1979–1989." *Asian Affairs: An American Review* 26, no. 3 (Fall 1999): 139–57.

Xu, Guoqi. *Olympic Dreams: China and Sports, 1895–2008.* Cambridge, MA: Harvard University Press, 2008.

Yu Fengzheng. *Gaizao* (Reform). Zhengzhou: Henan Renmin Chubanshe, 2001.

Yu Qi. "Changzheng Duiwai Xuanchuan De 'Sange Diyi' " (The Three Firsts in International Propaganda on the Long March). *Jundui Zhenggong Lilun Yanjiu* (Theoretical Studies of the Army Political Work) 17, no. 4 (August 2016): 51–52.

Zhai, Qiang. *China and the Vietnam Wars, 1950–1975.* Chapel Hill: University of North Carolina Press, 2000.

Zhang Pengyuan. "Cong Taiwan Kan ZhongMei Jin Sanshi Nian Zhi Xueshu Jiaoliu" (An Examination of Sino-American Academic Exchange in the Past Thirty Years from Taiwan's Perspective). *Hanxue Yanjiu* (Sinology Research) 2, no. 1 (June 1984): 23–56.

Zhang, Shuguang. *Economic Cold War: America's Embargo Against China and the Sino-Soviet Alliance, 1949–1963.* Stanford, CA: Stanford University Press, 2002.

Zhang Wei. "Kangzhan Shiqi De Guomindang Duiwai Xuanchuan Ji Meiguo Jizhe Qun" (Nationalist Government Foreign Propaganda and American Journalists in the War Against Japan). *Hangzhou Shifan Daxue Xuebao* (Shehui Kexue

Ban) (Journal of Hangzhou Normal University, Social Science Edition) 5 (September 2008): 39.

Zhang Xianqiu. *Nongfuhui Huiyi Lu* (A Memoir of the Joint Committee on Rural Reconstruction). Taipei: Xingzhengyuan Nongye Weiyuanhui, 1990.

Zhang Xizhe. *Zhonghua Minguo De Qiaosheng Jiaoyu* (Education for Overseas Chinese Students in the Republic of China). Taipei: Zhongzheng Shuju, 1991.

Zhao Jichang. *Meiyuan De Yunyong* (The Use of American Aid). Taipei: Lianjing Chubangshe, 1985.

Zhao Qina. "Meiguo Zhengfu Zai Taiwan De Jiaoyu Yu Wenhua Jiaoliu Huodong, (Yijiuwuyi Zhi Yijiuqiling Nian)" (The U.S. Government's Educational and Cultural Exchange Activities in Taiwan from 1951 to 1970). *OuMei Yanjiu* (Research on Europe and America) 31, no. 1 (March 2001): 79–127.

Zhongyang Dianshitai, ed. *Zhongyang Dianshitai De Diyi Yu Bianqian* (China Central Television's Firsts and Changes). Beijing: Dongfang Chubanshe, 2003.

Zhou Qingan and Di Wang. "Cong Waijiao Dangan Kan Zhongguo Zhengzhi Chuanbo Qibu: 1956–1957 Zhongguo Zhengfu Dui Waiguo Jizhe Guanli Zhidu Shi Chutan" (An Examination on the Beginning of China's Political Communication Based on Diplomatic Archives: A Preliminary History of the Management System Established by the Chinese Government for Foreign Journalists). *Xiandai Chuanbo* (Modern Communications) 34, no. 6 (2014): 29–30.

Zhu Jihua, ed. *Dangan Jiemi Waijiao Fengyun* (Exposing Secrecy in Diplomatic History Through the Archives). Shanghai: Xuelin Chubanshe, 2015.

Zhu Jingxian. *Huaqiao Jiaoyu* (Overseas Chinese Education). Taipei: Zhonghua Shuju, 1973.

Zhu Jiping. *Genxi Zhonghua: Zhuming Guiguo Kexuejia Caifeng* (Rooted in China: Reports on Famous Returned Scientists). Hefei: Anhui Jiaoyu Chubanshe, 1997.

Zulueta, Benjamin C. "Master of the Master Gland: Choh Hao Li, the University of California, and Science, Migration, and Race." *Historical Studies in Natural Science* 39, no. 2 (2009): 129–70.

Index

abortion, in China, 328
Acheson, Dean: dream of "peaceful evolution" in PRC, 329; protests received from Chinese students, 53; response to Sino-Soviet treaty, 48; thought reform at, 27; and U.S. policy on Taiwan, 125, 127–28, 370n5; and the U.S. trade embargo, 60; on U.S. vs. Chinese response to criticism, 25
ACLU. *See* American Civil Liberties Union
ACSW. *See* Association of Chinese Science Workers
acupuncture, 295, 313
Adams, Clarence, 232–34
Adkinson, Richard, 318
Adler, Solomon, 204
Advisory Committee on Emergency Aid to Chinese Students (ACEACS), 39
Africa: Du Bois and, 243, 248–49, 255–56; independence movements, 246; PRC and, 231, 239, 243, 247, 248–49; U.S. interventions in, 178. *See also specific countries*
African Americans: and armed struggle/revolution, 243, 250–54, 264, 266–70, 319 (*see also under* Williams, Robert F.); assassination plot against moderate Black leaders, 281–82; Beijing's alliance with radical leaders, 11, 242–43 (*see also specific individuals*); Black Nationalist movement, 268–70, 275–78 (*see also* Black Panther Party; Republic of New Africa; Revolutionary Action Movement); Black soldiers, 233–34; Chinese propaganda about, 46; civil rights (liberation) struggle, 235–39, 243, 254–55, 257, 268–69 (*see also* Civil Rights Act; *specific leaders*); encouraged toward armed revolution, 250–53; freedom from racism desired, 184, 214; Garvin's classes and lectures on, 235–39,

African Americans (*continued*)
393n133, 394n147; international support for, 257, 260; invited to visit PRC (generally), 11, 214–15, 242–43, 247 (*see also specific individuals*); journalists, 178 (*see also* Worthy, William); and the judicial system, 282, 287; liberation movement studied at Nankai Univ., 391n95; PRC support for struggle against discrimination, 257, 258–67, 269–71, 280, 286–87, 305, 319 (*see also* Mao Zedong — and the African American struggle); PRC visited (1970s), 304–5; racial struggle as class struggle, 258, 264–65, 278, 283–84; return to nonviolence, 281; violent protests, 269–70, 276, 277–78, 284; Williams on extent of U.S. racism, 264; working in PRC, 234–41. *See also specific organizations and individuals*

"Ain't Gonna Study War No More" (spiritual), 248

Allen, Ernest, 268

Allen, George, 36, 39–40

Alley, Rewi, 212, 226

ambassadorial talks (U.S.–PRC): cultural exchange discussed, 163–64, 176–77; interrupted following U.S. invasion of Cambodia, 294; on journalistic reciprocity, 195–97; PRC's goals and priorities for, 161, 163; repatriation of Chinese students and U.S. prisoners negotiated, 97, 99–100, 103–12, 118, 163–64 (*see also* Geneva Conference); restarted, 292–94

America as enemy: anti-American movements in PRC, 6, 50–66, 177, 207, 219–20 (*see also* Resist America and Aid Korea movement); during/after civil war, 14–16, 18, 26–27; Mao and, 16, 18, 26–27, 51–52, 54, 86, 164–65, 198, 202; primacy of Mao Zedong Thought and, 23; Strong on, 212; Taiwan issue and, 86, 162 (*see also* Taiwan; Taiwan Strait); after Tiananmen Square massacre, 329; U.S. accused of using biological weapons, 244. *See also* cultural aggression, American

American and Australian Affairs Division (under MFA), 53, 104–6, 165, 248, 379n23

American Civil Liberties Union (ACLU), 83, 282–83, 403n8

American Council of Learned Societies, 310

American cultural and educational institutions (in China): considered "cultural aggression," 6, 8, 27, 72, 202 (*see also* cultural aggression, American); registration of, 61–62; restrictions on, 14, 16–17, 19–21, 25–26; taken over, nationalized, and reformed by CCP/PRC, 3, 6, 7–9, 14, 50, 61–75. *See also* colleges and universities (China); hospitals; journalism in China; missionary colleges and universities; missionary schools; *specific institutions*

American imperialism. *See* America as enemy; cultural aggression, American

"American Imperialist Religious and Cultural Aggression in China" (Wei), 59

American journalists: authorized to visit PRC despite travel ban, 10, 161–62, 189–90, 193–94, 225–26, 229; Chinese visa applications, 169, 172, 178, 179; courted by CCP, during

[434] INDEX

civil war, 17–18, 165–66; invited to visit PRC in 1950s–60s (generally), 10, 161–62, 164–69, 177–78, 195–96, 198, 218–20, 380n31 (*see also* Snow, Edgar; Strong, Anna Louise; Worthy, William; *and other individuals*); PRC visited, as relations thawed, 301–3; reciprocity issue, 194–200, 217, 225–26, 229; refused admittance to PRC (1950s), 10, 196–200, 220–21; restricted/banned under CCP, 13, 17–20, 24, 165, 170; travel ban broken, 10, 161, 177–87; travel ban challenged, 169–72. *See also* journalism in China; news organizations, American; *specific individuals*
American Medical Association, 310
American Newspaper Guild, 190–91
Americans. *See* America as enemy; American cultural and educational institutions; American journalists; United States government; U.S. citizens in China; *specific organizations, institutions, and individuals*
American schools and universities (in China), 7–8, 9, 25–32, 57–58, 61–75. *See also* American cultural and educational institutions; colleges and universities (China); *specific institutions*
American Society of Newspaper Editors, 191
American students: in PRC, 318, 319; in Taiwan, 160. *See also* American Youth Delegation
American University, 318
American Youth Delegation, 10, 192–93, 195, 215–18
Anderson, Robert, 101
Andrus, J. Russell, 136, 142

Anti China Atrocities of the New Tsars (PRC film), 290
anticommunist efforts, U.S.: ideological campaign toward Chinese students, 8–9, 13, 33, 39–49; through education, in Taiwan, 141, 145–48, 151, 159–60 (*see also under* overseas Chinese)
Anti-Rightist movement (PRC), 191–92, 199. *See also* rectification movements
armed forces, Chinese. *See* Chinese military; Chinese People's Volunteer Army; People's Liberation Army
armed forces, United States. *See* United States military
Aronson, James, 210
art, American, 327–28
Asia. *See* Southeast Asia; *specific countries*
Asian Foundation, 153
Associated Press (AP): banned/regulated in China, 18–19, 24; reporters in or invited to China, 166, 168, 172–74, 301; reporting on U.S. detention of Chinese students, 98; and the travel ban, 171–73, 190
Association of Chinese Science Workers (ACSW), 44, 45, 45, 78, 82, 102
Association of Journalists (China), 165, 168
Atkinson, Brooks, 166
Atwood, William, 302–3
Austin, Warren, 57–59

Baltimore Afro-American, 167, 168, 186, 289. *See also* Worthy, William
Baltimore Sun, 166
Bandung Conference (1955), 103, 104, 163
Bantam Books, 275–76
Barnett, A. Doak, 228, 276

Bartholomew, Frank, 171, 174–75, 189–90
"bathing" (*xizao*), 72
Beam, Jacob D., 225, 229
Becker, Loftus, 193–94
Beijing (city): American cultural institutions allowed to operate in, 25–26; American journalists in, 24, 180–81, 183–84 (*see also* American journalists); BSO concert in, 322; International Bookstore, 209; model units in, 181; news organizations in, 20, 24; society for families of Chinese students in U.S., 118; USIS office shut down, 25. *See also* National Day celebrations; Tiananmen Square protests; *specific businesses and institutions*
Beijing (PRC government). *See* Chinese Communist Party; Chinese Communist Party Central Committee; People's Republic of China; *specific ministries, committees, and individuals*
Beijing First Textile Factory, 181, 184
Beijing Foreign Language Institute, 231, 234
Beijing Normal University, 56, 73
Beijing University. *See* Peking (Beijing) University
Berding, Andrew, 190
Bergman, Leibel, 238
Black Liberation Front, 269
"Black Militant in Red China Sizes Up 'Cultural Revolution'" (R. Williams), 289
Black Nationalist movement, 268–70, 275–78. *See also* Black Panther Party; Revolutionary Action Movement
Black Panther Party, 275, 305
Boggs, James and Grace, 269

Bo Gu, 166
Boston Symphony Orchestra, 322
Boxer indemnity, 3, 27
Brady, Anne-Marie, 204, 214
brainwashing. *See* propaganda, Chinese Communist; rectification movements; thought reform
Breen, Robert, 163
Brent, J. I., 149–50
Brick, R. M., 78
Brickley, James, 291
Bridgeman Middle School for Girls, 62–63
British Communist Party, 252–53
Brown, Elaine, 305
Brown, H. Emmett, 138, 146
Brownell, Herbert, Jr., 94, 363n36
Brucker, Herbert, 171, 175
Bureau of Publications, 28
Burger, Warren, 327–28
Burgess, Dwight, 285
Bush, George H. W., 326, 329
Byers, John, 48

Caldwell, Oliver J., 42
California Institute of Technology (CIT), 52, 102, 138, 359n99
Cambodia, 153, 156, 209, 257, 294, 298
Canada, 95, 160, 307, 317
Canham, Erwin, 171
Carmichael, Stokely, 277–78, 282
Carter, Jimmy, 317, 318–19, 325, 326, 328
CAS. *See* Chinese Academy of Science
Cash and Violence in Laos and Viet Nam (A. L. Strong), 209
CAST (China Association for Science and Technology), 310, 312
Catholic Church, 30–31. *See also* Gross, Fulgence, Fr.; Shanahan, Cormac, Fr.

CBS (Columbia Broadcasting Company). *See* Columbia Broadcasting Company
CCAS. *See* Committee of Concerned Asian Scholars
CCP. *See* Chinese Communist Party
CCPCC. *See* Chinese Communist Party Central Committee
CCPDWP. *See* Committee of the Chinese People Defending World Peace
Central Intelligence Agency (CIA), 312
Central Military Committee (CCP), 86
Chang, Iris, 53
Chang, T. K., 140
Chen Cheng, 146–47, 149, 150
Cheng, Tien-fong (Cheng Tianfang), 136, 147
Cheng Yan-fen (Zheng Yanfen), 145–46, 147. *See also* Overseas Chinese Affairs Commission
Chen Hansheng, 205, 244
Chen Shutong, 101, 108
Chen Tianchi (Chen Tien-Chih), 78
Chen Yi: and the African American struggle, 260; and Du Bois, 248, 261; and Pankey, 215; and Qian's return, 108; and M. Reiss, 203; and the Soviet threat, 293; and A. L. Strong, 206, 212
Chen Yuan, 30–31, 73. *See also* Fu Jen University
Chester, Christian, 208
Chiang Kai-shek. *See* Jiang Jieshi
Chiang Monlin (Jiang Menglin), 131, 142
Chicago Daily Tribune, 24
China (pre-revolution): American cultural institutions in (*see* American cultural and educational institutions; missionary colleges and universities); Communists' rise to power, 3–4 (*see also* Chinese Communist Party; civil war); democratic ideals accepted in principle, 3; first arrival of American merchants, sailors (1784), 57–57; modern education system [after American model], 3, 8; Qing government forced to pay Boxer indemnity, 27; science embraced, 3; war with Japan, 21 (*see also* World War II). *See also* civil war
China Aid Act (U.S., 1948), 37, 40
China Area Aid Act (U.S., 1950), 48–49, 76. *See also* Chinese students and scholars, in U.S.
China Association for Science and Technology (CAST), 310, 312
China Books & Periodicals (U.S. company), 209, 275
China Central Television, 322, 323
China Daily Distribution Corporation, 333
China Daily News (*Huaqiao Ribao*), 45
China Film and Exhibition Corporation, 322
China Global Television Network, 333
China Institute in America (CIIA), 34, 43, 46–47. *See also* Meng, Chih
China International Travel Agency, 168, 180, 182. *See also* interpreters
China International Travel Service, 316
"China: New Hope of Oppressed Humanity" (R. Williams), 267
China Pictorial (*Zhongguo Huabao*), 233, 249
China Reconstructs (*Zhongguo Jianshe*), 203, 205, 222
China's Red Army Marches (Smedley), 166
China Welfare Appeal Inc., 244
Chinese Academy of Science (CAS), 53, 108, 242–44, 310, 312, 318

Chinese Communist Party (CCP):
absolute control maintained, 309,
313–14, 321, 332; and the African
American struggle, 257, 258–61
(*see also* African Americans);
American ideals/culture deemed
threat to revolution, 6, 12, 14;
American influences rejected,
eradicated, 6–9, 16–17 (*see also*
American cultural and educational
institutions; cultural aggression); and
American journalists (*see* American
journalists); anti-American
movements launched, 6, 50–66, 219
(*see also under* America as enemy);
anti-intellectual movements
(generally), 121 (*see also* intellectuals,
Chinese); basic human rights denied
under, 23 (*see also* human rights);
break with Soviet-style Communism,
222; civil war characterized as
national revolution, 14–15;
Constitution (1945), 23; CPUSA
members/sympathizers invited to
PRC, 201–4, 221–25 (*see also* Strong,
Anna Louise); cultural and
educational institutions tightly
controlled, 8–9, 12, 50, 74–75 (*see also*
colleges and universities; education
[China]; missionary colleges and
universities); democracy, freedom
demanded of Nationalist
government, 23–24; under Deng
Xiaoping, 317; early foreign policy,
18–20; expansion of influence in
Southeast Asia, 143–44; foreign
policy rethought, 286–87, 304; Mao
Zedong Thought as guiding
principle, 14, 22–23, 320, 324 (*see also*
Mao Zedong Thought); members and
activities in the U.S., 44–45; news
media tightly controlled
(*see* journalism in China); Ninth CCP
Convention of the Fourth Army
(December 1929), 22; party hierarchy,
235; propaganda (*see* propaganda,
Chinese Communist; Propaganda
Department); reasons for success, 220;
and rectification movements, 14,
22–23, 121, 191–92, 357n2; Seventh
National Congress (March 1949), 21;
Soviet support sought (1949), 24–25;
split with CPSU, 222, 257; and the
Taiwan issue, 86; Third Plenary of
the Seventh National Congress, 30;
and the Tiananmen Square massacre,
321, 324, 329; "unification of
thoughts" under, 63 (*see also* thought
reform); U.S. characterized as enemy
(*see* America as enemy); World War II
collaboration with U.S., 15. *See also*
Chinese Communist Party Central
Committee; civil war; Mao Zedong;
People's Republic of China; *specific
agencies, committees, organizations, and
individuals*

Chinese Communist Party Central
Committee (CCPCC): 1949 Jan.
Politburo meeting and instruction,
18–20; and changing policy toward
U.S., 296; cultural and educational
institutions tightly controlled, 27–28,
30; Deng's address (1978), 320;
documents translated for U.S.-
resident Chinese, 45; educational
reforms instituted, 28–30 (*see also*
education [China]); foreign cultural/
educational institutions restricted,
nationalized, 14, 18–20, 25, 30–32
(*see also under* American cultural and
educational institutions); foreign
journalism banned, 17–20, 24–25

(*see also* journalism in China); and foreign journalists' visits, 17–18, 166–67 (*see also* American journalists); and improving Sino-American relations, 293; and invited Americans' visits, 215, 305; Oct. 26, 1950 directive, 54–57 (*see also* Resist America and Aid Korea movement); peaceful coexistence/transition position rejected, 257; people's communes a priority, 207–8; PLA instructed not to confiscate/destroy foreign institutions, 17; and rectification movements, 22–23 (*see also* rectification movements); "seven prohibitions" instruction, 332; and the Sino-Soviet conflict, 293; and thought reform, 71–72. *See also* Chinese Communist Party; People's Republic of China; *specific ministries, committees, and individuals*

Chinese Economy, The (Adler), 204

Chinese Industrial Cooperative, 224

Chinese Literature (*Zhongguo Wenxue*), 181, 184

Chinese military (under PRC), 293. *See also* Chinese People's Volunteer Army; People's Liberation Army

Chinese National Council of Professional Associations of Natural Science, 53

Chinese Nationalist government: and Chinese students in the U.S., 32–33, 35–36, 39, 102–3, 109–10, 113; cultural war against, in various cities, 22; and education of overseas Chinese, 145–50, 156, 158–59 (*see also under* overseas Chinese); espionage operations, 211; flight to Taiwan, 13, 125; political indoctrination courses, 27; reconquest of mainland China as goal, 140, 144; Sino-American Mutual Defense Treaty, 86, 162–63; and training/education programs for students from Taiwan, 10, 130, 131, 135; and training/education programs within Taiwan, 136; U.S. economic aid to, 6, 13, 27, 123, 128, 139–40; U.S. military aid to, 6, 13, 14–15, 27, 124–28, 144; U.S. objectives and actions regarding (1953), 144–45; U.S. recognition of, 93, 109–10; U.S. support for (generally), 6, 13, 14–16, 18, 27, 123–28. *See also* civil war; Jiang Jieshi; Taiwan; *specific ministries and individuals*

Chinese National Sports Commission (CNSC), 299

Chinese National Table Tennis Team (CNTTT): U.S. team hosted, 300; U.S. visited, 11, 280, 306–8, *308*, 310–11, 411n129; at world championships (1971), 298–300

Chinese People's Association for Friendship with Foreign Nations (CPAFFN), 300, 310, 312

Chinese People's Association for Cultural Relations with Foreign Nations (CPACRFN), 205, 246, 247–48, 304

Chinese People's Political Consultative Conference (CPPCC), 26, 27, 54, 71, 204

Chinese People's Volunteer Army (CPVA), 9, 50, 54, 360n1. *See also* Korean War

"Chinese Revolution and the Chinese Communist Party, The" (Mao), 214

Chinese students and scholars, in U.S.: after 1971, 316–20, 322, 324, 329–31; "adoption" by American families, 46, 47; American community groups

INDEX [439]

Chinese students and scholars (*continued*)
and, 43, 47; categories of, 41; CCP's ideological penetration of, 8–9, 44–45; CIIA and, 43, 46–47 (*see also* China Institute in America); communist sympathizers vetted, denied U.S. aid, 38–39; detained, arrested, or deported, 52–53, 77–80, 82–83, 84–85, 87–90, 92–98, 101–2, 350n4, 363n36; detention orders reviewed, rescinded, 84–85, 87, 90, 94–103, 105, 107, 109–10, 112, 364n53; enabled to remain in U.S., 9, 75–78, 358n91; financial distress, 32–34; Fulbright exchange, 327; information collected by PRC on, 104, 116, 118; letters from China, 117, 119–21; older students preferred by CCP, 330–31; perils of return, 9, 38, 82, 105–6, 119, 121, 369n122; as potential counter to communism in China, 40–42, 46; PRC campaign to get students to return, 114–22; PRC travel subsidies for, 105, 112–13, 117, 118; reluctant to return home, 85, 95, 100–101, 106, 116, 119–22; return home prohibited/allowed during Korean War, 7, 9, 50, 75–83, 79; statistics, 9; U.S. aid to stranded students, 3–4, 6–7, 8–9, 13, 32–40, 48–49, 78, 81, 102–3, 105, 126–27, 365n67 (*see also* Program of Emergency Aid to Chinese Students); U.S. anticommunist ideological campaign and, 8–9, 13, 33, 39–49. *See also specific individuals*
—repatriation conflict, 84–122; Chinese Nationalist government and, 109–10; financial aid for travel, 102–3, 365n67; Geneva Conference negotiations (1954), 84–97; names withheld from PRC, 110; negotiations after Geneva Conference, 97, 99–100, 104–12, 118, 365n74; petitions from students, 97–98; PRC skeptical of freedom to leave, 100, 104–9, 114; results of negotiations mixed, 112–22; return desired by Beijing, 9, 84–85, 114–22; U.S. detention orders reviewed, rescinded, 84–85, 87, 90, 94–103, 105, 107, 109–10, 112, 364n53; U.S. violation of agreement charged, 185

Chinese Students Christian Association in North America (CSCA), 44–45, 102

Chinese Students Protection Act (U.S., 1992), 329–30

Chinese Table Tennis Association, 310. *See also* Chinese National Table Tennis Team

Chou Wen-te, 119

Christian churches. *See* churches

Christians, Chinese, 58–59, 61, 67–68. *See also* churches; missionary colleges and universities; missionary schools

Christian Science Monitor, 166, 168, 171

Chu Anping, 199

Chu Bosheng, 205

Chung Hwa Correspondence School, 154

churches: in China, 17, 30–32, 58–59, 67–68 (*see also* Christians, Chinese; missionary colleges and universities; missionary schools); in U.S., 43, 47

CIA (Central Intelligence Agency), 312

CIIA. *See* China Institute in America

CIT. *See* California Institute of Technology

Civil Rights Act (1964), 237, 284

civil war, in China: 20th anniversary celebration, 293–294; about, 13;

American influences banned/ restricted in CCP-controlled areas, 3, 6, 8, 13–14; Du Bois's views on, 253; end of, 32; foreign journalists in CCP-controlled areas, 13, 17–20, 24, 165–66; Garvin's interest in, 240; impact on Chinese students in the U.S., 32–34, 38 (*see also* Chinese students and scholars, in U.S.); Soviet Republic of China, 264, 276; U.S. aid to Nationalists, 6, 13, 14–15, 16, 18, 27 (*see also* Jiang Jieshi); U.S. characterized as enemy by Mao/ CCP, 14–16, 18, 26–27, 32

class struggle (in U.S.), 237; racial struggle as, 258, 264–65, 278, 283–84

"cleaning house" metaphor, 19, 165

Cleveland, Harland, 35

Clough, Ralph N., 186

Clubb, Oliver, 80–81

CNSC (Chinese National Sports Commission), 299

CNTTT. *See* Chinese National Table Tennis Team

Coe, Frank, 203, 258, 260

Cohen, Robert, 218. *See also* American Youth Delegation

Cold War scholarship, cultural, 5

colleges and universities (China): administrative reforms, 74; American-subsidized institutions seized, nationalized, reformed, 7–8, 9, 30–32, 50, 61–75; graduate programs in Marxism, 332; reforms (1970s), 317; regulations and restrictions imposed, 28–31; and the Resist America and Aid Korea movement, 55–57; and the "seven prohibitions" (2010s), 332; thought reform at, 9, 69–72, 82, 121, 177.

See also missionary colleges and universities; *specific institutions*

colleges and universities (U.S.), 33, 39, 43–44, 47, 333. *See also* Chinese students and scholars, in U.S.; *specific institutions*

Colligan, Francis, 35

colonialism: African Americans and, 236–37, 249, 264, 278; Garvin on China and the struggle against, 236; and racism, in Mao's thought, 258–59, 278

Columbia Broadcasting Company (CBS), 168, 171, 290

Columbia University, 82, 135, 138, 177, 317

Committee of Concerned Asian Scholars (CCAS), 303–4, 314, 316

Committee of the Chinese People Defending World Peace (CCPDWP): and the Du Boises, 246, 247–48; and Pestana, 222; and A. L. Strong, 206; and H. Williams, 305; and R. Williams, 262, 264–65, 270–72

Committee on Friendly Relations Among Foreign Students, 43

Committee on Scholarly Communications with the People's Republic of China (CSCPRC), 310–12, 315, 328–30. *See also* Price, Frank

Common Program (PRC constitution), 26, 27–28, 29

communes, 207–8, 218–20

Communist parties, international, 221; and armed vs. peaceful revolution, 250–54 (*see also* African Americans). *See also* Chinese Communist Party; Communist Party of the Soviet Union; Communist Party of the U.S.A.

Communist Party of the Soviet Union (CPSU), 222, 252, 254, 257, 260. *See also* Soviet Union
Communist Party of the United States of America (CPUSA), 44–45; and the African American struggle, 252, 254, 260; Chinese scholars' involvement in, 52; members/sympathizers invited to PRC, 201–4, 221–25 (*see also* Strong, Anna Louise; *and other individuals*); Moscow sided with, 222; peaceful transition preferred over armed revolution, 254, 257; Pestana on state of, 223; Pu and, 398n58. *See also specific members*
Communist Youth League Central Committee, 217
Confucius Institutes, 333
Congress of Racial Equality (CORE), 268
Consultants, Incorporated, 133
"A Conversation with Mao Tse-tung" (Snow), 297. *See also* Snow, Edgar
Cook, Richard, 43
Cosin Commentator, 133–34
Council for United States Aid (CUSA), 126, 134
Cowen, Glenn, 299, 300
Cowles, Garner, 186, 225
CPACRFN. *See* Chinese People's Association for Cultural Relations with Foreign Nations
CPAFFN. *See* Chinese People's Association for Friendship with Foreign Nations
CPPCC. *See* Chinese People's Political Consultative Conference
CPSU. *See* Communist Party of the Soviet Union
CPUSA. *See* Communist Party of the United States of America
CPVA. *See* Chinese People's Volunteer Army
Crusader, The, 256, 266–68, 271, 274, 282–83. *See also* Williams, Robert F.
CSCA (Chinese Students Christian Association in North America), 44–45, 102
CSCPRC. *See* Committee on Scholarly Communications with the People's Republic of China
Cuba: revolution, 247, 251; R. Williams in, 256, 259, 266, 268, 272, 273
Cuban Missile Crisis, 233, 266
cultural aggression, American: American cultural institutions considered as, 6, 8, 27, 72, 202; American responses to charges of, 57–59; CCP actions to stop, 30–31, 51–65, 334; Christian churches considered as, 30–31; Lu Zhiwei on, 66, 69; Mao's attacks on, 26–27, 30; movement against, during Korean War, 9, 51–63, 65–69, 121 (*see also* Resist America and Aid Korea movement; thought reform); nationalization of American-subsidized institutions justified by, 7–8, 61–63, 65–69, 72–73; VOA as, 56 (*see also* Voice of America). *See also* America as enemy; American cultural and educational institutions
Cultural and Educational Commission (China), 61–62, 64, 67
cultural Cold War scholarship, 5
Cultural Revolution. *See* Great Proletarian Cultural Revolution
cultural systems (defined), 2
Culture, Ministry of, 28, 322, 323
CUSA (Council for United States Aid), 126, 134

Dalai Lama, 208
Dawn Over China (A. L. Strong), 209, 387n6
Dawson, Owen L., 129
Decker, Clarence R., 136
Decree on the Registration of the Foreign Subsidized and Managed Cultural, Educational, Relief Institutions and Religious Organizations, 61–62
Defense, Department of (U.S.), 60, 94, 101, 370n5. *See also* Joint Chiefs of Staff; United States military
Democratic Party, 237. *See also specific politicians*
demonstrations: in the PRC, 59, 219, 233, 321, 324, 326, 329; in the U.S., 221, 269–70, 276, 277–78, 284
Deng Jiadong, 72
Deng Jiaxian (Teng Chia-Hsien), 78–80, 79
Deng Xiaoping: and African Americans, 255, 256; BSO welcomed, 322; and China's modernization/reform, 317–20, 323–24, 330; commitment to CCP rule and ideology, 319–20, 323–25, 330; and human rights, 325–26; and J. Jackson, 221; and the nuclear test ban treaty, 257; removed from office, 284; and resumption of Sino-American cultural relations, 317–19, 321, 323–25, 327, 330; return to power, 317
Deng Yingchao, 206
Deng Zihui, 271
Dewey, John, 177
Ding Xilin, 247–48, 300
diplomatic relations (U.S.-PRC). *See* U.S.–PRC relations
documentary films, Chinese, 272–73, 289–90, 397n36

Dodd, Martha, 224
Dong Biwu, 44
Dong Xianguang. *See* Tong, Hollington
Drumright, Everett F., 91, 157, 174
Du Bois, Shirley Graham, 242, 245–49, 250, 255–56, 255, 261, 278–79. *See also* Du Bois, W. E. B.
Du Bois, W. E. B.: African countries called to turn to China, 243, 248–49; belief in Communism, 249, 253–54; books published in PRC, 245–46, 254–55; death, 261; invited to visit PRC, 242, 244–45; Mao and, 11, 249–51, 250, 256, 259, 261, 297, 397n36; views on revolution generally, 243, 250–51, 253–54, 259; visits to PRC, 246–51, 250, 253, 255–56, 255, 395n18, 396n28, 397n36; R. Williams's reception compared to, 262
Duggen, Laurence, 33
Dulles, John Foster: on communes, 207; Du Bois's appeal to, 244; on the future of Chinese communism, 192, 329; and overseas Chinese students in Taiwan, 155–56; and reciprocal visas for Chinese reporters, 196; and repatriation of Chinese and U.S. citizens, 87–88, 90–92, 94, 96–101, 104, 107, 110–11; and Taiwan's defense, 126, 163; and the travel ban, 170–71, 175, 187–94, 196, 200, 364n53 (*see also* travel ban, U.S.). *See also Kent v. Dulles*
Durdin, Tillman, 168
Dwight, William, 188–89, 191

Earnest, Morris L., 187
East China Normal University, 72–73
Eckstein, Alexander, 311. *See also* National Committee on United States-China Relations

Economic Cooperation Administration (ECA), 34–38, 123–36, 141. *See also* Mutual Security Agency; Program of Emergency Aid to Chinese Students

Editor & Publisher, 187–88

education (China): all media tightly controlled, 28–29; American model, 3, 8; Cultural Revolution's impact on, 284; curriculum reforms, 27–28, 29, 72; English- and foreign-language education, 231–33, 238, 317, 326–27, 331, 393n131; first national conferences on, 28–29; Garvin's courses, 235–39 (*see also* Garvin, Vicki); national defense education, 63; reform (1970s), 317; reform and reorganization (1950s), 69–75; Soviet model adopted, 3, 8, 69–70, 74–75; teaching methods, 238; thought-education movement, 69–73 (*see also* thought reform). *See also* colleges and universities (China); Ministry of Education, PRC; missionary colleges and universities; missionary schools; schools

education (Taiwan), 123–24; American students in Taiwan, 160; ECA/JCRR scholarship program, 129–34; overseas Chinese students in Taiwan, 7, 10, 142–60; students studying in U.S., 10, 123–24, 126, 128–35, 317, 371n23, 372(nn40, 50); vocational and engineering programs, 123–24, 135–42. *See also* Economic Cooperation Administration; Ministry of Education, Nationalist; Mutual Security Agency; *specific institutions*

Educational Exchange Office. *See* Office of Educational Exchange

Education Office (Office of Education; U.S.), 34

Egypt, 183

Eisenhower, Dwight D.: and the issue of detained Chinese and U.S. citizens, 83, 98, 100–101, 103, 119, 121; and Southeast Asia policy, 143, 145; and the travel ban, 169–71, 173–74, 188; and U.S. policy re Taiwan, 145, 296

Emergency Aid Program. *See* Program of Emergency Aid to Chinese Students

Engineering College of Taiwan. *See* Taiwan Engineering College

Epstein, Israel, 166, 167, 203, 212, 226, 228, 284

Epton, William Leo, Jr., 304–5

espionage, 52–53, 204, 211, 350n4

ethnic minorities, in China, 272

Evergreen People's Commune, 207

exchange students. *See* Chinese students and scholars, in U.S.; education (Taiwan)

Executive Council (of PRC), 61–62, 64, 67–68, 70

factories: in PRC, 181, 184, 219–20, 232, 265; in Southeast Asia, 209; in Taiwan, 125, 139

Fairbank, John King, 316

Fairfax-Cholmeley, Elsie, 203, 212

Fang Yi, 318

Far East Reporter, 224

"Farewell, Leighton Stewart" (Mao), 333

Federal Bureau of Investigation (FBI), 39, 44, 120–21, 277, 285

Federation of American Scientists, 302, 310

Feng Yidai, 180–81

Fenn, William P., 58, 60–61, 65

Feuerwerker, Albert, 315
films. *See* documentary films; movie and television industry; television
First Conference on Overseas Chinese Affairs (Nationalist Party, 1952), 145–46
Fisher, Thomas, 41, 44, 46, 76, 81
Fitzgerald, Dennis A., 152–53
Flieger, Howard, 380n31
FOA. *See* Foreign Operations Administration
Fontein, Jan, 327
Foreign Affairs, Ministry of. *See* Ministry of Foreign Affairs, Nationalist; Ministry of Foreign Affairs, PRC
Foreign Language Press, 168, 232–33, 238
Foreign Language Publication Administration, 239–40
Foreign Operations Administration (FOA), 124, 146, 149–52. *See also* International Cooperation Administration
Forman, Harrison, 166, 167, 168
Formosa. *See* Taiwan
Formosa Resolution, 163
Foster, William C., 130–31
Four Modernizations, 317, 319–21, 323–24, 334
France, 183, 317
Friend, Robert, 234
Fu Jen (Furen) University, 30–31, 56, 58, 60, 73
Fulbright Program: first U.S.-Chinese agreement, 3; with PRC, 326–27, 329, 330, 333; suspended after flight of Nationalist government, 32; with Taiwan, 125, 135, 160
Futureworld (film), 322
Fu Ying, 121

Fuzhou University, 73

Galston, Arthur W., 301–2
Gao Hua, 17
Garvin, Vicki, 234–41, 393n133, 394n147
General Relief Association for the Chinese People, 61
Geneva Conference (1954), 84–97
Georgetown University, 318
Ge Peiqi, 192
Gerlach, Talitha, 212, 246
Ghana: Du Bois and, 244, 255, 256; Garvin and, 234, 235; Pan-African People's Conference, 248; Strong's newsletters published, 211; R. Williams and, 257, 261–62, 273
Ginling College, 58
Ginling University, 73
Gong Peng, 168, 197, 226
Goodpaster, Andrew, 101
Gowen, Franklin, 99–100, 106
GPCR. *See* Great Proletarian Cultural Revolution
Graham, Shirley. *See* Du Bois, Shirley Graham
Great Britain, 103, 183, 257–58, 317, 370n5. *See also* Trevelyan, Humphrey
Great Leap Forward: Americans invited to PRC to show off, 218–25 (*see also* Snow, Edgar); hate-America campaign and, 219–20; Mao's predictions for, 227; people's communes, 207–8, 219–20; Strong's coverage of, 212 (*see also* Strong, Anna Louise). *See also* communes
Great Proletarian Cultural Revolution (GPCR): chaos caused by, 230, 231, 283, 284, 298, 317, 319; Garvin and, 239–40; Strohm on, 219–20; Strong on, 212–13
Green, Theodore Francis, 190

Griffin, R. Allen, 130, 141
Grondahl, Teg, 42–43
Gross, Fulgence, Fr., 182
Guanghua (Kuanghua) University, 72
Guangming Daily, 56, 59, 63, 69, 72, 199
Guangzhou, 2, 118, 168, 272, 301, 302, 314
guerrilla warfare, 243, 266, 267, 269–70, 274, 277, 283, 286
Guerrilla Warfare Advocates in the United States (Committee on Un-American Activities), 283
Guidance Committee for International Activities (of CCPCC), 165, 168
Guo Moruo: and the African American struggle, 260, 264; CSCPRC message to, 311; and Du Bois, 243–45, 247–49; and Resist America and Aid Korea movement, 53–54; and A. L. Strong, 213; and the takeover of American institutions, 61; and R. Williams, 262, 264
Guo Xiaochuan, 180–81
Guo Yonghuai, 102
Gu Weijun (V. K. Wellington Koo), 35

Habberton, Benjamin, 77
Hagerty, James, 91
Hai Tian Development U.S.A., 333
Hall, Gus, 254
Hall, Gwendolyn, 291
Hammarskjöld, Dag, 98
Hanyang Incident, 217–18
Harriman, W. Averell, 221
Harrington, Michael, 237
Harrington, Phillip, 177–87
Hartford Times, 24
Hatcher, Richard, 285
Hatem, George (Ma Haide), 212, 226
Health, Education, and Welfare, Department of, 323

Health, Ministry of, 65–66, 67
He Cheng, 65–66
He Guozhu, 78
He Long, 166, 206, 264
Henry, Milton (Gaidi Obadele), 276, 288
Henry, Richard (Imari Obadele), 276, 288
Herter, Christian A., 193, 200
Hessler, Peter, 333
Hightower, John, 172–73
Hinton, Carmelita, 304
Hinton, Joan, 212, 304
"History of the Negro in the U.S., The" (textbook; ed. Garvin), 238
Hoffman, Paul, 35
Hong Kong: American journalists in, 172–74, 179, 196–97, 199–200; applicants for colleges and schools in, 156; CCAS graduate students in, 303–4; Chou's family still in, 119; Communist-instigated riots and strikes in, 160; cultural war against Nationalists in, 22; under PRC rule, 333; and stranded Chinese students, 49, 78, 102, 113; students from, in PRC, 155–56, 159 (*see also under* overseas Chinese); students from, in Taiwan, 146, 147, 148, 151, 152–54, 156–57, 159–60
Hongxing Advanced Agricultural Production Cooperative, 183
Hoover, Herbert, Jr., 173
Hoover, J. Edgar, 277. *See also* Federal Bureau of Investigation
Hopkins, Mark, 329
hospitals (China), 20, 32, 57, 295, 312–13, 358n86. *See also* Peking Union Medical College
House Committee on Un-American Activities, 39, 277, 283

House Subcommittee on Internal Security, 222
Houston Press, 120
Hou Xianglin, 45
Hovde, Frederick L., 138
Howard University, 273
Huachung University, 65
Hua Nan College, 73
Huang Baotong, 45
Huang Fu, 65
Huang Hua, 87–89, 98, 226–27, 234, 239, 295
Huang Qibao, 94
Huang Xinxi, 255
Huang Zhen, 323, 327–28
Huan Xiang, 87–89
human rights: Chinese students on PRC's violations of, 120; confrontation over, 321, 329, 331; during Deng's leadership, 325–26; forced abortions, 328; in PRC generally, 7; U.S. detention of Chinese students claimed violation of, 53. *See also* Tiananmen Square protests
Human Rights Record of the United States (PRC report), 331
Hundred Flower campaign, 191–92, 199
Hurleigh, Robert, 188, 189, 191
Hurley, Patrick, 3, 15
Hu Shi, 121, 177
Hu Yaobang, 324

ICA. *See* International Cooperation Administration
IIE. *See* Institute of International Education
Immigration and Naturalization Service (INS); and Chinese students and scholars in the U.S., 49, 75–80, 82, 99, 101, 103, 107 (*see also* Chinese students and scholars: detention); ECA/JCRR scholarship students not required to register with, 133; Qian's deportation sought, 52
India: and return of Chinese students from the U.S., 105, 107, 110, 112–13, 117, 118, 120, 357n97; Sino-Indian relations, 165
Indonesia, 143, 153, 211, 257
Information and Educational Exchange Act (Smith-Mundt Act), 34, 36
Information Division (under MFA): and foreign and U.S. journalists' visits, 178–82, 230–31, 378n8; and invitations to U.S. journalists, 164–65, 167–68, 172, 175, 177–78
INS. *See* Immigration and Naturalization Service; International News Service
Inside the Red China (film; Cohen), 218
Institute of International Education (IIE), 33, 35, 37
Institute of Medicine (U.S.), 310
intellectuals, Chinese: American journalists met by, 180–81, 184; criticism of CCP and government by, 191–92, 199; instructed to denounce Hu Shi, 177; political campaigns against, 9, 85, 120, 121; support for Resist America and Aid Korea movement, 54–56; support for university reorganization, 73; thought reform and, 9, 69–72, 82, 121; U.S.-educated scholars treated poorly on return, 9, 82, 85, 106, 119–22. *See also* Chinese students and scholars, in U.S.; *specific individuals*
Interior Department (U.S.), 323
Internal Revenue Service (IRS), 113
International Broadcasting Act (1994), 331. *See also* Radio Free Asia

INDEX [447]

International Cooperation
    Administration (ICA), 152–55,
    157–58. *See also* Foreign Operations
    Administration
International News Service (INS), 120,
    168, 190
International Red Cross, 87
international relations, culture and
    (generally), 2
internet, 332
interpreters: for African American
    visitors, 247; for American
    journalists, 167, 168, 176, 180,
    182–83, *296*, 379n23; for the
    American youth delegation, 217, 218;
    for the CNTTT, in the U.S.,
    411n129; for A. L. Strong, 205; for
    Zhou and Mao, 80, *296* (*see also* Ji
    Chaozhu)
Investigation, Ministry of, 165, 168
IRS (Internal Revenue Service), 113
Ishibashi, Tanzan, 263
"Issues on War and Strategy" (Mao),
    252–53
Ivy, Jim, 129

Jackson, Ida, 214
Jackson, James, 221–22, 246
Japan: China's war against, 14–15, 125,
    214, 224, 240 (*see also* World War II);
    language instructors from, 317;
    Mao's meetings with Japanese
    citizens, 221, 263; pattern of
    invasions of China, 54; returning
    Chinese students detained in, 53; and
    Taiwan, 125, 129; World Table
    Tennis Championships in, 298–300
JCRR. *See* Joint Commission for Rural
    Reconstruction
Jenkins, Alfred, 97
Jessup, Philip, 41

Jiang Jieshi (Chiang Kai-Shek): Mao's
    attacks on, 23, 204–5; mutual defense
    treaty proposed, 86; and overseas
    Chinese, 145; reconquest of mainland
    China desired, 127, 140, 144; U.S.
    support for, 6, 13–16, 27, 127, 325,
    377n2; Worthy on, 185. *See also*
    Chinese Nationalist government;
    civil war; Taiwan
Jiang Nanxiang, 74–75
Jiang Yanshi, 129
Jiang Yinen, 71
Ji Chaoding, 226
Ji Chaozhu (Chi Chao-Chu), 78, 80, *296*
Jiefang Ribao, 22
Jin Yinchang (Chin Yin-Ch'ang), 78
John Brown (Du Bois), 245–46. *See also*
    Du Bois, W. E. B.
Johns Hopkins University Medical
    School, 66
Johnson, Louis A., 127–28
Johnson, Lyndon B., 284
Johnson, U. Alexis: journalistic
    reciprocity discussed, 195–96, 197;
    and negotiations over detained
    Chinese and U.S. citizens, 91–97,
    109–11, 163–64, 176–77; and PRC
    proposals for cultural exchange,
    163–64, 176–77
Johnstone, William C., Jr., 36, 43–44,
    46, 130
Joint Chiefs of Staff, 60, 128. *See also*
    Defense, Department of
Joint Commission for Rural
    Reconstruction (JCRR): ECA/
    JCRR scholarship program, 129–34;
    and education within Taiwan,
    136–37, 139
Joint Commission on Scientific and
    Technological Cooperation, 319
Jones, Jenkin, 186

journalism in China: all media tightly controlled, 20, 167, 180–81, 185, 329, 332–33; CCP publications in Nationalist-controlled areas, 22; censorship of Strong's work, 210–11; Chinese international news controlled from Xinhua headquarters, 18; Chinese journalists and U.S. assignments, 10, 161, 194–96, 197, 197, 385n5; foreign journalism banned by CCP, 17–20, 24–25; foreign journalists courted during civil war, 17–18, 165–67; journalists' criticism of CCP and government, 199; Maoist journalism, 17; MFA meeting on management of foreign reporters, 230–31; reciprocity issue, 194–200, 217; registration of institutions required, 62; VOA blocked, 331. *See also* American journalists; Association of Journalists; news organizations, American; *specific news organizations, publications, and individuals*

Judd, Walter, 40
Justice Department (U.S.), 75, 77, 98, 252. *See also* Immigration and Naturalization Service

Kang Sheng, 213, 225
Keatley, Robert, 302
Ke Bainian, 53, 379n23
Kefauver, Estes, 190
Kennedy, John F., 211, 229,
Kent v. Dulles, 205, 245
Ke Qingshi, 265
Khan, Yahya, 297, 408n79
Khanna, V., 283–84
Khrushchev, Nikita, 292, 390n78. *See also* Soviet Union
Kim Il-sung, 51

King, Martin Luther, Jr., 237–38, 277–79, 282, 285–86, 305, 319
Kissinger, Henry, 294, 298, 306, 307, 311–12
Knotkova, Marie, 215, *216*
Koo, V. K. Wellington (Gu Weijun), 35
Koop, Theodore, 191
Korean War: American POWs remaining in China, 232–34, 392n120; armistice, 51; beginning of, 127; Black soldiers in, 233–34; Chinese seizure of American assets/institutions during, 61–75; and Chinese students' return to China, 7, 9, 50–51, 75–83, 79 (see also Chinese students and scholars, in U.S.); Du Bois opposed to U.S. involvement, 244; impact on post-war U.S.-China relations, 85–86; Mao's son killed, 251; PRC's entry into, 3, 50, 51–54; PRC's need for medical services during, 66; PRC's warning to U.S. re, 228; U.S.-China cultural relations terminated during, 50–51; U.S. economic sanctions on PRC during, 59–61, 63; and U.S.-Taiwan relationship, 6, 10, 50, 123–27 (see also Taiwan)
Kreisberg, Paul H., 291

Land, S. Lewis, 136–37
Laos, 209
Lao She, 248
Lawton, Frederick, 48
Lee, Tsung-tao (Zhengdao Li), 82
Lee Teng-hui (Li Denghui), 131–32, 372n40
"Lei Feng's Diary," 233
Lei Yang, 294
Letters from China (A. L. Strong), 211–13

Liao Chengzhi, 210
Li Baokun, 80
Library of Congress, 323
Li Dequan, 248
Lieberman, Henry, 168–69
Li Fang-hsuen, 58
Life magazine, 166, 168, 297
Li Hengde, 78, 80, 82–83
Li Kenong, 166
Lin Biao, 166, 212–13, 274, 286, 294
Ling Qing, 53, 379n23
Ling Xianyang, 26
Link, Perry, 330
Little Red Book (Mao). See *Quotations from Chairman Mao*
Liu, Herman C. E., 246
Liu Bocheng, 166
Liu Ningyi, 244
Liu Shaoqi: and American visitors, 204, 206, 221, 263; elected president of PRC, 399n62; and the nuclear test ban treaty, 257; removed from office, 284; and the Soviet Union, 24–25, 32, 262; and thought reform, 70
Liu Xiyuan, 217
Liu Yandong, 332
Li Zhang, 199
Look magazine, 24, 178, 184–86, 225, 228. See also Harrington, Phillip; Snow, Edgar; Stevens, Edmund
Lotte, Jack, 120
loyalty movement, 71
Lucas, Scott, 39
Luce, Henry, 186
Lu Dingyi, 203, 204–7, 225
Luo Longji, 121
Luo Peilin, 359n99
Luo Ruiqing, 212, 260
Luo Shijun, 53
Lu Shanhua (Lu Shan-Hua), 78

Lu Zhiwei (Luh Chi-wei), 25–26, 57, 65–66, 69, 82. See also Yenching University

MacArthur, Douglas (Gen.), 128
Macau, students from, 146, 147, 148, 151, 152–53
Machenzie, Andy, 95
Mackensen, Paul, Rev., 182
Mackey, Cliff, 186
Ma Haide (George Hatem), 212, 226
Mallory, Mae, 276, 282
Man from Atlantis, The (television show), 322
Mansfield, Michael, 190
Mao Dun, 248
Mao Tse-tung's Quotations: The Red Guards' Handbook, 276. See also *Quotations from Chairman Mao*
Mao Zedong: and American communists, 221–22 (*see also specific individuals*); and the American youth delegation, 217; anti-rightist campaign against intellectuals, 121, 191–92, 199 (*see also* Anti-Rightist movement); campaigns against erroneous thoughts within CCP, 22–23; and Chinese Christians, 59; on "cleaning house," 19; on complete control over cultural institutions, 21; death, 317; democracy, freedom demanded of Nationalist government, 23–24; educational principles, 235; emergence as paramount leader of CCP, 14, 23–24; English interpreter for, 80 (*see also* Ji Chaozhu); foreign comrades ("true friends") welcomed, 19, 202; foreign press criticized, 25; goals, 220; and the GPCR (Cultural Revolution),

212, 239; and guerrilla warfare, 274, 277; Hu Shi's thought suppressed, 177; and the Korean War, 51–52; and missionary schools and colleges, 30–31; and the people's communes, 218; personality cult, 23–24, 220, 233, 295, 304; as president of PRC, 399n62; propaganda and the fight against Nationalist regime, 21–22; and rectification movements, 14, 22–23, 121, 191–92; Red Army established, 21; and a rising tide of socialism, 198; scholars' pledge of support sent to, 73; Soviet Republic of China established, 264, 276 (see also civil war); and thought reform, 70–71, 177, 220; and U.S. and PRC table tennis teams, 292, 298–300, 306–8, 310; and world revolution, 11, 259, 262, 287. See also Chinese Communist Party; Mao Zedong Thought

— and the African American struggle: Du Bois and Mao, 11, 249–51, 250, 256, 259, 261, 297, 397n36; Garvin and Mao, 235, 236–40; King's assassination denounced, 285; Mao's support (generally), 11, 242, 251–52, 258–61, 278; racial struggle as class struggle, 237, 239, 258; R. Williams and Mao, 11, 242–43, 258–63, 270–71, 273–74, 285–86, 297; H. Williams and Mao, 305

— and American journalists and writers: generally, 180, 185, 221; A. Smedley, 166; E. Snow, 166–67, 225–26, 227–28, 230, 294–98, 296; A. L. Strong, 16, 204–6, 213, 250, 250

— anti-American rhetoric: American reactionaries identified as threat, 16; campaign against American cultural influence, 9, 14, 27, 52, 59, 202 (see also cultural aggression, American); opposition to American imperialism called for, 16, 204–5, 236; on reactionary forces in missionary schools, 30; response to State Dept. *White Paper* (1949), 26–27; on U.S. (non)recognition, 198; on the weakness of American imperialism, 222. See also America as enemy

— and foreign policy/relations: 1949 directives, 18–19; cultural exchanges agreed to, 306; diplomatic relations with U.S. opposed, 192, 198; Geneva Conference negotiations (1954), 92 (see also Geneva Conference); Hurley's proposed agreement accepted, 3, 15; imperialist Japan deemed enemy, 15; improving Sino-American relations, 294–97; isolation of U.S. government as strategy, 164–65, 192; Nixon and Mao, 295–97, 306–8; nuclear weapons, 230, 257–58; Sino-Soviet conflict, 293–94; Taiwan issue, 86, 227, 296; Taiwan Strait Crisis, 162–63; on war with the U.S., 230, 360n1

— writings of: "The Chinese Revolution and the Chinese Communist Party" (Mao), 214; disseminated in U.S., 8, 11, 266; "Farewell, Leighton Stewart," 333; "On the Protracted War," 203; *Quotations from Chairman Mao (Little Red Book)*, 8, 11, 267, 274–76, 286, 298, 323; *Selected Works*, 203–4, 252–53; translated by Pu, 398n58. See also *Quotations from Chairman Mao*

Mao Zedong Thought: American ideals and values in opposition to, 23; and cultural exchanges (1970s), 316; Deng Xiaoping on, 320; Garvin and, 240 (*see also* Garvin, Vicki); as guiding principle of CCP and revolution, 14, 22–23, 320, 324; spread of, in U.S., 274–76; A. L. Strong and, 205, 213, 387n6 (*see also* Strong, Anna Louise); R. Williams and, 243, 266–67, 274–75, 286 (*see also* Williams, Robert F.). *See also* Mao Zedong; *Quotations from Chairman Mao*

Marshall, George, 34

Marxism: challenged by Xu, 121; courses in, 332; CPUSA and, 223; Garvin praised for studying, 240; implemented in higher education, 28, 70, 232; Mao as true follower of, 259; Mao on conflict with liberalism, 22; Mao Zedong Thought as, 23; PRC's adherence to, under Deng, 324, 332; revolutionary principle vs. peaceful coexistence/transition, 252–53, 257, 260–61. *See also* Mao Zedong Thought

Ma Xulun (minister of education), 29, 31, 53–54, 64, 66, 70. *See also* Ministry of Education

May, Timothy, 283

Ma Yinchu, 70

MCC. *See* Military Control Commission

McCardle, Carl W., 172–73

McConaughy, Walter, 186–87

McCune, Shannon, 131

McFall, Jack, 48–49

McWilliams, Carey, 210

media: Chinese state-run entities, in U.S., 333; social media, 332; state control over, in PRC, 20, 28–29, 167, 180–81, 185, 329, 331–32. *See also* American journalists; documentary films; journalism in China; movie and television industry; news organizations, American; television; *specific media organizations*

medicine, in China, 295, 312–13. *See also* hospitals

Mei, Y. C., 47

Mei Lanfang, 163

Meng, Chih, 34, 47, 246

Menon, Krishna, 107

Merchant, Livingston T., 131–32

Meyer, Hershel D., 223–24, 390n78

MFA. *See* Ministry of Foreign Affairs, Nationalist; Ministry of Foreign Affairs, PRC

Mikoyan, Anastas, 19, 202

military, Chinese. *See* Chinese military; Chinese People's Volunteer Army; People's Liberation Army

military, U.S. *See* Defense, Department of; Joint Chiefs of Staff; United States military

Military Control Commission (MCC), 20, 24–25

Miller, Robert, 174–75

Milliken, William, 291

Milton, David and Nancy Dall, 234, 284, 404n20

Mining and Metallurgy Institute (Changsha), 73

Ministry of Culture, 28, 322, 323

Ministry of Education (MOE), Nationalist, 33, 109, 131, 139, 145, 147–48, 154–55. *See also* education (Taiwan)

Ministry of Education (MOE), PRC: and American history research, 391n95; authority and mandate, 29, 346n59; and foreign language education, 231–32, 317; foreign-subsidized schools taken over, nationalized, 64–67, 69 (*see also under* colleges and universities [China]); and the get-students-back campaign, 117; private colleges and institutions under authority of, 31–32; reorganization of colleges and departments, 72–74; and schools of Marxism, 332. *See also* colleges and universities (China); education (China); schools (China)

Ministry of Foreign Affairs (MFA), Nationalist, 125

Ministry of Foreign Affairs (MFA), PRC: American and Australian Affairs Division, 53, 104–6, 165, 248, 379n23; and American journalists' visas, 169, 172, 179, 197; and American journalists' visits to PRC, 168, 176, 179–80, 295–96 (*see also* Information Division); and the CNTTT trip to the U.S., 307; and dissemination of Mao's thought outside China, 287; Division of European Affairs (*see* Huan Xiang); and Epstein, 203; and foreign journalists' visits (generally), 230–31, 378n8; and foreign language instruction, 317; information collected on Chinese students in U.S., 104–5; and Qian's case, 108; and the return of Chinese students from the U.S., 117–18; and A. L. Strong, 209; U.S. citizens invited (1971), 298; and U.S. detention of Chinese scholars, 53; and the USTTT visit to PRC, 299–300; and the VOA, 326; and R. Williams's travel documents, 404n26

Ministry of Health, 65–66, 67

Ministry of Investigation, 165, 168

Ministry of Public Security, 165, 168, 181–82

Mirsky, Jonathan, 314

missionaries, American, 60. *See also* hospitals; missionary colleges and universities; missionary schools; orphanages

missionary colleges and universities: Austin on, 57–58; CCP takeover of American-subsidized institutions supported, 62–63, 65; and charges of "cultural aggression," 57–59; operation allowed under CCP restrictions, 25–32; seized, nationalized, and reorganized, 7–8, 9, 30–32, 50, 61–75; thought reform at, 9, 70–72; Three-Self movement, 58–59. *See also* colleges and universities (China); education (China); *specific institutions*

missionary schools, 28–29, 58, 62–64. *See also* education (China); missionary colleges and universities

model units, 181, 230–31

MOE. *See* Ministry of Education, Nationalist; Ministry of Education, PRC

Mondale, Walter, 323, 325, 327

Mongolia, 293

Mosher, Steve, 328

Mote, Frederick, 315

movie and television industry: American movies shown in PRC, 322 (*see also* television); in PRC, 28, 55–56; in the U.S., 55–56

Moyer, Raymond T., 129, 130–31, 142

MSA. *See* Mutual Security Agency

Mullen, Bill V., 253

Murphy, Robert, 169–70

Museum of Fine Arts Boston, 327–28

Mutual Defense Assistance Act, 128

Mutual Security Act (1951), 128, 134, 140
Mutual Security Agency (MSA), 124, 128, 134–42

NAACP (National Association for the Advancement of Colored People), 237, 256, 281
NAFSA. *See* National Association of Foreign Student Advisors
Nanjing, 22, 25
Nankai University, 58, 82, 318, 391n95
NARCP (National Association of Relief for the Chinese People), 68
NAS. *See* National Academy of Science
Nason, John B., 129
NAST (National Association of Science and Technology), 118–19
Nathan, Andrew, 316
Nation, The, 168, 210
National Academy of Science (NAS), 310, 315, 329
National Advisory Commission on Civil Disorders, 284
National Art Gallery (Beijing), 327–28
National Association for the Advancement of Colored People. *See* NAACP
National Association of Foreign Student Advisors (NAFSA), 34–35, 43
National Association of Relief for the Chinese People (NARCP), 68
National Association of Science and Technology (NAST), 118–19
National Association of Writers, 181, 205
National Broadcasting Company. *See* NBC
National Committee on United States-China Relations (NCUSCR), 307, 310–13
National Conference on Higher Education (1950), 29

National Council of the Churches of Christ of the United States of America, 47
National Day celebrations (Oct. 1; PRC): African American leaders at, 242, 255, 256, 262–63, 270–71, 273–74, 305; American youth groups at, 217, 304; fear of Soviet attack on, 293–94; Snow at, 295
National Defense Authorization Act (Fiscal Year 2021), 333
National Endowment for the Arts, 323
National Endowment for the Humanities, 323
National Guardian, 203, 210, 253
Nationalist Party, 145. *See also* Chinese Nationalist government; Jiang Jieshi
National Jinling University, 73
National News Administration, 378n8
National News Association, 199
National Security Council (NSC), 128, 144–45, 307
National Taiwan University, 131, 138, 141–42, 146, 149–51, 155
National Urban League, 281
NBC (National Broadcasting Company), 168, 170, 171, 174, 301. *See also* Robinson, James
NCUSCR. *See* National Committee on United States-China Relations
Negroes with Guns (R. Williams), 257, 263, 275
Nehru, Jawaharlal, 103, 165
New China (journal), 239
New China News Agency. *See* Xinhua News Agency
New People in New China (Russell), 224
news media. *See* American journalists; journalism in China; media; news organizations, American
Newson, Moses, 289

news organizations, American: banned/regulated in China, 18–19; and Beijing's refusal to allow access, 199–200; Black press, 178 (see also *Baltimore Afro-American*; Worthy, William); and the travel ban, 169, 171–76, 186–91, 193–94. *See also* American journalists; United States Information Service; *specific news services, publications, and individuals*
Newton, Huey, 275, 305
New World Press (Chinese foreign-language publisher), 207, 209, 211
New York City, 269
New York Herald-Tribune, 166
New York Times: Galston and Signer's report, 302; on the GPCR, 212; journalists in or invited to China, 24, 166, 168, 169, 174–75, 302–3 (*see also* Epstein, Israel; Sulzberger, Cyrus); PRC retaliation against, 332; on the reciprocity issue, 196; reporting on U.S. detention of Chinese students, 98; and Snow's 1970 conversation with Mao, 297; on Snow's film, 230; surprised by China's refusal to admit journalists, 221; and the travel ban, 169, 171, 174–75; R. Williams and, 290
New Zealand, 211, 317
Nixon, Richard: and the Chinese table tennis team, 307–8, *308*, 411n129; efforts to improve Sino-American relations, 280, 293–94, 297, 306–7, 311; PRC visit, 280, 295–96, 304, 306–7, 314; Taiwan visit, 10, 86, 143–44, 146, 149; and R. Williams's return to the U.S., 285; and Zhou, 297, 408n79
nongovernmental organizations, and cultural exchange, 309–11. *See also specific organizations*

North Korea, 59–60. *See also* Korean War
North Vietnam, 209, 304. *See also* Vietnam; Vietnam War
Novak, Robert, 319
Noyes, Henry H., 209, 275
NSC. *See* National Security Council
nuclear weapons: Chinese program, 80, 229–30, 292; test ban treaty, 257–58; U.S. program, 204, 251

Obadele, Gaidi. *See* Henry, Milton
Obadele, Imari. *See* Henry, Richard
O'Brien, Lawrence, 282–83
Observer (Guanchazhe), 333
OCAC. *See* Overseas Chinese Affairs Commission
Office for the Reception of American Journalists, 168, 176
Office of Chinese Affairs (State Department), 77, 80–81, 96, 186–87
Office of Educational Exchange, 35–36, 43
Office of Policy Research, 164
Office of Religious Affairs, 67–68
Office of Strategic Service, 39
Office of the National Intelligence, 39
Office of the Reception of American Journalists, 168
Oksenberg, Michel, 322–23, 324
Olsen, John, 330
One Fourth of Humanity: The China Story (film; Snow), 230
"On Harvest Moon, U-2, Peace" (Strong), 211
"On the Platform with Mao Tse-tung" (R. Williams), 290
"On the Protracted War" (Mao), 203
opera exchange, 163
Organization of Mothers with Sons Lost in Korea, 163

orphanages, 57. *See also* relief institutions
Other America: The Poverty of the United States, The (M. Harrington), 237
Other Side of the River: Red China Today, The (Snow), 228
"Our Visit to China" (Du Bois), 249
overseas Chinese: education in PRC, 143, 146–47, 153, 156, 158–59, 159; education in Taiwan, 7, 10, 142–60; support for Nationalist government by, 145
Overseas Chinese Affairs Commission (OCAC; Taiwan), 145–49, 154, 159. *See also* Cheng Yan-fen; overseas Chinese: education in Taiwan
Overseas Chinese Daily, 117
Overseas Chinese Education Program. *See* overseas Chinese: education in Taiwan
Overseas Press Club, 187
Oyen, Meredith, 76
Ozawa, Seiji, 322

Pan-African People's Conference (1958), 248
Pan Gongyu, 333
Pankey, Aubrey, 215, *216*, 388n51
Paul Robeson (Graham), 246
Peace Conference of the Asian and Pacific Regions (Beijing, 1952), 244
Peace Corps, 331, 333
peaceful coexistence/transition (Communist concept): vs. armed revolution, 228, 252–53, 257, 260–61, 319; Williams on, 260–61, 264, 290, 291
peaceful evolution (American concept), 6, 7, 329
peace movement, 248, 250
Peking (Beijing) University: Du Bois's speech at, 248–49, 250, 253, 396n28;
editorial cartoon seen at, 183; Fulbright Program at, 326–27; Middle School Affiliated, 272; Mondale's speech at, 323, 325; students selected to study in U.S., 318; support for Resist America and Aid Korea movement, 55, 56; and thought reform, 70–71; Yenching Univ. schools absorbed, 73. *See also* colleges and universities (China); Fu Ying; Zhou Peiyuan
Peking Review, 203, 222, 238–40, 275
Peking Union Medical College (PUMC), 58, 65–66, 70, 72, 224, 358n86
Peng Dehuai, 166, 204–5, 206, 360n1
Peng Guiling, 133
Peng Zhen, 212, 225
Pennsylvania State College, 136, 138, 372n50
"People of Taiwan Are Our Brothers, The" (song), 313
People's China (*Renmin Zhongguo*), 203. *See also Peking Review*
People's Daily (*Renmin Ribao*): on the African American struggle, 252, 258, 269; on American-educated students' critique of the U.S., 45–46; American journalists denounced, 24; and the Anti-Rightist movement, 191–92, 199; on Chinese students in U.S., 114; and Du Bois, 246, 248–49, 255, 256; Fu forced to write article for, 121; journalist reviewed for U.S. assignment, 385n133; Mondale's speech covered, 323; on the nuclear test ban treaty, 258; Pankey's visit reported, 216; photo of Mao and Snow, 295, *296*; on Reiss's death, 203; on A. L. Strong, 206; Three-Self Declaration published, 59; U.S.

approval for journalists to visit PRC denounced, 194–95; VOA attacked, 329; and R. Williams, 260–61, 263, 271, 274, 278

People's Liberation Army (PLA): American military attachés put under house arrest, 19; Americans allowed to visit, observe, 166, 167, 227, 272, 313; and the first Taiwan Strait Crisis, 118; foreign institutions allowed to operate during civil war, 17, 25–26; H. Williams on, 313. *See also* Chinese military; Red Army

People's Republic of China (PRC): and Africa, 231, 239, 243, 247, 248–49; and African Americans (*see* African Americans; *specific individuals*); American journalists refused entry (1950s), 10, 161, 220–21, 226; Americans in (*see* African Americans; American journalists; U.S. citizens in China; *specific individuals*); anti-American campaigns/movements within, 6, 50–66, 177, 207, 219–20 (*see also* Resist America and Aid Korea movement); Anti-Rightist movement, 191–92, 199; citizens in U.S. jails, 185; "cleaning house" metaphor, 19, 165; Cultural Revolution (*see* Great Proletarian Cultural Revolution); demonstrations in, 59, 219, 233, 326; education in (*see* colleges and universities; education [China]); ethnic minority communities, 272; first government elected, 26; foreign passports invalid, 179; founding date, 40; human rights in (*see* human rights); intellectuals (*see* intellectuals, Chinese; universities and colleges [China]); journalism and media in (*see* journalism in China; media); and the Korean War, 3, 9, 50, 51–52 (*see also* Korean War); modernization and industrialization, 317, 319–21, 323–24, 334; nuclear weapons program, 80, 229–30, 292; patriotic celebrations (*see* National Day); people's communes, 207–8, 218–20; political study movement, 27–28; presidents, 399n62 (*see also* Liu Shaoqi; Mao Zedong; Xi Jinping); propaganda (*see* propaganda, Chinese Communist; Propaganda Department); rationing, 215; reasons for success, 220; relief institutions (*see* hospitals; relief institutions); and Southeast Asia (*see* Southeast Asia; *specific countries*); and the Soviet Union (*see* Sino-Soviet relations); students abroad (*see* Chinese students and scholars, in U.S.); superpower aspirations disavowed, 301–2; and Taiwan (*see* Taiwan)"unification of thoughts," 63 (*see also* thought reform); U.S. and its ideals seen as threat, 6–8, 13 (*see also* America as enemy; American cultural and educational institutions; cultural aggression, American); U.S. ban on travel to (*see* travel ban, U.S.); U.S. relations with (*see* Chinese students and scholars, in U.S.; United States government; U.S.–PRC relations); and the Vietnam War, 212, 308 (*see also* Vietnam War); visas, 179, 298 (*see also under* Ministry of Foreign Affairs). *See also* Chinese Communist Party; Chinese Communist Party Central Committee; Executive Council; *specific ministries, committees, organizations, locations, and individuals*

Pessin, Alan W., 329
Pestana, Frank, 222–23
Peterson, William, 244–45
Philippines, 156
Pickett, Clarence, 83
Pierson, Emily, 205, 224. *See also* Strong, Anna Louise
ping-pong teams. *See* Chinese National Table Tennis Team; United States Table Tennis Team
Pittsburgh Courier, 215, 249
PLA. *See* People's Liberation Army
Political Weekly (*Zhengzhi Zhoubao*), 21
Pollitt, Harry, 252–53
Pomfret, John, 329
Porgy and Bess, 163
Post Office, U.S., 282–83
Potter, Andrey A., 138
PRC. *See* People's Republic of China
press. *See* American journalists; journalism in China; news organizations, American; *specific journalists, publications, and news organizations*
Press Administration (China), 28
Price, Duane, 274–75
Price, Frank, 317–18
Problem of Education of Overseas Chinese, The (Office of Intelligence Research), 147
Program of Emergency Aid to Chinese Students: anticommunist ideological campaign and, 39–49; funding, 35–36, 38, 39–40, 49; origins and goals, 32–39; and U.S. policy on Chinese students' return home, 37–38, 40, 48–49, 76–78, 102–3
propaganda, Chinese Communist: and the fight against Nationalist regime, 21–22; Great Leap Forward and hate-America campaign, 219–20; in schools and colleges, 141 (*see also* colleges and universities); Strong's writings and, 208–13; U.S. characterized as enemy/threat, 15, 53–55, 198, 207 (*see also* America as enemy; cultural aggression, American; Resist America and Aid Korea movement); and the VOA, 326. *See also* Propaganda Department; *Quotations from Chairman Mao*; rectification movements; thought reform
— outside China: American journalists and, 167, 170, 176, 179–85 (*see also specific individuals*); American targets of, 8; armed revolution advocated, 252–53; Chinese Americans targeted, 45; cultural exchange programs used for, 312–14; documentary films as, 272–73, 289–90; English speakers needed for, 232; invited Americans and (generally), 11, 170, 176, 201–3, 214, 241 (*see also* American journalists; U.S. citizens in China; *specific individuals*); nonreciprocity for journalists used for, 198, 217; publications, 8, 203 (*see also Quotations from Chairman Mao*); publishing arms, 207; Snow as messenger, 294–97 (*see also* Snow, Edgar); Snow's recommendations for, 227; State Dept.'s ideological campaign spurred on by, 45–46 (*see also under* State Department); A. L. Strong and, 204–13 (*see also* Strong, Anna Louise); travel ban enforcement useful for, 186; in the U.S., 2020–present, 332–33; R. Williams as messenger (*see* Williams, Robert F.)
Propaganda Department: areas of responsibility/control, 28; Chinese

journalists considered for U.S. assignments, 197, 385n133; directors, 21, 205; Hu Shi's educational philosophy denounced, 177; and publications, 28, 253; and the Resist America and Aid Korea movement, 54–55; and schools of Marxism, 332; and the VOA, 326. See also propaganda, Chinese Communist
Pruitt, Ida, 224
"Psychological Warfare" (R. Williams), 267–68
Publications Administration, 28
Public Security, Ministry of, 165, 168, 181–82
PUMC. See Peking Union Medical College
Purdue University, 80, 138, 142
Pu Shan, 97
Pu Shouchang, 45, 258, 398n58
Pu Xixiu, 199

Qian Junrui, 66, 68–69
Qian Weichang, 121
Qian Xuesen (Tsien Hshue-shen): allowed to leave U.S., 101, 110, 114, 115; arrest and detention of, 52; desire to remain in U.S., 52–53; on PRC list of students detained in U.S., 94; PRC's attempt to secure return of, 108, 110, 118; travel aid not needed, 112; U.S. detention of students alleged, 101–2, 108
Qian Zhongjie, 159–60
Qing court, 2–3
Qinghua University: allowed to operate under CCP supervision, 26; American-educated scholars at, 80, 121; Austin on, 58; CCP's control over, 74–75, 185; CCP study camps at, 28; nationalized and reorganized, 73; scholars from, in U.S., 318; USTTT visit to, 300
Qin Jialin, 230–31
Quotations from Chairman Mao (Little Red Book), 8, 11, 266, 274–76, 286, 298, 323

racial discrimination: absent in China, 184, 185; in U.S. (see African Americans)
Radio Beijing, 326
Radio Free Asia, 331–32
Radio Free Dixie, 256, 266
RAM (Revolutionary Action Movement), 268–71, 277
Rankin, Karl L., 135, 146, 150–51
rationing, 215, 313–14
Reader's Digest, 218–20
Reap, John, 171
"Recognition of the People's Republic of China" (Snow), 225
rectification movements, 14, 22–23, 121, 191–92, 357n2
Red Army, 21–22. See also People's Liberation Army
Red Star Over China (Snow), 224. See also Snow, Edgar
Reed, Wayne O., 136
reeducation. See thought reform
Reiss, Manya, 203–4
relief institutions (in China), 61, 68. See also orphanages
religious institutions. See churches; missionary colleges and universities
Renmin University, 232
reporters. See American journalists; journalism in China; news organizations, American
"Report from Red China" (Snow), 228. See also Snow, Edgar
Republican Party, 237. See also specific politicians

INDEX [459]

Republic of China. *See* Chinese Nationalist government; Taiwan
Republic of New Africa (RNA), 276, 288–89
Resist America and Aid Korea movement, 53–63; American-subsidized institutions seized, nationalized, 61–75 (*see also under* American cultural and educational institutions). *See also* Chinese Communist Party: anti-American movement
Reston, James, 302–3, 313
Reuters, 159, 166, 179
revolution, Chinese. *See* Chinese Communist Party; civil war
Revolutionary Action Movement (RAM), 268–71, 277. *See also* Stanford, Maxwell C.
revolutions, communist (international). *See* world revolution
"Revolution Without Violence?" (R. Williams), 267, 268
Reynolds, Jack, 301
Rich, John, 301
Rise of the Chinese People's Commune, The (A. L. Strong), 207–8
Rittenberg, Sidney, 203–4, 212, 258, 284
RNA (Republic of New Africa), 276, 288–89
Robertson, Walter, 91, 186, 192
Robert Williams in China (documentary), 272–73
Robeson, Eslanda, 214–15
Robeson, Paul, 214
Robinson, James, 174
ROC (Republic of China). *See* Chinese Nationalist government; Taiwan
Rockefeller Foundation, 66, 224
Rockwell Kent v. John F. Dulles, 205, 245
Roderick, John, 172–74, 197, 301

Rogers, William, 291, 306
Ronning, Audrey, 302
Ronning, Chester, 95, 302
Roosevelt, Franklin, 3. *See also* Hurley, Patrick
Rubio, Marco, 333
Rusk, Dean, 60–61, 229
Russell, Maud, 224
Russia. *See* Soviet Union
Ruston, Maxwell, 326
Rutgers University, 291

Salisbury, Harrison, 290
Sargeant, Howland, 42
Sastroamidjojo, Ali, 163
Saturday Evening Post, 225
Sayre, Francis, 41–42
Schenck, Hubert G., 133, 140–41
scholars, Chinese. *See* Chinese students and scholars, in U.S.; intellectuals, Chinese
schools (China), 20, 58, 67, 217–18, 271–72. *See also* colleges and universities; education (China)
science and technology agreement, U.S.–PRC, 319–20
scientists, American, in PRC, 301–2, 310, 312, 315–16. *See also* social scientists
scientists, Chinese. *See* Chinese students and scholars, in U.S.; colleges and universities (China); intellectuals, Chinese; *specific organizations*
Scott, Rick, 333
Sea Breeze (*Haifeng;* student newspaper), 151
Seale, Bobby, 275. *See also* Black Panther Party
Sebald, William J., 170, 173
Selected Works of Mao Zedong, 203, 252–53

self-criticism, 72, 357n2
Senate Internal Security Subcommittee, 289
Shanahan, Cormac, Fr., 166
Shandong Field Research Project, 328
Shanghai: American journalists in (1950s), 180; American prisoners in, 181–82; American visitors to, 214–15, 216, 222–23; society for families of Chinese students in U.S., 118; USIS office shut down, 25; war against Nationalists in, 22, 125
Shanghai Filmmakers Union, 55–56
Shanghai Foreign Language Institute (SFLI), 234–39, 393(nn131, 133)
Shanxi, American journalists in, 165–66
Sheean, Vincent, 221
Sheldon, Eleanor, 315
Shen Jian, 248, 259, 261
Shen Ping, 99–100, 106–7
Shen Shanjong, 53
Shen Zonghan, 129
Shijingshan Iron and Steel Factory, 181
Shillock, John, 97
Shreve, R. Norris, 138
Signer, Ethan, 301–2
Singapore, 153, 159
Sino-American Conference on Vocational Industrial Education, 140–41
Sino-American Friendship Volunteers Program, 331
Sino-American Mutual Defense Treaty, 86, 162–63
Sino-American relations. See Taiwan; U.S.–PCR relations
Sino-Soviet relations, Soviet support sought by CCP (1949), 24–25
Sino-Soviet relations: CCP's break with Soviet Communism, 222, 257; escalating tensions and open conflict, 257–58, 290, 292–94; Pestana on importance of, 223; Russian experts withdrawn from China, 231, 257, 292; Treaty of Friendship, Alliance and Mutual Assistance (1950), 48. See also Soviet Union
Siu May Ting, Mrs., 44
Smedley, Agnes, 165–66, 379n16
Smith, Walter, 90–94
Smith-Mundt Act. See Information and Educational Exchange Act
Smithsonian Institution, 323
SNCC (Student Nonviolent Coordinating Committee), 268–69
Snow, Edgar, 15, 165–68, 224–31, 294–98, 296, 303
Snow, Helen Foster, 166
social media, 332
social scientists, 131, 312, 315–16, 321, 327, 328
Song Qingling, 68, 165, 214–15, 245, 261, 322
Song Zhong, 299. See also Chinese National Table Tennis Team
Souls of Black Folk, The (Du Bois), 254–55
sources, 6
Southeast Asia: Chinese Communist influence in, 10, 143–44, 146, 209; education of overseas Chinese from, 142–60; Nixon's trip to, 143–44; support for Nationalist government in, 145; U.S. presence and involvement in, 209 (see also Korean War; Vietnam War). See also overseas Chinese; specific countries
Southern Christian Leadership Conference, 305
South Vietnam, 209. See also Vietnam; Vietnam War

Soviet Republic of China, 264, 276. *See also* Chinese Communist Party; civil war

Soviet Union: American journalists and, 200; collapse, 331, 334; Cuban Missile Crisis, 233, 266; experts withdrawn from China, 231, 257, 292; Meyer and Teytelboym and, 224, 390n78; military clashes with PRC, 290, 292–94; nuclear test ban treaty signed, 257–58; and return of Chinese students from the U.S., 105; and revolutionary movements in Europe, North America, 262; revolution in, 252–53; A. L. Strong and, 205. *See also* Communist Party of the Soviet Union; Khrushchev, Nikita; Sino-Soviet relations; Stalin, Joseph

Special Work Group of Getting Students Back from the United States, 114–16. *See also* Work Group for the Return of the Students in Capitalist Countries

spies. *See* espionage

"spiritual aggression," 27. *See also* cultural aggression, American

SS President Cleveland, 78, 80, 115, 359n99

SS President Wilson, 78, 79, 113

Stalin, Joseph, 24–25, 32, 207. *See also* Soviet Union

Stalin Era, The (A. L. Strong), 207

Stanford, Maxwell C., 268–69, 277, 281–82. *See also* Revolutionary Action Movement

Stanford University, 328

Starzel, Frank, 171, 173–76

Stassen, Harold, 150–51

State Department (U.S.): American journalists authorized to visit PRC, 10, 193–94, 196–97, 225–26, 229 (*see also* American journalists; *specific individuals*); and China's Anti-Rightist movement, 192; China's human rights record criticized, 331; and the Chinese table tennis team, 307; Communists barred from entering U.S., 196; and cultural exchanges (1970s), 311–13; and Du Bois's travel, 244, 246; and economic sanctions against PRC, 59–61; and education of overseas Chinese in Taiwan, 147, 152, 154–55, 157–58; and Mao's desire to delay establishing diplomatic relations, 192; and negotiations over detained U.S. and Chinese citizens, 86, 89–101, 103–4, 109–14 (*see also* Chinese students and scholars, in U.S. — repatriation conflict); Office of Asian Communist Affairs, 290; Office of Chinese Affairs, 77, 80–81, 96, 186–87; reciprocal visas for PRC journalists refused, 194–96, 199–200; and A. L. Strong, 205; and training/education programs for students from Taiwan, 129–32, 135; and the travel ban, 169–76, 178, 186–94, 225–26, 229, 297 (*see also* travel ban, U.S.); and U.S.–Taiwan relations, 124–28 (*see also* Taiwan); *White Paper on U.S.-China Relations* (State Dept., 1949), 26–27; and R. Williams, 285, 287, 291–92. *See also* Acheson, Dean; Dulles, John Foster; *Kent v. Dulles*; Rusk, Dean; United States government; *specific individuals*

— and Chinese students/scholars: anticommunist ideological campaign, 8–9, 13, 33, 39–49; detentions reviewed, ended, 87, 97–103, 105;

negotiations over return of Chinese
students, 86, 89–101, 103–4, 109–14
(*see also* Chinese students and scholars
— repatriation conflict); students
desiring to remain, 119–20; students'
employment and immigration status,
48–49, 75–81, 358n91; students'
financial difficulties, 33–39, 76–78,
81, 102–3, 126–27 (*see also* Program of
Emergency Aid to Chinese
Students). *See also* Chinese students
and scholars, in U.S.
Steele, Archibald, 16
Steenhoven, Graham, 299, 307, 311.
    See also United States Table Tennis
    Team
Stein, Gunther, 166
Stern, Alfred, 224
Stevens, Edmund, 177–87
Stewart, Leighton, 69
Stockholm Peace Conference, 205
Stoessel, Walter, 294
Stokes, Carl, 285
Strohm, John, 218–20
Strong, Anna Louise: able to resume
    international travel, 205, 245; on the
    African American struggle, 260;
    considered friendly reporter, 168;
    Eighth Route Army headquarters
    visited, 166; other Americans'
    reception compared with, 226, 262,
    303; photos with Mao, 250, 297;
    relationship with CCP leaders, 16,
    204–6, 211–13, 250, *250*; resident in
    PRC (1950s-60s), 204–13; on Snow,
    224–25; writings, 206–13, *208*, 297,
    387n6
Strong, Robert C., 125, 127
Stuart, Leighton, 27
Student Nonviolent Coordinating
    Committee (SNCC), 268–69

students, American. *See* American
    students
students, Chinese: protests, 321, 324,
    326, 329. *See also* Chinese students
    and scholars, in U.S.; colleges and
    universities (China)
Subversive Control Act (U.S., 1950), 52
Sulzberger, Arthur Hays, 171
Sulzberger, Cyrus, 167–70
Sun Yat-sen, 145
Suo Libo, 272
Supreme Court, U.S. See *Kent v. Dulles*
"Surrender to the Truth" (Xiang Zhenli
    Touxiang) (Fu), 121
Suydam, Henry, 99
Suzhou (city), 183, 184

Taichung (Taizhong), College of
    Agriculture at, 139
Taiwan: agriculture, 128–29, 131, 134,
    141; as bastion against Chinese
    Communist regime, 123–24; Chinese
    students' return from U.S. to, 102–3;
    entry permits, 103, 146; Korean War
    and U.S.–Taiwan relations
    (generally), 6, 10, 50, 123–24 (*see also*
    specific aid agencies); leadership, 372n40
    (*see also specific individuals*); mutual
    defense alliance with U.S., 86,
    162–63, 377n2; National Long-Term
    Science Development Plan, 160;
    Nixon's visit to, 10, 86, 143–44, 146,
    149; and PRC policy toward U.S.
    (1950s–60s), 86, 104, 162–63, 227,
    229, 247; and PRC policy toward
    U.S. (1970s), 227, 229, 296, 302–3,
    309, 310, 313; PRC's claims not
    recognized by U.S., 226–27; PRC's
    use of force against, 217, 250, 252
    (*see also* Taiwan Strait); U.S. economic
    aid, 6, 128, 134, 139, 142–43, 148–51,

Taiwan (*continued*)
153, 155, 157–60, 371n23 (*see also* Economic Cooperation Administration; Mutual Security Agency); U.S. embassy in Taipei, 125, 127, 131, 149–50, 152–57 (*see also* Rankin, Karl L.); U.S. military aid, 6, 10, 50, 124, 125–28, 252, 370n5; U.S. military presence, 104, 162, 227, 228, 303; U.S. objectives regarding, 4, 144–45; U.S. "two China" policy, 198, 248. *See also* Chinese Nationalist government; education (Taiwan); *specific individuals, such as* Jiang Jieshi
Taiwan Engineering College, 137–41
Taiwan Strait: de-facto cease-fire, 103; Taiwan Strait Crisis (1954-55), 97, 118; Second Taiwan Strait Crisis (1958), 156, 219, 248, 252; U.S. military presence, 50, 54, 104, 227, 252
Taiwan Table Tennis Team, 307
Taiwan Teachers College, 136–39, 141, 149
Tang Mingzhao, 205, 211–12, 226, 248
Tannebaum, Gerald, 212
Tanzania, 276, 279, 285, 286, 289, 290, 404n26
Taylor, John (Mweusi Chui), 288
teacher-education programs, in Taiwan, 136–37
technology institutes, 73. *See also* colleges and universities (China)
television: American television, 272, 289–90, 322 (*see also* NBC); Chinese television, 314. *See also* media; *specific networks*
Templeton, Payne (Templeton report), 152–54
Temple University, 319

Temporary Regulations for Private Higher Education Institutions (1950), 29–31
Teng Chuan-kai (Deng Chuankai), 147
Terrel, C. L., 137
Teytelboym, Dora, 223–24, 390n78
Thailand, 153, 156
Thayer, Harry, 290–92
Thornburgh, Richard L., 329
thought-education (*sixiang jiaoyu*) movements, 69
thought reform (*sixiang gaizao*): Hu Shi's educational philosophy denounced, 177; Strohm on remolding of Chinese people, 220; of students and faculty members, 9, 69–72, 82, 121, 177; and total acceptance of Mao's thought, 220. *See also* rectification movements
thought struggle (*sixiang douzheng*), 22
Three-Self Reform movement, 58–59, 68
Tiananmen Square protests and aftermath, 321, 324, 329–31. *See also* student protests
Tianjin, 25, 58, 70, 82, 118. *See also* Nankai University
Tibetan Interviews (A. L. Strong), 208–9, 208
Time magazine, 166, 168
Today (Strong newsletter), 213
Tong, Hollington (Dong Xianguang), 126
Topping, Seymour, 302–3
Trading with the Enemy Act, 174
translators (of written works), 45, 203, 204, 232–33, 255, 263. *See also* interpreters
travel ban, U.S.: American journalists authorized to visit PRC despite, 10, 161–62, 189–90, 193–94, 225–26, 229

(*see also specific journalists*); Americans invited by PRC despite, 4, 161–62, 192–93, 215–17 (*see also* African Americans; American journalists; U.S. citizens in China); broken by American journalists, 10, 161, 177–87; broken by individual citizens, 245–46 (*see also specific individuals*); broken by youth group, 192–93, 215–18; challenged by American journalists, 169–76, 187–91; Du Bois on impact of, 249; exceptions considered, 189–94; imposed, 4, 7, 9, 50; maintained, 169–76, 186–89, 229; penalties for breaking, 171, 174, 186–87, 193; public support for allowing reporters to go to China, 190; relaxed/repealed, 292, 297; USTTT barred from 1961 world championships due to, 299

Treasury Department (U.S.), 60–61, 65, 171, 186, 194, 204. *See also* U.S.–PRC relations: U.S. economic sanctions

Trevelyan, Humphrey, 87–93, 96

Tripartite Treaty (nuclear test ban treaty), 257

Truman, Harry S.: Acheson's letter to, 25; and Chinese students, 40, 49, 53; Eisenhower's opinion of, 143; and the Korean War, 228; and U.S. policy re Taiwan, 125–28, 296

Trump, Donald, 333

Tsing, Ta-Kuin (Qin Dajun), 137, 140

Tsinghua Teaching and Research Fellowship Program, 47

Tucker, Shalby, 193

Tu Guangnan (Tu Kuang-Nan), 78

Tu Guangzhi (Tu Kuang-Chi), 45, 78

Tunghai University, 143

"two China" policy, 198, 248

Unfinished Revolution in China, The (Epstein), 203

"unification of thoughts," 63. *See also* thought reform

Union Hospital, 295, 313

United Board for Christian Higher Education in China (UBCHEC), 26, 32

United Board of Christian Colleges in China (UBCCC), 47, 58, 60–61, 65–66. *See also* Fenn, William P.

United Nations: Austin's speech on U.S.-China cultural relations, 57–58; Conference on International Organizations, 44; Conference on International Organizations (San Francisco, 1944), 44; and the Korean War, 31, 51; PRC's entry into, 305; Security Council, 57–58, 127; and the U.S. detention of Chinese students, 53, 98. *See also* Geneva Conference

United Press International (UPI): banned/regulated in China, 18–19, 24; on Pankey's arrival in Beijing, 388n51; reporters in or invited to China, 168, 174; reporting on U.S. detention of Chinese students, 98; and the travel ban, 171, 190–91. *See also* Bartholomew, Frank

United States (nation): Chinese students in (*see* Chinese students and scholars, in U.S.); citizens in China (*see* African Americans; American journalists; U.S. citizens in China; *specific individuals*); Garvin on class struggle in, 237; PRC perceptions of (*see* America as enemy; cultural aggression, American); racial discrimination in (*see* African Americans). *See also* United States government; United States military

United States Advisory Commission on Educational Exchange (USACEE), 37
United States government ("Washington"): and African American civil rights, 257 (*see also* African Americans); Beijing's strategy to isolate, 162, 164–65, 217; and the British and French invasion of Egypt, 183; and the Chinese Nationalist government (*see* Chinese Nationalist government; Jiang Jieshi; Taiwan); and Chinese students and scholars (*see* Chinese students and scholars; Fulbright Program); commitment to preserving American ideals and values, 12, 14; "cultural aggression" by (*see* cultural aggression); economic aid to China (statistics), 57; educational exchange goals, 37; education assistance for overseas Chinese in Taiwan (*see under* overseas Chinese); and human rights, 321, 329 (*see also* human rights); not recognized by PRC, 310; nuclear weapons program, 204, 251, 257–58; peaceful evolution encouraged, 6, 7, 329 (*see also* peaceful evolution); PRC's ideals and values seen as threat, 6; relations with PRC (*see* ambassadorial talks; U.S.–PRC relations); Sino-American Mutual Defense Treaty signed, 162–63; Southeast Asia involvement, 148, 209 (*see also* Southeast Asia; Vietnam War; *specific countries*); spread of Chinese Communism opposed, 6, 7, 40, 143–44 (*see also* anticommunist efforts, U.S.); and Taiwan (*see* Taiwan); travel ban (*see* travel ban); "two China" policy, 198, 248; and U.S.–China cultural relations before late 1940s, 2–3. *See also* United States military; *specific laws, agencies, and individuals*

United States Information Agency (USIA), 329. *See also* Fulbright Program

United States Information Service (USIS), 18–19, 25, 146, 152–54

United States International Communications Agency (USICA), 323, 327

United States military: attachés put under house arrest by PLA, 19; Black soldiers in, 233–34; Chinese communist cooperation with, during World War II, 15; Chinese propaganda about shellshock among, 46; and the Korean War, 50, 127; Korean War involvement seen by CCP as threat, 54; Mao on battling, 360n1; not to be involved in war in mainland China, 144, 145; personnel detained/imprisoned in China, 92, 95, 98, 100, 106, 113, 163 (*see also* U.S. citizens in China); PRC prepared to take on, 212; in Taiwan and Taiwan Strait, 50, 54, 104, 162, 227, 228, 252, 303; U-2 spy plane shot down by PRC, 211

United States Office of Education (USOE), 136, 372n50

United States Table Tennis Association, 307

United States Table Tennis Team (USTTT): invited to PRC, 292, 310; PRC visited, 11, 280, 298–301, 306, 311; at world championships (1971), 298–300. *See also* Chinese National Table Tennis Team

universities. *See* colleges and universities (China); colleges and universities (U.S.); *specific universities*

University of California, 138, 275
University of Iowa, 133
University of Michigan, 135, 290–91, 398n58
University of Nanking, 58, 73
University of Shanghai, 26, 72–73, 246
University of Utah, 275
UPI. *See* United Press International
Urban League, 237
USACEE (United States Advisory Commission on Educational Exchange), 37
U.S. Aid Technical Assistance Committee (USATAC), 134
"U.S.A: The Potential of a Minority Revolution" (R. Williams), 268
U.S.-China High-Level Consultation on People-to- People Exchange, 332, 417n45
U.S.–China People's Friendship Association (U.S.CPFA), 239, 240
U.S. citizens in China: before 1949, 202; American students (after 1971), 318, 319; American Youth Delegation, 10, 192–93, 195, 215–18; courted as influencers by PRC, 214–31, 241; CPUSA members/sympathizers invited to PRC, 201–4, 221–25 (*see also* Strong, Anna Louise; *and other individuals*); deported, 328–29; detained, 85–89, 91–100, 103–4, 113–14, 122, 181–82, 229; detainees and American journalists' visits to PRC, 171, 181–82, 187, 188; detainees' relatives invited to visit them in PRC, 163, 217; detainees released/expelled, 96–97, 100, 106, 113; detainees' release negotiated, 85–89, 91–97, 99–100, 103–4, 110–12, 163–64 (*see also* Chinese students and scholars —repatriation conflict);

employed as experts (1960s), 231–41, 404n20; few visas issued by PRC, 297–98; former Korean War POWs, 232–34, 392n120; invited to visit or work in PRC (generally), 4, 7, 10–11, 192–93, 201–2, 212, 214–18, 220–25 (*see also* African Americans; American journalists; *specific individuals*); scientists, 301–2; tight restrictions imposed on (late-1940s to 1950s), 16–17; visits in early 1970s, 301–6 (*see also* United States Table Tennis Team). *See also* African Americans; American journalists; travel ban, U.S.
USCPFA (U.S.-China People's Friendship Association), 239, 240
USIA (United States Information Agency), 329. *See also* Fulbright Program
USICA (United States International Communications Agency), 323, 327
USIS. *See* United States Information Service
U.S. News and World Report, 168, 380n31
USOE (United States Office of Education), 372n50
U.S.–PRC relations: American science, technology, capital sought by PRC, 6–7, 12, 317–21, 323, 330; delay in normalization preferred by PRC, 192, 198; Geneva Conference negotiations (1954), 84–97; negotiations over repatriation of citizens (*see* Chinese students and scholars — repatriation conflict); normalization of diplomatic relations, 318–19, 334; PRC journalists barred from U.S., 194–200; PRC not recognized by U.S. government, 7, 87, 90–93, 198;

U.S.–PRC relations (*continued*)
PRC policy toward U.S. (1960s), 212, 226–27, 229, 243, 247; PRC strategy to isolate U.S. government, 162, 164–65, 217; U-2 spy plane shot down, 211; U.S. ban on travel to PRC (*see* travel ban, U.S.); U.S. diplomats ejected from PRC, 48; U.S. economic sanctions against PRC, 9, 50, 59–61, 63; U.S. not recognized by PRC, 310. *See also* ambassadorial talks; *specific conflicts, topics of discussion, governmental agencies, and individuals*
USSR. *See* Soviet Union
USTTT. *See* United States Table Tennis Team
Utah Free Press, 274

"Vast Miracle of China Today, The" (Du Bois), 253
Vietnam, 153, 156, 209. *See also* North Vietnam; South Vietnam; Vietnam War
Vietnam War, 209, 212, 233–34, 283, 303, 308
vocational education, in Taiwan, 135–42
Vogel, Ezra F., 315
Voice of America (VOA), 41, 56, 326, 329–31
Votaw, Maurice, 166, 167
Voting Right Act (1965), 284

Wall Street Journal, 302, 332
Wang, David (Wang Kexin), 101
Wang Bingnan: cultural exchange discussed, 163–64, 176–77; letter to Chinese student, 120; and negotiations over detained Chinese and U.S. citizens, 92–96, 108–11, 113, 229, 365n74; and reciprocity regarding reporters, 195–97, 225–26, 229; and a U.S. diplomatic visit to China, 294
Wang Chuliang, 211–12
Wang Huanxun, 177
Wang Jiaxiang, 23
Wang Kunlun, 53–54
Wang Liangneng, 80, 94
Wang Ren, 117
Washington (U.S. government). *See* United States government
Washington, Walter, 284–85
Washington Post, 188, 230, 290
Waterloo University, Canada, 160
Watson, Cathryn, 253
Weatherly, Kathryn, 215
Wei Jingsheng, 325
Wei Zichu, 59
Wenhuibao (newspaper), 199
Wen Jiabao, 332
Wenkui, Bao, 350n4
When Serfs Stood Up in Tibet (A. L. Strong), 209, 211
Whipple, Dorothy, 146
White, Lincoln, 170, 194
White, Theodore, 23–24, 166–67
White, William, 232–33, 234
White Paper on U.S.-China Relations (State Dept., 1949), 26–27
Wick, Charles, 327
Wiggins, James Russell, 188, 191
Wilkins, Roy, 281–82
Williams, Hosea, 305, 313
Williams, John (son of R. Williams), 271–72, 284–85
Williams, Mabel (wife of R. Williams), 242, 262–65, 270, 284–85, 286. *See also* Williams, Robert F.
Williams, Robert F., 256–57; armed Black revolution advocated, 243, 261, 266–70, 274–77, 281, 283, 285–86;

armed revolution rhetoric abandoned, 285–86; armed self-defense advocated, 237, 243, 256–57, 261, 263, 275, 281; Chinese support sought for African American struggle, 257–61; decision to return to U.S., 279; documentary films, 272–73, 285, 289–90, 404n28; influence in U.S., 268–70, 274–78; international support sought for African American struggle, 257; invited to visit PRC (1960s), 242, 250, 261–62, 270–71; legal battles, 256, 279, 282–83, 287–89, 403n8; Mao and, 11, 242–43, 258–63, 270–71, 273–74, 285–86, 297; and Maoist thought, 243, 266–67, 274–75, 286; as messenger for PRC in U.S., 286, 289–92; PRC visited, 261–66, 270, 270–74, 278, 280, 283–84, 286; on racial struggle as class struggle, 264–65, 283–84; return to U.S., 11, 273, 279–88, 404(nn26–27)
Williams, Robert, Jr. (son of R. Williams), 271–72, 284–85
Wills, Morris, 232–34
Winnington, Alan, 213
Winter, Bob, 284
Women's International Democratic Federation Conference, 214
Wong Peng (Wang Peng), 147, 149
Wood, Shirley, 212
Woodcock, Leonard, 318
Work Group for the Return of the Students in Capitalist Countries, 118. *See also* Special Work Group of Getting Students Back from the United States
world order, post–World War II, 6
world revolution: African American struggle as part of, 242–43, 258, 273–74, 278 (*see also* African Americans; Williams, Robert F.); Beijing as leader of, 11, 243, 252–53, 257–59, 270, 273–74, 286–87; communist revolutions (generally), 250–53; Mao as leader of, 11, 259, 278, 287. *See also* Cuba; Soviet Union
World War II (war against Japan), 14–15, 21–22, 32, 214
Worthy, William, 167–68, 178–87, 272
writers, Chinese, 180–81
Writers Guild of America, 190
Wu, K. C. (Wu Guozhen), 126
Wuhan, 22, 25, 118, 232, 250
Wuhan University, 391n95
Wu Kuo-chen, 136, 137
Wu Lengxi, 203–4
Wu Liangkun, 82
Wu Liangyong (Wu Lianyong), 78
Wu Weiran, 313
Wuxi (city), 183
Wu Xiuquan, 57
Wu Xueqian, 204
Wu Xujun, 299
Wu Yaozong, 59
Wu Yi, 80
Wu Yifang, 58

X, Malcolm, 269
Xia Fei (Hsiah Fei), 97
Xian, 239, 313
Xiao Qian, 180
Xie Bingxin, 180
Xie Juezai, 68
Xi Jinping, 332
Xinhua Bookstore, 28
Xinhua News Agency (New China News Agency), 27, 28, 203, 210, 261, 333, 385n133
Xinhua Ribao (New China Daily), 22
Xu, Guangqiu, 327

Xu Min, 45
Xu Yingkui, 72
Xu Yongying, 44, 108, 116
Xu Zhangben, 121, 369n122

Yale-in-China (Changsha), 58
Yale Nursing School (Changsha, Hunan Province), 45–46
Yanan: CCP success in, 14; Epton in, 304; rectification movement in, 14, 22–23; Snow in, 226; A. L. Strong in, 204; U.S. and foreign journalists in, 17–18, 23–24, 165–66; U.S. military observers in, 15
Yanan Literature and Art Forum speech (Mao, 1949), 22
Yang, Chen-ning (Zhenning Yang), 82, 298
Yang Shangkun, 166
Yan Jingyao, 55
Yeh Kung-chao (Ye Gongchao), 125, 146
Ye Jianying, 166
Yen, James, 129
Yenching University: allowed to operate under CCP supervision/restrictions, 25–26, 27–28, 32; enrollment (1950), 31–32; faculty present at Zhou's address at Peking Univ., 70; nationalized, 65–69; political studies required, 27–28; reorganized and dismembered, 73–74; teachers' support for anti-American movement, 55, 58, 62; and thought education/reform, 69–72; U.S. subsidies, 57, 65, 66. *See also* colleges and universities (China); Lu Zhiwei
Yijiangshan Islands, 162–63. *See also* Taiwan Strait
Young, Whitney, 281–82

Zeng Zhaolun, 121
Zhang Bojun, 53–54, 199
Zhang Hanfu, 108
Zhang Jiafu, 108
Zhang Qingnian (Chang Ching-Nien), 78
Zhang Wen-tian, 166
Zhang Zichang, 113
Zhao Mindiao, 94
Zhao Zhongyao, 94, 350n4
Zhao Ziyang, 324
Zhou Enlai: 1975 report and goals, 317; and the African American struggle, 258; and American journalists, 164, 166, 169, 180, 195, 220, 301–3 (*see also* Snow, Edgar); and American visitors (early 1970s), 300–305; and the American youth delegation, 217; and the anti-American campaign, 53–54; and Chinese and U.S. table tennis teams, 307–8; and cultural exchanges (1970s), 312–13, 315; direct U.S.-China talks proposed, 103–4, 106–7; and Du Bois, 248–49, 256, 261; English interpreter for, 80 (*see also* Ji Chaozhu); and the First Taiwan Strait Crisis, 163; and foreign language education, 231; and the Geneva Conference (1954), 86, 88, 92; and the get-students-back movement, 114–16, 118; and the Korean War, 53–54, 55; at National Day celebrations, 256, 262; on need for thought reform, 70–71; and negotiations over detained citizens, 88, 92, 106–7, 108, 112, 118; and Nixon, 297, 408n79; and the nuclear test ban treaty, 257–58; on reciprocity, 195, 217; Reiss visited, 203; and E. Snow, 166, 225, 226–29, 295, 297; strategy to isolate U.S. government, 165; and A. L. Strong,

[470] INDEX

204–6, 211–13; subservience to Mao, 24; and the Taiwan issue, 86, 104, 299, 302–3; and the takeover of colleges and universities, 31; and thawing relations with the U.S., 295, 297, 300–303; and U.S. and PRC table tennis teams, 298–301; U.S. assets seized, 61; U.S. charged with violating Geneva Agreement, 185; and U.S. social scientists, 315; on war with the U.S., 212, 301–2; and R. Williams, 262, 265, 286, *286*, 290; and Yang Zhenning's parents, 298

Zhou Peiyuan, 318, *318*

Zhuang Zedong, 299

Zhu De, 21, 70, 166, 204, 206, 263

Zhu Kezhen, 108

Ziegler, Ron, 307

GPSR Authorized Representative: Easy Access System Europe, Mustamäe tee 50, 10621 Tallinn, Estonia, gpsr.requests@easproject.com

www.ingramcontent.com/pod-product-compliance
Lightning Source LLC
Chambersburg PA
CBHW031227290426
44109CB00012B/192